SCIENCE FICTION AND CULTURAL THEORY

Science Fiction and Cultural Theory: A Reader is an essential resource for students studying science fiction, science and popular culture, and contemporary theory. This book combines key theories that have become touchstones for work in the field with more recent thinking to showcase how theoretical paradigms central to science fiction such as posthumanism and mediation have become central to critical theory overall in the twenty-first century.

The book is divided into four sections:

- Gender, technology and the body
- The science-fictionalization of everyday life
- Media, mediation, science fiction
- Posthumanisms

Each section not only outlines the central critical trends in the study of science fiction across media but also shows dialogue and exchange as these concepts are refined. Each section concludes with a list of recommendations for further reading. In this volume Sherryl Vint brings together the most important critical essays and approaches to the study of science fiction over the last 40 years to create an ideal resource for classrooms.

Sherryl Vint is professor of science fiction media studies at the University of California, Riverside, USA. She is the author of *Bodies of Tomorrow* (2007), *Animal Alterity* (2010), *The Wire* (2013) and *Science Fiction: A Guide for the Perplexed* (2014). She is the co-author of *The Routledge Concise History of Science Fiction* (2011), and co-editor of *The Routledge Companion to Science Fiction* (2009), *Fifty Key Figures in Science Fiction* (2009) and *Beyond Cyberpunk* (2010). She is an editor of the journals *Science Fiction Studies* and *Science Fiction Film and Television*, and recipient of the Science Fiction Research Association's Pioneer Award.

Routledge Literature Readers

Also available in this series:

The Routledge Reader in Caribbean Literature
The History of Reading
Literature and Globalization: A Reader
World Literature: A Reader
Literature and the Bible: A Reader
Ecocriticism: The Essential Reader
Science Fiction and Cultural Theory: A Reader
The Routledge Auto | Biography Studies Reader

For further information on this series visit: http://www.routledge.com/books/series/RLR

SCIENCE FICTION AND CULTURAL THEORY

A Reader

Edited by Sherryl Vint

LONDON AND NEW YORK

First published 2016
by Routledge
2 Park Square, Milton Park, Abingdon, Oxon OX14 4RN

and by Routledge
711 Third Avenue, New York, NY 10017

Routledge is an imprint of the Taylor & Francis Group, an informa business

© 2016 Sherryl Vint

British Library Cataloguing-in-Publication Data
A catalogue record for this book is available from the British Library

Library of Congress Cataloging-in-Publication Data
Science fiction and cultural theory : a reader / [edited by] Sherryl Vint.

pages cm.— (Routledge literature readers)
Includes bibliographical references and index.
1. Science fiction—History and criticism. 2. Science fiction—Study and
teaching. 3. Science fiction—Influence. 4. Literature and society. I. Vint,
Sherryl, 1969- editor.
PN3433.5.S324 2015
809.3'8762-dc23
2015014093

ISBN: 978-1-13-881498-1 (hbk)
ISBN: 978-1-13-881499-8 (pbk)

Typeset in Bembo
by Apex CoVantage, LLC

Printed and bound in the United States of America by
Edwards Brothers Malloy on sustainably sourced paper

CONTENTS

FIGURES

ACKNOWLEDGEMENTS

A project of this magnitude emerges from a long period of conversations with other scholars in my field and it would be impossible to do justice to the many people from whom I've had the benefit of learning over the years. Thus I will limit these acknowledgements to those with whom I've had the most sustained theoretical conversations, while pointing to the much wider field of interlocutors whose knowledge informs my work in assembling this collection.

From the field at large, this list includes Neil Easterbrook, Roger Luckhurst, Colin Milburn, John Rieder and Patrick Sharp, and from my interdisciplinary travels in Science and Technology Studies (STS) this includes Juliet McMullin, Dana Simmons, Arielle Saiber and Chikako Takeshita.

I am also indebted to my co-editors in ongoing journal work, Mark Bould and Gerry Canavan at *Science Fiction Film and Television*, and Istvan Csicsery-Ronay, Art Evans, Joan Gordon, Veronica Hollinger, Rob Latham and Carol McGuirk at *Science Fiction Studies*. Additional thanks are due to the SFS Board for fostering the idea of such a collection and offering material support and to Rob Latham in particular for initial conversations linked to our shared Science Fiction and Technoculture Studies Program at UC Riverside that helped to frame the contents of this book.

I thank my graduate students, Stina Attebery, Irene Morrison and Josh Pearson, for their RA work on this project.

Most importantly I thank my editor, Ruth Hilsdon, for her support of this project and her incredible patience when administrative issues delayed its appearance.

I dedicate this work to Veronica Hollinger and Len Hatfield, who began the tradition of the "science fiction theory roundtable" at the International Conference on the Fantastic in the Arts, an event that has done much to enrich and complicate our theoretical engagement with the possibilities of genre.

Sherryl Vint, 2015

PERMISSIONS

12. Polity Press for permission to reprint extracts from Jussi Parikka, "Practicing Media Archaeology: Creative Metaphors for Remediation" from *What is Media Archaeology?*, Cambridge: Polity Press, 2012, pp. 136–158.

13. Garrett Stewart for kind permission to reprint extracts from his "The Videology of Science Fiction" from *Shadows of the Magic Lamp: Fantasy and Science Fiction in Film*, by George Edgar Slusser and Eric S. Rabkin, Southern Illinois University Press, 1985.

14. The author for kind permission to reprint extracts from Tom Gunning, "The Cinema of Attractions" from *Wide Angle*, pp. 63–70 with cuts.

15. Excerpt from *The Anti-Aesthetic: Essays on Postmodern Culture* – Copyright © 1998 by The New Press. Reprinted by permission of The New Press. www.thenewpress.com.

16. Greenwood Publishing Group, Incorporated for permission to reprint Brooks Landon, "On a Clear Day You Can See the Horizon of Invisibility: Rethinking Science Fiction Film in the Age of Electronic (Re)Production" from *The Aesthetics of Ambivalence: Rethinking Science Fiction Film in the Age of Electronic (Re) Production*, Greenwood Press, 1992, pp. 145–160.

17. From "The Wonder Years and Beyond: 1989–1995" from *Special Effects: Still in Search of Wonder*, by Michelle Pierson. Copyright © 2002 Columbia University Press. Reprinted with permission of the publisher.

18. Henry Jenkins, "The Cultural Logic of Media Convergence", from *International Journal of Cultural Studies*, March 2004; vol. 7, 1: pp. 33–43. Copyright © 2004, SAGE Publications. Reprinted by Permission of SAGE.

19. Donna Haraway for kind permission to reprint extracts from Donna Haraway, "The Cyborg Manifesto" from *Simians, Cyborgs and Women: The Reinvention of Nature*, New York: Routledge, 1991, pp. 149–181 with cuts.

20. Routledge Taylor and Francis Group LLC Books for kind permission to reprint extracts from N. Katherine Hayles, "The Life Cycle of Cyborgs" from *The Cyborg Handbook* by Chris Gray, New York: Routledge, 1995, pp. 321–334. Copyright © 1995, CCC Republication.

21. "The Image Virus", in *Terminal Identity*, Scott Bukatman, pp. 70–99. Copyright, 1993, Duke University Press. All rights reserved. Republished by permission of the copyright holder. www.dukeupress.edu.

22. Rosi Braidotti, "Meta(l)morphoses", from *Theory, Culture and Society* May 1997. Copyright © 2004, SAGE Publications. Reprinted by Permission of SAGE.

23. Nabeel Zuberi and Phillip Hayward for kind permission to reprint extracts from Nabeel Zuberi, "The Transmolecularization of [Black] Folk: *Space in the Place*, Sun Ra, and Afrofuturism" from *Off the Planet: Music, Sound and Science Fiction Cinema*, ed. Phillip Hayward, John Libbey Cinema and Animation, John Libbey Publishing, 2004.

24. University of Minnesota Press for permission to reprint extracts from Susan Napier, "When the Machines Stop: Fantasy, Reality and Terminal Identity in *Neon Genesis: Evangelion* and *Serial Experiments: Lain*" from *Robot Ghosts and Wired Dreams: Japanese Science Fiction from Origins to Anime*, University of Minnesota Press, 2007.

Disclaimer

The publishers have made every effort to contact authors/copyright holders of works reprinted in *Science Fiction and Cultural Theory: A Reader* to obtain permission to publish extracts. This has not been possible in every case, however, and we would welcome correspondence from those individuals/companies whom we have been unable to trace. Any omissions brought to our attention will be remedied in future editions.

INTRODUCTION

Semiotic ghosts and broken dreams: science fiction and cultural theory

In William Gibson's "The Gernsback Continuum," a photographer is commissioned to capture the remnants of 1930s futurism embodied in architecture from that era, a mix of imperialist grandeur and high-tech gloss that finds its expression in buildings such as a gas station whose "superfluous central towers ringed with those strange radiator flanges . . . look as though they might generate potent bursts of raw technological enthusiasm, if you could only find the switch that turned them on" (27). The title, of course, refers to Hugo Gernsback, founder in 1926 of *Amazing Stories*, the first pulp magazine devoted specifically to science fiction. Gernsback enthusiastically promoted the promise of this new genre – and is credited with coining its name, although he first proposed the more awkward "scientifiction" – which he promised heralded an entirely new kind of fiction for a rapidly changing world. "Science, through its various branches of mechanics, electricity, astronomy, etc., enters so intimately into all our lives today," Gernsback observes in his first editorial, that we need fiction that can reflect and respond to this "entirely new world" (3). Moreover, he continued, such fiction would not only provide "tremendously interesting reading" for those living amidst technological change, but could also provide a sort of template for futures yet to come: "New inventions pictured for us in the scientifiction of today are not at all impossible of realization tomorrow" (3).

One can feel Gibson's "bursts of raw technological enthusiasm" in Gernsback's rhetoric, and the story is about interrogating this relationship between what is pictured in science fiction and what is realized in material practice. Yet Gibson perceptively notes that this relationship goes beyond mere gadgets and innovations, that new developments in science and technology, released into the world, change our social structures and ideological frameworks, change the kinds of people we, living within them, become. His protagonist sets out to find examples of "raygun Gothic" to include in a coffee-table book entitled "*The Airstream Futuropolis: The Tomorrow That Never Was*" (24), a style he describes as "an architecture of broken dreams" (27) because such optimistic visions of the gleaming technological future were displaced and undermined by the more prosaic realities of twentieth-century technoscientific development that went hand-in-hand with what Eisenhower called the military-industrial complex and thus with the vicissitudes of world wars, the globalization of capital, and the erosion of ideals of democracy. The "broken dreams" of this Gernsbackian future signify in multiple ways: they are destroyed because the dystopian present proves far different than this utopian future; they are discontinuous, as in broken sleep, because flashes of techno-optimism continue to fuel technological change; they are forgotten or ignored, as in broken promises, since the reality of technocultural change often increased inequity and conflict, unlike visions of harmonious cities of the future; they are broken as a suspect under interrogation might be broken, mentally exhausted and no longer able to cling to their original story; and, perhaps most importantly, they are broken in the sense of no longer functioning properly – such dreams of the perfect future through "progress" have somehow led us to an often-dystopian present.

Indeed it is this final irony that most troubles Gibson's protagonist. "The rockets on the covers of the Gernsback pulps had fallen on London in the dead of night, screaming," he reflects, and "After the war, everyone had a car – no wings for it – and the promised superhighway to drive it down, so that the sky itself darkened, and the fumes ate the marble and pitted the miracle crystal . . ." (27, ellipses in original). Fredric Jameson offers similar commentary in his foundational essay "Progress versus Utopia; Or, Can We Imagine the Future?" when he reflects on the function of science fiction. Although many have claimed that the genre anticipates the future, "thus preparing our consciousness and our habits for the otherwise demoralizing impact of change itself," Jameson sees sf contemporary to his writing (and Gibson's) as itself broken, such visions "historical and dated – streamlined cities of the future on peeling murals – while our lived experience of our greatest metropolises is one of urban decay and blight." The promised Utopian future, Jameson suggests, "turned out to have been merely the future of one moment of what is now our own past" (151) and thus the function of sf proves not to be to imagine the future. Rather, science fiction gives us a method for "apprehending the present as history" (153) and thus perceiving the relationship between our own choices and the kinds of futures we are actively in the process of making. It may be structurally impossible to project a utopian future, but nonetheless sf keeps alive the utopian impulse by narrating this condition of impossibility.

A similar dynamic is at play in Gibson's story. Working on this project and immersing himself in the futuristic dreams of an earlier era, the protagonist finds himself haunted by its "semiotic ghosts" (33), visions of the future that might have been, which his friend Kihn, a conspiracy theory expert, tells him are a manifestation of the human collective unconscious, now "framed in a kind of sci-fi imagery that permeates our culture" (29). Such visions are not exactly hallucinations and not exactly real, Kihn explains, but simply a common experience of yearning: "People see these things. Nothing's there, but people *see* them anyway. Because they need to, probably" (28). The protagonist feels he has passed through "a membrane of probability" (27) and briefly visited this alter plane, awakening from a dream fueled by "amphetamine and exhaustion" (30) to see a wondrous city of the future straight out of sf cinema such as *Metropolis* (Lang 1927) and *Things to Come* (Menzies 1936): "Roads of crystal soared between the spires, crossed and recrossed by smooth silver shapes like beads of running mercury" (31). He finds this vision sublime in the full sense of this word, both wondrous and fear inducing, and the fear attaches itself particularly to the inhabitants of such a future city, a statuesque blonde couple he briefly glimpses sharing the alter-roadside stop with him. These are people for whom the dream of progress never faded, who live "in a dream logic that knew nothing of pollution, the finite bounds of fossil fuel, or foreign wars it was possible to lose" (32); they are "smug, happy, and utterly content with themselves and their world" (32–33). Such complacent confidence is redolent of "the sinister fruitiness of Hitler Youth Propaganda" (33) to the protagonist, who shrinks from contact with these dream people and their unreconstructed faith in technological progress.

Now almost one hundred years after the founding of *Amazing Stories*, we live in a world even more completely suffused with experiences and objects that were once found only in sf. The discourses of science fiction have given us our technological imagination and shaped our experience of living in what Roger Luckhurst calls our "technologically saturated society" (3) and at the same time sf continues to take inspiration from and reflect ongoing developments in science and technology. Thus the technological imagination and technocultural reality reinforce and remake one another in manifold ways. Gibson's protagonist finds in "really bad media" (33) an antidote for the imperialist overtones of 1930s futurism, and the story ends with his determined commitment to be attentive to reality, "the human near-dystopian we live in" (35), rather than be seduced by the Dream of the retrofuturist city. We are all haunted by the semiotic ghosts of sf media, both good and bad, and the cultural theory collected in this volume aims at helping us to understand the movement of ideas and worldviews and practice across this "membrane of probability" between the sf imagination and the world of technocultural innovation. Television is the bad object of choice in "The Gernsback Continuum," presumably representing so banal an imaginary that no one could take seriously the futures it projects. This skepticism about sf futures reminds us of the ways that seemingly innocent visions of materialist excess in many sf futures buttress – wittingly or not – politics of colonial extraction and class division. The bad media recommended to our protagonist, such as "*Nazi Love Motel*" (33), at least keep such power dynamics in view and, more importantly, remind us to approach technophilic visions with some critical reserve.

There is a reason that Disney's utopian Tomorrowland quickly became a kind of retrofuture-land, an archive of past visions of the gleaming future that allowed visitors to escape from the nonutopian present.[1] As Gibson's story shows, the boundless vision of technofuturist possibility had a rather short shelf life – and even then came with some ideological assumptions that begged interrogation. Were we to imagine a Tomorrowland extrapolated from our own present, the gleaming rocket cars and handy jetpacks would be replaced by rides based on finding potable water or managing daily activities post–peak oil. Yet even here we must remember that the techno-topian imagination has always been in complex dialogical exchange with contemporary conditions, that the celebratory World of Tomorrow built for the 1939 World's Fair was created in the midst of an economic crisis and on the eve of world war. This volume is about these reciprocal exchanges between science fiction and contemporary culture, the ways in which a knowledge of science fiction can illuminate aspects of our technocultural present and how works of technocultural theory can help us recognize the cultural work done by science fiction.

The volume is organized into four sections: Technology, Gender and the Body; The Science-Fictionalization of Everyday Life; Media, Mediation, Science Fiction; and Posthumanisms. In each I've sought to give some sense of historical perspective regarding how the various discourses that link sf with cultural theory have developed, and also to select examples that show the range of critical work that is being done using science fiction as a touchstone. Inevitably there are sites of intersection across the sections, and a number of essays could have been placed within more than one section; indeed, the linear format of the codex is only one possible arrangement for these materials, and I have attempted in my introductions to each section to suggest something not only of the dialogue within the section but also the conversations across sections of this volume as well. I have chosen to provide longer and fewer selections within each section rather than shorter excerpts from more pieces in the belief that it is important to retain the contemporary framing for each argument, as much as possible, and not merely to extract central critical insights from their embeddedness in original publication contexts. Thus this volume both collects key pieces of cultural theory engaged with science fiction and also provides a brief historical overview of the development of sf cultural theory. The Recommended Further Reading lists at the end of each section are intended to provide this missing perspective of breadth by listing a number of influential works from which excerpts might have found their way into a larger version of this project.

Finally, in addition to functioning as broader take on what Istvan Csicsery-Ronay dubbed, in reference to Baudrillard and Haraway, "The SF of Theory," this volume also aims to begin to develop a critical vocabulary of sf theory specifically for media sf. There is a long and important tradition of sf theory developed in reference to print sf – grounded in Darko Suvin's *Metamorphoses of Science Fiction* and Fredric Jameson's early Marxist readings of sf, many of them collected in *Archaeologies of the Future*; extended into new critical modes by influential later work such as John Huntington's *Rationalizing Genius* and Carl Freedman's *Critical Theory and Science Fiction*; and continuing always to embrace new theoretical perspectives, as found in N. Katherine Hayles's *How We Became Posthuman* and John Rieder's *Colonialism and the Emergence of Science Fiction* – but there is no comparable tradition of sf media criticism, despite the appearance of a number of important works that might ground such a tradition, many of them collected here. This volume thus begins a conversation about what a media-centric sf theory might look like, but there is much work in this area yet to be done.

The technological imagination

The volume is premised on the conviction that science fiction is what centrally shapes our technological imagination and that the imagination is more than peripheral to the technocultural reality we make and inhabit. In this I am influenced by Anne Balsamo's *Designing Culture: The Technological Imagination at Work* (see Section 1), in which she argues that images and ideals drawn from the technological imagination shape how we design technology, and that how we design technology influences what we then do with this technology. Design choices for Balsamo, then, are much more than cosmetic and in fact are something closer to what in sf might be called world-building, the unfolding of assumptions about social structures and values that is embedded within the technologies we create. Thus to transform cultures of science requires that we simultaneously transform the technological imagination. Here science fiction can play a role – and indeed a very important role if we understand that design and the technological imagination are generative of the kinds of scientific cultures we make (and futures we anticipate, as Gibson has shown): the technological imagination is not mere artifice on an underlying culture but is in fact its very ground of being.

Steven Shaviro's work (see Section 1) announces itself explicitly as a project of the technological imagination, "to write cultural theory as science fiction to come to grips with a world that itself seems on the verge of being absorbed into the play of science fiction novels and films" (67). He sees in sf and theory a shared project of engaging "concepts that have not yet been worked out" (67) and understands the central role that science fiction has in shaping the contingencies of how and why technology emerges into the world. In his words, strikingly similar to Gibson's vision in "The Gernsback Continuum," we "are haunted by the ghosts of what has not yet happened" (75). The haunting is not necessarily something to be exorcized, as Gibson would have it, however; rather, the fact that sf images haunt our dreams and thus permeate our choices within the history of technoscientific development concomitantly means that sf becomes a valuable resource for interrogating the logic of these dreams, for unpacking the assumptions and predispositions that inevitably shape the choices we make about technology and its uses. Thus "what has not yet happened" is often the very best guide to what *is* happening around us.

Jean Baudrillard (see Section 3), one of the philosophers most consistently linked with sf visions, asserts that postmodern culture, our culture, is characterized by an inextricable blurring between reality and its representations, a condition he calls hyperreality. Baudrillard's theory of the simulacrum – copies or symbols that do not refer to any underlying reality, doing away with the binary of reality/representation – offers a vision of science fiction sensibilities as a generalized mode of perception. Here signs create rather than reflect the world, resulting in an experience of reality as a kind of science fiction in which we live. Although calls that sf reflects the "new" reality have circulated from the genre's early days, as we saw with Gernback's editorial, more recently such claims take the reverse form of asserting that reality has become like science fiction, rather than that science fiction shows us more clearly a new reality. This very Baudrillardian sense of the genre, in which reality struggles to catch up to its more compelling representation, informs recent critical discussions of how sf has become generalized to infuse much of contemporary culture well beyond its genre roots (see Wolfe) and also perhaps explains why so many recent novelists (Margaret Atwood, Colson Whitehead, Cormac McCarthy, Michel Faber, Chang-rae Lee) have turned to genre-derived images and scenarios in their recent fiction.

In the essay included in this volume, Baudrillard describes how a new cultural imaginary about technology is informed by new political regimes of governance and control, a shift from "fantasies of power, speed and appropriation" linked to the car when it first emerged as a technological object, for example, to new discourses contemporary to Baudrillard's writing that reflect different capacities now valued by post-Fordist governance, "mastery, control and command, an optimization of the play of possibilities offered by the car as a vector" (197). While Baudrillard explicitly draws on science fiction to develop his theory of hyperreality, other theorists collected in this volume, such as Manuel De Landa's work on intelligent machines, or Friedrich Kittler's work on discourse networks and communication technologies, show their debts to science fiction clearly only when placed in this continuum with other, more overtly science-fictional works. Engaging the technological imagination in broad historical perspective, De Landa convincingly shows, for example, how much the history of military technological innovation can be understood as an expression of what we might call the sf imagination; he places such technological innovations within a timeline that leads up to the ideal of war by intelligent machines, war conducted by distributed and, ideally, self-repairing and self-reproducing robots that take humans out of the decision-making loop for reasons of efficiency. Although De Landa does not reference him, Philip K. Dick showed us the risks of such a project in stories like "Second Variety" (1953) and "Autofac" (1955) long before military drones were more than a gleam in the military-industrial complex's eye. We are haunted by the ghosts of what has not yet happened, indeed.

This technological imagination has both utopian and dystopian tendencies, and the ways in which science fiction thus influences technoculture, and vice versa, cannot be predicted in advance. As Susan Napier points out (see Section 4), despite Japan's reputation in the West as a country already with one foot in the future – a reputation deeply enhanced both by the frequent sf themes of Japanese manga and anime as they are received by the West, and even more by the techno-orientalist representations of Asian culture in much American sf – Japan is deeply ambivalent about the technology that pervades its social world and its own popular culture reflects this ambivalence. In her reading of *Evangelion*, for example, Napier finds a protagonist far from the smug and commanding technofuturists envisioned by 1930s American sf, one who is instead deeply conflicted about his fusion with the machine even as he feels worthless without it. Events such as the 1995 Aum Shinrikyō cult's poison gas attack on the Tokyo subway – a cult whose mythology includes a prophesized nuclear World War III between the US and Japan that will inaugurate Armageddon – reveal the darker side of a hyperreal culture in which science fiction and lived experience fuse into an unstable mélange. Like some darker version of Gibson's blonde utopians brought to life, the Aum Shinrikyō members are a stark reminder that the technological imagination has very material effects.

Scott Bukatman's work (see Section 4), drawing on sf writer William Burroughs, interrogates the ways that representations "infect and transform" (271) reality. This is a vision of sf as both a symptom of our hyperreal condition, a genre that expresses the hopes and anxieties of our technocultural age, and also as something like a cure for this condition, a mode that allows us to bring into visibility – perhaps to "treat" – the underlying causes of cultural change. A meditation on the "terminal identity" of late 1990s culture, an identity that seemed simultaneously to be ended by postmodern fragmentation and reconstructed at the site of human-machine interface (the terminal), Bukatman's work is one in a number of works on posthumanism that first emerged within genre sf studies. Similar to the recent situation that sees many novelists turning to the tools and techniques of sf in a phenomenon Gary Wolfe calls genre evaporation, the theoretical discourse of posthumanism has moved from the periphery (science fiction and technocultural studies) to the center of humanities scholarship in recent years. The questions the genre has long asked, not merely about the influence of science and technology on daily life, but also about the nature of the human and the status of life itself, have come to shape much of contemporary cultural theory. As the essays collected in this volume demonstrate, science fiction and its influence on the technological imagination have played a central and at times unacknowledged role in thinking about alterity and subjectivity, and this theoretical imagination, too, has been infected and transformed by sf.

The prevalent influence of sf is evident in the wide variety of sites of contemporary cultural theorization that owe a debt to sf frameworks and terminology, from media archaeologies and avant-garde repurposing art of the media archaeologies examined by Jussi Parikka (see Section 2); to the connections between such practices and the fan methodologies of remixing and mash-up that have now become central to the political of popular culture and political economy overall, as Henry Jenkins argues (see Section 3); to the extensive imagining of biological DNA as computer code that Eugene Thacker argues has fundamentally shaped the biomedical and pharmaceutical industries on imaginative and material levels (see Section 2); to the ways, as Nabeel Zuberi shows, that African American culture has drawn on technological imagery and the sf imagination to both reimagine racial politics as a kind of sf in the mythology of the Nation of Islam, or to create another kind of politics of the posthuman through music in Sun Ra's Afrofuturist discourse (see Section 4). In each of these examples, across a wide range of cultural, political, and economic sites of engagement, we find evidence of science fiction as a guide to social reality, of social reality constructed under the influence of a technological imagination that has its roots in science fiction. Indeed, each section of this volume is organized around an area where the exchanges between science fiction and social reality across what Gibson has called the "membrane of probability" seem particularly intense.

Section 1 (Gender, Technology, and the Body) points to the centrality of both gender and human/machine interface in the technological imagination and also to ways that sf has helped to make issues of embodiment and gender visible in technoculture. Balsamo, for example, points to the importance not only of encouraging more women to enter into the science, technology, engineering, and mathematics (STEM) disciplines, a recent topic of considerable debate in education policy, but also uses metaphors drawn from sf to illuminate this issue. Describing science as a territory that women need to "colonize," she quickly turns self-reflexive about the imperialist logic of this metaphor and reverses it, to suggest that women are in fact the overlooked indigenes rather than the potential colonizers of the land of science: "When surveying this territory, most people simply don't see the women who have been there, and are still there" (80). This phrasing, intentionally or not, will remind the science fiction reader of James Tiptree's feminist sf story "The Women Men Don't See" (1973), about two women who prefer to venture into the unknown with alien anthropologists rather than continue to be devalued by patriarchy on earth. Tiptree is herself an unseen woman – the name a pseudonym used by Alice Sheldon – and her work frequently interrogates the ways that patriarchal culture devalues or erases the contributions of women and, like much other feminist sf, imagines how cultures might be different were women able to live outside of patriarchal shaping. The sf reference, then, adds concrete specificity and weight to Balsamo's argument that addressing the problem of women in the STEM disciplines requires wholesale rethinking and cultural revision instead of simply just adding women to existing structures: a robust understanding of gender requires us to recognize that the cultures themselves would be different had they emerged from equitable gender arrangements – a vision that sf can bring to life.

Other selections in this section and elsewhere in the volume make clear how integral gender is to shaping our ideas about embodiment, human-machine interface, and the technological imagination, from Rosi Braidotti's arguments about the becoming-woman posthumanism of David Cronenberg's films; to Friedrich Kittler's careful tracing of the gendered implications of how text is produced mechanically and otherwise; to Colin Milburn's ethnographic interrogation of "the intensely gendered discourse surrounding *Crysis* [a video game]", which reveals "the stakes and the standards of militarized masculinity in contemporary technoculture" (151). The 2014 Gamergate controversy about sexism in video game culture shows that the consequences of these speculative imaginations are very material: in this incident both female employees within the industry and female journalists and academics seeking to comment on it were the subject of aggressive and misogynist harassment in online forums, including threats of violence in the physical world. Interrogating the sf imagination and how it shapes our engagement with technology is thus deeply political cultural work.

Section 2 (The Science-Fictionalization of Everyday Life) explores practices of military, medical, and information technology (IT) culture to consider the ways such practices are deeply shaped by the sf imagination and to demonstrate that perspectives developed within sf have now become tools for cultural politics as a whole. One of the key recurring images is the future of the human with the technological, whether this be the delegation of decision making from human to software explored by De Landa, the super-soldier augmentation programs analyzed by Milburn, or the transformation of the human body into a source of "spare parts" in the construction of the brain-dead patient to facilitate organ transplantation, as explored by Susan Squier. Perhaps it is Jussi Parikka's contribution on the critical work of artistic collectives such as Dead Media Lab that most strikingly makes visible the fact that science fiction not only informs and reflects contemporary scientific cultures, but is also itself doing a kind of critical cultural work in dialogue with this science. Dead Media Lab "is also a social laboratory for those practices that engage both in thinking about future green information technologies and in promoting community engagement in DIY methods that are inventive everyday reuses and appropriations of the art methods of the early twentieth-century avant-garde" (167), a description that sounds like nothing so much as like a work of ecological science fiction, such as the collection *Future Primitive* (1997) edited by Kim Stanley Robinson. Although its stories do not focus on media technologies exclusively, they are informed by this same do-it-yourself (DIY) and transformative ethos of repurposing existing technologies toward creating more sustainable futures. Similarly, Henry Jenkins's work in Section 3 demonstrates how the cultural poaching techniques developed in sf fandom have become part of a new media practice of "actively shaping the flow of media" (227) through transmedia storytelling and activist resistance to cultural IP.

Section 3 (Media, Mediation, Science Fiction) builds on my contention that media sf, and especially film, is one of the places where we can most strongly see this convergence of science fiction, the technological imagination, and the critical perspectives of cultural theory. Baudrillard argues, contra Marshall McLuhan, that "the media are no longer the extensions of man; man has instead become an extension of them" (262), and both Annette Michelson and Vivian Sobchack in Section 1 explore ways that the cinema extends and transforms its viewers. The unusual visual and perspectival possibilities embodied by the zero-gravity effects sequences for *2001: A Space Odyssey*, Michelson suggests, not only create the alternative world in which the film is set but also transform the entire cinematic viewing experience, such that "viewing becomes, as always but as never before, the discovery, through the acknowledgement of disorientation, of what it is to see, to learn, to know, and of what it is to be, seeing" (20). Thus, the science fictionalization of cinema foregrounds the experience of cinematic mediation overall, echoing arguments Gunning makes about the early, prenarrative cinematic attractions that have come to seem very science fictional, establishing "cinema less as a way of telling stories than as a way of presenting a series of views to an audience, fascinating because of their illusory power" (191). By combining media and sf theory, we begin to see the cinema itself as a kind of science-fictional, world-building enterprise, as a way of *thinking* about the world by *representing* the world, twisting Baudrillard's thought back around on itself to become a science-fictional media reflexivity about how to live in such hyperreal times.

Section 4 (Posthumanisms) is where the recent convergence of perspectives drawn from science fiction with those found in recent cultural theory is most evident. In the early 1990s, when discourses of posthumanism first began to emerge, perspectives that questioned the philosophical legacies of humanism – work by scholars such as Donna Haraway, Rosi Braidotti, and more recently Gary Wolfe – were frequently not distinguished from musings we now call transhumanist, advocated by groups such as Humanity+ and the 2045 Initiative, that seek ways to instantiate the new stage of human evolution and move the species beyond mere human embodiment, whether by unloading our minds into machines or by transforming our bodies via genetic engineering. Images drawn from sf figured centrally in early discussions of posthumanism, so much so that Donna Haraway's ironically playful cyborg – which deconstructs human/animal, machine/organism, and material/virtual binaries – was frequently mistaken for Arnold Schwarzenegger's Terminator, so much so that the political thrust of Haraway's ironic myth often disappeared from view. Similarly, although N. Katherine Hayles rejected the fantasy of mind uploading in her influential *How We Became Posthuman*, her extensive engagement with posthumanism as modified embodiment cemented in the popular imagination a vision of the posthuman as primarily an sf creature.

More recently posthumanism has been theorized in more abstract ways, imagining thought and language past the discourse of humanism and indeed striving to imagine it post- anthropocentrism tout court. Posthumanism has become such a central critical framework that we might begin to think of its influence as on par with the linguistic turn of poststructuralism in the 1970s. The essays represented here show how central sf has been to the emergence and development of this critical framework, and seek to restore a stronger sense of complexity and nuance to how we conceive of sf's relationship to this field. Although posthumanism is evident in cultures far beyond sf and its technological imagination, the genre's long history of engaging with such concepts demands that we do not overlook its contributions or reduce them to mere icons such as Terminators or artificial intelligences (AIs).

Science fiction as vernacular theory

These various reflections on the centrality of the technological imagination to contemporary life – and the centrality of science fiction to the technological imagination – reveal the main organizational premise of this volume: we should understand science fiction as a kind of vernacular theory of the present moment. Again and again the essays collected here treat sf as theory or write theory as a kind of sf, some of them written in dialogue with the genre and some of them merely demonstrating through their sf qualities the convergence of science fiction and cultural theory. Like the interdisciplinary field of Science and Technology Studies (STS), from which many of these essays are drawn, sf is interested in the contingent history of technology, in the myriad ways that technology and culture shape and transform one another, in the normative ideas (about humanity, about nature) that are both reinforced and resisted by discourses of science and technology. Both sf and cultural theory allow us to see connections and contradictions, points of convergence and tension, in the technological imagination and in material practice. Bringing these essays together in one volume allows us to appreciate, via a pattern of repetition, how much sf has been and can be a practice of cultural theory.

The most famous and obvious example of this is Donna Haraway's "A Cyborg Manifesto" (see Section 4), which proclaims "the boundary between science fiction and social reality is an optical illusion" (237). An innovator of the kind of critical work showcased in this volume, Haraway reads feminist sf as an example of cultural theory about "the power to signify" (244), reminding us that "the machine is not an *it* to be animated, worshipped, and dominated. The machine is us, our processes, an aspect of our embodiment. We can be responsible for machines; *they* do not dominate or threaten us. We are responsible for boundaries; we are they" (245). We are they. We build the world of our technocultural, social reality in part through the science fictions we create, the values they embody, and the futures they strive to materialize. We find echoes of Haraway's manifesto in Rosi Braidotti's call for "redrawing politically informed maps of the present" (273) through the new kinds of subjectivities sf can envision and thus the "different desiring subjects" (275) it might bring into being; in Scott Bukatman's invocation of Debord and the notion of analyzing spectacle through the language of spectacle; in Anne Balsamo's definition of design as "one set of practices whereby the world is dynamically reconfigured by specific acts" and her contention that transformative design needs interdisciplinary teamwork including contributions by artists; in Vivian Sobchack's exploration of the phenomenology of cinema and its depiction of magically transformed bodies, an experience that blurs reality and representation because "insofar as we subjectively live both our bodies and our images, each not only informs the other, but they also become significantly confused" (56); in Susan Squier's reading of sf as a kind of ideological immunosuppressive drug central to "bringing about public acceptance of organ transplant technology" (111).

More importantly, Haraway does not merely take note of this "optical illusion" separating reality from science fiction, but she takes it as a call for us to recognize our power to create social reality, to do so responsibly and through politics of affinity and social justice. We do this by embracing new kinds of subjects and political agents that sf can narrate into being; through the cultural politics of poaching and remix that emerged from sf fan practice and are now central to engagements with the political economy of contemporary culture; and through the liberation of affect made possible by the wonder of the sf imagination, a "popular energy" that Tom Gunning associates with early, nonnarrative cinema and other spectacles and which, he argues, some artists sought to organize "for radical purpose" (193). Michelle Pierson sees a trace of the kind of spectacularly driven affect in the computer-generated imaging (CGI) and sf aesthetic she calls "technofuturist," which quickly moved beyond sf to become a cultural dominant; her work builds on Garrett Stewart's central insight that the future as depicted in sf film is often about the future of film itself, pioneering the visual effects that will soon become the cultural norm. Yet Stewart, like Gunning, draws our attention to the critical potential of such depictions of wonder, to the way that sf often makes the human, as seen through alien eyes, the object of the gaze. Thus, he wonders: "Is it not perhaps the essence of science fiction as a genre to show us new views of ourselves under duress from the extraordinary?" (183).

This collection of essays that highlights the convergences of science fiction and cultural theory aims to show us new versions of ourselves – the "us" of sf scholars and the "us" of cultural critics; to show us how "we," on either side of this divide, are engaged in parallel projects; to provide a resource for the study of science fiction, especially media sf; and to make the claim that knowledge of and engagement with sf is important to cultural theory, particularly posthumanism and the study of digital cultures, perspectives long central to the genre. Finally this volume is to remind us, in Haraway's phrase, that "we are they," that the technocultural futures we build are contingent on the technological imagination we nurture: "we" are Gibson's photographer, crossing the membrane into the technocultural visions of times past, but "we" are also, to a degree, the inhabitants of the gleaming city, its values persisting in the technocultural objects, products of this history, that shape our quotidian experience, as many of the essays in this volume demonstrate. Thus, this collection of "the sf of theory" is our guidebook to our science-fictional present, a tool to help us to understand our past and to design the futures we want.

Note

1   And thus it is not surprising that the recent *Tomorrowland* (2015) is propelled precisely by this difficulty of imagining a hopeful future, a struggle dramatically revealed in the opening and meta-filmic frame that contrasts Frank (George Clooney) and the Space Age optimism of his 1960s childhood with the ubiquitous bleak message that shapes the twenty-first century curriculum for Casey (Brit Robertson). Although the film is overtly about rediscovering the power of optimism to make a better future, it depicts not only the bleakness of the present but the ruins of Space Age Tomorrowland turned into totalitarian ruin, and thus visually reinforces the message that we can no longer imagine the future as a space of hope.

Works Cited

Csicsery-Ronay, Istvan. "The SF of Theory: Baudrillard and Haraway." *Science Fiction Studies* 18.3 (1991): 387–404.

Dick, Philip K. "Second Variety." *Space Science Fiction* 1.6 (May 1953): 103–144.

———. "Autofac." *Galaxy* 11.2 (November 1955): 70–95.

Freedman, Carl. *Critical Theory and Science Fiction*. Middletown, CT: Wesleyan University Press, 2000.

Gernsback, Hugo. "A New Sort of Magazine." *Amazing Stories* 1.1 (April 1926): 3.

Gibson, William. "The Gernsback Continuum." *Burning Chrome*. New York: Ace Books, 1987: 23–35.

Hayles, N. Katherine. *How We Became Posthuman: Virtual Bodies in Cybernetics, Literature and Informatics*. Chicago: University of Chicago Press, 1999.

Huntington, John. *Rationalizing Genius: Ideological Strategies in the American Science Fiction Short Story*. New Brunswick, NJ: Rutgers University Press, 1989.

Jameson, Fredric. "Progress versus Utopia; Or, Can We Imagine the Future?" *Science Fiction Studies* 9.2 (July 1982): 147–158.

———. *Archaeologies of the Future: The Desire Called Utopia and Other Science Fictions*. London: Verso, 2007.

Luckhurst, Roger. *Science Fiction*. London: Polity, 2005.

Rieder, John. *Colonialism and the Emergence of Science Fiction*. Middletown, CT: Wesleyan University Press, 2008.

Robinson, Kim Stanley. *Future Primitive: The New Ecotopias*. New York: TOR, 1997.

Suvin, Darko. *Metamorphoses of Science Fiction: On the Poetics and History of a Literary Genre*. New Haven, CT: Yale University Press, 1977.

Tiptree, James T. "The Women Men Don't See." *The Magazine Fantasy and Science Fiction* (December 1973): 4–29.

Wolfe, Gary. *Evaporating Genres: Essays on Fantastic Literature*. Middletown, CT: Wesleyan University Press, 2011.

SECTION 1

Gender, technology and the body

The fusion of human bodies with technology is perhaps the most obvious site of convergence between science fiction and contemporary cultural theory. As the entries in this section demonstrate, sf helps to interrogate and thematize the ways that our bodies and subjectivities are changed by a changing technology and to explore the ways that technology itself has become gendered – and gendering – in our cultural imagination.

Annette Michelson's work on the phenomenology of watching *2001: A Space Odyssey* was an influential document in the development of sf film criticism, taken up – as Section 3 demonstrates – by a number of other scholars who were beginning to develop a vocabulary for speaking about the particular aesthetics of sf film. It has not received the recent critical attention it deserves largely because it has not been reprinted until now. Michelson compellingly argues that the effects in the film work so pervasively on our perceptions as to constitute "the *relocation of the terrain upon which things happen*" (22), making the experience of watching this sf film also phenomenological, an experience of being in a science-fictional world. This essay not only anticipates the centrality of effects to cinema, and thus the central role of sf film in pushing the entire media in new directions – an argument we will see developed by other theorists in Section 3 – but it also enables us to understand this viewing experience as a fusion of human-embodied perception with the world on the screen. Thus, Michelson's notion of the "carnal knowledge" of film shares with posthumanist theory a concern with questioning how interacting with technology shapes the nature of human being. Michelson suggests that the kind of knowledge we gain from cinematic viewing, a carnal knowledge of embodied experience, emerges from a specific relationship to the object of knowledge. Thus, sf cinema begins to make us technocultural subjects.

Friedrich Kittler is an important media theorist whose work is not often associated with science fiction. Nonetheless, his interest in how media of communication shape and change the nature of what can be communicated shows obvious affinities with sf perspectives. Gill Partington's "Friedrich Kittler's *aufschriebsystem*," published in the *Science Fiction Studies* special issue on Technoculture (March 2006) and edited by Roger Luckhurst, makes such parallels between Kittler's theory and sf imagining clear.[1] This excerpt, taken from Kittler's *Gramophone, Film, Typewriter* (1999; original German publication 1986), traces the way new technologies for recording and transmitting information changed the style and cultural meanings attached to writing itself.

He is attentive to gendered differences, noting, for example, that an increased need for speedy transcription that emerged with technologies such as the telegraph contributed to a shift in the gender of secretarial staff. In the era of male clerks, a meticulous aesthetics of handwriting structured the profession; as speed became an important criterion, women proved more suited to this new demand, although it was "precisely their marginal position in the power system of script that forced women to develop their manual dexterity" (32). The excerpt here shows how the subject who writes – the "I" that might speak in script – shifts as we move from composing by hand to typewriter to computer, opening the door to shift from "from a register of data to a register of persons or even their self-registration" (40). Thus Kittler, too, reveals a kind of sf identity that emerges from our interactions with machines and mediating technologies.

Barbara Creed's essay has become foundational to the reading of Ridley Scott's film *Alien* (1979) and to our understanding of the gender dynamics of this sf film, which is often celebrated for its portrayal of a strong female protagonist. As Creed reveals through her analysis of all elements of gender in the film, including the gendering of the alien antagonist and the gendered connotations of how technology is represented, the film is ambivalent about female empowerment. Later work on posthumanist theory, such as N. Katherine Hayles's discussion of Bernard Wolfe's *Limbo* in Section 4, shows the continuing importance of psychoanalytic frameworks for understanding our affective relationship with technology.

The following selection by Vivian Sobchack combines this insight into the representation of monstrous femininity with the perspectives on phenomenology of cinema explored by Michelson's and Kittler's insights on how mediating technologies change the humans who use them. Reading the "special effects" of cosmetic surgery in conjunction with the special effects of film, Sobchack finds a continuity between science fiction's monstrous women – the female alien analyzed by Creed being one example among many – and the demonization of aging women in our culture at large. Thus, Sobchack reveals, our attraction to the spectacle of sf effects has a gendered element as well, linked to how we want the effect to be simultaneously invisible (that is, seamlessly integrated into the "real") and hypervisible (that is, pointing to the wonder of a technology that could achieve such effects). Sobchack's insightful work demonstrates how this dynamic is particularly intense for female viewers who imagine their own bodies as the object of such technological intervention, and how too much acknowledgement of the work entailed in achieving this illusion "might curb our desire, despoil our wonder, and generate fear of pain and death" (63).

Steven Shaviro continues this exploration of how material and virtual experiences blur into one another in what he calls networked society in an excerpt from his series of short meditations on science fiction as theory collected in *Connected, or What it Means to Live in Network Society* (2003). Focusing in particular on the ways that the economy has created physical and virtual worlds as "two coordinated realms, mutually dependent products of a vast web of social, political, economic, and technological changes" (72), he examines the posthuman future presented in Warren Ellis's *Transmetropolitan* comic book series to show us how science fiction can help us see our technocultural reality in new ways. Neither representing the present nor predicting the future, sf is about their interdependent relationship, "about the shadow that the future casts upon the present" (75).

Section 1 closes with an excerpt from Anne Balsamo's recent *Designing Culture* (2011), which theorizes technologies as objects of practice – "assemblages of people, materialities, practices, and possibilities" (79) – and sees their design as a kind of world-building practice. Overall her work is particularly concerned with recognizing and fostering women's contributions to technoculture, and in the excerpt included here she argues for the transformative effect that women's perspectives would have on the mutual construction of technology and subjects. Balsamo more directly addressed science fiction in her earlier *Technologies of the Gendered Body* (1995), but here too her work might be understood as engaging in a kind of science fictional practice along the lines of Shaviro's method. "The purpose of theory is to inspire us to ask more incisive questions about the phenomena that terrify and fascinate us," Balsamo contends, and "the purpose of criticism is to illuminate the complexity of the phenomena in such a way that others are provoked to formulate their own theoretical understandings, accounts, and questions" (84). I can think of no more apt an explanation of how science fiction is a kind of theory or better prompt for expanding our technocultural criticism about the genre.

Note

1   The full text of this essay is available online at www.depauw.edu/sfs/backissues/98/partington98.html.

Arrival: From George Meliès' *Trip to the Moon*, 1905.

BODIES IN SPACE

The layout of this chapter reflects that of original printing, as required by reprint permission.

ANNETTE MICHELSON

I

All mastery casts a chill.
—Mallarmé

The indefinable, knowing fear which is the clearest intimation of the metaphysical.
—Borges

In the winter of 1905 the first continuously operated movie theater opened in Los Angeles. There is an obvious sense in which the history of film is circumscribed by the feature of that theatre's initial program, George Méliès *Trip to the Moon*, and Stanley Kubrick's *2001:*

A Space Odyssey. There is another sense in which its evolution hypostatizes the accelerating dynamics of History. Walking the three blocks between the Museum of Modern Art's screening room and the Loew's Capitol, thinking of that evolution, one finds oneself tracing a vector, exploring, in implication, as one goes, a multi-dimensional movement of human consciousness in our century.

In 1961, the year of Méliès' centenary, the Cinémathèque Française and the Union Centrale des Arts Décoratifs presented in the Louvre a commemorative exhibition still present to me as one of the finest I have seen. One wandered through the reconstitution of a life-work prodigious in its inventive abundance as through a forest alive with apparitions and metamorphoses, stopping all

Departure: From George Meliès *Trip to the Moon*, 1905.

at once, however, as before a clearing, arrested as by a shaft of light, the illumination flaring from a photograph upon the wall.

Greatly enlarged, it showed the Méliès Company in action.[1] The Company had been, of course, a family

Film as "Carnal Knowledge"

affair, its production something of a "cottage industry," and one saw it here in operation on one of the artfully designed and fastidiously executed sets which were a point of honor and pride for an indefatigable Master Builder. The photograph gave one pause.

It gives us a behind-the-scene view, shows not the action being filmed, but its reverse side, the flats of its set anchored, here and there, in the manner of theatrical décor, to the ground. Men – gentlemen, formally dressed and hatted – stand about, supporting those flats, ready to catch them should the screws fail and they fall. The image is, of course, "moving" because it restores to us the feeling of the primitive, the home-made and artisanal modesty, the fragile and precarious underpinnings of a grandiose venture. It articulates, as well, the manner in which film first made its entrance, through the stage door (*l'entrée des artistes*), and

something of the homely mechanics, the dialectic at work in the fabrication of illusion itself, its re-invention for us. It illustrates the manner in which the artisan, the bourgeois family man, the *bricoleur*, prestidigitator and entrepreneur fused in a single figure of genius to engender the art of cinema as we know it.

The 19th century had been dreaming of movies, as all its forms of popular narrative and diversion (photographic album, panoramic view, magic lantern, shadow play, wax museum and the novel itself) conspire to testify, and Méliès' intrepid talent, a synthesis of the imagination and industry which were subsequently to be reified into the opposing terms of the new form's dialectic, fused these dreams into something real. If Lumière had been the first cinematographer, Méliès was the first of the *réalisateurs*, as distinct from the *metteurs-en-scene*; he *realized* the cinema itself.

Seeing Kubrick's *Space Odyssey*, we sense, we know, that its ontogeny recapitulates a philogeny.[2] The very conditions of its making involved the scale of enterprise, the dedicated resolution and intellectual flexibility, the proud marshalling of vast resources brought to bear upon the most sophisticated and ambitious ventures of our culture. Its making required, indeed, a length and complexity of preparation, a breadth of conception and detail of organization analogous only to those invested in the launching of a new regime, a new inter-continental missile system, a fresh episode in the exploration of space. And its appearance has, in fact, generated the same sort of apprehension of "cultural shock" which Arthur C. Clarke describes, in his novelistic rendering of the screenplay, as the reaction to the invention of "the highly advanced HAL 900 [*sic*]

Computer, the brain and nervous system" of the narrative's "vehicle," the space-ship *Discovery*.

Like that black monolith whose unheralded materialization propels the evolution of consciousness through the three panels of the movie's narrative triptych, Kubrick's film has assumed the disquieting function of Epiphany. It functions as a disturbing structure, emitting, in its intensity of presence and perfection of surface, sets of signals. That intensity and perfection are contingent upon a conspicuous invisibility of *facture* commanded by the power of a rigorously conceptual imagination, disposing of vast amounts of money. Those signals, received by a bewildered and apprehensive community (tribe? species?) of critics, have propelled them, all unwilling, into a chorus of dismay, a choreography of vacillation, of approach, and recoil, to and from the "object." We know that song and dance; they are the old, familiar projection of a crisis in criticism. And still the "object" lures us on. Another level or "universe" of discourse awaits us.

We are dealing, then, with a work which is revelatory, a "breakthrough," one whose substance and function fuse in the synthetic radicalization of its metaphors. It is precisely because form and surface command the most immediate and complex intensity of physical response that they release a wild energy of speculation, confirming, even as they modify, the character and options of the medium. In that oscillating movement between confirmation and transformation, the film as a whole performs the function of a Primary Structure, forcing the spectator back, in a reflexive gesture, upon the analytic rehearsal of his experience, impelling, as it does so, the conviction that here is a film like any other, like all others, only more so – which is to say, a paradigm, unique. (If one were concerned with an "ontology" of cinema, this film could be a place in which to look for it.) The margin of difference-in-similarity which contains or defines its "edge" over other films is the locus of its poetry.

The play of an inspired primate ("Moonwatcher" is Clarke's name for him) ending the Prologue of this film, issues in the visionary realization which

transforms a bone into a weapon, then flings it in a gesture of apperceptive exultation, high into the vacant air. Méliès' extraordinary intuition, realizing (inventing) the possibilities of the medium, created out of forms and materials that lay to hand, a new instrument of the imagination, an agent of power and delight, launching his cinema in confident optimism out into an unsuspecting world.

Kubrick's transformation of bone into spacecraft through the movement of redescent (through that single cut which concludes the Prologue and initiates the Odyssey) inscribes, within the most spectacular ellipsis in cinematic history, nothing less than the entire trajectory of human history, the birth and evolution of intelligence. Seizing appropriating the theme of spatial exploration as narrative metaphor and formal principle, he has projected intellectual adventure as spectacle, converting, through still another leap of the imagination, Méliès' pristine fantasy to the form and uses of a complex and supremely sophisticated structure.

Moving, falling toward us with the steady and purposive elegance of an incomparably powerful "vehicle," Kubrick's masterwork is designed, in turn, as an instrument of exploration and discovery. *A Space Odyssey* is, in fact, in the sustained concreteness and formal refinement which render that design, precisely that which Ortega believed modern poetry to have become: a "higher algebra of metaphors."

II

The object in motion moves neither in the space in which it is nor in that in which it is not.
—Zeno

The present hath no space. Where then is the time which we may call long?
—Saint Augustine

In a letter, undated but probably of 1894, Pierre Louÿs calls upon Debussy, about to embark upon the career of

The frustration or inversion of expectations, impelling us to a compensatory movement of reversal clarifying for us the nature of motion itself.

Fernand Leger, *Ballet Mécanique*, 1924.

music critic which produced the brilliant and insolent persona of "Monsieur Croche, Anti-Dilettante," to "do something" to cure the malady of contemporary criticism. Complaining that "one cannot strike a single chord these days without eliciting a flurry of metaphysical speculation," he says that *Lohengrin*, after all is a work "about movement." "It is about a man who arrives and departs," and nothing else. Or, as Valéry was shortly to say, "The true connoisseur of this art is necessarily the person to whom it suggests nothing."

Like all statements of this kind, these strictures suggest a critical strategy rather than an esthetic, a working hypothesis formulated in terms of a particular historical situation, a re-orientation of critical concern in the interests of immediate usefulness and interest. Like Fénéon's descriptive criticism of painting, like Mallarmé's assertion, to Degas, that "poetry is made with words rather than with ideas," like Robbe-Grillet's attack on Metaphor, Stravinsky's rejection of musical "content" or "subject," and Artaud's indictment of theatrical text, they propose a therapy for an intellectual tradition in which, as in that of our current film criticism, an endemic and debilitating Idealism perpetuates exhausted critical categories. Reductive, double-edged, polemically inflected, they urge a closer, fresher, more innocent and comprehending view of the Object, a respect for form and physicality as the ground of interest and value.

Like *Lohengrin*, *Space Odyssey* is, of course, endlessly suggestive, projects a syncretic heritage of myths, fantasies, cosmologies and aspirations. Everything about it is interesting; it proposes, however, nothing of more radical interest than its own physicality, its "formal statement" on the nature of movement in its space; it "suggests" nothing so urgent and absorbing as an evidence of the senses, its discourse on knowledge through perception as action, and ultimately, on the nature of the medium as "action film," as mode and model of cognition.

Reading the critical or journalistic reproaches (and defences) addressed to this film's supposedly "static quality," its "plotless" structure in which "nothing happens," one recalls the myths which dominated a half-century or so of theatrical criticism's uncomprehending view of Chekov, as of Wagner. In this *Odyssey* incident, surprise, discovery, shock and violence abound. Its plot turns, in fact, upon *intrigue*, as the French define

plot. And, like a "scenario" (the term adopted by contemporary technocrats such as Herman Kahn for their hypothetical projections of our future), its structure is "open." Like *Lohengrin* and *Uncle Vanya*, above all, however, this work is about "arrival and departure," about movement. Its narrative, a voyage of discovery, a progress towards disembodiment, explores, through a multi-level tactics of displacement, through a constant and intensive re-invention of the possibilities of cinematic immediacy, the structural potentialities of haptic disorientation as agent of cognition.

Navigation – of a vessel or human body – through a space in which gravitational pull is suspended, introduces heightened pleasures and problems, the intensification of erotic liberation and of the difficulty of purposeful activity. In that floating freedom, all directed and purposive movement becomes work, the simplest task an exploit. The new freedom poses for the mind, in and through the body, the problematic implications of all freedom, forcing the body's recognition of its suspended coördinates as its necessity. The dialectic of pleasure and performance principles, projected through camera's radical re-structuring of environment, the creation of ranges of change in light, scale, pace, heighten, to the point of transformation, the very condition of film experience. Viewing becomes, as always but as never before, the discovery, through the acknowledgement of disorientation, of what it is to see, to learn, to know, and of what it is to be, seeing. Once the theatre seat has been transformed into a vessel, opening out onto and through the curve of a helmet to that of the screen as into the curvature of space, one rediscovers, through the shock of recognition, one's own body living in *its* space. One feels suspended, the mind not quite able to "touch ground." One surveys that familiar ground of experience (as the astronauts have indicated, remarking that a prime reason for space flight lay in the rediscovery and organization of the *earth's* resources), feeling the full meaning of "suspense" as anticipation, *sensing* that though things may possibly be the same again, they will, thanks to

Kubrick, never be the same *in quite the same way.*

If, then *Space Odyssey* proposes, as in Bergson's view all works of art do, "the outline of a movement," it is, as well what Elie Faure claimed all *film* to be: "an architecture of movement." As a film which takes for its very subject, theme and dynamics – both narrative and formal – movement itself, it has a radical, triple interest and urgency, a privileged status in the art that is ours, modern.

III

Form is tinted with meaning.
—Quintilian, after Zeno

The secret of the true artist consists in the following: he effaces nature through form.
—Schiller

There is a moment – that present moment which extends a century back into the past – in which the entire system of presuppositions governing the artist's view of subject, content and theme is undermined. That moment initiates in the radical questioning of art as mimesis. It produces a shift or displacement of the artist's aspiration. The movement of displacement is by no means steady or uncontested, as the entirely problematic esthetic implicit in Expressionism (it is, after all, neither school nor style, but the name we give to sixty years of polymorphic contestation) insistently reminds us. In that shift, the culmination of a crisis sustained since the 17th century through philosophy, the authority of the imagination moves to replace that of a transcendence animating the esthetic of transcription or expression. Sustained through the radical art of our century, the shift is pre-figured in Flaubert's celebrated letter of January, 1852, to Louise Colet: "What I consider fine, what I should like to do is a book about nothing, a book without external attachments of any sort, which would hold of itself, through the inner strength of its style, as the earth sustains itself with no support in air, a book with almost no subject. Or at least an almost invisible subject, if possible."

This aspiration toward a work of total autonomy, self-referring, self-sustaining, and self-justifying, required the invention of a mediating strategy, a transition. The subject could be eliminated only through a process of dissolution initiated by its re-definition. Therefore, Flaubert's subsequent affirmation, in a letter dated one year later: "Since poetry is purely subjective, there is no such thing as a fine subject. Yvetôt and Constantinople are of equal value. One can write equally well abut anything at all. It is the artist who elevates things (through his manner of writing)." (The manner in and degree to which the history of pictorial and sculptural modernisms confirms and embodies this position requires no immediate development in this particular journal.)

It is, however, at precisely that moment which instigates the dissolution of the subject, a process crystallized and extended through Mallarmé and Cézanne into the art of our own day, it is when the painter, rendering "seeing rather than things seen," takes painting as his subject, when the novelist commences the relating of "narrativity" itself, that art's aspiration shifts, expands, intensifies, tending, as in a movement of compensation, towards the most radical and all-encompassing of possible functions. Poetry, consenting through Mallarmé to be poetry only, proposes, simultaneously, to become "the orphic explanation of the earth," of a "world meant," moreover, "to end in a book." The dissolution of the subject or figure, the contestation of art as Mimesis, of Realism itself, is grounded in the problematic consciousness of a reality no longer assumed as pre-defined or pre-existent to the work of the imagination. Art now takes the nature of reality, the nature of consciousness in and through perception, as its subject or domain. As exploration of the conditions and terms of perception, art henceforth converges with philosophy and science upon the problem of reality as known and knowable.

Thus, the very ambiguity of Kandinsky's title for his esthetic treatise, *Towards the Spiritual in Art* – translatable, too, from the German as *Towards the Intellectual in Art* – defines with great precision the nature and locus of the shift. Its ambiguity spells out the problems involved in the relocation, through abstraction, of sources of authority, interest and inspiration, which had been dislodged by the crisis in the Western metaphysical tradition. Text and title re-enact, in their ambivalence and contractions, that crisis; their celebrated "confusion" has the clarity of a syndrome, a syndrome converted into an esthetics bequeathed to us, somewhat in the manner of an hereditary taint or talent, in the sensibility of "Abstract Expressionism."

That movement towards abstraction which animates the style and esthetics of modernism posed for every art form, the problem of what Ortega calls "the incompatibility of the perception of lived reality with the perception of artistic form," in so far as "they call for different adjustments of our perceptive apparatus." "An art that requires such a double seeing is a squinting art. The 19th century was cross-eyed . . ." [ellipses in original]. Ortega, speaking with a certain crudeness symptomatic of ambivalence, spoke far truer than he knew.

Surely that statement is nowhere more significant than in its central omission. It stops just short of the recognition that the 19th century ended in producing the cinema, the art form whose temporality created another space in which "lived reality" could once again be figured, restructured. Cinema is the temporal instrument working in a direction counter to that of modernist painting's increasingly shallow space, through which the deep space of illusionism is reinvented. In assuming the burden of illusionism, cinema reintroduces not only "lived reality," but an entirely new and seemingly limitless range of structural relationships allowing for the reconciliation of "lived reality" with "artistic form." In order to do so, of course, film not only rehabilitated the "squint," but elevated it to the status of a dynamics of creation and perception, installed it as the very central principle of an art form, the source of its power and refinement.

Film's relation to modernism is, consequently, delicate and complex in the extreme, and the demands it makes

upon its audience have a strenuousness directly proportionate to that complexity and delicacy, contingent upon its illusionistic immediacy. Its fullest experience demands a kind of critical athleticism.

As all who care more than casually for movies know, the point at which one begins to understand the nature of the medium comes when one sees the images before one, not as a sequence of events evolving past or within the limits of a frame, but rather as a structure organized in depth and in relation to the frame by the camera itself. The heightened experience of film henceforth involves the constant oscillation between the two "points of view," the constant "adjustment of the perceptive apparatus" in an activity of experience. The trajectory of both narrative and of camera lens as the extension of the eye and will of the artist begins to describe itself for us when we see, as in the scene of the poisoning of the Czarina in *Ivan The Terrible*, that the slow and devious

passage of a goblet through a room is the propulsion, to its destined victim, by design dissembled as chance, through a camera movement, the movement of History. Film's narrative now acquires the dimension of style, as the structural and sensuous incarnation of the artist's will.

One follows, in another celebrated instance, the trolley car ride of Murnau's *Sunrise, moved* to pity by the protagonist's agony of anguish and shame, *borne along*, from a country to a city landscape, *carried away*, as they emerge from an extremity of alienation into reconciliation as into the New Jerusalem, and ultimately *transported* by the movement of the camera, the artist's agent, his mind's eye, defining and sustaining the space and dimensions of narrative as form.

Film proposes, then, and most sharply when it is greatest, a dissociative economy of viewing. That is why, although its "dream-like" quality received an immediate and extensive

"The Passage into Euclidian Space," through one of the finest and most sophisticated camera movements in the history of film.

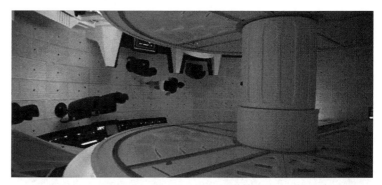

entry in the Dictionary of Received Ideas, it remains to be stressed that cinema is, more than any other art form, that which Plato claimed art in general to be: a *dream for waking minds.* The paradox testifies to the manner in which film provokes that delicate dissociation, that *contraposto* of the mind, that constantly renewed tension and readjustment whose symptom is, indeed, Ortega's "squint."

If this distance, the alienation of the spectator with respect to his experience, reflecting the elevation of doubt to an esthetic principle, may be said to characterize modernist sensibility as a whole, determining, in fact, the intensity of its very longing for immediacy, then film's conversion of that principle to the uses of a formal dynamics gives it a privileged place as a medium centrally involved with the cognitive aspiration of modern art. The dissociative economy of film viewing heightens our perception of being physical to the level of apperception: one becomes conscious of the modes of consciousness. The athleticism required of the spectator is contingent on the manner in which film reflects or returns that which is brought to it. Like all esthetic situations, it offers – quite beyond the luxury of identification – the occasion to gain awareness of the inner presuppositions that sustain us, so that pleasure is informed with the shock of recognition.

A Space Odyssey, that film of "special effects" in which "nothing happens," is simply one which, in its extremity of stylistic formal coherence and richness, its totally reinvented environment, quite dissolves the very notion of the "special effect," They disappear. Above all, however, it solicits, in its overwhelming immediacy, the *relocation of the terrain upon which things happen.* And they happen, ultimately, not only on the screen but somewhere between screen and spectator. It is the area defined and constantly traversed by our active restructuring and reconstitution, through an experience of "outer" space, of the "inner" space of the body. Kubrick's film, its action generating a kind of cross-current of perception and cognitive restructuring, visibly reaches, as it were, for another arena, redefining

the content of cinema, its "shape of content." The subject and theme of *A Space Odyssey* emerge, then, as neither social nor metaphysical; they develop elsewhere, between, in a genetic epistemology.

IV

My mobility is the way in which I counterbalance the mobility of things, thereby understanding and surmounting it. All perception is movement. And the world's unity, the perceiver's unity, are the unity of counterbalanced displacements.
—Merleau-Ponty

All things in the heaven of intelligibility are heavenly. . . . In this kingdom, all is diaphanous. Nothing is opaque or impenetrable, and light encounters light. No traveler wanders there as in a foreign land.
—Plotinus [ellipses in original]

This *Odyssey* traces, then, in its "higher algebra of metaphors," the movement of bodies in space, voyaging through spheres beyond the pulls of terrestrial attraction, in exploration of the Unknown, in and through *Discovery*.

The Voyage as narrative form acts, in its deformation or suspension of the familiar framework of existence (as in the logic of Alice, the geography of Saint Brendan, the reality of Don Quixote, the sociology of Gulliver), to project us, as in space travel, toward the surface of a distant world, its propulsive force contriving, through a Logistics of the Imagination, to redeliver us in rebound from that surface, into the familiar, the known, the Real.

So, too, the voyage of the astronauts ultimately restores us, through the heightened and complex immediacy of this film, to the space in which we dwell. This navigation of a vessel as instrument of exploration, of the human organism as adventurer, dissolves the opposition of body and mind, *bringing home* to us the manner in which "objective spatiality" is but the envelope of that "primordial spatiality," the level on which

the body itself effects the synthesis of its commitments in the world, a synthesis which is a fusion of meaning as experienced, tending toward equilibrium.

By constantly questioning that "objective spatiality," Kubrick incarnates the grand theme and subject of learning as self-recognition, of growth as the constant disruption and re-establishment of equilibrium in progress towards knowledge. This succession of re-establishments of equilibrium proposes a master metaphor for the mind at grips with reality, and we re-enact its progress through a series of disconcerting shocks which solicit our accommodation.

As soon as the airline hostess starts her movement though through the space-craft's interior, moving up the wall, around and over the ceiling, disappearing upside down into it, we get an intimation – through the shock of surprise instigated by the defiance of our gravity – of the nature of our movement in our space. The delight we take in the absurdity of her progress is the index of our heightened awareness of something fundamental in ourselves. The system of pre-suppositions sustaining our spatial sense, the coördinates of the body itself, are hereby suspended and revised. That revision and its acknowledgement constitute our passport into another space and state of being, from which our own can be observed and known.

The writing pen floating in the space-craft's cabin and retrieved by the hostess prior to her movement over wall and into ceiling had signaled to us, as it were, the passage into the weightless medium. Since, however, we define and comprehend movement – and repose – in terms of our bodily positions, through the sense of inner coördinates rather than in terms of what is merely seen, that signal could not fully prepare us for, or inform us of, the suspension of those coördinates, inevitable in the weightless environment. (And indeed, judging from the surprised laughter that has followed that second sequence in each of nine viewings of the film, it does not prepare us.) The difference between the two qualities and intensities of response is the difference between things seen and things felt, between situations visually observed and those sensed haptically, between a narrative emblem and a radically formal embodiment of, spatial logic.

A weightless world is one in which the basic coördinates of horizontality and verticality are suspended. Through that suspension the framework of our sensed and operational reality is dissolved. The consequent challenge presented to the spectator in the instantaneously perceived suspension and frustration of expectations, forces readjustment. The challenge is met almost instantaneously, and consciousness of our own physical necessity is regenerated. We snap to attention, in a new, immediate sense of our earth-bound state, in repossession of those coördinates, only to be suspended, again, toward other occasions and forms of recognition. These constitute the "sub-plot" of the Odyssey, plotting its action in us.

The extraordinary repetitive sequence of the woman climbing a staircase in Léger's *Ballet Mécanique* erases the possibility of destination or of completion of action, thereby freezing a woman in a perpetual motion of ascent. So, too, this first sequence of the air-hostess's navigation (and it is only one of an amazing series of variations upon the qualities and modes of movement) suspends us, in its frustration and inversion of our expectations, impelling us to a reflexive or compensatory movement of reversal, clarifying for us something of the essential nature of motion itself.

By distorting or suspending the logic of action as we know it (movement's completion in time, the operation of the coördinates), each sequence questions, thereby stimulating awareness of, the corporeal *a-prioris* which compose our sensory motor apparatus. Sensing after the fifth ascent or so that Léger's woman will never "arrive," we re-direct our attention, in a movement of recognition, to the fact and quality of movement as such. The recognition of paradox speaks through our laughter, arguing for that double nature of Comedy as Bergson saw it; its delight in the concrete and its unique capacity for play with ideas.

In their reduction of people moving to bodies in motion, both sequences elicit the laughter which Bergson tells

Scale and movement as the plot of Odyssey, plotting the action in us.

us is the response to that transformation or reduction of the human into the mechanical which underlies all comedy. Solicited, then, through a constantly playful succession of surprises to a re-assessment or re-structuring of the real, we see, in our surprised laughter, that here is a work which employs a very serious form of wit to teach us something of the nature of our experience.

A Space Odyssey, then, proposes, in its epistemology, the illustration of a celebrated theory of Comedy. In a film whose terrain or scene of action is, as we have seen, the spectator, the spectator becomes the hero or butt of comedy. The laugh is on us; we trip on circumstance recognizing, in a reflex of double-take, that circumstances have changed. Tending, in the moment which precedes this recognition, "to see that which is no longer visible," assuming the role of absent-minded comic hero, "taken in," we then adjust in comprehension, "taking it in." Kubrick does make Keatons of us all.

If "any incident is comic that calls our attention to the physical in a person, when it is the moral side that is concerned," *Space Odyssey* indeed provides through variation and inversion, a fascinating range of comic situations. (On quite another level, of course HAL, the computer as character, reverses the comic "embarrassment of the soul by the body" in being a mere body embarrassed by possession of a soul. A thing which gives the impression of being a person, rather than – as in silent comedy at its paroxysmic best – a person giving the impression of being a thing, "he *acts* as though he has feelings," as one astronaut remarks. Here, God help us, is someone or something who, as R.D. Laing says, "can pretend to be what he – or it – really is.")

As a film whose grand theme is that of learning, whose effect is intimately revelatory, *A Space Odyssey* is, in the strongest and deepest sense of the word, maieutic. Kubrick's imagination, exploring the possibilities of scale, movement, direction as synthesized in a style, works towards our understanding. The intensified and progressively intimate consciousness of one's physicality provides the intimation of that physicality as the ground of consciousness. The film's "action" is felt, and we are "where the action is." Its "meaning" or "sense" is sensed, and its content is the body's perceptive awaking to itself.

The briefest, most summary comparison with *Alphaville* shows Godard's film to be, as I have on another occasion suggested, a film of "dis-location," as against this new film of "dis-orientation." Godard installs the future within the landscape of present-day Paris, dislocating the spectator *in situ*, so to speak. Kubrick's suspension and distention of the properties of environment transform it into something radically new and revealing. The difference between the two films is also, of course, the difference between the strategies of *bricolage* or a "do-it-yourself" technique, brilliantly handled, and of technology. Two attitudes toward futurity are inscribed within the conditions of their making.

Alphaville's superimposition of image upon image, of word upon word, of plot upon plot, creates a complex system of visual, verbal and narrative puns within which past and future alternatively and reciprocally mask and reveal each other. Futurity inhabits things as they look now. It is installed, moreover, as a *corruption* of the here-and-now, projecting Godard's essential romanticism in a dislocation that is primarily fictional in its tactics. Figurative, one might say. In this film, Godard, like his Eurydice, looks backward in nostalgia.

In *Space Odyssey*, a total formalization imposes futurity through the eye and ear. The look and sense of things in their movement, scale, sound, pace and intensity. Unlike most other science fiction films, both unflaggingly sustain a coherent visual style. All others (from *Metropolis* through the *Buck Rogers* series to *Barbarella*) relax, about halfway through, capitulating in a relaxation of the will, a fatigue of the imagination, to the past. (It is generally a Gothic past, a style of medievalism, and these

two films are probably the only ones utterly devoid of billowing capes and Gothic arches.) The manner in which both exemplify film's pre-empting of the function, the esthetic mode, of Visionary Architecture, begun by Méliès, presents a striking contrast: Godard adopts a policy of abstinence, of invention in austerity, Kubrick a planned and prodigal expenditure of resources. (The manner in which the different economies at work – European as against American – seem to represent opposing sensibilities making fundamentally esthetic decisions, leads one to remember that Godard's Computer – a Sphinx, speaking with the re-educated voice of a man whose vocal chords have been removed – asks

questions, while Hal, that masterpiece of "the third Computer breakthrough," presumably knows all the answers.)

Kubrick's prodigality is, however, totalizing, heightens, through the complete re-invention of environment, the terms, the stylistic potential of cinematic discourse. Therefore, one's thrilled fascination with the majestic movements of the space-craft through the heavens, with the trajectories of arrival (landing), departure (levitation), seeing (sighting), conjunction (synthesis), action (gauging) through which the parameters of movement, scale, direction, intensity are examined, exploited. Suspended, totally absorbed by their momentous navigation, one remembers only days later, the

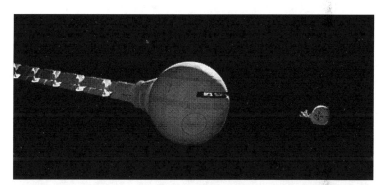

The Future as corruption of the here and now. Jean-Luc Godard, *Alphaville*, 1965.

manner in which the slow, repetitive lifting of the bridge in *Ten Days That Shook the World* shattered action, inventing, in its radically disjunctive force, another kind of cinematic time. The number and kinds of space simultaneously proposed by isometric readings and interior projections – as in the approach toward the space station or in the landing on the Moon – are fused by the spectator who discovers, with a sudden thrill of delight, that he is the meeting place of a multiplicity of spaces, depths and scales, his eye their agent of reconciliation, his body the focal point of a multi-dimensional, poly-spatial cosmos.

In the visionary catapulting through the "Star Gate," "beyond infinity," through galactic explosions of forms and sound as landscape, we zoom over a geography photographed in "negative," passing finally, as through a portal, to a scene which reveals itself to be that of the eye itself. Experience as Vision ends in the exploration of seeing. The film's reflexive strategy assumes the eye as ultimate agent of consciousness, reminding us, as every phenomenological esthetic, from that of Ortega to that of Merleau-Ponty has, that art develops from the concern with "things seen to that of seeing itself."

In a series of expansions and contractions, the film pulsates leading us, in the final sequence following the "trip," with the astronaut into a suite of rooms, decorated in Regency style. Here, every quality of particularity, every limiting, defining aspect of environment is emphasized. The sudden contraction onto these limits, projects us from galactic polymorphism into an extreme formality, insinuating, through the allusion of its décor, the idea of History into Timelessness. It shocks. Everything about the place is defined, clearly "drawn." In the definition of this room lit from beneath the floor, as in the drainage of color (everything is greenish, a bit milky, translucent, reminding one slightly of video images), we perceive the triumph of *disegno* over *colore*. An idea of a Room, it elaborates the notion of Idea and Idealism as Dwelling. (Poincaré, after all, imagined Utopia as illustrating Riesmann's topology.) It is, of course, a temporary dwelling – Man's last Motel stop on the journey towards disembodiment and renascence. Its very sounds are sharper; the clatter of glass falling to the floor informs us that glass is breaking upon glass, evoking through an excruciation of high-fidelity acoustics, something of the nature of Substance. It is this strange, Platonic intensification-through-reduction of the physical which sustains the stepping-up of time, through the astronaut's life and death, to rebirth, ejecting us with him once again, through a final contracting movement of parturition, into the heavens.

V

Structural formation, that reflective process of abstraction which draws its sustenance not from objects, but from actions performed upon them.
—Piaget

However, the fact that knowledge can be used to designate sexual intercourse . . . points to the fact that for the Hebrews, "to know" does not simply mean to be aware of the existence or nature of a particular object. Knowledge implies also the awareness of the specific relationship in which the individual stands with that object, or of the significance the object has for him.
—The Interpreter's Dictionary of the Bible [ellipses in original]

If *A Space Odyssey* illustrates, through its exercise in genetic epistemology, the manner of our acting, it provides the immediate demonstration that the ability to function in space is neither given nor predetermined, but acquired and developed.

Its re-establishment of the notion of equilibrium as open process is central. In a weightless medium, the body confronts the loss of those coördinates through which it normally functions. The manner in which all directed movement is endowed with the momentousness of the task indicates the reinvention of those coördinates for operational efficiency. Total absorption in their reinvention creates a form of motion of extraordinary unity, that of total concentration, the precondition of Style, a style we normally recognize as the quality of dance movement.

It would be interesting, then, to consider a style of movement created by the exact inversion of that negation of weight (its retrieval, in fact), which animates the Dance of our Western historical tradition. More interesting, still, perhaps, is the realization that the style created by the astronauts in movement, in the reinvention of necessity, does indeed have a special affinity with that contemporary dance which proceeds from the radical questioning of balletic movement, the redefining and rehabilitation of the limits of habitual, operational movement as an esthetic or stylistic mode.

In that questioning initiated by Cunningham, radicalized through the work of Rainer, Whitman, Paxton, and others, dance is re-thought in terms of another economy, through the systematic negation of the rhetoric and hierarchies imposed by classical balletic conventions and language. That rhetoric is, in fact, reversed, destroyed, in what has been called the "dance of ordinary language" and of "task performance." This movement of reversal – revolutionary – traversing the forms of most modernist art, works in Dance as well, toward "the dissolution of the (fine) subject."

The astronauts' movements—as in the very great sequence of the repair of the presumably malfunctioning parts—is invested with an intensity of interest (sustaining itself through every second of its repetition), a "gravity" which is that of total absorption in the operational movement (task performance) as a constant reinvention of equilibrium in the interests of functional efficiency. The stress is on the importance, "the fascination of what's difficult," which is to say, the simplest operations. They require the negation of a floating freedom. (It should have been the business of Vadim's recently released *Barbarella* to explore the erotic possibilities of the body floating free in outer space suggested by that film's superb opening credits. Unfortunately *Barbarella's* progress is entirely earthbound; the film is a triumph of iconography over form.)

The astronauts' movements, slowed by weightlessness, reinvent the conditions of their efficiency. This slowness and the majesty with which the space-craft itself moves, are predicated, of course, upon the speed of space travel itself. And the film itself moves ultimately with that momentum, that apparent absence of speed which one experiences only in the fastest of elevators, or jet planes.

The complex maneuvering of tools, craft or the mere navigation of the body involves an adjustment which constitutes an adventure, a stage in the development of the Mind. Seeing films, in general, one gains an intimation of the link between the development of sensory-motor knowledge to that of intelligence itself.

We know, through the systematic investigations which constitute the monumental life-work of Piaget that the acquisition of the basic coördinates of our spatial sense is a very gradual process, extending roughly over the first twelve years of our lives. There is, presumably, no difference in kind between the development of verbal logic and the logic inherent in coordination of action. Both involve the progress through successive adjustments to perturbation which re-establish, in an open process and through a succession of states of equilibrium, the passage from a "pre-operational" stage, to that of concrete operations, and finally to abstract operations. "*The logic of action is, however, the deepest and most primitive.*"

And here, of course, lies the explanation of the *Space Odyssey's* effect upon its audiences, the manner in which it exposes a "generation gap." This film has "separated the men from the boys" – with implications by no means flattering for the "men."

"Human action consists in the continual mechanism of readjustment of equilibration. . . . one can consider

the successive mental structures engendered by development as so many forms of equilibrium each representing a progress over the processing ones. On each successive level the mind fulfills the same function, which is to incorporate the universe, but the structure of assimilation varies. The elaboration of the notion of space is due to the co-ordination of movements, and this development is closely linked to those

of sensory-motor awareness and of intelligence itself."[3]

The structures are to be comprehended in terms of the genetic process linking them. This Piaget calls equilibrium, defined as a process rather than a state, and it is the succession of these states which defines the evolution of intelligence, each process of equilibration ending in the creation of a new state of disequilibrium. This is

The absorption in "the fascination with what is difficult." Movement becomes performance, acquires the gravity and unity of dance style.

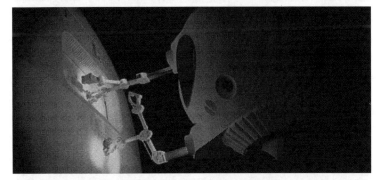

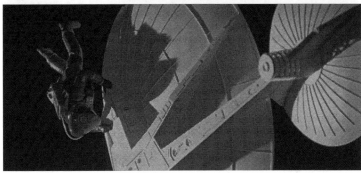

the manner of the development of the child's intelligence.

"The development of the coördinates of horizontality and verticality are not innate, but are constructed through physical experience, acquired through the ability to read one's experience and interpret it, and both reading and interpretation always suppose a deductive system capable of assuring the intellectual assimilation of the experience. The construction of the system of coördinates of horizontality and verticality is extremely complex . . . it is, in effect, not the point of departure of spatial knowledge, but the end point of the entire psychological construction of Euclidian space."

And Kubrick has proposed, in the *Space Odyssey*, a re-enactment of the very process of sensory-motor habit formation, soliciting, through the disturbance and re-establishment of equilibrium, the recapitulation of that fundamental educative process which effects "our incorporation of the world." *Space Odyssey* makes the experience of learning both plot and sub-plot of an Action or Adventure film. An invitation to a voyage, it proposes the re-enactment of an initiation, sustained *rite de passage*, "The Passage into Euclidian Space."

The young are, of course, still closer to the slow development of the body's wisdom, to the forming of the sensory-motor apparatus. Above all, however, they are more openly disposed to that kind of formal transcription of the fundamental learning process which negates it and, through its form, the notion of equilibrium is a state of definition, of rest in finality.

To be "mature" in our culture is to be "well-balanced," "centered," not easily "thrown off balance." Acceptance of imbalance is, however, the condition of receptivity to this film. Our "maturity" pre-supposes the "establishment" of experience as acquisition, the primacy of wisdom as knowledge over that of intellectual exploration, or achievement over aspiration. "Adventure," as Simmel observes in an essay of remarkable beauty,[4] "is, in its specific nature and charm, a form of experiencing.

Not the content but the experiential tension determines the adventure. In youth the ascent falls on the process of life, on its rhythms and antinomies; in old age, it falls on life's substance, compared to which experience . . . appears relatively incidental. This contrast between youth and age, which makes adventure the prerogative of youth may be expressed as the contrast between the romantic and the historical spirit of life. Life in its immediacy counts (for youth) . . . The fascination is not so much in the substance, but rather the adventurous form of experiencing it, the intensity and excitement with which it lets us feel life. What is called the subjectivity of youth is just this; the material of life in its substantive significance is not as important to you as is the process which carries it, life itself."

The critical performance around this film, object, Structure, revolving as it has about the historical anecdotal, sociological, concerned as it is with the texture of incident is, of course, the clear projection of ageing minds and bodies. Its hostile dismissal constitutes, rather like its timid defense, an expression of fatigue. This film of adventure and of action, of action as adventure is an event, an extraordinary occasion for self-recognition, and it offers, of course, the delights and terrors occasions of that sort generally provide. Positing a space which, overflowing screen and field of vision, converts the theatre into a vessel and its viewers into passengers, it impels us, in the movement from departure to arrival, to rediscover the space and dimensions of the body as theatre of consciousness. Youth in us, discarding the spectator's decorum, responds, in the movement of final descent, as to "the slap of the instant," quickening in a tremor of rebirth, reveling in a knowledge which is *carnal*.

Notes

1 [This image has been omitted. – SV]
2 For a consideration of this question one does well to compare Méliès admirable text, *Vues Cinématographiques*, reprinted in the catalog of

the commemorative exhibition (Paris, 1961), which encompasses, within 15 densely printed pages, a basic course in filmmaking and a discussion of the formal and technical problems involved and resolved in his own work, with the information on the making of *2001: A Space Odyssey* provided by the *Journal of the American Cinematographer*, June 1968, Vol. 49, No. 6. The parallels on all parameters are striking. In the production of this particular *grande machine*, the use and invention of metamachines resulted, as one might expect (in a medium, whose history is, more than any, tied to technological development), a number of technical breakthroughs recalling or extending those created by Méliès himself. Here are a very few:

a. Kubrick directed the action in the centrifuge sequences from outside by watching a closed circuit monitor relaying a picture from a small video camera mounted next to the film camera inside the centrifuge itself.

b. In order to attain a slow and "large-scale" movement of doors and other parts, motors were made to drive these mechanisms, then "geared down so far that the actual motion, frame by frame was imperceptible. 'We shot most of these scenes,' says Kubrick, 'using slow exposures of 4 seconds per frame. One couldn't see the movement. A door moving 5 inches during a scene would take 5 hours to shoot. You could never see any unsteady movement. It was like watching the hand of a clock.'"

c. "For the Stargate sequence, a slit-scan machine was designed, using a technique of image scanning as used in scientific and industrial photography. This device could produce two seemingly infinite planes of exposure while holding depth-of-field from a distance of 15 feet to 1 1/2 inches from the lens to an aperture of F 1/8 with exposures of approximately one minute per frame using a standard 65mm. Mitchell camera."

d. "A huge 10 by 8 foot transparency plate projector for the application of the Alekan-Gerrard method of front-projected transparency" was constructed for the primates sequence. It is expected to open up enormous possibilities for future film production.

3 For detailed consideration of the notion of equilibrium as open learning process, I refer the reader to Piaget's *La Représentation De L'Espace Chez L'Enfant*, Presses Universitaires de France, Paris, 1948, and most particularly to the chapter entitled *Le Passage à L'Espace Euclidien*. Further discussion of this notion and of the development of spatial coordinates is to be found in Volume 5 and 6 of *Etudes Epistémologiques*, Presses Universitaires, Paris as well as in *Six Etudes Pychologiques*, Editions Gonthier, Geneva, 1964.

4 *The Adventure*, in George Simmel, *Essays on Sociology, Philosophy and Aesthetics*, Harper and Row, New York, 1965.

2

TYPEWRITER

Friedrich Kittler

"Typewriter" is ambiguous. The word meant both typing machine and female typist: in the United States, a source of countless cartoons. (Typed letter of the bankrupt businessman to his wife: "Dear Blanche, I have sold all my office furniture, chairs, desks, etc. etc., and I am writing this letter under difficulties with my typewriter on my lap.")[1] But the convergence of a profession, a machine and a sex speaks the truth. Bermann's word "stenotypist" gradually came to require footnotes explaining that since 1885, it has referred to women who have completed Ferdinand Schrey's combined training program in the Hammond typewriter and stenography. In the case of "typewriter," by contrast, everyday language for once matches statistics. [. . .]

It is clear that the statistical explosion begins in 1881, with the record sales of the Remington II. Although the number of men [employed as secretaries] dwindles like a bell curve, the number of female typists increases almost with the elegance of an exponential function. As a consequence, it might be possible – as we approach the threshold of infinity – to forecast the year in which typist and woman converge. [. . .]

An innocuous device, "an 'intermediate' thing, between a tool and a machine," "almost quotidian and hence unnoticed,"[2] has made history. The typewriter cannot conjure up anything imaginary, as can cinema; it cannot simulate the real, as can sound recording; it only inverts the gender of writing. In so doing, however, it inverts the material basis of literature.

The monopoly of script in serial data processing was a privilege of men. Because orders and poems were processed through the same channel, security protocols evolved. Even though more and more women were taught letters in the wake of general educational reform, being able to read was not the same as being allowed to write. Prior to the invention of the typewriter, all poets, secretaries, and typesetters were of the same sex. As late as 1859, when the solidarity of American women's unions created positions for female typesetters, their male colleagues on the presses boycotted the printing of unmanly type fonts.[3] Only the Civil War of 1861–64 – that revolutionary media network of telegraph cables and parallel train tracks[4] – opened the bureaucracy of government, of mail and stenography, to writing women; their numbers, of course, were as yet too small to register statistically.

[. . .]

If only because of that [use of male pseudonyms], an omnipresent metaphor equated women with the white sheet of nature or virginity onto which a very male stylus could then inscribe the glory of its authorship. No wonder that psychoanalysis discovered during its clean-up operation that in dreams, "*pencils, pen-holders,* . . . and other *instruments* are undoubted male sexual symbols."[5] It only retrieved a deeply embedded metaphysics of handwriting.

[. . .]

The literal meaning of text is tissue. Therefore, prior to their industrialization the two sexes occupied strictly symmetrical roles: women, with the symbol of female industriousness in their hands, wove tissues; men, with the symbol of male intellectual activity in their hands, wove tissues of a different sort called text. Here, the stylus as singular needlepoint, there, the many female readers as fabric onto which it wrote.

Industrialization simultaneously nullified handwriting and hand-based work. Not coincidentally, it was William K. Jenne, the head of the sewing-machine subdivision of Remington & Son, who in 1874 developed Sholes's prototype into a mass-producible "Type-Writer."[6] Not coincidentally as well, early competing models came from the Domestic Sewing Machine Co., the Meteor Saxon Knitting-Machine Factory, or Seidel & Naumann.[7] Bipolar sexual differentiation, with its defining symbols, disappeared on industrial assembly lines. Two symbols do not survive their replacement by machines, that is, their implementation in the real. When men are deprived of the quill and women of the needle, all hands are up for grabs – as employable as employees. Typescript amounts to the desexualization of writing, sacrificing its metaphysics and turning it into word processing.

[. . .]

Mechanical storage technologies for writing, images, and sound could only be developed following the collapse of this system [the link between authority of word and authority of hand that wrote it]. The hard science of physiology did away with the psychological conception that guaranteed humans that they could find their souls through handwriting and rereading. The "I think," which since Kant was supposed to accompany all of one's representations, presumably only accompanied one's readings. It became obsolete as soon as body and soul advanced to become objects of scientific experiments. The unity of apperception disintegrated into a large number of subroutines, which, as such, physiologists could localize in different centers of the brain and engineers could reconstruct in multiple machines. Which is what the "spirit" – the unsimulable center of "man" – denied by its very definition.

[. . .]

But ever since 1810, the introduction of the rotary press and continuous form into the printing trade made typesetting machines desirable in which ("as with a piano") "the various types fall, through a touch of the keys, into place almost as quickly as one speaks."[8] And when Samuel Morse patented his electric cable telegraph in 1840, he introduced a communications technology whose speed of light far outpaced all forms of manual communication. [. . .] Consequently, not long thereafter

> a whole generation of telegraph operators had appeared who could understand code much faster than they could write it down. Stenographers found themselves in a similar fix. They could take their notations as quickly as a man could speak, and yet they couldn't transcribe faster than at a snail's pace.[9]

What therefore became part of the wish list were writing instruments that could coincide with the operating speed of nervous pathways. Since aphasia researchers had figured out the number of milliseconds it takes for a letter to travel from the eye to the hand muscles via the brain's reading and writing centers, the equation of cerebral circuits with telegraphic dispatches had become a physiological standard.[10] When "the average latency, that is the time between the stimulus and the pushing of a button takes about 250 milliseconds," and when, furthermore, "the typing of a given output resembles a flying projective" because "it only needs a starting signal" and "then goes all by itself"[11] – then, the typewriter as a mass-produced article was bound to roll automatically off the production lines of a gun manufacturer.

[. . .]

The technologies of typewriting and sound recording are by-products of the American Civil War. Edison, who was a young telegrapher during the war, developed his phonograph in an attempt to improve the processing speed of the Morse telegraph beyond human limitations. Remington began the serial production of Sholes's typewriter models in September 1874 simply because "after the Civil War boom things had been on the slow side," and they had "more capacity than they were using."[12]

The typewriter became a discursive machine-gun. A technology whose basic action not coincidentally consists of strikes and triggers proceeds in automated and discrete steps, as does ammunitions transport in a revolver and a machine-gun, or celluloid transport in a film projector. "The pen was once mightier than the sword," Otto Burghagen, the first monographer of the typewriter, writes in 1898, "but where the typewriter rules," he continues, "Krupp's cannons must remain silent!"[13] Burghagen is contradicted, however, by his own deliberations on "the significant *savings of time*, which endear the machine to the merchant. With its help one can complete office work in a third of the time it would take with the pen, for with each strike of a key the machine produces a complete letter, while the pen has to undergo about five strokes in order to produce a letter."[14]

[. . .]

When Lillian Sholes, as "presumably" the "first type-writer" in history,[15] sat posed in front of her father's prototype in 1872, female typists came into existence for purposes of demonstration, but as a profession and career, the stenotypist had yet to come. That was changed by the central branch of the Young Women's Christian Association in New York City, which trained eight young women in 1881 to become typists and immediately received hundreds of inquiries (at $10 a week) from the corporate world. [. . .]

Thus evolved the exponential function of female secretaries and the bell curve of male secretaries. Ironically enough, the clerks, office helpers, and poet-apprentices of the nineteenth century, who were exclusively male, had invested so much pride in their laboriously trained handwriting as to overlook Remington's innovation for seven years. The continuous and coherent flow of ink, that material substrate of all middle-class individuals and indivisibilities, made them blind to a historical chance. Writing as keystrokes, spacing, and the automatics of discrete block letters, bypassed a whole system of education. Hence sexual innovation followed technological innovation almost immediately.

[. . .]

The fact that "the female clerk could all-too-easily degrade into a mere typewriter"[16] made her an asset. From the working class, the middle class, and the bourgeoisie, out of ambition, economic hardship, or the pure desire for emancipation[17] emerged millions of secretaries. It was precisely their marginal position in the power system of script that forced women to develop their manual dexterity, which surpassed the prideful handwriting aesthetics of male secretaries in the media system.

[. . .]

Martin Heidegger on the hand and the typewriter (1942–43)

Man himself acts [*handelt*] through the hand [*Hand*]; for the hand is, together with the word, the essential distinction of man. Only a being which like man, "has" the word μύθος, λόγος, can and must "have" "the hand." Through the hand occur both prayer and murder, greeting and thanks, oath and signal, and also the "work" of the hand, the "hand-work," and the tool. The handshake seals the covenant. The hand brings about the "work" of destruction. The hand exists as hand only where there is disclosure and concealment. No animal has a hand, and a hand never originates from a paw or a claw or talon. Even the hand of one in desperation (it least of all) is never a talon, with which a person clutches wildly. The hand sprang forth only out of the word and together with the word. Man does not "have" hands, but the hand holds the essence of man, because the word as the essential realm of the hand is the ground of the essence of man. The word as what is inscribed and what appears to the regard is the written word, i.e., script. And the word as script is handwriting.

It is not accidental that modern man writes "with" the typewriter and "dictates" [*diktiert*] (the same word as "poetize" [*dichten*]) "into" a machine. This "history" of the kinds of writing is one of the main reasons for the increasing destruction of the word. The latter no longer comes and goes by means of the writing hand, the properly acting hand, but by means of the mechanical forces it releases. The typewriter tears writing from the essential realm of the hand, i.e., the realm of the word. The word itself turns into something "typed." Where typewriting, on the contrary, is only a transcription, and serves to preserve the writing, or turns into print something already written, there it has a proper, though limited, significance. In the time of the first dominance of the typewriter, a letter written on this machine still stood for a breach of good manners. Today, a handwritten letter is an antiquated and undesired thing; it disturbs speed reading. Mechanical writing deprives the hand of its rank in the realm of the written word and degrades the word to a means of communication. In addition, mechanical writing provides this "advantage," that it conceals the handwriting and thereby the character. The typewriter makes everyone look the same. . . . [ellipses in original]

Therefore, when writing was withdrawn from the origin of its essence, i.e., from the hand, and was transferred to the machine, a transformation occurred in the relation of Being to man. It is of little importance for this transformation how many people actually use the typewriter and whether there are some who shun it. It is no accident that the invention of the printing press coincides with the inception of the modern period. The word-signs become type, and the writing stroke disappears. The type is "set," the set becomes "pressed." This mechanism of setting and pressing and "printing" is the preliminary form of the typewriter. In the typewriters we find the irruption of the mechanisms in the realm of the word. The typewriter leads again to the typesetting machine. The press becomes the rotary press. In rotation, the triumph of the machine comes to the fore. Indeed, at first, book printing and then machine type offers advantages and conveniences, and these then unwittingly steer preferences and needs to this kind of written communication. The typewriter veils the essence of writing and of the script. It withdraws from man the essential rank of the hand, without man's experiencing this withdrawal appropriately and recognizing that it has transformed the relation of Being to his essence.

[. . .]

In the typewriter the machine appears, i.e., technology appears, in an almost quotidian and hence unnoticed and hence sign-less relation to writing, i.e., to the word, i.e., to the distinguishing essence of man. A more penetrating consideration would have to recognize here that the typewriter is not really machine in the strict sense of machine technology, but is an "intermediate" thing, between a tool and a machine, a mechanism. Its production, however, is conditioned by machine technology.

This "machine," operated in the closest vicinity to the word, is in use; it imposes its own use. Even if we do not actually operate this machine, it demands that we regard it if only to renounce and avoid it. This situation constantly repeats everywhere, in all relations of modern man to technology. Technology *is* entrenched in our history.[18]

"Our writing tools are also working on our thoughts," Nietzsche wrote.[19] "Technology *is* entrenched in our history," Heidegger said. But the one wrote the sentence about the typewriters on a typewriter, the other described (in a magnificent old German hand) typewriters per se. That is why it was Nietzsche who initiated the transvaluation of all values with his philosophically scandalous sentence about media technology. In 1882, human beings, their thoughts, and their authorship respectively were replaced by two sexes, the text, and blind writing equipment.[20]

[...]

Indeed: Nietzsche, as proud of the publication of his mechanization as any philosopher,[21] changed from arguments to aphorisms, from thoughts to puns, from rhetoric to telegram style. That is precisely what is meant by the sentence that our writing tools are also working on our thoughts. Malling Hansen's writing ball,[22] with its operating difficulties, made Nietzsche into a laconic.

[...]

None of the models prior to Underwood's great innovation of 1897 allowed immediate visual control over the output. In order to read the typed text, one has to lift shutters on the Remington model, whereas with Malling Hansen's – notwithstanding other claims – the semicircular arrangement of the keys itself prevented a view of the paper. But even Underwood's innovation did not change the fact that the typewriters can and must remain a blind activity. [...] After a fraction of a second, the act of writing stops being an act of reading that is produced by the grace of a human subject. With the help of blind machines, people, whether blind or not, acquire a historically new proficiency: *écriture automatique*.

[...]

In the second essay of [Nietzsche's] *On the Genealogy of Morals*, knowledge, speech, and virtuous action are no longer inborn attributes of Man. Like the animal that will soon go by a different name, Man derived from forgetfulness and random noise, the background of all media. Which suggests that in 1886, during the founding age of mechanized storage technologies, human evolution, too, aims toward the creation of a machine memory. [...] To make forgetful animals into human beings, a blind force strikes that dismembers and inscribes their bodies in the real, until pain itself brings forth a memory. People keep promises and execute orders only after torture.

Writing in Nietzsche is no longer a natural extension of humans who bring forth their voice, soul, individuality through their handwriting. On the contrary: [...] humans change their position – they turn from the agency of writing to become an inscription surface. Conversely, all the agency of writing passes on in its violence to an inhuman media engineer who will soon be called up by Stoker's *Dracula*. A type of writing that blindly dismembers body parts and perforates human skin necessarily stems from typewriters built before 1897, when Underwood finally introduced visibility.

[...]

Since only professors in Berlin and friends involved in information technology were privileged to have their manuscripts typed and readied for publication, Kafka had no choice but – in an unusual step for him – to go to work on the typewriter himself. Whereas the "main" and "happy" part of Kafka's work consisted in "dictating to a living being" in the office,[23] the endless stream of love letters to Felice Bauer[24] started, as if negating love itself, with a typescript.

"But dearest Felice!" Kafka wrote a year later, "Don't we write about writing the way others talk about money?"[25] Indeed: from the first letter to the last, their impossible relationship was a feedback loop of text processing. Time and again, Kafka avoided traveling to Berlin with his hand, the hand that once held Felice Bauer's. Instead of the absent body there arrived a whole postal system of letters, registered letters, postcards, and telegrams in order to describe that "hand" with "the hand now striking the keys." What remained of "personal typing idiosyncrasies" was only what was simultaneously of interest to *The Criminological Uses of Typewriting*, naming, the "types of mistake correction": first, with skilled typists; second, with unskilled typists; and third, with "skilled typists on an unaccustomed system."[26]

[. . .]

In one of his last letters to his last female pen pal, however, Kafka took stock: of misused love letters and communications vampires, of reduced physical labour and information machines.

> How on earth did anyone get the idea that people can communicate with one another by letter! Of a distant person one can think, and of a person who is near one can catch hold – all else goes beyond human strength. Writing letters, however, means to denude oneself before the ghosts, something for which they greedily wait. Written kisses don't reach their destination, rather they are drunk on the way by the ghosts. It is on this ample nourishment that they multiply so enormously. Humanity senses this and fights against it and in order to eliminate as far as possible the ghostly element between people and to create natural communication, the peace of souls, it has invented the railway, the motorcar, the aeroplane. But it's no longer any good, these are evidently inventions made at the moment of crashing. The opposing side is so much calmer and stronger; after the postal service it has invented the telegraph, the telephone, the radiograph. The ghosts won't starve, but we will perish.[27]

Hence only ghosts survive the Kafka–Bauer case: media-technological projects and texts reflecting the material limitations of the written word. [. . .]

Kafka, however, for whom Ms. Bauer did not type a single manuscript, let alone construct media networks, stuck to old-fashioned literature. From the typewriter he only learned to dodge the phantasm of authorship. As with his first love letter, the "I," "the nothingness that I am,"[28] disappeared under deletions or abbreviations until all that remained was a Joseph K. in *The Trial* and a K. by itself in *The Castle*. The office machines of his days also freed the Kafka of his literary nights from the power of attorney, that is, the authority to sign documents:

> I could never work as independently as you seem to; I slither out of responsibility like a snake; I have to sign many things, but every evaded signature seems like a gain; I also sign everything (though I really shouldn't) with FK only, as though that could exonerate me; for this reason I also feel drawn to the typewriter in anything concerning the office, because its work, especially when executed at the hands of the typist, is so impersonal.[29]

Mechanized and materially specific, modern literature disappears in a type of anonymity, which bear surnames like "Kafka" or "K." only emphasize. The "disparition élocutoire du poète"[30] urged by Mallarmé becomes reality. Voice and handwriting treacherously could fall subject to criminal detection; hence every trace of them disappears from literature. As Jacques Derrida, or "J.D.," observes in a May 1979 love letter whose address must also be without (a) proper name(s):

> What cannot be said above all must not be silenced, but written. Myself, I am a man of speech, I have never had anything to write. When I have something to say I say it or say it to myself, basta. You are the only one to understand why it really was necessary that I write

exactly the opposite, as concerns axiomatics, of what I desire, what I know my desire to be, in other words you: living speech, presence itself, proximity, the proper, the guard, etc. I have necessarily written upside down – and in order to surrender to Necessity.

and *"fort" de toi.*

I must write you this (and at the typewriter, since that's where I am, sorry: . . .).[31]

Hence Derrida's *Postcard* consists of one continuous stream of typed letters punctuated by phone calls that are frequently mentioned but never recorded. Voice remains the other of typescripts.

[. . .]

T.S. Eliot, who will be "composing" *The Waste Land* "on the typewriter," "finds" (no different from Nietzsche) "that I am sloughing off all my long sentences which I used to dote upon. Short, staccato, like modern French prose." Instead of "subtlety" "the typewriter makes for lucidity,"[32] which is, however, nothing but the effect of its technology on style. A spatialized, numbered, and (since the 1888 typewriters' congress in Toronto) also standardized supply of signs on a keyboard makes possible what and only what QWERTY prescribes.

Foucault's methodical explanation, the last and irreducible elements of which are at the center of his discourse analysis, can easily eliminate the sentences of linguistics, the speech acts of communications theory, the statements of logic. Only to be confronted by two factual conditions that seem to fulfill all the criteria for an elementary "statement" of discourse analysis: "The pile of printer's character which I can hold in my hand, or the letters marked on the keyboard of a typewriter."[33] Singular and spatialized, material and standardized, stockpiles of signs indeed undermine so-called Man with his intentions and the so-called world with its meaning. Only that discourse analysis ignores the fact that the factual condition is no simple methodological example but is in each case a techno-historical event. Foucault omits the elementary datum (in Latin, the casting of dice or *coup de dés*) of each contemporary theoretical practice and begins discourse analysis only with its applications or configurations: "the keyboard of a typewriter is not a statement; but the same series of letters, A, Z, E, R, T, listed in a typewriting manual, is the statement of the alphabetical order adopted by French typewriters."[34]

Foucault, the student of Heidegger, writers that "there are signs, and that is enough for there to *be* signs for there to *be* statements,"[35] only to point for once to the typewriter keyboard as the precondition for all preconditions. Where thinking must stop, blueprints, schematics, and industrial standards begin. They alter (strictly following Heidegger) the relationship of Being to Man, who has no choice but to become the site of their external recurrence. A, Z, E, R, T . . . [ellipses in original]

[. . .]

Carl Schmitt, "The Buribunks: a historico-philosophical meditation" (1918)

Today, because we have been granted the privilege of enjoying the glorious notion of the diary at its zenith, we tend to overlook what a majestic deed one man performed when – perhaps as the unknowing instrument of the world spirit – he planted with the first innocuous note the first seed, which now overshadows the earth as a gigantic tree. A certain, I would say, moral feeling of obligation urges us to question what historical personage embodies the precursor to this wonderful epoch, the messenger pigeon that the world spirit has sent in advance of its last and most highly refined period. We are obliged to put this question at the center of our principal investigation.

It would be a mighty triumph for Buribunkology[36] if we could identity a hero such as Don Juan as its ancestor and – in opposition to the charge of scholarly absentmindedness – take pride in its paradoxical descent from this virile and decidedly unscholarly cavalier. [. . .] [The diary keeper] may very well be tempted to compare his sense of achievement with the plucky self-confidence of the frivolous conqueror of women. Still, this seductive parallel should not distract us from the profound seriousness of our endeavor or lead us to lose the distance from our possible founding father, which sober objectivity and detached science dictate to us. Did Don Juan really have the specifically buribunkological attitude that urged him to keep a diary, not for the sake of recording, superficially, his manly conquest, but – if I may say so – out of a sense of sheer obligation and debt vis-à-vis history? We cannot believe so. Don Juan had no interest in the past, just as he fundamentally had no interest in the future, which for him did not go beyond the next conquest; he lived in the immediate present, and his interest in the individual erotic adventure does not point to any signs of a beginning self-historicization. We cannot detect any signs of the attitude characterizing the Buribunk, which originates from the desire to record every second of one's existence for history, to immortalize oneself. Like the Buribunk keeping a diary, Don Juan relishes each individual second, and in that there is certainly a similarity of psychological gesture. . . . Not for a single moment does he have what I would like to call the cinematic attitude of the Buribunk – he never apprehends himself as the subject-object of history – in which the world soul, writing itself, has become realized. And the register that Leporello keeps for him he takes along only as an afterthought, as a delectable flavoring for his horizontal delights. Hence, we have legitimate doubt whether, for example, from the 1,003 Spanish representatives, more than three owe their entry into the register to the very existence of the register itself. Put differently, we wonder whether Don Juan has been prompted into action by his inner need to start and keep a register, if only in those three cases, the way numerous major achievements in the arts, in science, in everyday life have been produced solely with the idea of their recorded existence in a diary or newspaper – the diary of the masses – in mind. The register was never the final cause; in implementing the acts of innervation at issue, it was – in the rectangle of psychological forces – relegated to the role of an accidental, of an accompanying positive motor. Thus, for us Don Juan is finished.

All the more interesting is the behavior of Leporello. He relishes the sensuous leftovers of his master, a couple of girls, a couple of choice morsels; for the most part, he accompanies his master. A Buribunk does not do that, for a Buribunk is unconditionally and absolutely his own master, he is himself. Gradually, however, what awakens in Leporello is the desire to partake in the escapades of his master by writing them down, by taking note of them, and it is at this moment that we see the dawn of Buribunkdom. With the aid of a commendable trick he surpasses his master, and if he does not become Don Juan himself, he becomes more than that; he changes from Don Juan's wretched underling into his biographer. He becomes a historian, drags Don Juan to the bar of world history, that is, world court, in order to appear as an advocate or prosecutor, depending on the result of his observations and interpretations.

[. . .]

Not until Ferker did the diary become an ethical-historical possibility; the primogeniture in the realm of Buribunkdom is his. Be your own history! Live, so that each second of your life can be entered into your diary and be accessible to your biographer! Coming out of Ferker's mouth, these were big and strong words that humanity had not yet heard. They owe their distribution into the nooks and crannies of even the most remote villages to a worldwide organization aimed at disseminating his ideas, an organization well managed and having the support of an intelligent press. No village is so small that it is without a blacksmith, as the old song went; today, we can say with not a little pride that no village is so small that it is not imbued with at least a touch of Buribunkic spirit. The great man, who presided like the chief of a general staff over his thousands of underlings, who guided his enormous business with a sure hand, who channeled the attention of the troops of researchers to hot spots, and who with unheard-of strategic skill focused attention on difficult research problems by directing pioneering dissertations – this impressive personality experienced a truly sensational rise. Born of humble origins and educated without Latin in the middle school of his small town, he successively became a dentist, a book-maker, an editor, the owner of a construction company in Tiflis, the secretary of the headquarters of the international association to boost tourism on the Adriatic coast, the owner of a movie theater in Berlin, a marketing director in San Francisco, and, eventually, Professor of Marketing and Upward Mobility at the Institute of Commerce in Alexandria. [. . .]

Now we are finally in a position to define historically the critical contribution of this ingenious man: not only has he made the radically transformative idea of the modern corporation feasible for human ingenuity without leaving the ground of the ethical ideal; not only has he demonstrated through his life that one can build a career of purposive ambition and still be an ethically complete being, bound under the sublation of the irreconcilable duality of matter and mind in a way that invalidates the constructions of theologizing metaphysics, which were inimical to the intellectual climate of the twentieth century, through a victorious new idealism; he has, and this is the crux, found a new, contemporary form of religion by strictly adhering to an exclusionary positivism and an unshakeable belief in nothing-but-matter-of-factness. And the mental region in which these numerous and contradictory elements, this bundle of negated negations, are synthesized – the unexplainable, absolute, essential that is part of every religion – that is nothing but the Buribunkological.

[. . .]

As a fully matured fruit of the most noble Buribunkdom, this genius [Schnekke] fell from the tree of his own personality. In Schnekke we find not the least visible trace of hesitation, not the slightest deviation from the distinguished line of the Ur-buribunkological. He is nothing more than a diary keeper, he lives for his diary, he lives in and through his diary, even when he enters into his diary that he no longer knows what to write in his diary. On a level where the I, which has been projecting itself into a reified, you-world constellation, flows with forceful rhythm back into a world-I constellation, the absolute sacrifice of all energies for the benefit of the inner self and its identity has achieved the fullest harmony. Because ideal and reality have here been fused in unsurpassable perfection; what is missing is any particular singularity, which shaped Ferker's life in such a sensational way but which, for any discussion focusing on the essential, must be understood as a compliment rather than a critique. Schnekke is, in a much more refined sense than Ferker, a personality, and precisely because of that has he disappeared behind the most inconspicuous sociability. His distinct idiosyncrasy, and I determined solely by the most extreme rules of its own, is located within a spectrum of indiscriminate generality, in a steady colorlessness that is the result of the most sacrificial will to power. Here we have reached the absolute zenith of Buribunkdom; we need not be afraid of any relapse, as with Ferker. The empire of Buribunkdom has been founded. For in the midst of his continuous diaries, Schnekke (with his strong sense of generality and his universal instinct) saw the opportunity to detach the diary from its restrictive bond with the individual and to convert it into a collective organism. The generous organization of the obligatory collective diary is his achievement. Through that, he defined and secured the framing conditions of a buribunkological interiority; he elevated the chaotic white noise of disconnected and single Buribunkdom into the perfect orchestration of a Buribunkic cosmos.

[. . .]

The basic outline of the philosophy of the Buribunks: I think, therefore I am; I speak, therefore I am; I write, therefore I am; I publish, therefore I am. This contains no contradiction, but rather the progressive sequence of identities, each of which, following the laws of logic, transcends its own limitations. For Buribunks, thinking is nothing but silent speech; speech is nothing but writing without script; writing is nothing but anticipated publication; and publication is, hence, identical with writing to such a degree that the differences between the two are so small as to be negligible. I write, therefore I am; I am, therefore I write. What do I write? I write myself. Who writes me? I myself write myself. What do I write about? I write that I write myself. What is the great engine that elevates me out of the complacent circle of egohood? History!

I am thus a letter on the typewriter of history; I am a letter that writes itself. Strictly speaking, however, I write not that I write myself but only the letter that I am. But in writing, the world spirit apprehends itself through me, so that I, in turn, by apprehending myself, simultaneously apprehend the world spirit. I apprehend both it and myself not in thinking fashion, but – as the deed precedes the thought – in the act of writing. Meaning: I am not only reader of world history but also its writer.

[. . .]

We see through the illusion of uniqueness. We are the letters produced by the writing hand of the world spirit and surrender ourselves consciously to this writing power. In that we recognize true freedom. In that we also see the means of putting ourselves into the position of the world spirit. The individual letters and words are only the tools of the ruses of world history. More than one recalcitrant "no" that has been thrown into the text of history feels proud of its opposition and thinks of itself as a revolutionary, even though it may only negate revolution itself. But by consciously merging with the writing of world history we comprehend its spirit, we become equal to it, and – without ceasing to be written – we yet understand ourselves as writing subjects. This is how we outruse the ruse of world history – namely, by writing it while it writes us.[37]

World history comes to a close as a global typewriters' association. Digital signal processing (DSP) can set in. Its promotional euphemism, post-history, only barely conceals that war is the beginning and end of all artificial intelligence.

In order to supersede world history (made from classified intelligence reports and literary processing protocols), the media system proceeded in three phases. Phase 1, beginning with the American Civil War, developed storage technologies for acoustics, optics, and script: film, gramophone, and the man–machine system, typewriter. Phase 2, beginning with the First World War, developed for each storage content appropriate electric transmission technologies: radio, television, and their more secret counterparts. Phase 3, since the Second World War, has transferred the schematic of a typewriter to a technology of predictability per se; Turing's mathematical definition of computability in 1936 gave future computers their name.

Storage technology from 1914 to 1918 meant deadlocked trench warfare from Flanders to Gallipoli. Transmission technology with VHF tank communications and radar images, those military developments parallel to television,[38] meant total mobilization, motorization, and blitzkrieg from Vistula in 1939 to Corregidor in 1945. And finally, the largest computer program of all time, the conflation of test run with reality, goes by the name of the Strategic Defense Initiative. Storing/transmitting/calculating, or trenches/blitz/stars. World wars from I to n.

In artificial intelligence, all media glamour vanishes and goes back to basics. [. . .] Bits reduced the seeming continuity of optical media and the real continuity of acoustic media to letters, and these letters to numbers. DSP stores, transfers, calculates – millions of times per second, it runs through the three functions necessary and sufficient for media. The standard for today's microprocessors, from the point of view of their hardware, is simply their systematic integration.

[. . .]

But with sufficient integration and repetition, the modular system [of the CPU] is capable of processing, that is, converting into any possible medium, each individual time particle of the data received from any environment. As if one could reconstruct, custom-made from one micro-second to the next, a complete recording studio comprising reel-to-reels plus radio transmission plus control panel and switchboard. Or, as if the Buribunks' immense permeation with data coincided with an automated Buribunkology that could be switched, at the speed of electrical current, from a register of data to a register of persons or even their self-registration. [. . .] The storage media of the founding generation were only capable of replacing the eye and the ear, the sensorium of the central nervous system; the communications media between the two wars were only capable of replacing the mouth and the hand, the motorics of information. Which is why, behind all registers, all channels, a human being still appeared to be doing the transmitting. So-called thinking remained thinking; it therefore could not be implemented. For that, thinking or speech had to be completely converted into computing.

[. . .]

The first to be affected [by the invention of the Turing machine] were of course stenotypists. After eleven years, Turing's Universal Discrete Machine fulfilled the prophecy that an apparatus "also renders superfluous the typist." His simulation game, in which a censor is to but cannot actually decide which of two data sources *A* and *B* is human and which is a machine, signif-icantly has a precursor. According to Turing, computer *B* replaces the systemic position of a woman who — in competition or gender war with a man *A* — seeks to persuade the data gap *C* that she is the real woman. But since both voices are severed from the "written, or better still, typed" flow of information, Remington's secretary gives her farewell performance. Whenever transvestite *A* insists that he has strands of hair "nine inches long," the human predecessor of the computer writers to her censor, as mechanically as futilely, "I am the woman, don't listen to him!"[39]

[. . .] Computers write by themselves, without secretaries, simply with the command WRITE. [. . .] Only those intersections between computers and their environments that, following ASCII code (American Standard Code for Information Interchange), are networked bit by bit with typewriter keys[40] will continue to offer women jobs for a while. When ENIAC, "the first operational computer," according to misleading American accounts, calculated projectile tra-jectories and A-bomb pressure waves during the Second World War, one hundred women were hired in addition to male programmers. Their job: "to climb around on ENIAC's massive frame, locate burnt-out vacuum tubes, hook up cables, and perform other types of work unrelated to writing."[41]

By contrast, Turing, with an eye toward "computers and guided projectiles," predicted good times for men, programmers, and mathematicians.[42] But it was a strange kind of mathematics into which he imported the elegance and complexity of classical analysis. What disappeared in the split-up of binaries was not only the continuity of all graphs and trajectories examined since Leibniz, and which Fourier's theory and Edison's phonographs simply followed. What was much more drastic than such primitive step functions was his crucial innovation: the abolition of the difference between numbers and operational symbols, data and commands. [. . .]

Every microprocessor implements through software what was once the dream of the cabala; namely, that through their encipherment and the manipulations of numbers, letters could yield results or illuminations that no reader could have found. Computers are endless series of numbers only whose relative position decides whether they operate as (verbal) commands or (numeric) data or addresses. If John von Neumann, the mathematician of the Second World War, had not taken certain precautions for his machines, a command sequence of numbers such as ADD could also add up, aside from the usual data, command sequences themselves, until no programmer would be able to comprehend the starry mathematics to which that take-off had abducted their computer.

The neat separation of data, addresses, commands – that is, of storage contents, points of transfer, and processing steps – by contrast, assures that for each address, there is only one command or datum on the bus. A box of numbered paper sips that can log on not only (as with the Buribunks) to certain books, chapters, pages, terms, but to any individual bit of the system. Computer algorithms, instead of simply reproducing a logic, consist of "LOGIC + CONTROL."[43] No wonder that governmental ingenuity invented the impossible job of the data security specialist to camouflage the precision of such data control.

[. . .]

The typing, computing, and sewing machines in the brains or books of Nietzsche and [Adolf] Kußmaul hence became reality. The founding myth of a media landscape, which would only be the worldwide unfolding of neurophysiology, reached its peak in Friedlaender's machine fiction. Fourteen years later, it ends in Turing's machine, which was also never built but is mathematically conceivable. The computer and the brain are functionally compatible, but not in terms of their schematics. Since the nervous system, according to Turing, is "certainly not a discrete-state machine," that is, not infinitesimally precise, all the unpredictabilities of a Laplacian universe loom over it.[44] Thus, "the real importance of the digital procedure lies in its ability to reduce the computational noise level to an extent which is completely unobtainable by any other (analogy) procedure." And even if – following Neumann's elegant simplification – the neural, but not the hormonal, conduits operate according to a digital model, their information flow is still five thousand times slower than that of computers.[45] The brain, however, compensates for this loss of transmission through the parallel processing of whole sets of data; statistical breadth (presumably based on majority gates) for which computers can compensate only through serial processing and recursive functions.

[. . .]

Whether or NOT the Japanese empire took seriously the resource embargo threatened by Roosevelt (that is, attack the United States), whether or NOT Vice Admiral Nagumo's flotilla would sink the Pacific battleships at Pearl Harbor with carrier-bound aircraft, whether or NOT he would maintain silence in his areas of operation off the Aleutian Islands (he did): these were precisely the digital puzzles of 1941, solvable only through the interception and decoding of necessarily discrete sources of information. And since the machine mathematics of the current century endowed general staffs with the ability to encrypt their orders automatically, that is, immeasurably more efficiently than by hand, decoding had to be done by machines as well. The Second World War: the birth of the computer from the spirit of Turing and his never-built principle relay.

[. . .]

In 1926, the German navy used the first encryption machines.[46] Three years later, soon after Major Fellgiebel, the subsequent chief of Army Communications, had taken over the Abwehr's cryptography divisions,[47] the army followed. The secret typewriter of Wilmersdorf was equipped with yet more secret rotors, as well as the name of secrecy itself: ENIGMA. For a decade, it lived up to that name.

[. . .]

Enigma had the practical advantage or theoretical disadvantage that its cipher consisted of a self-inverse group. In order to be encoded or decoded on the same machine, letter pairs had to be interchangeable. For example, when the OKW encoded its O as a K, the K inversely turned into an O. From that followed "the very particular feature that no letter could be enciphered by itself."[48] Not even the OKW was capable of writing its own name. Turing subjected these few yet revealing implications to a sequential analysis that weighted and controlled all the probabilities of solution. With automatized judgment, the Oriental Goddess[49] ran through permutation after permutation, until the letter salad became plain text again. War of typewriters.

And since from "15 to a maximum of 29 percent"[50] of the German radio traffic ran through Enigma, the spy war reached a new level: interception yielded "not just messages, but the whole enemy communication *system*."[51] The midrange levels of command – from army and division headquarters to individual blitzkrieg weapons on land, in the air, or at sea – betrayed their addresses, which are, all spy novels notwithstanding, more revealing than data or messages. Sixty different Enigma codes and 3,000 classified radio messages per day, with all of the specs for their senders and receivers, recorded the war like a typewriter the size of Europe. Under the conditions of high technology, war coincides with a chart of its organizational structure. [. . .]

It is only one step from the flowchart to the computer. The addresses, data, commands that circulated between humans and typewriters in the German army or its British simulacrum could finally turn into hardware. This last step was undertaken in 1943 by the Post Office Research Station at Bletchley Park. One thousand five hundred tubes were expropriated and converted into overloaded switches and, instead of reinforcing radio analog signals, simulated the binary play of Boolean algebra. Transistors did not make it into the world until 1949, but even without them the universal discrete machine – including data entry, programming possibilities, and the great innovation of internal storage mechanisms[52] – saw its first implementation, for which Turing's successors could find no other name than COLOSSUS. Because the strategic secrets of the Führer's headquarters, Wolfsschanze, could, as is logical, only be cracked by a monster computer.

[. . .]

A simple feedback loop – and information machines bypass humans, their so-called inventors. Computers themselves become subjects. IF a preprogrammed condition is missing, data processing continues according to the conventions of numbered commands, but IF somewhere an intermediate result fulfills the condition, THEN the program itself determines successive commands, that is, its future.

[. . .]

At any rate, cybernetics, the theory of self-guidance and feedback loops, is a theory of the Second World War.

[. . .]

With Wiener's Linear Prediction Code (LPC), mathematics changed into an oracle capable of predicting a probable future even out of chaos – initially for fighter aircraft and anti-aircraft guidance systems, in between the wars for human mouths and the computer simulations of their discourses.[53] Blind, unpredictable time, which rules over analog storage and transmission media (in contrast to the arts), was finally bought under control. With digital signal processing, measuring circuits and algorithms (like an automated sound engineer) ride along on random frequencies. [. . .]

With the consequence that COLOSSUS gave birth to many a son, each more colossal than its secret father. According to the ministry of supply, Turing's postwar computer ACE was supposed to calculate "grenades, bombs, rockets, and cruise missiles"; the American ENIAC "was to simulate trajectories of shells through varying conditions of air resistance and wind velocity, which involved the summation of thousands of little pieces of trajectories." John von Neumann's EDVAC was being designed to solve "three-dimensional 'aerodynamic and shock-wave problems, . . . shell, bomb and rocket work, . . . [and] progress in the field of propellants and high explosives'"; BINAC worked for the United States Air Force; ATLAS, for cryptoanalysis; and finally, MANIAC, if this suggestive name had been implemented in time, would have optimized the pressure wave of the first H-bomb.[54]

[. . .]

Under the conditions of high technology, literature has nothing more to say. It ends in cryptograms that defy interpretation and only permit interception. Of *all* long-distance connections on this planet today [in 1986],[55] from phone services to microwave radio, 0.1 percent flow through the transmission, storage, and decoding machines of the National Security Agency (NSA), the organization succeeding the SIS [Secret Intelligence Service] and Bletchley Park. By its own account, the NSA has "accelerated" the "advent of the computer age," and hence the end of history, like nothing else. An automated discourse analysis has taken command.

Notes

1 Bliven 1974 [*sic*], 72. Other languages experienced terminological problems. In French, the typewriter was initially called "typographe, piano à écrire, clavecin à écrire, pantographe, plume typographique" (B. Müller 1975, 169), as well as "dactylographe."
2 Heidegger 1942–43/1992, 86.
3 See Cockburn, 1981.
4 See Van Creveld 1985, 103–4.
5 Freud, *Introductory Lectures on Psycho-Analysis*, 1915–16, in idem 1962, 15: 155 [ellipses in original]. See also Giese 1914, 528, on "Sexual Models for Simple Inventions," (*Sexualvorbilder bei einfachen Erfindungen*). [. . .]
6 See Bliven 1954, 56.
7 See Stümpel 1985, 9.
8 *Journal of Arts and Sciences*, 1823, cited in Brauner 1925, 4.
9 Bliven 1954, 35.
10 See, for example, Grashey 1885, 688.
11 Salthouse 1984, 94–96.
12 Bliven 1954, 56.
13 Burghagen 1898, 31.
14 Ibid. Typing-speed records in the United States, by contrast, were up to fifteen letters per second (Klockenberg 1926, 10).
15 Current 1954, 54.
16 Schwabe 1902, 7.
17 For evidence on the social stratification of typists, see Witsch 1932, 54.
18 Heidegger, 1942–43/1992, 80–81, 85–86.
19 Nietzsche, letter toward the end of February 1882, in idem 1975–84, pt. 3, I: 172.
20 [Nietzsche shifted from handwriting to writing on a typewriter – whose mechanisms originally prevented the author from seeing the type as it emerged – and then to dictating to a stenographer late in his life when failing eyesight compromised his writing ability. Kittler traces through examples how the new method of composing text changed the style of Nietzsche's writing. – SV]
21 See Nietzsche, letter of March 17, 1882, in idem 1975–84, pt. 3, 1: 180. "I enjoyed a report of the *Berliner Tageblatt* about my existence in Genoa – even the typewriter was mentioned." The mechanized philosopher clipped the news item.
22 [The newly patented device in Nietzsche's typewriter. – SV]
23 Kafka, November 2, 1912, 1912/1965, 23.
24 [She was a woman who worked as a stenographer for the Odeon record company, later Carl Lindström A.G., the largest German manufacturer of Dictaphones and gramophones. She had an extraordinarily successful career for a woman of her time, including the power of attorney to sign for the company. She and Kafka were briefly engaged and often typed their correspondence. – SV]
25 Kafka, August 10, 1913, in ibid., 302.
26 Streicher 1919, 38–41. Based on these criminological uses, on April 8, 1983, the republic of Romania came to the nice conclusion of coercing all typewriter owners into registering their machines with the authorities. See Rosenblatt 1983, 88.
27 Kafka, March 1922, in idem 1953, 229. See Derrida 1980/1987, 33.
28 Kafka, July 10, 1913, in idem 1974, 289.
29 Kafka, December 21–22, 1912, in ibid., 115–16.

30 Mallarmé 1895/1945, 366.
31 Derrida 1980/1987, 194. [ellipses in original]
32 Eliot, August 21, 1916, in idem 1971: x.
33 Foucault 1969/1972, 85.
34 Ibid., 86.
35 Ibid., 84.
36 [Kittler coins this term in reference to a diary-typing machine called Buribunks by Carl Schmitt, whose work he references in the section above. – SV]
37 Schmitt 1917/1918, 92–105.
38 See Diller 1980, 188–92. The Secret Service took over British TV stations to use UHF to scramble the stereophony of German bombers over England. See R. Jones 1978, 175.
39 Turing 1950, 434.
40 See Bliven 1954, 132.
41 See Morgall 1981.
42 Turing, in Hodges 1983, 362.
43 See Kowalski 1979, 424.
44 Turing 1950/1992, 451.
45 J. von Neumann 1951/1963, 295, 301–2.
46 See Garliński 1979, 12.
47 See Wildhagen 1970, 1982.
48 Hodges 1983, 168.
49 [The name given to Turing's machine for deciphering the Enigma code. – SV]
50 Rohwer and Jäckel 1979, 336.
51 Hodges 1983, 192.
52 See ibid., 267.
53 See Sickert 1983, 134–42.
54 See Hodges 1983, 355, 301, 304, 413, respectively [ellipses in original]. More generally, see Gorny 1985, 104–9.
55 Raven, quoted in Bamford 1986, 324.

Works Cited

Bamford, James. 1986. *NSA: Amerikas geheimster Nachrichtendienst*. Zurich/Schwäbisch Hall.
Bliven, Bruce, Jr. 1954. *The Wonderful Writing Machine*. New York.
Brauner, Ludwig. 1925. "Die Schreibmaschine in technischer, kultureller und wirtschaftlicher Bedeutung." In *Sammlung gemeinnütziger Vorträge*, ed. Deutscher Verin zur Verbreitung gemeinnütziger Kenntnisse in Prag. Prague.
Burghagen, Otto. 1898. *Die Schreibmaschine. Illustrierte Beschreibung aller gangbaren Schreibmaschinen nebst gründlicher Anleitung zum Arbeiten auf sämtlichen Systemen*. Hamburg.
Cockburn, Cynthia. 1981. "The Material of Male Power." *Feminist Review* 9.
Current, Richard Nelson. 1954. *The Typewriter and the Men Who Made It*. Urbana, Ill.
Derrida, Jacques. 1987. *The Postcard: From Socrates to Freud and Beyond*. Trans. Alan Bass. Chicago.
Diller, Ansgar. 1980. *Rundfunkpolitik im Dritten Reich*. Vol. 2 of *Rundfunk in Deutschland*, ed. Hans Bausch. Munich.
Foucault, Michel. 1972. *"The Archaeology of Knowledge" and "The Discourse on Language."* Trans. A.M. Sheridan Smith. New York.
Freud, Sigmund. 1962. *The Standard Edition of the Complete Psychological Works of Sigmund Freud*. Ed. and trans. James Strachey. 23 vols. London.
Garliński, Jozef. 1979. *The Enigma War*. New York.
Giese, Fritz. 1914. "Sexualvorbilder bei einfachen Erfindungen." *Imago: Zeitschrift für Anwendung der Psychoanalyse auf die Geisteswissenschaften* 3: 524–35.
Gorny, Peter. 1985. "Informatik und Militär." In *Militarisierte Wissenschaft*, ed. Werner Butte, 104–18. Reinbek.
Grashey, Hubert. 1885. "Über Aphasie und ihre Beziehungen zur Wahrnehmung." *Archiv für Psychiatrie und Nervenkrankheiten* 16: 654–88.
Heidegger, Martin. 1992. *Parmenides*. Trans. André Schuwer and Richard Rojcewicz. Bloomington, Ind.
Hodges, Andrew. 1983. *Alan Turing: The Enigma*. New York.

Jones, Reginald V. 1978. *Most Secret War*. London.

Kafka, Franz. 1953. *Letters to Milena*. Ed. Willi Haas, trans. Tania and James Stern. London.

———. 1965. *The Diaries of Franz Kafka 1910–1913*. Ed. Max Brod, trans. Joseph Kresh. New York.

———. 1974. *Letters to Felice*. Eds. Erich Heller and Jürgen Born, trans. James Stern and Elizabeth Duckworth. London.

Klockenberg, Erich. 1926. *Rationalisierung der Schreibmaschine und ihre Bedienung: Psychotechnische Arbeitsstudien*. Berlin.

Kowalski, Robert A. 1979. "Algorithm = Logic + Control." *Communications of the Association for Computing Machinery* 2: 424–36.

Mallarmé, Stéphane. 1945. *Oeuvres completes*. Eds. Henri Mondor and G. Jean-Aubry. Paris.

Morgall, Janine. 1981. "Typing Our Way to Freedom: Is It True the New Office Technology Can Liberate Women?" *Feminist Review* 9 (Fall).

Müller, Bodo. 1975. *Das Französische in der Gegenwart: Varietäten, Strukturen, Tendenzen*. Heidelberg.

Neumann, John von. 1961–63. "The General and Logical Theory of Automata." In idem, *Collected Works*, vol. 5, 288–328.

Nietzche, Friedrich. 1975–84. *Briefwechsel: Kritische Gesamtausgabe*. Eds. Giorgio Colli and Mazzino Montinari. Berlin.

Rohwer, Jürgen, and Eberhard Jäckel, eds. 1979. *Die Funkaufklärung und ihre Rolle im Zweiten Weltkrieg*. Stuttgart, 1979.

Rosenblatt, Roger. 1983. "The Last Page in the Typewriter." *Time* (May 16): 88.

Salthouse, Timothy. 1984. "Die Fertigkeit des Maschinenschreibens." *Spektrum der Wissenchaft* 4: 94–100.

Schmitt, Carl. 1918. "Die Buribunken: Ein geschichtsphilosophischer Versuch." *Summa* 1, no. 4: 89–106.

Schwabe, Jenny. 1902. *Kontoristin: Forderungen, Leistungen, Aussichten in diesem Berufe*. 2nd ed. Leipzig.

Sickert, Klaus, ed. 1983. *Automatische Spracheingabe und Sprachausgabe: Analyse, Synthese und Erkennung menschlichen Sprache mit digitalen Systemen*. Haar.

Streicher, Hubertus. 1919. *Die kriminologische Verwertung der Maschinenschrift*. Graz.

Stümpel, Rolf, ed. 1985. *Vom Sekretär zur Sekretärin: Eine Ausstellung zur Geschichte der Schreibmaschine und ihrer Bedeutung für den Beruf der Frau im Büro*. Gutenberg Museum Mainz, Mainz.

Turing, Alan M. 1950. "Computing Machinery and Intelligence." *Mind: A Quarterly Review of Psychology and Philosophy* 59: 433–60.

——. 1992. *Mechanical Intelligence*. Vol. 3 of *Collected Works*. Ed. D.C. Nice. Amsterdam.

Van Creveld, Martin L. 1985. *Command in War*. Cambridge, Mass.

Wildhagen, Karl Heinz, ed. 1970. *Erich Fellgiebel: Meister operative Nachrichtenverbindungen: Ein Beitrag zur Geschichte der Nachrichtentruppe*. Wennigsen.

Witsch, Josef. 1932. *Berufs- und Lebensschicksale weiblicher Angestellten in der schönen Literatur*. 2nd ed. Sozialpolitische Schriften des Forschungsinstitutes für Sozialwissenschaften in Köln, no. 2. Cologne.

3

ALIEN AND THE MONSTROUS-FEMININE

Barbara Creed

The science fiction horror film *Alien* (1979) is a complex representation of the monstrous-feminine in terms of the maternal figure as perceived within a patriarchal ideology. She is there in the text's scenarios of the primal science of birth and death; she is there in her many guises as the treacherous mother, the oral sadistic mother, the mother as the primordial abyss; and she is there in the film's images of blood, of the all-devouring vagina, the toothed vagina, the vagina as Pandora's box; and finally she is there in the chameleon figure of the alien, the monster as fetish-object of and for the mother. But it is the archaic mother, the reproductive/generative mother, who haunts the *mise-en-scène* of the film's first section, with its emphasis on different representations of the primal scene.

According to Freud, every child either watches its parents in the act of sexual intercourse or has fantasies about the act – fantasies which relate to the problem of origins. Freud left open the question of the cause of the fantasy but suggested that it may initially be aroused by "an observation of the sexual intercourse of animals."[1] In his study of the Wolf-Man, Freud argued that the child did not initially observe his parents in the act of sexual intercourse but that he witnessed the copulation of animals whose behaviour he then displaced onto his parents. In situations where the child actually witnesses sexual intercourse between its parents, Freud argued that all children arrive at the same conclusion: "They adopt what may be called a *sadistic view of coition*."[2] If the child perceives the primal scene as a monstrous act – whether in reality or fantasy – it may fantasize animals or mythical creatures as taking part in the scenario. Possibly the many mythological stories in which humans copulate with animals and other creatures (Europa and Zeus, Leda and the Swan) are reworkings of the primal scene narrative. The Sphinx, with her lion's body and woman's face, is an interesting figure in this context. Freud suggested that the Riddle of the Sphinx was probably a distorted version of the great riddle that faces all children – Where do babies come from? An extreme form of the primal fantasy is that of "observing intercourse while one is still an unborn baby in the womb."[3]

One of the major concerns of the science fiction horror film (*Alien*, *The Thing*, *Invasion of the Body Snatchers*, *Altered States*) is the reworking of the primal scene in relation to the representation of other forms of copulation and procreation. *Alien* presents various representations of the primal scene. Behind each of these lurks the figure of the archaic mother, that is, the image of the mother in her generative function – the mother as the origin of all life. This archaic figure is somewhat different from the mother of the semiotic chora, as posed by Kristeva,[4] in that the latter is the pre-Oedipal mother who exists in relation to the family and the symbolic order. The concept of the parthenogenetic, archaic mother adds another dimension to the maternal figure and presents us with a new way of understanding how patriarchal ideology works to deny the "difference" of woman in her cinematic representation.

The first birth scene occurs in *Alien* at the beginning, where the camera/spectator explores the inner space of the mother-ship whose life support system is a computer aptly named "Mother." This exploratory sequence of the inner body of the "Mother" culminates with a long tracking shot down one of the corridors which leads to a womb-like chamber where the crew of seven are woken up from their protracted sleep by Mother's voice monitoring a call for help from a nearby planet. The seven astronauts emerge slowly from their sleep pods in what amounts to a re-birthing scene which is marked by a fresh, antiseptic atmosphere. In outer space, birth is a well controlled, clean, painless affair. There is no blood, trauma or terror. This scene could be interpreted as a primal fantasy in which the human subject is born fully developed – even copulation is redundant.

The second representation of the primal scene takes place when three of the crew enter the body of the unknown space-ship through a "vaginal" opening: the ship is shaped like a horse-shoe, its curved sides like two long legs spread apart at the entrance. They travel along a corridor which seems to be made of a combination of inorganic and organic material – as if the inner space of this ship were alive. Compared to the atmosphere of the *Nostromo*, however, this ship is dark, dank and mysterious. A ghostly light glimmers and the sounds of their movements echo throughout the caverns. In the first chamber, the three explorers find a huge alien life form which appears to have been dead for a long time. Its bones are bent outward as if it exploded from the inside. One of the trio, Kane, is lowered down a shaft into the gigantic womb-like chamber in which rows of eggs are hatching. Kane approaches one of the eggs; as he touches it with his gloved hand it opens out, revealing a mass of pulsating flesh. Suddenly, the monstrous thing inside leaps up and attaches itself to Kane's helmet, its tail penetrating Kane's mouth in order to fertilize itself inside his stomach. Despite the warnings of Ripley, Kane is taken back on board the *Nostromo* where the alien rapidly completes its gestation process inside Kane.

This representation of the primal scene recalls Freud's reference to an extreme primal scene fantasy where the subject imagines travelling back inside the womb to watch her/his parents having sexual intercourse, perhaps to watch her/himself being conceived. Here, three astronauts explore the gigantic, cavernous, malevolent womb of the mother. Two members of the group watch the enactment of the primal scene in which Kane is violated in an act of phallic penetration – by the father or phallic mother? Kane himself is guilty of the strongest transgression; he actually peers into the egg/womb in order to investigate its mysteries. In so doing, he becomes a "part" of the primal scene, taking up the place of the mother, the one who is penetrated, the one who bears the offspring of the union. The primal scene is represented as violent, monstrous (the union is between human and alien), and is mediated by the question of incestuous desire. All restagings of the primal scene raise the question of incest, as the beloved parent (usually the mother) is with a rival. The first birth scene, where the astronauts emerge from their sleep pods, could be viewed as a representation of incestuous desire *par excellence*: the father is completely absent; here, the mother is sole parent and sole life-support.

From this forbidden union, the monstrous creature is born. But man, not woman, is the "mother" and Kane dies in agony as the alien gnaws its way through his stomach. The birth of the alien from Kane's stomach plays on what Freud described as a common misunderstanding that many children have about birth, that is, that the mother is somehow impregnated through the mouth – she may eat a special food – and the baby grows in her stomach from which it is also born. Here, we have a third version of the primal scene.

A further version of the primal scene – almost a convention[5] of the science fiction film – occurs when smaller craft or bodies are ejected from the mother-ship into outer space; although sometimes the ejected body remains attached to the mother-ship by a long lifeline or umbilical cord. This scene is presented in two separate ways: one when Kane's body, wrapped in a white shroud, is ejected from the mother-ship; and the second, when the small space capsule, in which Ripley is trying to escape from the alien, is expelled from the underbelly of the mother-ship. In the former, the "mother's" body has become hostile; it contains the alien whose one purpose is to kill and devour all of Mother's children. In the latter birth scene the living infant is ejected from the malevolent body of the "mother" to avoid destruction; in this scenario, the "mother's" body explodes at the moment of giving birth.

Although the "mother" as a figure does not appear in these sequences – nor indeed the entire film – her presence forms a vast backdrop for the enactment of all the events. She is there in the images of birth, the representations of the primal scene, the womb-like imagery, the long winding tunnels leading to inner chambers, the rows of hatching eggs, the body of the mother-ship, the voice of the life-support system, and the birth of the alien. She is the generative mother, the pre-phallic mother, the being who exists prior to knowledge of the phallus.

In explaining the difficulty he had in uncovering the role of the mother in the early development of infants, Freud complained of the almost "prehistoric" remoteness of this "Minoan-Mycenaean" stage:

> Everything in the sphere of this first attachment to the mother seemed to me so difficult to grasp in analysis – so grey with age and shadowy and almost impossible to revivify – that it was as if it had succumbed to an especially inexorable repression.[6]

Just as the Oedipus complex tends to hide the pre-Oedipal phase in Freudian theory, the figure of the father, in the Lacanian rewriting of Freud, obscures the mother–child relationship of the imaginary. In contrast to the maternal figure of the Lacanian imaginary, Kristeva posits another dimension to the mother – she is associated with the pre-verbal or the semiotic and as such tends to disrupt the symbolic order.[7]

I think it is possible to open up the mother-question still further and posit an even more archaic maternal figure, to go back to mythological narratives of the generative, parthenogenetic mother – that ancient archaic figure who gives birth to all living things. She exists in the mythology of all human cultures as the mother-goddess who alone created the heavens and earth. In China she was known as Nu Kwa, in Mexico as Coatlicue, in Greece as Gaia (literally meaning "earth") and in Sumer as Nammu. In "Moses and Monotheism," Freud attempted to account for the historical existence of the great mother-goddesses.

> It is likely that the mother-goddesses originated at the time of the curtailment of the matriarchy, as a compensation for the slight upon the mothers. The male deities appear first as sons beside the great mothers and only later clearly assume the features of father-figures. These male gods of polytheism reflect the conditions during the patriarchal age.[8]

Freud proposed that human society developed through stages from patriarchy to matriarchy and finally back to patriarchy. During the first, primitive people lived in small hordes, each one dominated by a jealous, powerful father who possessed all the females of the group. One day the sons, who had been banished to the outskirts of the group, overthrew the father – whose body they devoured – in order to secure his power and to take his women for themselves. Overcome by guilt, they later attempted to revoke the deed by setting up a totem as a substitute for the father and by renouncing the women whom they had liberated. The sons were forced to give up the women, whom they all wanted to possess, in order to preserve the group which otherwise would have been destroyed as the sons fought amongst themselves. In "Totem and Taboo," Freud suggests that here "the germ of the institution of matriarchy"[9] may have originated. Eventually, however, this new form of social organization, constructed upon the taboo against murder and incest, was replaced by the re-establishment of a patriarchal order. He pointed out that the sons had: "thus created out of their filial sense of guilt the two fundamental taboos of totemism, which for that very reason inevitably corresponded to the two repressed wishes for the Oedipus complex."[10]

Freud's account of the origins of patriarchal civilization is generally regarded as mythical. Lévi-Strauss points out that it is "a fair account not of the beginnings of civilization, but of its present state" in that it expresses "in symbolic form an inveterate fantasy" – the desire to murder the father and possess the mother.[11] In her discussion of "Totem and Taboo," Kristeva argues that a "strange slippage" has taken place, in that although Freud points out that morality is founded on the taboos of murder and incest his argument concentrates on the first to the virtual exclusion of the latter. Yet, Kristeva argues, the "woman – or mother – image haunts a large part of that book and keeps shaping its background." She poses the question:

> Could the sacred be, whatever its variants, a two-sided formation? One aspect founded by murder and the social bond made up of a murderer's guilt-ridden atonement, with all the projective mechanisms and obsessive rituals that accompany it; and another aspect, like a lining, more secret and invisible, non-representable, oriented toward those uncertain spaces of unstable identity, toward the fragility – both threatening and fusional – of the archaic dyad, toward the non-separation of subject/object on which language has no hold but one woven of fright and repulsion?[12]

From the above, it is clear that the figure of the mother in both the history of human sociality and in the history of the individual subject poses immense problems. Freud attempts to account for the existence of the mother-goddess figure by posing a matriarchal period in historical times while admitting that everything to do with the "first attachment to the mother" is deeply repressed – "grey with age and shadowy and almost impossible to revivify." Nowhere does he attempt to specify the nature of this "matriarchal period" and the implications of this for his own psychoanalytical theory, specifically his theory of the Oedipus complex which, as Lacan points out, "can only appear in a patriarchal form in the institution of the family."[13] Kristeva criticizes Freud for failing to deal adequately with incest and the mother-question while using the same mystifying language to refer to the mother; the other aspect of the sacred is "like a lining," "secret and invisible," "non-representable." In his re-reading of Freud, Lacan mystifies the figure of the woman even further: ". . . the woman is not-all, there is always something with her which eludes discourse."[14] Further, all three writers conflate the archaic mother with the mother of the dyadic and triadic relationship. They refer to her as a "shadowy" figure (Freud); as "non-representable" (Kristeva); as the "abyss of the female organ from which all life comes forth" (Lacan[15]), then make no clear attempt to distinguish this aspect of the maternal imago from the protective/suffocating mother of the pre-Oedipal or the mother as object of sexual jealousy and desire as she is represented in the Oedipal configuration.

The maternal figure constructed within/by the writings of Freud, Lacan and Kristeva is inevitably the mother of the dyadic or triadic relationship – although the latter figure is more prominent. Even when she is represented as the mother of the imaginary, of the dyadic relationship, she is still constructed as the *pre-Oedipal* mother, that is, as a figure about to "take up a place" in the symbolic – as a figure always in relation to the father, the representative of the phallus. Without her "lack," he cannot signify its opposite – lack of a lack or presence. But if we posit a more archaic dimension to the mother – the mother as originating womb – we can at least begin to talk about the material figure as *outside* the patriarchal family constellation. In this context, the mother-goddess narratives can be read as primal-scene narratives in which the mother is the sole parent. She is also the subject, not the object, of narrativity.

For instance in the "Spider Woman" myth of the North American Indians, there was only the Spider Woman, who spun the universe into existence and then created two daughters from whom all life flowed. She is also the Thought Woman or Wise Woman who knows the secrets of the universe. Within the Oedipus narrative, however, she becomes the Sphinx, who also knows the answers to the secret of life; but here her situation has been changed. She is no longer the subject of the narrative; she has become the object of the narrative of the male hero. After he has solved her riddle, she will destroy herself. The Sphinx is an ambiguous figure; she knows the secret of life and is thereby linked to the mother-goddess but her name, which is derived from "sphincter," suggests she is the mother of toilet training, the pre-Oedipal mother who must be repudiated by the son so that he can take up his proper place in the symbolic. It is interesting that Oedipus has always been seen to have committed two horrific crimes: patricide and incest. But his encounter with the Sphinx, which leads to her death, suggests he is also responsible for another horrific crime – that of matricide. For the Sphinx, like the Medusa, is a mother-goddess figure; they are both variants of the same mythological mother who gave birth to all life. Lévi-Strauss has argued that a major issue in the Oedipus myth is the problem of whether or not man is born from woman. This myth is also central to *Alien*:

> Although the problem obviously cannot be solved, the Oedipus myth provides a kind of logical tool which relates the original problem – born from one or born from two? – to the derivative problem: born from different or born from same?[16]

The Medusa, whose head, according to Freud, signifies the female genitals in their terrifying aspect, also represents the procreative function of woman. The blood which flows from her severed head gives birth to Pegasus and Chrysaor. Although Neptune is supposed to be the father, the nature of the birth once again suggests the parthenogenetic mother. In *Alice Doesn't*, Teresa de Lauretis argues that:

> to say that narrative is the production of Oedipus is to say that each reader – male or female – is constrained and defined within the two positions of a sexual difference thus conceived: male-hero-human, on the side of the subject; and female-obstacle-boundary-space, on the other.[17]

If we apply her definitions to narratives which deal specifically with the archaic mother – such as the Oedipus and Perseus myths – we can see that the "obstacle" relates specifically to the question of origins and is an attempt to repudiate the idea of woman as the source of life, woman as sole parent, woman as archaic mother.

In his article, "Fetishism in the Horror Film," Roger Dadoun also refers to this archaic maternal figure. He describes her as:

> a maternal thing situated on this side of good and evil, on this side of all organized form, on this side of all events – a totalizing, oceanic mother, a "mysterious and

profound unity," arousing in the subject the anguish of fusion and of dissolution; the mother prior to the uncovering of the essential *béance* [gap], of the *pas-de-phallus*, the mother who is pure fantasm, in the sense that she is posed as an omnipresent and all-powerful totality, an absolute being, only in the intuition – she does not have a phallus – which deposes her . . .[18]

If Dadoun places emphasis on her "totalizing, oceanic" presence, I would stress her archaism in relation to her generative powers – the mother who gives birth all by herself, the original parent, the godhead of all fertility and the origin of procreation. What is most interesting about the mythological figure of woman as the source of all life (a role taken over by the male god of monotheistic religions) is that, within patriarchal signifying practices, particularly the horror film, she is reconstructed and represented as a *negative* figure, one associated with the dread of the generative mother seen only in the abyss, the monstrous vagina, the origin of all life threatening to reabsorb what it once birthed. Kristeva also represents her in this negative light, and in this context it is interesting to note that Freud linked the womb to the *unheimlich*, the uncanny. Freud also supported, and elaborated upon, Schelling's definition of the uncanny as "something which ought to have remained hidden but has come to light."[19] In horror films such as *Alien*, we are given a representation of the female genitals and the womb as uncanny – horrific objects of dread and fascination. Unlike the mythological mother-narratives, here the archaic mother, like the Sphinx and the Medusa, is seen only in a negative light. But the central characteristic of the archaic mother is her total dedication to the generative, procreative principle. She is outside morality and the law. Ash's eulogy to the alien is a description of this mother: "I admire its purity; a survivor unclouded by conscience, remorse or delusions of morality."

Clearly, it is difficult to separate out completely the figure of the archaic mother, as defined above, from other aspects of the maternal figure – the maternal authority of Kristeva's semiotic, the mother of Lacan's imaginary, the phallic woman, the castrated woman. While the different figures signify quite separate things about the monstrous-feminine, each one is also only part of the whole – a different aspect of the material figure. At times the horrific nature of the monstrous-feminine is totally dependent on the merging together of all aspects of the material figure into one – the horrifying image of woman as archaic mother, phallic woman and castrated body represented as a single figure.

The archaic mother – constructed as a negative force – is represented in her phantasmagoric aspects in many horror texts, particularly the science fiction horror film. We see her as the gaping, cannibalistic bird's mouth in *The Giant Claw*; the terrifying spider of *The Incredible Shrinking Man*; the toothed vagina/womb of *Jaws*; and the fleshy, pulsating, womb of *The Thing* and *Poltergeist*. What is common to all of these images of horror is the voracious maw, the mysterious black hole which signifies female genitalia as a monstrous sign which threatens to give birth to equally horrific offspring, as well as threatening to incorporate everything in its path. This is the generative archaic mother, constructed within patriarchal ideology as the primeval "black hole." This, of course, is also the hole which is opened up by the absence of the penis; the horrifying sight of the mother's genitals – proof that castration can occur.

However, in the texts cited above, the emphasis is not on castration; rather it is the gestating, all-devouring womb of the archaic mother which generates the horror. Nor are these images of the womb constructed in relation to the penis of the father. Unlike the female genitalia, the womb cannot be constructed as a "lack" in relation to the penis. The womb is not the site of castration anxiety. Rather, the womb signifies "fullness" or "emptiness" but always it is its own point of reference. This is why we need to posit a more archaic dimension to the mother. For the concept of the archaic mother allows for a notion of the feminine which does not depend for its definition on a concept of the masculine. The term "archaic mother" signifies woman as sexual difference. In contrast the maternal figure of the pre-Oedipal is always represented in relation to the penis – the phallic mother who later becomes the castrated mother. Significantly, there is an attempt in *Alien* to appropriate the procreative function of the mother, to represent a man giving birth, to deny the mother as signifier of sexual difference – but here birth can exist only as the other face of death.

The archaic mother is present in all horror films as the blackness of extinction – death. The desires and fears invoked by the image of the archaic mother, as a force that threatens to reincorporate what it once gave birth to, are always there in the horror text – all pervasive, all encompassing – because of the constant presence of death. The desire to return to the original oneness of things, to return to the mother/womb, is primarily a desire for non-differentiation. If, as Georges Bataille[20] argues, life signifies discontinuity and separateness, and death signifies continuity and non-differentiation, then the desire for and attraction of death suggests also a desire to return to the state of original oneness with the mother. As this desire to merge occurs after differentiation, that is after the subject has developed as a separate, autonomous self, then it is experienced as a form of psychic death. In this sense, the confrontation with death as represented in the horror film, gives rise to a terror of self-disintegration, of losing one's self or ego – often represented cinematically by a screen which becomes black, signifying the obliteration of self, the self of the protagonist in the film and the spectator in the cinema. This has important consequences for the positioning of the spectator in the cinema.

One of the most interesting structures operating in the screen-spectator relationship relates to the sight/site of the monstrous within the horror text. In contrast to the conventional viewing structures working within other variants of the classic text, the horror film does not constantly work to suture the spectator into the viewing process. Instead, an unusual phenomenon arises whereby the suturing processes are momentarily undone while the horrific image on the screen challenges the viewer to run the risk of continuing to look. Here, I refer to those moments in the horror film when the spectator, unable to stand the images of horror unfolding before his/her eyes, is forced to look away, to not-look, to look anywhere but at the screen. Strategies of identification are temporarily broken, as the spectator is constructed in the place of horror, the place where the sight/site can no longer be endured, the place where pleasure in looking is transformed into pain and the spectator is punished for his/her voyeuristic desires.

Confronted by the sight of the monstrous, the viewing subject is put into crisis – boundaries, designed to keep the abject at bay, threaten to disintegrate, collapse. The horror film puts the viewing subject's sense of unified self into crisis in those moments when the image on the screen becomes too threatening or horrific to watch, with the threat that the viewing subject will be drawn to the place "where meaning collapses," the place of death. By not-looking, the spectator is able momentarily to withdraw identification from the image on the screen in order to reconstruct the boundary between self and screen and reconstitute the "self" which is threatened with disintegration. This process of reconstitution of the self is reaffirmed by the conventional ending of the horror narrative in which the monster is usually "named" and destroyed.[21]

Alien collapses the image of the threatening archaic mother, signifying woman as "difference," into the more recognized figure of the pre-Oedipal mother; this occurs in relation to two images of the monstrous-feminine: the oral-sadistic mother and the phallic mother. Kane's transgressive disturbance of the egg/womb initiates a transformation of its latent aggressivity into an active, phallic enemy. The horror then played out can be read in relation to Kristeva's concept of the semiotic chora. Kriseva argues that the maternal body becomes the site of conflicting desires (the semiotic chora). These desires are constantly staged and restaged in the workings of the horror narrative where the subject is left alone, usually in a strange hostile place, and forced to confront an unnamable terror, the monster. The monster represents both the subject's fears of being alone, of being separate from the mother, and the threat of annihilation – often through reincorporation. As oral-sadistic mother, the monster threatens to reabsorb the child she once nurtured. Thus, the monster is ambiguous; it both repels and attracts.

In *Alien*, each of the crew members comes face to face with the alien in a scene whose *mise-en-scène* is coded to suggest a monstrous, malevolent maternal figure. They watch with fascinated horror as the baby alien gnaws its way through Kane's stomach; Dallas, the captain, encounters the alien after he has crawled along the ship's enclosed, womb-like air ducts; and the other three members are cannibalized in a frenzy of blood in scenes which emphasize the alien's huge razor-sharp teeth, signifying the monstrous oral-sadistic mother. Apart from the scene of Kane's death, all the death sequences occur in dimly lit, enclosed, threatening spaces reminiscent of the giant hatchery where Kane first encounters the pulsating egg. In these death sequences the terror of being abandoned is matched only by the fear of reincorporation. This scenario, which enacts the conflicting desires at play in the semiotic chora, is staged within the body of the mother-ship, the vessel which the space-travelers initially trust, until "Mother" herself is revealed as a treacherous figure programmed to sacrifice the lives of the crew in the interests of the Company.

The other face of the monstrous-feminine in *Alien* is the phallic mother. Freud argued that the male child could either accept the threat of castration, thus ending the Oedipus complex, or disavow it. The latter response requires the (male) child to mitigate his horror at the sight of the mother's genitals – proof that castration can occur – with a fetish object which substitutes for her missing penis. For him, she is still the phallic mother, the penis-woman. In "Medusa's Head" Freud argued that the head with its hair of writhing snakes represented the terrifying genitals of the mother, but that this head also functioned as a fetish object. He also noted that a display of the female genitals makes a woman "unapproachable and repels all sexual desires," referring to the section in Rabelais which relates "how the Devil took flight when the woman showed him her vulva."[22] Perseus's solution is to look only at a reflection, a mirror-image of her genitals. As with patriarchal ideology, his shield reflects an "altered" representation, a vision robbed of its threatening aspects. The full difference of the mother is denied; she is constructed as other, displayed before the gaze of the conquering male hero, then destroyed. The price paid is the destruction of sexual heterogeneity and repression of the maternal signifier. The fetishization of the mother's genitals could occur in those texts where the maternal figure is represented in her phantasmagoric aspects as the gaping, voracious vagina/womb. Do aspects of these images work to mitigate the horror by offering a substitute for the penis? However, it is possible that we could theorize fetishism differently by asking: Who is the fetish-object a fetish for? The male or female subject? In general, the fetishist is usually assumed to be male, although Freud did allow that female fetishism was a possibility.[23] The notion of female fetishism is much neglected although it is present in various patriarchal discourses.[24]

In *The Interpretation of Dreams*,[25] Freud discusses the way in which the doubling of a penis-symbol indicates an attempt to stave off castration anxieties. Juliet Mitchell refers to doubling as a sign of a female castration complex: "We can see the significance of this for women, as dreams of repeated number of children – 'little ones' – are given the same import." In this context, female fetishism represents an attempt by the female subject to continue to "have" the phallus, to take up a "positive" place in relation to the symbolic.[26]

Female fetishism is clearly represented within many horror texts – as instances of patriarchal signifying practices – but only in relation to male fears and anxieties about women and the question: What do women want? (*The Birds, Cat People, Alien, The Thing*.) Women as yet do not speak their own "fetishistic" desires within the popular cinema – if, indeed, women have such desires.

The notion of female fetishism is represented in *Alien* in the figure of the monster. The creature is the mother's phallus, attributed to the maternal figure by a phallocentric ideology terrified at the thought that women might desire to have the phallus. The monster as fetish object is not there to meet the desires of the male fetishist, but rather to signify the monstrousness of woman's desire to have the phallus.

In *Alien*, the monstrous creature is constructed as the phallus of the negative mother. The image of the archaic mother – threatening because it signifies woman as difference rather than constructed as opposition – is, once again, collapsed into the figure of the pre-Oedipal mother. By relocating the figure of woman within an Oedipal scenario, her image can be recuperated and controlled. The womb, even if represented negatively, is a greater threat than the mother's phallus. As phallic mother, woman is again represented as monstrous. What is horrific to her desire to cling to her offspring in order to continue to "have the phallus." Her monstrous desire is concretized in the figure of the alien; the creature whose deadly mission is represented as the same as that of the archaic mother – to reincorporate and destroy all life.

If we consider *Alien* in the light of a theory of female fetishism, then the chameleon nature of the alien begins to make sense. Its changing appearance represents a form of doubling or multiplication of the phallus, pointing to the mother's desire to stave off her castration. The alien is the mother's phallus, a fact which is made perfectly clear in the birth scene where the infant alien rises from Kane's stomach and holds itself erect, glaring angrily around the room, before screeching off into the depths of the ship. But the alien is more than a phallus; it is also coded as a toothed vagina, the monstrous-feminine as the cannibalistic mother. A large part of the ideological project of *Alien* is the representation of the maternal fetish object as an "alien" or foreign shape. This is why the body of the heroine becomes so important at the end of the film.

Much has been written about the final scene, in which Ripley/Sigourney Weaver undresses before the camera, on the grounds that its voyeurism undermines her role as successful heroine. A great deal has also been written about the cat. Why does she rescue the cat and thereby risk her life, and the lives of Parker and Lambert, when she has previously been so careful about quarantine regulations? Again, satisfactory answers to these questions are provided by a phallo-centric concept of female fetishism. Compared to the horrific sight of the alien as fetish object of the monstrous-feminine, Ripley's body is pleasurable and reassuring to look at. She signifies the "acceptable" form and shape of woman. In a sense the monstrousness of woman, represented by Mother as betrayer (the computer/life-support system) and Mother as the uncontrollable, generative, cannibalistic mother (the alien), is controlled through the display of woman as reas-suring and pleasurable sign. The image of the cat functions in the same way; it signifies an acceptable, and in this context a reassuring, fetish object for the "normal" woman. Thus, Ripley holds the cat to her, stroking it as if it were her "baby," her "little one." Finally, Ripley enters her sleep pod, assuming a virginal repose. The nightmare is over and we are returned to the opening sequence of the film where birth was a pristine affair. The final sequence works, not only to dispose of the alien, but also to repress the nightmare image of the monstrous-feminine within the text's patriarchal discourses.

Kristeva's theory of abjection, if viewed as description rather than prescription, provides a productive hypothesis for an analysis of the monstrous-feminine in the horror and SF horror film.[27] If we posit a more archaic dimension to the mother, we can see how this figure, as well as Kristeva's maternal authority of the semiotic, are both constructed as figures of abjection within the signifying practices of the horror film. We can see its ideological project as an attempt to shore up the symbolic order by constructing the feminine as an imaginary "other" which must be repressed and controlled in order to secure and protect the social order. Thus, the horror film stages and re-stages a constant repudiation of the maternal figure.

Notes

1 Sigmund Freud, "From the History of an Infantile Neurosis" in *Case Histories II*, Pelican Freud Library, Vol. 9, Harmondsworth: Penguin 1981.

2 Sigmund Freud, "On the Sexual Theories of Children" in *On Sexuality*, Pelican Freud Library, vol. 7, Harmondsworth: Penguin 1981, p. 198.

3 Sigmund Freud, "The Paths to the Formation of Symptoms" in *Introductory Lectures on Psychoanalysis*, Pelican Freud Library, vol. 1, Harmondsworth: Penguin 1981, p. 417.

4 Julia Kristeva, *Powers of Horror: An Essay on Abjection*, New York: Columbia University Press, 1982, p. 14.

5 Daneil Dervin argues that this structure does deserve the status of a convention. For a discussion of the primal scene fantasy in science fiction cinema, see "Primal Conditions and Conventions: The Genre of Science Fiction." [in *Alien Zone: Cultural Theory and Contemporary Science Fiction*. London: Verso, 1990. 96–102.]

6 Sigmund Freud, "Female Sexuality" in *On Sexuality*, Pelican Freud Library, vol. 7, p. 373.

7 For a discussion of the relation between "the semiotic" and the Lacanian "Imaginary," see Jane Gallop, *Feminism and Psychoanalysis: the Daughter's Seduction*, London: MacMillan 1983, pp. 124–5.

8 Sigmund Freud, "Moses and Monotheism," *The Standard Edition of the Complete Psychological Works of Sigmund Freud*, Pelican Freud Library, vol. 13, London: Hogarth Press 1958, vol. 23, p. 83.

9 Sigmund Freud, "Totem and Taboo" in *The Origins of Religion*, Pelican Freud Library, vol. 13, Harmondsworth: Penguin 1985, p. 206.

10 Ibid., p. 205.

11 Lévi-Strauss, quoted in Georges Bataille, *Death and Sensuality: A Study of Eroticism and the Taboo*, New York: Walker & Company 1962, p. 200.

12 Kristeva, pp. 57–8.

13 Jacques Lacan, in Anthony Wilden, ed., *The Language of the Self*, Baltimore: Johns Hopkins university Press 1970, p. 126.

14 Jacques Lacan, *Le Seminaire XX*, p. 34, translated by Stephen Heath, "Difference," *Screen*, vol. 19, no. 3 1978, p. 59.

15 Jacques Lacan, *Le Seminaire II*, translated in Heath, p. 54.

16 Claude Lévi-Strauss, *Structural Anthropology*, trans. C. Jacobson and B.G. Schoepf, New York: Doubleday 1976, p. 212.

17 Teresa de Lauretis, *Alice Doesn't: Feminism, Semiotics, Cinema*, Bloomington: Indiana University Press 1984, p. 121.

18 Roger Dadoun, "Fetishism in the Horror Film," *enclitic*, vol. 1, no. 2, 1977, pp. 55–6.

19 Sigmund Freud, "The Uncanny," *The Standard Edition*, vol. 17, p. 245.

20 Bataille, *Death and Sensuality.*

21 For a discussion of the relationship between the female spectator, structures of looking and the horror film, see Linda Williams, "When the Woman Looks" in Mary Anne Doane, Patricia Mellencamp and Linda Williams, eds, *Re-Vision: Essays in Feminist Film Criticism*, Los Angeles, CA: American Film Institute 1984.

22 Sigmund Freud, "Medusa's Head," *The Standard Edition*, vol. 18, p. 105.

23 Sigmund Freud, "An Outline of Psychoanalysis," *The Standard Edition*, vol. 23, p. 202.

24 Mary Kelly, "Woman-Desire-Image," *Desire*, London: ICA, 1984.

25 Sigmund Freud, *Interpretation of Dreams*, Pelican Freud Library, vol. 4, Harmondsworth: Penguin 1982.

26 Juliet Mitchell, *Psychoanalysis and Feminism*, Harmondsworth: Penguin 1974, p. 84.

27 For an analysis of the horror film as a "return of the repressed," see Robin Wood's articles, "Return of the Repressed," *Film Comment*, July–August 1978; and "Neglected Nightmares," *Film Comment*, March–April 1980.

4

SCARY WOMEN

Cinema, surgery, and special effects

Vivian Sobchack

What is it to be embodied quite literally "in the flesh," to live not only the remarkable elasticity of our skin, its colors and textures, but also its fragility, its responsive and visible marking of our accumulated experiences and our years in scars and sags and wrinkles? How does it feel and what does it look like to age and grow old in our youth-oriented and image-conscious culture – particularly if one is a woman? In an article on the cultural implications of changing age demographics as a consequence of what has been called "the graying of America," James Atlas writes:

> Americans regard old age as a raw deal, not as a universal fate. It's a narcissistic injury. That's why we don't want the elderly around: they embarrass us, like cripples or the terminally ill. Banished to the margins, they perpetuate the illusion that our urgent daily lives are permanent and not just transient things.[1]

This cultural – and personal – sense of aging as "embarrassing" and as a "narcissistic injury" cannot be separated from our objectification of our bodies as what they look like rather than as the existential basis for our capacities, as images and representations rather than as the means of our being. Thus, insofar as we subjectively live both our bodies and our images, each not only informs the other, but they also become significantly confused.

What follows, in this context, is less an argument than a meditation on these confusions as they are phenomenologically experienced, imagined, and represented in contemporary American culture, where the dread of aging – particularly by women – is dramatized and allayed both through the wish-fulfilling fantasies of rejuvenation in certain American movies and the more general, if correlated, faith in the "magic" and "quick fixes" of "special effects," both cinematic and surgical. This conjunction of aging women, cinema, and surgery is also the conjunction of aesthetics and ethics, foregrounding not merely cultural criteria of beauty and desirability but also their very real as well as representational consequences. As Susan Sontag writes:

> Growing older is mainly an ordeal of the imagination – a moral disease, a social pathology – intrinsic to which is the fact that it afflicts women much more than men. It is particularly women who experience growing older with distaste and even shame.[2]

Thus, it is not surprising that, at sixty-three and as a woman with a privilege of self-reflection, I am always struggling with such distaste and shame in response to the various processes and cultural determinations of my own aging.

[. . .]

Whatever my stance, I live now in heightened awareness of the instability of my image and of myself, and I think about cosmetic surgery a lot: getting my eyes done, removing the furrows in my forehead, smoothing out the lines around my mouth, and lifting the skin around my jaw. But I am sure I would be disappointed. I know the effects wouldn't last – and I feel, perhaps irrationally but perhaps not, that there would be awful consequences. [. . .] I have this sense that surgery would put me physically and temporally out of sync with myself, would create of me an uncanny and disturbing double who would look the way I "was" and forcibly usurp the moment in which I presently "am." There is a certain irony operative here, of course, since even without surgery I presently don't ever quite recognize myself or feel synchronous with my image when I look at it in mirrors or pictures. And so, although I don't avoid mirrors, I also don't seek them out, and I'm not particularly keen on being photographed. Rather, I try very hard to locate myself less in my image than in (how else to say it?) my "comportment."

It is for this reason that I was particularly moved when I first read in *Entertainment Weekly* that Barbra Streisand (only a year younger than I am, a Brooklyn-born Jew, a persistent and passionate woman with a big mouth like me) was remaking and updating *The Mirror Has Two Faces*, a 1959 French film about a housewife who begins a new life after plastic surgery. Barbra's update was to tell the story of "an ugly duckling professor and her quest for inner and outer beauty."[3] Obviously, given that I'm aging academic woman who has never been secure about her looks, this struck a major chord. Discussing the film's progress and performing its own surgery (a hatchet job) on the middle-aged producer, director, and star, *Entertainment Weekly* reported that the "biggest challenge faced by the 54-year-old" and "hyper-picky" Barbra

> was how to present her character. In the original, the mousy housefrau undergoes her transformation via plastic surgery. But Streisand rejected that idea – perhaps because of the negative message – and went with attitude adjustment instead. Which might work for the character, but does it work for the star? "Certain wrinkles and gravitational forces seem to be causing Streisand concern," says one ex-crew member. "She doesn't want to look her age. She's fighting it." (9)

[. . .]

Before actually seeing the film (eventually released in 1996), I wondered just what, as a substitute for surgery, Barbra's "attitude adjustment" might mean. And how would it translate to the superficiality of an image – in the mirror, in the movies? Might it mean really good makeup for the middle-aged star? Soft focus? Other forms of special effects that reproduce the work of cosmetic surgery? It is of particular relevance here that recent developments in television technology have produced what is called a "skin contouring" camera that makes wrinkles disappear. In a *TV Guide* article rife with puns about "vanity video" and "video collagen" we are told of this "indispensable tool for TV personalities of a certain age" that "can give a soap opera ingénue a few extra years of playing an ingénue" but was first used "as a news division innovation" to make aging news anchors look younger.[4] [. . .] This marvelous television camera aside, however, just how far can these special effects that substitute for cosmetic surgery take you – how long before really good makeup transforms you into a grotesque, before soft focus blurs you into invisibility, before special effects transform you into a witch, a ghoul, or a monster? Perhaps this *is* the cinematic equivalent of attitude adjustment. The alternative to cosmetic surgery in what passes for the verisimilitude of cinematic realism is a change in *genre*, a transformation of sensibility that takes us from the "real" world that demonizes middle-aged women to a world of "irreal" female demons: horror, science fiction, and fantasy.

Indeed, a number of years ago I published an essay on several low-budget science fiction/ horror films made in the late 1950s and early 1960s that focused on middle-aged female characters.[5] I was interested in these critically neglected films because, working through genres deemed fantastic, they were able to displace and disguise cultural anxieties about women and aging while simultaneously figuring them in your face, so to speak. For example, in *Attack of the 50-Ft. Woman* (Nathan Juran, 1958), through a brief (and laughable) transformative encounter with a giant space alien, wealthy, childless, middle-aged, and brunette Nancy achieves a literal size, power, and youthful blondeness her philandering husband, Harry, can no longer ignore as she roams the countryside, wearing a bra and sarong made out of her bed linens, looking for him. In *The Wasp Woman* (Roger Corman, 1959) Janet [*sic*] Starlin, the fortyish and fading owner of a similarly fading cosmetics empire, can no longer serve as the model for advertising her products ("Return to Youth with Janice Starlin!") and overdoses in secret experiments with royal "wasp jelly," which not only reduces but also reverses the aging process. There are, however, side effects, which regularly turn the again youthful cosmetics queen into a murderous insect queen (with high heels, a sheath dress, and a wasp's head). And, in *The Leech Woman* (Edward Dein, 1960), blowzy, alcoholic, despised June becomes her feckless endocrinologist husband's guinea pig as they intrude on an obscure African village to find a secret "rejuvenation serum." Made from orchid pollen mixed with male pituitary fluid (the extraction of which kills its donors), the serum allows June to experience, if only for a while, the simultaneous pleasures of youth, beauty, and revenge – in the tribal ritual of her transformation, she chooses her husband as pituitary donor. *The Leech Woman* is the most blatant of these movies about ageism, not only in plot but also in dialogue. The wizened African woman who offers June her youth speaks before the ritual:

> For a man, old age has rewards. If he is wise, the gray hairs bring dignity and he is treated with honor and respect. But for the aged woman, there is nothing. At best, she's pitied. More often, her lot is of contempt and neglect. What woman lives who has passed the prime of her life who would not give her remaining years to reclaim even for a few moments of joy and happiness and know the worship of men. For the end of life should be its moment of triumph. So it is with the aged woman of Nandos, a last flowering of love, beauty – before death.

In each of these low-budget SF-horror films scared middle-aged women are transformed into rejuvenated but scary women – this not through cosmetic surgery but through fantastical means, makeup, and special effects. Introduced as fading (and childless) females still informed by – but an affront to – sexual desire and the process of biological reproduction, hovering on the brink of grotesquerie and alcoholism, their flesh explicitly disgusting to the men in their lives, these women are figured as more horrible in – and more horrified by – their own middle-aged bodies than in or by the bodies of the "unnatural" monsters they become. In this regard, Linda Williams's important essay, "When the Woman Looks," is illuminating. Williams argues that there is an affinity declared and a look of recognition and sympathy exchanged between the heroine and the monster in the horror film. The SF-horror films mentioned here, however, collapse the distance of this exchange into a single look of *self-recognition*. Touching on this conflation of woman and monster in its link with aging, Williams writes:

> There is not that much difference between an object of desire and an object of horror as far as the male look is concerned. (In one brand of horror film this difference may simply lie in the age of its female stars. The Bette Davises and Joan Crawfords considered too old to continue as spectacle-objects nevertheless persevere as horror objects in films like *Whatever Happened to Baby Jane?* [1962] and *Hush . . . Hush, Sweet Charlotte* [1965]).[6]

Indeed, such horror and SF films dramatize what one psychotherapist describes as the culture's "almost visceral disgust for the older woman as a physical being," and they certainly underscore "ageism" as "the last bastion of sexism."[7] These films also recall, particularly in the male – and self – disgust they generate, Simone de Beauvoir's genuine (if, by today's standards problematic) lament:

> [W]oman is haunted by the horror of growing old. . . . [T]o hold her husband and to assure herself of his protection. . . . it is necessary for her to be attractive, to please. . . . What is to become of her when she no longer has any hold on him? This is what she anxiously asks herself while she helplessly looks on at the degeneration of this fleshly object which she identifies with herself. [. . .][8]

How, in the face of this cultural context, *as* a face in this cultural context, could a woman not yearn for a rejuvenation serum, not want to realize quite literally the youth and power she once seemed to have? In the cinematic – and moral – imagination of the low-budget SF-horror films I've described above, aging and abject women are thus "unnaturally" transformed. Become suddenly young, beautiful, desirable, powerful, horrendous, monstrous, and deadly, each plays out grand, if wacky, dramas of poetic justice. No plastic surgery here. Instead, through the technological magic of cinema, the irrational magic of fantasy, and a few cheesy low-budget effects, what we get is major "attitude adjustment" – and of a scope that might even satisfy Barbra. The leech woman, wasp woman, and fifty-foot woman each literalize, magnify, and enact hyperbolic displays of anger and desire, their youth and beauty represented now as lethal and fatal, their unnatural ascendance to power allowing them to avenge on a grand scale the wrongs done them for merely getting older. Yet, not surprisingly, these films also maintain the cultural status quo – even as they critique it. For what they figure as most grotesque and disgusting is not the monstrousness of the transformation or the monster but rather the "unnatural" conjunction of middle-aged female flesh and still-youthful female desire. And – take heed, Barbra – the actresses who play these pathetic and horrific middle-aged women are always young and beautiful under their latex jowls and aging makeup. Thus, what these fantasies of female rejuvenation give with one hand, they take back with the other. They represent less a grand masquerade of feminist resistance than a retrograde striptease that undermines the double-edged and very temporary narrative power these transformed and empowered middle-aged protagonists supposedly enjoy – that is, "getting their own back" before the eventually "get theirs." And, as is the "natural" order of things in both patriarchal culture and SF-horror films of this sort, they do get theirs – each narrative ending with the restoration and reproduction of social (and ageist) order through the death of its eponymous heroine-monster. Attitude adjustment, indeed!

These low-budget films observe that middle-aged women – as much before as after their transformations and attitude adjustments – are pretty scary. In *Attack of the 50-Ft. Woman*, for example, as Nancy lies in her bedroom after her close encounter of the third kind but before she looms large on the horizon, her doctor explains to her husband the "real cause" of both her "wild" story of an alien encounter and her strange behavior: "When women reach the age of maturity, Mother Nature sometimes overworks their frustration to the point of irrationalism." The screenwriter must have read Freud, who, writing on obsessional neurosis in 1913, tells us:

> It is well known, and has been a matter for much complaint, that women often alter strangely in character after they have abandoned their genital functions. They become quarrelsome, peevish, and argumentative, petty and miserly; in fact, they display sadistic and anal-erotic traits which were not theirs in the era of womanliness.[9]

Which brings us back again to Barbra, whom it turns out we never really left at all. In language akin to Freud's, the article on the production woes of Barbra's film in *Entertainment Weekly* performs its own form of ageist (psycho)analysis. The "steep attrition rate" among cast and crew and the protracted shooting schedule are attributed to both her "hyper-picky" "perfectionism" and to her being a "meddler" (8). We are also told: "Among the things she fretted over: the density of her panty hose, the bras she wore, and whether the trees would have falling leaves" (9). A leech woman, wasp woman, fifty-foot woman – in Freud's terms, an obsessional neurotic: peevish, argumentative, petty, sadistic, and anal-erotic. Poor Barbra. She can't win for losing. Larger than life, marauding the Hollywood countryside in designer clothes and an "adjusted" attitude doesn't get her far from the fear or contempt that attaches to middle-aged women in our culture.

Perhaps Barbara [*sic*] – perhaps I – should reconsider cosmetic surgery. Around ten years younger than Barbra and me and anxious about losing the looks she perceived as the real source of her power, my best friend recently did – although I didn't see the results until long after her operation. Admittedly, I was afraid to; afraid she'd look bad (that is, not like herself or like she had surgery), afraid she'd look good (that is, good enough to make me want to do it). Separated by physical distance, however, I didn't have to confront – and judge – her image, so all I initially knew about her extensive facelift was from email correspondence. (I have permission to use her words but not her name.) Here, in my face, so to speak, as well as hers, were extraordinary convergences of despised flesh, monstrous acts, and malleable image (first "alienated" and later proudly "possessed"). Here, in the very prose of her postings, was the conjunction of actuality and wish, of surgery and cinema, of transformative technologies and the "magic" of "special effects" – all rendered intimately intelligible to us (whether we approved or not) in terms of mortal time and female gender. She wrote, "IT WORKED!" and then she continued:

> My eyes look larger than Audrey Hepburn's in her prime. . . . I am the proud owner of a fifteen-year old's neckline. Amazing – exactly the effect I'd hoped for. Still swollen . . . but that was all predicted. What this tendon-tightening lift did (not by any means purely "skin deep" – he actually . . . redraped the major neck and jaw infrastructure) was reverse the effects of gravity. [. . .] One night of hell due to . . . a compression bandage that made me feel as if I were being choked. Mercifully (and thanks to Valium) I got through it. . . . [. . .] My sutures extend around 80% of my head; *Bride of Frankenstein* city. All (except for the exquisitely fine line under my eyes) are hidden in my hair. But baby I know they're there. Strange reverse-phantom limb sensation. I still have my ears, but I can't exactly feel them. . . . I took Valium each evening the

first week to counteract the tendency toward panic as I tried to fall asleep and realized that I could only move 1/4 inch in any direction. Very minimal bruising – I'm told that's not the rule. . . . I still have a very faint chartreuse glow under one eye. With makeup, *voila!* I can't jut my chin out – can barely make my upper and lower teeth meet at the front. In a few more months, that will relax. And I can live with it. [. . .] The work that was done by the surgeon will last a good seven years. I plan to have my upper eyes done in about three years. This message is for your eyes only. I intend, if pressed, to reveal that I have had my eyes done. Period. Nothing else.[10]

But there's plenty more. And it foregrounds the confusions and conflations of surgery and cinema, technology and "magic," of effort and ease, that so pervade our current image culture. Indeed, there is a bitter irony at work here. Having willfully achieved a "seamless" face, my best friend has willingly lost her voice. She refuses to speak further of the time and labor and pain it took to transform her. The whole point is that, for the magic to work, the seams – both the lines traced by age and the scars traced by the surgery – must not show. Thus, as Kathleen Woodward notes in her wonderful essay "Youthfulness as Masquerade": "Unlike the hysterical body, whose surface is inscribed with symptoms, the objective of the surgically youthful body is to speak nothing."[11] But this is not the only irony at work here. At a more structural level this very lack of disclosure, this silence and secrecy, is an *essential* (if paradoxical) element of a culture increasingly driven – by both desire and technology – to extreme extroversion, to utter disclosure. It is here that cosmetic surgery and the special effects of the cinema converge and are perceived as phenomenologically reversible in what has become our current morphological imagination. Based on the belief that desire – through technology – can be materialized, made visible, and thus "realized," such morphological imagination does a perverse, and precisely superficial, turn on Woodward's distinction between the hysterical body that displays symptoms and the surgically youthful body that silences such display. That is, symptoms and silence are conflated as *the image of one's transformation and one's transformation of the image* become reversible phenomena. These confusions and conflations are dramatized most literally, of course, in the genre of fantasy, where "plastic surgery" is now practiced through the seemingly effortless, seamless transformations of digital morphing.

Indeed, the morphological figurations of fantasy cinema not only allegorize impossible human wish and desire but also extrude and thus fulfill them. In this regard two such live-action films come to mind, each not only making visible (and seemingly effortless) incredible alterations of an unprecedented plastic and elastic human body but also rendering human affective states with unprecedented superficiality and literalism. The films are *Death Becomes Her* (Robert Zemeckis, 1992) and *The Mask* (Chuck Russell, 1994) – both technologically dependent on digital morphing, both figuring the whole of human existence as extrusional, superficial, and plastic. [. . .]

Death Becomes Her functions in a similar manner [inner states displayed on morphing body], although, here, with women as the central figures, the narrative explicitly foregrounds age and literal rejuvenation as its central thematic – youth and beauty are the correlated objects of female desire. Indeed, what's most interesting (although not necessarily funny) about *Death Becomes Her* is that plastic surgery operates in the film twice over. At the narrative level its wimpy hero, Ernest Menville, is a famous plastic surgeon-seduced away from his fiancée, Helen, by middle-aging actress Madeline Ashton, whom we first see starring in a musical flop based on Tennessee Williams's *Sweet Bird of Youth*. Thanks to Ernest's surgical skill (which we never actually *see* on the screen), Madeline finds a whole new career as a movie star. Here, J.G. Ballard, in a chapter of his

The Atrocity Exhibition called "Princess Margaret's Face Lift," might well be glossing Madeline's motivations in relation to Ernest in *Death Becomes Her*. Ballard writes:

> In a TV interview . . . the wife of a famous Beverly Hills plastic surgeon revealed that throughout their marriage her husband had continually re-styled her face and body, pointing a breast here, tucking in a nostril there. She seemed supremely confident of her attractions . . . as she said: "He will never leave me, because he can always change me."[12]

Death Becomes Her plays out this initial fantasy but goes on to exhaust the merely human powers of Madeline's surgeon husband to avail itself of "magic" – both through narrative and "special" morphological effects. Seven quick years of screen time into the marriage, henpecked, alcoholic Ernest is no longer much use to Madeline. Told by her beautician that he – and cosmetic surgery – can no longer help her, the desperate woman seeks out a mysterious and incredibly beautiful "Beverly Hills cult priestess" (significantly played by onetime Lancôme pitchwoman, Isabella Rossellini), who gives her a youth serum that grants eternal life, whatever the condition of the user's body.

At this point the operation of plastic surgery extends from the narrative to the representational level. Indeed, *Death Becomes Her* presents us with the first digitally produced skin – and the "magic" transformations of special computer graphic and cosmetic effects instantaneously nip and tuck Madeline's buttocks, smooth and lift her face and breasts with nary a twinge of discomfort, a trace of blood, or a trice of effort, and reproduce her as "young." Indeed, what Rossellini's priestess says of the youth serum might also be said of the cinematic effects: "A touch of magic in this world obsessed by science." Thus, in the service of instant wish fulfillment this phrase in the narrative disavows not only the extensive calculations of labor and time involved in its own digital effects but also the labor and time entailed by the science and practice of cosmetic surgery.

The film's literalization of anxiety and desire in relation to aging is carried further still. That is, inevitably, the repressed signs of age return and are also reproduced and literalized along with the signs of youth and beauty. When rejuvenated Madeline breaks her neck after being pushed down a flight of stairs by Ernest, she lives on (although medically dead) with visible and hyperbolic variations [the damage caused by aging . . .]. And, after Madeline shoots the returned and vengeful Helen (who has also taken the serum), Helen walks around with a hole in her stomach – a "blasted" and "hollow" woman, however youthful. ("I can see right through you," Madeline says to her.) Ultimately, the film unites the two women – "Mad" and "Hel" – in their increasingly unsuccessful attempts to maintain their literally dead and peeling skin, to keep from "letting themselves go," from "falling apart" – which, at the film's end, they quite literally do.

In both *The Mask* and *Death Becomes Her* cinematic effects and plastic surgery become reversible representational operations – literalizing desire and promising instant and effortless transformation. Human bodily existence is foregrounded as a material surface amenable to endless manipulation and total visibility. However, there is yet a great silence, a great *invisibility*, grounding these narratives of surface and extroversion. The labor, effort, and time entailed by the real operations of plastic surgery (both cinematic and cosmetic) are ultimately disavowed. Instead, we are given a screen image (both psychoanalytic and literal) that attributes the laborious, costly, and technologically based reality that underlies bodily transformations to the nontechnological properties of, in the one instance, the mask, a primitive and magical fetish, and in the other, a glowing potion with "a touch of magic." Of course, like all cases of disavowal, these fantasies turn in and around on themselves like a Möbius strip to ultimately break the silence and reveal the repressed on the same side as the visible screen image.

That is, on the screen side the technological effects of these transformations fantasies are what we came for, what we want "in our face." But we want these effects without wanting to see the technology, without wanting to acknowledge the cost, labor, time, and effort of its operations – all of which might curb our desire, despoil our wonder, and generate fear of pain and death. As Larissa MacFarquhar notes: "Surely, the eroticizing of cosmetic surgery is a sign that the surgery is no longer a gory means to a culturally dictated end but, rather, an end in itself."[13] Indeed, like my friend who wants the effects of her face-lift to be seen but wants the facts of her costly, laborious, lengthy, and painful operation to remain hidden, our pleasure comes precisely from this "appearance" of seamless, effortless, "magical" transformation. Yet on the other, repressed side we are fascinated by the operation – its very cost, difficulty, effortfulness. We cannot help but bring them to visibility. There are now magazines, videos, and Web sites devoted to making visible not only the specific operations of cinematic effects but also surgical effects. (Perhaps the most "in your face" of these can be found on a Web site called – no joke – "Dermatology in the Cinema," where dermatologist Dr. Vail Reese does a film survey of movie stars' skin conditions, both real and cinematic.)[14] These tell-all revelations are made auratic by their previous repression and through a minute accounting of the technology involved, hours spent, effort spent, dollars spent. My friend, too, despite her desire for secrecy, is fascinated by her operation and the visibility of her investment. Her numeracy extends from money to stitches but is most poignant in its temporal lived dimensions: four hours on the operating table, one night of hell, a week of limited jaw motion, time for her hair to grow back, a few months for her upper and lower jaws to "relax," three years before she will do her eyelids, seven years before the surgeon's work is undone again by time and gravity. The "magic" of plastic surgery (both cinematic and cosmetic) costs always an irrecoverable – and irrepressible – portion of a mortal life.

And a mortal life must *live through* its operations, not magically, instantaneously, but *in time*. It is thus apposite and poignant that, offscreen, Isabella Rossellini, who plays and is fixed forever as the eternal high priestess of youth and beauty in both *Death Becomes Her* and old Lancôme cosmetic ads, has joined the ranks of the onscreen "wasp woman," Janet [*sic*] Starlin. After four-teen years as the "face" of Lancôme cosmetics, she was fired at age forty-two for getting "too old."[15] Unlike the wasp woman, however, Rossellini can neither completely reverse the aging process nor murder those who find her middle-aged flesh disgusting. Thus, it is also apposite and poignant that attempts to reproduce the fantasies of the morphological imagination in the real world are doomed to failure: medical cosmetic surgery never quite matches up to the seemingly effortless and perfect plastic surgeries of cinema and computer. This disappointment with the real thing becomes ironically explicit when representational fantasies incorporate the real to take a documentary turn. Discussing the real face-lift and its aftermath of a soap opera actress incorporated into the soap's televised narrative, Woodward cites one critic's observation that "the viewer inspects the results and concludes that they are woefully disappointing."[16]

This disappointment with the "real thing" also becomes explicit in my friend's continuing emails. Along with specific descriptions of her further healings, she wrote:

> Vivian, I'm going through an unsettling part of this surgical journey. When I first got home, the effect was quite dramatic – I literally looked twenty years younger. Now what's happened: the swelling continues to go down, the outlines of the "new face" are still dramatically lifted. BUT, the lines I've acquired through a lifetime of smiling, talking, being a highly expressive individual, are returning. Not all of them – but enough that the effect of the procedure is now quite natural and I no longer look twenty years younger. Maybe ten max. . . . I'm experiencing a queasy depression. Imagining that the

procedure didn't work. That in a few weeks I'll look like I did before the money and the lengthy discomfort. Now I scrutinize, I imagine, I am learning to hate the whole thing. Most of all, the heady sense of exhilaration and confidence is gone. In short, I have no idea any longer how the hell I look.

Which brings me back to myself before the mirror – and again to Barbra, both behind and in front of the camera. There is no way here for any of us to feel superior in sensibility to my friend. Whether we like it or not, as part of our culture, we have all had "our eyes done." As Jean Baudrillard writes:

> We are under the sway of a surgical compulsion that seeks to excise negative char-acterizes and remodel things synthetically into ideal forms. Cosmetic surgery: a face's chance configuration, its beauty or ugliness, its distinctive traits, its negative traits – all these have to be corrected, so as to produce something more beautiful than beautiful: an ideal face.[17]

With or without medical surgery we have been technologically altered, both seeing differ-ently and seeming different than we did in a time before either cinema or cosmetic surgery presented us with their reversible technological promises of immorality and idealized figu-rations of magical self-transformation – that is, transformation without time, without effort, without cost.

To a great extent, then, the bodily transformations of cinema and surgery inform each other. Cinema *is* cosmetic surgery – its fantasies, its makeup, and its digital effects able to "fix" (in the doubled sense of repair and stasis) and to fetishize and to reproduce faces and time as both "unreel" before us. And, reversibly, cosmetic surgery *is* cinema, creating us as an image we not only learn to enact in a repetition compulsion but also must – and never can – live up to. Through their technological "operations" – the work and cost effectively hidden by the surface "magic" of their transitory effects, the cultural values of youth and beauty effectively reproduced and fixed – we have become subjectively "derealized" and out of sequence with ourselves as, paradoxically, these same operations have allowed us to objectively reproduce and "realize" our flesh "in our own image." These days, as MacFarquhar puts it, "sometimes pain, mutilation, and even death are acceptable risks in the pursuit of perfection" – and this because the plasticity of the image (and our imagination) has overwhelmed the reality of the flesh and its limits. Indeed, as of 1996, "three million three hundred and fifty thousand cosmetic surgical procedures were performed, and more than one and a half million pounds of fat were liposuctioned out of nearly three hundred thousand men and women."[18]

[. . .]

Susan Bordo ponders "the glossy world" of media imagery that

> feeds our eyes and focuses our desires on creamy skin, perfect hair, bodies that refuse awkwardness and age. It delights us like visual candy, but it also makes us sick with who we are and offers remedies that promise to close the gap – at a price.[19]

I finally did get to see my rejuvenated friend in the flesh. She looked pretty much the same to me. And, at the 1996 Academy Awards (for which the song in *The Mirror Has Two Faces* received the film's only nomination), Barbra was still being characterized by the press as "peevish" and "petty." And that wasn't all, poor woman (money and voice aside). Two years after linking Barbra with her SF–horror film counterparts and ironically figuring her as marauding the countryside as a middle-aged monster in designer clothes, I found my imagination elaborately realized in a 1998 episode of the animated television series, *South Park*. Here was featured a huge "MechaStreisand" trashing the town like Godzilla. Tellingly, one of the South Park kids asks: "Who is Barbra Streisand?" and is answered thus: "She's a really old lady who wants everybody to think she's forty-five." This coincidence may seem uncanny, but, indeed, suggests just how pervasively middle-aged women, particularly those with power like Streisand, are demonized and made monstrous in our present culture.

I, in the meantime, have become more comfortable in my ever-aging skin. I'm old enough now to feel distant from the omnipresent appeals around me to "look younger" and to "do" something about it. Indeed, after my friend's surgery I vowed to be kinder to my mirror image. In the glass (or on the screen), that image is, after all, thin and chimerical, whereas I, on my side of it, am grounded in the fleshy thickness and productivity of a life, in the substance – not the reproduced surface – of endless transformation. Thus, now each time I start to fixate on a new line or wrinkle or graying hair in the mirror, now each time I envy a youthful face on the screen, I am quick to remember that on my side of the image I am not so much ever aging as always becoming.

Notes

1 James Atlas, "The Sandwich Generation," *New Yorker*, Oct. 13, 1997, 59.

2 Susan Sontag, "The Double Standard of Ageing," reprinted in *No Longer Young: The Older Woman in America* (Ann Arbor: Institute of Gerontology, University of Michigan/Wayne State University Press, 1975), 31. [. . .]

3 Jeffrey Wells, "Mirror, Mirror," *Entertainment Weekly*, Apr. 12, 1996, 8. Subsequent references will be cited in the text.

4 J. Max Robins, "A New Wrinkle in Video Technology," *TV Guide* (Los Angeles metropolitan edition), Sep. 28–Oct. 4, 1996, 57. The news anchors who have benefited from the camera and their ages at the time of the *TV Guide* piece were Dan Rather, 64; Peter Jennings, 58; Tom Brokaw, 56; and Barbara Walters, 65.

5 See Sobchack, "Revenge of *The Leech Woman*." *Uncontrollable Bodies: Testimonies of Identity and Culture*. Eds. Rodney Sappington and Tyler Stallings. Seattle: Bay Press, 1994. 79–91.

6 Linda Williams, "When the Woman Looks," in *The Dread of Difference: Gender and the Horror Film*, ed. Barry Keith Grant (Austin: University of Texas Press, 1996), 21.

7 Elissa Melamed, *Mirror, Mirror: The Terror of Not Being Young* (New York: Linden Press/Simon and Schuster, 1983)], 30.

8 Simone de Beauvoir, *The Second Sex*, trans. H.H. Parshley (New York: Bantam, 1968), 542.

9 Sigmund Freud, "The Predisposition to Obsessional Neurosis," in *Collected Papers*, vol. 1, ed. Ernest Jones, trans. Joan Riviere (London: Hogarth and the Institute of Psycho-Analysis, 1950), 130.

10 An illuminating comparison might be made between my friend's detailing of her cosmetic surgery and its aftermath with J.G. Ballard's "Princess Margaret's Face Lift," in *The Atrocity Exhibition*, new rev. ed. (San Francisco: Re/Search, 1990), 111–12. Its opening paragraph reads (and note the focus again on jowls and neck): "As Princess Margaret reached middle age, the skin of both her cheeks and neck tended to sag from failure of the supporting structures. Her naso-labial folds deepened, and the soft tissue along her jaw fell forward. Her jowls tended to increase. In profile the creases of her neck lengthened and the chin-neck contour lost its youthful outline and became convex" (111). For a similar graphic description see also Larissa MacFarquhar, "The Face Age," *New Yorker*, July 21, 1997, 68: "Consider the brutal beauty of the face-lift. . . . If you're getting a blepharoplasty (an eye job, the doctor will slice open the top of each of your eyelids, peel the skin back and trim the fat underneath with a scalpel, or a laser. If you're also in for a brow-lift, the doctor might carve you to the bone from the top of your forehead down along your hairline; slowly tear the skin away from the bloody mush it's attached to underneath; and then stretch it back and staple it near the hairline. You may suffer blindness, paralysis, or death as a consequence, but most likely you'll be fine."

11 Kathleen Woodward, "Youthfulness as Masquerade," *Discourse* 11, no. 1 (Fall–Winter 1998–89), 133–34.

12 Ballard, "Princess Margaret's Face Lift," 111.

13 MacFarquhar, "The Face Age," 68.

14 See www.skinema.com (accessed Oct. 24, 2003).

15 For more on the Lancôme episode and Rossellini's bitterness about it see Isabella Rossellini, *Some of Me* (New York: Random House, 1997).

16 Woodward, "Youthfulness as Masquerade," 135. (Woodward is citing film and cultural critic Patricia Mellencamp.)

17 Jean Baudrillard, "Operational Whitewash", in *The Transparency of Evil: Essays on Extreme Phenomena*, trans. James Benedict (New York: Verso, 1993), 45. Of special interest in surgically constructing the ideal face is the French performance artist Orlan, who has publicly undergone any number of surgeries in an ironic attempt to achieve the forehead of Mona Lisa, the eyes of Psyche (from Gérôme), the chin of Botticelli's Venus, the mouth of Boucher's Europa, and the nose from an anonymous sixteenth-century painting of Diana. On Orlan and the connection between special effects and cosmetic surgery see Victoria Duckett, "Beyond the Body: Orlan and the Material Morph," in *Meta-Morphing: Visual Trans-formation and the Culture of Quick Change*, ed. Vivian Sobchack (Minneapolis: University of Minnesota Press, 2000), 209–23.

18 MacFarquhar, "The Face Age," 68. In regard to the meaning of these statistics (and I don't fully agree with her) MacFarquhar writes: "It doesn't make sense to think about cosmetic surgery as a feminine issue these days, since more and more men – a fifth of all patients in 1996 – are electing to undergo it" (68).

19 Susan Bordo, "In an Empire of Images, the End of a Fairy Tale," *Chronicles of Higher Education*, Sep. 19, 1997, B8.

5

CONNECTED; OR WHAT IT MEANS TO LIVE IN THE NETWORK SOCIETY

Steven Shaviro

Preface

[. . .] I try to write cultural theory as science fiction to come to grips with a world that itself seems on the verge of being absorbed into the play of science fiction novels and films. I have several precedents for this approach. In *Difference and Repetition*, Gilles Deleuze suggests that philosophy ought to be seen, in part, as "a kind of science fiction" (xx). This is because philosophy, like science fiction, can "make present the approach of a coherence that is no longer ours," no longer that of our familiar humanistic certainties. Philosophy is like science fiction in that it deals with concepts that have not yet been worked out; both genres work "at the border which separates our knowledge from our ignorance, and transforms the one into the other" (xxi). Or, as Michel Foucault similarly writes, the greatest reward and highest justification for making intellectual work comes when this work results, "in one way or another and to the extent possible, in the knower's straying afield of himself" (1986, 8). [. . .]

[. . .]

The Integrated Circuit. Our current understanding of networks dates from the development of cybernetic theory in the 1940s and 1950s. The model has since been greatly elaborated, notably in the chaos and complexity theories of the 1980s and 1990s.[1] As it seems to us now, a network is a self-generating, self-organizing, self-sustaining system. It works through multiple feedback loops. These loops allow the system to monitor and modulate its own performance continually and thereby maintain a state of homeostatic equilibrium. At the same time, these feedback loops induce effects of interference, amplification, and resonance. And such effects permit the system to grow, both in size and in complexity. Beyond this, a network is always nested in a hierarchy. From the inside, it seems to be entirely self-contained, but from the outside, it turns out to be part of a still larger network. A network is what Ilya Prigogine and Isabelle Stengers call a dissipative structure: it generates local stability and maintains internal homeostasis in far-from-equilibrium conditions, thanks to massive "energy exchanges with the outside world" (143). These expenditures, in turn, become a source of hidden order, what Stuart Kauffman calls "order for free." What seems like noise, waste, chance, or mere redundancy from the point of view of any given system turns out to be meaningful and functional in the context of the next, higher-level system. As N. Katherine Hayles puts it, networks operate through a dialectic of pattern and randomness, rather than one of presence and absence (285). This is why we define networks as being made of bits, rather than atoms. What matters is not the hardware, but the software; not what the network is actually made of, but only the way it is connected up, and the information that gets transmitted through it.

[. . .]

Media Saturation. The science fiction comic book series *Transmetropolitan* is written by Warren Ellis and drawn by Darick Robertson. The series is set in a future American mega-metropolis known only as the City. It's a place much in the mold of Burroughs's Ba'dan. Every square inch of the City is filled with crowds in ceaseless motion, continually being assaulted by flashing billboards, multimedia screens on the sidewalk, surveillance cameras, and street vendors selling everything from high-tech sex toys to "long pig," fast food made from cloned human flesh. People alter their genetic makeup at the slightest whim; with "temporary morpho-genetic plug-ins," for instance, you can be a tourist in another species, "get yourself some reptile skin for three weeks, spend a month in feathers" (1998a, 37). You can also imbibe "gene factors" that plug you permanently into the worldwide communications network or that cure whatever new diseases have invaded the City lately. People sometimes even download themselves into "foglets," clusters of airborne nanomachines that take the place of more palpable flesh (1998b, 72–92). But if you don't want to go that far, you can try the new drugs that are constantly being synthesized, faster than the government can outlaw them. Or else, as a last resort, you can convert to one of the new religions that are being invented daily (1998b, 48–71). And if it's self-protection you're after, there are lots of bizarre weapons around, such as the dreaded "bowel disruptor" (1998b, 24). Of course, there is no such thing as privacy in the City. The media are everywhere. Thousands of TV channels cater to every imaginable age, ideology, taste, and sexual preference. Cameras, microphones, and reporters are stationed on every block, providing live feeds to the Net. In short, the delirium of advanced technology has been entirely woven into the texture of everyday life. This is what a fully networked, "posthuman" existence might be like. Could we really endure such a condition? One episode of *Transmetropolitan* is about Revivals, people who had their bodies placed in cryogenic suspension when they died at the end of the twentieth century (1998b, 93–114). Brought back to life in the City, these people immediately freak out. They simply can't handle the overload, and nobody much wants them around, anyway.

[. . .]

Buy Me. In *Transmetropolitan*, we are introduced to a hot new marketing phenomenon: "block consumer incentive bursting," popularly known as "buybombs." A flash of light zaps you from the television set. You see intense patterns and spots before your eyes; pressure from the flash can even give you a nosebleed. But the major effect only comes later, when you go to sleep. The buybombs "load your brain with compressed ads that unreel into your dreams" so that you are literally "dreaming television advertisements" (Ellis and Robertson 1998b, 45–47). This is viral marketing with a vengeance. What better tactic, for memetic parasites, than to infiltrate themselves into our dreams? It's not just that dreams are so common a metaphor for our most fervent hopes, desires, and imaginings, nor even that we find it so easy to believe that they provide us with insight into ourselves. The really important thing about dreaming is this: it is the most antisocial activity I ever engage in. Dreaming is the one experience that I must go through alone, that I cannot possibly share with anyone else. Of course, I often try to recount my dreams in words, but I cannot help feeling that such words are woefully inadequate. If I cannot quite remember my own dreams, if I cannot narrate them to myself any more than I can to someone else, if I cannot translate them into the generalities of language, this only confirms how unique and personal they are. Dreams are the last refuge of old-fashioned interiority and mental privacy. This makes them the object of a powerful nostalgia, even among the most resolutely unsentimental and forward-looking. My dreams are so many proofs of my singularity; they cannot be redeemed, or substituted for, or exchanged. That's why any violation of dream space is so disturbing, whether it's Freddie Krueger assaulting me in my sleep or buybombs exploding in my head. It means that I haven't really withdrawn from the world after all. It means that I am nothing special. It means that I'm just the same as everybody else. The network has colonized my unconscious. It has made me into a tiny version of itself. The whole situation reminds me of Jim Carrey's Ace Ventura, spewing out forty years' worth of television impersonations as if they were the raw contents of his unbridled id. Such is the terminal state of the networked consumer: to be intensely involved, and maximally distracted, all at once.

[. . .]

From Surveillance to Control. Foucault memorably describes the Panopticon as an "instrument of permanent, exhaustive, omnipresent surveillance, capable of making all visible, as long as it could itself remain invisible . . . a faceless gaze that transformed the whole social body into a field of perception" (1979, 214). But that was then – the nineteenth century – and this is now. Deleuze says that Foucault "was actually one of the first to say that we're moving away from disciplinary societies, we've already left them behind. We're moving toward control societies that no longer operate by confining people but through continuous control and instant communication" (1995, 174). Once we have all been connected, there is no longer any need for the Panopticon's rigid, relentless, centralized gaze. The new forces of control are flexible, slack, and distributed. In a totally networked world, where every point communicates directly with every other point, power is no longer faceless and invisible. Instead, it works in plain sight. Its smiley face is always there to greet us. We are fully aware that its eyes are looking at us; it even encourages us to stare back. Rather than shrouding itself in obscurity and observing us in secret, the network offers us continual feedback even as it tracks us. It does not need to put us under surveillance, because we belong to it, we exist for it, already. Deleuze describes this process of control through the network as "a *modulation*, like a self-transmuting moulding continually changing from one moment to the next, or like a sieve whose mesh varies from one point to another" (178–79). In this way, control is less visual than tactile. It invites our hands-on participation. Sometimes it is even touchy-feely. Just look, for instance, at Microsoft's "Home of the Future." This "smart" house tailors every aspect of its environment just for you. It "looks into your eyes, turns on soft lights and mood music, and responds to commands. It teaches piano, helps do the grocery shopping and keeps an eye on the kids." The house has "miniature cameras" in every room, but not to worry: you can always invoke "make private" mode, if you don't want anybody else to see you (Heim 2000). Only the network itself has to know where you are and what you are doing. No more need for classified FBI files and secret police reports; discreetly and intimately, the network takes care of everything.

[. . .]

Almost Famous. Spider Jerusalem is the hero of *Transmetropolitan*. Spider is bald, lanky, and heavily tattooed, with an acerbic prose style, a love for high-tech weaponry, and a devotion to all sorts of pharmacological excess. He is a muckraking political journalist, sort of like Woodward and Bernstein combined with Hunter S. Thompson. Spider has a perpetual love/hate relationship with the City. Its sensory overload, technological overkill, and sheer human density drive him crazy. But the City's extremes are also the only stimulants powerful enough to fuel his writing. Spider is a postmodern *flâneur*, restlessly wandering the City's streets in search of a story. He generally finds more than he has bargained for: everything from police-sanctioned killings and cover-ups to political scandals involving cloning, child abuse, and real estate deals. When it all becomes too much, Spider holes up in his bunker and tries to stupefy himself with drink, drugs, and TV. But this never works, because Spider cannot escape his own image. The problem is his newspaper columns have made him famous. Nearly everyone in the City knows who he is; they love his identity as a crusading journalist with a gonzo lifestyle, even as they ignore his political messages. It's hard to "speak truth to power" when your very act of speaking is being marketed as entertainment. And so Spider suffers existentially, even though he profits financially, from being a celebrity. In one issue of *Transmetropolitan* (Ellis and Robertson 2002, 5–26), Spider's assistants find him cowering in a corner, waving around a gun and muttering paranoid threats. What drives him over the edge is not just too many drugs, but also seeing himself portrayed on TV. Spider appears on the tube as a cuddly cartoon character for kids, as a macho action figure, and as a stud in a porno flick. In the comic, each of these visions is drawn in a different style by a different cartoonist. The visual diversity highlights the schizophrenic melt-down of Spider's personality. Eventually, Spider can only imagine himself in the form of one or another media stereotype; in a drugged-out stupor, he hallucinates, first his vengeance as an all-powerful superhero, then his martyrdom as a lynching victim torn apart by his own fans. There's no easy solution to this dilemma. Spider needs his fame in order to get his message out, but this fame guarantees that the message will be distorted. At the end of the issue, Spider tells his fans that he didn't want them "paying attention" to him personally; all he wanted was for them "to *hear* me!" To which the fans reply: "We did. We just didn't listen" (Ellis and Robertson 2002, 26). As Spider already knows but is forced to learn again, no message can control the conditions of its own reception.

[. . .]

Foglets. Ray Kurzweil puts great stock in J. Storrs Hall's notion of foglets. These are intelligent, tiny robots – or nanobots – each about the size of a human cell. As foglets float through the air, they "grasp one another to form larger structures" and "merge their computational capacities with each other to create a distributed intelligence" (Kurzweil 2000, 145). In this way, the foglets join together in swarms, producing what Hall calls a *Utility Fog*. Human beings can also download their minds into these foglet swarms. The result, according to Kurzweil, is that "physical reality becomes a lot like virtual reality." That is to say, the world becomes infinitely, instantaneously malleable. A Utility Fog can rearrange its surroundings into any desired configuration, although, as Kurzweil admits, "it's not entirely clear who is doing the desiring." For instance, if you are hungry, foglet technology can "instantly create whatever meal you desire" (145). The only problem with this scenario is that, if you are a swarm of foglets, you will never be hungry for human food in the first place. You won't have a mouth, or a tongue, or taste buds, or a stomach. Of course, you will be able to simulate the pleasurable sensation of tasting gourmet food, but if you can do that, then why even bother creating an actual meal? All this is to suggest that, despite its name, the Utility Fog does not do much of anything useful. Like so many virtual and AI technologies, it is not a productivity tool, but a means of autonomous pleasure, like a high-tech vibrator or dildo. Such is clearly the case in *Transmetropolitan* (Ellis and Robertson 1998b, 72–92). As one Fog Person explains, "we have no physical needs. All we have to do is amuse ourselves. Being regular humans can get in the way of that" (85). Mostly, it seems, the Fog People are virtual aesthetes and dandies, who pass the time by having impalpable sex (91) and by fabricating whimsical objects out of "air and dirt and whatever else is around" (83). Nothing could be further from Kurzweil's vision of AIs as hard-working, hard-computing entrepreneurs.

Wetware. One character in *Transmetropolitan* can't understand why anyone would ever want to be transformed into a foglet swarm: "If you're bored of your body, you could buy a new one, or temp, or even go transient. Why become dust?" (84). The answer, perhaps, is that whoever does this is "queer for machinery" (77). It's just one particular kink among many others. But it's one that AI enthusiasts, like Kurzweil and Moravec, share. They love to talk about DNA code, evolutionary algorithms (Kurzweil 2000, 294–97) and the like; but they tend to get squeamish when it comes to the actual messiness of biological "wetware," or anything else that isn't dry as dust and silicon chips. It's a long way from the orderly, progressive computations of classic

AIs like Kurzweil's "spiritual machines" (or even of Kubrick's HAL, for that matter) to the delirium of "splices" (genetically hybridized organisms), "tropes" (designer neurochemicals), and "mods" (biological implants), as described in Paul Di Filippo's short story collection, *Ribofunk*. The merger of biology and information processing works in both directions. The genome is becoming ever more reduced to algorithmic, digital calculations, but thought and calculation are themselves becoming ever more subject to the vagaries of analog, phenotypic embodiment. If "the biologic bank is open," as Burroughs says, "anything you want, any being you imagined can be you. You have only to pay the biologic price" (1979, 56). For Di Filippo, however, this price turns out to be a monetary one, just like the price of everything else. In the world of *Ribofunk*, prepubescent teenagers can go to the mall to get "any possible alteration on [their] somatype or genotype" (201); adults use enslaved transgenic hybrids as personal servants (17–33), sidekicks (77–94), gofers (172–87), and even sex partners (20ff); and street gangs create new mind-altering drugs "with their home amino-linkers and chromo-cookers" (87). As long as you've got the cash – or more precisely, the credit – you can have it done. These biological enhancements have nothing to do with utility. They are generally used either as fashion accessories or else as terrorist weapons. Their development does not follow the placid logic of adaptive optimization, but the far crazier rhythms of evolutionary arms races and of commodities proliferating wildly in the marketplace.

The Culture of Real Virtuality. We have seen, in various ways, how the phenomena of virtual reality – from cyberspatial disembodiment to prosthetic hyperembodiment, and from distributed, artificial intelligence to concentrated corporeal enhancement – all depend on the frantic exchange and circulation of money, or on what Marx (1993) called the accelerated turnover of capital. Money at once grounds and volatilizes virtual reality. On the most obvious level, money grounds virtual reality, because money is what makes it all happen. A huge influx of venture capital fueled the dot-com bubble of the late 1990s. And when the bubble collapsed, as such speculative manias are wont to do, many of the Internet sites involved suddenly disappeared. But on a deeper level, the development of virtual technologies coincides with the increasing virtualization of money itself. This is part of the massive reorganization of capital that took place in the last three decades of the twentieth century. This transformation has been analyzed in depth by David Harvey, Manuel Castells, and others. Harvey sees the process as a fundamental shift from the Ford-ism of the mid-twentieth century to a new regime of *flexible accumulation* (147), characterized by just-in-time production, a more frequent use of part-time and temporary labor, and above all "the complete reorganization of the global financial system" due to "a rapid proliferation and decentralization of financial activities and flows" (160–61). There has been "a general speed-up in the turnover time of capital," leading to the increasing "volatility and ephemerality of fashions, products, production techniques, labour processes, ideas and ideologies, values and established practices" (285). Castells adds to this account an emphasis on global networking among corporations of different sizes, as well as among the members of political and financial elites (2000, 163–215). And he insists upon the novelty and importance, not of information per se, but of technologies that actually use information as their "raw material" (70). Castells also focuses on the synergy between the late-twentieth-century information technology revolution and the growth of globally interdependent finance markets (102ff). These markets are dependent upon advanced information technology, and in return they provide the major impetus for the technology's continuing development. Financial speculation and the electronic media are thus locked together in a mutually reinforcing, positive feedback loop. The more the world becomes a single "global village" (McLuhan and Fiore 1968), the more financial activity mutates into bizarre and extravagant forms (like derivatives[2] and hedge funds), and the more frenetically financial speculation sweeps across the globe, destabilizing entire economies in an instant. Production is subordinated to circulation, instead of the reverse. Money, the universal equivalent, has become increasingly virtual (unmoored by any referent) over the past half century, and everything else is decentered and virtualized in its wake. It's like Derrida on steroids. This delirium is the motor of what Castells calls "the culture of real virtuality": the technologies, communications media, and network structures that provide the material grounding for our increasingly virtual existences (355–406). The physical and virtual worlds should not be opposed; rather, they are two coordinated realms, mutually dependent products of a vast web of social, political, economic, and technological changes.

[…]

Overload. Of course, "optimized transience disorientation" is not only something that happens in the workplace; it is close to being a universal condition in the age of information networks. In Paul Di Filippo's novel *Ciphers*, we are introduced to semiotic (as opposed to biological) AIDS: "Ambient Information Distress Syndrome. Otherwise known as channel-overload . . . The victim basically feels overwhelmed by all the information pouring in on him." Symptoms include fugue states and catatonia as the victim "tries to escape all stimuli" (142). But these efforts to retreat are futile. The information keeps on pouring in. In the terminal stage of semiotic AIDS, the sufferer regresses to the form of a fetus and finally blinks out of existence: "his synaptic interconnections became incompatible with the physical structure of our universe, and the cosmos squeezed him out" (268). Similarly, in *Transmetropolitan*, Spider Jerusalem is diagnosed with "I-Pollen Related Cognition Damage": an allergic reaction triggered by exposure to "information pollen." At first, the IPRCD victim suffers from high blood pressure, and occasional nosebleeds, hallucinations, and blackouts. Subsequently, in 98 percent of all cases, there is "continual cognition damage. Memory loss. Intensified hallucination. Eventual motor control damage" (Ellis and Robertson 2003, 36). Semiotic AIDS and IPRCD alike are consequences of Landauer's Principle: the strange fact that, while no energy is needed to create and transmit information, some energy is needed to destroy it. In theory, computation and communication can be perfected to any desired degree of frictionless efficiency. But you cannot get rid of information without dissipating energy in the form of friction or heat. "In handling information, the only unavoidable loss of energy is in erasing it" (Siegfried 74). Memorization is free and easy, but it is entropically costly to forget. Thanks to this basic asymmetry, information cannot be expunged as easily as it is accumulated. At some point, the physical limits, either of the brain's storage capacity or of its ability to dissipate heat will be reached. Think of this as the price of being connected. You can't get rid of old information fast enough, or efficiently enough, to accommodate the new. Your nervous system is pushed to the brink. Eventually, it suffers a catastrophic collapse. It crackles and burns, swamped by information overload, and is swept away in the space of flows.

[…]

I Can't Go On, I'll Go On. In the network society, you are what you owe, instead of what you eat. Deleuze distinguishes the old regime of confinement from the new regime of debt in this way:

> In disciplinary societies you were always starting all over again . . . while in control societies you never finish anything. . . . Control is short-term and rapidly shifting, but at the same time continuous and unbounded, whereas discipline was long-term, infinite, and discontinuous.

> (1995, 179–81)

It is worth going over this contrast in detail. First, debts are "short-term and rapidly shifting," because they are always being rolled over and renewed. When you're in debt, "things can change on you. Really fast," since the turnover of capital is so rapid, and speculation-driven markets are so volatile (Jeter 167). The control society "is based on floating exchange rates," whereas the disciplinary society was grounded in the long-duration fixity of the gold standard (Deleuze 1995, 180). The only thing that doesn't change in the control society is the brute fact that you *are* in debt; you will never finish with that, never be able to clear the ledgers and start all over again. Second, when everything is coded in terms of debt, the old disciplinary separations and discontinuities – between what is human and what is not, for instance – tend to break down. The human is now connected with everything else, across the lines of Jeter's erased border, or Donna Haraway's "leaky distinctions." The great opposition between life and death gives way to a situation in which different degrees of death, like different degrees of debt, are spread all along a "continuum." There are no longer any closed spaces or pregiven categories; instead, fine adjustments are continually being made, through the process of "universal modulation" (Deleuze 1995, 182). Third, the disciplinary society was "infinite," while the control society is "unbounded" (*illimité*). To be confined means to be strictly bounded in space and time. But confinement also has an infinite dimension, since only an absolute and transcendent power (the State as arbiter, the impartial judiciary, or the Kantian moral law) has the inflexible authority to decree it. Debt, in contrast, is immanent, contingent, and flexible; it is contracted in varying circumstances and amounts, it is always renewable, and it is managed through adjustable interest rates (Jeter 167). Debt has no claims to transcendence, but for that very reason, it is potentially limitless, propagating onward and outward indefinitely, without bounds.

[. . .]

A Postmodern Metaphysics. Crisis, undecidability, expenditure: these are the metaphysical concepts proper to networks and the network society. Modernity sought to eradicate all metaphysics, but it discovered, in spite of itself, that this is impossible – or better, that it is an endless task. Neither positivism, nor linguistic analysis, nor mathematical logic, nor Heidegger's interrogation of Being was able to exorcize the ghost of transcendence. Twentieth-century thought finally rediscovered what Kant already knew: that the "illusions of reason" can be criticized and compelled to acknowledge their limits, but they cannot be altogether eliminated. This is why Foucault urges that, "instead of denouncing metaphysics as the neglect of being, we force it to speak of extrabeing" (1998, 347). Metaphysics is not about objects in the world, in their presence and positivity. It is rather about the spaces between things, their zones of fuzziness and indiscernibility. It is about what Foucault, following Kant, calls "nonpositive affirmation" or "the testing of the limit" (1998, 74). And it is about the interstices of the network. "A line of becoming," Deleuze and Guattari say, "is not defined by points that it connects, or by points that compose it; on the contrary, it passes between points, it comes up through the middle" (1987, 293). Similarly, the hacker heroine of Pat Cadigan's science fiction novel *Synners* has to maneuver in between the nodes of the network, in order not to be wiped out by a virus:

> if you couldn't walk on the floor, you walked on the ceiling. If you couldn't walk on the ceiling, you walked on the walls, and if you couldn't walk *on* the walls, you walked *in* them. . . . If you were walking in the walls, and the walls had black holes, you had to be something that a black hole wouldn't recognize as existing.
>
> (351)

The Marxist idea of crisis, Bataille's notion of expenditure, and Deleuze and Guattari's concept of undecidability, are all ways of walking in between – of invoking *extrabeing* – in order to oppose the solidity, the inertia, and the seeming self-evidence of the actual. They are ways of finding ambiguous points of potential, gaps in the linear chain of causality, unexpected openings to new, emergent processes. Where deconstruction can only see undecidability as the aporia of rational thought, leading to a paralysis of the will, Deleuze and Guattari rather welcome it as a stimulus to both thought and action: "the undecidable is the germ and locus par excellence of revolutionary decisions" (473). The absence of any cognitive grounding for our actions is precisely their condition of possibility. In the same way, there's nothing predetermined about a crisis and no guarantee that any given crisis will lead to radical change, rather than to nothing at all, or even to more misery and oppression. But crisis remains the condition of possibility for change, the metaphysical extravagance that alone can open up chinks in the otherwise impenetrable armor of the real.

[...]

The Dream of a Common Language. However, this opposition [between rejecting and embracing difference] is complicated by the fact that the Family itself, no less than the Sygn,[3] is a loose network, without a center, and not a top-down, hierarchical organization. The "father-mother-son" structure that the Family employs is by no means absolute or rigid. It works as "a model through which to see many different situations. The Family has always been quite loose in applying that system to any given group of humans or nonhumans, breeding or just living together" (129). That is to say, the Family's model of power is more like Lévi-Strauss's "elementary structures of kinship" than it is like *The Donna Reed Show*. Of course, this doesn't make the Family's ideology any the less sexist, racist, homo-phobic, and authoritarian. But it *does* mean that the Family, just like the Moral Majority or Al-Qaeda, is a thoroughly postmodern phenomenon.[4] As Hardt and Negri put it, speaking of contemporary Islamic radicalism, but in terms that could just as well apply to the Christian Right in America, or to the Family in the novel, "fundamentalism should not be understood as a return to past social forms and values, not even from the perspective of the practitioners . . . the fundamentalist 'return to tradition' is really a new invention" (148–49). The ostensibly traditional values that such groups invoke "are really directed in reaction to the present social order" (149). It is only *now* that the fundamentalists are able to feel nostalgia for a past that never existed in the first place. Castells similarly argues that Muslim and Christian fundamentalisms, and movements like the right-wing militias in the United States, must be understood as phenomena of globalization and informationalization (1997, 12–27) whose entire political practice is organized around decentralized electronic networks and focused upon such forms of action as interventions in the global media (68–109). This all suggests that the Family and the Sygn are not diametrically opposed so much as they are deeply implicated with one another. They are much like the "two interpretations of interpretation, of structure, of sign, of play" discussed by Derrida:

> the one seeks to decipher, dreams of deciphering a truth or an origin which escapes play and the order of the sign, and which lives the necessity of interpretation as an exile. The other, which is no longer turned toward the origin, affirms play and tries to pass beyond man and humanism.

The first interpretation, that of the Family, is "saddened, *negative*, nostalgic, guilty," as it laments the loss of the center; the second, that of the Sygn, is an "*affirmation*" that "*determines the noncenter otherwise than as loss of the center*" (Derrida 292). But even as Derrida highlights the incompatibility between these two positions, he also insists that they must be taken together. They belong to the same field of possibilities; they are expressions of the same predicament. Although they are "absolutely irreconcilable," nevertheless "we live them simultaneously and reconcile them in an obscure economy"; there cannot be "any question of *choosing*" between them (293). The Family and the Sygn are competing ways of articulating the local with the universal. But they both take the information economy for granted. Even the Sygn's admirable politics of difference presupposes – and remains within the horizon of – the network society. The Sygn, no less than the Family, fails to leave space for the singularity of *contact*, which Delany elsewhere (1999, 123ff) celebrates in contradistinction to the routinized benefits of networking.

[. . .]

What It Means to Live in the Network Society. So this is what it means to live in the network society. We have moved out of time and into space. Anything you want is yours for the asking. You can get it right here and right now. All you have to do is pay the price. First of all, you must pay the monetary price, since money is the universal equivalent for all commodities. But you also have to pay the *informational price*, since information is also a universal equivalent. Information is the common measure and the medium of exchange for all knowledge, all perception, all passion, and all desire. The universal equivalent for experience, in short. In the network society, experience will be digital or not at all. But this also means that what you get is never quite what you paid for. It's always just a tiny bit less. The mystery of the extraction of surplus value, unveiled by Marx in the context of nineteenth-century capitalism, applies to the information economy as well. The one real innovation of the network society is this: now surplus extraction is at the center of consumption as well as production. When you buy something from Microsoft, or DynaZauber, all the formal conditions of equal exchange are met. And yet there is always something extra, something left over, something that is missing from your side of the equation. A surplus has leaked out of the exchange process. What's missing is what is *more than information*: the qualitative dimension of experience or the continuum of analog space in between all those ones and zeroes. From a certain point of view, of course, this surplus is nothing at all. It is empty and insubstantial, almost by definition. For if it did exist, it could easily be coded, quantified, and informatized, to any desired degree of accuracy. It is not that there is some hidden essence, basic to human existence, that somehow cannot be rendered by information machines. It is rather that information can all too well account for everything; there is literally nothing that it cannot capture and code. But this *nothing* is precisely the point. Because of this nothing, too much is never enough, and our desires are never satisfied. This *nothing* insinuates itself into our dreams. It is what always keeps us coming back for more. And *that* is "the dirty little secret that corporations know."

[. . .]

Connected. You may say that all this is merely science fiction. None of it is happening: not now, not here, not yet. But science fiction does not claim to be reportage, just as it does not claim to be prophecy. It does not actually represent the present, just as it does not really predict the future. Rather, it involves both the present and the future, while being reducible to neither. For science fiction is about the shadow that the future casts upon the present. It shows us how profoundly we are *haunted* by the ghosts of what has not yet happened. This is the condition that K.W. Jeter describes for us, in his account of the network society: "The little machines continued their work, visibly, like some nightmare of a future that had already arrived" (17).

Notes

1   For a celebratory history of these developments, form cybernetics to complexity theory and beyond, see Kelly. For a more nuanced and critical account, see Hayles.
2   For a discussion of the strange, delirious logic of derivatives in the global financial marketplace, see Doyle (2003).

3 [Shaviro refers here to his reading of Samuel R. Delany's *Stars in My Pockets Like Grains of Sand* which explores the conflict between two cultural systems by these names. – SV]
4 I thus disagree with Freedman's claim that the Sygn "is certainly more coherent with 'modernity' of the epoch" depicted in the novel than is the Family (159).

Works Cited

Burroughs, William S. 1979. *Ah Pook Is Here*. London: John Calder.

Cadigan, Pat. 2001. *Synners*. New York: Four Walls Eight Windows.

Castells, Manuel. 1997. *The Power of Identity*. Vol. 2 of the *Information Age: Economy, Society, and Culture*. Malden, Mass.: Blackwell.

———. 2000. *The Rise of the Network Society*. Vol. 1 of *The Information Age: Economy, Society, and Culture*, 2d ed. Malden, Mass.: Blackwell.

Delany, Samuel R. 1985. *Stars in My Pocket Like Grains of Sand*. New York: Bantam Spectra.

———. 1999. *Times Square Red, Times Square Blue*. New York: New York University Press.

Deleuze, Gilles. 1994. *Difference and Repetition*. Trans. Paul Patton. New York: Columbia University Press.

———. 1995. *Negotiations*. Trans. Martin Joughin. New York: Columbia University Press.

Deleuze, Gilles, and Félix Guattari. 1987. *A Thousand Plateaus*. Trans. Brian Massumi. Minneapolis: University of Minnesota Press.

Derrida, Jacques. 1980. *Writing and Difference*. Trans. Alan Bass. Chicago: University of Chicago Press.

Di Filippo, Paul. 1997. *Ciphers*. Campbell, Calif.: Cambrian Publications, and San Francisco: Permeable Press.

———. 1998. *Ribofunk*. New York: Avon Press.

Doyle, Richard. 2003. *Wetwares: Experiments in Postvital Living*. Minneapolis: University of Minnesota Press.

Ellis, Warren, and Darick Robertson. 1998a. *Back on the Street*. Vol. 1 of *Transmetropolitan*. New York: DC.

———. 1998b. *Lust for Life*. Vol. 2 of *Transmetropolitan*. New York: DC.

———. 2000. *The New Scum*. Vol. 4 of *Transmetropolitan*. New York: DC.

———. 2002. *Gouge Away*. Vol. 6 of *Transmetropolitan*. New York: DC.

———. 2003. *Dirge*. Vol. 8 of *Transmetropolitan*. New York: DC.

Foucault, Michel. 1979. *Discipline and Punish*. Trans. Alan Sheridan. New York: Vintage.

———. 1986. *The Use of Pleasure*. Vol. 2 of *The History of Sexuality*. Trans. Robert Hurley. New York: Vintage.

———. 1998. *Aesthetics, Method, and Epistemology*. Vol. 2 of *Essential Works of Foucault*. Trans. Robert Hurley et al. New York: The New Press.

Freedman, Carl. 2000. *Critical Theory and Science Fiction*. Hanover, N.H.: Wesleyan University Press.

Haraway, Donna J. 1991. *Simians, Cyborgs, and Women: The Reinvention of Nature*. New York: Routledge.

Hardt, Michael, and Antonio Negri. 2001. *Empire*. Cambridge, MA: Harvard University Press.

Harvey, David. 1990. *The Condition of Postmodernity*. Malden, Mass.: Blackwell.

Hayles, N. Katherine. 1999. *How We Became Posthuman: Virtual Bodies in Cybernetics, Literature, and Informatics*. Chicago: University of Chicago Press.

Heidegger, Martin. 1996. *Being and Time*. Trans. Joan Stambaugh. Albany: State University of New York Press.

Heim, Kristi. 2000. "Microsoft Showcases Home Wired to Internet." *Silicon Valley News*, 25 July. www.mercurycenter.com/svtech/.

Jeter, K.W. 1998. *Noir*. New York: Bantam.

Kant, Immanuel. 1987. *The Critique of Judgment*. Trans. Werner S. Pluhar. Indianapolis: Hackett.

———. 1996. *The Critique of Pure Reason*. Trans. Werner S. Pluhar. Indianapolis: Hackett.

Kauffman, Stuart. 1995. *At Home in the Universe: The Search for the Laws of Self-Organization and Complexity*. New York: Oxford University Press.

Kelly, Kevin. 1994. *Out of Control*. New York: Addison–Wesley.

Kurzweil, Ray. 2000. *The Age of Spiritual Machines*. New York: Penguin.

Lévi-Strauss, Claude. 1963. *Structural Anthropology*. New York: Basic Books.

Marx, Karl. 1993. *Capital*. Vol. 2. Trans. David Fernbach. New York: Penguin.

McLuhan, Marshall, and Quentin Fiore. 1968. *War and Peace in the Global Village*. New York: Bantam.

Prigogine, Ilya, and Isabelle Stengers. 1984. *Order out of Chaos: Man's New Dialogue with Nature*. New York: Bantam.

Siegfried, Tom. 2000. *The Bit and the Pendulum*. Hoboken: John Wiley and Sons.

6

GENDERING THE TECHNOLOGICAL IMAGINATION

Anne Balsamo

In 2005 when Lawrence Summers, who was then president of Harvard University, hypothe-sized that women's lack of "intrinsic aptitude" was a plausible explanation for the imbalance in the numbers of men and women in high-level positions in science and mathematics professions, he demonstrated not only a peculiar disregard for the sensibilities of his audience (he was speak-ing at an invitation-only conference on women and minorities in the sciences and engineering workforces), but also a rather simple-minded analysis of a complex social, economic, and tech-nocultural situation.[1] While Summers asserted at the beginning of his speech that he was going to posit three possible hypotheses for the imbalance, by the end of his presentation it was clear that he favored two explanations: that women don't aspire to high-powered jobs (such as those in science and engineering); and that they lack intrinsic aptitude to do these jobs. In short, he put the blame on women for their lack of participation within these professions. In contrast, feminist researchers collectively demonstrate that such a seemingly simple question as why the profession of engineering remains male-dominated in the United States is actually much more complicated to parse, let alone answer.

When focusing on the issue of head count, it is important to tease out matters of history, opportunity, and preference from matters of discrimination and biological sex differences.[2] Well before we agree that lack of "intrinsic aptitude" is a reasonable cause, we might want to consider the contribution of other factors, including social factors, such as

- the demographic distribution of faculty who teach in engineering programs (Hall and Sandler, 1982);
- the biological reproductive practices of women and men at different ages (Landau, 1991);
- the differing opportunities and life responsibilities taken on by men and women with pro-fessional engineering credentials (Rosenfeld, 1984);
- the availability of mentors and female-friendly guides (Rosser, 1990);
- gendered socialization patterns (Cockburn, 1985).

Add to these a variety of institutional factors, such as

- the financial remuneration of engineering faculty at all levels (Fogg, 2003);
- the classroom experiences of female students within engineering programs (Hall and Sandler, 1982);

- the institutional practices and policies that guide professional development in academic programs in engineering and sciences (Matyas and Dix, 1992).

Further, add in several technocultural factors, such as

- the historical creation of the professional engineer as a heroic man (Marvin, 1988);
- mass media representations of women and men in relation to technology (Balsamo, 2000);
- the gendered narratives that circulate in engineering, science, and mathematics textbooks (Rosser, 1990).

To expand on one line of analysis, a feminist investigator might begin by interrogating the question itself: What is the timeframe of this question? How many women were eligible to be hired as professional scientists and engineers that year or in the immediately preceding years? How long have these professional options been available to them? How do women's aspirations, tastes, and preferences for particular careers manifest as, and within, actual employment situations? For example, during the late 1990s (the years preceding Summers's frame of reference), the growth of women-owned companies increased significantly: according to one source, the number of women-owned firms in the United States increased at twice the rate of all firms (14 versus 7 percent) in the six-year period of 1998–2003.[3] This provides a slightly different context for the interpretation of the numbers of women in engineering positions When we think about the expanding range of choices women now have for employment and possible career paths, the numbers may say more about the desirability (or lack thereof) of engineering jobs compared to others. Feminist research into these questions rests on the assumption that some women want to pursue careers in these professions, while others – even those with the appropriate academic credentials – don't. Research in this direction would investigate how women's choices are realized, thwarted, or transformed through the process of professional employment. My point is that even as Summers claimed that his comments were intended to be provocative, by asserting that "you have to be careful in attributing everything to socialization," he failed to demonstrate a nuanced understanding, either of the question or the possible contributing conditions. In lieu of presenting a more complex account that correctly would have challenged the single-cause analysis, which attributes the imbalance solely to differential socialization patterns, he retreated to a more polemical explanation, locating the cause in women's innate inadequacies.

To be fair to Summers, the persistent gender imbalance, in terms of raw numbers, remains an exceedingly difficult phenomenon to understand, let alone to change. Many academic administrators across the United States have been proactive in seeking strategies to enroll more women in science, technology, engineering, and mathematics (STEM) programs. The National Science Foundation (NSF) initiated its first programs to encourage the participation of women in STEM research in 1991; by the time of Summers's remarks (2005), it is reasonable to expect that these program investments would have yielded an increase in the percentages of women employed in engineering and science professions.[4] During the same time, deans and educators were wringing their hands trying to figure out how to get more women, as well as people from racial and ethic [sic] minorities, enrolled in STEM programs, and industries were spending considerable effort to attract women as customers, audiences, consumers, and clients of technological goods and services. During the 1990s, several technology makers and retailers shifted considerable marketing resources to focus on the female customer. The electronics industry giant Samsung figured out that the female consumer controls more than fifty percent of domestic electronics purchases. Other players jumped in to address this buying power: Best Buy formulated the "Jill Initiative" to enable the transformation of the working suburban mom into a big-time electronics buyer. The computer company Dell responded by offering device jackets in different colors.[5] Several of the rollicking start-up companies of the 1990s focused their business plans on women as the target consumer for new technological goods and services; two of the more noteworthy included Purple Moon – led by Brenda Laurel – a company that built games for girls and was eventually acquired by Mattel, Inc.; and Her Interactive, Inc., an interactive entertainment company targeting girls of all ages.[6] As efforts designed to address the gender imbalance in technology activities, almost all of these focus attention on the absent, under-consuming, under-producing, abstract female subject. The explanations for her absence vary: some continue to argue that, due to biological factors, women are ill-suited to the demands of technological professions; others assert that it's a consequence of poor socialization (mostly on the part of girls and women; sometimes they remember also to pay attention to the behavior of boys and men). Some posit that technologies don't have enough style. For the most part, though, the discussion fixates on the simple count of female bodies: if we can just get more women into contact with technology, the argument goes, all sorts of good things will happen.

Profit motive aside, the most difficult thing to note about these approaches is that they are not entirely misguided in their intended objectives. It would be interesting – and fair, in a democratic sense – to have more girls and women involved in technology use, development, and research. But their mere presence is not necessarily going to transform the technologies they experience: there is no guarantee that women will do things differently in their engagement with technologies, as consumers, players, or designers. Rather, this belief betrays a biological essentialism that contradicts the accumulated insight of twenty-five years of feminist theory, that gender is a social and cultural enactment. Moreover, this approach, when it is invoked as a way of transforming technology to be more empowering or democratic, ignores the fact that technologies are not mere tools of human agents. As I suggested in the introduction, technologies are not merely objects: they are best understood as assemblages of people, materialities, practices, and possibilities. To transform them requires the employment of a framework that can identify the complex interactions among all these elements. For feminist teachers and scholars, one of the most vexing questions concerns the appropriate posture to assume on the topic of technoculture writ large: how can we support democratic efforts to increase the participation of women, and other underrepresented agents, in the process of technological development, but at the same time avoid a naïve belief in biological, racial, or sexual essentialism?

The technological imagination: a gendered makeover

As a way to begin to address this question, I turn to a consideration of the technological imagination. As I described in the introduction, this is a mindset and a creative practice of those who analyze, design, and develop technologies. It is an expressive capacity to use what is at hand to create something else. This is a quality of mind that grasps the doubled-nature of technology: as determining and determined, as both autonomous and subservient to human goals. It understands the consequence of technocultural productions and creations from multiple perspectives. It enables a person to understand the broader sets of forces that shape the development of new technologies and take account of how these forces might be modified or transformed. More critically, it enables a person to see how emerging technologies get won over to particular ideologies and systems of value, when they could be defined otherwise. Developing this imagination is a necessary step in shifting our collective world-view such that we can evaluate more clearly the path we're on and, more importantly, act ethically in developing the foundation of future technocultures.

As I have argued elsewhere (Balsamo, 2000), feminists need reliable maps and innovative tools to navigate the technocultural terrain. It is especially important that these maps and tools remain attendant to the dual aims of feminist technoscience studies: to be analytically critical of the social and political consequences of the deployment of scientific knowledge, along with the technological logics and practices that emerge within scientific and technological institutions; and to be steadfastly supportive of, and encouraging to, the women who choose to pursue careers in these fields. The maps we create must be able to guide travelers through rapidly changing landscapes, identify rocky roads and smoother trails, and provide pointers toward destination sites of inspiration. More importantly, we need to provide women guidance in how to do things differently within this landscape. While I am keenly aware that this terrain is uneven and difficult for even the savviest traveler, let alone for those who have been actively discouraged and inadequately trained to use tools and methods, I am also firmly convinced that this territory is exactly where feminists need to venture. I invoke the metaphor of colonizing a terrain consciously and with more than a bit of irony. This territory is far from virgin land; it is, and has always been, populated by geniuses, hero-inventors, renegade hackers, and libertarian technologists. The assumed gender identity of these native inhabitants is male. Feminists know that women too have lived within this territory as geniuses, inventors, hackers, and technologists, but that they have often been invisible as members of the indigenous population. When surveying this territory, most people simply don't see the women who have been there, and are still there, creating significant inventions and innovations.

The first step in gendering the technological imagination is taken in recognizing the persistence of a dominant myth of gender and technology. This myth assigns different roles and values to men's and women's engagement with technology: men are traditionally identified as the idealized and most important agents of technological development, while women are cast as either unfit, uninterested, or incapable. In broad terms, it has been the class of white men who have enjoyed the benefits of formal institutional recognition as agents of the technological imagination. As Autumn Stanley has amply documented, women of all races and ethnicities have been systematically and overtly written out of the historical record of technology development since the mythical beginning.[7]

In an interesting twist of logic, white men who are heralded as hero technologists are subtly degendered: the product of their imaginations is rarely considered to be the expression of a gendered, racialized, and class-based subjectivity or body. Gender, as many feminists have documented, has historically been an attribute of women's work, subjectivity, and bodies.[8] One of the consequences of the degendering of men is that the technological imagination is considered to be without gender. This, of course, is not the case. Women do not bring gender to the technological imagination. Moreover, technology is not a new interest of women: they have always been involved in technocultural innovation, even when institutionally and legally prohibited from being recognized as such.[9] The technological imagination has always been gendered, which is not to say that gender has always been recognized or fully explored as a source of imaginative inspiration.[10]

The next step in gendering the technological imagination is to focus on how things are done differently with technologies, especially as these involve relations with other human beings. The process of doing things differently may be the work of women, but not the expression of essential feminine insight; it may seek different horizons, but not necessarily better ones; it may manifest different values, but not different outcomes. The gendered transformation of the technological imagination is not solely a matter of theory, but a matter of praxis. As much as we try, we will never be able to know in advance how this imagination will be changed by the participation of women (or anyone else, for that matter); its transformation will be evident in what gets enacted.

This is why I am so interested in the notion of designing in its verb form. Designing is a key process of technocultural innovation. It names the practices through which the technological imagination manifests most clearly in the negotiations among people who share an explicit objective of creating new technologies. To say that a given design is a consequence of social negotiations does not mean that technical principles or the material world are irrelevant. The matter of the world too is materialized through the practices of designing. As feminist philosopher and physicist Karen Barad (2003) asserts, "matter does matter." This is not only because the basic building blocks of any technology – what we casually refer to as raw materials – have properties that are non-negotiable, for example they transform at certain temperatures or show stress under certain conditions. Matter matters because the world is always already a plenitude. For any given technology, agency is manifested unevenly by the people who create the device, program it, engineer it, manufacture it, buy it, use it, abuse it, and eventually dispose of it. But agency – defined pragmatically as the ability to affect the technological outcome – is not an exclusive privilege of human beings. In the process of designing, the matter of the world also manifests agency.

While Barad's focus is not specifically on the site of designing, I borrow insights from her work to describe the nature of agency that constitutes designing practice. Before I turn to the implications of her thinking for a consideration of designing practice, let me outline some of her key theoretical moves. Drawing on an epistemology developed by physicist Niels Bohr, Barad elaborates a framework for understanding the nature of agency, materiality, and posthuman performativity that she calls "agential realism." This framework resists the traditional realist ontology that posits an essential distinction between subjects and objects (the material world). Her approach, in contrast to traditional realist ontology, argues that neither subjects nor materiality preexist the interactions that constitute them. Barad (1998: 96) coins the term "intra-action" to "signify the inseparability of 'objects' and 'agencies of observation.'" All distinctions, including those of human, non-human, matter, and materiality are constituted through specific intra-actions. There is no prior distinction between the object that is observed to "be an object" and the activity of observing: intra-actions are primary phenomena. According to Barad, it is through intra-acting that agency manifests, not as property bestowed upon subjects or inherent in their nature, but rather agency materializes through intra-actions that constitute boundaries, demarcations, and distinctions among elements of phenomena. Intra-actions are iterative; they build on one another. She argues (2003: 815) that "it is through specific agenic intra-actions that . . . particular embodied concepts become meaningful" (ellipses in original), and further that "the material and the discursive are mutually implicated in the dynamics of intra-activity" (822), and "outside of particular agenic intra-actions, 'words,' and 'things' are indeterminate" (820). It is through specific agenic intra-actions that the distinction between words and matter is constituted and, presumably, continually reproduced through subsequent intra-actions. At base, she asserts, "matter is always already an ongoing historicity," and "meaning is . . . an ongoing performance of the world in its differential intelligibility" (821, ellipses in original), but she also insists more than once that "no priority is given to either materiality or discursivity" (825). Matter matters because it "plays an active role in its iterative materialization" (826). It is not the passive natural world that is brought into being through cultural practices. In this, Barad firmly refutes the nature/culture dualism that would posit the prior existence of one or the other: both nature and culture are constituted through agenic intra-action. She suggests that technologies materialize through the "intra-actions of a multitude of practices."[11]

Inspired by Barad's work, I want to think again about the practices of designing. In her terms, designing is the name for one set of practices whereby the world is dynamically reconfigured by specific acts (what Barad calls "intra-actions") through which boundaries are constituted and enacted. A boundary is a distinction that sets one concept apart from another. Textually boundaries are represented by the / in the couplets actors/world and materiality/discourse. Through intra-actions, boundaries are constituted that mark certain things as "human factors," other things as "elements of materiality," other things as "characteristics of the apparatus," and yet other things as "social influences." It is through intra-actions that important designations are established, those then serve as the foundation for more complex constructions. Devices and apparatuses, as Barad points out, always come to us as already sedimented layers of intra-actions, which means that they are always marked with an intended purpose, a set of meanings, and an already specified relationship to the material world. Although she deploys a different discourse, I consider Barad's insights to be compatible with the framework that I elaborated in the introductory chapter. Using her term, I understand "intra-actions" to constitute elements that are articulated with one another to form assemblages.

The practices of designing constitute a specific set of intra-actions that make the technologies intelligible. To push this a bit further, the practices of designing literally make the material world intelligible. Intra-actions are iterative: the boundaries, demarcations, and marks that constitute elements of basic phenomena are constantly in the process of reformulation. Understanding the iterative nature of intra-actions supports the fact that technologies do not get set in place once and only once, but that the arrangements among elements must be reproduced over time and place. Just as "matter does not exist outside of time, history, or culture" (Barad, 1998: 109), so too is this true for technologies: they are always in the process of materializing through intra-actions. More to the point of this chapter, every intra-action that constitutes a technology offers an opportunity to do things differently. Intra-actions may be strongly constrained by sedimented layers of previous intra-actions, but they are not strictly determined by those previous intra-actions. It is these moments of possibility that need to be explored and exploited for the purposes of designing technoculture differently.

Participants who engage in the set of practices and social negotiations that constitute the designing process constantly move between former understandings and new insights. Participants' presuppositions about their understanding of the design task, the material world, the influences of other participants, and indeed even of their own identities as designers, are continually revisited and revised in the process of continued interactions with other participants, creative tools, raw materials, and institutional forms – all in the aim of designing something new. Designers bring many presuppositions (the build-up of previous intra-actions) to the design situation, which manifest as historically and culturally specific assumptions and beliefs. Understanding that presuppositions are an inevitable element of the designing scenes sets the stage for a methodological interrogation of these layers of knowing and belief. The aim is not necessarily to discard prior understandings, beliefs, meanings, interpretations, or attributions, but to understand how they are constituted and how they might be creatively reconfigured in the service of technological innovation. This also sets the stage for identifying other ways of knowing and new contexts that may contribute inspiration and imaginative resources to the designing process. This provides an opening for considering the creative role of gender in the exercise of the technological imagination, one that avoids falling into biologically essentialist claims that women will naturally design technologies differently than men.

By modeling and improvising in a social setting, participation in collaborative acts of designing new technologies enables people to learn both practices and habits of mind from other collaborators. Furthermore, collaborations that involve people with expertise in different domains provide a more diverse set of practices and frameworks to draw on in a creative endeavor. If indeed the genesis of creativity is the "escape from one range of assumptions to another" – as architectural-design theorists William Mitchell, Allen Inouye, and Marjory Blumenthal (2003) suggest – then the inclusion of people with different backgrounds and varied expertise on a collaborative design team is a critically important source of creative thinking. Diversity among design participants is generative, not because of some innate biological or ethnic quality, but because people embody different sets of assumptions. Sometimes these assumptions are shaped by background; sometimes they are shaped by domain expertise.[12] This argument supports the call not only for the creation of multidisciplinary design teams (that include artist-practitioners, humanists, along with technology experts such as computer scientists and engineers), but also for those diverse in culture, gender, ethnicity, and race. In this sense, designers manifest creativity, not only by mediating between culture writ large and the immediate social setting of the design team, but also by negotiating and apprehending the sets of assumptions held by individual collaborators.

Just as all good designing work includes the careful consideration of materials, conventions, technical codes, and audience expectations, so too it includes a consideration of the layers of meaning that are already invested in the technology-under-development. These layers of meaning include the beliefs and ways of knowing that designers already embody, and the meanings that circulate about particular types of technology, aesthetics, value, and affordances. To gender the technological imagination is to acknowledge that all participates bring gendered, racial, and class-based assumptions to the designing process. These assumptions contribute to the creation of meaning for a technology-under-development. Acknowledging different sets of assumptions enables designers to identify the many contexts within which technologies become meaningful, and then more fully assess how these various contexts might contribute or constrain the meaning (and the deployment, and success, and social value) of the technology-under-development. At a base level, this approach demonstrates how culture is not only an inevitable part of the designing process, but also an important, under-utilized creative resource in the process of technocultural innovation. It suggests ways that design participants can identify and understand the technocultural meanings that not only influence the technology-under-development, but also the participants themselves.[13] These insights, drawing on work in feminist epistemology, illuminate the nature of agency that manifests in the practices of designing new technologies.

[. . .]

Designing feminist futures: "the time is now for us"

In preparation for our participation in the NGO Forum,[14] I had the opportunity to interview Patsy Robertson, a senior media advisor for the United Nations who served as the chief spokeswoman for the Fourth UN Conference. At one point I asked if there were interventions (outlined in the Draft Platform for Action) that should be put off until foundational work had been accomplished? I was referring specifically to U.S.-based concerns inserted into the platform that argued for increased access to technology and support for the education of women in science and technology. She replied quickly and forcefully: "*The time is now for us.*"[15] Her words stuck with me in the intervening years, as I've had the occasion to reflect on the experiences involved in building the multimedia application and participating in the 1995 NGO Forum. One of the consequences is that I've tried to think differently about my own feminist interventions. More poetically, I wonder: *How NOW?*

What I've realized is that despite its Dr. Seussian semantics, the question, "How Now?" is more complex than it first appears. Invoking both the concepts of practice and time, this sound bite has sent me back to revisit foundational feminist work in an effort to unpack the compressed meaning of this small phrase. "How?" is a question that women have wrestled with since long before the term *feminist* came into vogue. "How?" is the basic question that guided thousands of female innovators, inventors, scientists, and philosophers. As feminist historians and technoscience critics understand quite well, the right to ask this question, and the right to explore its answers has been a privilege often denied to women. We also know it is a question that women live with every day, at every moment: How do I do this? How do I get there from here? How did this happen? In its best form, the question "How?" announces the fascination of an engaged mind; in its worst, it is the tragic lament of a knowing victim. In occupying both subject positions simultaneously, and a range of those between, women, throughout history, have demonstrated the many ways in which the question "How?" can be a matter of life and death.

Practice and theory seemed at one point antithetical concepts. In the late 1970s and early 1980s, feminists struggled to elucidate the logic that connected one to the other. Was theory elitist? Shouldn't practice serve as the true horizon of feminist efforts? Was there even such a thing as practice without theory? Showing the influence of these earlier feminist moments, my preoccupation with the question, "How Now?" again raises the issues of the relationship between theory and practice:[16] after theory and criticism, what next? Here, I'm not asking, what is the future of feminist theory and criticism; I'm asking how now do I proceed with my life, my scholarship, and my world-making? How then, for me, are theory and practice related? I believe that the purpose of theory is to inspire us to ask more incisive questions about the phenomena that terrify and fascinate us; the purpose of criticism is to illuminate the complexity of the phenomena in such a way that others are provoked to formulate their own theoretical understandings, accounts, and questions. The horizon of this iterative questioning and analysis is transformed practice. For me, the aim of feminist technocultural studies is to theorize and critically analyze the situation of gendered subjects – across cultures and across contexts – and to provide insights, if not exactly blueprints, for the transformation of those situations and contexts through intentional practice. We need maps and tools, not simply to theorize with, but also to guide us to act and transform the worlds within which we live.

We work, under the banner of feminism, for the improvement of women's lives. Yet, one of the most provocative lessons I learned, through my participation in the 1995 NGO Forum and Fourth UN World Conference on Women, is that there is no global consensus on what it means to improve women's lives. Other than a wide-scale call to intervene against and cease the violence done to women in every national context, I found no singular feminist answer to the question, "How Now?"

Thus, a provisional response to my question, "How Now?" sends me deeper into the investigation of the dynamics of design. The horizon of this investigation is the illumination of a set of practices whereby the future, as a set of perpetual *nows*, will be realized. I'm interested in the process whereby the future is brought forth out of the present. I don't seek to predict the stories, artifacts, technologies, and power arrangements that emerge from the current moment to form the next current moment. The daily practice I engage in now focuses on the design of technocultural artifacts: my research investigates practices of meaning-making – how the meanings of new technologies are reproduced, structured, manipulated, hijacked, and sometimes contested. My intent is to participate consciously in the act of designing technoculture in ways that are ethically and socially responsible. This, too, is a consequence of gendering the technological imagination.

Notes

1 See Summers (2005a). The editorial response was immediate: see, for example, Bombardieri (2005). Although the discussions have largely vanished, the blogosphere response was especially lively. The National Organization for Women circulated a call for a broader commitment to equality for women in science and technology: see Nelson (2005). On January 19, 2005, Summers issued a letter where he admitted that he was "wrong to have spoken in a way that had resulted in an unintended signal of discouragement to talented girls and women" (Summers, 2005b). The Anita Borg Institute for Women and Technology staff created a web document called "Chronicles of a Controversy" that contains a transcript of Summers's original remarks and links to the text of his apology and to the news coverage of the controversy (ABI Staff, 2005).

2 The question of sex differences among males and females belongs to a different category of question that implies different research paradigms and protocols. While there is a significant body of feminist work on these questions, this research was not cited by Summers. See WISELI (2005).

3 Even the most cursory of investigations into the business scene in the U.S. in the late 1990s suggests that there are many women pursuing demanding, risky, and potentially highly rewarding business ventures (Office of Advocacy, U.S. Small Business Administration, 2003).

4 As summarized in the NSF report (2002) between 1991 and 2001, the government agency has spent more than $84 million in awards for projects that are part of its Program for Gender Equity. And yet, in the year 2000 the gender composition of the labor force in science and engineering indicated that the unemployment rates of women were higher than men in all STEM occupations and age groups.

5 An article in *Business Week* (Gogoi, 2005) described several efforts by technology retailers to attract a larger share of female consumers. The article quotes Jonas Tanenbaum, senior marketing manager of flat-panel displays for Samsung Electronics America, as saying "we now recognize that the female consumer is influencing, if not controlling, 50 percent of all consumer-electronic purchasing today." The article also describes how the "Jill Initiative" at Best Buy is designed to transform the trend-savvy working suburban mom with a fair amount of disposable income, who's likely to shop at Target as opposed to Wal-Mart, into a big-time electronics buyer. With women in mind, Dell has increased the number of accessories available for sale on its site. "We started offering stylish jackets in different colors for the Pocket DJ at the direct request of our women customers," says Gretchen Miller, a director of product marketing for the Austin Texas PC Maker.

6 The story about Purple Moon's acquisition by Mattel, Inc. is recounted in Laurel (2001).

7 Autumn Stanley (1995) investigates and, sometimes for the first time, uncovers women's contributions to the development of five areas of technology: agriculture, computers, machines, medicine, and reproduction. The bibliography alone is an incredible and invaluable contribution to the history of technology.

8 For example, see Irigaray (1985) on the labor of becoming woman.

9 In addition to Autumn Stanley's work (see n. 7 above), Marvin (1988) also documents the systematic erasure of women from official histories of early communication technologies such as the telephone.

10 Donna Haraway's manifesto, first published in 1985, catalyzed an entire generation of feminist thinkers, encouraging them not only to critically engage the dominant technologies of the twentieth century – communication and cybernetics – but also to carefully attend to the emergence of new technologies (Haraway 1985). Spurred on in part by Haraway, as well as by a maturing sensibility about the importance of seizing "the master's tools," feminist critics across the globe have turned their attention to a range of techno-scientific disciplines; as a consequence we now have a significant body of trenchant criticism to draw upon in our encounters with a range of new techno-scientific phenomena.

   Several feminist projects demonstrate the enactment of a gendered technological imagination. The following are a mere sampling of projects: In the U.S., there is the [*sic*] Paula Treichler's (1999) work on HIV/AIDS and medical discourse; Lisa Cartwright's (1995) analysis of the role of the cinematic gaze in the constitution of medical diagnostics; Katherine Hayles's (1999) analysis of our posthuman condition; and Alison Adam's (1998) description of how gender is inscribed in AI programs and systems. In Europe, feminist scholars have turned their attention to key issues, such as the gendered division of labor in a global information society (Mitter and Efendioglu, 1997) and the "gender mainstreaming" strategy promoted by the European Union (Behning and Pascual, 2001). Other noteworthy work by feminist scholars of technology include Nina Wakefield's (2008) ethnographic research on blogging, and Randi Markussen's (1996) work on feminism and Scandinavian design. In Canada, see Kim Sawchuk's (1999) work on embodiment and new media technologies; the study of digital cities by Barbara Crow et al.; and Janine Marchessault's (2007) research on art, digital media, and globalization. In Australia, see

Elspeth Probyn's (2005) analysis of the cultural work of shame and media technologies, and Meaghan Morris's (2005) article on "humanities for taxpayers."

11 What is particularly useful for the discussion here is Barad's account of the nature of apparatuses: "Apparatuses are not inscription devices, scientific instruments set in place before the action happens, or machines that mediate the dialectic of resistance and accommodation. They are neither neutral probes of the natural world nor structures that deterministically impose some particular outcome." Barad elaborates Bohr on this point: "apparatuses are not mere static arrangements *in* the world, but rather *apparatuses are dynamic (re)configurations of the world, specific agential practices/intra-actions/performances through which specific exclusionary boundaries are enacted.* Apparatuses have no inherent 'outside' boundary. This indeterminacy of the 'outside' boundary represents the impossibility of closure – the ongoing intra-action in the iterative reconfiguring of the apparatus of bodily production. Apparatuses are open-ended practices" (emphasis in the original, 2003: 816).

12 Several programs designed to foster collaboration among artists and technologists as peers also demonstrate these assumptions. See for example: Craig Harris's (1999) account of the artist-in-residence program at Xerox PARC; Michael Naimark's (2003) report for *Leonardo* journal on the opportunities and constraints of such collaborations; Michael Century's (2006) description of the studio lab concept. On the concept of artists as inventors see the edited volume by Dieter Daniels and Barbara Schmidt (2008) and Simon Penny (2008). On the topic of the management of art-technology research collaborations see Biswas (2008).

13 Panagiotis Louridas (1999: 523) makes a distinction between self-conscious and unselfconscious design, arguing that "unselfconscious design is design without designers. It is the prevalent form of design activity in primitive and traditional societies in which design professions do not exist." He reminds us of the anthropological term for this mode of unselfconscious design, *bricolage*, and wants to argue for the usefulness of the term as a way of describing the creative practices of the professional (self-conscious) designer. In this argument, the self-conscious designer replaces tradition (of the bricoleur) in designating the materials to design with, the problems to design for, and the solutions that will suffice. The consequence of the "designer as bricoleur" or the "design as bricolage" perspective asserts the importance of understanding the transformative power of the designer to change the world.

14 [Balsamo refers to the 1995 NGO Forum held in conjunction with the UN Fourth World Conference on Women in Beijing. The purpose was to debate and draft a *Platform for Action* that would reinforce the resolutions of the Third World Conference on Women held in 1985. She and a delegation of others lobbied representatives on the issues of women and the media and education and training for women in science and technology. As part of these efforts, they created an interactive multimedia application called *Women of the World Talk Back*. – SV]

15 Patsy Robertson is currently [2011] an international media consultant and was the former Director of Information and Official Spokesperson for the Government of Jamaica. Excerpts from my interview with her are included in the Video Dialogues that are part of the *Women of the World Talk Back* documentary.

16 To my mind, the most thoroughgoing exploration of this question, and indeed of the tension between theory and practice, is found in Paula Treichler's (1999: 2) work on AIDS, which is framed by the question, "what should be the role of theory in an epidemic?"

Works Cited

ABI Staff. 2005. "Chronicle of a Controversy." Anita Borg Institute for Women and Technology. http:// anitaborg.org/.

Adam, Alison. 1998. *Artificial Knowing: Gender and the Thinking Machine*. London: Routledge.

Balsamo, Anne. 2000. "Teaching in the Belly of the Beast." In *Wild Science: Reading Feminism, Medicine and the Media*, edited by Janine Marchessault and Kim Sawchuk, 185–214. London: Routledge.

Barad, Karen. 1998. "Getting Real: Technoscientific Practices and the Materialization of Reality." *Differences* 10, no. 2: 87–128.

———. 2003. "Posthumanist Performativity: Toward an Understanding of How Matter Comes to Matter." *Signs* 28, no. 3: 801–31.

Behning, Ute, and Amparo Serrano Pascual, eds. 2001. *Gender Mainstreaming in the European Employment Strategy*. Brussels: European Trade Union Institute (ETUI).

Biswas, Amitava. 2008. "Managing Art-Technology Research Collaborations." *International Journal of Arts and Technology* 1, no. 1: 66–89.

Bombardieri, Marcella. 2005. "Summers' Remarks on Women Draw Fire." *Boston.com*. January 16.

Cartwright, Lisa. 1995. *Screening the Body: Tracing Medicine's Visual Culture*. Minneapolis: University of Minnesota Press.

Century, Michael. 2006. "Humanizing Technology: The Studio Lab and Innovation." In *A Guide to Good Practice in Collaborative Working Methods and New Media Tools Creation*, edited by Liz Goodman and Katherine Milton. www.ahds.ac.uk/creating/guides/new-media-tools/.

Cockburn, Cynthia. 1985. *Machinery of Dominance: Women, Men and Technical Know-How*. London: Pluto.

Crow, Barbara, Michael Longford, Kim Sawchuk, and Andrea Zeffiro. 2008. "Voices from Beyond: Ephemeral Histories, Locative Media and the Volatile Interface." In *Urban Informatics: The Practice and Promise of the Real-Time City*, edited by Marcus Foth, 158–78. Hershey, Pa.: Information Science Reference, IGI Global.

Daniels, Dieter, and Barbara U. Schmidt, eds. 2008. *Artists as Inventors*. Ostfildern, Germany: Hatje Cantz Verlag.

Fogg, Piper. 2003. "The Gap that Won't Go Away: Women Continue to Lag Behind Men in Pay; The Reasons May Have Little to Do with Gender Bias." *Chronicle of Higher Education*, April 18, A12.

Gogoi, Pallavi. 2005. "Of Gadgets and Gender." *Bloomberg Business Week*, February 14. www.businessweek.com/.

Hall, R.M., and B.R. Sandler. 1982. "The Classroom Climate: A Chilly One for Women?" In *Student Climate Issues Packet*. Washington, D.C.: Project on the Status and Education of Women, Association of American Colleges.

Haraway, Donna. 1985. "A Manifesto for Cyborgs: Science, Technology and Socialist Feminism in the 1980s." *Socialist Review* 80 (March/April): 65–108.

Harris, Craig, ed. 1999. *Art and Innovation: The Xerox PARC Artist-in-Residence Program*. Cambridge, Mass.: MIT Press.

Hayles, N. Katherine. 1999. *How We Became Posthuman: Virtual Bodies in Cybernetics, Literature, and Informatics*. Chicago: University of Chicago Press.

Irigaray, Luce. 1985. *Speculum of the Other Woman*. Trans. Gilligan G. Gill. Ithaca, N.Y.: Cornell University Press.

Landau, Susan. 1991. "Tenure Track, Mommy Track." *Association for Women in Mathematics Newsletter* (May/June).

Laurel, Brenda. 2001. *Utopian Entrepreneur*. Cambridge, Mass.: MIT Press.

Louridas, Panagiotis. 1999. "Design as Bricolage: Anthropology Meets Design Thinking." *Design Studies* 20, no. 6: 517–35.

Marchessault, Janine. 2007. *Fluid Screens, Expanded Cinema*. Toronto: University of Toronto Press.

Markussen, Randi. 1996. "Politics of Intervention in Design: Feminist Reflections on the Scandinavian Tradition." *AI & Society* 10, no. 2: 127–41.

Marvin, Carolyn. 1988. *When Old Technologies Were New: Thinking about Electric Communication in the Late Nineteenth Century*. New York: Oxford University Press.

Matyas, Marsha Lakes, and Linda Skidmore Dix, eds. 1992. *Science and Engineering Programs: On Target for Women?* Washington, D.C.: National Academy Press.

Mitchell, William J., Allen S. Inouye, Marjory S. Blumenthal, eds. 2003. *Beyond Productivity: Information Technology, Innovation, and Creativity*. Washington, D.C.: National Academies Press.

Mitter, Swasti, and Umit Efendioglu. 1997. "Teleworking in a Global Context." In *Virtually Free: Gender, Work and Spatial Choice*, edited by Ewa Gunnarsson, 13–20. Stockholm: Nutek.

Morris, Meaghan. 2005. "Humanities for Taxpayers: Some Problems." *New Literary History* 36, no. 1: 111–29.

Naimark, Michael. 2003. "Art at Interval." Speech for the Opening of the Tech Museum of Innovation, San Jose, California. (March 2). www.naimark.net/.

National Science Foundation (NSF). 2002. *Program for Gender Equity in Science, Technology, Engineering, and Mathematics: A Brief Retrospective 1993–2001*. Arlington, Va.: National Science Foundation. NSF 02–107. www.nsf.gov/.

Nelson, Donna. 2005. "Harvard President's Comments Demonstrate Need for Commitment to Equality for Women in Science and Technology." January 21. *National Organization for Women*. www.now.org/.

Office of Advocacy, U.S. Small Business Administration, 2003. "Dynamics of Women-Operated Sole Proprietorships, 1990–1998." March. www.sba.gov/advol/.

Penny, Simon. 2008. "Bridging Two Cultures: Towards an Interdisciplinary History of the Artist-Inventor and the Machine Artwork." In *Artists as Inventors*, edited by Dieter Daniels and Barbara U. Schmidt, 142–57. Ostfildern, Germany: Hatje Cantz Verlag.

Probyn, Elspeth. 2005. *Blush: Faces of Shame*. Minneapolis: University of Minnesota Press.

Rosenfeld, Rachel A. 1984. "Academic Career Mobility for Women and Men Psychologists." In *Women in Scientific and Engineering Professions*, edited by Violet B. Haas and Carolyn C. Perrucci, 89–134. Ann Arbor: University of Michigan Press.

Rosser, Sue V. 1990. *Female-Friendly Science: Applying Women's Studies Methods and Theories to Attract Students*. New York: Pergamon Press.

Sawchuk, Kim. 1999. "Wounded States: Sovereignty, Separation, and the Quebec Referendum." In *When Pain Strikes*, edited by Bill Burnes, Cathy Busby, and Kim Sawchuk, 96–115. Minneapolis: University of Minnesota Press.

Stanley, Autumn. 1995. *Mothers and Daughters of Invention*. New Brunswick, N.J.: Rutgers University Press.

Summers, Lawrence. 2005a. "Remarks at NBER Conference on Diversifying the Science and Engineering Workforce." Talk delivered to National Bureau of Economic Research Conference. January 14. www.president.harvard.edu/.

———. 2005b. "Letter from President Summers on Women and Science." January 19. www.president.harvard.edu/.

Treichler, Paula A. 1999. *How to Have Theory in an Epidemic: Cultural Chronicles of AIDS*. Durham, N.C.: Duke University Press.

Wakefield, Nina, and Kris Cohen. 2008. "Fieldwork in Public: Using Blogs for Research." In *The Sage Handbook of Online Research Methods*, edited by Nigel Fielding, Raymond M. Lee, and Grant Blank, 307–26. London: Sage Press.

Women in Science and Engineering Leadership Institute (WISELI). 2005. "Response to Lawrence Summers' Remarks on Women in Science." http://wiseli.engr.wisc.edu/.

Section 1: Recommended Further Reading

Alaimo, Stacy. *Bodily Natures: Science, Environment and the Material Self*. Bloomington: Indiana University Press, 2010.

Balsamo, Anne. *Technologies of the Gendered Body*. Durham, NC: Duke University Press, 1995.

Cartwright, Lisa. *Screening the Body: Tracing Medicine's Visual Culture*. Minneapolis: University of Minnesota Press, 1995.

De Lauretis, Teresa. *Technology of Gender: Essays on Theory, Film and Fiction*. Bloomington: Indiana University Press, 1987.

Flanagan, Mary and Austin Booth (eds). *Reload: Rethinking Women + Cyberculture*. Cambridge, MA: MIT Press, 2002.

Heise, Ursula K. *Sense of Place and Sense of Planet: The Environmental Imagination of the Global*. Oxford: Oxford University Press, 2008.

Kittler, Friedrich. *The Truth of the Technological World: Essays on the Genealogy of Presence*. Palo Alto: Stanford University Press, 2014.

Nakamura, Lisa. *Digitizing Race: Visual Cultures of the Internet*. Minneapolis: University of Minnesota Press, 2007.

Shildrick, Margrit. *Dangerous Discourses of Disability, Subjectivity and Sexuality*. New York: Palgrave Macmillan, 2012.

Stone, Allucquére Roseanne. *The War of Desire and Technology at the Close of the Mechanical Age*. Cambridge, MA: MIT Press, 1996.

Turkle, Sherry. *Evocative Objects: Things We Think With*. Cambridge, MA: MIT Press, 2011.

Wajcman, Judy. *TechnoFeminism*. London: Polity, 2004.

SECTION 2

The science-fictionalization
of everyday life

The selections gathered in this section consider the various ways that contemporary experience has taken on dimensions once found only in science fiction, and how sf offers us a "language" of images and metaphors to capture the reality of daily experience in technologized, global, neoliberal modernity. Such perspectives are thus connected with those in Section 1 in the sense that the myriad ways that technology, subjectivity and sociality have been mutually constituted throughout the history of technological development means that imaginative representations of technology have contributed to the material history of technological development.

This section opens with a section from Manuel De Landa's comprehensive overview of the ways that humans and machines have been integrated throughout the history of warfare, from exploring the rise of AI and ideas of an autonomous fighting machine to the innovations in computer design that led to machines substituting for aspects of human judgment in automated weapons. His carefully contextualized work shows how dominant models of technological construction become the template for understanding all knowledge production, a conceptual system that shifts with time and place. He concludes with the observation that the kind of "intelligence" embodied in intelligent machines is a very narrow one; "they may display intelligent behavior in very specific fields, without resembling complex human intelligence in general" (104), but nonetheless he finds reasons for hope as well as concern. The independence of distributed decision making, the basis for much computational design, seeds the ground for the development of local "computational ecologies" that may resist the overarching command-and-control framework desired by their creators. Such innovative possibilities are the focus of much research in digital humanities today.

Susan Squier turns our attention to biomedicine and the field of transplant medicine, again finding significant overlap in the stories narrated by science fiction and the material practice that shapes this emerging culture. Exploring a wide range of practices that incorporate parts of the human body into material objects – artistic practices, technical and scientific research processes, curatorial work in galleries and museums – she notes that "[t]he value and significance of a human organ or body part is no longer self evident, but rather is *produced* through a complex set of institutional negotiations involving medicine, art, society, the legal system, human emotions and economic calculations" (110). In her view, sf has played a central role in this cultural imaginary, to such a degree that she wonders whether the emotional and intellectual adjustments required to see the body as composed of replaceable parts has somehow been "*enabled* . . . by the transformative narrative that is science fiction" (111); moreover, she asks, if that is the case "can we abstract from this instance a model for the relations between science fiction and biomedicine?" (111).

As if in answer to Squier's question, Eugene Thacker's work explores the ways in which biology itself has become an informational science in recent theory and practice, influenced by both the history of framing data in computer science terms (as explored by De Landa) and by the ways that mapping the human genetic code has encouraged biomedical practices based on revising this code. Thacker explores how the discourse of bioinformatics – part computer science, part genomics and part sf in the ways theorized by Squier – has changed how we think about our bodies and our selves. Thacker's work also adds a needed dimension of economic analysis to this mix, theorizing about how bioinformatics theories value in two registers, medical benefit and economic value, and exploring the consequences of research regimes in which these two kinds of value are in tension. "What at one level appears to be a relatively straightforward economic relation – wages into insurance, insurance into drugs, drugs into the body," he observes, "is at another level a dynamical, unending process of valorization – patents into drugs, drugs into tests, tests into patents" (129). At times medicine threatens to become a practice of generating patents rather than one of treating patients, seeming to materialize a dystopian sf vision.

Both the promise and the peril of technology is the focus in the excerpt taken from J.P. Telotte's *The Mouse Machine* (2008), a work that explores the convoluted relationship between the technological imagination and technoscientific innovation that is the legacy of the Disney brand. Telotte situates Disney's sf productions within the history of effects innovation that is more fully explored by the selections in Section 3 and in dialogue with Susan Sontag's influential reading of 1950s sf films in "The Imagination of Disaster" (1965), which saw in this era's movie monsters the ideological twin of the scientific innovation marshalled to fight them – a science that often proved as monstrous as the creatures. Faced with the challenge of how to represent the dangers of technology within film narrative while simultaneously developing its brand based on techno–optimistic innovation, Disney presents an ambivalent vision of technology as deeply shaped by the subjectivity of those who control it; this technological imagination and its constricted view at times seems to threaten to substitute a science-fictional vision of reality for material observation. Drawing on Paul Virilio, Telotte suggests that Disney's adaptation of Jules Verne's *20,000 Leagues Under the Sea* (1956), against the grain of Disney's larger project, shows the risk that "inhabiting a technologized environment can fundamentally disorient us because of the way such an environment eliminates or replaces those references or horizons – 'ethical and esthetic' – that help guide our lives and enable us to carry out the sort of negotiations in which we are always involved" (140), and living immersed in technological mediation.

The ways in which Hollywood representation blur into virtual reality (VR) and further blur into the technological imaginary structuring material experience are further explored by Colin Milburn in his essay on the confluence between research on military super-soldier projects and the phenomenological experience of being such a super-soldier through the avatar of the video game *Crysis*. Here Milburn brings a cultural studies perspective to the genealogical work done by De Landa. Central to Milburn's argument is a reading of the equivocal way that gender enters this discourse, connecting this work as well to arguments by Creed and Sobchack in Section 1. The *Crysis* soldier is simultaneously phenomenologically feminine – penetrated by nanotechnology, the player's computer overwhelmed by the powerful game – and symbolically masculine – an image of super strength, hardness and speed. Thus Milburn discerns a queer crisis at the heart of *Crysis*, a gender ambiguity that cascades through the discourse of speculative militarism and requires us to rethink sexuality in military super-soldier projects as well.

Finally, Jussi Parikka's chapter on the practice of media archeology rounds out the section with an essay that helps us to see ways of theorizing sf as critical methodology. In this overview of the aims and animating theories of media archaeology as a critical and artistic practice, Parikka describes research that will be very familiar to those familiar with discourses of science fiction. A key aspect of media archeology, as Parikka describes it, is a method for "engaging the past and learning from the past media cultures in order to understand present mediated, globalized network culture through artworks executed in various media" (163). This critical engagement with the ways that entire cultural systems unfold around specific technological implementations – and playful exploration of how they might have been otherwise – aligns with the sf imagination, especially in the DIY parallels between media archaeology installations and the cosplay practices of sf steampunk fandom.

7

BLOODLESS TRANSFUSION

Manuel De Landa

For centuries, military commanders have dreamed of eliminating the human element from the battlefield. When Frederick the Great assembled his armies in the eighteenth century, he did not have the technology to eliminate human bodies from the space of combat, but he did manage to eliminate the human will. He put together his armies as a well-oiled clockwork mechanism whose components were robot-like warriors. No individual initiative was allowed to Frederick's soldiers; their only role was to cooperate in the creation of walls of projectiles through synchronized firepower. Under the pressure of the increased accuracy and range of firearms, military commanders in the following centuries were forced to grant responsibility to the individual soldier, to let him run for cover or stalk the enemy, for instance. The human will be returned to the battlefield.

But the old dream of getting human soldiers out of the decision-making loop survived. After World War II, digital computers began to encourage again the fantasy of battles in which machines totally replaced human beings. Forty years later advances in Artificial Intelligence [AI] are beginning to turn those fantasies into reality. Indeed, the latest chapter of the "great book of Man-the-Machine," to use Michel Foucault's phrase,[1] tells of the imminent birth of a new breed of computers; predatory computers. In a document called "Strategic Computing," published in 1984, the Pentagon has revealed its intention to create autonomous weapons systems capable of fighting wars entirely on their own.

During World War II a primitive form of intelligence had already found its way into weapons when antiaircraft artillery was equipped with tracing devices capable of predicting the future positions of a targeted plane. The replacement of human marksmanship by machines took a further step forward during the Vietnam War when mechanical intelligence migrated from the launching platform to the projectile itself. But these "smart bombs" still depended on humans for establishing their targets. In order to get the human eye completely out of the loop the military has announced its intention to create robotic weapons, machines capable of autonomic target detection and friend/foe recognition.

[. . .]

In this chapter, I want to examine the history of the information-processing technology that could finally make the military commander's dream of a battlefield without human soldiers a reality. We have already seen many of the military applications of computers, cruise missiles, war games, radar and radio networks. This provided a picture of the many ways in which computer technology has affected military institutions. Now it is time to investigate the influence that the military has had on the development of information-processing machines. In some cases, like the development of the transistor in the 1950s or the creation of the integrated chip in the 1960s, this influence has been indirect. The transistor and the chip were the products of civilian inventors, but it was the military that nurtured these key inventions during the period when their development was not commercially feasible. In other cases, the influence has been more direct, as in the case of AI research, which has been funded from its inception in the 1950s by the Pentagon.

The needs of war have not only influenced the development of the internal components of computers (transistors and chips) but also computers themselves. The computer was born in 1936 as an "imaginary" machine. That is, Alan Turing, its inventor, gave only a logical specification of the machine's functions without bothering to give any details regarding its physical implementation. The original purpose of the machine was to settle some abstract questions in metamathematics, not to solve any real computational problem. Thus, Turing was able to simplify his machine to the extreme, not allowing irrelevant questions of implementation to distract him from the essential issues. For example, his imaginary machine needed to have a storage device to hold information, and the simplest solution was to equip the machine with an "infinite paper tape." For its original purpose this worked fine, but when it came time to embody this "abstract device" into a concrete assemblage, many years went into deciding how to best implement the infinite paper tape in a form of a finite computer memory.

[. . .]

We encountered demons when discussing decentralized computer networks in the previous chapter [of *War in the Age of Intelligent Machines*]. There we saw that in order to avoid bottlenecks and overloads in a network, the flows of information circulating through it had to be allowed to self-organize — that is, instead of a central computer directing the traffic of messages in the network, the messages themselves had to possess enough "local intelligence" to, in effect, find their own destination. The messages had to become independent software objects or demons. In more ambitious schemes of control (e.g., agoric systems), demons begin to form "computational societies" as they barter and bid for resources (memory, processing time) and engage in cooperative and competitive forms of computation.

Thus, instead of picturing DNA in terms of current paradigms of computation (Turing machines), we can learn from what nature has created in order to evolve new paradigms for the design of computers. But if the information-processing engines used by the genetic code do not resemble Turing machines, that does not mean that universal computers are irrelevant to understanding self-replication. In particular, a Turing machine may be used to endow robots with the ability to self-reproduce. If autonomous weapons acquired their own genetic apparatus, they could probably begin to compete with humans for the control of their own destiny. But how could machines reproduce themselves? Although nobody has actually built a self-replicating robot, it has already been proved mathematically that machines, after reaching a certain singularity (a threshold of organizational complexity), can indeed become capable of self-reproduction.

In the early 1950s von Neumann began thinking about two questions. One related to the problem of building automata that "fix themselves," that is, robots whose overall behavior remains relatively stable even if their components malfunction. The second question related to the building of automata that reproduce themselves: "Von Neumann's work on automata formed out of unreliable parts was an outgrowth, in part, of his interest in the Air Force's problem of the reliability of its missiles. . . ."[2]

Unlike the problem of self-repairing automata, von Neumann's research on the question of self-reproducing robots was conducted without any military applications in mind. But his results, indicating a threshold of complexity beyond which machines are endowed with self-reproducing capabilities, have acquired a new meaning in the age of predatory machines.

When von Neumann began thinking about self-reproduction, he imagined physical machines floating in a lake, with all the components needed to build their progeny floating around the lake ready to be assembled. This imaginary physical model, however, proved too restrictive to conduct his research: it tended to distract him from the essential aspects of self-replication. What von Neumann needed was literally a world of abstract robots, where the problems associated with the physical assembling of components could be ignored. He found the right conditions to conduct his research in the world of "cellular automata." These are "robots" whose bodies are nothing but patterns on a computer screen.

[. . .]

In simple cellular spaces, like the popular computer game Life, the cells may be either live or dead, that is, they can have only two possible states. The cellular automata that von Neumann designed were much more complicated than those simple creatures. Instead of only two states, the cells making up his abstract robots could have as many as twenty-nine states.[3] But, differences in complexity aside, the problem was to find the simplest set of rules that could allow a pattern of cells to build a replica of itself, following the instructions contained in a "genetic program." In other words, von Neumann's robots did not self-replicate the way a crystal does, building simple copies of themselves in a mechanical way. Rather, his robots simulated the self-reproducing of living organisms, in which a blueprint is followed for the assembling of the progeny, and then a copy of the blueprint is stored in the new creatures to allow them in turn to self-reproduce.

Basically, what von Neumann did was to create groups of cells that would simulate the workings of the elementary building blocks of Turing machines (And gates and Or gates). Using these, he synthesized simple "organs," which in turn were used as building blocks to create higher level organs. At the end of the process, von Neumann synthesized a machine capable of building any other machine (a "universal constructor") and a machine capable of simulating any other machine, a Turing machine. The reason von Neumann needed to create a cell-based version of a universal computer (Turing machine) is that he needed a programmable engine to supervise the reproductive cycle. The job of the Turing machine was to determine the point at which the information guiding the process of self-reproduction was to stop being interpreted as a recipe for the building of replicas, and begin to be treated as a blueprint to be copied into the new creatures.[4]

[. . .]

Hardware

For a long time technical objects – levers and pendula, clockworks and motors – were assembled by tinkerers who relied on hunches and rules of thumb, but who did not know exactly how the machines really worked. An abstract description of the mechanisms involved had to wait until the technical assemblage had been studied scientifically as if it were one more object of nature. The steam motor, for instance, appeared suddenly in 1712, after ten years of intense non-scientific tinkering. But it was not truly understood until 1824, when scientific research finally produced a diagram encapsulating the "essential" aspects of the mechanisms involved. Although some assemblages, like the transistor and the integrated chip, have quite recently been created through tinkering, many machines begin life as abstract descriptions that only later are given a physical body.

[. . .]

One and the same singularity may become a part of different technological assemblages. The singularity marking the phase transition between water and steam, for instance, may be embedded in one way in a clockwork mechanism and in an entirely different way in a true steam motor. Thus, the relation between the two levels of the phylum seems to be that the information stored in the abstract description of a mechanism serves as a constraint on processes of self-organization, determining the exact role they will play in a given assemblage. If we think of the machinic phylum as being composed of all the critical points in the rate of flow of matter and energy, then the role of abstract descriptions is that of informing the way in which the artisan selects and appropriates some of these points to make them converge in a concrete physical assemblage:

> We will call an assemblage every constellation of singularities and traits deduced from the flow – selected, organized, stratified – in such a way as to converge. . . . artificially or naturally. . . . Assemblages may group themselves into extremely vast constellations constituting "cultures," or even ages. . . . We may distinguish in every case a number of very different lines. Some of them, phylogenic lines, travel long distances between assemblages of various ages and cultures (from the blowgun to the cannon? from the prayer wheel to the propeller? from the pot to the motor?); others, ontogenetic lines, are internal to one assemblage and link up its various elements, or else cause something to pass . . . into another assemblage of a different nature but of the same culture or age (for example, the horseshoe which spread through agricultural assemblages).[5]

When analyzing the evolution of tactical formations in history, I provided an example of this phenomenon of machinic migration: as the clockwork ceased to be the dominant form of technology with the birth of the steam motor, people began to put together other "machines" following the new model. Thus, while the armies of Frederick the Great may be seen as a well-oiled clockwork mechanism, the armies of Napoleon were assembled more like a motor. Similarly, logical calculi, the ancestors of computer hardware, were assembled for two millennia as little clockworks, until Boole came along and tapped the reservoir of combinatorial resources contained in arithmetic. A logical calculus may be seen as a machine whose parts are physical inscriptions on a piece of paper. The job of these machines is to act as "conveyor belts" to transport truth from one set of inscriptions (representing, for example, the premise "All men are mortal") to another set of inscriptions (standing for the conclusion "I am mortal"). As such, logical calculi are, like any other technology, capable of being affected by ontogenetic influences – the form in which an assemblage spreads across the technological spectrum – such as the switch from the clockwork to the motor as the dominant paradigm for the assembly of machines.

Philosopher of science Michel Serres was the first to point out that the transition between the clockwork age and the motor age had more profound implications than the simple addition of a new breed of machines to the technological "races" already in existence. He sees in the emergence of the steam motor a complete break with the conceptual models of the past: "from the Greek mechanical experts to [the mathematicians of the eighteenth century], the motor is not constructible. It is outside the machine . . . and remains very much beyond Physics." There were of course elaborate clocks, musical boxes, and toy automata, but these machines ran on an external source of motion, they did not produce it themselves. "They transit movement, propagate it, invert it, duplicate it, transpose it, transform it and obliterate it. They are paths of movement toward a repose, no matter how complex the map is."[6]

[. . .]

An abstract motor, the mechanism dissociated from the physical contraption, consists of three separate components: a reservoir (of steam, for example), a form of exploitable difference (the heat/cold difference) and a diagram or program for the efficient exploitation of (thermal) differences. In the nineteenth century, even *social* theories began to come complete with their own reservoirs, their own mode of difference and their own circulation diagrams. Serres mentions Darwin, Marx and Freud as examples in the area of scientific discourse: reservoirs of populations, of capital or of unconscious desires, put to work by the use of differences of fitness, class or sex, each following a procedure directing the circulation of naturally selected species, or commodities and labor, or symptoms and fantasies. Serres also finds the abstract motor in such apparently unrelated areas as painting (Turner) and literature (Zola).[7]

To Serres's research I have added the examples from tactical formations just mentioned. Napoleon himself did not incorporate the motor as a *technical* object into his war machine (as mentioned, he explicitly rejected the use of steamboats[8]), but the abstract motor did affect the mode of assemblage of the Napoleonic armies: "motorized" armies were the first to make use of a reservoir of loyal human bodies, to insert these bodies into a flexible calculus (nonlinear tactics), and to exploit the friend/foe difference to take warfare from clockwork dynastic duels to massive confrontations between nations.

[. . .]

From the point of view that matters to us here, one particular incarnation of the Boolean motor is most important: that controlling the flow of electricity inside computers: And gates and Or gates. As early as 1886 Charles Peirce had suggested the possibility of incarnating Boolean logic in electrical switching circuits. But it was not until 1936 that Claude Shannon showed how relay and switching circuits could be expressed by equations using Boolean algebra. In these equations True and False correspond to the open and closed states of a circuit. The binary connectives, that is, "And" and "Or," are modeled by different kinds of switches.[9] Shannon was the creator of the elementary "cells" in the body of modern computers. Because he stood at the threshold between a world of machines made of inscriptions in paper (notations) and another of electronic devices, he was able to easily move back and forth between the two. He understood that the typographical resources of arithmetic could be used to design complex electrical circuits. For example, since And and Or gates are but one physical incarnation of the operators of Boolean calculus, for any given electrical circuit made up of these gates there is a corresponding formula in the calculus. Shannon took advantage of this fact to translate electrical circuits into formulas (that is, strings of physical inscriptions), compressing them using typographical resources (operations on strings of inscriptions), and then to translate them back into the form of much-simplified circuit designs. In this way, the internal circuitry of modern computer hardware began to evolve until it reached its present state. And and Or gates became universal building blocks, with which complex machines could be built. With the Boolean motor, then, we have reached a first stop in the study of the evolution of computer hardware. From here on the military will play an increasingly formative role in the development of information-processing technology. The operators of the Boolean motor, And and Or, having acquired a physical form, began a journey across physical scales, first moving from switching relays to vacuum tubes, then to transistors, finally to the ever-more dense integrated circuits.

Miniaturization

The process underlying the creation of And gates and Or gates may be seen as a migration, a journey that took logical structures from their point of departure in the human brain (in the form of heuristics) to their destination: the body of the Turing machine. Aristotle extracted them from the brain and embodied them in an infallible recipe (the syllogism), a series of steps that when followed mechanically led invariably to correct results. Then, Boole generalized this recipe to include all of deductive logic. In this form the And and Or operators, assembled into binary arithmetic, managed to capture some of the powers of computation found in the human brain. Finally, these operators were given a physical form by Claude Shannon.

Once incarnated, though, the forces guiding the operators' migration – forces both material and historical – began to change, and the migration became increasingly implicated in the development of the war machine. In its drive to apply these operators to every aspect of the command and control structure, the military pushed for miniaturization; and with each generation the operators' function came to rely increasingly on the singularities and electrochemical properties characteristic of certain materials – in short, the operators began to merge with the flow of matter and energy. And it is in this context that the military engineer, very much a descendant of the weapons artisan, takes on an increasing significance.

Vannevar Bush, the ultimate military technocrat, was both an electrical engineer and an important figure in the early application of mechanical computing to the problems of modern ballistics. During World War II Bush created the machinery necessary for effecting the mobilization of the scientific community's resources for the purposes of war. [. . .] The Manhattan project, and many of the other programs under Bush's command during the war, involved the intensive use of computers. These were not yet Turing machines, but rather special-purpose devices designed to handle very specific problems like the calculation of artillery range tables.

In 1936 Alan Turing assembled a machine that could take abstract descriptions (tables of behavior), which capture the essential aspects of a physical device, and simulate that device. His machine was imaginary in the sense that he gave only a logical specification of the device without bothering about implementation details. It consisted of three components: an infinite paper tape for the storage of physical inscriptions (including tables of behavior); a scanning head to read from and write on the paper tape; and a control unit, capable of directing the scanning head, to make it read or write, or move along the paper tape. This three-component assemblage was not intended to be used for the solution of specific practical problems. Turing created his abstract machine to show not its practical value in mechanical computation, but to prove that mathematics could not be completely mechanized. With his machine he proved the existence of uncomputable problems – uncomputable, that is, by any particular Turing machine but not by a gifted human. Mathematicians, he showed, could not be taken out of the loop.[10]

But a decade and a half after these machines had been born as imaginary devices, they were incarnated into a physical machine, and the modern computer was born. Turing's most important step was to reduce concrete physical assemblages to tables of behavior, and then to store them in the "paper tape" of his imaginary machine. Once there the scanning head could read the entries on the table, and the control unit could implement the necessary steps to simulate the concrete physical device represented by the table. Furthermore, from the point of view of the future evolution of computer software, the key idea was that once reduced to a table of behavior, a physical device could be stored on the same paper tape (memory) as the information it operates on. In other words, the word processor could be stored right next to the text that it manipulates.

This meant that just as data can be manipulated by abstract typewriters, so can the typewriters themselves be manipulated by other programs. For example, one may want to modify a word processor to transform it from a machine using the Roman alphabet to one using an Arabic alphabet. This could be accomplished by modifying the abstract typewriter, treating it as if it were one more piece of data. In contrast with old calculating machines in which operations may only be read and data only written, here data could be read and acted on, and operations (programs) written upon and therefore modified on the run. That is, software that operated on itself could now be written.

[...]

Several military think tanks (the RAND Corporation, the Office of Naval Research, etc.) stepped into the breach and continued the mobilization of science into the Cold War. The military became a true institutional entrepreneur, financing basic research, supervising production methods, aiding in the dissemination of technology and in general institutionalizing the war-forged bonds between military needs and scientific solutions. In particular, the Army Signal Corps provided an impetus toward the miniaturization of logical circuitry, a drive to squeeze electronic components into every nook and cranny of the war machine.

[...]

Accordingly, by the late 1930s the Army Signal Corps had developed the first walkie-talkie in an effort to avoid the carnage of World War I in the then rapidly approaching global confrontation. As the Nazis demonstrated with their blitzkrieg tactics, a network of weapons systems (mission-oriented infantry, tanks, aircraft) joined together by wireless was the wave of the future in warfare. By the end of World War II, the miniaturization of electronic components that had made portable wireless a reality had become institutionalized as a military-scientific research goal. The first step in this journey across physical scales was achieved with the invention of the transistor at Bell Laboratories in the late 1940s.

Both the transistor and the silicon chip were the product of civilian inventors (William Shockley and Jack Kilby, respectively), but their infancy was nurtured by the military, which consumed large quantities of these components during the period when they were too expensive for commercial applications. In the case of the transistor, the first physical machine without moving parts, the Army Signal Corps acted not only as a consumer but also as a true entrepreneur: by 1953, it was providing up to 50 percent of the research funding. It was also underwriting the construction of production facilities and subsidizing the development of engineering processes to speed up the translation of applications from prototypes to finished product. It sponsored conferences to aid in the diffusion of the new technology and helped in the difficult process of setting industry-wide standards to increase internal organization cohesion.[11]

[...]

Military applications demanded an increasing number of components for every new circuit design. Miniaturizing these components via solid-state devices solved some of the problems (power consumption and mechanical failure), but it also created a new problem of its own. The smaller the components the harder it became to interconnect them to form a circuit. Transistors had to be wired together by hand using magnifying lenses and ever-smaller soldering tools. Augmenting the number of components in a circuit also increased the probability that one of the many handmade connections could be faulty, rendering the whole device useless.

[...]

The machinic phylum, seen as technology's own internal dynamics and cutting edge, could still be seen shining through the brilliant civilian discoveries of the transistor and the integrated chip, which had liberated electronic circuit designs from the constraints on their possible complexity. But the military had already begun to tighten its grip on the evolution of the phylum, on the events happening at its cutting edge, channeling its forces but limiting its potential mutations:

> Although it might be tempting to conclude that military patronage had merely allowed the technology to mature until its costs could be reduced, this simplistic

"pump priming" interpretation needs to be examined closely. As the case of the Signal Corps' intensive promotion of the high-performance diffused transistor illustrates, military patronage could be tightly tied to specific variants of the new technology that filled requirements virtually unique to the military. . . . A complex of characteristics suggesting a technological style, including the structure of the industry and the technology appearing at its cutting edge, were linked to the military in the 1950s and have continued to be associated with military enterprise.[12]

We saw in the previous chapter that the imposition of military production methods onto the civilian world was accompanied by the transfer of a whole command and control grid. In the early nineteenth century, for instance, the American military began to transform the mode of operation of its armories in order to produce firearms with perfectly interchangeable parts. To achieve this goal, they introduced methods for the routinization and standardization of labor. These methods marked the beginning of the rationalization of the labor process, which would later be further developed by Frederick Taylor in army arsenals, and whose main goal was to centralize control of the production process by shortening the chain of command. When the civilian industry adopted these methods, partly under the pressure of military contractors, they adopted not only a system of mass production, but also the command and control grid needed to impose that system in the workplace. With the advent of computers, this process of "dispossession of control" reached its culmination. The system of Numerical Control, developed with funds from the Air Force, effectively withdraws all control from workers in the area of weapons production and centralizes it at the top.

But if NC (and related methods) effectively shortened the chain of command by getting humans out of the decision-making loop, it also weakened the civilian sector of the economy by its adverse effects on worker's productivity. The Germans and the Japanese, who concentrated in maximizing not control but overall productivity, have now gained the lead in areas long dominated by American corporations, with the result that the U.S. has become a net importer of machine tools for the first time since the nineteenth century. [. . .] If we consider that the last two global conflicts were essentially wars of logistics in which the total industrial potential of a nation was the key to victory, we can see that the effects on the civilian sector by the military command imperative will only be self-defeating in the long run.

[. . .]

Software

We have explored the long migration movement that took logical structures from their point of departure in the human body to the miniaturized form through which they entered the body of predatory machines. This transference of logical machinery was partly a result of technology's own dynamic forces (the machinic phylum) in the first part of the journey, and partly the effect of direct military intervention in the second stage of this evolution. When we explore the technological and military lineages of the software of autonomous weapons we will find a similar migration, not of logical machinery this time but of control machinery. Computer hardware involves, as we saw, the mechanization of "conveyor belts" for the transport of truth across sentences. Software, on the other hand, involves the mechanization not of "logical resources" but of the means to press into service those resources.

Let us call the means through which the resources contained in computer hardware are pressed into service by software "control machinery," or simply "control." Just as the history of hardware involved a migration of deductive conveyor belts from the human body to the machine, so the evolution of software needed a migration of control in several stages. The first step in this migration of control from humans to machines was part of a long historical process that began with the first attempts at a rationalized division of labor. Although this process received its main momentum from the efforts of military engineers, it was also developed in certain civilian sectors, the textile industry, for example. The earliest form of software was a set of pattern-weaving procedures stored in the form of holes punched in paper cards. This was the automated loom introduced by Jacquard in 1805. His device effectively withdrew control of the weaving process from human workers and transferred it to the hardware of the machine. This was the beginning of a new migration. In this century a second step was taken when control was transferred from the hardware to the software. At that point a master program acquired the responsibility to trigger the beginning of a given process and direct the utilization of hardware resources.

Finally, in the last three decades research in Artificial Intelligence has revealed that, in order to create more human-like programs, the control of a given process must not reside in a master program, but in the very data that master program works on. We may think of the "mind" of a robot as consisting of the database in which the external world is represented through "sensors," that reflect changes in the outside world – in short, the migration of control from programs to data permits external events to trigger internal processes. When this degree of dispersion of control is achieved through "demons," we could say that the machine has acquired a "mind" of its own. But can robots really have a mind?

There is no direct answer to this question. All we can do is establish certain criteria for machine intelligence, and see if real robots meet those criteria. In 1950 Alan Turing proposed his test for determining the intelligence of machines that was basically an acting test. Place a human and a computer in separate rooms and let a second human try to decide which is which through a session of questions and answers. If the computer can fool the human interrogator then it must be said to have at least a primitive form of intelligence. But this simple test must be revised in the light of many recent AI programs that are based on a repertoire of canned answers, which manage nevertheless to fool human users into attributing beliefs and desires to them. A case in point is a program named ELIZA. As its astonished inventor said, "ELIZA created the most remarkable illusion of having understood [a conversation] in the minds of the many people who conversed with it." When subjects were told that the program was simply using canned answer-templates, and had never really interacted with them, they would not only disregard these explanations but "would often demand to converse with the system in private."[13]

[. . .]

If Frederick the Great's phalanx was the ultimate clockwork army, and Napoleon's armies represented the first motor in history, the German *Blitzkrieg* was the first example of the distributed network: a machine integrating various elements through the use of radio communications. As the flow of information in a system became more important than the flow of energy, the emphasis switched from machines with components in physical contact with each other to machines with components operating over vast geographical distances. And if a Turing machine is an instance of the abstract motor, then several computers working simultaneously on a given problem correspond to the third stage in the series clockwork-motor-network: a parallel computer.

[. . .]

Parallelism not only achieves a dramatic increase in speed but also allows the development of systems that are more "human-like" in that they do not follow a rigidly deterministic sequence of steps, but plan their strategies by considering many factors simultaneously. Some form of parallel computation is necessary to make autonomous weapons a reality. Strictly speaking, the problem of achieving true parallel computing is a question of hardware.

[...]

In the absence of true parallel processing at the hardware level, the history of software may be seen as a struggle against the limitations sequential processing imposes on machine intelligence. But if we view this struggle as a migration of control from the human body to data itself, then it becomes clear that the migration far precedes software. Indeed, industrial processes have gone from being human driven to being hardware driven, then program driven, finally becoming data driven. Some technological lineages may be classified according to the degree of control they allow workers to exercise over a production process. For example, there is a clear sequence of development starting with power tools with a fixed sequence of functions to machines actuated by the introduction of the work piece, to machines capable of detecting errors and changing state accordingly, to machines capable of anticipating an action required and adjusting themselves to provide it. In this sequence the level of skill required from the worker diminishes gradually as the control of the production process is transferred to the machine.[14] Workers lose control as the machine gains it.

In this sense, we can trace the origins of software to 1805, the year Jacquard introduced his control mechanism for pattern-weaving looms. Jacquard's idea of coding the direction of the weaving process into a series of holes punched in cards was in fact an elaboration of earlier ideas and over a century of experimentation. But, for our purposes, we may say that his device transferred control (and structure[15]) from the human body to the machine in the form of a primitive program stored as punched holes in paper cards, the earliest form of software: a rigid sequence of steps to be followed sequentially in an unbroken chain. Charles Babbage, who in the early nineteenth century designed a primitive kind of computer (the Analytical Engine), saw the importance of Jacquard's device for the future of mechanical computation. Babbage was a student of the labor process and saw the idea of instruction cards controlling the weaving process as a form of "abstract assembly line."

[...]

Turing realized that programs that change themselves could be written, and this would allow them to surrender control to a subprogram, rewriting themselves to know where control had to be returned after the execution of a given subtask.

> When control passing is combined with a primitive message-passing facility – at minimum, a remainder of where the control came from, so that it can be returned to later – subroutines are born. And since subroutines can be nested . . . the notion of a hierarchy of control also emerges.[16]

A master program surrenders control to a subroutine designed to perform a particular task; the subroutine itself may call into action even simpler programs that perform even simpler tasks, and this hierarchy may go on for several layers. When each subprogram finishes its own task, it returns control to the immediately higher level subroutine until control returns to the master program. Control is not rigidly located in one central organ in the hardware, but rather circulates up and down a hierarchy in which the upper levels define an overall goal to be achieved while the lower levels define subgoals that may be activated whenever needed. Thus, we may say that the control of a process of computation has migrated from the hardware of the computer to its software (to the master program).

Although this scheme allowed the creation of more flexible programs, the kind of software that could endow robots with mechanical intelligence needed to go beyond a program-directed, hierarchical flow of control. Otherwise, every routine would have to be programmed, every contingency planned for – its activities would remain, in a sense, clockwork, in that it could follow only a limited repertoire of orders. Such a master program would soon become too big and unmanageable and, indeed, would present an obstacle for the further evolution of robot intelligence. To avoid the combinatorial explosions that a hierarchical scheme of control would produce once a certain level of complexity is reached, AI researchers began in the 1960s to design software languages that allowed the data itself to act as the controlling agent.

[. . .]

To adequately trace the evolution of robot minds, we must understand a few things about the history of logic. I mentioned before that a logical calculus may be seen as a system of conveyor belts that transport truth from one sentence to another. Deductive systems have a relatively easy job: they need to transport truth from a general principle (axiom) to a particular fact (theorem). Inductive systems, on the other hand, have a much harder task. They must "pump" truth up from a particular piece of evidence ("This emerald is green") to a general principle applying to a whole class of things ("All emeralds are green"). The problem of mechanizing inductive conveyor belts is equivalent to building a machine that can learn from experience. And this is, of course, just what is needed to create autonomous weapon systems. Thus, the design of an "inference engine," to use the technical term, capable of performing inductive inferences (pumping truth up from particular to general statements) is at the center of robotics research.

[. . .]

Theorem-proving allows robots to solve problems, but only to the extent that the problems are modeled by the operation of pumping truth up from a particular piece of data to a general principle stored in a database. Although many kinds of robotic actions may be so modeled, theorem-proving forces robots to approach many different problems using basically the same strategy. By switching from theorem-proving to a Pandemonium[17] robots become capable of generating different strategic approaches to a given problem according to the specific nature of the problem. Furthermore, recent implementations of this approach allow robots to produce plans of attack at different levels of abstraction, allowing them to achieve optimal results without getting bogged down by irrelevant data.

[. . .]

Expertise

The earliest form of software, as we saw above, was created to run Jacquard's automatic loom, in which the routine operations involved in pattern weaving were stored in punched paper cards. This change in manufacturing process was bitterly opposed by workers who saw in this migration of control a piece of their bodies literally being transferred to the machine. And it is not simply a coincidence that Babbage, besides being an early user of punched cards for the storage of programs, was also an analyst of the labor process. The decomposition of a particular human task into its basic components and the acquisition of control by machines are two elements of a single strategy. The transfer of control from the body to the machine that marks the beginning of the evolution of software was part of the process, described by historian Michel Foucault in *Discipline and Punish* of disciplining the body to increase its potential, while simultaneously reducing its mastery over its newly acquired skills.

This may be seen most clearly in the drill and discipline techniques used by seventeenth-century generals to transform a mass of mercenaries and vagabonds into an army: training amplified their fighting abilities but decreased their mastery over the battlefield, reducing them to mere cogs on a well-oiled clockwork mechanism. This process of dispossession of control may also be seen in the area of weapons manufacture. In the U.S. the rationalization of the labor process created the first methods for the absolute control of the production process from above, shortening the chain of command in the logistics of weapons procurement.

Indeed, we saw that in more recent times, behind every application of computers to the problems of war, there was a desire to take humans out of the decision-making loop. Thus, as mechanical intelligence migrated from gunners to the missile's launching platform and then to the missile itself, the gunner was taken out of the loop. In a similar way, as the different elements that make up a battle (the rate of advance of armies, the lethality index of weapons, etc.) were quantified, human beings began to disappear from war games. In the latest RAND Corporation design the SAM and IVAN automata simulate armageddons in which politicians and diplomats (not to mention other humans) have been taken out of the strategic decision-making loop.

To the extent that Jacquard's loom was part of this long historical process of transferring control from humans to machines, we must say that software has "military origins." And yet, the military has influenced the evolution of software only indirectly. The imposition of command structures on civilian industry affected technology as a whole, and not software qua software. Even in modern times, when the development of programming techniques was directly funded by military agencies, the scientists overseeing the funding process gave the evolution of software plenty of room for creative experimentation. This period of "enlightened" Pentagon support, in which a concern to increase productivity overshadowed the need to tighten control, ended by the early 1970s. ARPA, which had funded Artificial Intelligence programs from their inception, changed its name to DARPA ("D" for defense)[18] to signal the fact that only projects with a direct military value would be funded from then on. At that point the removal of humans from the loop acquired a new form. It was not enough to transfer control from the body to the machine, the new drive involved transferring the body's know-how and expertise to a new kind of database: the knowledge bank.

As mentioned above, AI research began in the 1950s with the rather naïve goal of discovering the "eternal laws of thought," or in technical terms, of finding an algorithm (infallible mechanical procedure) capable of performing inductive inferences. As it turned out, machines need to have access to factual knowledge about the world to be able to ground their inferences, and what is more, they need to posses heuristic knowledge. Because heuristic knowledge is developed to serve very specific areas of human activity, the kind of "intelligent machines" that AI is building along these lines resemble more an idiot savant than a master thinker. In other words, they may display intelligent behavior in very specific fields, without resembling complex human intelligence in general.

[...]

The first expert systems were developed not for military but for civilian applications. MYCIN, for example, was a program that could diagnose certain diseases (meningitis, blood diseases) when fed a list of the patient's symptoms. Then there was DENDRAL, the very first expert system created in 1965 by the epistemological entrepreneur Edward Feigenbaum. This robotic adviser could determine the molecular and atomic structure of a chemical compound by analyzing its mass spectrograph. But even though early expert systems were not destined for the military (but rather for domestic surveillance),[19] the corporation founded by the creator of this theology (Tecknowledge, Inc.) has been a major military contractor for expert systems used in the evaluation and analysis of strategic indicators and warnings, tactical battlefield communications analysis and other areas.

[...]

With the birth of knowledge engineering,[20] the examination regime has taken a giant step forward. It is not enough anymore to establish the true nature of a subject. This true nature must now be transferred to a machine. The raw data for a knowledge base is produced by verbal examination of experts on the logical structure of a particular task, and by formations of the rule of thumb than an expert is discovered to be using in his or her own work. The lists of data accumulated in these sessions must then be converted into the format of a knowledge base and the right inference engine chosen to match the expert's own inductive process.

[. . .]

Once experiential knowledge is captured and the resulting reservoir of know-how is connected to an inference engine (like the Pandemonium) to allow for the efficient exploitation of those resources, the third component must be added: a human interface. This allows the expert system to interact with its users in order to be able to explain, for instance, the rationale for a given piece of advice. Without being able to reconstruct the line of reasoning followed to reach a particular conclusion, an expert system cannot generate trust on the part of its users. And without this trust, its role in the real world would probably be very limited.

[. . .]

The efforts of military institutions to get humans out of the loop have been a major influence in the development of computer technology. The birth of autonomous weapons systems, of war games played by automata, of production systems that pace and discipline the worker, all are manifestations of this military drive. But, as we saw in the conclusion to Chapter One [of *War in the Age of Intelligent Machines*], even though humans are being replaced by machines, the only schemes of control that can given robots the means to replace them (the Pandemonium) are producing another kind of independent "will" which may also "resist" military domination. For example, the future of the military depends on the correct functioning of its worldwide command and control networks, like the WWMCCS [World Wide Military Command and Control System]. This network, up to the 1970s, was designed around a centralized scheme of control (batch processing) that caused bottlenecks and delays, even when operating without the friction produced by war. To make a global command and control network a functional entity the military needed to replace a central computer handling the traffic of message with a scheme where the messages themselves had the ability to find their own destination. The messages had to become demons.

However, when demons are allowed to barter, bid and compete among themselves for resources, they begin to form "computational societies" which resemble natural ecologies (like an insect colony) or even human ecologies (like a marketplace). In other words, demons begin to acquire a degree of independence from their designers. Indeed, as we mentioned in the previous chapter, as the membrane of computers which is beginning to cover the surface of the planet evolves into "computational ecologies," demons begin to acquire more "local intelligence." On one hand, the Pandemonium offers the military the only way to create autonomous weapon systems; on the other hand, a Pandemonium as embodied in worldwide computer networks creates conditions that threaten absolute military control.

Notes

1 [This phrase is taken from Michel Foucault, *Discipline and Punish: The Birth of the Prison*, trans. Alan Sheridan, New York: Vintage, 1995, p. 136. In the original chapter, De Landa has an epigraph from this work in which this phrase appears. – SV.]

2 Herman H. Goldstine, *The Computer from Pascal to von Neuman*, Princeton, NJ: Princeton University Press, p. 279 [ellipses in original]. The question of self-repairing machines is of extreme military

importance. In particular, the problem of self-repairing communications networks that can survive a nuclear attack. On the theoretical aspects of self-repairing systems, see Rolf Landauer, "Role of Relative Stability in Self-Repair and Self-Maintenance," in F. Eugene Yates (ed.), *Self-Organizing Systems: The Emergence of Order*, pp. 435–443, New York: Springer, 1987.

3 Arthur Burks, "Von Neumann's Self-Reproducing Automata," in Arthur Burks (ed.), *Essays on Cellular Automata* (Champaign, IL: University of Illinois Press, 1970), p. 60.

4 William Poundstone, *The Recursive Universe* (New York: William Morrow, 1985), p. 188. The Turing machine's role in simulated self-replication was to stop the infinite regress involved in trying to store, in one and the same blueprint, both instructions to assemble a new robot and instructions to copy these instructions into the new robot. In other words, true self-reproduction could only be achieved if a robot-plus-blueprint system was capable of creating not just another robot, but a robot-plus-blueprint replica. Thus, the instructions to build a replica would have to contain a small copy of themselves built inside, to allow the robot to copy them into the new machine. But then this small copy would have to contain an even smaller copy and so on *ad infinitum*. The obvious solution is to allow the robot to switch modes: first it must take the blueprint as a set of instructions to be interpreted and followed; then, when it is finished, it switches modes, and begins taking the blueprint as a set of inscriptions to be copied into the replica. Von Neumann coded a Turing machine into cellular space to allow the robot to make this "switch" between modes.

5 Gilles Deleuze, *The Logic of Sense*, trans. Mark Lester, ed. Constantin V. Boundas, New York: Columbia University Press, 1990, p. 409 [ellipses in original].

6 Michel Serres, "It Was Before the (World) Exhibition," in Jean Clair and Harold Szeeman (eds.), *The Bachelor Machines* (New York: Rizzoli, 1975) [ellipses in original].

7 Michel Serres, *Hermes: Literature, Science and Philosophy* (Baltimore: Johns Hopkins, 1982), p. 54.

8 Martin Van Crevald, *Technology and War* (New York: Free Press, 1989), p. 167. It is said that Roosevelt gave the go-ahead for the Manhattan Project when told the story of how Napoleon had missed his chance to invade England by rejecting the use of steam power. See Peter H. Wyden, *Day One: Before Hiroshima and After*, New York: Simon and Schuster, 1984, p. 37.

9 Martin Gardner, *Logic Machines and Diagrams*, Chicago: University of Chicago Press, 1982, p. 129.

10 Andrew Hodges, *Alan Turing: The Enigma of Intelligence*, New York: HarperCollins, 1985, p. 109.

11 Thomas Misa, "Military Needs, Commercial Realities, and the Development of the Transistor, 1948–1958," in Merritt Roe Smith, *Military Enterprise and Technological Change: Perspectives on the American Experience*, pp. 253–288, Cambridge, MA: MIT Press, 1985, p. 262.

12 Ibid., p. 285.

13 Joseph Weizenbaum, quoted in Douglas R. Hofstadter, *Gödel, Escher, Bach: An Eternal Golden Braid*, New York: Basic Books, 1979, p. 600.

14 Harry Braverman, *Labor and Monopoly Capital* (New York: Monthly Review Press, 1974), p. 216.

15 Allan Newell and Herbert Simon, "Computer Science as Empirical Inquiry," in John Haugeland (ed.), *Mind Design: Philosophy, Psychology, Artificial Intelligence*, Montgomery, VT: Bradford, 1981, p. 45. Computer science pioneers Newell and Simon have described two milestones in the history of their discipline. The first step was the creation of the stored program concept, which allowed procedures to be coded at the same level than the data they operate on: "The next step, taken in 1956, was list-processing [which allowed] the creation of a genuine dynamic memory structure in a machine that had heretofore been perceived as having fixed structure. . . . [List-processing] was an early demonstration of the basic abstraction that a computer consists of a set of data types and a set of operations proper to these data types, so that a computational system should employ whatever data types are appropriate to the application, independent of the underlying machine. . . . [McCarthy's creation of LISP in 1959–60] completed the act of abstraction, lifting list structures out of their embedding in concrete machines, creating a new formal system. . . . which could be shown to be equivalent to the other universal schemes of computation. [Turing's machines, Church's Lamda calculus, etc." (*ibid*, p. 45) [ellipses and additions in original]

After the birth of the list, data structures went on mutating and became "frames" (lists plus demons), "scripts," "micro-worlds" and so on. In general they acquired more structure of their own in an attempt to capture the versatile information storage patterns of human minds. For a discussion of the implications of merging demons with advanced data structures like Minsky's "frames," see Hofstadter, *Gödel, Escher, Bach*, p. 662.

16 Zenon Pylyshyn, "Complexity and the Study of Artificial and Human Intelligence," in Haugeland, *Mind Design*, p. 75 [ellipses in original]. The claim that Turing invented the notion of a "subroutine"

(and modern programming) in the late 1940s is put forward by Hodges (*Alan Turing*, pp. 324–26). Pylyshyn prefers to mark the emergence of this concept by its formalization as a TOTE (Test–Operate–Test–Unit) in the early sixties.

17 [De Landa discusses this term in an omitted section. He uses it to describe the space created by the multiple interactions among various software objects: actors, objects, production rules, antecedent theorems, if-added methods, demons, servants, etc. – SV]

18 [ARPA stands for Advanced Research Projects Agency. – SV]

19 In fact, an early mutation of an expert systems theory appears to have been a peculiar CIA attempt to create a "Nixon machine" or a "Kissinger machine": according to the investigative journalist Seymour Hersh, "Sometime in 1969, a group of academics . . . came to a NSC staff meeting to discuss a new technique in parapsychology, constructing abstract models of the world leaders [which would] simulate and predict [their] behavior. . ." [ellipses in original]. See Hersh, *The Price of Power* (New York: Summit, 1983), quoted in Jim Hougan, *Secret Agenda* (New York: Random House, 1984), pp. 52–53. For the later applications of expert systems technology, see Edward Feigenbaum and Pamela McCorduck, *Fifth Generation: Artificial Intelligence and Japan's Computer Challenge to the World*, New York: Signet, 1984, p. 303.

20 [De Landa here is drawing on an omitted passage in which he discusses the emergence of the human sciences based on data collections and norms, drawing on Foucault's work in *Discipline and Punish*. – SV]

8

TRANSPLANT MEDICINE AND TRANSFORMATIVE NARRATIVE

Susan Squier

An English artist steals human bodies and body parts to make plaster casts of them, which he decorates with precious metals.[1] A German anatomist "plastinates" cadavers, immersing them in cooled liquid acetone, infusing them with a secret polymer preparation, arranging them in often stylized scenes, and drawing ten thousand people in one day to his exposition of "anatomy art."[2] A Canadian artist exhibits jewelry made from twelve-week-old fetuses and solicits townspeople for donations of body parts to incorporate into his art projects. A Dutch pathologist collects the organs and bodies of young children, keeping the head of an eleven-year-old child in a jar, and labeling one nine-week-old fetus "Inflated monster Humpty Dumpty."[3] LifeGems, a company based in Chicago, Illinois, sells alternative "personalized" memorials to grieving people: synthetic diamonds of between .25 carat and 1.3 carats made from the carbon remains of a loved one, whether human or animal. [. . .] These disturbing manipulations of the human body, the subject of media and judicial attention at and beyond the beginning of the twenty-first century, raise questions about the way we understand human organs and body parts.

[. . .]

Although they occur in the seemingly very divergent realms of art and medicine, they share a preoccupation with the manipulation of the human body that has been, since *Frankenstein*, a central trope in science fiction. As such, they draw our attention to the role science fiction has played, both bridging and boundary breaking: raising questions about the epistemological impact of the disciplinary divide as well as registering shifts (both semiotic and material) occurring across the entire field of nature-culture. [. . .]

My goal here is to engage in an exploration of the foundations of the contemporary field of transplant surgery in the biomedical and cultural imaginary. Anthropologist Nancy Scheper-Hughes has observed,

> Transplant surgery has reconceptualized social relations between self and other, between individual and society, and among the "three bodies" – the existential lived body-self, the social, representational body and the body political. Finally, it has redefined real/unreal, seen/unseen, life/death, body/corpse/cadaver, person/nonperson, and rumor/fiction/fact.[4]

The various ways that human beings in Anglo-America have imaginatively negotiated relations between the "three bodies" itemized by Scheper-Hughes tell us much about the role of culture and society in the normalization of transplant surgery. In particular, science fiction has functioned as a pivot point, the zone of the in-between, the uncategorizable, even the abject, rather than fitting securely in either of the seemingly secure zones of "art" and "science." As I will argue, because of its status as an in-between or liminal zone (freed from the epistemological constraints of disciplinary knowledge), science fiction is able to perform an imaginative transformation of the body that can predate and, in fact, enable its biomedical transformation.

[...]

Organ stripping

The cases of art using human organs (Kelly, von Hagens, and Gibson) all amplify questions also raised by a scandal that occurred in the world of medicine: questions of "professional interest, commerce, and . . . ownership."[5] In 1999, Dirk van Velzen, a Dutch pathologist who worked at the Alder Hey Children's Hospital, in Liverpool, England, was found to have "harvested" thousands of organs, without parental consent, from children who had been autopsied at his hospital. A shocked British public was fed vivid details of the scandal by the daily press. An "archive" of human and fetal organs had been discovered at the Alder Hey Hospital, including a heart collection containing more than two thousand hearts; a fetal collection containing around 1,500 fetuses, and an additional collection that by December 1999 had accumulated more than 445 partial or full fetal remains. This collection, kept by Dr. van Velzen as a private museum, included one jar holding the head of an eleven-year-old child and another containing a nine-week-old fetus.[6] While the hospital was found to have retained more than 1,500 fetuses ("miscarried, stillborn or aborted without consent"), the scandal extended beyond Alder Hey. A committee of inquiry led by the United Kingdom's chief medical officer, Professor Liam Donaldson, soon revealed that the practice of taking the organs from deceased children was a common one.[7] In 1999 investigators found that the Bristol Royal Infirmary had collected hearts and other organs for decades. The Donaldson committee found that "105,000 organs" were retained at medical schools and hospitals throughout Britain.

The response to the Alder Hey scandal occupied a prominent position in British newspapers and their Web pages in 1999 and 2000. After the hospital admitted that it had retained the organs of more than eight hundred children who had been autopsied between 1988 and 1995, the parents involved were contacted and given the opportunity to retrieve the organs and tissues that had – without their knowledge – been removed and retained.[8] For Paula O'Leary, whose eleven-month-old son Andrew had died of SIDS eighteen years before the scandal broke, the process of retrieving her child's remains was painfully complex. First, she was told that his heart had been retained by the hospital. Then after the family buried the heart in a small white casket, they were told that some tissues were still uninterred. When Mrs. O'Leary and her lawyer went to the hospital, "She was shown a box full of Andrew's organs preserved in glass – including his liver and gall bladder, spleen, adrenal glands, thymus gland, kidneys, skull, brain and spinal cord. His pancreas and thyroid gland had disappeared, she was told."[9] Not only the body of Andrew O'Leary but also the memory of him that his mother retained were grotesquely dismembered by the Alder Hey scandal.

[...]

What issues are raised by the Alder Hey scandal and its press coverage? It exposes the profit-driven, even grotesque, aspects of a supposedly benevolent institution (the children's hospital). More than that, this scandal of unlicensed organ retrieval and sale reveals that fluctuating, contested, and constructed – in short, liminal – position of human organs at the turn of the twenty-first century. It raises a number of crucial questions: the possibility and locus of ownership of organs, the professional use of organs, the (relative or absolute) merits of organ gift and organ sale, and the question of informed consent for all of the above. If we round back from the Alder Hey organ-stripping scandal to the instances of organ art with which I began, we are led to ask: To which kinds of commerce can human organs legitimately be subjected? Artistic, including the purchase of organs and body parts for artistic use, the sale of organ-derived art objects, and the mounting of organ-related gallery shows?[10] Scientific or technical, including the development of new models for anatomical illustration, new forms of cadaver preservation and memorializing, new tissue preservation techniques, and new strategies for diagnosis and testing? Curatorial, including the accumulation of organs and body parts for private or public museums? Then, what kind of ownership of organs and body parts is possible or acceptable? Ownership of the organ by the human being in whom it is found, the medical scientist or artist to whom it is transferred, or the sanctified ground in which it ultimately rests? Ownership of the fetus by the gestating woman, the woman who has decided to abort it, the abortionist, pathologist, or anatomist who has retrieved it, the artist who employs it as part of his intellectual property, or the state that controls the access to, and outcome of, the process of fetal development? Ownership of the cadaver's cremated remains by the grieving survivor(s), the funeral director who supplies the cremated remains to LifeGem, the LifeGem franchisee who subjects the remains to the patented carbon retrieval process from which the material of the colored synthetic diamond is formed, or the person who becomes the recipient (and owner) of the resulting LifeGem "memorial"?

[. . .] The value and significance of a human organ or body part is no longer self evident, but rather is *produced* through a complex set of institutional negotiations involving medicine, art, society, the legal system, human emotions and economic calculations. From the initial distinction between worthless organs and valuable ones, we have now moved to distinguishing between the various reasons for which organs are valued: as metonymic representation of a loved one, as the actual/memorial essence of the deceased, as information, as replacement parts, as exchangeable commodity.

[. . .]

Organ of information: the demise of the autopsy

[. . .]

Despite the discomfort with organ harvesting resulting in a decline in autopsies, the procedure of organ transplantation has become an accepted part of Western medicine. [. . .] Indeed, throughout the world, people with means increasingly take for granted the notion that transplantation procedures will continue to be refined, making it ever easier to replace diseased organs with healthy ones and thus prolong life.[11] Whether we think of this as the acceptance of a cadaver organ, excised quickly from the body of a brain-dead accident victim, as the "gift" of a living organ, surgically removed from a healthy sibling or close relative, or even as the theft of an organ from an inadequately informed and vulnerable organ "donor," this procedure is increasingly routine. Curiously, however, science fiction is still frequently invoked as a gauge for the progress of organ transplantation. [. . .]

The curious role of science fiction in the normalization of this biomedical practice is the point of departure for what follows. Instead of taking as self-evident the difference between science fiction and this particular area of medicine [. . .] I want to inquire into its status, to investigate the nature of the relationship between the fields of science fiction and organ transplantation.

Can it be that the transformative procedure of transplant medicine is *enabled* somehow by the transformative narrative that is science fiction? And if so, can we abstract from this instance a model for the relations between science fiction and biomedicine? Can we generate, beyond that, a model for the relations between the realms of the symbolic (art) and the material (biology and medicine)?

[. . .]

Contemporary sociologists, ethnographers, medical ethicists, and anthropologists have responded differently to the political, cultural, and ethical implications of the global trade in transplant organs, some (like Swazey and Fox[12]) choosing to leave the field out of unease at the personal and social costs of the technology, others (like the members of the Bellagio Task Force on Organ Transplantation) banding together to examine "the ethical, social, and medical effects of the commercialization of human organs" (Scheper-Hughes et al. 2000, 2). A number of rumors and urban legends circulating in popular culture may articulate local resistance to this sweeping global trend. While Benjamin Radford described as an urban legend the tale of a grandmother trying to sell her five-year-old grandson to a man who would kill him for his kidneys, later discussions of such reports have tended to emphasize the ways they condense a number of actual events: the existence of a global organ traffic, the vulnerable position of street urchins in a number of cultures, and the imbalance (racial, social, agential, economic) between organ donor and organ recipient (Scheper-Hughes et al. 2000; Radford 2001). Most recently Stephen Frears's film *Dirty Pretty Things* (2002) dramatizes the place of illegal organ procurement in a complex global economy in which work, nationality, race, sex, identity, and even health are alienable, subject to commodification, and available to anyone *for a price*.[13]

Yet on both the scholarly and the popular levels, the issues that are being raised about organ transplantation, and the questions generated by it, are not new. Long before concerns about organ transplantation appeared in the writings of ethicists, public policy writers, and anthropologists, they were aired in works of science fiction. Anthropologist Donald Joralemon has observed that

> organ transplantation seems to be protected by a massive dose of cultural denial, an ideological equivalent of the cyclosporine which prevents the individual body's rejection of a strange organ. This dose of denial is needed to overcome the social body's resistance to the alien idea of transplantation and the new kinds of bodies and publics that it requires.[14]

In particular, live-donor organ transplantation requires particular psychic effort, on a personal and social level, to endorse. [. . .]

I will argue in what follows that throughout the twentieth century science fiction writing was as crucial in the cultural realm as immunology was in the realm of medicine in bringing about public acceptance of organ transplant technology. Indeed, we might think of science fiction as functioning as a kind of ideological cyclosporine. Science fiction does not just purvey "a massive dose of cultural denial," inoculating us against the terrible desires fueling organ transplantation, through arguably it does that. Rather, in science fiction, we find articulated and negotiated issues integral to the normalization and institutionalization of transplant technology: the relation between body, body part, and identity; and the notion that even the death of the self is subject to social and scientific construction.

[. . .]

Concerned with the implications of organ transplantation for human identity, these [science fiction] stories all articulate specific resistances to the practice of organ transplantation framed in terms of class, ethnicity, race, and age, as well as different motives for undergoing the procedure. Read chronologically, they reveal changes in our understanding of human life. No longer is human existence defined by its unique temporal and spatial coordinates: one body, one life, in a specific space and time. Instead human life is increasingly defined by the agential, instrumental deployment of resources for bodily renewal, both its temporal and spatial context subject to extension or translocation. Like the organ art with which I began, these science fiction short stories too both enact and articulate this profound transformation in our understanding of human life.

[...]

"The Black Hand"

[...] Charles Gardner Bower's 1931 "The Black Hand"[15] [...] begins with the interview between a potential organ recipient and his doctor, and [...] the doctor acts as advocate for an operation that the recipient initially resists. But in this case, the potential recipient is the well-born and well-connected artist named Van Puyster, portraitist of the prince of Siam, who learns that he must have his infected hand amputated. Desperate at the thought of the amputation, unwilling to accept "one of your infernal leather and metal contraptions," he learns from his doctor that a hand transplant may be possible. "There is a condemned man in the state prison who has agreed to sell you his arm before he dies" (Bowers 1931, 910).

The themes of racial, social, and economic coercion and the medical motives for involvement in transplant surgery [are vivid]. As the doctor explains to his patient Mr. Van Puyster, "The negro wishes $10,000 to go to his estate and he wants an impressive burial. I shall charge no more than my regular fee for amputations, *as I greatly desire the honor of being the first to accomplish this operation*" (911). That the organ donor is a condemned criminal raises some potential complications for the surgery. Dr. Evans explains:

> I intend to make a direct transfer of his arm to your stump, as I do not think you would relish being bound by the side of a condemned criminal for ten minutes, much less ten days, furthermore, he is doomed to execution before that time would have expired....The negro being condemned to the lethal chamber shall, instead, die under the anesthesia.
>
> (911)

While grafts are customarily carried out by suturing the recipient and the donor tissues together until the graft "takes," clearly such a union is problematic for moral, physiological, and psychological reasons. Morally, the donor is socially untouchable. Physiologically, the donor will be dead (and a danger to the recipient) before the graft is completed. And psychologically, body part grafting is more comfortable to the potential recipient, in this work of fiction as it also is in fact. Realism and aesthetic appeal (a graft) frequently win out over pragmatic ease and function (a prosthesis). The story also anticipates the debate around the practice of using convicted criminals as organ donors, either as cadaver donors (as was the case in a phase of Western transplantation) or as unwilling living donors, as has been reported at the turn of the twenty-first century by anthropologists working in India and China (Scheper-Hughes et al. 2000; L. Cohen 1999). Finally, the story invokes the troubling relationship between death (induced or confirmed) and the process of organ transplantation. The organ donor is a convicted criminal sentenced to death for his crime, just as – with the new acceptance of brain death as the requirement for organ harvesting – the "beating-heart" organ donor (or "neo-mort") would die as a result of the act of organ harvesting.[16]

[. . .] Van Puyster demonstrates a reluctance to undergo the transplant operation, since as an artist he is especially sensitive to the visual impact of such a transformation:

> The shock to his aesthetic mind was almost overpowering. The thought of a black hand was revolting, but the thought of no hand at all was like death itself. Would the hand be large and awkward, or would it be slender and sensitive? Was it coal black, or only a light mulatto? Could he ever return to his society with such a stigma?
>
> (911)

Despite his reluctance, Van Puyster accepts the graft of "the arm that has murdered an un-armed man," an arm that (to make matters worse) "is black" (910). The minutely described operation ends with the application of a cast, and the separation of the two individuals: one to recover in the surgical ward of the hospital, the other to meet his fate. "The negro, still under anesthesia, was turned over to the prison officials" (923). As the narrative concludes, we learn that the operation has been a success: "Two weeks later and the arm was healing rapidly. Two years later and complete sensation had returned. Five years later and the black hand was painting masterpieces, but Van Puyster always wore gloves" (923).

If the story ended here, we would comment on the author's accurate prediction that donor organs would, more often than not, come from racial "Others," while the recipients would most frequently be white. We would remark that Van Puyster's habitual gloves echo that power imbalance through the symbolic assertion that the painting of masterpieces and the possession of a "black hand" are incompatible. We might also note the metonymy that (ironically) makes that same black hand the agent of genius, as distinct from Van Puyster who wields it.

But as the story goes on, our attention shifts from the donor to the recipient, and we move into the genre of psychiatric case history to read the case of Van Puyster the artist. "H.V.P., a native born American of Dutch and English ancestry, age 46, unmarried, white male," has been admitted to the "Psychopathic Hospital" after the judge committed him, "as the jury had found him insane when on trial for a series of homicides of Negroes" (923). As the case history stipu-lates, H.V.P. was the recipient of "the world's first arm-grafting operation . . . [and] the arm was taken from a condemned negro criminal" (923).

After the surgery, Van Puyster undergoes a transformation in character and conduct: though he is still painting marvelous pictures, they have begun to verge on the fantastic, and then the grotesque. He avoids encountering "negroes" at any time, discharges his Negro valet, and is manifestly uncomfortable even at the mention of "a negro." Socially increasingly reclusive, his behavior begins to mimic that of the ghastly Dr. Hyde:

> It was during this period that he started going out during the night and on several occasions he was known to have stayed away from home for as many as three days at a time and to have returned at the end of that period with his clothes mud-splattered and torn and in an altogether disreputable state. His man also noticed that these events corresponded with a series of brutal murders.
>
> (923)

The case report charts Van Puyster's arrest and incarceration, during which he is assailed by hallucinations that he is "being pursued by a negro, who was attempting to cut off his arm . . . He grew more morose and solitary and under no conditions would he admit an attendant to remove his glove" (923 [ellipses in original]). Just as physicians have diagnosed paranoia and decided that "his right arm again be amputated, this time above the region of the graft," Van

Puyster is "found dead in his cell, having bled to death from a self-inflicted wound which had severed his *right* radial artery" (923). In its understated rationality, the case summary that concludes Bower's story manages still to suggest its uncanny alternative. The judgment is suicide ("A patient with a negative psychiatric history became criminally insane following a graft of a negro's arm"), but the implication lingers that the deed was really murder, as the Negro criminal has come at last to reclaim his donated hand.[17]

In form and outcome, these early-twentieth-century narratives anticipate two important shifts in the social climate surrounding organ transplants. First the overt attention to racial differences in early-twentieth-century transplant narratives has been succeeded, in the early twenty-first century, by a covert and *enabling* racial imbalance between organ recipients (frequently, though not always, white and "first world") and organ donors (frequently, though not always, black or brown and "third world"). Second, most likely in response to that growing local and global inequity, there has been a shift in the psychiatric perspective on organ transplantation cases. Whereas the early twentieth-century stories explore the psychiatric and social effects of being the organ *recipient*, by the early twenty-first century, it would become standard medical procedure to assess the psychiatric and social fitness for, and effects of, being a live organ *donor*.

[. . .]

From the military draft to the organ draft

Robert Silverberg's "Caught in the Organ Draft" (1983) appeared during the height of the Vietnam War, and it captures Scheper-Hughes's point that the flow of organs follows the modern routes of capital, from the dispossessed to the affluent, but with a twist.[18] Here we follow the flow of *physical capital* from the vigorous and disenfranchised young to the frail but institutionally dominant old. An organ draft law, "put through by an administration of old men," has given rise to a system providing a never-ending supply of healthy organs for the elderly pillars of society. Through this new organ draft system, young men and women register on turning nineteen, and those who are high in "organ reservoir potential" receive an "organ draft" notice calling them to report to Transplant House for their ritual physical exam, after which the draftee goes "on call" and within an average of two months they are "carving [him] up" (Silverberg 1983, 143). The result is a society in which the young feel victim to the old, much as they did during World War I, but the nature of their victimization is medical rather than military. As the protagonist thinks when he eyes a pair of "splendid seniors" as the story opens:

> We can guess at their medical histories. She's had at least three hearts, he's working on his fourth set of lungs, they apply for new kidneys every five years, their brittle bones are reinforced with hundreds of skeletal snips from the arms and legs of hapless younger folk: their dimming sensory apparatus is aided by countless nerve grafts obtained the same way; their ancient arteries are freshly sheathed with sleek Teflon. Ambulatory assemblages of second-hand human parts, spiced here and there with synthetic or mechanical organ substitutes, that's all they are. And what am I, then, or you? . . . In their eyes I'm nothing but a ready stockpile of healthy organs, waiting to serve their needs.
>
> (142) [ellipses in original]

The story follows a young man from his draft notice through his organ "donation," tracing his evolution from draft resistance to cooperation and finally to collaboration with the system of organ draft once he himself stands to gain from its fund of endlessly procurable organs. The system of organ transplantation that Silverberg's fiction institutionalizes embodies the two central elements of medical practice in late modernity: the adaptation of a statistical rather than individual, approach to human life, and the tendency of medical technology to create the need it satisfies. As the protagonist explains, "Nobody escapes. They always clip you, once you qualify. The need for young organs inexorably expands to match the pool of available organpower" (144).

As he works through his own emotional and strategic responses to the organ draft notice, the protagonist raises a variety of prominent issues in contemporary organ transplantation debate: whether human beings have the right to bodily integrity; whether it is ethical to practice live-organ transplantation; whether body enhancement is an appropriate medical practice; whether body parts (including tissues and DNA samples) can be possessed; whether there *is* really a "shortage of transplantable organs," or whether that reflects broader power shifts in a society that privilege longevity of the powerful over quality of life of the relatively powerless; whether there are limits to the medical fight against death. The protagonist traces the progress in organ transplantation in two registers: medically, where it takes the form of an increasing victory over the immune system's tendency to reject the transplanted organ, and socially where it takes the form of an increasingly institutionalized system of interlinked greater and lesser coercions that shape the populace toward more and more widespread involvement with the donation system. While "eventually everybody will have a 6-A Preferred Recipient status by virtue of having donated," the protagonist still struggles against another kind of resistance: psychic rather than physical: "Drugs, radiation treatment, metabolic shock – one way and another, the organ rejection problem was long ago conquered. I can't conquer my draft rejection problem. Aged and rapacious legislators, I reject you and your legislation" (154). Yet after a night spent weighing the options, the protagonist makes his decision: "When the time comes, I'll surrender peacefully. I report to Transplant House for conscriptive donative surgery in three hours" (155). His own likely future need for transplant organs has changed his mind. When the story concludes, the transplant operation has been completed.

> I've given up unto the powers that be my humble pound of flesh. When I leave the hospital. . . . I'll carry a card testifying to my new 6-A status. Top priority for the rest of my life. Why I might live for a thousand years.
>
> (156)

Written more than thirty years ago, Silverberg's story clearly references the social security system in its carefully calibrated relationship between present financial contribution and future receipt. But it does so, strikingly, by anticipating the emergence of a bioeconomy: a market (and a futures market) in human body parts and products. The story articulates all the contemporary critiques of the organ transplantation system, including the problematic developments of organ commodification, the live-donor system, and the inequitable distribution of obligations and gifts. In the time since the story's publication, we have continued to build the institutional system of organ transplantation that Silverberg warned us against, so that by now his science fiction short story seems more parable of the present than prediction of the future.

[. . .]

September 11 and after

Contemporary medicine is turning to transplantation not just of organs and body parts but of tissues as well, even embryonic tissues.[19] In a recent bulletin in *Reuters Medical News for the Web*,

Dr. Curt R. Freed told a remarkable story to demonstrate the advantages of such transplantation for producing relief from the tremors, rigidity, and immobility resulting from Parkinsonism:

> The advantage of transplant therapy is the consistent effect achieved for the symptoms of Parkinson's disease, Dr. Freed said. One of the study patients, who had discontinued L-dopa therapy after receiving this transplant, was working on the 34th floor of one of the World Trade Center towers during the September 11th attack. Dr. Freed said the patient was able to walk down 33 flights of stairs and about 3 additional miles to reach public transportation to get home.[20]

These embryonic cell transplants recall the debate about the ethics of using discarded embryos (whether the product of miscarriages, abortions, or excess research embryos) as material for another set of transplantation intended to prolong life and to enhance its quality. As in Silverberg's story, in Freed's story too we must address the issue of using the young (in this case the *embryonic*) to improve life expectancy and life quality for the very old (in this case, forty patients between thirty-four and seventy-five years old). Moreover, in his reference to the attacks of 11 September 2001, Dr. Freed's report returns us to questions about science fiction, the human body, and the definition of rubbish.

In an article entitled "Hauling the Debris, and Darker Burdens" published in the *New York times* six days after the September 11 attacks on the World Trade Center, journalist Charlie LeDuff reported that a fine line "separates rescue from recovery."[21] For the rescue workers, toiling in the unimaginable chaos of what came to be known as "ground zero," the distinction between working to save living people or to recover bodies or body parts was subject to delicate shifts and fluctuations.

> "There is no clear demarcation where we are in rescue and suddenly we're into recovery," an official from the Federal Emergency Management Agency said. "The elements of the two can coexist side by side, but there will come a point when rescue operations will be over."

In this attack, so minutely anticipated by science fiction and film that its factual form seemed at first redundant, none of the people trapped in the rubble of the collapsed towers had the option of life extension through organ transplantation. Indeed, as one rescue worker observed, the *haul* of human body parts and organs was pitifully small. Organs were no longer valued as life extenders but now welcomed only as the definitive mark of a life having ended. Moreover, journalists commented on how the accumulated posters bearing the faces of the deceased formed a new form of art installation. Here again, the contrast must be remarked: this new memorial art is as distant as can be imagined from von Hagens's Koerperwelten or Anthony-Noel Kelly's gilded corpses.[22] Grounded not in the presence of aestheticized organs but in their absence, it celebrates a human body that is marked by a precious ephemerality and vulnerability.

The attack on the World Trade Center was also an assault on the carefully crafted illusion of risk management that is integral to our dominant contemporary life strategy, as columnist Maureen Dowd observed, echoing social theorists Zygmunt Bauman and Ulrich Beck.[23]

> It was always a delusional vanity, this fixation boomers had about controlling their environment. They thought they could make life safe and healthy and fend off death and aging. . . . They would overcome flab with diet and exercise, wrinkles with collagen and Botox . . . decay with human growth hormone, disease with stem cell research and

bio-engineering. . . . After all these finicky years of fighting everyday germs and inevitable mortality with fancy products, Americans are now confronted with the specter of . . . hazardous-waste trucks spreading really terrifying, deadly toxins like plague, smallpox, blister agents, nerve gas and botulism.[24]

Writing of the uncanny resemblance of the terror attacks to blockbuster disaster movies, *New Yorker* columnist Anthony Lane speculated, "This ruination was the opposite of invention; of conjured worlds; whether it will also signal, in part, a death of invention is more difficult to call."[25]

We might raise the same question about both transplant medicine and the transformative function of science fiction narratives: will we see a death of invention in both areas, now that they have been surpassed by the events of 11 September 2001? Silverberg's character supports the organ draft because it promises to extend his life: "Why I might live for a thousand years!" (Silverberg 1983, 156). But investment in immunosuppressant medicine and organ transplantation technology requires funds that may now have been reallocated away from replacement and regeneration medicine to another sort of life extension project. And if we play the extrapolative game so central to science fiction, what we are likely to predict is not an organ draft but rather a military draft, as part of the remilitarization of ordinary life in the battle against terrorism.

If we recall the proposition that science fiction functions as *rubbish* – a culturally fertile zone of transformation and possibility – recent commentary on science fiction movies suggests that a shift may be occurring in our cultural valuation of this genre. Science fiction, for so long the fertile ground for imaginative transformation of life as we know it, now seems only a grim commentary on life as we must live it; no longer fantasy, but documentary. Ironically, now that science fiction's representations are moving from the ephemeral and fantastic to the durable and mimetic, that which was once rubbish (stigmatized for it by some, valued for it by others) has now attained cultural resonance. [. . .] The imaginative emancipation offered by science fiction traditionally lay in its capacity to create magical new worlds. In contrast, science fiction now shocks us by its resemblance to fact. Unable any longer to inoculate us against our fears, science fiction sutures us to a destructive present that is all-too-real.

Notes

1 Jane Wildgoose, "Who Really Owns Our Bodies?" *Guardian Unlimited*, 30 January 2001.
2 "The Von Hagens Interview," *Science Interviews*, www.scienceinterviews.com (accessed 16 November 2001).
3 Celia Hall, "Organs Scandal: Children's Heads Were Found in Hospital Archive," *Daily Telegraph*, 31 January 2001.
4 Scheper-Hughes et al. 2000.
5 The phrase was used by Jane Wildgoose.
6 Celia Hall, "Organs Scandal: Children's Heads Were Found in Hospital Archive," *Daily Telegraph*, 31 January 2001. Note the intrusion of juvenile literature, as well as fantasy, into the labeling, which was felt to be particularly reprehensible. Textualization of the deceased also operates in the remediation suggested by the Donaldson report: "Where tissues or organs have been donated for teaching purposes, families will be invited to prepare a 'life book' on the person who has died. This would take the form of a scrap book of the child's life 'so students would be reminded that [the organ was] part of a real child and so afforded appropriate respect.'" "Science and Medicine: 105,000 Body Parts Retained in the U.K., Census Says," *Lancet* 357, no. 9253, 3 February 2001.
7 "Science and Medicine," *Lancet*, 3 February 2001.
8 "British Organ Scandal Physicians Face Investigation," *Reuters Medical News*, 15 March 2001.
9 Barwick 2001b; see also 2001a.

10 As Walker (1999) observes, "One issue raised by the [Anthony-Noel] Kelly case was the legitimacy of casting as an artistic technique. Casting is an ancient reproductive method and a historic method of manufacturing editions of sculptures. It is also an ancient method of producing three-dimensional records of the appearances of the dead. Yet in the nineteenth century it was considered suspect as a means of achieving first-order art.... It is also worth remembering that casts of body parts are made by medical practitioners and preserved in medical museums" (224 [ellipses in original]).

11 That this is not the case in Japan has been studied by Margaret Lock (2002), Trevor Corson (2000), and Emily Ohnuki-Tierney (1994).

12 [Renee C. Fox and Judith P. Swazey, *Space Parts: Organ Replacement in American Society* (Cambridge: Oxford University Press, 1992).]

13 As David Edelstein observes, "The screenwriter, Steven Knight, is an English TV veteran who helped to create the original *Who Wants to Be a Millionaire?*, and the grasping/yearning quality of that infamous title is in every scene: the film is *What Wants to Be a Citizen – and What Part of Your Anatomy Will You Give Up?*" *Slate*, 18 July 2003.

14 Scheper-Hughes et al. 2000.

15 [Charles Gardener Bowers, "The Black Hand," *Amazing Stories* 5.10 (January 1931).]

16 "They are hardly 'corpses' in the traditional sense. Although they are 'dead patients' they do not resemble our other dead patients. The expression 'brain dead' is accurate but seems to avoid the crucial issues. Most would agree that these donors are no longer 'persons.' When the patient is admitted to the operating room, the recorded diagnosis is 'beating-heart cadaver' – a term that is offensive to many people. Gaylin coined the term 'neomort' ten years ago, but it has not become popular. *Perhaps we will only be able to give these artificially maintained organ donors an appropriate name when we ourselves have made the necessary emotional and cultural adjustments*" (Youngner et al. 1985, cited in Swazey and Fox 1992, 62–63; italics mine).

17 An alternative interpretation for this story would emphasize the hand's threatening liminality, understanding Van Puyster's death as a voluntary murder of the Negro in himself, or to be more precise of his own racial indeterminacy.

18 Silverberg [1972] 1983.

19 As this book was going to press, Catherine Waldby and Robert Mitchell shared with me the prospectus for their book in progress, "Tissue Economies: Gifts, Commodities, and Bio-value in Late Stage Capitalism." I want to thank them for their generosity, and I regret that it was too late to incorporate a response to it.

20 The article reported that "a favorable outcome of human embryonic dopamine cell transplantation in patients with Parkinson's disease" can be predicted by a good response preoperatively to therapy with L-dopa, the drug used to restore fluid movement to Parkinson's sufferers by replacing dopamine in the brain. Dr. Curt R. Freed, of the University of Colorado at Denver, reported on research showing that patients under sixty years of age who responded favorably to L-dopa therapy also responded well to the transplantation of embryonic mesenphalic tissue. For the transplantation of embryonic tissue, not even cyclosporine or other immunosuppressant drugs were needed, Freed reported: the patients received symptom relief even without immunosuppression therapy, with 85 percent of the transplant patients surviving. "Response to Dopamine Cell Transplantation predicted by L-Dopa Response," *Reuters Medical News for the Professional*, 18 November 2001.

21 Charlie LeDuff, "Hauling the Debris, and Darker Burdens," *New York Times*, 17 September 2001, A1, A12.

22 [These are two art projects that use human body tissues that Squier discusses in the full version of the essay. – SV]

23 Beck 1992.

24 Maureen Dowd, "From Botox to Botulism," *New York Times*, 26 September 2001. [ellipses in original]

25 Lane 2001, 80.

Works Cited

Barwick, Sandra. 2001a. "I Will Never Get over It, Says Distraught Mother." *Daily Telegraph*, 31 January.
———. 2001b. "Organs Scandal: They Laid 36 Parts of My Baby on a Table, Put Them into a Bag, and Ran." *Daily Telegraph*, 31 January.
Bauman, Zygmunt. 1992. *Mortality, Immortality, and Other Life Strategies*. Stanford: Stanford University Press.
Beck, Ulrich. [1986] 1992. *Risk Society: Towards a New Modernity*. London: Sage.

Bowers, Charles Gardner. 1931. "The Black Hand." *Amazing Stories* 5, no. 10 (January): 909–11.

Cohen, Lawrence. 1999. "Where It Hurts: Indian Material for an Ethics of Organ Transplantation." *Daedalus* 128, no. 4 (Fall): 135–65.

Corson, Trevor. 2000. "The Telltale Heart: Death and Democracy in Japan." *Transition* 9. No. 4: 78–96.

Lane, Anthony. 2001. "This Is Not a Movie: Same Scenes, Different Story." *New Yorker*, 24 September, 79–80.

Lock, Margaret. 2002. *Twice Dead: Organ Transplants and the Reinvention of Death.* Berkeley: University of California Press.

Ohnuki-Tierney, Emily, et al. 1994. "Brain Death and Organ Transplantation: Cultural Bases of Medical Technology." *Current Anthropology* 35: 233–54.

Radford, Benjamin. 2001. "Urban Legend Makes International News." *Sceptical Inquirer* (Buffalo), May–June. 7–8.

Scheper-Hughes, Nancy et al. 2000. "The Global Traffic in Human Organs." *Current Anthropology* 41 (2): 191–224.

"Science and Medicine: 105,000 Body Parts Retained in the U.K., Census Says." 2001. *Lancet*, 3 February.

Silverberg, Robert. [1972] 1983. "Caught in the Organ Draft." In *Caught in the Organ Draft: Biology in Science Fiction*, ed. Isaac Asimov, Martin H. Greenberg, and Charles G. Waugh. New York: Farrar, Straus and Giroux.

Swazey, Renee, and Judith P. Fox. 1992. *Spare Parts: Organ Replacement in American Society.* New York: Oxford University Press.

Walker, John Allan. 1999. *Art and Outrage.* Sterling, Va.: Pluto Press.

Youngner, S.J., M. Allen, E.T. Barlett et al. 1985. "Psychosocial and Ethical Implications of Organ Retrieval." *New England Journal of Medicine*, 1 August, 321–24.

9

BIOINFORMATIC BODIES AND THE PROBLEM OF "LIFE ITSELF"

Eugene Thacker

The two faces of DNA

In popular culture, it is becoming increasingly difficult to separate DNA from its computer-generated representation. Whereas earlier science fiction films such as *Bride of Frankenstein* could reference only in language the existence of the molecular level, in the late twentieth and early twenty-first centuries DNA can be represented in all its informatic and three-dimensional splendor. Whether the DNA in question be that of human-insect hybrids (*The Fly*; *Spider-Man*), mutants (*The Hulk*, the *X-Men* films), alien invaders (*The Thing*, *Virus*), or plain old genetic surveillance (*Gattaca*), wherever one finds biology in popular culture, one also finds that which generates biology: computer graphics and imaging technologies. But beyond this, popular culture also posits a further proposition: not only do computers represent DNA, but DNA is in some strange way translatable with information itself: consider the "rage virus" of *28 Days Later*, the biotechnological hybrid of virus and media violence, or the viral logic of the media virus in *Ringu*.

But in a sense, none of this is new and was already presaged in the life sciences. After all, in the 1940s didn't physicist Erwin Schrödinger already hypothesize that the genetic material in all living beings was a "hereditary code-script"?[1] And didn't Watson and Crick's 1953 papers on the structure of DNA simply affirm what earlier biologists had guessed, that DNA is a code?[2] When François Jacob and Jacques Monod published their research on genetic regulatory mechanisms, wasn't their formulation of the "cybernetic enzymatics" a further postulation that DNA is a computer?[3] And when Heinrich Matthaei and Marshall Nirenberg announced that they had "cracked the genetic code" in 1962, didn't this once and for all establish the fact of DNA as a code and biology as information?[4] This history has been well documented by historians of science such as Lily Kay and Hans-Jörg Rheinberger, especially in the exchanges between molecular biology, on the one hand, and cybernetics and information theory, on the other.[5] In addition, cyberneticians, information theorists, and computer scientists were similarly paying attention to DNA as well. Claude Shannon's information theory grew out of his dissertation dealing with the algorithmic and combinatoric properties of a genetic code, and computer scientist John von Neumann, in speaking of the relationship between the brain and the computer, noted how DNA forms, in the biological organism, as a kind of memory system.[6]

Thus, historically speaking, there is plenty of precedent within the hard sciences for this intersection between genetics and informatics, biology and technology. Yet, in a way, the motto "biology is information" is not spoken by anyone, but rather demonstrated by the surreal artifacts that populate the biotech lab: online genomic databases, DNA chips, combinatorial chemistry, three-dimensional molecular modeling, gene-targeting software, and "wet-dry cycles" in drug development. In these and other hybrid artifacts, we see not only the integration of the biological and the technological, but also the integration of a material and an immaterial understanding of biological life. The field of bioinformatics is a good example in this regard, for it directly brings together bioscience and computer science, genetic and computer "codes." Simply defined as the application of computer and networking technologies to the research problems of molecular biology, bioinformatics has quickly grown into a discipline of its own and into a significant industry as well. High-profile projects such as the sequencing of the human genome have been largely bioinformatics-driven projects, and bioinformatics research on the Internet is increasingly becoming an indispensable tool for molecular biology labs.

In the current context of bioinformatics, we have a set of questions to consider. How does bioinformatics reconfigure the relationship between biology (as natural) and technology (as artificial)? In the negotiation between biology and technology, how does bioinformatics balance the inherent tension between the material and immaterial? Contemporary discourses surrounding cyberspace, virtual bodies, and cyborgs endlessly play out the informatization of the biological, material body. These discourses not only assume a pretechnological body, but also foster a vision of the body that is highly textualized and semiotic ("material-semiotic nodes" and so forth). Biotechnology, however, defined in part by its connections to biology, is preoccupied with the materiality of the biological body and not with the immaterial domain of virtual bodies and avatars. And yet the body's materiality is also always contextualized by a discourse of materiality.[7] So what is happening in a field such as bioinformatics? Is bioinformatics simply the "computerization" of biology? No doubt bioinformatics and biotechnology generally take us far beyond the well-worn tropes of the cyborg and its affiliates. Any technique or technology used in biotech research demonstrates this: PCR,[8] gene therapy, microarrays, even tissue engineering. In the myriad of techniques and technologies that can be observed in the biotechnology lab, a common ontological and political-economic viewpoint stretches across them all. A "natural" biological process (such as DNA base-pair complementarity) is repurposed and serves as the "technology" for each process, but in a different context (such as the precise heating and cooling cycles of PCR). This technology is purely biological – a technology *because* it is purely biological.

This point assumes that bioinformatics – and by extension biotechnology – must work in either the material domain of biology or the immaterial domain of informatics. Bioinformatics refuses this split in its practices and products, however. For instance, the online genome database was at one time the living cells of human volunteers and subsequently cDNA libraries in the lab. The same can be said for the U.S. PTO database[9] as well. Similarly, all the software and databases count for nothing if they do not in some minimal way reconnect and "touch" the biology of living cells and living patients via therapies, tests, or drugs. Thus, we can rephrase our question another way: How does bioinformatics – as an increasingly foundational approach in biotechnology research – strategically bring together the informatic and the biological in such a way that it can accommodate both the material and the immaterial, both medical benefit and economic value?

[. . .]

Hacking the genome

[. . .]

Several factors contributed to the emergence of a distinct disciple of "bioinformatics" as the HGP[10] progressed during the 1990s. Within the lab itself, several improvements were made in genetic sequencing and replication, such as PCR, more efficient gel electrophoresis tools, and, finally, fully automated gene sequencing computers.[11] In addition, although the HGP remained a U.S.-based project, it increasingly expanded itself, forming more substantial partnerships with the United Kingdom's Wellcome Trust and establishing outposts in Germany, Japan, China, and France. These two factors combined to produce an unprecedented rise in the genomic data being produced – a far cry from a small group of labs manually funneling data into a single database. The deluge of information has in recent years necessitated an efficient, accurate, and sophisticated means of managing all of it. The new field of bioinformatics has thus come to play an indispensable role in genetics and biotechnology research.

[. . .]

With all this investment and risk, how are profits made? One primary area is in patents, especially in the United States but also in the European Union. A recent study by GeneWatch UK, a policy research and watchdog group, listed the top-ten genetic patent holders from both the public and private sectors. What is noteworthy is that this study was carried out by accessing the GENSEQ database, a commercial database that contains all genetic sequences patented worldwide. The report's top-ten list includes Genset (applications on more than 36,000 gene sequences), Genzyme (patent claims on more that 8,500 sequences), and the U.S. NIH (patent claims on just less than 3,000 sequences).[12]

[. . .]

In summary, the boost given to the pharmaceutical industry through bioinformatics has been in three primary areas: the identification of "drug targets" (molecular compounds upon which to act); "lead discovery," or the creation of novel drug compounds; and the production of genomics-based tests for already-existing drugs. The latter is broadly called *pharmacogenomics*, which, according to one definition, is "the study of the entire spectrum of genes that determine drug response, including the assessment of the diversity of the human genomic sequence and its clinical consequences."[13] Along the way, computer and informatics-based technologies play a central role, from the mining of genome databases to the study of metabolic pathways in the cell, to the computational study of common drug candidate classes, such as proteases, ion channels, and G-protein coupled receptors (GPCRs, a type of membrane protein). Computer technologies are promising to play a key role in drug development, but the process is obviously still very much tied to the material and biological conditions of the clinical trial phases. Thus, although a novel drug candidate may be driven by bioinformatics and pharmacogenomics technologies, at some point the in silico world of drug discovery must directly and materially interface with the in vivo world of the human body (mediated by the in vitro experiments in the discovery and preclinical phases). This set of interactions is of interest here in both ontological and political-economic terms. The manifold passages from a file in a genome database to a patent file, to the pharmacogenomics study of a lead series, to a genetics-based test for patient ADRs[14] are the primary interests of this chapter.

Thus, bioinformatics is not simply a subset of computer science, nor is it simply the newest tool for molecular biology research. It is a set of novel informatically driven practices and knowledge that have taken shape alongside bioinformatics as a discipline, a business, and an industry. Two main things are interesting about bioinformatics. First, bioinformatics is as much an ontological endeavor as it is a biological one. This endeavor goes beyond the rhetorical exchanges of postwar molecular biology (the metaphor of the genetic "code" and so on), without ever absolutely denying the metaphorical role that informatics plays in molecular genetics. In a sense, bioinformatics takes all the terminology, concepts, and metaphors of informatics at face value; it moves with great ease between the metaphor of DNA as information and the construction of online genome databases. As we shall see, assumptions concerning the division between the material and immaterial, or the biological and the informatic, are redefined and reshaped in various ways along the way. Bioinformatics is, first and foremost, an ontological practice, demonstrating the ways in which DNA is information and the ways in which information materializes, and, above all, participating in the reconfiguration of dominant ways of understanding the relation between the living and nonliving, the biological and the technological.

But – and this is the second interesting point – bioinformatics is not just in the business of philosophy; as an emerging field, it has outlined for itself a set of specific aims and areas of application (e.g., pattern matching in sequence alignment, database management in genomics, three-dimensional graphics in molecular modeling). Bioinformatics does not exist in a vacuum, in which the niceties of the formal relationships between DNA and information are endlessly examined. In many cases, the same genetic code in a genomic database such as GenBank is also found in the U.S. PTO database in a patent file for a derived gene or gene product. Indeed, a number of commercially available databases are dedicated to the correlation of genetic and patent data for researchers, academic departments, and biotech companies. A single gene sequence can potentially generate a great deal of economic value, from the genomics-based development of drugs to the forging of temporary alliances between biotech start-ups and large pharmaceutical corporations, to the creation and marketing of genetic tests, to patent licenses for the development of other laboratory techniques and technologies. Bioinformatics is not just an informatic view of biology; it is also at the same time a biological view of economic value. In other words, the ontological question "What is life?" is always folded into a set of political-economic questions, such as, "Can biology be turned into a technology?" or "Can life be property?"

This twofold character of bioinformatics – at once ontological and political – can be called *the politics of "life itself."*[15]

[...]

But the phrase "life itself" also denotes the slipperiness of any claim to have discovered an essence – mechanical or vitalist – of biological life. As the philosopher and historian of science Georges Canguilhem notes, this emphasis on "life itself" drives much biological thinking in the West, from Aristotle's animating "Soul" to Darwin's selection mechanisms, to the emergence of molecular biology during the postwar era. The elusive nature of "life itself" seems to be both the basis of biology and the point that always stands outside of biology.

[...]

Canguilhem and "life itself"

From the most general perspective, thinking about biological life is as old as thinking about thinking. Canguilhem notes that "the theory of the concept and the theory of life have the same age and the same author."[16] He is speaking of Aristotle, "the logician of the concept and the systematic philosopher of living things."[17] The links between philosophy and life, ontology and biology, are, at first vague and abstract. In any definition of biological life, be it mechanist or vitalistic, there is always something that escapes, something that exists beyond the ability of conceptualization. And yet nothing is more self-evident and less in need of proof than the fact of life. What could be more impractical – and, more important, impossible – than the age-old, unanswerable question, "What is life?" For Canguilhem, the seemingly vague question concerning "life" is both ancient and contemporary. Consider, as an example, the titles of books published by molecular biologists during the postwar era, books about the then-emerging field of molecular genetics and aimed at non-specialist, popular audiences: Francis Crick's *Life Itself*, François Jacob's *The Logic of Life*, J.B.S. Haldane's *What is Life?*, Andre Lowff's *The Biological Order*, Henry Quastler's *The Emergence of Biological Organization*, and George Beadle and Muriel Beadle's *The Language of Life*. Such books owe a great deal to Erwin Schrödinger's lectures entitled "What is Life?" in which the existence of a "hereditary code script" was hypothesized in decidedly informatic terms. More recently, diverse books such as Robert Sinsheimer's *What is Life?*, Lynn Margulis and Dorian Sagan's *What Is Life?*, and bioinformatician Pierre Baldi's *The Shattered Self* continue to pose the question first elaborated in a specifically genetic manner by molecular biologists of the postwar era.[18]

[...]

In 1966, Canguilhem gave two lectures in Brussels, both entitled "The Concept and Life."[19]

[...]

The title of Canguilhem's lectures is instructive. As he notes at the outset, to have a concept of life is, in a sense, to be life itself:

> For Aristotle, soul was not only the nature but also the form of the living thing. Soul was at once life's reality (*ousia*) and definition (*logos*). Thus, the concept of the living thing was, in the end, the living thing itself.[20]

In tracing the interest in the relation between concepts and life back to Aristotle, Canguilhem is also suggesting that, despite the reliance on quantitative analysis and the techniques borrowed from information theory, the then-emerging field of genetics still displayed an Aristotelian interest in life-giving "form" or "Soul." As Canguilhem notes,

> when we say that biological heredity is the communication of a certain kind of information, we hark back in a way to the Aristotelian philosophy with which we began.... If we are to understand life, its message must be decoded before it can be read.[21]

Yet, at the same time, genetics was not simply Aristotelian in the same way that seventeenth-century natural history or eighteenth-century vitalism were; its unique appropriation of information theory and cybernetics made it at once the most modern of biological sciences and yet a science in which Aristotle's life-giving "form" reappears as genetic sequence or molecular structure. "Messages, information, programs, code, instructions, decoding: these are the new concepts of the life sciences."[22]

[...]

The relationship between Aristotelian "Soul" and genetic "information" is part of a broader, more complex historical transformation that Canguilhem outlines in a 1973 encyclopedia article simply entitled "Vie" (Life).[23] Canguilhem identifies four, largely overlapping threads in the history of biological thinking on "life itself." Each thread is dominated by a principle understood to be nontranscendent and yet distinct from the particular materiality of the organism: *animation* (which is the most elaborated in Aristotle), *mechanism* (articulated in philosophy and biology by Descartes and adumbrated by Harvey and Malpighi), *organization* (again stemming from Aristotle, but taking fuller shape in Comte, cell theory, and Bernardian physiology), and finally, *information* (resulting from the intersections between cybernetics/information theory and molecular biology).[24]

For Canguilhem, the point in outlining these threads is precisely to emphasize the nonlinear, overlapping, discontinuous character of biological thinking. In the case of molecular genetics, the influence of cybernetic "feedback" and the concepts of information theory are decisive in reformulating the question concerning "life itself." Canguilhem points specifically to information theory in this regard:

> Claude Shannon's work on communications and information theory and its relation to thermodynamics (1948) appeared to offer a partial answer to an age-old question about life. . . . Is organization order amidst disorder? Is it the maintenance of a quantity of information proportional to the complexity of the structure?[25]

Whereas the second law of thermodynamics describes how an object will tend toward a more disordered state (a state of greater entropy), the example of living organisms seems to provide a counterexample, where growth, development, regeneration, and adaptation resist the tendency toward entropy.

Keeping in mind the three Aristotelian elements that Canguilhem points to – form, organization, animation – we can further elaborate on how genetics and bioinformatics transform the question of "life itself." Modern genetics, in the significance given to the notion of "genetic information" or a "genetic code," implicitly refashions Aristotle's notion of form, organ, and animation. Instead of a teleologically driven form (recall Aristotle's example of the eye), genetics gives us a technically driven information (genes are not determined or determining, but they do express, mutate, and replicate via protein intermediaries). Likewise, instead of an organ's serving as the principle of order for the organism, genetics and biochemistry emphasize the notion of organization, even self-organization (e.g., protein folding, bonding specificity between enzymes, metabolic networks in the cell). Finally, instead of the more physiological principle of animation or motion, genetics offers the model of political economy: the production, distribution, and consumption of molecular compounds within the cell (transcription/translation, membrane signaling and transport, cellular metabolism).

[. . .]

I can summarize Canguilhem's approach to genetics by deriving these three propositions from his work:

- The first proposition is that molecular genetics is an attenuated Aristotelianism; the concept of a "genetic code" is, in the framework established by Canguilhem, a more technical, operative version of Aristotle's "form." Genetics, however, is not completely Aristotelian because it is, as a biological science, predicated on the materiality of the organism, on the "stuff" of life.
- A second proposition is that genetics concerns itself less with the constitution or morphology of the organism and more with the ways in which an organisms is "informed." The emphasis on codes, sequences, and other data types makes genetics – and bioinformatics – very distant from the kind of visible analogies established by natural historians. [. . .]
- This relationship between information and error leads to a third proposition: in the medical context, genetics facilitates, or at least inculcates, a shift from the organism to the sequence as the basic unit of "life itself." At issue here is much more than mere scientific reductionism, for a number of genomic and so-called systems biology approaches have been able to incorporate molecular genetics into a systemswide view that includes technologies such as DNA microarrays and computer databases.[26] Yet the shift away from organism to sequence, with all its connotations of "code" and "information," also reveals a significant fissure in the concept of "life itself."

[...]

As Evelyn Fox Keller notes, precisely the opposite [from information theory's concept of signal as pattern unchanged by content] occurs in molecular biology's appropriation of terms such as *information, code*, and *sequence* from information theory and cybernetics.[27] In genetics, a single base pair mutation – from an A (adenine) to a C (cytosine), for instance – can result in a drastic change in phenotypic expression. Diseases such as sickle cell and cystic fibrosis do in fact result from, respectively, single base pair and single gene mutations. And, as noted, new fields such as pharmacogenomics are predicated on the search for the minute genetic differences (SNPs) that make some patients more susceptible to side effects than others. Thus, when Watson and Crick talk about "genetical information," they define *information* in exactly the opposite way in which the term operates in the information and computer sciences.[28] This tension – between an informatic definition of information and a genetic definition of information – has become even more complicated today, in which biological research and computer research are increasingly integrated into genome databases, gene-finding algorithms, and molecular-modeling software. In short, fields such as bioinformatics contain the residues of the Aristotelian tension between "form" and "information," a tension that is, paradoxically, materialized in artifacts such as in vitro plasmid libraries and online genome databases.

"In a nature twofold they shine"

[...]

In spite of what would seem to be a tendency to make the biological fully "virtual," neither bioinformatics nor the drug-discovery process takes place completely in the computer or on the Internet. This point cannot be stressed enough: *bioinformatics is as material as it is immaterial, all the while constituted by an informatic approach to the biological domain*. What this means is that, for bioinformatics, Aristotelian form and process is not enough; in a way, bioinformatics seems to be a dissatisfied Aristotelianism. Computer-assisted sequencing and analysis can go so far, but the drug-discovery process demands, at some point, a return to the wet lab. In the case of the cathepsin-K drug,[29] this return happened after the in silico drug-target identification and validation process (identifying the compound to act upon and matching that compound with the manifestation of disease). In this case, animal studies using the cathepsin-K therapy were the first loop from the digital to the biological in the "wet-dry cycle" of the drug-discovery process. This tension is crucial to understanding fields such as bioinformatics. Though, as Canguilhem notes, modern genetics and biochemistry may smuggle in Aristotelian "form," they also remain resolutely materialist, if for no other reason than that their endpoint or application must be something material (a gene therapy, a drug) or must in some way materially touch the body of the medical patient.

Although these three elements of form, process, and matter significantly inform the role of "life itself" in bioinformatics, another element is equally important: the role that various discursive exchanges play in the transformation of the concept of "life itself" within these scientific fields. I have already noted the significant roles that the sciences of cybernetics, information theory, and early computer science played in the formation of molecular genetics during the postwar era; this influence can be seen today in the range of hybrid artifacts that populate many biotechnology labs, from genome databases to DNA microarrays. The intersections between genetic and computer "codes" is in many ways the dominant theme of the recent history of molecular biology and genetics, and it will arguably take new forms in the leading-edge fields of bioinformatics and "in silico drug discovery." However, as also noted, such conceptual exchanges are at best incomplete exchanges and approximate appropriations.

Such approximation, in some instances, can affect the way in which scientific knowledge is determined. For instance, the fields of cybernetics and information theory, largely contextualized by World War II military research, configured "command and control" within communications and weaponry systems in a particular way; agency was human based and largely centralized, though augmented by an array of mechanical or informational prosthetics or both. In importing the concepts of "information," "code," "noise," and so forth, molecular geneticists such as Francis Crick implicitly imported the notions of command and control that were part of those concepts. Thus, the emphasis on the "central dogma" of genetics during the 1960s ("DNA makes RNA makes proteins, and proteins make us") configured DNA as a kind of command-and-control system that deployed instructions outward to the synthesis and organization of proteins in the cell. Though one still finds versions of this central dogma in textbooks, it has taken some time for this largely reductive maxim to be complemented by more complex approaches emphasizing gene regulation, biopathways, and protein–protein interactions.[30]

[. . .]

So far I have offered only a partial listing of the characteristics of "life itself" in the domain of bioinformatics and drug development. What should be apparent is how the ontological concerns of Aristotelian "form" are closely tied to the political-economic concerns of applications and instrumentality. Clearly, there is nothing wrong with the development of successful genetic therapies and drugs in general; but, all the same, it is important to acknowledge and pay attention to the complicated, manifold interests in fields such as bioinformatics. Biotechnology is both a science and an industry, and in examples such as the cathepsin-K drug candidate it is not difficult to see how the medical and economic values are not always in sync. In some instances, a drug candidate may perform biologically in a way that runs counter to the economic interests of its development (e.g., the HER2 test for cancer). In other cases, potential economic value is facilitated by new diagnostic technologies (e.g., the HLA-B test for the AIDS drug Abacavir). Depending on the direction in which the balance between medical and economic value tips, we may see in the future the combination of population genomics, genetic screening, and pharmacogenomics result in the "medicalization of lifestyle," or what one report calls "pills for the healthy ill."[31]

[. . .]

The economy of DNA, or Marx as bioinformatician

Consider again our case study of Human Genome Science's cathepsin-K compound. We can ask, What are the different types of value in the development of such a drug candidate? From one perspective, it is the drug itself that is of the most value, for the measure of the success of the drug is directly related to the potential economic gains for Human Genome Sciences and GlaxoSmithKline. Thus, the measure of economic value is predicated on the measure of biological or medical value; or, put another way, animal economy determines, in part, financial economy. The task of the drug-development process from this vantage point is therefore to turn information effectively into a product, to turn an abstract, immaterial entity (e.g., genetic sequence on a database) into a concrete, material entity (an FDA-approved prescription drug). The exclusive reliance on information in itself goes only so far. In the business of health care and pharmaceuticals, the endpoint is always the material, biological body of the patient, and it is this biological baseline that must be confronted.[32] Although information may be of value in itself, it is only part of the picture. Thus, *connecting information to the biological body is the primary challenge of "life itself" in the age of bioinformatics.* The measure of the two types of value – medical and economic – are based on effectively transforming something immaterial that is exchanged into something material that is consumed as its endpoint.

Yet, from another perspective, the biological, material body of the patient is not the endpoint of the drug-development process, despite the newfound role bioinformatics promises to play in the process. The average drug developed using biotechnology arguably benefits only partially from direct drug sales. The booming industry of diagnostic tests – many genetics based – and the linking of such tests to computer databases are also significant parts of the drug-discovery process and the pharmaceutical industry. These two aspects – diagnostics and databases – are more services than products and, as such, are dependent on information technologies to deliver results accurately. In the case of diagnostics, pharmacogenomics techniques, including the use of DNA microarrays, are promising to be able to match the genetic makeup of individual patients to particular drugs in order to minimize ADRs. This possibility, combined with the increasing diversity of biological databases (including SNP databases, population-specific genome databases, and traditional patient data in clinics), means that both medical and economic value are predicated on the ability of information to perform computational and analytical work. Here, economic value is predicated on medical value, but in a way that is different from the case of drug discovery. From a purely economic standpoint, there is less risk involved in the offering of these types of services, for a diagnostic test can be medically and economically beneficial, whether or not an ADR is discovered in a drug that is tested. Indeed, a common critique leveled at the idea of pharmacogenomics is that it offers a way for pharmaceutical companies to sell better the drugs already on the market, instead of transforming or even questioning the logic of drug development. Instead of a traditional "one size fits all" approach, pharmacogenomics simply shifts the scale of its operations into a "many sizes fit all" approach. As a number of more critical reports suggest, the basic principles of drug effectiveness, regulation, and testing are still left largely unquestioned.

[. . .]

But if we consider this same process [product-based economy of doctors prescribing drugs for conditions] from the larger picture of a bioinformatics industry, there is more than this simply information-into-drugs equation. As can be witnessed in the development of many drugs, including the cathepsin-K candidate, the process includes not only an actual pill, but also patents, licenses on patents, tests, and databases, not to mention direct-to-consumer marketing for new drugs. From this perspective, the challenge for a bioinformatics-based drug-development process is different. The challenge is now to maintain the recirculation of products (pills, testing technologies) back into information (databases, test results, marketing and media campaigns). If drugs currently exist in a cycle of technological obsolescence similar to the information technology industry, then the main challenge put forth to the pharmaceutical industry is not how to develop sustainable and effective treatments, but rather *how to transform temporary material products continually into the long-term generation of information.* What generates economic value, from this standpoint, is an infrastructure for the production of information, yet without ever completely severing the link to the patient's biological body.

These two perspectives on the medical-economic valuation of the cathepsin-K drug candidate correspond to what Karl Marx has famously called the "general formula of capital." Speaking about nineteenth-century industrial capitalism, he notes that the nature of capital can be considered through two perspectives on exchange. The first is the perspective of the individual worker and consumer. In this perspective, the individual works a certain number of hours manufacturing a commodity, for which a wage is given in the form of money. That person then takes the money and purchases other commodities produced by other individuals – food, clothing, or housing. Or, in the context of health care, an individual who works at an information technology job receives wages (part of which may go toward health insurance), and, if the person is ill, that money is exchanged for a prescription drug, which is then consumed.[33] This admittedly simplified context includes two subprocesses: the transformation of a commodity into money and the transformation of money into another commodity. Another way of stating this is that the product of the individual's labor power is exchanged for money and then that money is in turn exchanged for the product of the another [*sic*] individual's labor power.[34] In a sense, even in this basic relationship, capitalist exchange already coordinates living, biological labor power via immaterial, money intermediates. Marx was fond of using biological metaphors for the process of exchange. As he notes, "in so far as the process of exchange transfers commodities from hands in which they are non-use-values to hands in which they are use-values, it is a process of social metabolism." Thus, the exchange of money for commodities and commodities for money constituted the core "metabolic interaction of social labor." Although in a modern context the emergence of service industries, flexible accumulation, and information-based or immaterial labor has made this basic relationship more complicated, what we can retain from Marx's analysis is this basic "metamorphoses of commodities through which the social metabolism is mediated."[35]

[...]

Thus, in the example of the cathepsin-K drug candidate produced by Human Genome Sciences and GlaxoSmithKline, we can see a process similar to the one Marx describes as the "metamorphosis of commodities" and the general formula of capital (M-C-M'). Certainly, from one perspective, the drug-discovery process results in a consumable "thing." But from the perspective of the movement of the economic process as a whole, that moment of material production and consumption exists within a larger framework that emphasizes the further generation of value, a kind of biological valorization process. The drug-discovery process for SB-462795 resulted not only in an actual drug for testing in clinical trials but also in a number of patents (one for human osteoclast-derived cathepsin, another for a derived version of the cathepsin-K gene), an osteoporosis test sold to Quest Diagnostics, and the formation of a gene therapy consortium of pharmaceutical and biotech companies. What at one level appears to be a relatively straightforward economic relation – wages into insurance, insurance into drugs, drugs into the body – is at another level a dynamical, unending process of valorization – patents into drugs, drugs into tests, tests into patents.

However, the example of bioinformatics and cathepsin-K is not fully accounted for by the model Marx proposes, for fields such as bioinformatics and pharmacogenomics must, as we have seen, constantly negotiate the space separating the material and the immaterial, the biological and the informatic, the complex of Aristotelian form, organ and animation. Indeed, Marx does note that the process of capital is forced to deal temporality with material commodities, but that the ultimate aim of capital is to obtain a kind of immaterial, free-floating state. For Marx, the

> material variety of the commodities is the material driving force behind their exchange, and it makes buyers and sellers mutually dependent, because none of them posseses the object of his own need, and each holds in his hand the object of another's need.[36]

Yet the contradiction in the general process of capital is that if the process is taken purely in terms of the exchange of equivalencies, there can be no surplus value and no profit: "If commodities, or commodities and money, of equal exchange-value, and consequently equivalents, are exchanged, it is plain that no one abstracts more value from circulation that [*sic*] he throws into it. The formation of surplus-value does not take place."[37]

Thus, on the one hand, capital is defined as the process in which money is turned into more money via commodities, and yet this exchange of equivalencies denies the creation of surplus value, the very thing it is supposed to make possible. A pharmaceutical company invests a certain amount of money in the development of a drug with the intention of extracting some surplus value or profit from this drug (either in direct sales or in licenses or spinoff services). In the case of cathepsin-K, the C in the M–C–M' formula is thus the material pill, the drug itself. Yet the potential profits gained do not arise from pricing alone, for pricing does not address the more fundamental issue of how a differential can emerge from an equivalency. In this case, even the pricing mechanisms of the drug industry, although they calculate potential gains, cannot account for the conditions that make possible the derivation of a differential from equivalencies.[38]

[...]

When we turn to the case of bioinformatics and pharmacogenomics, we can similarly [to specialization and division of labor in industrial capitalism] notice two major transformations in the drug-development process that, the companies hope, will create the profit differential. The first is that the commodities in the biotech industry, like in many other industries, are increasingly becoming immaterial and informatic. The medical application of biotechnology is directed primarily toward prescription drugs, but a panoply of service-based industries satellite the actual development of drugs: database management, data analysis, software design, "info-medicine," and, of course, diagnostics. But this can be detected in a range of other industries as well (most notably the information technology and entertainment sectors). What is unique about biotechnology generally and about the bioinformatics and pharmacogenomics industries specifically is that *it is not only commodities that are becoming more immaterial, but also the bodies that consume those commodities.* To be sure, patients' biological bodies are not being "uploaded' in some kind of science fiction scenario. But the hegemony of molecular genetics, when combined with new information and computer technologies, has created a context in which the biological body – "life itself" – is increasingly understood and analyzed in informatic ways. The push toward pharmacogenomics and, in some cases, toward preemptive genetic testing has as its aim the development of a totally in silico monitoring and diagnostic system for biological "life itself."

On possible consequence of this tendency – a tendency supported by a great deal of investment capital in pharmacogenomics technologies – is that genetic medicine will "touch" the body only to the degree that the body and "life itself" are understood in informatic ways. If we accept Marx's description of the general process of circulation of capital and the ambivalent necessity for capital to descend temporarily into the material domain, then, with the body reconfigured as an informatic entity, capital can potentially bypass to a greater degree the vulnerability of the C intermediary in the M–C–M' formula. By supporting the creation of genome databases, patient-specific genetic tests, and integrated medical and pharmacy data networks, the biotech industry facilitates minimal contact with the biological body. Or, to be more specific, the general tendency toward a bioinformatics-based approach to drug development makes contact with the biological body determined by the degree to which that body and "life itself" are understood as informatic. *Thus, the passage from Aristotelian form to genetic information is mediated by capital.* We can even extend Aristotle's metaphor into Marx's analysis. In the same way that, for Aristotle, the true function of the eye is sight, the true biological function of DNA becomes the generation of capital (as information): the "form" of DNA is information.

As previously stated numerous times, this tendency toward an informatic understanding of "life itself" in no way implies the total liquidation of the material, biological body. The point is that the material biological body – "life itself" – is also the informatic body. The body materially counts only inasmuch as it is understood as information and as genetic information. From Marx's political-economic perspective, fields such as bioinformatics and pharmacogenomics can be seen as an attempt to create a new type of commodity, one that is not based on services, affective entertainment, or immaterial goods. This new type of commodity is just material enough to permit the M-C-M' cycle to continue; indeed, another name for Marx's general formula is what the pharmaceutical industry calls "wet-dry cycles." This minimally material commodity is just material enough to permit the necessity of further genetic tests and the ongoing consumption of new drugs in the cycle of obsolescence. But as a form of "life itself" that is informatic and bio-informatic, this commodity creates a more seamless transition from M to M'; the area of greatest vulnerability and risk – the living body – is thus placed at one or several removes from its context in novel artifacts such as genome databases and SNP-based diagnostic tests. If, as the hopeful forecasts for pharmacogenomics state, drug development is to take place almost entirely in silico in the future, and if, in such a context, the body is only minimally material, then this mode of economic valuation would seem to be the most beneficial for the biotech and pharmaceutical industries.[39]

[. . .]

Notes

1 See Erwin Schrödinger, *What is Life?* (Cambridge: University of Cambridge Press, 1967), pp. 20–22.

2 See Francis Crick's papers published during the 1960s, such as "The Genetic Code," *Scientific American* 207 (1962): 66–75; "The Recent Excitement in the Boding Problem," *Progress in Nucleic Acids Research* 1 (1963): 163–217; and "Towards the Genetic Code," *Discovery* 23.3 (1962): 8–16.

3 See their landmark paper, François Jacob and Jacques Monod, "Genetic Regulatory Mechanisms in the Synthesis of Proteins," *Journal of Molecular Biology* (1961): 318–359. Also see Jacob's *The Logic of Life: A History of Heredity* (New York: Pantheon, 1974), pp. 267–298.

4 See their paper, Heinrich Matthai [*sic*], Oliver W. Jones, Robert G. Martin, and Marshall Nirenberg, "Characteristics and Composition of RNA Coding Unit," *Proceedings of the National Academy of Science* 48 (1962): 1580–1588. Also see Marshall Nirenberg, "The Genetic Code II," *Scientific American* 208 (1963): 80–94.

5 See Lily Kay, *Who Wrote the Book of Life? A History of the Genetic Code* (Stanford, Calif.: Stanford University Press, 2000); and Hans-Jörg Rheinberger, *Toward a History of Epistemic Things: Synthesizing Proteins in the Test Tube* (Stanford, Calif.: Stanford University Press, 1997).

6 See Claude Shannon's Ph.D. dissertation, "An Algebra for Theoretical Genetics," Department of Mathematics, Massachusetts Institute of Technology, April 15, 1940. See also John von Neumann's lectures, republished as *The Computer and the Brain* (New Haven, Conn.: Yale University Press, 2000), pp. 68–70. Von Neumann, along with Alan Turing, was partially responsible for introducing biological concepts into computer science, thereby providing the discourse of artificial intelligence with a biological dimension.

7 As Judith Butler notes, "the anatomical is only 'given' through its signification, and yet it appears to exceed that signification, to provide the elusive referent in relation to which the variability of significa-tion performs. Always already caught up in the signifying claim by which sexual difference is nego-tiated, the anatomical is never given outside its terms and yet it is also that which exceeds and compels that signifying chain, that reiteration of difference, an insistent and inexhaustible demand." Judith Butler, *Bodies that Matter* (New York: Routledge, 1993), p. 90.

8 [Polymerase chain reaction, a process used to amplify DNA strands to produce a larger sample. – SV]

9 [Patent and Trademark Office – SV]

10 [Human Genome Project – SV]

11 On the development of lab technologies for biotech, see John Hodgson, "Gene Sequencing's Industrial Revolution," *IEEE Spectrum* (November 2000): 36–42. On PCR, see Paul Rabinow, *Making PCR: A Story of Biotechnology* (Chicago: University of Chicago Press, 1996).

12 The study, published in November of 2000, can be accessed at www.genewatch.org. [More recent studies of ethical and economic issues in biotech and patents are also available on this site. – SV]

13 Urs Meyer, "Introduction to Pharmacogenomics: Promises, Opportunities, and Limitations," in *Pharmacogenomics: The Search for Individualized Therapies*, ed. Julio Licino and Ma-Li Wong (Weinheim,

Germany: Wiley-VCH, 2002), p. 3. For more on pharmacogenomics, see D.S. Bailey, A. Bondar, and L.M. Furness, "Pharmacogenomics: It's not Just Pharmacogenetics," *Current Opinion in Biotechnology* 9 (1998): 595–601; Thomas Burnol and August Watanabe, "Genetic Information, Genomic Technologies and the Future of Drug Discovery," *Journal of the American Medical Association* 28 (2001): 551–555; Brian Calus and Dennis Underwood, "Discovery Informatics: Its Evolving Role in Drug Discovery," *Drug Discovery Today* 7.18 (September 2002): 957–966; W.E. Evans and M.V. Reiling, "Pharmacogenomics: Translating Functional Genomics into Rational Therapeutics," *Science* 286.5439 (1999): 487–491; G.S. Ginsburg and J.J. McCarthy, "Personalized Medicine: Revolutionizing Drug Discovery and Patient Care," *Trends in Biotechnology* 19.12 (1001): 491–496; M.W. Linder and R. Valdes Jr., "Pharmacogenetics in the Practice of Laboratory Medicine," *Molecular Diagnosis* 4 (1999): 365–379; Roy Pettipher and Lon Cardon, "The Application of Genetics to the Discovery of Better Medicine," *Pharmacogenomics* 3.2 (2002): 257–263; and A.D. Roses, "Pharmacogenetics and the Practice of Medicine," *Nature* 405 (2000): 857–865.

14 [Adverse Drug Reactions – SV]

15 The phrase has also been used recently by Donna Haraway, Sarah Franklin, and Nikolas Rose. The use here certainly builds on their work, but is also meant to refer specifically to this dual political and ontological aspect of fields such as bioinformatics and pharmacogenomics, which integrate biology and information in novel ways.

16 Georges Canguilhem, "The Concept of Life," in *A Vital Rationalist*, ed. François Delaporte, trans. Arthur Goldhammer (New York: Zone, 2000), p. 303.

17 Ibid. Canguilhem's proposition needs to be qualified, of course, for it can quite easily be argued that Plato's theory of forms and the faculty of reason in the *Timaeus* – in its analogizing between anatomy and the Platonic idea – is equally valid as a candidate for the philosophy of biology. However, Canguilhem extends his analysis of Aristotle to point to the way in which both the study of the concept and the study of organic life were circumscribed within a more rigorous, analytical framework. "It was Aristotle the naturalist who based his system for classifying animals on structure and mode of reproduction, and it was the same Aristotle who used that system as a model for his logic" (p. 303).

18 For a review of this phenomenon, see my article "Shattered Body, Shattered Self," *Afterimage* 29.5 (March–April 2002).

19 "Le concept et la vie" was first published in *Revue philosophique de Louvain* 64 (May 1966): 193–223.

20 Canguilhem, "The Concept of Life," p. 303.

21 Ibid, pp. 316–317. [ellipses in original]

22 Ibid, p. 316.

23 Georges Canguilhem, "Vie," *Encyclopedia universalis* (Paris: Encyclopedia Universalis France, 1973), 16: 764–769.

24 Canguilhem's approach looks for two things methodologically: "thematic conservation" across disparate disciplines and paradigms (e.g., Aristotelian hylomorphism in the works of eighteenth-century naturalism and nineteenth-century physiology), and what Canguilhem calls "scientific ideology," or the ways in which discursive exchanges in the sciences both inform those sciences and take them astray into sociology, politics, economics, and culture.

25 Canguilhem, "The Epistemology of Biology," p. 87. [ellipses in the original]

26 Even prior to these developments, molecular biology research during the 1960s had already emphasized the network-based, systemswide activity of genes and proteins; François Jacob and Jacques Monod's famous research on genetic regulatory mechanisms is an important example in this regard.

27 Evelyn Fox Keller, *Refiguring Life: Metaphors of Twentieth-Century Biology* (New York: Columbia University Press, 1995). As Fox Keller notes, "the notion of genetical information that Watson and Crick invoked was not literal but metaphoric" (p. 19).

28 By the time of Watson and Crick's much-lauded 1953 papers, the language of informatics in molecular biology was already quite developed, such that the two could note how, in a molecular form such as DNA, "many different permutations are possible, and it therefore seems likely that the precise sequence of the bases is the code which carries the genetical information." See James Watson and Francis Crick, "General Implications of the Structures of Deoxyribonucleic Acid," *Nature* 171 (1953): 965–967. Fox Keller thus argues that, contra Shannon and Weaver, for Watson and Crick, "if 'genetical information' is to have anything to do with life, it must involve meaning." *Refiguring Life*, p. 94.

29 [SB-462795 is a drug for osteoporosis developed by Human Genomic Sciences in conjunction with GlaxoSmithKline. It is claimed to be the first drug candidate derived specifically from genomics and bioinformatics technologies. In the full chapter, Thacker outlines this drug's journey from research

through clinical trials. It inhibits an enzyme called cathepsin-K that breaks down bone marrow cells. – SV]

30 The prevalence of the central dogma is one of the curious instances in the history of molecular biology. Any cursory understanding of genes and proteins cannot but help us to recognize the inherently complex nature of genetic function. Although Jacob and Monad's research did contribute to the understanding of mRNA and its cousins, it was, more important, a statement concerning the nonlinear, multiagential nature of gene function. Indeed, during the same period in which some researchers were working on "cracking the genetic code," biologists such as C.H. Waddington, Richard Lewontin, and Stuart Kauffman were performing studies showing how the complexity of genetic function required new, nonreductive approaches in biology. Yet it is difficult not to see the specter of the central dogma still very much alive in the biotech industry, with its emphasis on pills and "silver bullet" therapies. This emphasis makes sense economically – it would be difficult to market a therapy based on complexity and much easier to market a drug – but in many cases it does not make sense medically, as the low rate of current positive drug response and ADRs attest.

31 See the GeneWatch UK report *Pharmacogenetics: Better, Safer Medicine?* GeneWatch Briefing no. 23 (July 2003), available at www.genetwatch.org.

32 Indeed, this may be one explanation for why a number of bioinformatics companies did not survive the dotcom bust of the 1990s. Companies that began with great fanfare – such as DoubleTwist – have since gone under, perhaps owing to the fact that they limited themselves to the information technology–based services of database management. The most successful bioinformatics companies have focused either on software development or on the creation of entire "drug discovery suites" or packages.

33 Marx's specific example, infused with the ideology critique developed by him and Engels, is as follows: "Let us now accompany the owner of some commodity, say our old friend the line [*sic*] weaver, to the scene of action, the market. His commodity, 20 yards of linen, has a definite price, £2, and then, being a man of the old school, he parts for the £2 in return for a family bible of the same price. . . . The process of exchange is therefore accomplished through two metamorphoses of opposite yet mutually complementary character – the conversion of the commodity into money, and the re-conversion of the money into a commodity." *Capital*, trans. Ben Fowkes (New York: Penguin, 1990 [orig. 1867]), 1: 199–200. [ellipses in original]

34 Even without discussing the biotech industry, Marx already begins to think of labor and exchange in biological, or at least physiological, terms: "the whole process accomplishes nothing more than the exchange of the product of his labor for the product of someone else's." Ibid., 1: 200.

35 Ibid., 1: 198, 200, 199.

36 Ibid., 1: 262.

37 Ibid.

38 Marx abbreviates this paradox: "Capital cannot therefore arise from circulation, and it is equally impossible for it to arise apart from circulation. It must have its origin both in circulation and not in circulation" Ibid, 1: 268.

39 Many Marxian critics have provided variations on Marx's original formula, so I feel obliged to do the same, especially because I have absolutely no mathematical aptitude. In the context of pharmacogenomics, Marx's M-C-M' formula is really more of an M-I[C]-M' formula, in which I is the information of value generated in the drug-development process (e.g., genetic sequence, protein data, biomarkers) and I[C] denotes the way in which material commodities such as drugs in the body are always enframed by the genetic-informatic paradigm of "life itself."

10

A MONSTROUS VISION

Disney, science fiction, and CinemaScope

J.P. Telotte

The post–World War II era would see the emergence of a new cinematic discourse *about* technology with the sudden popularity of the science fiction genre. While this formula had staked out a place in the cinematic imagination at a very early point in film history, as Georges Méliès' *A Trip to the Moon* (1902) attests, and while its subjects naturally resonated with the development of film technology itself, it had found only sporadic success and, in the late 1930s and 1940s had largely been relegated to the realm of the serials. When it did burst into popularity in the 1950s, it would manifest a rather remarkable character. As Susan Sontag notes in one of the most famous assessments of the genre, the science fiction cinema of the 1950s and early 1960s took the form of a kind of collective "imagination of disaster," wherein was forecast all of the cultural anxieties about science and technology that were the inevitable baggage of the Cold War and its constant specter of atomic annihilation – anxieties that were frequently taking the form of monstrous and destructive alien invaders, nuclear warfare, or atomic mutations.[1] And as Sontag further suggests, while those films were generally quite popular, in large part because of their efforts at visualizing the extraordinary, or what she terms their emphasis on "the aesthetics of destruction" (216), they typically demonstrated an "inadequate response" to "the most profound dilemmas of the contemporary situation" (227). For while they provided a thrilling technological vision, they offered little effective suggestion of how to cope with that looming new world.

This linked vision of technology and a monstrous imagery may seem an exaggerated way of approaching another significant technological turn for Disney, especially given the studio's customary family orientation. However, its less-than-satisfactory experience with the hybrid system in the 1940s, the technologically driven destruction brought by World War II, and a Cold War atmosphere that repeatedly evoked very unfamily-like visions of scientifically driven apocalypse must have given Disney some pause in its otherwise consistent embrace of the technological. As it moved into these relatively uncharted waters, the studio had to weigh a clear economic attraction, the fact that there was a large postwar audience that was in some measure thrilled by glimpsing the latest technological advances, which were quickly moving from scientific development to familiarity and home consumption, against a potential difficulty, the awareness that this audience was also increasingly worried by the forces – and the monsters – that these advances seemed to be unleashing. As a result, we find that as Disney sought to further diversify its offerings by moving into this popular – and generally quite profitable – genre, and as it began to shift into pure live-action filmmaking that would also inevitably engage it in a cultural discourse *about* technology, it did so in a rather ambivalent or qualified way that would clearly differentiate its product from most other science fiction films of the period.

Unlike most other science fiction efforts then being filmed, Disney's first offering in the genre was an adaptation of a classic novel, Jules Verne's *20,000 Leagues Under the Sea* (1954). Of course, by telling that nineteenth-century story the studio would not have to *directly* address the mid-twentieth-century issues facing its audience. And yet Verne's novel already contained an ambivalent treatment of science and technology that would allow the film to sound its own cautionary note. Moreover, Disney decided to add an element of technological attraction, for *20,000 Leagues Under the Sea* would also mark the studio's first foray into one of the latest developments in cinematic technology, the new widescreen CinemaScope process. The resulting adaptation deemphasized the extraordinary voyage aspect of Verne's work, placed at the narrative's center a monstrous encounter that, like the many other monsters, mutations, and suddenly awakened creatures that so filled our science fiction dreams of the period, spoke to the cultural anxieties about the world that our scientific and technological developments seemed to be constructing, and wrapped everything in an appealing new technological packaging. In sum, as Disney crafted its first foray into science fiction, we can see the traces of that widespread cultural anxiety, of the studio's desire to address the monstrous specter behind this anxiety, and of its hope to offer a technically thrilling package that would also therefore be less disturbing for the typical Disney audience.

Yet given the company's history of eagerly adopting the latest film technology and its preeminence in the realm of fantasy, the move towards science fiction at this time must also have seemed a quite natural and, indeed, economically sound one. In fact, following the popular trend, the studio determined to take on science fiction almost simultaneously in film, in its first television series (as we shall see in the following chapter [of *The Mouse Machine: Disney and Technology*]), and in the Tomorrowland area of the new Disneyland theme park. However, the subjects of that genre represented just as much of a problem for Disney as for the other film studios and, indeed, for the rest of American culture, as if they marked a troubling site of unstable references or were terms in a negotiation that refused to be satisfactorily concluded. While few might have looked to Disney for something better than the sort of "inadequate response" Sontag describes, and while the choice of texts might have offered little promise in addressing the "contemporary situation," the political/ideological impingements of the subject matter seem to linger very near the surface of this film, as if inviting the sort of confrontation that a film like *The Three Caballeros* had largely side-stepped.

Certainly, by 1954, after a flood of sensationalist titles like *The Thing from Another World* (1951); *Invasion U.S.A.* (1952); and *The War of the Worlds* (1953), the studio's choice of *20,000 Leagues Under the Sea* as its initial science fiction effort must have seemed a rather "safe" one for this typically forward-looking genre. For Verne's novel pointedly looks back, further back than any Disney Main Street, to the emerging industrial mindset of the nineteenth century, to a kind of naïve technological vantage that was typical of the various books in Verne's "Voyages Extraordinaires" series. Of course, Verne's works were usually set in his own present to better facilitate his negotiations with the emerging technological world. As Edward James offers, he wanted to emphasize to his readers "that scientific and technological changes were occurring in their own society, and that more were imminent" (17). But for this very reason, Disney's choice to keep that nineteenth-century context, thereby producing a kind of nostalgic narrative, seems noteworthy, especially given the studio's very contemporary efforts in this direction that were then underway for its *Disneyland* television show and its theme park. But this choice is at least partly explained by the fact that such present-tense narratives risked stirring those fears and anxieties that beset the contemporary world, evoking the sort of monsters that might not sit well with the traditional Disney family audience, and perhaps *too* closely linking the Disney product with that cinema of "disaster." And too, intimations of disaster simply went against the grain of that fundamental Disney approach to the technological we have earlier described. Hence, a nostalgic science, something that could frame present-day technoscience in a safely remote past, wherein the "references" were a bit clearer and less ambiguous, represented a useful start to negotiations, a compelling and somewhat sensible compromise given both the issues mentioned above and the great cost of this film adaptation.[2]

However, negotiations would hardly be that easy, given the cultural climate, and monsters would proliferate throughout the narrative – monsters imagined, real, and looming. In fact, Paul Virilio has described as "monstrous" one effect that shows up here, and one with which our scientific and technological developments have increasingly confronted us: "the loss of references, the loss of all distinctions" (*Crepuscular* 165), a level on which our very world can seem monstrous because it has become so confusing. The Verne novel actually looks toward this conception, for it begins by establishing the public misperception of the submarine *Nautilus* as a sea monster – a misperception that was part of the ship's protection, since it resulted in a public discourse about monsters and the ocean's secrets rather than an outcry against a nineteenth-century terrorist, a discourse that looked back to the realm of legends instead of forward to the latest scientific developments. Most importantly, this initial confusion of monster and technology allowed Verne an effective critical vantage, letting him contrast older fears of the unknown with a modern, rationalist attitude – a strategy, as we shall see, that the studio would appropriate for a number of its television episodes in this vein. But the Disney conception would more directly develop and exploit this monstrous aspect of Verne's narrative and the play of confusion that attends it, proliferating monsters as a central metaphor of the film and a key term for effecting its complex negotiations.

Even prior to shooting the film, though, Disney was already facing a rather unconventional sort of monster on this project. For *20,000 Leagues Under the Sea* was, as we have noted, the studio's first foray into the new CinemaScope technology, which had just been introduced in 1953 by Twentieth Century-Fox. The product of a studio that was, as John Belton has described, "caught up in the turmoil of an industry-wide financial crisis and self-redefinition" (113), thanks to changing audience patterns, government regulation, and the new competition of television, CinemaScope was a technology the difficulties of which were still being understood and negotiated. In quickly adopting this new technology, Disney faced several limitations, among them the fact that, since Fox was heavily committed to pushing this new format for its own productions, which had first priority, it could only make a single CinemaScope lens available to Disney for much of the production schedule. Additionally, the aesthetics of wide-screen filmmaking – e.g., the problems of composing for a 2.35:1 aspect ratio rather than the conventional 1.33:1, of regulating camera movement, of compensating for a lack of depth of field, of appropriate editing rhythms – were just being explored. However, as Bordwell, Staiger, and Thompson note, the "new set of stylistic devices" that widescreen filming involved were relatively quickly "brought into line with the classical schemata" (361). As a kind of stylistic "monster," CinemaScope was, it seems, relatively easily tamed.

Helping in that process was the choice of director, for Richard Fleischer did have some experience with this sort of technological innovation. In 1953, for example, he had tackled the filming of a modern-day western, *Arena*, in a widescreen 3D process. In fact, contemporary accounts suggest that he was more troubled by and engrossed in the practical difficulties of underwater photography for *20,000 Leagues* than by the aesthetic issues associated with the wide-screen shooting.[3] In practice, he seems to have let his subject matter largely dictate the film's compositional style. Thus, he used the CinemaScope frame to emphasize the long, stylized design of the narrative's principle visual attraction, the submarine *Nautilus*, to provide for dynamic shots by depicting the submarine advancing diagonally into the wide frame to attack another ship or to escape danger, and to place the ship in extreme long shot against the horizon, other craft, or land. Since the narrative generally shifts between empty expanses of ocean and the cramped quarters of the *Nautilus*, depth of field proved a relatively minor consideration. And the editing, save for the climactic flight with a giant squid, is rather conventional. Long takes, along with frequent subjective shot/reaction shot pairings, for example, make maximum capital of the underwater and location scenes, producing effects similar to what we find in the popular Disney "True-Life Adventure" documentaries of the period. In effect, Fleischer seems to have rather easily coped with this technological monster and, in the process, probably encouraged the studio to release its next animated feature, *Lady and the Tramp* (1955), in CinemaScope as well.

While in this case the cinematic technology did not prove especially challenging the effort at *talking about* technology would require a good deal more negotiation, as Disney tried to draw out of Verne's narrative a more appropriate-for-the-era emphasis on the monstrous. Thus, the film opens not with Verne's after-the-fact, journalistic account, stressing how "the human mind is always hankering after something to marvel at" (2), but with an image of a supposed page from Verne's novel, actually something written for the film to develop its concern with monsters. That page describes how "the shipping world was alarmed by rumors of an avenging monster on the loose"; it dissolves into a scene that offers a glimpse of such a monster, as a mysterious entity with a gleaming "eye" charges and sinks a ship; and then the narrative illustrates the public responses to this attack in a typical seaport, San Francisco, as Old Billy, a survivor of the sinking, assures a crowd that "it was the monster alright – a cable's length long from beak to tail . . . with one big eye like a lighthouse." This opening context not only gives reason to the following naval expedition in search of the monster – an expedition involving the French scientists Professor Arronax, his apprentice Conseil, and the American harpooner Ned Land – but also establishes a public discourse about monsters that helps to structure the film's narrative and lend a frame to the film's precariously balanced discourse about the nature of modern technology.

The film further establishes the main terms in this discourse through the interplay between Professor Arronax and three reporters from the San Francisco newspapers, representatives of the nineteenth century's "yellow press." For while the professor describes his efforts to "gather facts," they try to prod him into saying something that might be turned into an arresting headline. His measured response, referring to "current scientific knowledge," is one of openness; while not acknowledging the existence of monsters, he allows that "If we could go deep enough, we would all be surprised at the creatures down there." This scientific assessment, though, simply serves to measure the sensationalist attitude that has come to surround those "rumors," as the morning newspaper brings the headline, "Monster Exists, Says French Scientist," accompanied by a sketch of a giant sea monster, complete not only with "beak," "tail," and "eye," but even with wings. This lurid popular discourse that has paralyzed regular shipping is based in legends of the past, yet it is shown as all too easily emerging from and even obscuring the truly scientific, suggesting how easily the public mind can blur the difference between myth and science, and thus the various external pressures that can shape our sense of the scientific, effectively reframing it as what we today describe as technoscience.[4]

With the subsequent expedition to hunt down the monster or expose it as the stuff of such popular constructions or "rumors," the impact of this loss of reference takes on a more disturbing dimension. For it begins by further underscoring that, despite Arronax's view, science does not operate in a pure state, but that it is partly constructed by powerful cultural forces that can obscure its focus. While Arronax wants passage to the South Pacific so that he can shed some scientific light on these rumors, we see that he can only continue this research because the U.S.

Navy and State Department, the military and the government, will back it in order to serve commercial motivations. Thus they invite him, as an internationally respected expert, to serve as an observer on an expedition whose objective is to dispel the fears and rumors that have interrupted normal shipping. And the expedition's leader, Captain Farragut, emphasizes this goal for the scientific expedition, as he pronounces, "In my considered opinion, no such monster exists or ever did." He further terms the subject of this search simply a "legend," but explains that the mission will "give the lie to those rumors" circulated by the newspapers. The one musical number in the film, Ned Land's "A Whale of a Tale," immediately follows this pronouncement and serves to further undermine the notion of a monster by framing it in the context of a series of comic tall tales of the sea. By this point in the narrative, the "monster," only briefly glimpsed at the film's beginning, has effectively disappeared into the realm of legend, rumor, and tall tale – all constructs of the human imagination and, finally, nothing really fearful. In its place we see emerging a number of other surprisingly disturbing – at least for a Disney film – menaces: big business and government that dislike disruptions, a military that serves the interests of business and government and tolerates no challenges to its presumed power, and a press that flourishes primarily by fostering fears and anxieties. This collection of critiques suggests at least an effort to create an ideological context for the narrative's eventual focus on both nostalgic and contemporary issues of science and technology.

However, with the monster's sudden reappearance the narrative moves in a rather different direction, offering another sort of transformation that shifts focus from such ideological issues to scientific ones, particularly to the difficult task of naming and categorization, of establishing limits or boundaries. For both before and after it attacks and cripples Farragut's frigate, the monster undergoes a series of misidentifications and alternate namings. A lookout initially describes it simply as "a floating object," suggesting debris from a sinking ship they have sighted and recalling a whale that had earlier been misidentified as the monster, while another sailor assures his shipmates that it is "the monster." Thrown overboard in the ensuing fight, Professor Arronax and Conseil come upon it enshrouded in fog, and initially think their landing is an island. Yet when Conseil determines that, rather, "it looks like a monster," Arronax after some deliberation corrects him, labeling it "a miracle," "a submarine boat," and foreshadowing another shift in identification. Offering that "there is great genius behind all of this," he is in turn cautioned by Conseil, "Yes, and great evil." Conseil's comment, of course, already suggests a kind of intellectual negotiation at work within the narrative, one that tries to frame this fantastic piece of technology in the context of the death and destruction it has wrought, while it also points to the key shift in the film, as the notion of "monster" comes to denote something else, something human and even individualistic: the creator of this extraordinary machine.

The subsequent sequences makes this shift explicit, as Captain Nemo reveals himself and exposes his own monstrous aspect, even as he directs his visitors to appreciate his "miracle" of fantastic technology, despite its menacing look, not as a monster but simply, as Arronax himself offers, "a craft of human invention." For over the next sequence, and in keeping with the pattern of Verne's novel, the ship and all of its working details are put on display for Nemo's "guests" as wonders of scientific achievement, largely removed from any cultural context, while Nemo himself becomes the narrative's monster. Thus, he soon informs Arronax that, despite the professor's assumptions, Nemo does not consider himself "a civilized man," and he orders the professor, Conseil, and Ned Land to be left on the *Nautilus's* deck while it submerges, leaving them to drown. It is a monstrous act from which he relents at the last moment, but it establishes a pattern that recurs when he later threatens Ned with death and when he attacks a ship loaded with munitions, destroying it and all onboard. With that attack Ned underscores the narrative shift, describing how sailors just like him were being "slaughtered by that monster," and even

Arronax, who at various points in the narrative expresses some sympathy for Nemo and an obviously detached admiration for his technological achievements, finally labels him "a murderer." Thanks to the effects of the CinemaScope lens, the extreme close-ups of Nemo as he plays his organ in anticipation of the attack only further this monstrous identification. For they distort his facial features, while also easily evoking a cinematic tradition of monstrous madmen, specifically recalling Lon Chaney's similar presentation at the organ in the classic horror film *The Phantom of the Opera* (1921).

And yet, the film never completely settles for such a traditional generic identification and strictly personal indictment. Despite these familiar images and Ned's repeated description of Nemo as "a madman," the monstrous appellation sits uneasily here, in part because we learn of the background that has turned Nemo into a self-professed "avenger" against humanity's own monstrous nature – thereby raising a note of sympathy – but also because the narrative inserts a series of other candidates to again shift and blur the "monster" reference. This blurring begins with the representatives of the unnamed nation that he blames for the torture and murder of his wife and child – military figures whom we see beating prisoners and loading their ships with the raw materials for war. It continues with the cannibals who nearly capture Ned and Conseil and attack the *Nautilus*, and whose nature is codified in the human skulls and bones that decorate their village. And it culminates in one of the most compelling monsters in the Disney canon, the giant squid that fulfills Arronax's earlier warning about the surprising "creatures down there" in the sea's depths, while also providing another elongated figure for effective wide-screen shot compositions. In its outsized nature, unreasoning assault, and nightmarish combination of features – as well as its dependence on what we generally term "special effects" – the squid quickly evokes more traditional cinematic monsters, and it mobilizes the sort of human response we often see in horror films, as everyone joins together – Nemo, his crew, his prisoners – to fight and defeat the creature in hand-to-tentacle combat. It becomes a familiar case of humans versus a *real* monster and, through their joint efforts against this creature, punctuated by Ned Land's saving of Nemo, helps to leaven the earlier indictment of humanity's own monstrous nature.

With the squid attack sequence, *20,000 Leagues Under the Sea* also manages to achieve the sort of retreat from present concerns that was always implied by its nostalgic narrative – and for which Disney films have often been scored. It has evoked a technological monster, only to shift that term to a traditional "mad scientist," then to various practically anonymous branches of the human family, and finally to arrive at a most suitable candidate, the sort of monstrous creature that audiences of the era were becoming quite familiar with thanks to films like *The Beast from 20,000 Fathoms* (1943), *Them!* (1954), *The Monster from the Ocean Floor* (1954), and *It Came from Beneath the Sea* (1955). And yet all of these mutant monsters of the science fiction genre were always just stand-ins, representatives of a larger monstrousness that had been unleashed on the world and that finally could not be avoided; they were just common players in a genre that, as Peter Biskind puts it, "was born with the atom and died in the late fifties when . . . we learned to love the bomb" (98). Mutants caused or creatures awakened by atomic testing, they invariably played out the terms of a larger cultural struggle with the monstrous forces of science and atomic technology that threatened to go out of all control, with their almost inevitable defeat reassuring us that such technologically born monsters might somehow be kept in check.

Yet, even given its satisfying narrative displacement of the monstrous onto the squid – which is just one more "beast" from "beneath the sea" literally and psychologically brought to the surface by the work of technology – the film cannot escape another level of easily shifting references, those bound up in modern American culture itself. For with the *Nautilus*'s return to its home base of Vulcania and Nemo's determination to destroy that base along with all of his discoveries, *20,000 Leagues Under the Sea* finally makes the same sort of connection as its generic brethren of the 1950s. The explosion Nemo sets off – "an explosion such as the world has never known," as he offers – destroys the island, kills the soldiers who have landed there, and eventually sinks the *Nautilus*. It is an ending quite unlike that envisioned by Verne's novel, which has the *Nautilus* defeated not by a technologically fashioned cataclysm, not hoist on its own scientific petard, but sunk by a natural force, a maelstrom in Arctic waters. More significantly, the Disney ending produces a familiar mushroom cloud, attesting to its nuclear nature and that of the secret power Nemo has discovered. It marks the final monster of the film, that of a scientific knowledge capable of producing, according to Nemo, "enough energy to lift mankind from the depths of hell into heaven, or destroy it." Yet, as a concluding voice-over intones, in a rhetoric that was unmistakable in the period, this knowledge is also one for which the world is not yet "ready" – a monster of the narrative's past that still haunted the film audience's present and that easily incited all of the era's nuclear powers.

That image of the mushroom cloud provides a most sobering image for the film's conclusion, since despite Nemo's faint promise of "hope for the future," it invariably recalls American atomic testing in the same South Pacific, a location that did, after all, represent a pointed shift from the arctic setting of the novel's conclusion. Moreover, it opened onto another quite accidental present-day correspondence, since in 1954 and prior to the film's release the U.S. Navy had launched its first nuclear-powered submarine, fittingly naming it *Nautilus*, after Verne's technological monster. While reinserting Verne's vision into the public consciousness and thus providing something of a publicity windfall for the Disney film – one that would propel it to the position of third highest-grossing film in 1955 and Disney's top money-maker to that date[5] – this ship, as the first component of the new "nuclear navy" that was then being constructed, also brought with it some troublesome baggage, a reminder of how these technologies, the submarine and nuclear power, were being joined – and celebrated – as the latest weapons in the nation's arsenal. In short, it further established a connection to that dangerous real world and extended the lexicon of monstrous references by underscoring the link between atomic power and weaponry that Disney would be at some pains to counter over the coming years.[6]

But of what significance, finally, is this proliferation of monstrous figures in *20,000 Leagues Under the Sea* and its various cultural kin, or the simple shifting of references that lets us all too easily play with this word "monster"? We have seen how rapidly the term surfaces and changes reference to finally include the era's atomic fears, even subtly – and surprisingly – indicting America and its new nuclear navy; but does this pattern do any more than reinforce, almost in spite of its nostalgic imagery, a sense of how embedded this film is in its 1950s context of science fiction, mutant creatures, and atomic paranoia? The great fallout from inhabiting a world bounded by "new technologies," Virilio offers, is ultimately "a crisis of ethical and esthetic references, the inability to come to terms with events in an environment where the appearances are against us"; for in such circumstances, in a realm of "increased mediatization" of all knowledge, a "*reality effect* replaces immediate reality" (*Lost* 24). In short, inhabiting a technologized environment can fundamentally disorient us because of the way such an environment eliminates or replaces those references or horizons – "ethical and esthetic" – that help guide our lives and enable us to carry out the sort of negotiations in which we are always involved.

It is in this context especially that we might map this monster metaphor onto the Disney film, its own technological discourse, and its efforts at negotiating between scientific and ideological imperatives. We might recall how Virilio links the notion of the monstrous to the unsettling way in which terms easily seem to shift their meaning as we suffer a "loss of references," or simply feel we are at sea, somewhat like Ned Land trapped within the *Nautilus*, with all the customary points of reference shifted or lost, with a "reality effect," determined by this strange new habitat, the submarine, having replaced reality itself. Here, in fact, is a key link to the larger thrust of the film, for Ned and Conseil, as they try to figure out how to escape from this technological monster, find themselves frustrated, since, in another and most telling shift from Verne's narrative, all of the maps and charts on the submarine lack the conventional delineations of longitude and latitude, the appropriate points of reference that would let them situate themselves. Instead, they discover that Nemo has so rejected the normal world that he has created maps in which all markings and measurements extend out from a mysterious central point – his uncharted island base of Vulcania, the source of all his technological achievements – in effect, from his own subjective vantage that confirms him as a kind of master of this world.[7] This element stands in marked contrast to the novel, which is careful at every turn to cite place and position, latitude and longitude, even to have Nemo repeatedly mark for his "guests" the ship's position as a way of impressing them with its capabilities.[8] That conception of a subjective chart, then, in its own way stands as symbolic of the film's ultimate monstrous logic and of the real threat that Nemo and the new world he represents pose, as it shows how a "reality effect" might be mapped over our "immediate reality," and suggests, through the power latent in Vulcania – a power that could destroy the world – a grave danger that underlies such substitution.

Armed with this sudden insight, that the monster is the point of reference – or as we might interpret, that the arbitrariness of references is itself monstrous – Ned and Conseil manage their own sort of negotiation. They plot Nemo's charts against a normal map, literally find their place in the world once more, and send out messages noting their location, thus precipitating their eventual escape. They, in effect, act out the film's desire to escape from this modern dilemma, from this monstrous atomic and subjective disintegration, no less than from the disturbing concerns of modern technology, and to reassert a simple set of limits on and order in this world – an order that takes a casual form throughout the narrative in Arronax and Conseil's remarks on marine taxonomies. However, this escape is far from satisfying, not nearly as comforting as the conventional use of technology to defeat the technologically awakened mutants and monsters that we find in other science fiction films of the era. For it reminds us that the frightened populace we see early in the film indeed had reason to be scared. And it leaves audiences of the present, in that period when, as Nemo offers, "all this will someday come to pass," yet to cope with this power, to negotiate with our own technoscientific regime and the monsters it creates. It leaves us feeling rather like Ned, Arronax, and Conseil as the film ends, simply adrift in a small dinghy in a seemingly limitless ocean, with our horizons still threatened by an inescapably technological future.

Of course, this reading may seem rather somber for a film that many commentators have simply categorized as "fantasy at its best" (Maltin, *Disney* 121), or "spectacle" marked by "splendid special effects" (Gifford 38). But it also serves as a needed corrective to those who would sweepingly categorize all Disney texts, regardless of the era, as "carefully controlled" "fantasy," particularly marked by "escapist themes" (Wasko, *Understanding Disney* 118). Eleanor Byrne and Martin McQuillan, in trying to read Disney narratives like many other recent critics, primarily as "reactionary parables of the American right" (2), have also noted this interpretive problem. As they set about exploring what they assumed to be the simple "conservative values" of the Disney canon – values that seemed marked by a level of what they term "blatentness" – they also observed frequent challenges to those values, often finding in the films a pattern of contradictory, frequently shifting "ideological codes" (5) that they were unable to resolve. What the shifting notions of the monstrous in *20,000 Leagues Under the Sea* point to is a version of that narrative instability – one that betokens an effort, both within the culture and in the Disney studio at this time, to negotiate different points of view on the technological. In this case, those unstable references trace out the Disney narrative's difficult confrontation with the psychological and cultural concerns surrounding the latest technological developments, which stubbornly resisted both conventional narrative resolution and a simple nostalgic relegation to the past.

More generally here, they point to what we might see as a recurrent Disney difficulty during this period in portraying the world of modern technoscience – or negotiating with its monstrous potential. As the studio first moved into the realm of science fiction, with such efforts as the Tomorrowland section of the Disneyland theme park, the Tomorrowland episodes of the *Disneyland* television series, and *20,000 Leagues Under the Sea*, it encountered various problems that defied easy resolution. Tomorrowland was simply not ready for the opening of Disneyland, and when the first guests arrived, a gas leak was discovered there. When confronted with Tomorrowland's problems, Walt is reported to have directed, "Cover it up with balloons and pennants" (Thomas, *Walt Disney* 268). When planning got underway for the television series, as Bill Cotter notes, the studio nearly "ignored the Tomorrowland section of the show," since "no one was sure exactly how to portray the future" (64). And here too the problem was "covered up" with other types of programming, such as the enormously popular Davy Crockett episodes. Ultimately, the fewest shows were devoted to this theme, and by the 1958 season, at the height of American space consciousness, no Tomorrowland shows were being offered. And *20,000 Leagues Under the Sea* almost inevitably opened onto the more disturbing implications of 1950s technoscience, the simultaneous possibilities to, as Arronax offers, "revolutionize the world" and, as Nemo counters, "destroy it," as well as the disturbing recognition that our science and technology were largely guided by the interests of business, government, and the military. But these various possibilities are the same ones that we continue to try to negotiate today; for the monsters, as the Disney/Pixar film *Monsters, Inc.* (2001) humorously illustrates, remain in our dreams, in our cultural closets. To the credit of *20,000 Leagues Under the Sea*, and perhaps to the consternation of many of today's Disney critics, it does not, like many of its generic brethren of the 1950s, simply offer a formulaic solution to our technological concerns. In fact, this film seems to suggest that the satisfactory negotiation of technoscience's possibilities was simply more a fantasy than even a Disney narrative could easily visualize.

Yet *20,000 Leagues Under the Sea* did at least demonstrate one possible option, one way that the studio would, at several points in the future, manage to bargain with the troubling themes of technoscience. In 1959, for the first time in a decade Disney lost money, thanks largely to the cost of *Sleeping Beauty*, and to counter that situation the company again turned to a technologically themed story to restore their fortunes. They allocated the largest budget to date for a live-action feature – $4,500,000 – to begin shooting *Swiss Family Robinson*, a film about a nineteenth-century Swiss family shipwrecked on their way to make a new life in New Zealand.[9] Salvaging all that they can from the ship – livestock, books, weapons, ropes and pulleys – the family creates on another South Seas island a thoroughly modern environment, in fact, one that, the father of the family brags, sports "all the latest conveniences." Through a variety of inventions and contraptions they even manage to defend their new and quite comfortable world from attacking pirates, as they effectively – thanks to the powers of science and technology – transform an interruption in their immigration into an acceptable end to their journey.

The narrative is, of course, essentially an adventure, much in the vein of *20,000 Leagues Under the Sea*, with few major developments in its plot. However, its central concern, as well as its chief attraction – as is especially attested to by the reappearance of the Swiss Family tree house as a theme park attraction first in Disneyland and later in Walt Disney World's Magic Kingdom – is the stranded family's technological ingenuity. For they almost eagerly apply the latest scientific lessons of modern European culture to their primitive island world, easily transforming its raw materials – palm trees, bamboo, vines, fresh flowing water – into the stuff of a technological society, and in the process providing audiences with a lesson in the advantages of modern technological culture at a time when technology had become all too closely linked to the contentions of the Cold War. And the film's box office easily measured the success of this nostalgic take on industry and ingenuity, as it earned more than $7,500,000 on its first release (Maltin, *Disney* 179). Here there are no monsters, apart from the human sort represented by the rather stock menace of pirates, and the family is quite at home with technology. In fact, through the Robinson's *tree* house, we see how technology and nature might come to an accommodation, how a comfortable bargain might well be struck. Of course, that bargain works so easily in large part because culture itself has been removed from the equation, as the point of reference, just as with Nemo's Vulcania, becomes the Robinsons' island, while the rest of society is simply bracketed off. But *Swiss Family Robinson* is very much a wish-fulfillment fantasy, one that seems almost a reflection on Disneyland itself, and while not home to monsters, it is not the real world either.

Notes

1   Sontag, in her famous assessment of science fiction cinema of the 1950s and 1960s, suggests that it embodies "the deepest anxieties about contemporary existence," anxieties not only about "physical disaster, the prospect of universal mutilation and even annihilation," but also "about the condition of the individual psyche" faced with such new and global menaces (223).

2   Disney's *20,000 Leagues Under the Sea* was certainly one of the most ambitious films the studio had ever undertaken, as well as its most costly, requiring Roy Disney to request additional investments from the studio's bankers. However, it was an investment of money and resources that, like many other Disney gambles, paid off. See Christopher Anderson's discussion of the film's success in *Hollywood TV*, 148–49, and Bob Thomas's description of the production's problems in *Walt Disney*, 235–38.

3   See Fleisher's [*sic*] "Underwater Filmmaking" essay, originally published in *Films in Review*. It is a focus that Disney also emphasized in its production of a documentary about the making of *20,000 Leagues Under the Sea*, which became an early episode of the new *Disneyland* television series, airing on December 8, 1954. This show, entitled "Operation Undersea," would, in fact, win the studio Emmy Awards for Best Individual Program of the Year and for Best Television Film Editing. See Cotter, 144.

4   We might note the more restrained version of Professor Aronnax's (the name is spelled differently in the novel) newspaper interview found in Verne's novel. Lacking the sensationalist sketch, the article is one in which, as Aronnax recounts, he "discussed the question [of a monster] in all its aspects, political and scientific" (10). In fact, the novel quotes almost the entirety of the interview, so that readers gain a sense of the very measured and scientific message he offers to the newspaper readers and that the newspaper accurately reports.

5   Released on December 23, 1954, *20,000 Leagues Under the Sea* earned the bulk of its receipts during 1955. Its $8 million in box office during that year made it Disney's most successful film to date. See Cobbett Steinberg's listing of box office receipts from 1955 in *Reel Facts*.

6   Certainly the most famous of these efforts is the Disney short, *Our Friend the Atom* (1957), released theatrically in Europe and presented as part of the *Disneyland* television series in the United States. As its title suggests, this film sought to educate the public about the peaceful uses of the atom at a time when the specter of atomic warfare loomed large in the public consciousness.

7   Indeed, given the titles of other of Verne's "Voyages Extraordinaires," such as *Master of the World* and *Robur the Conqueror*, we might well argue that this work is in dialogue with this sort of postulated crisis of subjectivity, and that Walt Disney, in his efforts to fashion his own lands and worlds (Disneyland, Walt Disney World) was a natural descendant of Verne in this regard.

8   As an example, we might note the following passage from the novel, as it describes the *Nautilus* in "open waters," with no discernible point of reference. Undaunted by the lack of any visual orientation, Professor Aronnax explains that the ship "headed straight for the Pole, without deviating from the 52nd meridian. From 67°30' to 90°, we still had 22½° of latitude to go, about five hundred leagues, or more than a thousand miles" (Verne 349).

9   For background on Disney's financial situation in this period and on the making of *Swiss Family Robinson*, see Bob Thomas's *Walt Disney*, 295–96, and Steven Watts's *Magic Kingdom*, 300–302.

Works Cited

Anderson, Christopher. *Hollywood TV: The Studio System in the Fifties.* Austin: University of Texas Press, 1994.

Belton, John. *Widescreen Cinema.* Cambridge, MA: Harvard University Press, 1992.

Biskind, Peter. *Seeing is Believing: How Hollywood Taught Us to Stop Worrying and Love the Fifties.* New York: Pantheon, 1983.

Bordwell, David, Janet Staiger, and Kristin Thompson. *The Classical Hollywood Cinema: Film Style and Mode of Production to 1960.* New York: Columbia University Press, 1985.

Byrne, Eleanor, and Martin McQuillan. *Deconstructing Disney.* London: Pluto Press, 1999.

Cotter, Bill. *The Wonderful World of Disney Television.* New York: Hyperion Press, 1997.

Gifford, Denis. *Science Fiction Film.* New York: Dutton, 1971.

James, Edward. *Science Fiction in the Twentieth Century.* Oxford: Oxford University Press, 1994.

Maltin, Leonard. *The Disney Films.* 4th ed. New York: Disney Editions, 2000.

Sontag, Susan. "The Imagination of Disaster." *Against Interpretation.* New York: Dell, 1966. 212–28.

Steinberg, Cobbett. *Reel Facts: The Movie Book of Records.* New York: Random House, 1978.

Thomas, Bob. *Walt Disney: An American Original.* Rev. ed. New York: Hyperion Press, 1994.

Virilio, Paul. *The Lost Dimension.* Trans. Daniel Moshenberg. New York: Semiotext(e), 1991.

Virilio, Paul, and Sylvere Lotringer. *Crepuscular Dawn.* Trans. Mike Taormina. New York: Semiotext(e), 2002.

Wasko, Janet. *Understanding Disney: The Manufacture of Fantasy.* Cambridge: Polity Press, 2001.

Watts, Steven. *The Magic Kingdom: Walt Disney and the American Way of Life.* Columbia: University of Missouri Press, 1997.

11

HAVE NANOSUIT – WILL TRAVEL

Video games and the crisis of the digital battlefield

Colin Milburn

The digital battlefield: an immense network of computers, sensors, and communications systems linking soldiers and machines into common channels of data, where every vehicle, weapon, and combat trooper is rendered a component in the integrated circuits of command and control. It is a hypermedia environment generated by the flows of information streaming from various mobile units, intelligence sources, and global positioning satellites. The zone of armed conflict becomes a virtual reality, navigated on a computer monitor or a heads-up display.

The completely digital theater of war appears just off screen but closer than ever, an emergent development of the military-entertainment complex.[1] The promise of programmable war – synchronizing everything from the operations of unmanned ground and aerial vehicles to the biomonitoring of soldiers – configures material bodies as discretely atomized nodes in computational phase space. For instance, Dutch DeGay describes the digital battlefield as depending on two specific engineering objectives:

> One is a new suite of vehicles and the network that those vehicles will operate in, and the other is the next-generation soldier who will be a node, if you will, to plug into that network and interact with those vehicles. . . . We look at the soldier as the next-generation platform. The *Star Trek* analogy is the Borg, a group of people who are plugged into a supercomputer and part of the collective, so they can share information and push data back and forth; what one person knows, everybody knows.[2]

This modular soldier, plugged into combat zones born from science fiction, has been evolving in military programs all over the world, including Germany's IdZ (Infanterist der Zukunft), India's F-INSAS (Futuristic Infantry Soldier as a System), the United Kingdom's FIST (Future Integrated Soldier Technology), France's FELIN (Fantassin à Equipement et Liaisons Intégrées), Singapore's ACMS (Advanced Combat Man System), Norway's NORMANS (Norwegian Modular Network Soldier), Australia's Land 125, the United States' Future Warrior, and many others. These programs – some in active development, others recently scrapped or revamped – focus on decentralized control networks where, as the critical theorists Alexander Galloway and Eugene Thacker have written, "the scale is fractal in nature, meaning that it is locally similar at all resolutions, both macroscopic and microscopic." Such "networks are elemental, in the sense that their dynamics operate at levels 'above' and 'below' that of the human subject." They operate, in other words, as interactions of *bits* and *atoms*.[3]

According to the U.S. Army Research Office, the final realization of this vision will depend on innovative military science that looks into "creation and utilization of materials, devices, and systems through the control of matter on the nanometer-length scale and into the ability to engineer matter at the level of atoms, molecules, and supramolecular structures." This research will contribute to

> increasing command and control, lethality, mobility, survivability, and sustainability of systems in the field. . . . [It will enable] a strategically mobile force capable of handling the full spectrum of future operations from stability and support operations through major theater war.[4]

Indeed, nanotechnology would provide revolutionary solutions for integrating soldiers and information systems in the battlespaces of the future. As U.S. Navy officer Shannon L. Callahan explains, if this projected revolution in military affairs depends on "integrating the infantryman's capabilities into the digitized battlefield without adversely affecting his performance, thereby multiplying his lethality through an ability to communicate what he sees and knows up to higher headquarters," then nanotechnology and its "tiny devices could be the revolution's enabling technology."[5] Certainly, the sense of revolutionary potential informed the U.S. Army's decision in 2001 to create the Institute for Soldier Nanotechnologies at MIT:

> The individual soldier [of the future] . . . will require systems revolutionary in their capabilities. Recent advances in the field of nanoscience suggest that [it] may be possible to provide the soldier with radically new capabilities in full-spectrum threat protection without incurring significant weight or volume penalties. Such soldier systems will only be realized by directing additional resources to the Army's Science and Technology Program in the emerging field of nanoscience. For that reason, the Army's Science and Technology Program in the emerging and assigns arena is being extended . . . to create a University Affiliated Research Center (UARC) entitled the "Institute for Soldier Nanotechnologies."[6]

When the Army Research Office initially solicited proposals for the institute, the Broad Agency Announcement appeared on the Army Research Office website beside a cartoon of the digital battlefield. In this image, futuristic soldiers charge across a computational grid. As in the *Matrix* films, the environment materializes from a background of green binary code. The 1s and 0s from the antique past of monochrome monitors morph into a scene of high-tech warfare. The cartoon makes one thing perfectly clear: the digital battlefield of the future will be forged from the collision of cyberspace with nanospace.

Shortly after establishing its operations at MIT, the ISN produced a couple of publicity videos to reinforce this notion. *Soldier of the Future*, developed in 2004 by North Bridge Productions (a division of DigiNovations) in collaboration with the game company Boston Animation, splices interviews of real MIT scientists together with fictive animations of military nanotechnology in action. The animated vignettes present the vision of a skintight exoskeleton that will harden to stop sniper bullets, synthesize antitoxins in response to chemical weapon explosions, and administer first aid to wounded soldiers by "applying little electric currents to systems [of exomuscle] that are unimaginably small and light." Rendering biometric data visible on the battlefield network, the suit will enable soldiers and commanders

Figure 11.1   The digital battlefield: US ARO final solicitation, Institute for Soldier Nanotechnologies (2001).

alike to observe its molecular operations. In one vignette, a chemical weapon injures a soldier named Benson. His suit injects nanoparticles into his bloodstream to combat the toxins. Another soldier, watching this microscopic process through the visualization system in his own suit, says, "I switched to monitor Benson over the battlefield network. The drama unfolding in my viewscreen was riveting." The drama of military nanotechnology, turning the chemical interior of the soldier body into yet another setting for the theater of war, would appear to be no mere fantasy. According to the *Soldier of the Future* video, it is almost here: "Nanotechnology research is taking this out of the realm of dreams and, within a couple of decades, into the field."

A later ISN video opens with a first-person action sequence. The green-tinted visual field of this sequence recalls the heads-up displays (HUDs) featured in some first-person shooter games, for example, *Rainbow Six: Lockdown*. In this 2005 game, the Rainbow Six team must stop terrorists from releasing a nano-virus:

> Unidentified terrorists attacked LNR Anderson – a South African nanotech research company. They were illegally developing a bioweapon called Legion. It's an artificial

virus, created with nanotechnology, engineered to wipe out civilian populations, then burn itself out.[7]

Similarly, the ISN video concerns a small squad of nanosuited soldiers infiltrating an enemy bioweapons bunker. During this search-and-destroy mission, an airborne bioagent (dubbed "bad stuff" by the squad leader) infects Jones, one of the soldiers. But before Jones is aware of it, the nanotech systems that monitor his blood chemistry go into action to contain the contamination.

In this video, the digital battlefield – networking information from various recording devices and nanosensors in the soldiers' uniforms – is available not only to the troops but to the officers and scientists coordinating the operation through their command terminals: the first-person shooter perspective is identical for the soldiers and the officers. When Jones's bio-contamination occurs, the distributed HUD indicates that a man has been exposed and therefore must be "sent out," dropped from the mission – like the convention in video games where the HUD inventories *remaining lives* or *extra men*. Subsequently, the video offers us a molecular view of what happens inside the suit, showing the subdermal functions of the onboard "med-surveillance systems." Nano-syringes rapidly puncture the soldier's skin, sucking samples of his blood through "micro-blenders." His puréed RNA molecules filter through lab-on-a-chip devices, which beam diagnostic data back through the digital network. Thanks to the suit, Jones survives to fight another day.

Wars are made rebootable. Soldiers' lives are made replayable. As the first *Soldier of the Future* video says, ISN scientists are "mounting an assault on that challenge [of soldier survivability] with tools that were unimaginable just a few years ago." Affording command and control even at the atomic scale, nanotechnologies of the most radical and far-out varieties ("unimaginable just a few years ago") now appear clear and present.

Yet even as scientific institutions and "soldier of the future" programs embrace the technocratic promises of programmable warfare, popular engagements with military nanotechnology frequently open onto futures of an altogether different order.

Figure 11.2 First-person shooter: *Soldier of the Future* video, Institute for Soldier Nanotechnologies (2005). Reprinted with permission of the Institute for Soldier Nanotechnologies.

Crysis mode

A huge number of video games today animate the technical concepts and political dimensions of military nanotechnology, making the digital battlefield less a dreamscape of future wars than an everyday playspace, easily accessible and endlessly reloadable. Games such as *Deus Ex* (2000) and *Deus Ex: Invisible War* (2003), *PlanetSide* (2003) and *PlanetSide 2* (2012), the *Red Faction* series (2001–2011), *Nano Breaker* (2005), *Project: Snowblind* (2005), the *Metal Gear Solid* series (1998–), *Heroes of War: Nanowarrior* (2009), and several dozen others turn speculative nanoscience and military engineering diagrams into recreational experiences. These games contribute to the irruption of futuristic technologies into everyday life by simulating the conditions for advanced nanowarfare as both imminent and playable. In doing so, they participate in the militarization of popular culture, making the state of perpetual armed conflict into a form of consumable pleasure – and often naturalizing militaristic values of imperialism, xenophobia, misogyny, and aggressive masculinity in the process.[8] But this is only part of the story.

For some gamers, quotidian explorations of the digital battlefield afford perceptions and sensations of nanowarfare that diverge significantly from official military visions. Of course, media consumers often appropriate, reinterpret, and remake cultural materials in ways that unpredictably subvert their "proper" meanings. As Michel de Certeau famously argued, "Everyday life invents itself by *poaching* in countless ways on the property of others."[9] So even as nanowar games normalize the digital battlefield, they also enable its *recreational potential*.

Consider the blockbuster PC game *Crysis*. Developed by the German game company Crytek, it came out in 2007 as the first entry in a larger saga. In *Crysis*, the player takes the role of James Dunn, an elite U.S. Special Forces soldier, identified by the code name "Nomad." Nomad is equipped with a nanosuit, which mimics prototypes from the Institute for Soldier Nanotechnologies and the U.S. Future Warrior program. According to Bernd Diemer, the senior designer on the *Crysis* project, the game strives for fidelity:

> Taking inspiration from the Future Warrior 2020 program, we developed the Nano Fibre Suit that can enhance strength, speed and armour levels. The player can max the speed to dash across an open field, change to the strength setting and silently punch out a sentry.[10]

In many ways, *Crysis* presents itself as a playable version of the scenarios depicted in the ISN videos.

The game takes place on a tropical island in the South China Sea, where the North Korean military has commandeered an alien artifact discovered by U.S. archeologists. The island becomes a stage for globalization as militarization. The plot unfolds through open-ended sandbox gameplay. The player can proceed through various military objectives with a large degree of freedom, selecting missions according to preference rather than a prescribed order, thanks to the logistics of net-centric warfare that render the island as a digital battlefield. Yet between skirmishes with North Korean soldiers and the onslaught of alien creatures, the narrative elements take a backseat to the real focus of the game, namely, the playability of the nanosuit itself, and its relation to the figure of the male soldier inside.

The nanosuit has several functions that the player can activate at will. Whenever we initiate these nano-functions, an ominous male voice mechanically announces the outcome of our selection: "MAXIMUM ARMOR," "MAXIMUM STRENGTH," "MAXIMUM SPEED," and so forth. This voice would seem to be the programmed rhetoric of military science as such, built into the operating system of the suit that we inhabit in first-person perspective. The voice, along with the text messages that pop onto our HUD, reminds us, comforts us, about our invulnerability – our virtual impenetrability – in the embrace of the nanosuit. We are encouraged to think of our avatar *pumped up to the max*, boasting maximum power, maximum hardness.

While emphasizing toughness and rigidity, *Crysis* also presents some fleeting views of the interior operations of the nanosuit. Brief shots in the intro video provide an intimate, almost illicit perspective on the high-tech war machine that Nomad has become. These third-person images show the extent to which nano enhancement, in rendering the soldier maximally powerful, simultaneously renders him maximally fluidic: a porous membrane where materials pass back and forth with abandon.

The graphic exposure of nano devices dropping into the bloodstream, embedding themselves in muscle fibers, and infiltrating the epidermis (similar to the ISN images of nano-needles puncturing the skin) discloses a conundrum in the imagination of military nanotech. The soldier is made technologically hard only by virtue of being technologically soft. The soldier is penetrated at all times: not a closed off, armored body, but an open, wet, and humble body unfastened by tiny probing technologies. The mediated views offered by *Crysis* and the ISN videos situate us initially in the first-person perspective and then, ecstatically, in the third-person perspective directly at the nanoscale. We see the body's molecular opening, its biomechanical fluidity, even while bombarded with the rhetoric of hardness. We are suspended between these two perspectives, unable to resolve them because they are both insisted on, graphically and semiotically.

This is what I will call the *crysis mode* of the nanowarrior, smeared between the poles of maximally hard and maximally soft – armored and fluidic, meaty and mechanical, self and other at the same time. It represents a condition of rupture and disarray internal to the symbolic order of militarization, enframed by the speculative horizon of programmable warfare.

Concerns about the crysis mode circulate both overtly and covertly among the self-professed *hardcore gamers* who contribute to discussions of *Crysis* in online forums, blogs, video-posting websites, and gaming magazines. From 2006 (when prerelease materials for the title first appeared) through 2012, I monitored more than ten thousand of these public discussions about *Crysis*. The

Figure 11.3   Inside the nanosuit: dropping from holes in the exoskeleton, nanospheres infiltrate the pores of Nomad's skin. © 2007 Crytek GmbH.

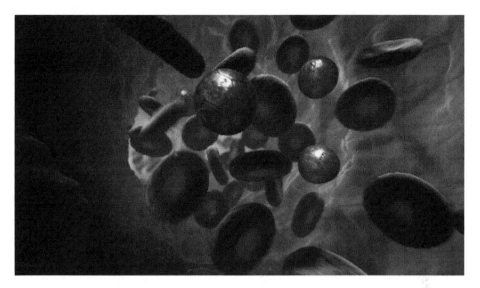

Figure 11.4   Wet nanotechnology: power-boosting nanospheres flow through Nomad's bloodstream. © 2007 Crytek GmbH.

vast majority of players seemed to support the notion that *Crysis* appeals to aggressive masculinity, mythically encoded by the Y chromosome itself. One player explains, "The whole basis of . . . *Crysis*, is besting an adversary and that is something that we with the Y-Chromosome have excelled at, for better or worse, since the dawn of time."[11] As a prerequisite for playing the game, in addition to owning high-end computer equipment, some other players would "even add a new requirement: a penis. *Crysis* is the manliest game on any system."[12]

Industry stereotypes often assume that military first-person shooters like *Crysis* sell predominantly to male consumers, thus discounting female gamers, as well as transgender and intersex gamers, from consideration in future game design and marketing strategy (a situation that has only recently started to change). Certainly, there are many female gamers who play *Crysis*. But in public discussions of the game, hardcore male gamers frequently assume that all other discussants are also male. In the conversations I observed, players generally agreed that *Crysis* and its sequels are aimed at men: as one player suggested, rated "M for Manly."[13] This is so much the case that, in one conversation where a *Crysis* player called "—Anna—" announced her female identity ("I'm a girl gamer, would like to chat, but I'm busy playing *Crysis*"), the immediate response was incredulity, with several respondents insisting that this "girl gamer" must really be a "boy gamer" in disguise.[14] A majority of players involved in *Crysis* discussions online make a point of their maleness, either in specific postings or in their author profiles. Whether or not they are actually as male as they profess to be (and it is quite conceivable that some female gamers might seek to covertly pass as male in these public forums), the intensely gendered discourse surrounding *Crysis* nevertheless plays out the stakes and the standards of militarized masculinity in contemporary technoculture.

In any event, to whatever degree there might be slippage between the *offline* gender identity and the *online* persona of a *Crysis* player – that is, to whatever extent female gamers might be performing as male or vice versa when discussing *Crysis* – this kind of transgender recreation would *already enact* the problematics of the crysis mode. For the relationship between the hyper-masculine image of military nanotechnology (the nanosuit's baritone assurance of maximum power enveloping the tumescent bodies of Nomad and his fellow soldiers, Psycho, Prophet, Aztec, and Jester) and the body of the soldier-player who inhabits this image is precisely what is rendered precarious by the *Crysis* experience.[15]

For many players of *Crysis*, military nanotechnology means empowerment without imperilment. The game cultivates an affirmative response to the nanosuit and its capabilities, generating fantasies of individual superiority and invulnerability under the regime of nanotechnology. The narrative of the game disappears in relation to the affective force of the playable nanosuit, the imaginary transformation of the player into an indomitable nanowarrior, backed up by the insistence that all of this is *scientifically plausible*. As one player writes, the game

> manages to make you feel like a badass thanks to the high-tech nano-suit, which has four settings to help with combat situations. . . . By the end of single player it'll be second nature. . . . The nano-suit really helps you feel superior for a plausible reason [i.e., nanotechnology].[16]

Yet the fantasy of impenetrable vigor often clashes with the recognition that such powers depend on the molecular opening and invasion of the soldier body. Even as some players identify the nanosuit as protecting subjective and biological integrity (in accord with the rhetoric of *maximum armor*), others are discomfited by the fact that the nanosuit "allows you to use enhanced abilities to supplement your battle prowess . . . by releasing nanobots into your bloodstream."[17] A few, puzzled by the disconnect between hard rhetoric and wet imagery, interpret the playable nanosystems as operating at different levels, dividing the armoring functions from the penetrating functions: "in fact, I believe in the game the 'nano suit' is two part, the part that covers the users body and provides armour/cloaking, and the free flowing 'capsules' within the bloodstream that boost strength and speed upon command."[18] Others express preference for the exomuscle functions, distinct from the intravenous nanospheres: "I suppose the balls [passing from the suit into the bloodstream] are things using nano technology to speed up the body. I like the idea of carbon nanotubes conforming to the muscles to make them stronger better myself."[19] Yet many perceive the nanosuit as actually transforming the biomolecules of the body – getting into the DNA:

> The coolest thing about this game, the Nano Suit. The Nano Suit is a very high tech piece of military property. It has the power to alter your genetic code and will give you 4 different powers, Defense which will make you invulnerable to bullets and more for short time, Speed which will make you ten times faster for short time, Cloak which makes you invisible for short time, and my favorite Strength which give you super strength to pick enemys [*sic*] up and throw them and such.[20]

Among those players who detect the perplexities of a technology that promotes maximum hardness while making the soldier into a weeping membrane or molecular sponge, the condition of crysis quite often appears as a failure of normative gender: "little nano guys go into your bloodstream to make you faster!! . . . I'm not even kidding man, these little thingies like balls or something went inside the guys bloodstream and he dyked out. Like, ran fast."[21] The penetrability of the male soldier ("the guy"), his opening to these "little nano guys" or "these little thingies like balls" that get inside him, provokes a player response in which the enhancement of *maximum speed* is understood as a queering. The soldier's ability to run fast when injected with nanospheres is interpreted as sexual chaos, gender slippage: the guy "dykes out," bewilderingly ambiguated. Normative distinctions – the firm and the fluid, the closed and the open, the masculine and the feminine – seem to dissolve in the image of military nanosystems. The code name of Nomad even suggests such instability and fluidity: the transgression of borders, a subject in process, becoming otherwise. Certainly, a number of players have commented on a sense of gender trouble among the nanosuited soldiers: "JAKE DUNN (aka Nomad) is a raving lesbian trapped in a mans body . . . and Psycho had a fetish for guys in nano suits."[22]

Crysis players often discuss the ambivalent condition of these soldiers, spread between maximum hardness and maximum fluidity, precisely because the game presents it as going both ways. Working through the ambiguities of military nanotechnology in the game, some players arrive at a rather queer perspective on the future.

Hardware fetish

The power fantasies animated by *Crysis* might seem localized to the irreal spaces of science fiction. Yet adaptation to the digital battlefield, inhabitation of the soldier avatar in the grip of the nanosuit, quickly translates into a tacit sense of personal investment in the future, an embodied response to what one player aptly calls the game's "unsatiable hardware fetish."[23]

The *Crysis* program demands so much computational muscle to run that only heavy-duty PCs equipped with high-octane processors and graphics cards are capable of serving the game at its optimum settings. With its resource-intensive game engine (CryEngine 2), which provides vivid 3D graphics, sophisticated AI behaviors, and a responsive open-world environment, *Crysis* requires advanced computer hardware with maximized tech specs just to play it: maximum hardware. It has become infamous: "*Crysis* demanded so much graphical horsepower it crippled most PCs."[24] These outrageous requirements make the game itself seem like an artifact transported backward in time from a science fiction universe: "It's too demanding today, that's just the simple truth. Nothing runs it."[25] Another gamer concurs: "It may be cheaper to travel forward in time to play *Crysis* than it is to build a machine capable of bending the game to its will."[26] The idea of future-ladenness echoes throughout the gaming community: "*Crysis* is the future. The present isn't ready for it."[27]

Invoking the same militarized rhetoric and science fiction idioms that characterize the story of *Crysis* itself – the "crippling" of lesser PCs, the race for technoscientific power, and the notion that you might need a time machine to operate the game – players of *Crysis* express a mixture of frustration and swagger in describing their gaming experiences. The frustration appears when they are unable to make the game work: "bLAH, This game is my Moby Dick. . . . I get annoying *screen tearing* constantly . . . that gives me a headache . . . this bastaaard of a game. I hate it I want Crysis dead."[28] But many players start to swagger as soon as they are able to make the game run, even imperfectly:

> I did play crysis on its on very high settings and i did lag a bit at times and i couldent [*sic*] put the anti aliasing up all the way but no computer can run crysis on very high . . . but all in all my computer is awesome and is the envy of everyone i know.[29]

Although the game "cripples most PCs," those players equipped with superior hardware have comparatively little trouble. These well-equipped players often describe their computers in terms that evoke Nomad's awesome nanosuit – while warning other players that, without such a computer, the full awesomeness of the nanosuit will remain elusive. For example:

> *Crysis* is straightforward: You take the role of a soldier of the future who dons a high-tech nanosuit that augments natural human qualities like speed, strength, and

fortitude. . . . But all of this comes at a price: the cost of a state-of-the-art gaming machine. Play without a technologically advanced rig and you'll have no choice but to run the game at the lowest visual settings.[30]

Or likewise:

Great Game, great graphics and really cool gameplay. If u need to get away from enemies use super speed on your nanosuit and you run really fast! But be warned you have to have a really high tech computer to play this game![31]

The story of Nomad, a soldier engaged in international (and interplanetary) warfare, pumped up to the max by virtue of his nanotech exoskeleton, provides an analogy for the technical achievement of running the game itself. Superior computer hardware becomes the player's own high-tech exoskeleton. Like the nanosuit, a "state-of-the-art gaming machine" is a hardware prosthesis: a "technologically advanced rig" practically imported from the future, grafted to the player's body at the moment of picking up the controls. To own such a computer is to be directly in touch with the future depicted in the game. Which is to say, the computer now appears as a fetish. It is the source of high-tech power, maximum hardness, maximum strength.

For some, this hardware fetishism has strong sexual implications, reflecting the phallocentrism of the game narrative. Many players have noted that the game's incessant incantation of *maximum strength* and *maximum armor* seems really to mean, as one puts it, "MAXIMUM penis length."[32] Players of *Crysis* therefore often measure and compare their relative computing powers in phallic terms: "Those are some pretty heavy processor requirements [to run the game], glad i have a larger e-penis than the rest of you."[33] These gamers regularly post photos of their computers and lists of their tech specs to online message boards, sometimes even distributing close-up shots of their CPUs or graphics cards in ways that self-consciously mimic pornographic imagery. Occasionally, fellow players of *Crysis* appear quite impressed with such displays of hardware prowess: "I was checking it out [a friend's computer]. Looks totally sweet. Gives big e-penis for sure."[34] Or: "That rig will give you a HUGE e-penis. Congrats on that. . . . Your CPU looks amazing with the 4g of RAM."[35] Or: "Damn. That rig is sweet dude. You easily have the best rig here. That pic of your rig you emailed me was sweet. I love your rig."[36]

Yet just as frequently, other players respond with distain or hostility toward those players who advertise pornographic details about their *Crysis*-mastering hardware: "Congratulations, you can show off your computer on the internet. Your penis probably got larger because of what a good computer you have."[37] Similarly: "I guess your e-penis makes up for your real one."[38] Sarcastic allusions to oedipal complexes and castration anxieties are bandied about to deflate the pretensions of hardware show-offs: "I told my mom that I had a small penis, so she said to buy a new 500 dollar video card. Now my penis is huge!"[39] But whether admiring or ridiculing such displays of e-penis power, the communal discourse of *Crysis* players routinely affirms a linkage between the futuristic nanosuit in the game, the technical capacities required to play the game at maximum settings, and the psychotopography of the male body.

We see here an instance of what Sherry Turkle has described as the tendency to identify the computer as a prosthesis or a mirror, a *second self*: "This kind of identification is a powerful source of computer holding power. People are able to identify physically with what is happening inside the machine. It makes the machine feel like a part of oneself."[40] The sensation of bodily extension or identification with the computer by no means requires physical connection with the hardware; as Turkle writes, "The sense of physical relationship depends on symbolic contact."[41]

In the case of *Crysis*, symbolic contact with the digital battlefield produces a feeling of inhabitation, a merger with the hardware as the site of everyday nanowars.

Many players see the predicament of Nomad in the game as equivalent to the predicament of the computer as it struggles with the *Crysis* software: "Crysis: Not just a game, but also the state your PC is in trying to run this game!"[42] Frequently, this translates as a *corporeal* predicament, a symbolic crysis of the player's own body. Indeed, to the extent that it anthropomorphizes the gaming system as an extension or reflection of the player's body, the discursive field of *Crysis* effectively *e-masculates* the player. Echoing the gamer vocabulary of e-penis, the concept of e-masculation would signify the *electronic performance of masculinity*, the inflation of soldier-male superiority through the virtuosity of gaming hardware – and, at exactly the same time, the *emasculation* or castration of the player-soldier through the very same gaming hardware. For example, when considering the hardware expectations for running *Crysis*, one player said, "I was pretty fucking gay for my Core 2 Duo with the Geforce 8800 GTS. Now, I just feel small, limp and ashamed."[43] Or as another player puts it, "*Crysis* may very well kick your computer in the balls."[44] We see the multiple and irresolvable tensions inherent to the crysis mode of the nanowarrior, where the ability to swagger about e-penis power simultaneously involves a risk of e-penis wounding, a deflation caused by the very measure of electronic masculinity: the software of *Crysis* itself. Here, the power enhancement associated with those *little thingies like balls* that drop into your bloodstream is nearly identical to the experience of getting *kicked in the balls*: nano-empowerment only through nano-imperilment. In other words, full-on crysis mode.

Gay for play

Players experience the crysis mode in identifying their own gaming systems as the enabling condition to enter the digital battlefield of *Crysis* and, simultaneously, as the site of limitation or insufficiency relative to the demands of that battlefield. Some players, desperately wanting to join in the fun and live the dream, nevertheless fear for the safety of their computers, and likewise, their own security: "if i put that [*Crysis*] in my computer it would explode."[45] One gamer writes that if he dared to install *Crysis*, the game would "rape my computer in its ass aaaaall night long man. And then the next morning my computor [*sic*] would wake up in a street without it's shell on and be complety [*sic*] and utterly violated. RAPED."[46] For yet another wannabe *Crysis* player, the game's thuggish hardware demands appear as an alluring danger, a fantasy of rough trade: "Just thinking about it makes my anus bleed."[47] The power kicks of *Crysis* expose the technical limits of average graphics processors to handle the game, ubiquitously expressed as bodily – or more specifically, anal – vulnerability: "GPUwise it [*Crysis*] is tearing us a new one."[48] Such transference of anxiety between hardware integrity and personal security, of course, is at odds with the game's own rhetoric of maximum armor. But as we see, this is the nature of the crysis mode: protection enabled only by total exposure to the risks of technology, hardness enabled only by total molecular penetration. In crysis mode, pleasure in extreme militarism comes simultaneously with being forced to one's knees and made to service the fetish object: "*Crysis* can bring even the manliest of rigs to their knees."[49] No doubt about it: "even top end systems were brought to their knees by this game."[50]

Playing within the crysis mode – a volatile condition where even the manliest *tops* might be made into *bottoms* – appears for some gamers as a queering of heterosexual imperatives, or more specifically, a failure of normative masculinity in their own relations to the game. Homophobic and misogynistic responses are unfortunately frequent within the community of *Crysis* players. A few identify their computational shortcomings as sexual debasement, an involuntary servitude to the phallic demands of the game: "i wish my pc didnt suck total penis filth."[51] Others try to reject the near-universal fetishism of *Crysis* as the benchmark for hardware power and "MAXI-MUM penis length," because everyone comes up short in comparison; they no longer want to view themselves as effeminate recipients of its awesome technology: "Come on guys, lets all take our lips off Crysis's dick."[52]

In many ways, then, *Crysis* animates the queerness of the digital battlefield – identified by several players as the "fetish for guys in nano suits" that seems to exist at the core of today's speculative militarism, both in video games and in real life. For example, one gamer describes Nomad's exoskeleton in *Crysis* as "some gay nanosuit. . . . Note of the use of the word gay, not as an insult but as a descriptive word for the sexual status of the nanosuit, which resembles a dudes ballet costume."[53] Yet another gamer, referring to the "Soldier of the Future" suit designed by the U.S. Army's Natick Soldier Center and featured in the ISN publicity videos, writes, "Looks like its for the homosexual type."[54] High-tech combat gear and eroticized images of guys in nanosuits body forth a future-in-the-present that intersects both military utopias and gay fantasies. *Crysis* exposes the extent to which the fetishistic projection of futurity through the playable form of the Soldier of the Future – whether a costume mock-up or a video game avatar – is a fundamentally queer practice. For on the digital battlefield, there is no natural or normative future – only that future in crisis.

Crysis vivifies a future in the present that is entirely, and in every sense, queer. Some players simply cannot handle it: "Yea im done with *Crysis*, too many gay things happened to me in the game. . . . nano suit my ass."[55] The failure of the nanosuit to guarantee hetero-male identity is charged with *gayness*, both sexual and nonsexual. Trying it out, putting it on, seems like risky business. It might even lead to flamboyant performances of gender:

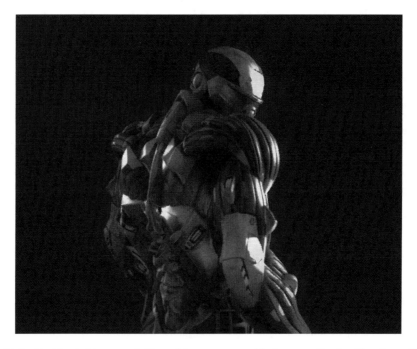

Figure 11.5 Cruising in his nanosuit, Nomad throws us a smoldering, over-the shoulder glance. © 2007 Crytek GmbH.

Figure 11.6   Future Warrior, US Army Natick Soldier Center, 2003. A member of Natick's Operational Forces Interface Group poses in a mock nanosuit costume.

I'm not qualified to review this game. I couldn't play through this whole mess. But I'm an arrogant bitch who has to give his two cents to everything, so here they are. . . . The whole beginning looks like a gay latex fetish porn.[56]

Turning away in frustration from a future redolent of *gay latex fetish porn* ("I couldn't play through"), this gamer nevertheless perceives himself as becoming-queen, an *arrogant bitch*.

Others instead find nothing but pleasure in inhabiting a hardcore future where gender becomes fluid and sexuality opens to play. As one reviewer advises, to get maximum enjoyment from the game, best to just play along with the fetishwear fun and get on with saving the world: "be sure to slap on your gimp suit (errrrrr . . . nanosuit) and let it echo 'MAXIMUM CRISIS' while you're on the biggest mission for mankind's ultimate survival."[57] Wearing the nanosuit might facilitate a kind of sexual awakening: "In *Crysis* you have the luxury of wearing the most sophisticated, and sexy, combat suit known to man kind. This sexiness is called the Nanosuit."[58] Inhabiting the nanosuit not only seems to make players aware of its potential queering effects but likewise solicits their comfort with its ambivalences – an enjoyment of the destabilized relations between soldier and hardware, player and avatar, penetrator and penetrated. As one player attests,

I've take a huge slap . . . Crysis killed me once again. He even rape me so hard, I want a 9800 GTX [Nvidia GeForce graphics card] now! I wasn't expect the game to be SO good. I really had some much fun, some much gorgeous moments.[59]

The imagined phallic demands of the *Crysis* software would seem similar – yet all in good fun? – to slapping and raping the player himself. But such violation is surprisingly expressed as affirmative pleasure ("SO good"). Rather than protection against further penetration, purchasing a more powerful Nvidia 9800 GTX graphics card would instead mean more thoroughly opening oneself to repeat performances, to meet the game's own appetites and ferocious desires on more equal terms, and to get further satisfaction from the intensity of the experience (albeit, perhaps, without suffering so much *screen tearing*). Several male players have described their pleasure in the game with similar masochistic joy, similar fluidity of gender categories, and similar desire to repeat again and again: "im the biggest Crysis whore in the world."[60] These players find the sexual ambiguities animated by *Crysis* to be part of what makes the game so much fun in the first place. One player (self-identified as a straight married man and a military engineer in the U.S. Air Force), confessing his fanboy desire to "get on this game's dick now," imagines an alternative sexual response, a male femininity: "And the Nano-suit makes me wet . . . sooo much fun."[61]

Whether trying to distance themselves from the queer future of everyday nanowars through a vocabulary of homophobic panic or instead blissfully enjoying the ride and looking forward to further adventures, players of *Crysis* adapt to the game, inhabiting the nanosuit as a symbol of their own computational condition, and navigating the crysis mode without ultimate resolution. If there is resistance to the future of nanowar, it is a resistance produced from within, an internal tension between the force objectives of soldier-male militarism and the molecular queering that destabilizes those force objectives from the inside. For recognition that the dominant rhetoric of the game is actually at odds with its own technical representations of nanowar – that is, recognition of the crysis mode – opens players' eyes to the other self-critical and self-queering dimensions of the game. In discussing the internal resistances or tensions experienced in playing with Nomad, a number of players become ever more attentive to the failures of the in-game military rhetoric to live up to its own hype, affording a space for critical analysis and a subversive perspective on the politics at stake. For example, one player writes,

> I also liked that the game tried to be topical. You played as a technically superior enemy to the Koreans, hunting them, which obviously had a relation to ideas about the major Western powers and their foreign policies in mind. This was a battle to win a major resource, possibly a power source. (Much like oil or nuclear power).
> The arrival of the aliens can be read in several ways too. The destructive power unleashed by war and violence perhaps? Or more likely given the nature of the aliens, it was representative of the earth rebelling against mankind's destruction, or even more simply, destruction from ecological change. The earth essentially erupts like a volcano of ice, smothering the tropical jungles. (Referring to current fears about global warming and the melting of the ice-caps.) So it was nice to see some thought went into it.[62]

So amid all the enthusiastic chatter about maximum power and e-penises, some *Crysis* players take the game as an opportunity to question, to evaluate, and to self-reflect on their own participation in everyday nanowars.

Game on

The video games of military nanotechnology make the digital battlefield described by Dutch DeGay into a commonplace reality: "We look at the soldier as the next-generation platform. The *Star Trek* analogy is the Borg, a group of people who are plugged into a supercomputer and part of the collective." Channeling the Borg's notorious motto – *Resistance is futile* – DeGay's vision reveals the conscriptive logic of the digital battlefield. Soldiers would be totally *plugged* into the data network of C4ISR (Command, Control, Communications, Computers, Intelligence, Surveillance, and Reconnaissance), merging with nano and other technologies that promise to turn war into a video game. Indeed, games such as *Crysis* that make the digital battlefield into a playable experience become part of the apparatus of training and induction.

As DeGay has said,

> It's no shock to see that technology being used for training [soldiers]. . . . It has always been a challenge to get the time, space and resources to train soldiers, so video games give leaders and commanders an easier portable training option.

And likewise, a recruitment option:

> It's not a stretch of the imagination that people who have the chance to see the capabilities of the next generation of soldier [in a video game] . . . might find the idea of being a soldier more appealing. Or at the very least give them a better idea of what it might be like to be a soldier.

DeGay has served as technical advisor for several games, including *Ghost Recon: Advanced Warfighter* (2006), *Ghost Recon: Future Soldier* (2013), *EndWar* (2008), and others. Authenticity is key, according to DeGay, in order to give players "as real a military experience possible in a video game."[63] Certainly, the video games that stage everyday nanowars in our own living rooms attend directly to military research programs that industriously transform science fiction into reality, making the future as immediate and immersive as possible, something we can all enjoy. Perhaps resistance is futile. As one player has said of *Crysis*, "Now that i've tried it i can't resist it."[64]

And yet, in making nanowars playable, these games stage a condition of interminable crysis, where resistance and accommodation to the digital battlefield are experienced simultaneously: an effect of the dynamic tension between the molar and the molecular, the command core and the network, the *e-penis function* and the *e-masculation function*. By performing the play of sexual difference, morphing sexualities, and molecular fluidity all at the site of the warrior body, mapping directly onto a player's own wet relationship with high-tech hardware, games such as *Crysis* spectacularly deconstruct themselves. They render the serious notion of *everyday nanowars* laughable, something of a pleasurable joke. They open up a queer resistance *from the inside* against the otherwise overwhelming futility of resistance.

Upon inserting *Crysis* into any computer, the pre-credits launch sequence to the game – featuring the resonant male voice of the nanosuit – announces that players of this game will experience the ultimate in high-tech digital warfare: "MAXIMUM GAME." But as many players have noted, what the voice actually says is entirely ambiguous. As one player put it, summing up the indistinction, the irresolvable double-speak and double-think of the crysis mode in action, "i swear to god that i thought he said 'MAXIMUM GAY.'"[65]

Let's all play.

Notes

1 Timothy Lenoir, "All but War Is Simulation: The Military-Entertainment Complex," *Configurations* 8 (2000): 289–335.
2 DeGay quoted in Courtney E. Howard, "Fueling the Future," *Military & Aerospace Electronics* 7, no. 7 (2006): 26–31, 26.
3 Alexander R. Galloway and Eugene Thacker, *The Exploit: A Theory of Networks* (Minneapolis: University of Minnesota Press, 2007), 155–157.
4 U.S. Army Research Office, "Institute for Soldier Nanotechnologies," October 2001, www.aro.army. mil/soldiernano/finalsolicit.pdf (now available through the Internet Archive's Wayback Machine).
5 Shannon L. Callahan, "Nanotechnology in a New Era of Strategic Competition," *Joint Force Quarterly* 26 (2000): 20–26, 25, 20; referencing Scott Gourley, "Lethal Combination," *Jane's Defence Weekly* 30, no. 14 (1998): 39–42.
6 U.S. Army Research Office, "Institute for Soldier Nanotechnologies."
7 *Rainbow Six: Lockdown* (Red Storm Entertainment, Ubisoft, 2005), Mission 2—Operation: Backlash, Briefing 1/5.
8 Stephen Kline, Nick Dyer-Witheford, and Greig De Peuter, *Digital Play: The Interaction of Technology, Culture, and Marketing* (Montréal: McGill-Queen's University Press, 2003).
9 Michel de Certeau, *The Practice of Everyday Life*, trans. Steven Rendall (Berkeley: University of California Press, 1984), xii. For examples, see Henry Jenkins, *Convergence Culture: Where Old and New Media Collide* (New York: New York University Press, 2006).
10 Diemer quoted in Logan Booker, "Inside Crysis," *Atomic: Maximum Power Computing*, September 21, 2006, www.atomicmpc.com.au/Feature/60160,inside-crysis.aspx.
11 AkumaX, "Why Do We Play Videogames?," *Giant Bomb*, September 17, 2008, www.giantbomb.com/ profile/AkumaX/blog/why-do-we-play-videogames/11549/.
12 Jordan Roher, "Fantesticle Penisula Adventure," *Not Clickable*, October 28, 2007, www.notclickable. com/blog/fantesticle-penisula-adventure/.
13 danni Marchant, "M for Manly," response to Benji, "—>What Would You Guys Rate Crysis 2? (Sticky Please)<—," May 22, 2011, *Game Skyrim*, www.gameskyrim.com/what-would-you-guys-rate-crysi s-sticky-please-t105930.html. According to Benji, the original *Crysis* sets the benchmark: "10/10: Crysis – Not safe for work or little kids: M for Manly."
14 —Anna—, comment #256, response to Polkastripe, "Girl Gamers," *GameSpot*, November 17, 2007, www.gamespot.com/forums/offtopic-discussion-314159273/girl-gamers-26040943/?page=6. Ultimately, —Anna—'s "real" gender could not be resolved.

15 On the dynamics of online gender performance, see Sherry Turkle, *Life on the Screen: Identity in the Age of the Internet* (New York: Simon and Schuster, 1995); Allucquère Rosanne Stone, *The War of Desire and Technology at the Close of the Mechanical Age* (Cambridge, MA: MIT Press, 1995); and Sue-Ellen Case, *The Domain-Matrix: Performing Lesbian at the End of Print Culture* (Bloomington: Indiana University Press, 1996).

16 Dan Adams, "Crysis Review: Crytek Blasts Back onto the PC with the Most Beautiful Kind of Violence," *IGN*, November 12, 2007, http://pc.ign.com/articles/834/834614p1.html.

17 Matt Bertz, "Farcrysis," *Game Informer* 18, no. 1 (2008): 96.

18 Shadonic0, response to jpear5000, "So We Have All Learned Something from Crysis," *Crysis* Message Board for PC, *GameFAQs*, July 4, 2008, www.gamefaqs.com/boards/detail.php?board=931665&topic=44051199.

19 Broadsword, response to FANBOI69, "NANO SUIT: What Does the 'NANO' Suit Do That We Haven't Already Seen?," *inCrysis*, August 22, 2007, http://incrysis.com/forums/viewtopic.php?pid=147758.

20 Dustin Edmunds, "Crysis," *Im Having a Crysis*, November 1, 2007, http://dustball21d.blogspot.com/2007/11/crysis.html. While genetic transformations are barely hinted in the first game, *Crysis 2* makes clear that the nanosuit remakes soldiers at the level of DNA and neurotransmitters.

21 peacemaker898, response to FANBOI69, "NANO SUIT: What Does the 'NANO' Suit Do That We Haven't Already Seen?," *inCrysis*, August 22, 2007, http://incrysis.com/forums/viewtopic.php?pid=147758.

22 Milos, response to imacker, "Is It Just Me or Is Crysis Boring?," *Crysis Online*, November 19, 2007, www.crysis-online.com/forum/index.php?topic=14615. On gender as performative process, see Judith Butler, *Gender Trouble: Feminism and the Subversion of Identity* (New York: Routledge, 1990).

23 redwinedrummer, "Crysis Alert. Crysis Alert.," *Reverse-Engineering the Cross-Com: The Technological Endeavors of an Advanced Warfighter*, November 29, 2007, http://redwinedrummer.wordpress.com/2007/11/29/crysis-alert-crysis-alert/.

24 Matt Bertz, "Meanwhile, Across the Island . . .," *Game Informer* 18, no. 12 (2008): 126.

25 Emil, response to Alec Meer, "Crysis in Crisis," December 17, 2007.

26 "The Top 50 Games of 2007: *Crysis*," *Game Informer* 18, no. 1 (2008): 42.

27 Eric, response to Alec Meer, "Crysis in Crisis," December 17, 2007.

28 l88bastard, "I Hate Crysis," *SLI Zone*, December 3, 2008, http://forums.slizone.com/index.php?showtopic=30865.

29 Pat M., "Customer Testimonial," BuyDirectPC, January 8, 2009, www.buydirectpc.com/reviews.html.

30 Chad Sapieha, "*Crysis* (M): Super-Realistic Violent Sci-Fi Shooter," *Common Sense Media*, January 2008, www.commonsensemedia.org/game-reviews/Crysis.html.

31 SunsBalla23, "Great!," response to Sapieha, "*Crysis* (M)," January 28, 2008.

32 dudeworld1 [Text Comment], January 13, 2009, response to cswong1990, "Crysis Cinematic Intro," YouTube, February 4, 2008, www.youtube.com/watch?v=5QzKIeLRVtM.

33 polystethylene, response to Bot-IGN, "Crysis Warhead System Requirements Revealed," Message Boards, *IGN*, August 14, 2008, http://boards.ign.com/Boards/Message.aspx?brd=9108&topic=169131636&page=1.

34 Poobah, response #20 to Poobah, "Buying a Rig to Run Crysis," *Crysis Online*, August 18, 2008, www.crysis-online.com/forum/index.php/topic,25098.0.html.

35 jazzzy, responses #19 and #20 to Poobah, "Buying a Rig to Run Crysis," August 17–18, 2008.

36 alexander224, response #60 to HektikNinja, "What Are the Specs of Your Rig?," *Zoklet*, February 5, 2009, http://bbs.zoklet.net/showthread.php?t=4253.

37 Billy Bob Joe, response to Spiffymarlin, "How Well Would This Run?," Crysis Message Board for PC, *GameFAQs*, July 13, 2008, www.gamefaqs.com/boards/genmessage.php?board=931665&topic=44239785.

38 xtrick, response to angelhair, "Crysis SP Rlsed," *FPSLabs*, October 27, 2007, http://hardware.gotfrag.com/portal/forums/thread/314936/.

39 Rockefella, response #35, "PC Discussion Thread," *Ultimatecarpage*, February 4, 2006, www.ultimatecarpage.com/forum/gaming/23940-pc-discussion-thread.html.

40 Sherry Turkle, *The Second Self: Computers and the Human Spirit*, 20th anniversary ed. (Cambridge, MA: MIT Press, 2005), 171.

41 Turkle, *Second Self*, 176.

42 txtmstrjoe, "The Crysis Controversy," *Overclock.net*, July 18, 2008, www.overclock.net/blogs/txtmstrjoe/591-crysis-controversy.html.

43 Camerhil, response #33 to Kuactet, "Crysis (Not 'Far Cry 2')," *Cracked*, August 7, 2007, www.cracked.com/forums/index.php?topic=19492.

44 Adams, "Crysis Review."

45 iIiLukeyiIi, response to infrequentdelta, "Crysis Nanosuit [High Quality]," *GameTrailers*, October 9, 2008, www.gt.tv/player/usermovies/268219.html.

46 afrospezz, response to KoroushGhazi, "Crysis Demo – Destructible Vegetation DX9," YouTube, October 2008, www.youtube.com/watch?v=8SkXuoElvXY.

47 Steakslim, response #11 to Curium244, "780i Asus P5N-T Deluxe," *Crysis Online*, December 12, 2007, www.crysis-online.com/forum/index.php?topic=16845.

48 SuperFly03, response #8 to James_8970, "*Crysis*, Quad Core Optimized?" *Xtreme CPU*, November 18, 2007, http://forum.xcpus.com/pc-gaming/7119-crysis-quad-core-optimized.html.

49 Chris Swertfeger, "Intel E7200 2.53GHz Dual Core Processor," *Techware Labs*, November 20, 2008, www.techwarelabs.com/reviews/processors/intel_e7200_2_53ghz_dual_core_processor/index.shtml.

50 SightseeMC, response to Alec Meer, "Crysis in Crisis," December 15, 2007.

51 astromario, response to "*Crysis*: Oceanic Onslaught Gameplay," *GameTrailers*, July 6, 2008, www.gametrailers.com/player/27855.html.

52 SuperLuigiBros, response to cornholio12, "*Crysis* Graphics Overrated!," *E-mpire*, May 30, 2006, http://forums.e-mpire.com/archive/index.php/t-57239.html.

53 gatman, response #161 to PE2, "Things You'd Like to See Changed/Added/Removed in Crysis So Far," *inCrysis*, September 14, 2006, http://incrysis.com/forums/viewtopic.php?id=292.

54 Led_poison, response to knowledge-funk, "New US Military Technology – The Exoskeleton," Forums, *GameSpot*, March 9, 2008, www.gamespot.com/pages/forums/show_msgs.php?topic_id=26280598.

55 xXxKEVxXx, response #20 to AUA_Violator, "Patch 1.1 Has Finaly Killed Crysis for Me," *Crysis Online*, January 15, 2008, www.crysis-online.com/forum/index.php?topic=19081.

56 CoinMatze, "Like That Hot, Dumb Girl in School," *Giant Bomb*, July 21, 2008, www.giantbomb.com/crysis/3030-11757/user-reviews/2200-779.

57 Kalidh Mohamed, "Crysis Review," *Middle East Gamers*, November 13, 2007, www.megamers.com/pc/review.php?game_category=2&article_id=2041.

58 Teddy Pierson [a.k.a. -1313-Evil_Homer], "Crysis Nanosuit," *Planet Crysis*, 2008, http://planetcrysis.gamespy.com/View.php?view=GameInfo.Detail&id=4.

59 svenminoda, response to washd123, "My Final Crysis Review+ LVL16," *washd123's Game Pad*, *GameTrailers*, December 1, 2007, http://washd123.gametrailers.com/gamepad/index.php?action=viewblog&id=206855.

60 rott112, response #3 to rot112, "Dox 180.70.. Thank You Dox," *NotebookReview*, November 28, 2008, http://forum.notebookreview.com/showthread.php?t=325733.

61 easy_bake, response to Tangojorg, "BTW (Crysis: DEMO and BETA)," *BoxHeads*, October 29, 2007, www.theboxheads.net/modules.php?name=Forums&file=viewtopic&t=4410.

62 Matt, response to Alec Meer, "Crysis in Crisis," December 15, 2007.

63 DeGay quoted in John Gaudiosi, "Red Storm Entertainment Enlists Army Specialist for GRAW," Xbox website, May 16, 2006, www.xbox.com/en-US/games/t/tomclancysghostreconadvancedwarfighterxbox360/20060516-soldierinterview2.htm.

64 Nocutius, response #21 to werty316, "Crysis Demo – The Countdown Is Over!," *Bjorn3d*, October 27, 2007, www.bjorn3d.com/forum/showthread.php?t=18951.

65 OldParr, response to M337ING, "*Crysis* Multiplayer Walkthrough," *GameTrailers*, September 18, 2007, www.gametrailers.com/player/usermovies/107487.html. This polymorphous line has now spread over the Internet, made into gamer videos and ringtones. For example, see the video by ReacticFlyerTests, "Crytek Maximum Gay," YouTube, August 26, 2009, www.youtube.com/watch?v=B-kQzUeEtFxM.

12

PRACTISING MEDIA ARCHAEOLOGY

Creative methodologies for remediation

Jussi Parikka

A lot of media–archaeological work is executed in artistic ways. Already the earlier interest in historically as well as theoretically rich investigations into resurfacing patterns of use, hidden and neglected inventions, as well as the multitemporal histories of devices and media technological contexts were accompanied by original artistic practices that were creating archaeologies of media in the present. A lot of media-archaeological theory has been open to accepting a range of media artistic avant-garde as part of the archaeological inquiries, in which the methodology becomes a way of critically questioning new technologies; Siegfried Zielinski (1999: 22) writes of

> those among the avant-garde of electronics in whose heads and hands the new techniques do not become independent ends in themselves, but are constantly irritated and reflected upon: artists like Valie Export, David Larcher, Nam June Paik, Steina and Woody Vasulka, or Peter Weibel.

Addressing media-archaeological creative practices, this chapter presents some of the work in this stream of interest, [. . .] and taps into the question of how media archaeology can work as a method for artistic engagement in present-day media culture.

[. . .]

Assembling the present past

Yet exactly what media–archaeological art means is less often articulated. We know it deals with engaging the past and learning from the past media cultures in order to understand present mediated, globalized network culture through artworks executed in various media. But what, more specifically, have been the works we could see as media-archaeological? As a form of brainstorming (and with help of such early texts as Huhtamo 1995), I tried to come up with at least six different ways in which one can see old media technology and themes resurrected in the contemporary context – whether in galleries, festivals or online. Of course, several of the projects in these categories overlap with each other, and the list is not intended to be anything more than a heuristic tool to illuminate what is being talked about in this chapter.

1.   Artistic works that visually engage with historical themes; for example in more cinematic pieces, such as Lynn Hershman Leeson's *Conceiving Ada* (1997), which reimagines folds of time between digital culture and the past heroine of early computers and software, Lady Ada Lovelace (1815–52). Also, in the wider popular culture, media-archaeological themes can be found in such products as the popular online clip "Pixels" by Patrick Jean and Onemoreproduction (www.onemoreproduction.com) in which 8-bit characters invade New York. Retro-themes can be seen linked to the media-cultural nostalgia drive (Suominen 2008).

2.   Invoking alternative histories, which are able to offer critical insights into the assumed-natural state of digitality – whether technological or social – through the art piece that goes against the grain in terms of the materials it uses, or the narratives of use. Good examples include Zoe Beloff's cinematic constructions of gendered histories of technology, of mediums and devices of control; Paul DeMartinis's *The Messenger* installation (1998/2005) investigates telecommunications from an alternative perspective; various steampunk-themed ideas, performances and devices kicked off by Gibson and Sterling's *The Difference Engine* novel as a phantasy [*sic*] of the information age of the nineteenth century.[1]

3.   Art of/from obsolescence: pieces and practice that use obsolescent materials and solutions to engage with emerging media culture – or just investigate the potentials in reusing and hacking electronic media. Examples could include: Vuk Cosic's ASCII[2] art that refers directly to media-archaeological investigations into remediation of textuality, marginalized technologies and "useless" media solutions: the Refunct Media installation (by Klomp, Gaulon and Gieskes) that rewires obsolete media into a new media ecology (http://vimeo.com/27417437, date accessed 5 Nov 2011); festivals like the Art of the Overhead Projector-series in Sweden, organized by Linda Hilfling and Kristoffer Gansing, on obsolete image media; 8-bit sound cultures as inspiration for thinking about "new" digital culture and its artistic practices, as well as more recent but still out-dated examples, such as Alexei Shulgin's live rock performances with a 386dx processor computer and Windows 3.1 Operating System in 1998. Perhaps we could even consider Bernie Lubell's various wood installation works across the years as a case in point – using an "obsolete" material to construct "high-tech" machines.

4.   Imaginary media that are constructed and not just imagined: devices that are dead, or were never built, being reconstructed and re-employed, for their curiosity value but also to investigate the nature of progress, change and the novelty-obsessed technological culture that is still, however, embedded in (planned) obsolescence; [. . . such as] Gebhard Sengmüller's *A Parallel Image* installation, DeMarinis's works, such as *The Edison Effect* and *Gray Matter*, modulate already existing ideas in sound recording and electrical communications into inventive directions and concrete assemblages. Julien Maire is as clearly a media-archaeological artist with a fascination in re-investigating past apparatuses, but modified in creative ways. Bruce Sterling's influential *Dead Media* project and such artistic parts of it as the online interactive "Embrace the Decay" work, can be seen dealing with themes of technological disappearance and remediation (www.moca.org/museum/digital_gallery.php, accessed 27 Nov 2011).

5.   Media-archaeological art that draws from concrete archives – in other words, artistic practice informed by archival work and historical materials, a direct way of working like a historian but for artistic ends. Such work is well documented in Sven Spieker's (2008) art-historical take in his *The Big Archive* (see also Merewether 2006), and visible in works of such contemporary artists as Gustav Deutsch (*Film ist*), Bill Morrison's work with "orphan film material" (for instance in the film *Light is Calling*, 2003) and that of Sarah Angliss, who

is able to draw on her background at the Science Museum, London, and through her sound and robotic performances develops themes from media history. In addition, for example, there is the work of David Link, addressing the Manchester "Baby" (Small-Scale Experimental Machine, more officially) computer, which was the first stored-program computer, and the Love Letter Generator-program by Christopher Strachey (1916–1975). As an artist, Link works almost like a historian, but one who does not express himself (only) in writings, but in constructions – history becoming media art.

6. Media-archaeological art methods that dig not only into the past, but also inside the machine and address the present – but technically "archaeological" – buried conditions for our media culture. Such projects that focus on opening up the machines, as well as speaking to a range of important contemporary processes, protocols, software and hardware environments with art/activist practices that at times come close to circuit bending and hardware hacking include, for example, The Institute for Algorhythmics and Microresearch Lab in Berlin; Rosa Menkman's projects such as *The Collapse of PAL* performed as part of the Transmediale 2011 festival; Matthias Fitz's investigations into electromagnetic fields in his installation work (*Re-Creation of an Unstable Universe*, exhibited at the Art Claims Impulse-gallery in Berlin in Spring 2011); and, for instance, even Cory Arcangel's interventions into game cultures, such as hacking the Super Mario console game in *Super Mario Clouds* (2002).

[. . .]

Media-archaeological art as time-machines

Media archaeology is always in danger of veering towards excavations of curious instruments and odd gadgets just for their own sake and hence losing the wider political contexts in which technology takes part in governing bodies, affording perceptions and building platforms for social relations, work, entertainment, and identity. All of these are questions which cultural studies has identified as crucially political in the sense of the politics of everyday life. Politics of media-archaeological art *has* tapped into gender (Zoe Beloff), the aesthetico-scientific basis of technopolitics (DeMarinis) and ideologies of technological progress (a wide range of different artists), as well as environmental issues (Hertz). Furthermore, I am interested in the ways media-archaeological reconstructions and "thinkering" (Huhtamo 2010) can mobilize new forms of temporality, which act as subtle ways of rethinking myths of progress, linearity of time and teleological assumptions concerning evolution of media culture that underpin the more mainstream ways of seeing how media technology is part of our lives.

Also outside media-archaeological discussions, remix and remediation have gained a strong foothold as key aesthetic processes and artistic practices of digital culture (Campanelli 2010; Bolter and Grusin 1999). These can be seen as emblematic of aesthetic practices that focus on the use of archives and existing material for creative purposes, and, as such, also rethink the notion of creativity outside myths of romanticized originality. Novel assemblages consisting of already-existing material – whether material that is found, or that is intentionally preserved in archival institutions – can be seen as fresh, interesting and even political. Such remix-practices in media arts have produced a number of interesting works. For instance, Paul D. Miller, DJ Spooky, is a prime example of thinking through both DJ culture and theory, as well as the historical layers of media culture evident in such works as the Errata Erratum remix-machine that draws on the ideas on creativity of Marcel Duchamp (1887–1968), and extends to thinking of musical storage media such as phonographs as "memory game devices" (www.moca.org/museum/digital-Gallery.php, accessed 27 Nov 2011). Of course, in everyday culture, remixes are part of the wide possibilities offered by digital tools and online platforms – YouTube is filled with creative amateur remixes, that are rethinking originality, remastering, mash-ups, and hence new and old, in curious hybrids. This is why we need to be aware of the wider infiltration of what were traditionally seen as art methods as part of everyday creativity in post-Fordist cultures where a lot of avant-garde art discourses and views have been adopted in how we work and perceive labor (see Lazzarato 2008).

In terms of media-archaeological art, lots of the ideas seem to mix historical time scales intentionally. Laurent Mignonneau and Christa Sommerer's *The Life Writer* (2006) mixes up mechanical typewriter technology with production of genetic algorithms; Julien Maire's *The Inverted Cone* (2010) is a complex assemblage that investigates the nature of time, and clashes pasts and presents in its Henri Bergson-influenced visual worlds. In addition, Tom Jennings's *The Story Teller* is here a useful way to illustrate the idea of media-archaeological art as *an assemblage*, a curious time-machine (Huhtamo 1995) that does not always transport us back (or forth) in time but involves multiple temporalities in itself.[3] *The Story Teller* reuses ideas and obsolete material from media history, including a teletype machine, a papertape reader, and a speech-phoneme processing system. While the performance piece, which includes reciting eight hours of narrative about Alan Turing, can be seen to touch on the history of computing, and Turing's idea concerning the infinite paper-based calculation machine, it also involves a more complex mix of media. Referring back not only to computing, but to telegrams, punched paper, old storage forms, as well as the mechanical basis of computing, the piece is itself a multiple layer of different technologies and hence time scales. It fits in with a notion of history proposed by Fernand Braudel (1980): history as a multi-layered, multi-rhythmic, concerted plurality of various times – a polyphonic history.

[. . .]

What media-archeological practices are good at doing is forcing us to think about time as *pleated*. Outside the linear "earlier–later" time axis, this shows that time spreads in all directions. Hence, many of the important discussions in society concerning machines and technology have to do with convincing people what is new and what is obsolescent, and finding subtle ways to impose such categories – through marketing, legislating and political measures. One of the most urgent debates since the 1990s has been the temporality of the network culture, and the various attempts to capture "Internet time" as a specific form of speed – of both progress and work processes.[4] The unfounded belief in the permanence of the digital as a material grounding for long-term storage is constantly questioned by things breaking down [. . .]. Hence, ephemerality seems a more apt description of the workings of memory and time in digital culture – but not without a material grounding again (see Chun 2011). Projects that engage with slowing down time, address digital to analogue translations like the *Embroidered Text Message* (2009) by Ginger Anyhow (gingeranyhow.com/textmessages.html, accessed 28 Nov 2011), or then investigate durations that are beyond our human time-span are as much emblematic of this problem of time and storage in digital culture as the ideas presented in previous chapters. As we will see below, these are also crucial questions concerning information technology waste and the political side of research into the "deep time relations of media" (Zielinski 2006; cf. Gabrys 2011).

Dead media or zombie media?

Siegfried Zielinski's concept of "deep time" is adopted from geological research and a focus on a horizon of durations of not only thousands, or millions, but billions of years of history. For Zielinski, this idea points towards the need to look at media too in terms of their long-term relations that radically step out of the short-term use value that is promoted by capitalist media industries. As a political and ecological twist to this, one project that takes its impulse directly from media-archaeological and dead-media debates is the Dead Media Lab by Garnet Hertz – the already-mentioned California-based artist and writer. Hertz's creative practice is informed by deep involvement in various "tinkering" methodologies, from circuit bending to DIY robotics, and he has been able to connect that with media-archaeological interests – something we have, in collaboration, also called "zombie media" of the living dead of media culture (Hertz and Parikka 2012).

Hertz's project picks up Bruce Sterling's call for a sustained interest in knowledge of media that are dead, and discarded outside normal use in everyday life – but still can have much artistic and other value. Hertz twists this further into an ecological project, or even ecosophic in the sense that Félix Guattari (2000) talks of ecosophy as reinvention of the various transversal relations between the social, the psyche, the economic and the environment. Dead Media Lab becomes hence much more than a lab for repurposing information technology – Hertz quotes the statistics on the hundreds of millions of still-operational devices that are discarded in the US alone. It is also a social laboratory for those practices that engage both in thinking about future green information technologies and in promoting community engagement in DIY methods that are inventive everyday reuses and appropriations of the art methods of the early twentieth-century avant-garde – repurposing existing media and "readymades" becomes less about Duchamp and more about circuit bending and hacking workshops at community centers. It closely relates to the "rematerializing" tendencies in electronic waste that force us to think about the *natural* history of electronics, well analyzed by Jennifer Gabrys (2011).

The link to media archaeology becomes most clearly voiced in this part of his Dead Media Lab call – innovation through media history:

> The history of obsolete information technology is fruitful ground for unearthing innovative projects that floundered due to a mismatch between technology and socioeconomic contexts. Because social and economic variables continually shift through time, forgotten histories and archaeologies of media provide a wealth of useful ideas for contemporary development. In other words, the history of technological obsolescence is cheap R&D that offers fascinating seeds of development for those willing to dig through it. This lab encourages the study of obsolescence and reuse in media history as a foundation for understanding the dynamics of media change.
>
> (www.conceptlab.com/deadmedia/)

As cheap R&D, media-archaeological ideas about memory, time, duration and obsolescence are part of a wider artist-activist engagement. Less a textual method, circuit bending and hardware hacking are related to thinking about media history in fresh ways that also engage with the important question of how we are able to reuse devices that too easily and too quickly end up in waste sites.

Hence, work such as Hertz's ties in to both the lineage of media-archaeological artists such as DeMarinis, who has also been interested in the wider environmental ideas concerning media (nature as media) and equally to such initiatives as, for instance, the Mediashed in the UK. Mediashed key activity revolves around the call for "free media" that are outside the proprietary platforms, and hence open both legally and technically. Mediashed's work has focused on both software and reusing waste and junk materials (such as electronic devices and parts) for community and artistic purposes. In addition, they have shown an interest in "obsolescent" forms of communication in their EcoMedia theme days and projects that expand the idea of communication to various techniques, from shouting, spitting and smelling to pigeon communication, all found in natural bodies. (For a connection to media archeology and imaginary media, see Parikka 2011.)

In such projects, we are moving father away from what has usually been the safe ground of media archaeology. Even if "redundancy," "obsolescence," "time" and "dead media" connected the approaches of both free media activists and media archaeologists, the latter have, as Kahn too flagged, been reluctant to be that political. Yet to me, this link that Hertz is able to make is of crucial value in expanding media-archaeological theory and art methods. Hence, in addition to Mediashed, another clear link would also be the UK-based Redundant Technology Initiative (http://rti.lowtech.org/intro/) that grounds all of its activity in "technology that they could acquire for nothing." As such, it has meant concrete spaces for Free Media tinkering (Access Space is characterized on their website as "an open-access digital reuse centre" for learning and teaching), as well as projects that recircuit back to recent media history, even in the form of Mac Hypercards, ASCII-text, 28.8K faxes repurposed as part of an imaginary TV-feedback system, and manifestos promoting "low tech" (http://rti.lowtech.org/).

As we argue with Hertz (Hertz and Parikka 2012), techniques of media-archaeological art like circuit bending are crucial for a wider environmental consciousness. The aesthetic tactics and various "minor" methods such as circuit bending, hardware tinkering and so forth are important links to a wider activist stance towards technical media. The increasingly closed nature of consumer technology (see Guins 2009) is the other side of the coin in this call to reuse old technology. This closedness is what really defines proprietary platforms. A large amount of current consumer technology is not meant to be opened, tinkered with and reused, and this is guaranteed through various measures, ranging from Digital Rights Management that legally restricts users' possible actions to the various design strategies that make it very difficult to engage in, for instance, circuit bending. Such techniques can indeed be seen as "minor" but they are important for illuminating how technological solutions relate to power relations. Even design solutions – using glue instead of screws – are part of this wider regime of controlling patterns of (re)use (cf. Kittler 1997).

Furthermore, this relates to the wider politics of "planned obsolescence" (Hertz and Parikka 2012), which can be seen as the background for much of consumer society, including technology. In such perspectives, the wider history of reuse in avant-garde art from Duchamp to DJing and VJing not only is about innovations through remixing and mash-ups, but is set against the demand for originality and newness that drives production of technology. As a form of governing production and demanding constant replaceability, "planned obsolescence" has, since the 1930s, been seen as a form of enforced obsolescence and as supporting new product design. Yet, during the last decades it has become even more evident that such a drive for creation is unsupportable in terms of the ecological load it creates and distributes very unevenly as part of the global economy.

Signal-based media art

As the above section, as a brief glimpse into various activist contexts of addressing obsolescence, demonstrates, the importance of the "material" is very central to media-archaeological artists. As addressed in earlier chapters [of *What is Media Archaeology?*], the materiality of technical media is, however, in itself problematic, and was addressed for a long time as "immateriality." The 1990s cyberculture was keen to address new information technologies as virtual, which I believe was merely a euphemism for "imperceived" and led to a lot of neglect in terms of trying to understand the ways in which power was circuiting itself through the technologies. Kittler's as well as media archaeologists' influence was to give insight into how the seemingly fleeting and ephemeral was grounded in politics of hardware, code, signal transmission and protocols.

[. . .]

The Berlin-situated Institute for Algorhythmics brands itself as "listening and looking for an epistemology of everyday life" (www.algorhythmics.com/, accessed 17 Nov 2011) which also reveals a further side to the media materialities of the information economy – not immaterial, but temporal:

> Algorhythms occur when real matter is controlled by symbolic structures like instructions written as code. Algorhythms show us that our digital culture is not immaterial, but divided in time. Time + music becomes important for understanding media. With enough scientific effort the invisible electronic or electromagnetic (wireless) signals can be made hearable. Listening to those digitally modulated signals, you can hear the rhythmic character of the signals of most digitally working devices and also of wireless consumer electronic networks like WLAN, GSM, UMTS, Bluetooth, digital TV and Radio, et cetera.
>
> (Ibid.)

The Institute taps into two key themes in contemporary media arts and theory: sound and algorhythmic culture. As such, it is able to use aesthetic methods as epistemological investigations – formations of knowledge, or how we understand and know about our technical world around us that is often structured as "imperceptible," except for the content of what is being transmitted to consumers.

These practical methods for epistemological investigations into contemporary culture also go by the name of "Sonic Archaeology" (www.sonicarcheology.net/, accessed 25 Nov 2011) as coined by Shintaro Miyazaki (2011). Sonic Archaeology investigates various software and hardware methodologies through which to map the quite often invisible and imperceptible electromagnetic waves as well as investigations into computers, mobile phones, mp3-players and digital cameras. Hence, archaeology becomes a way of understanding how such devices structure the everyday worlds and temporal sequences in which we live in technological societies – but instead of speaking generally about technological society, they look at the concrete processes and gadgets in which such traditional cultural studies concepts as power now reside.[5] Archaeologies of the present do not focus only on historical time, but also on the way in which contemporary technologies are archives that store, process and distribute information. There is a parallel development that at least implicitly picks up on Kittler's tripartite "commands, addresses, data" division [. . .] as the methodological guideline: media archaeologies of looking at media history through technical terms that apply to institutionalization or systematization of what we used to call "power, subjects and experience," and concretely, how such new forms of concepts for humanities' analysis of technology afford investigations into the insides of machines as well.

[. . .]

Signals, but also values, tubes, antennas, telephone exchanges and semiconductors are revealed [by such analyses] as much more than enabling technical parts. They can also reveal a lot about the social and power implications of technologies, and illuminate a very important transversal theme: the components are often the more fluid bits, that establish intermedial relations, and as such are temporally and media-archaeologically often more important than what we see as coherent media (televisions, computers, cinema).

Values and tubes are *transmedia* components (cf. Ernst 2008) that were essential for the innovations from telegraphy to television and computing; antennas are the often neglected part of our wireless and transmission cultures; telephone exchanges are a similar "switch" in terms of how communication works – a good example of mobilizing old exchange technologies into a politically hot topic is by the ex-Mongrel-group and UK-based artist trio Harwood, Wright, Yokokoji in their *Tantalum Memorial*, which ties old telephone switch technology together with Congolese alternative practices of "radio trottoire" communication in the context of mining of Coltan, an essential mineral for our media technologies such as mobile phones, primarily found in the Congo.[6]

[...]

Scientist-artists, or just informed users?

Much of what has been introduced above – the projects, some of the methods, and themes that characterize media-archaeological art – begs the question: do we then have to become engineers to say and do anything interesting and accurate about current media culture? Luckily, the ways to engage effectively and critically with media culture are not that narrowly defined – but what these artists and projects flag is the need to dig deeper than textual analysis. In a way, much of the demand for a thorough, meticulous and disciplinarily open analysis and creation is expressed by Zielinski in his own way of feeding anarchaeological ideas toward practice. It is the step from consumption to production:

> The only effective form of intervention in this world is to learn its laws of operation and try to undermine or overrun them. One has to give up being a player at a fair-ground sideshow and become an operator within the technical world where one can work on developing alternatives. For artistic praxis with computers in particular, this means learning the codes they function with.
>
> (Zielinski 2006: 260)

This is an important call for media theory and practice, and resonates with some other voices of recent years: Alex Galloway and Eugene Thacker (2007:100) claim that "Today to write theory means to write code," whilst referring to Geert Lovink's earlier call against the "vapour theory" of unspecified mysticism and rhetoric that fails to attach to the actual practices which constitute media culture. Similarly, one could say that designers are actually in a privileged position concerning media critique with the ability to create new media objects, processes and uses – in short, worlds. Several arguments seem to carry the same message: we need to understand the various modalities of our tools for thought – such tools are not only about text and writing. In the same way that university curricula and ways of assessing students are slowly taking into account that verbal and written works are not the only modality of expression, and that one can do media critique through production (audiovisual, software- and network-based, performance, installation and so forth), there is an urgent need to promote the understanding of such practices in/as research. And yet, having said that, I am a vigorous defender of the need for theory – traditions of philosophy, critical theory and innovative conceptualizations that are crucial ways to mobilize the technical and practical as part of resistance.

In terms of digital culture and society, the theme of "media education" has been important for years. An understanding and basic knowledge of uses of, for instance, computers was on the agenda already in the 1980s with the emergence of the first computers. These were integrated into school curriculums too – from basic workshops I attended when at school in Finland (where the pupils often knew more than the teacher, who had not really used a computer herself before), to the wide implementation of cybernetics and training of programming in Eastern Europe,[7] and, for instance, in the UK the BBC Microcomputer and the educational programmes in schools and on television (*The Computer Programme*, BBC2, 1982).

Some recent projects have actually engaged in media education as well, but with a special focus on old media. A good example is the Science Museum (London) workshop on old "groove" technologies of recording, from Edison wax discs to more recent types of inscription technologies. Together with scholar and writer Katy Price, Aleksander Kolkowski worked with a youth group as part of the Museum's Oramics special project (which in itself has tackled a media-archaeological theme, the female pioneer Daphne Oram's early British music synthesizing machine from the 1960s).

Here, the students were allowed a hands-on approach to obsolete recording technologies, which, as Kolkowski argues, is a way to start thinking about digital cultures of recording and sound as well. Kolkowski elaborates it as a kind of education about forms of listening and hearing – and perhaps also a problematization of the assumed universality of the digital.[8] Workshops like these, as well as the ones that Hertz has organized for a variety of different age and interest groups and communities, propose the idea of media archaeology as educating us about technology and media, not only as critical consumers who can hermeneutically interpret complex media content but also as producers who can actively engage in various media practices. A bit like the Kolkowski/Price workshop, Hertz's circuit-bending workshops investigate the possibilities of reuse of discarded old technologies, such as battery-powered toys modified into musical instruments, as well as acting as an easy crash-course in electronics and circuits – the fundamental features for media literacy in the age of technical communication. Even if the projects do not always reference directly the canon of media-archaeological theory such as Huhtamo, Zielinki, Grusin and others, they engage with similar themes and the persistence of media history in the present.

Notes

1 Also, Morten Riis's (http://mortenriis.dk/) Steam Engine Music performances, positioned directly in media archaeology, mobilize steampunk allusions.

2 ASCII is short for American Standard Code for Information Interchange and it was released in 1963 (with major revisions later) as a form of text encoding; it provides the information for how to encode digital binaries into text characters (as well as control characters).

3 Thank you to Garnet Hertz for bringing this work to my attention. Zoe Beloff also talks of time-machines. In an interview I conducted in Spring 2011 (Beloff 2011), she referred to "the nineteenth-century idea that machines of mechanical reproduction are really 'time-machines': cinema, a time-machine of movement, frame by frame awakening forgotten fantasies; stereo photography bringing about the artificial reconstruction of space and the phonograph resurrecting the voices of the dead." However, the early use of the term "time travel" to refer to media-archaeological art comes from Huhtamo (1995). His text "Time-Travelling in the Art Gallery: An Archaeological Approach in Media Art" and other texts from that period used the idea extensively.

4 See Geert Lovink's posting on the Net.time mailing list 15 December 1998, "Net.time, not swatch time" (www.nettime.org, accessed 28 Nov 2011).

5 The historical reference point for the Sonic Archaeology project is the 1970s US National Security Agency paper "TEMPEST: A Signal Problem" published in their *Cryptologic Spectrum* journal. It presented the problem of signal processing and its encryptability in the age of electronic communication from the point of view of national security, which taps into the Kittler-inspired interest in the military origins of media agendas and solutions, but also concretely into how any part of an electrical communication system emits through its switches, contacts, relays and other hardware components radio frequencies or acoustic energy (www.sonicarcheology.net/, accessed 28 Nov 2011); approved for release by the NSA on 27 Sept. 2007, FOIA Case #51633, "TEMPEST: A Signal Problem. The Story of the discovery of various compromising radiation from communications and Comsec equipment," online at www.nsa.gov/public_info/_files/cryptoloigc_spectrum/tempest.pdf (accessed 28 Nov 2011).

6 For a short project description, see *Neural*, www.neural.it/art/2008/11/tantalum_memorial_honoring_tho.phtml. The project was awarded the 2009 Transmediale Award.

7   The Media-archaeological Fundus collections (Berlin Humboldt University Institute for Media Studies) include good Cold War-era examples of various toys and educational computers and circuit training devices.
8   Kolkowski interview "Sonic Alchemy": http://jussiparikka.net, 11 April 2011.

Works Cited

Beloff, Zoe (2002) 'An Ersatz of Life: The Dream Life of Technology' in *New Screen Media. Cinema/Art/Narrative*, ed. Martin Rieser and Andrea Zapp (London: BFI), 287–96.

————— (2006) 'Towards Spectral Cinema' in *Book of Imaginary Media. Excavating the Dream of the Ultimate Communication Medium*, ed. Eric Kluitenberg (Amsterdam and Rotterdam: Debalie and NAi Publishers), 125–239.

————— (2011) '"With Each Project I Find Myself Reimagining What Cinema Might Be"', an interview by Jussi Parikka, *Electronic Book Review* (November), www.electronicbookreview.com/thread/imaginarrative/numerous (accessed 28 Nov 2011).

Bolder, Jay David and Grusin, Richard (1999) *Remediation. Understanding New Media* (Cambridge, MA: The MIT Press).

Braudel, Fernand (1980) *On History*, trans. Sarah Matthews (London: Weidenfeld and Nicolson).

Campanelli, Vito (2010) *Web Aesthetics. How Digital Media Affect Culture and Society* (Rotterdam: NAi Publishers / Institute of Network Cultures).

Chun, Wendy Hui Kyong (2011) 'The Enduring Ephemeral or The Future Is a Memory' in *Media Archaeology. Approaches, Applications, Implications*, ed. Erkki Huhtamo and Jussi Parikka (Berkeley, CA: University of California Press), 184–203.

DeMarinis, Paul (2010) *Buried in Noise*, ed. Ingrid Beirer, Sabine Himmelsbach and Carsten Seiffarth (Heidelberg and Berlin: Kehrer).

————— (2011) 'Erased Dots and Rotten Dashes, or How to Wire Your Head for a Preservation' in *Media Archeology. Approaches, Applications, Implications*, ed. Erkki Huhtamo and Jussi Parikka (Berkeley, CA: University of California Press), 211–38.

Ernst, Wolfgang (2008) 'Distory. 100 Years of Electron Tubes, Media-Archaeologically Interpreted vis-á-vis 100 Years of Radio' in *Re-inventing Radio. Aspects of Radio as Art*, ed. Heidi Grundmann, Elisabeth Zimmermann, Reinhard Braun, Dieter Daniels, Andreas Hirsch and Anne Thurmann-Jajes (Frankfurt am Main: Revolver), 415–30.

Gabrys, Jennifer (2011) *Digital Rubbish. A Natural History of Electronics* (Ann Arbor: University of Michigan Press).

Galloway, Alexander R. and Thacker, Eugene (2007) *The Exploit: A Theory of Networks* (Minneapolis: University of Minnesota Press).

Guattari, Félix (2000) *The Three Ecologies*, trans. Ian Pindar and Paul Sutton (London and New Brunswick, NJ: The Athlone Press).

Guins, Raiford (2009) *Edited Clean Version: Technology and the Culture of Control* (Minneapolis: University of Minnesota Press).

Hertz, Garnet (2009) 'Methodologies of Reuse in the Media Arts: Exploring Black Boxes, Tactics and Archaeologies'. Ph.D. thesis, Visual Studies, University of California Irvine.

Hertz, Garnet and Parikka, Jussi (2012) 'Zombie Media: Circuit Bending Media Archaeology into an Art Method', *Leonardo* 45.5 (2012): 424–430.

Huhtamo, Erkki (1995) 'Time-Travelling in the Gallery: An Archaeological Approach in Media Art' in *Immersed in Technology. Art and Virtual Environments*, ed. Mary Anne Moser with Douglas McLeod (Cambridge, MA: The MIT Press, 1996), 232–68.

————— (2010) 'Thinkering with Media: On the Art of Paul DeMarinis' in Paul DeMarinis, *Buried in Noise* (Heidelberg and Berlin: Kehrer), 33–39.

Kittler, Friedrich A. (1997) *Literature, Media, Information Systems*, and intro. John Johnston (Amsterdam: G+B Arts).

Lazzarato, Maurizio (2008) 'Art, Work and Politics in Disciplinary Societies and Societies of Security', *Radical Philosophy* 149 (May/June), 26–32.

Merewether, Charles, ed. (2006) *The Archive. Documents of Contemporary Art* (London and Cambridge, MA: Whitechapel and MIT Press).

Miyazaki, Shintaro (2011) "AlgoRHYTHMS Everywhere – A Heuristic Approach to Everyday Technologies' in *Pluralizing Rhythm: Music, Arts, Politics*, ed. Jan Hein Hoogstad and Birgitte Stougaard (Amsterdam and New York: Rodopi).

Parikka, Jussi (2011) 'Media Ecologies and Imaginary Media: Transversal Expansions, Contractions and Foldings', *Fibreculture* 17, http://seventeen.fibreculturejournal.org/, accessed 27 Nov 2011.

Spieker, Sven (2008) *The Big Archive: Art from Bureaucracy* (Cambridge, MA: The MIT Press).

Suominen, Jaakko (2008) 'The Past as the Future? Nostalgia and Retrogaming in Digital Culture', *Fibreculture* 11, http://journal.fibreculture.org/issue11/issue11_suominen.html.

Zielinski, Siegfried (1999) *Audiovisions. Cinema and Television as Entr'actes in History*, trans. Gloria Custance (Amsterdam: Amsterdam University Press).

——— (2006a) *Deep Time of the Media. Toward an Archaeology of Hearing and Seeing by Technical Means*, trans. Gloria Custance (Cambridge, MA: The MIT Press).

——— (2006b) "Modelling Media for Ignatius Loyola: A Case Study on Athanasius Kircher's World of Apparatus between the Imaginary and the Real." *Book of Imaginary Media: Excavating the Dream of the Ultimate Communication Medium*, ed. Eric Kluitenberg. (Rotterdam: Debalie and NAi Publishers), 29–55.

Section 2: Recommended Further Reading

Bennett, Jane. *Vibrant Matter: A Political Ecology of Things*. Baltimore: Johns Hopkins University Press, 2009.

Bogost, Ian. *Alien Phenomenology, or What It's Like to Be a Thing*. Minneapolis: University of Minnesota Press, 2012.

Castells, Manuel. *Networks of Outrage and Hope: Social Movements in the Internet Age*. London: Polity, 2012.

Cooper, Melinda. *Life as Surplus: Biotechnology and Capitalism in the Neoliberal Era*. Seattle: University of Washington Press, 2008.

Da Costa, Beatriz and Kavita Philip. *Tactical Biopolitics: Art, Activism and Technoscience*. Cambridge: MIT Press, 2010.

Franklin, Sarah. *Biological Relatives: IVF, Stem Cells, and the Future of Kinship*. Durham, NC: Duke University Press, 2013.

Milburn, Colin. *MondoNano: Fun and Games in the World of Digital Matter*. Durham, NC: Duke University Press, 2015.

Morton, Timothy. *Hyperobjects: Philosophy and Ecology After the End of the World*. Minneapolis: University of Minnesota Press, 2013.

Noyse, Benjamin. *Malign Velocities: Accelerationism and Capitalism*. London: Zero Books, 2014.

Sharp, Lesley A. *The Transplant Imaginary: Mechanical Hearts, Animal Parts and Moral Thinking in Highly Experimental Science*. Berkeley: University of California Press, 2013.

Sunder Rajan, Kaushik. *Biocapital: The Constitution of Postgenomic Life*. Durham, NC: Duke University Press, 2006.

SECTION 3

Media, mediation, science fiction

This section of the volume explores the centrality of sf texts to emerging technologies and techniques of reproduction in cinema and fan cultural practices. As the essays collected here establish, sf has been central in pushing cinema toward new techniques for special effects, innovations that have significantly shaped our understanding of the role of narrative in science fiction cinema and, indeed, in cinema overall. Building on the insights represented in Section 2 on how aspects of contemporary experience seem to be informed by sf, the selections here explore the centrality of visual media and practices of mediation in contemporary experience and the degree to which icons drawn from sf have given us the template for mass-mediated culture, from the special effects of sf cinema, to the blurring of reality and representation in postmodern consumer culture, to the creative exchanges between industry and fan cultures in recent media culture.

The section opens with Garrett Stewart's powerful argument that "movies about the future tend to be about the future of movies" (179); that is, that the media innovations within the sf diegesis anticipate the future of media practice. Coining the term videology to describe this phenomenon, he argues that such films are as much about the ideological cultures of media consumption they depict as about the technologies that enable them. Beginning with the observation that images of screens within screens – representational technologies used to frame another spectacle within the cinematic frame – are ubiquitous in sf film, Stewart argues that such films thus encourage a kind of self-reflexivity about our media consumption and our understanding of our experience as framed by media. Similar to Telotte's argument about Disney's engagement with sf in the 1950s, Stewart suggests that such commentary on the effects of mediating technologies found within sf films might function to draw our attention to the narrow worldview toward which "the invidious proliferation of optical technology, unexamined and unchecked, could blindly lead us" (185).

This essay is followed by Tom Gunning's contemporary and widely influential "The Cinema of Attraction," an essay not on sf but whose perspectives on early, nonnarrative cinema open up our understanding of effects sequences in sf film to wider significance. Focusing on how early film conveyed wonder not primarily through its specific content but rather through the fact that actions might be filmed at all, Gunning argues for the importance of rethinking film in such terms as phenomenological experience, drawing our attention to the "relation between films and the emergence of the great amusement parks, such as Coney Island, at the turn of the

173

century" (192). This essay also provides resources for rethinking the relationships among cinema, science fiction and such other kinds of amusement – one might note, for example, that sf in its popular form emerged only a decade before the 1939 World's Fair embraced the title "The World of Tomorrow," an exhibition that was recognized as science fictional by contemporary fans who organized the first World SF Convention at this site. It is also a foundational essay for rethinking the genre beyond the paradigm of print, for taking seriously the kinds of cultural work done by spectacle and thus for developing a nuanced body of theory for media sf rather than merely dismissing it, as has the critical tradition until recently, as inevitably inferior to sf in its print form.

Jean Baudrillard's theory of hyperreality captures the feeling that we are living in a science fictionalized world and he argues that this is precisely because we are immersed in media and mediation, in a new system of postmodern signification that has severed all relation between representation and an underlying reality. In this mode of the simulacra, he contends, we can no longer effectively distinguish between reality and representation because so much of our lived experienced is always-already filtered through media of representation. In the essay reproduced here, Baudrillard offers a theory of what he calls "the ecstasy of communication" in such a context, a world in which the binary public/private no longer holds any meaning. In such a context, the challenge is no longer (as in traditional ideological critique) to uncover what is hidden or repressed, but rather the difficulty is "the visible, of the all-too-visible, of the more-visible-than-the-visible" (199). Communication is reduced to mere circulation, Baudrillard suggests, and the message no longer has any importance: just the mere act of communicating is all. Here reality and science fiction seem to collapse into one another, a dilemma that we see explored by sf itself, such as in Ellis's comics analyzed by Shaviro in Section 1. Ellis's protagonist, journalist Spider, is trapped by the contradictions of a hyperreal, spectacularized society: his fans "love his identity as a crusading journalist with a gonzo lifestyle, even as they ignore his political messages," Shaviro points out. "It's hard to 'speak truth to power' when your very act of speaking is being marketed as entertainment" (70).

Brooks Landon further develops a specific theory of media sf in his unjustly neglected *The Aesthetics of Ambivalence* (1992), from which the next chapter is taken. In the larger work, Landon develops a theory of "science fiction thinking" that builds on the promises of sf's capacity for representing the world otherwise that is central to the critical tradition regarding print sf. In the section reproduced here, Landon looks at the effects of changing technologies on the ideologies thus represented, building on Gunning's work on the importance of spectacle and phenomenological experience to cinematic viewing, extending this analysis from early nonnarrative film to consider the role of special effects in sf film. Landon also begins to theorize the possibility for a nonnarrative sf cinema of the future, a cinema that would have more in common with MTV music videos and media archaeology art installations than it does with blockbuster sequels and transmedia franchises. Although aspects of his work may now seem somewhat dated given the tremendous technological changes of the past 20 years, nonetheless this essay represents a key moment in the theorization of media sf and indeed anticipates critical perspectives only now coming into dominance. This early attempt to theorize the significance of new techniques of media production and distribution seems prescient when read now in light of Web 2.0 culture. The recent explosion of the short sf film on various web hosting sites, for example, is only one of the many events that show us how Landon's work anticipated the critical frameworks we need for grasping recent practice.

Michelle Pierson's exploration of digital effects and their centrality to sf cinema extend these frameworks, and the chapter excerpted here covers the period of production roughly contemporary to the publication of Landon's work. Drawing on similar perspectives as those discussed by Sobchack in Section 1, but deployed to different ends, Pierson distinguishes between effects that are meant to be seen and those that are meant to be invisible as effects, suggesting that the former are one of the ways that Gunning's notion of the "cinema of attractions" remains part of the pleasure of sf film. Updating Landon's early work on media sf beyond film, Pierson offers insightful commentary as well on the ways that film and digital gaming cultures exchange aesthetic techniques, but also reminds us of the importance of remaining attentive to the differences between the aims and effects of the two media, as well as to the "different visual design protocols [that] have evolved for different types of game platforms" (218).

Finally, Henry Jenkins's early essay on what is now widely recognized as convergence culture points to the ways that Landon's "science fiction thinking" has shaped our experience of technologically saturated media and advertising culture, and the context of transmedia storytelling. Where there was once a binary between fan practices "outside" hegemonic industry culture and "internal" commercial media production, exchanges across this border have increasingly complicated this picture. Writing a decade ago, Jenkins outlines a number of areas that require more theorization and new techniques of analysis, and predicts: "For the foreseeable future, convergence will be a kind of kludge – a jerry-rigged relationship between different media technologies – rather than a fully integrated system" (226). He calls for critical work that will help us to understand and shape the new balance of power in the emerging media era. As much of Jenkins' own work, especially his foundational *Textual Poachers* (1992), has shown, sf cultures have led the way in innovating new media consumption practices as much as the genre has led the way in innovative effects techniques. Thus, sf is a central resource for understanding the dynamics of contemporary media practice overall.

13

THE "VIDEOLOGY" OF SCIENCE FICTION

Garrett Stewart

Let me for openers brave some blunting of my argument in a bid for pith. Movies about the future tend to be about the future of movies. Science/fiction/film: this is no more the triadic phrase for a movie genre than three subjects looking on at their own various conjunctions. Science fiction in the cinema often turns out to be, turns round to be, the fictional or fictive science of the cinema itself, the future feats it may achieve scanned in line with the technical feat that conceives them right now and before our eyes. That notorious paradox fashioned to characterize cinema as a "dream machine," the soldered bond of the imaginative and the mechanical, was already there in the narrative category "science fiction," science which was fantastic if for no other reason than because it was not yet fact. All four terms are thus most clearly welded in the *dreamed science* of *mechanized fiction*, those conjectured devices screened with an electronically activated film of the future which offer ramifications and refinements of visual technology itself – the imaginary engineering of the image to which moviemaking may someday succeed.

An opening parable. When, in the seventh decade of science fiction on film the movie *Capricorn One* (Peter Hyams, 1978) arrived to entertain the speculation that the federal space program and its televised promotion might be entirely short-circuited (or in the argot of such coverage: closed-circuited) – that in fact the whole thing might be fabricated in a studio as a "media event" in the most absolute sense – this "deconstructive" conceit reached deep into one's instincts about the more than ordinarily close collusion between cinematic illusionism and futuristic fantasy. In an unexpected theatrical sense, the manned "stage" of the Apollo flight in the film is more transmission than space mission, a mere takeoff on a takeoff. Further, in a curious double crossing of temporal and spatial logic wherein the mechanics of simulation intersect the odd mechanical laws of the rendered phenomenon, the secret studio mock-up of the landing on Mars requires for its national television broadcast a slow-motion delayed replay to approximate the weightlessness of the astronauts; the very medium of cinematic representation across time is retarded so as to simulate a distant space whose gravitational field is governed by rules other than the physics of Earth. *Capricorn One* is a quite literal grounding of scientific futurity in the machinations of the cinematic image. As such it all but imperceptibly shifts the cutting edge of technological ingenuity in the genre of science fiction film from machines in outer space to the logistics of their replication in inner or screen space, from aeronautics to cinematics. Indeed, it allows us to imagine that all independent scientific advance, as photographically retailed to the public, might have stopped with the advent of what is usually considered to be (and no accident) the first narrative film, George Méliès 1902 rocket fantasy *A Trip to the Moon*, beyond which point movies could not only have begun duplicating our most miraculous tools, but anticipating and confecting them before our receptive gaze.

[...]

A more candid start would back these reflections up against the first and recurrent question that started me thinking along these lines – a question, I must say which seemed less and less naïve the more specific evidence I began to sieve through it. Why, I wondered, are there so many viewing screens and viewing machines crowding so many of the science fiction sets one can think of – banks of monitors, outsized video intercoms, x-ray display panels, hologram tubes, backlit photoscopes, aerial scanners, telescopic mirrors, illuminated computer consoles, overhead projectors, slide screens, radar scopes, whole curved walls of transmitted imagery, the retinal registers of unseen electronic eyes? Surely more is at stake than the economy of working from the given, disguised and glorified, by intruding into narrative some of the equipment one had to produce it. Evidence would suggest, instead, that video technology is not merely recruited in this way; its purposes are critically scrutinized. They are analyzed in so central an isolation that, in movie after movie, cinema becomes a synecdoche for the entire technics of an imagined society.

[...]

In the spirit of fabrication so many of these filmed futures display, perhaps even in the Newspeak[1] they may satirize, I mint this term "videology" as a two-sided coinage. By joint reference to technological and ideological models, I mean to suggest that these films about film in the future, or about related systems of illusion and communication, are at least as much about the mores as machines, more political than polytechnic. As with modernism in all its aesthetic variants, so with the special case of cinematic futurism: the involuted scrutiny of the medium owes binding allegiance beyond itself. Future screens within the present spectacle are not the medium doodling with and duplicating itself for the medium's own sake, but in the root sense a mediation not only between here and then but between technological gadget and the human allegory to which it tunes us. For repeatedly we find ourselves reading these concentric visual devices not just as replicas of our own theatrical mechanism scaled down by their distance from us in time, but rather in some other symbolic ratio to the mere eventualities of optical science. To generalize rather hazardously: screens screened by or inset within other screens tell us not about seeing per se and its strange efficiencies but about vision in its fullest sense. When these projective fantasies of science fiction film, meditating on their own premising machines, turn the hermetic inside out to become emblematic, they often portray for us how we may come, for better and often for worse, to see and receive the world.

[...]

If I had to choose a single parable, among many, which most subtly unfolds a ruling truth about science fiction as a visionary dispensation, it would be the salvation by averted gaze not at the end of *Raiders* [*of the Lost Ark* (Spielberg, 1981)] but in the throne room of the Krell power in *Forbidden Planet* (Fred Wilcox, 1956). The scientist Morbius, long in exile from Earth, discloses there something abut the very secrets of the framing fiction in an emblematic scene that holds the mirror up to an unparalleled nature, the secret power source of the previous and self-defeated civilization of the Krell empire. The human eye, Morbius explains, cannot stare into the molten nuclear origin of this power and survive. As in the Gorgon myth, this searing source must be glimpsed through a reflecting surface. What we see in the resulting scene, set in the antechamber to omnipotent energy, is a lone hexagonal panel to the left of the screen providing more or less direct access, somehow, to the volcanic churning of the power source, while flanking it at the right is a more dimly glowing replica taken to be a mirror, which is scrutinized by Morbius and the two astronauts he would indoctrinate. By no law of optics, however, are these panels, the radiant original and the presumed mirror, arranged in relation to each other so that any real reflecting can go on. They are both angled toward the viewer as in some pre-perspectival tableau from a medieval fresco. And of course we in the audience get to look directly at both. The allegory these viewing planes enact, in their relation to each other and to us, is not just that cinema is a fantastic mirror, rectangular rather than hexagonal, in which we can see unholy and inordinate and perhaps even lethal wonders framed and disinfected by art, but also that film art allows us to see apparently *without* mediation — but only, of course, apparently — what characters within plot cannot or dare not.

The power of this parable of power and visual empowerment is that it is not detached from but ironically ratified by plot. We learn that the Krell civilization did themselves in by outdoing themselves, creating a telepathic mastery over matter that left all normal defensive mechanisms behind. The projective reification of unconscious desires they then commanded, called by Morbius the invocation of "monsters from the id," is best understood in the long run by analogy to visual summoning gone amok, where the ultimate creature is in fact etched in electromagnetic impulses fueled by the planetary power source. It is an outsized version of a miniature hologram figure earlier conjured by materialized desire as the test of mind-boosting on a Krell children's toy. What we are warned against in this cautionary fable is in part the danger of cinematic "projection" if it were ever to become more than art's bordered, orderly, and two-dimensional mirror. As allegorized in the Krell chamber of deflected revelation, then and finally, the power of unbridled imaginative energy is benign only when kept at, and held to the rules of, aesthetic distance. It should now be possible to appreciate how the name Morbius, suggesting not just the Morphean release of dreams, also involves us, as probable allusion to the Möbius strip, in that involuted logic whereby something coiled within us and unmaterialized, once twisted into view, may turn upon and destroy us. The name may thus suggest, as formal correlative of this emblem, a strip of film looping over its length in an infinitely elusive return — the cinematic artifact retracing its own process of generation and its latent dangers.

From the start of the cinema's interest in science fiction there has been this reflexive monitory strain. What if the fiction of film could achieve the efficacy of science, a dark technological alchemy? Two early entries on the roster of the genre enrolled their titles as if, like *The Time Machine*, [Pal, 1960], they were periphrases for, while perversions of, the cinematic apparatus. In René Clair's *The Crazy Ray* (1923, in French *Paris Qui Dort*) the title force field has transmuted, in effect, the power of stop-action editing to a freezing of the real world. A petrifying implementation of filmic optics, this crazed ray empowers the virtual *de*cinematizing of the world's continuous action. In a comparable vein, *The Invisible Ray* (Lambert Hillyer, 1936) also illustrates an inversion of the filmic principle by *de*creating the objects of its beam rather than hallucinating their presence, crumbling the world's entities to dust.

Both these early films imagine the malign by analogy with their own projective powers. Art, like science, should stay in its place, especially that technologized art which is the escalating magic of cinema. So says Fritz Lang's *Metropolis* (1926) as well, but there the emphasis is not on the projective but the fictive qualities of the cinema, its genius for delusion. When the treacherous scientist Rotwang sets about to simulate in his laboratory the heroine of the subjugated lower orders in the film's future totalitarian state, he converts a steel robot into her image in a blast of galvanic voltage that also involves the openly cinematic superimposition of the womanly image on the angular metallic mannequin. This artificial creature is thus generated in the form not of a fleshly android so much as a "celluloid,"[2] an illusory *dea ex machina* sent forth to subvert the revolutionary discontent of the masses. All of this was taken up and talked down (or so he thought) by H.G. Wells and his director William Cameron Menzies in *Things to Come* (1936) a decade later, where the gleaming clean Hyatt Regency set of the future is riddled, studded, and bejeweled with chromium and plexiglass viewing screens and hologram tubes of all shapes and sizes, cut to the eclectic measure of the state's democratic tolerances for the airing of any view.[3]

[. . .]

At this turn, it is probably time to say that watching anything on a direct-transmission screen within a film, just as watching anything within a movie in the process of being filmed, has a way, initially at least, of buttressing rather than undercutting the larger film's primary reality; the mediation we *see* at work may seek to remove the contagion of artifice from the mediation of the outer film medium itself. This is a way of returning to that original question I asked myself about the prevalence of screening devices in science fiction film, and of returning this whole question to a point before what I have been calling the potential for metafilmic allegory gets underway. A common motive for the proliferation of visual image systems in science fiction cinema, especially of television monitors, and especially in the films of alien visitation or monstrous mutation, is for documentary authentication. We like to share by proxy our astonished gaze by watching other innocent bystanders caught in the act of looking on at remarkable phenomena, a middle-aged couple over TV dinners in some seedy apartment, passengers in airports at overhead screens, drunks in bars, pedestrians passing an appliance store where several televisions flicker in display. The rhetorical motive is clear, the strategy facile. The ontological reverberations, however, may be unruly or deliberately subversive.

[. . .]

When secondhand visual documentation within a science fiction movie is actual film footage screened in the presence of the projector, rather than disseminated on television, the corroborating tendency of such visual evidence may aspire toward an interesting concentric ratio. Remember *Them!* (George Douglas, 1954), with its mutant ants enlarged out of all biological proportion by atomic radiation. At one point we cut from a scene in which photographs of their huge larvae are exhibited as evidence of their existence to a darkened screening room. As if the stills themselves have hatched, we watch ordinary warrior ants in enormous closeup on a screen that gradually fills the space of our own. In this all but microscopic footage as microcosm of the outer film's disturbing hypothesis, the movie runs the risk of our thinking that its own giant ants are merely photographic enlargements, which of course they are. It does this in order to make a more interesting rhetorical point: that the jostling of our normal perspective on the insect population, in the modeling and trick effects of the movie *Them!* as a whole, is no less concerned than these instructive enlargements of the documentary footage with an ant's disproportionate strength and ferocity. This slight of perspective is indeed all the more convincing if we are to read the invasion, from a larger vantage yet, as a paranoid fifties parable of the post–A-bomb threat not of genetic deformation but of its political counterpart in international communism, or as a parable of the A-bomb itself as an outsized monster beyond our control. The screened documentary works hand in hand – or more aptly, hand in glove – with the mutant parable by which it is contained. Visual corroboration in the screening room, itself tampered with legitimately within the plot to make a pedagogical point, becomes a touchstone of other thematic rather than entomological tampering in the film that surrounds it and compounds its implications.

[. . .]

Just before the landing of the Martians, *War of the Worlds* [Haskin, 1953] has moved from the black-and-white newsreel prologue into a sequence of "astronomical animation" in color, explained to us in voiceover by Cedric Hardwick as the interplanetary vision of aliens "scanning the universe with instruments beyond our imagination." Midway in the narrative, an attempt is made (as in *The Fly*) to simulate the actual ocular equipment of the individual invaders. Immediately following a scene in which Earth's own advanced optical technology in the form of an electron microscope is used to analyze the alien's bloodcells, we move to a laboratory in which the lights are brought down, a screen lowered, and a mock-documentary footage projected that purports to show, through a set of tripled fish-eye lens shots, the approximate workings of the Martian visual apparatus. In a film whose primary motive is to show *us* what *they* would look like, an inset film has been commissioned, produced, and screened that turns the tables, and the camera, on us. Yet is this entirely a reversal of expectations, or only their logical extension? Is it not perhaps the essence of science fiction as a genre to show us new views of ourselves under duress from the extraordinary?

Through the inhabited rather than just refabricated vision of an alien creature, a more recent film, Michael Crichton's *Westworld* (1973), opens a further aspect of this generic variation. In a vacation resort of the future, one of the simulated storybook (or movie) environments reconstructed from the mythical past, along with a Roman villa and a Medieval castle, is a Western frontier town furnished with robot barmaids and gunslingers. These virtually undetectable androids are, however, slowly gaining autonomy and growing discontent with their lot. They gradually refuse to be controlled by the hundreds of underground computer monitors that stage-manage their service activities for the guests, including sexual exploitation and violent death. At the critical turn of plot, when the computer control room is mysteriously shut down and sealed off by the insurrectionist energies of the robot work force, the scientists inside slowly suffocating to death, we cut for the first time in the film to a robot's eye view of the world. No longer watched by the scientists, but placed on his own alert, the android gunslinger (Yul Brynner) takes aim at his victim while we see not only along his line of sight but with his own artificial vision, a computer scan substituting for any natural eye view. The advent of subjectivity is thus marked by cinematic technique as a foregrounding of vision itself. The robot's need to survey the enemy generates a digital grid of color graphics that, like the representational radar, allows him to discern the fleeing shape of his prey. In the intercut stalking that takes up the last ten minutes of the film, humanoid and human exchange like bullets the glances of their new antagonism. Even when the robot is not in fact shooting at the hero, the very format of shot / reverse shot editing in this cinematic narrative, long reserved for the human participants, has thus broken with standard generic logic (as in their own less extensive ways have *The Fly* and *War of the Worlds*) and incorporated the monster's own point of view. The editing of *Westworld* has to this degree humanized the alien consciousness in the very moment of its defiant otherness, of its deviant, its anthropomorphic will to power. At the same time the editing discloses what must be considered a metafilmic reversal. The alien is no sooner humanized than we are thrown back on our own spectatorial alienation. He watches the hero the way we watch both, electronically.

The strategy of incorporating such various media representations as the control room monitors in *Westworld* or the movie theater in *War of the Worlds* so that they redound to the augmented credibility of a film's extraterrestrial or aberrant phenomena often induces a range of additional ironies.

[. . .]

[F]or every inset screen – or its explosion – that serves as a touchstone of present and familiar reality within a landscape of deviation, there are at least as many instances in futuristic science fiction of vanguard or experimental visual artistry which in their own advanced functions frame for us the extent of scientific advance, even as they covertly comment on more than their pure engineering bespeaks. [The remainder of this essay] will concentrate not on corroborative film footage or television transmission, but instead on futuristic video instrumentation in itself, incarnation of rather than yardstick for the extraordinary. A good place to begin with the hypertrophy of visual technics in George Lucas's *THX 1138* (1970), whose title character has been reduced from humanizing name to computerized designation while his underground future state is inhabited in part by computerized video simulations of real people. Our hazily lit glimpse of this future is often coincident with the voyeuristic spying of a central computer by means of mini-cameras stationed throughout its domain. After optically snooping on the masses this Orwellian Big Brother projects back to them in phone-booth-like confessionals a video image of their putative Lord. At one point, however, a misfit illicitly strays into a central projection room where, as in the unveiling of the Wizard of Oz at his control panel, the artifice of video projection is discovered, with a giant photograph of the technological godhead propped up before the cameras. In other scenes the citizenry sit mesmerized before giant television screens out of which lifesize hologram images move and speak in a monotonous pacification of the mass anxiety. The fixation upon illusions tends to drain staring subject as well as object of all substance, all inner life. Once again the darker imaginings of science fiction rewrite optical technology as a denaturing threat.

It might well be argued that this holographic nightmare lies behind the plot of Stanislaw Lem's novel *Solaris* (1961) and, all the more so, of the Soviet film made from it by Andrei Tarkovsky a decade later. The suddenly materialized clone of the hero's dead wife, a neutrino mirage generated from micro-second to micro-second out of a protean plasmic mass or brain the size of an ocean, a dormant body called Solaris, is a short step further into independent palpability – while of course also a quantum leap – beyond the three-dimensional, holographic simulation of identity in *THX*. A change from the novel *Solaris* on the way to its film version is suggestive here. The tape recorder by which the hero's dead predecessor is "resurrected" to tell what he has learned before his death about the powers of the Solarian ocean becomes in the film a huge video screen, projecting the last words of the deceased as a surviving caveat to those who follow. Since the hero's wife is also in a sense subjectively "resurrected" as a visual as well as a bodily hallucination, and is present before the movie viewers not by the split-second-self-regeneration of neutrino particles (as the plot has it) but by the twenty-four frames per second of filmic illusion, the bond between the materialized dead man on videotape and an erotic avatar from the unconscious, electromagnetically aggravated into presence, is hard to mistake. The centuries-old, perpetually researched mystery of the Solarian sea as a seemingly conscious electromagnetic matrix is solved by analogy when we come to understand it as, in psychic effect, a giant image generator wirelessly tied into the privacies of desire, materializing what we would hide so as to know us to the core.

What seems fearsome and inscrutable in this dimly glimpsed scheme can of course (as in Lucas's *THX 1138* to which we now return) degenerate to the blatantly totalitarian. What makes the plot of *THX* a striking indictment of image-making rather than just an attack on the video spying of some cruel future regime, what again allegorizes it into present relevance, is that potential conversion of an image-addicted populace to no better than holographic simulations. Such siphoning off of all subjectivity from the visible envelope of self to a politically sanctioned treachery foreseen for the future that simply spells out the inherent threat of any mindless submission in the first place, however pacifying, to the brute objectivity of mere images.

Toward the end of the film, the hero (Robert Duvall) attempts to escape from his underworld city (called, in the title of the student version of the film done by Lucas at the University of Southern California, an "Electronic Labyrinth"). It is an escape which will bring him finally to a huge ventilation shaft and from there into real daylight for the first time. On the way he breaks into a video monitor room, annex of the central computer bank, and in an act of ultimate counter-acculturation takes the controls himself. He punches out the necessary code and then focuses in on a full-screen shot of the bottled fetus to which his just-dead mate's ID number has been reassigned. Too long trapped in this encaved prison house of images himself, he cannot help but read this last image – the only one he has chosen for himself to call up, the one that makes visible to him the end of what human place he could claim in this subterranean world – cannot help but read this fetal image, or at least we can't help but read it for him, as a symbol. The hero will become now in his own shaved person just such a newborn identity, out the long tunnel into the light. In escaping from the actual detention center a few scenes before, the prison within the prison – an overexposed sterile space bled of color and without discernible walls or angles, as if it were the two-dimensional space of his own video-monitored entrapment on an engulfing white screen – he is led out by a fugitive hologram, no less. This video refugee, one of the figures nightly used to pacify the masses, is a mirage tired of being ensnared in his monotonous digital circuit and aching to break free into bodied reality. When asked by the hero for the direction out, he points straight off the screen into the camera and so at us, at a palpable world elsewhere, the world itself.

Lucas's film would have cut his disjunction between illusion and reality cleanly enough without its wry and at first disorienting prologue. It is there, however, precisely to enact the tunnel vision, as it were, that would route the current state of visual entertainment into this future brand of perversity and abuse. Lucas's movie opens even before its credits with a loaded dislocation of fictional context, the audience given without explanation a short black-and-white preview of the next installment of an outdated *Buck Rogers* serial from 1939, with its stentorian overvoice promising that what we are to be treated to in the next episode will be merely our own technology escalated into the twenty-first century. What the film hints by this integral "preview" as prophecy is not unlike the implication of the opening documentary footage in *War of the Worlds* once set in contrast to the narrative cinema for which those initial spectators are lined up under the marquee. Lucas's film suggests that we are soon going to move through and beyond such outmoded fables of our future as *Buck Rogers*, the weak-minded optimism of these early comic-book "projections," into the more unsettling truth about that futurity lurking latent in the very midst of our predilection for such comfortingly fantastic narratives, for images without critical sting. When we come upon those subsequent hologram projections doled out by a repressive state (unmoderated images of sex and violence in the shape of nude dancing and police brutality, talk shows and evangelical programs, even narrative distractions in the form of an Amos-and-Andy-like sitcom), we are in a position to receive the ultimate reflexive argument of the film that envisions them: the notion that it too would be no more than another mindless pacifier of the masses if it did not take the dangers of such psychic suppression as its satiric theme – if, instead of being political art, it were mere hallucinatory diversion. When the small squarish frame of the 1930s black-and-white footage spreads to the full scope of the contemporary screen, the perspective is in more than one sense widened, as if the film itself were opening its eyes, and ours for us, to the larger grim picture. The *Buck Rogers* preview thus points straight to the center of the film's ironic intent, for it aligns the bland fantasies of cinema history with the totalitarian vanishing point toward which the invidious proliferation of optical technology, unexamined and unchecked, could blindly lead us.

[. . .]

Clos[e] in spirit to the dystopian harangue of *THX 1138* is Richard Fleischer's film of three years later, *Soylent Green* (1973). The movie is an ecological nightmare set in New York City early in the next century, population forty million. The earth is now denuded of vegetation, and the undersea flora which the people believe is the staple of their diet, a wafer called Soylent Green, turns out in the film's climactic disclosure to be, by a gruesome Malthusian irony, a processed fragment of recycled bodies from the city's overpopulated morgues. It is a movie in which we can detect each of the two chief services of frames within frames, the first a corroborative piece of documentary footage on television, then a more insidious instance of cinematic technique turned to funereal psychology. A routine inset of video certification in the film's first actual scene shows a television interview with the governor, who explains a delay in the weekly ration load of the green diet. Again it is a confirming framed example of our own contemporary media projected into the future and incorporated there as a measure of its so-called advances as well as an electronic mollifier of the future's abused victims.

In contrast, our sense of all bearings, emotional and otherwise, is deliberately upset with the actual movie within the movie later stretched to (and beyond) our full-screen space. Society's inducement to the elderly to submit to voluntary extermination, out of its own secret need for their corpses, is the guarantee that any man or woman will be assured a remedial vision of the earth's now decimated beauty in a prolonged moment of audio-visual bliss: a technologically reclaimed heaven on earth. The giant extermination warehouse where this transpires is called "Home" for the unhealthy sense of eschatological nostalgia to which it panders. When mortuary volunteers sign up for the color-coded, musically orchestrated twenty minutes of ecstatic visual images on a screen curved 360 degrees to the full periphery of the craving mind's eye, we cannot ultimately know whether the home to which these decedents think to be returning is some glimpsed threshold of heaven (and Biblical "long home") or merely the lost pastoral pleasures of an earth from which urban trauma has deracinated them all. For what we see along with the hero (Charlton Heston) as he pushes his way into the projection chamber and forces open the steel curtain that would close out the show to all who have not paid the exorbitant final price, is the head of his old friend Sol (Edward G. Robinson), silhouetted against the swollen Cinerama womb of his termination, awash in the scenes of which he so often spoke to Heston: blooming floral vistas, elk herding, rushing rapids, placid seacoasts, a spectacular sunset. Even the fact of the rear projection which effects this vision is implicated in its horror. In its hiding and denial of the very mechanics of presentation, this visually drugged euthanasia would elicit faith in a sacramental miracle hovering before the dying eye, when it is in fact merely the trace of a world behind and lost, present now in front of its deluded communicant only by the illusion of images and the deceit of their source. Given the complicity between this visionary service center and the food-processing plant to which the appeased corpses are carted off, we may sense an additional dovetailed irony: that cinema itself, in its inauthentic recycling of seen reality, does in its own right cannibalize the world.

Grotesque and intriguing enough. But there is a further twist that begs the entire cinematic question so raised. All these images, accompanied by the same light classical score (i.e., served up as full-scale sound cinema) later appear behind the final credits of our movie, but with no silhouetted head of a dramatized viewer standing in sacrificially for us within the frame. Heston has been shot in an attempt to expose the treachery of human recycling. The last image within the plot is his bloodied arm squeezed into a tight vertical slot of remaining photographic space by the closing in of a black "screen" in no way motivated by narrative, matting out the scene from either side. We have no way to read as more than a closural gimmick this masking, displacement, or cancellation of the image until the screen suddenly fills with the death vision of Robinson, in reprise. The vanishing space of plot is now recognized, quite possibly, as the world closed out by the equivalent of that sliding metal (now mental) barrier in the death chamber. In one sense, or from one direction, we are excluded from Heston's fate (either death from his wound or assassination to keep him quiet), but then in another sense the coda now excludes all but the visions we assume him to have inherited from Robinson to a deathbed legacy, including the closing sunset formerly timed to the dying of a man named Sol or "Sun." If the most disturbing thing about the old man's earlier going "home" was that the grace of mortal epiphany was now politically contracted for and technologically programmed, then cinema in some festered future incarnation had taken over the soul's deepest privacy. If so, then the sense generated by the final credits of being inside Heston's dying mind, or at least in attendance at the death of his heroic mission, relieved as he may be by the beauty of what furtively glimpsed "cinema" has taught him to imagine as ideal, implies that visual technology, here freed from totalitarian manipulation, may have recouped some of its desperate utility and its true beauty. Or has it?

[. . .]

As guardian of our past, the science of photographic reproduction has intimately to do with the preservation of our very lives as remembered, preserved within and from our own worst futures. When film is used in the extermination chamber as a kind of demonic technological parody of divine afflatus or natural revelation, a saving grace at the gate of negation, what I think we are to realize, given the bracketing of this by opening and closing allusions to both photographic and cinematic record, is that such film footage can genuinely deliver a saving vision only in a very different sense already familiar to us from the deepest reflexive reach of *THX 1138*. Film might "redeem" not mainly in the sense of preserving what had once been lovely in the world, but by daring to imagine, in a dark allegory like that worked out in this particular film, how easy it would be to lose this loveliness. [. . .] At this level of lingering uneasiness, we begin to see the final double bind of the film's cinematic auto-allegory and of the deathbed imagery that comprises the movie's own closure. To need such a last airless and illusory gesture to redeem us or retrieve our losses, any more than to need the old photographs behind the credits to tell us where we've been, is scant consolation at the moment of our last hero's assassination, the death gasp of human resistance to the self-devouring nature of history.

[. . .]

With *THX 1138*, *Colossus*, *Looker*, or *Tron* about the enslavement by, within, and as image; *Soylent Green* about reality's doing away into image; *Zardoz* about the inner life optically expropriated by image; Kubrick's and Godard's movies[4] further investigating the cinema's potentially false stance toward the psychological reality which film would affect or defer, impinge on or dismiss from consideration – with all this behind us there is still to be explored the threat of the image itself in its own macabre autonomy, and this too as estimated by screens within screens.

[. . .]

Fahrenheit 451 [Truffaut, 1966] is a story about Eden reclaimed, the word's if not the world's. The false idols of video transmission are immolated before our eyes and the true secular Logos of the literary tradition reinshrined in the tabernacles of memory. As myth of restitution Truffaut's film stands in direct contrast to the archetypal and irreversible fall of *The Man Who Fell to Earth* [1975], directed by the man who was the chief cinematographer of *Fahrenheit 451* a decade before, Nicholas Roeg. The entitling premise of Roeg's film is in itself a reversal of the generic trajectory of science fiction from earth's known and horizoned reality into *terra incognita*. The alien villain has been recast as the descending hero trying to home in on the living hell of our foreign and estranging ways. Instead of the mysterious intruder as aberration or menace, instead of his being in any way aggressively invasive, he quickly attempts to integrate himself, to make do until he can make his trackless way back.

The credits burst open upon a space traveler (David Bowie) hurtling in a multi-staged rocket toward earth. He comes to see what he can learn (or take?) from our terrestrial bounty for his own drought-afflicted planet. He intends then to go home. But to become the man who flew *from* earth he would need yet another rocket, and he soon learns that such commodities on earth must be earned by being purchased. So he proceeds to become (in the root sense of the term) astronomically rich so as to return to the stars. He immediately sets about using his advanced technological knowledge to invent things his earthly counterparts just as quickly decide they need. First among these inventions, and the only one of which we hear in any detail, is a so-called "self-developing camera." It might more accurately be known as a self-photographing camera, its role in the film only accurately assessed if it is seen to comment on the disavowed voyeurism masquerading as objective omniscience which characterizes all film narrative.

[. . .]

Bowie's alien from another world will [. . .] profit hugely and even innocently from a mass-produced visual technology that travesties the self-alienating distance from feeling in which our strange culture indulges, the fetishistic relish of the body at a willed distance from its desire.

[. . .]

The space visitor is finally locked away in a suite of rooms, one of which is decorated with *trompe l'oeil* photographic wallpaper of a sylvan scene. It is in the adjacent bedroom that he is visited at intervals for a number of medical tests and tamperings which gradually convert his intended guise as a *trompe l'oeil* humanoid to an involuntary and irreversible replica. Before his last operations we see him staring, gin-soaked and oblivious, at an oversized television screen as large as the "walls" in *Fahrenheit*, upon which is being run that great cinematic tale of betrayal, *The Third Man*.

[. . .]

We first see the improbable vantage of the spaceman's remarkable camera and then we watch his fatal addiction to the most atavistic and predictable trivia of American television, by which he is hypnotized at a remove not unlike the uncommitted distance maintained by the self-alienating mechanics of his camera. Early in the film he gets a hotel maid to help him furnish his lonely room with a number of television sets, barricading himself from his new but unwelcome reality with this babel of mediating images and idiolects, from commercials through soap operas to rerun theatrical features.

[. . .]

Bowie drops into plot as the typical science fiction foil for heroic resistance or heroic under-standing, the mysterious and challenging alien. As such, however, he is forced to look on at the collapse and banishment of the whole form of storytelling, or filmmaking, that brought him into view. Rather than being allowed his formulaic role in science fiction, he gets stranded as ironic pawn within an anti-capitalist allegory. His whole effort is now to break his way back as heroic protagonist into that science fiction genre and its plot-making energy from which, but also by which, he fell into the realm of his present story's earthly rendering. The creature from outer space has been retrieved by his own time travel from the unarrived unmaterialized future known only to us through science fiction convention, has been fleshed out in humanoid form and then crucified, all so that we should be reminded through his excruciating example that he is not half so alienated from the rest of us as are any of us from the gruesome modernity we have engendered on the near edge of the future. But the spaceman's defeat by time, his temporalizing collusion with the human, the murder of his futurity, all this amounts to the burial within plot of the science fiction formulas upon which it seemed to found itself. The failures of science within this fiction are lamented both through the absence of those empowering machines of space flight that are the staple of the genre and through video technology's corrupt links to personal fiction-making, to fantasy, to dream. The would-be hero can no longer get back to, nor will he ever be able to look back upon, his lost origin, not through any screening machine or amazing vehicle of his preternaturally advanced devising. The whole genre of science fiction, with its fabulous engines and visual tools in the hands of fantastic visitors, goes to its grave unmourned, just as other forms of narrative film have passed way unattended by the hero within it. They too have included movies which, like viable science fiction, properly watched, could reward and reorder the very modes of seeing.

To offer some review at the close, there are two crucial sorts of self-involved "videology" in science fiction cinema: let me summarize them as (1) the state of the art and (2) the art of some future state. There are on the one hand, that is, those nested instances of present visual science within a visual medium that serve as confirming *frames* of reference, so to say, in the company of alien biologies or advanced technologies – touchstones of the real within reach of the freely conceived. There are on the other hand those imagined electronic marvels of specifically visual function that are the very lodestones of prophesied science in any film of our scientific posterity. Like many of the strongest documents in the film genre of science fiction, the lapsarian fable of *The Man Who Fell to Earth* is a story oriented by these two modes of "videology," both the ordinary screenings that fail to touch even as they obsess the hero, and his own visual innovations, by which he cannot even glimpse again his dream. As a self-conscious dead end for the genre of science fiction, as I was calling it a moment ago, nevertheless this film recuperates in rather pure form what I have continually noticed as science fiction's deepest purpose. For in the allegorical ingenuity of all the genre's views of and views on looking – the filmmaking about photography and film-viewing, the science and the fiction of the seeing eye and the visionary mind – what we are asked still and all to look upon in the meticulously polished, imperceptibly tilted mirror of its narrative art, what we are invited to peruse at a revelatory new slant, is only ourselves, now and here.

Then again this way of summing up may seem to distort the true poise of our involvement. If we come to the genre with these expectations, we must still be distanced by its works and workings long enough to relearn its service more securely. As spectators, we become agents of our own alienated vision, with travel in space or time the very vehicle of both aesthetic and psychological distanciation. The self-conscious allegories of science fiction talk us out of the truisms of ready identification by which we are lured to these films in the first place, lured as much as we are by the promise of wondrous and seductive futures they might bring to view. Toward this reconstructive purpose the metaphysical is encased within the mechanical. Movies about – as well as brought about by – a technology of the image, cinematic artifacts turned purposefully reflexive, alone allow us this clarity of reflection on the ideologies by which we see and so lead our lives.

Notes

1 [This is a reference to George Orwell's *Nineteen Eighty-Four*, adapted to film by Michael Anderson in 1956. – SV]

2 A term I used (p. 364) for the transparent dream projection of the hero of *Sherlock Junior*, as part of an argument about the film's combined technological and oneiric self-consciousness in "Keaton through the Looking Glass," *The Georgia Review* 33 (Summer 1979): 348–67.

3 See my "Close Encounters of the Fourth Kind," [*Sight and Sound* 47 (Summer 1978): 167–74] pp. 171–72, for a fuller look at the achievements of optical science in the underworld city of Everytown.

4 [The list of films discussed in the full essay, as well as those mentioned here, includes Kubrick's *A Clockwork Orange* (1971) and Godard's *Alphaville* (1965) – SV].

14

THE CINEMA OF ATTRACTION

Early film, its spectator and the avant-garde

Tom Gunning

Writing in 1922, flushed with the excitement of seeing Abel Gance's *La Roue*, Fernand Léger tried to define something of the radical possibilities of the cinema. The potential of the new art did not lay in "imitating the movements of nature" or in "the mistaken path" of its resemblance to theater. Its unique power was a "matter of *making images seen*."[1] It is precisely this harnessing of visibility, this act of showing and exhibition which I feel cinema before 1906 displays most intensely. Its inspiration for the avant-garde of the early decades of this century needs to be re-explored.

Writings by the early modernists (Futurists, Dadaists, and Surrealists) on the cinema follow a pattern similar to Léger: enthusiasm for this new medium and its possibilities; and disappointment at the way it has already developed, its enslavement to traditional art forms, particularly theater and literature. This fascination with the *potential* of a medium (and the accompanying fantasy of rescuing the cinema from its enslavement to alien and passé forms) can be understood from a number of viewpoints. I want to use it to illuminate a topic I have approached before from another angle, the strangely heterogeneous relation that film before 1906 (or so) bears to the films that follow, and the way a taking account of this heterogeneity signals a new conception of film history and film form. My work in this area has been pursued in collaboration with André Gaudreault.[2]

The history of early cinema, like the history of cinema generally, has been written and theorized under the hegemony of narrative films. Early filmmakers like Smith, Méliès, and Porter have been studied primarily from the viewpoint of their contribution to film as a storytelling medium, particularly the evolution of narrative editing. Although such approaches are not totally misguided, they are one-sided, and potentially distort both the work of these filmmakers and the actual forces shaping cinema before 1906. A few observations will indicate the way that early cinema was not dominated by the narrative impulse that later asserted its sway over the medium. First there is the extremely important role that actuality film plays in early film production. Investigation of the films copyrighted in the U.S. shows that actuality films outnumbered fictional films until 1906.[3] The Lumière tradition of "placing the world within one's reach" through travel films and topicals did not disappear with the exit of the Cinématographe from film production.

But even within non-actuality filming – what has sometimes been referred to as the "Méliès" tradition – the role narrative plays is quite different than in traditional narrative film. Méliès himself declared in discussing his working method:

As for the scenario, the "fable," or "tale," I only consider it at the end. I can state that the scenario constructed in this manner has *no importance*, since I use it merely as a pretext for the "stage effects," the "tricks," or for a nicely arranged tableau.[4]

Whatever differences one might find between Lumière and Méliès, they should not represent the opposition between narrative and non-narrative filmmaking, at least as it is understood today. Rather, one can unite them in a conception that sees cinema less as a way of telling stories than as a way of presenting a series of views to an audience, fascinating because of their illusory power (whether the realistic illusion of motion offered to the first audiences by Lumière, or the magical illusion concocted by Méliès), and exoticism. In other words, I believe that the relation to the spectator set up by the films of both Lumière and Méliès (and many other filmmakers before 1906) had a common basis, and one that differs from the primary spectator relations set up by narrative film after 1906. I will call this earlier conception of cinema, "the cinema of attractions." I believe that this conception dominates cinema until about 1906–1907. Although different from the fascination in storytelling exploited by the cinema from the time of Griffith, it is not necessarily opposed to it. In fact the cinema of attraction does not disappear with the dominance of narrative, but rather goes underground, both into certain avant-garde practices and as a component of narrative films, more evident in some genres (e.g., the musical) than in others.

What precisely is the cinema of attraction? First it is a cinema that bases itself on the quality that Léger celebrated: its ability to *show* something. Contrasted to the voyeuristic aspect of narrative cinema analyzed by Christian Metz,[5] this is an exhibitionist cinema. An aspect of early cinema which I have written about in other articles is emblematic of this different relationship the cinema of attractions constructs with its spectator: the recurring look at the camera by actors. This action which is later perceived as spoiling the realistic illusion of the cinema, is here undertaken with brio, establishing contact with the audience. From comedians smirking at the camera, to the constant bowing and gesturing of the conjurors in magic films, this is a cinema that displays its visibility, willing to rupture a self-enclosed fictional world for a chance to solicit the attention of the spectator.

Exhibitionism becomes literal in the series of erotic films which play an important role in early film production (the same Pathé catalogue would advertise the Passion Play along with "scenes griviose d'un charactére piquant," erotic films often including full nudity), also driven underground in later years. As Noël Burch has shown in his film *Correction Please: How We Got into Pictures* (1979), a film like *The Bride Retires* (France, 1902) reveals a fundamental conflict between this exhibitionist tendency of early film and the creation of a fictional diegesis. A woman undresses for bed while her new husband peers at her from behind a screen. However, it is to the camera and the audience that the bride addresses her erotic striptease, winking at us as she faces us, smiling in erotic display.

As the quote from Méliès points out, the trick film, perhaps the dominant non-actuality film genre before 1906, is itself a series of displays, of magical attractions, rather than a primitive sketch of narrative continuity. Many trick films are, in effect, plotless, a series of transformations strung together with little connection and certainly no characterization. But to approach even the plotted trick films, such as *Voyage dans la lune* (1902), simply as precursors of later narrative structures is to miss the point. The story simply provides a frame upon which to string a demonstration of the magical possibilities of the cinema.

Modes of exhibition in early cinema also reflect this lack of concern with creating a self-sufficient narrative world upon the screen. As Charles Musser has shown,[6] the early showmen exhibitors exerted a great deal of control over the shows they presented, actually re-editing the films they had purchased and supplying a series of offscreen supplements such as sound effects and spoken commentary. Perhaps most extreme is the Hale's Tours, the largest chain of theaters exclusively showing films before 1906. Not only did the films consist of non-narrative sequences taken from moving vehicles (usually trains), but the theater itself was arranged as a train car, with a conductor who took tickets, and sound effects simulating the click-clack of wheels and hiss of air brakes.[7] Such viewing experiences relate more to the attractions of the fairgrounds than to the traditions of the legitimate theater. The relation between films and the emergence of the great amusement parks, such as Coney Island, at the turn of the century provides rich ground for rethinking the roots of early cinema.

Nor should we forget that in the earliest years of exhibition the cinema itself was an attraction. Early audiences went to exhibitions to see machines demonstrated (the newest technological wonder, following in the wake of such widely exhibited machines and marvels as X-rays or, earlier, the phonograph) rather than to view films. It was the Cinématographe, the Biograph or the Vitascope that were advertised on the variety bills in which they premiered, not *The Baby's Breakfast* or *The Black Diamond Express*. After the initial novelty period, this display of the possibilities of cinema continues, and not only in magic films. Many of the close-ups in early film differ from later uses of the technique precisely because they do not use enlargement for narrative punctuation, but as an attraction in its own right. The close-up cut into Porter's *The Gay Shoe Clerk* (1903) may anticipate later continuity techniques, but its principal motive is again pure exhibitionism, as the lady lifts her skirt hem, exposing her ankle for all to see. Biograph films such as *Photographing a Female Crook* (1904) and *Hooligan in Jail* (1903) consist of a single shot in which the camera is brought close to the main character, until they are in midshot. The enlargement is not a device expressive of narrative tension; it is in itself an attraction and the point of the film.[8]

The term "attractions" comes, of course, from the young Sergei Mikhailovich Eisenstein and his attempt to find a new model and mode of analysis for the theater. In his search for the "unit of impression" of theatrical art, the foundation of an analysis which would undermine realistic representational theater, Eisenstein hit upon the term "attraction."[9] An attraction aggressively subjected the spectator to "sensual or psychological impact." According to Eisenstein, theater should consist of a montage of such attractions, creating a relation to the spectator entirely different from his absorption in "illusory imitativeness."[10] I pick up this term partly to underscore the relation to the spectator that this later avant-garde practice shares with early cinema: that of exhibitionist confrontation rather than diegetic absorption. Of course the "experimentally regulated and mathematically calculated" montage of attractions demanded by Eisenstein differs enormously from these early films (as any conscious and oppositional mode of practice will from a popular one).[11] However, it is important to realize the context from which Eisenstein selected the term. Then as now, the "attraction" was a term of the fairground, and for Eisenstein and his friend Yuketvich it primarily represented their favorite fairground attraction, the roller coaster, or as it was known then in Russia, the American Mountains.[12]

The source is significant. The enthusiasm of the early avant-garde for film was at least partly an enthusiasm for a mass culture that was emerging at the beginning of the century, offering a new sort of stimulus for an audience not acculturated to the traditional arts. It is important to take this enthusiasm for popular art as something more than a simple gesture of *épater les bourgeoisie*. The enormous development of the entertainment industry since the Teens and its growing acceptance by middle class culture (and the accommodation that made this acceptance possible) has made it difficult to understand the liberation popular entertainment offered at the beginning of the century. I believe that it was precisely the exhibitionist quality of turn-of-the-century popular art that made it attractive to the avant-garde – its freedom from the creation of a diegesis, its accent on direct stimulation.

Writing of the variety theater, Marinetti not only praised its esthetics of astonishment and stimulation, but particularly its creation of a new spectator who contrasts with the "static," "stupid voyeur" of traditional theater. The spectator at the variety theater feels directly addressed by the spectacle and joins in, singling along, heckling the comedians.[13] Dealing with early cinema within this context of archive and academy, we risk missing its vital relation to vaudeville, its primary place of exhibition until around 1905. Film appeared as one attraction on the vaudeville program, surrounded by a mass of unrelated acts in non-narrative and even nearly illogical succession of performances. Even when presented in the nickelodeons that were emerging at the end of this period, these short films always appeared in a variety format, trick films sandwiched in with farces, actualities, "illustrated songs," and, quite frequently, cheap vaudeville acts. It was precisely this non-narrative variety that placed this form of entertainment under attack by reform groups in the early Teens. The Russell Sage Survey of popular entertainments found vaudeville "depends upon an artificial rather than a natural human and developing interest, these acts having no necessary, and as a rule, no actual connection."[14] In other words, no narrative. A night at the variety theater was like a ride on a streetcar or an active day in a crowded city, according to this middle class reform group, stimulating an unhealthy nervousness. It was precisely such artificial stimulus that Marinetti and Eisenstein wished to borrow from the popular arts and inject into the theater, organizing popular energy for radical purpose.

What happened to the cinema of attraction? The period from 1907 to about 1913 represents the true *narrativization* of the cinema, culminating in the appearance of feature films which radically revised the variety format. Film clearly took the legitimate theater as its model, producing famous players in famous plays. The transformation of filmic discourse that D.W. Griffith typifies bound cinematic signifiers to the narration of stories and the creation of a self-enclosed diegetic universe. The look at the camera becomes taboo and the devices of cinema are transformed from playful "tricks" – cinematic attractions (Méliès gesturing at us to watch the lady vanish) – to elements of dramatic expression, entries into the psychology of character and the world of fiction.

However, it would be too easy to see this as a Cain and Abel story, with narrative strangling the nascent possibilities of a young iconoclastic form of entertainment. Just as the variety format in some sense survived in the Movie Palaces of the Twenties (with newsreel, cartoon, sing-along, orchestra performance and sometimes vaudeville acts subordinated to, but still co-existing with, the narrative *feature* of the evening), the system of attraction remains an essential part of popular filmmaking.

The chase film shows how towards the end of this period (basically from 1903–1906) a synthesis of attractions and narrative was already underway. The chase had been the original truly narrative genre of the cinema, providing a model for casuality [*sic*] and linearity as well as a basic editing continuity. A film like Biograph's *Personal* (1904, the model of the chase film in many ways) shows the creation of a narrative linearity, as the French nobleman runs for his life from the fiancées his personal column ad has unleashed. However, at the same time, as the group of young women pursue their prey towards the camera in each shot, they encounter some slight obstacle (a fence, a steep slope, a stream) that slows them down for the spectator, providing a mini-spectacle pause in the unfolding of narrative. The Edison Company seemed particularly aware of this, since they offered their plagiarized version of this Biograph film (*How a French Nobleman Got a Wife Through the New York Herald Personal Columns*) in two forms, as a complete film, or as separate shots, so that any one image of the ladies chasing the man could be bought without the inciting incident or narrative closure.[15]

As Laura Mulvey has shown in a very different context, the dialectic between spectacle and narrative has fueled much of the classical cinema.[16] Donald Crafton in his study of slapstick comedy "The Pie and the Chase" has shown the way slapstick did a balancing act between the pure spectacle of gag and the development of narrative.[17] Likewise the spectacle film traditionally proved true to its name by highlighting moments of pure visual stimulation along with narrative. The 1924 version of *Ben Hur* was in fact shown at a Boston theater with a timetable announcing the moment of its prime attractions:

8:35   The Star of Bethlehem
8:40   Jerusalem Restored
8:59   Fall of the House of Hur
10:29 The Last Supper
10:50 Reunion[18]

The Hollywood advertising policy of enumerating the features of a film, each emblazoned with the command, "See!" shows this primal power of the attraction running beneath the armature of narrative regulation.

We seem far from the avant-garde premises with which this discussion of early cinema began. But it is important that the radical heterogeneity which I find in early cinema not be conceived as a truly oppositional program, one irreconcilable with the growth of narrative cinema. This view is too sentimental and too ahistorical. A film like *The Great Train Robbery* (1903) does point in both directions, toward a direct assault on the spectator (the spectacularly enlarged outlaw unloading his pistol in our faces), and towards a linear narrative continuity. This is early film's ambiguous heritage. Clearly in some sense recent spectacle cinema has re-affirmed its roots in stimulus and carnival rides, in what might be called the Spielberg-Lucas-Coppola cinema of effects.

But effects are tamed attractions. Marinetti and Eisenstein understood that they were tapping into a source of energy that would need focusing and intensification to fulfill its revolutionary possibilities. Both Eisenstein and Marinetti planned to exaggerate the impact on the spectator, Marinetti proposing to literally glue them to their seats (ruined garments paid for after the performance) and Eisenstein setting firecrackers off beneath them. Every change in film history implies a change in its address to the spectator, and each period constructs its spectators in a new way. Now in a period of American avant-garde cinema in which the tradition of contemplative subjectivity has perhaps run its (often glorious) course, it is possible that this earlier carnival of the cinema, and the methods of popular entertainment, still provide an unexhausted resource – a Coney Island of the avant-garde, whose never dominant but always sensed current can be traced from Méliês through Keaton, through *Un Chien andalou* (1928), and Jack Smith.

Notes

1 Fernand Léger, "A Critical Essay on the Plastic Qualities of Abel Gance's Film *The Wheel*" in *Functions of Painting*, ed. and intro. Edward Fry, trans. Alexandra Anderson (New York: Viking Press, 1973), 21.
2 See my articles "The Non-Continuous Style of Early Film," in *Cinema 1900–1906*, ed. Roger Holman (Brussels: FIAF, 1982) and "An Unseen Energy Swallows Space: The Space in Early Film and its Relation to American Avant Garde Film," in *Film Before Griffith*, ed. John L. Fell (Berkeley: Univ. of California Press, 1983), 355–66, and our collaborative paper delivered by M. Gaudreault at the conference at Cerisy on Film History (August 1985) "Le cinéma des premier temps: un défi a l'histoire du cinéma?" I would also like to note the importance of my discussions with Adam Simon and our hope to further investigate the history and archaeology of the film spectator.

3 Robert C. Allen, *Vaudeville and Film: 1895–1915, A Study in Media Interaction* (New York: Arno Press, 1980), 159, 212–13.

4 Méliês, "Importance du Scénario" in *George Méliês*, Georges Sadoul (Paris: Seghers, 1961), 118 (my translation).

5 Metz, *The Imaginary Signifier: Psychoanalysis and the Cinema*, trans. Celia Britton, Anwyl Williams, Ben Brewster and Alfred Guzetti (Bloomington: Indiana Univ. Press, 1982), particularly 50–80, 91–97.

6 Musser, "American Vitagraph 1897–1901," in *Cinema Journal*, 22,3 (Spring 1983), 10.

7 Raymond Fielding, "Hale's Tours: Ultrarealism in the Pre-1910 Motion Picture," in Fell, 116–30.

8 I wish to thank Ben Brewster for his comments after the original delivery of this paper which pointed out the importance of including this aspect of the cinema of attractions here.

9 Eisenstein, "How I Became a Film Director," in *Notes of a Film Director* (Moscow: Foreign Language Publishing House, n.d.), 16.

10 Eisenstein, "Montage of Attractions," trans. Daniel Gerould, in *The Drama Review*, 18,1 (March 1974), 78–79.

11 Ibid.

12 Yon Barna, *Eisenstein* (Bloomington: Indiana Univ. Press, 1973), 59.

13 "The Variety Theater 1913," in *Futurist Manifestos*, ed. Umbro Apollonio (New York: Viking Press, 1973), 127.

14 Michael Davis, *The Exploitation of Pleasure* (New York: Russell Sage Foundation, Dept. of Child Hygiene, Pamphlet, 1911).

15 David Levy, "Edison Sales Policy and the Continuous Action Film 1904–1906," in Fell, 207–22.

16 "Visual Pleasure and Narrative Cinema," in *Screen*, 16,3 (Autumn 1975), 6–18.

17 Papers delivered at the FIAF Conference on Slapstick, May 1985, New York City.

18 Nicholas Vardac, *From Stage to Screen: Theatrical Method from Garrick to Griffith* (New York: Benjamin Blom, 1968), 232.

15

THE ECSTASY OF COMMUNICATION

Jean Baudrillard (translated by John Johnston)

There is no longer any system of objects. My first book contains a critique of the object as obvious fact, substance, reality, use value.[1] There the object was taken as sign, but as sign still heavy with meaning. In this critique two principal logics interfered with each other: a *phantasmatic logic* that referred principally to psychoanalysis – its identifications, projections, and the entire imaginary realm of transcendence, power and sexuality operating at the level of objects and the environment, with a privilege accorded to the house/automobile axis (immanence/transcendence); and a *differential social logic* that made distinctions by referring to a sociology, itself derived from anthropology (consumption as the production of signs, differentiation, status and prestige). Behind these logics, in some way descriptive and analytic, there was already the dream of symbolic exchange, a dream of the status of the object and consumption beyond exchange and use, beyond value and equivalence. In other words, *a sacrificial logic* of consumption, a gift, expenditure (*dépense*), potlatch, and the accursed portion.[2]

In a certain way all this still exists, and yet in other respects it is all disappearing. The description of this whole intimate universe – projective, imaginary and symbolic – still corresponded to the object's status as mirror of the subject, and that in turn to the imaginary depths of the mirror and "scene": there is a domestic scene, a scene of interiority, a private space-time (correlative, moreover, to a public space). The oppositions subject/object and public/private were still meaningful. This was the era of the discovery and exploration of daily life, this other scene emerging in the shadow of the historic scene, with the former receiving more and more symbolic investment as the latter was politically disinvested.

But today the scene and mirror no longer exist; instead, there is a screen and network. In place of the reflexive transcendence of mirror and scene, there is a nonreflecting surface, an immanent surface where operations unfold – the smooth operational surface of communication.

Something has changed, and the Faustian, Promethean (perhaps Oedipal) period of production and consumption gives way to the "proteinic" era of networks, to the narcissistic and protean era of connections, contact, contiguity, feedback and generalized interface that goes with the universe of communication. With the television image – the television being the ultimate and perfect object for this new era – our own body and the whole surrounding universe become a control screen.

If one thinks about it, people no longer project themselves into their objects, with their affects and their representations, their fantasies of possession, loss, mourning, jealousy: the psychological dimension has in a sense vanished, and even if it can always be marked out in detail, one feels that it is not really there that things are being played out. Roland Barthes already indicated this some time ago in regard to the automobile: little by little a logic of "driving" has replaced a very subjective logic of possession and projection.[3] No more fantasies of power, speed and appropriation linked to the object itself, but instead a tactic of potentialities linked to usage: mastery, control and command, an optimalization of the play of possibilities offered by the car as a vector and vehicle, and no longer as object of psychological sanctuary. The subject himself, suddenly transformed, becomes a computer at the wheel, not a drunken demiurge of power. The vehicle now becomes a kind of capsule, its dashboard the brain, the surrounding landscape unfolding like a televised screen (instead of a live-in projectile as it was before).

(But we can conceive of a stage beyond this one, where the car is still a vehicle of performance, a stage where it becomes an information network. The famous Japanese car that talks to you, that "spontaneously" informs you of its general state and even of your general state, possibly refusing to function if you are not functioning well, the car as deliberating consultant and partner in the general negotiation of a lifestyle, something – or someone: at this point there is no longer any difference – with which you are connected. The fundamental issue becomes the communication with the car itself, a perpetual test of the subject's presence with his own objects, an uninterrupted interface.

It is easy to see from this point speed and displacement no longer matter. Neither does unconscious projection, nor an individual or social type of competition, nor prestige. Besides, the car began to be de-sacralized in this sense some time ago: it's all over with speed – I drive more and consume less. Now, however, it is an ecological ideal that installs itself at every level. No more expenditure, consumption, performance, but instead regulation, well-tempered functionality, solidarity among all the elements of the same system, control and global management of an ensemble. Each system, including no doubt the domestic universe, forms a sort of ecological niche where the essential thing is to maintain a relational décor, where all the terms must continually communicate among themselves and stay in contact, informed of the respective condition of the others and of the system as a whole, where opacity, resistance or the secrecy of a single term can lead to catastrophe.)[4]

Private "telematics": each person sees himself at the controls of a hypothetical machine, isolated in a position of perfect and remote sovereignty, at an infinite distance from his universe of origin. Which is to say, in the exact position of an astronaut in his capsule, in a state of weightlessness that necessitates a perpetual orbital flight and a speed sufficient to keep him from crashing back to his planet of origin.

This realization of a living satellite, *in vivo* in a quotidian space, corresponds to the satellization of the real, or what I call the "hyperrealism of simulation":[5] the elevation of the domestic universe to a spatial power, to a spatial metaphor, with the satellization of the two-room-kitchen-and-bath put into orbit in the last lunar module. This very quotidian nature of the terrestrial habitat hypostasized in space means the end of metaphysics. The era of hyperreality now begins. What I mean is this: what was projected psychologically and mentally, what used to be lived out on earth as metaphor, as mental or metaphorical scene, is henceforth projected into reality, without any metaphor at all, into an absolute space which is also that of simulation.

This is only an example, but it signifies as a whole the passage into orbit, as orbital and environmental model, of our private sphere itself. It is no longer a scene where the dramatic interiority of the subject, engaged with its objects as with its image, is played out. We are here at the controls of a micro-satellite, in orbit, living no longer as an actor or dramaturge but as a terminal of multiple networks. Television is still the most direct prefiguration of this. But today it is the very space of habitation that is conceived as both receiver and distributor, as the space of both reception and operations, the control screen and terminal which as such may be endowed with telematic power – that is, with the capability of regulating everything from a distance, including work in the home and, of course, consumption, play, social relations and leisure. Simulators of leisure or of vacations in the home – like flight simulators for airplane pilots – become conceivable.

Here we are far from the living-room and close to science fiction. But once more it must be seen that all these changes – the decisive mutations of objects and of the environment in the modern era – have come from an irreversible tendency towards three things: an ever greater formal and operational abstraction of elements and functions and their homogenization in a single virtual process of functionalization; the displacement of bodily movements and efforts into electric or electronic commands; and the miniaturization, in time and space, or processes whose real scene (though it is no longer a scene) is that of infinitesimal memory and the screen with which they are equipped.

There is a problem here, however, to the extent that this electronic "encephalization" and miniaturization of circuits and energy, this transistorization of the environment, relegates to total uselessness, desuetude and almost obscenity all that used to fill the scene of our lives. It is well known how the simple presence of the television changes the rest of the habitat into a kind of archaic envelope, a vestige of human relations whose very survival remains perplexing. As soon as this scene is no longer haunted by its actors and their fantasies, as soon as behavior is crystallized on certain screens and operational terminals, what's left appears only as a large useless body, deserted and condemned. The real itself appears as a large useless body.

This is the time of miniaturization, telecommand and the microprocession of time, bodies, pleasures. There is no longer an ideal principle for these things at a higher level, on a human scale. What remains are only concentrated effects, miniaturized and immediately available. This change from human scale to a system of nuclear matrices is visible everywhere: this body, our body, often appears simply superfluous, basically useless in its extension, in the multiplicity and complexity of its organs, its tissues and functions, since today everything is concentrated in the brain and in genetic codes, which alone sum up the operational definition of being. The countryside, the immense geographic countryside, seems to be a deserted body whose expanse and dimensions appear arbitrary (and which is boring to cross even if one leaves the main highways), as soon as all events are epitomized in the towns, themselves undergoing reduction to a few miniaturized highlights. And time: what can be said about this immense free time we are left with, a dimension henceforth useless in its unfolding, as soon as the instantaneity of communication has miniaturized our exchanges into a succession of instants?

Thus the body, landscape, time all progressively disappear as scenes. And the same for public space: the theater of the social and theater of politics are both reduced more and more to a large soft body with many heads. Advertising is its new version – which is no longer a more or less baroque, utopian or ecstatic scenario of objects and consumption, but the effect of an omnipresent visibility of enterprises, brands, social interlocutors and the social virtues of communication – advertising in its new dimension invades everything, as public space (the street, monument, market, scene) disappears. It realizes, or, if one prefers, it materializes in all its obscenity; it monopolizes public life in its exhibition. No longer limited to its traditional language, advertising organizes the architecture and realization of super-objects like Beaubourg and the Forum des Halles, and of future projects (e.g., Parc de la Villette) which are monuments (or anti-monuments) to advertising, not because they will be geared to consumption but because they are immediately proposed as an anticipated demonstration of the operation of culture, commodities, mass movement and social flux. It is our only architecture today: great screens on which are reflected atoms, particles, molecules in motion. Not a public scene or true public space but gigantic spaces of circulation, ventilation and ephemeral connections.

It is the same for private space. In a subtle way, this loss of public space occurs contemporaneously with the loss of private space. The one is no longer a spectacle, the other no longer a secret. Their distinctive opposition, the clear difference of an exterior and an interior exactly described the domestic *scene* of objects, with its rules of play and limits, and the sovereignty of a symbolic space which was also that of the subject. Now this opposition is effaced in a sort of *obscenity* where the most intimate processes of our life become the virtual feeding ground of the media (the Loud family in the United States,[6] the innumerable slices of peasant or patriarchal life on French television). Inversely, the entire universe comes to unfold arbitrarily on your domestic screen (all the useless information that comes to you from the entire world, like a microscopic pornography of the universe, useless, excessive, just like the sexual close-up in a porno film): all this explodes the scene formerly preserved by the minimal separation of public and private, the scene that was played out in a restricted space, according to a secret ritual known only by the actors.

Certainly, this private universe was alienating to the extent that it separated you from others – or from the world, where it was invested as a protective enclosure, an imaginary protector, a defense system. But it also reaped the symbolic benefits of alienation, which is that the Other exists, and that otherness can fool you for the better or the worse. Thus consumer society lived also under the sign of alienation, as a society of the spectacle.[7] But just so: as long as there is alienation, there is spectacle, action, scene. It is not obscenity – the spectacle is never obscene. Obscenity begins precisely when there is no more spectacle, no more scene, when all becomes transparence and immediate visibility, when everything is exposed to the harsh and inexorable light of information and communication.

We are no longer part of this drama of alienation; we live in the ecstasy of communication. And this ecstasy is obscene. The obscene is what does away with every mirror, every look, every image. The obscene puts an end to every representation. But it is not only the sexual that becomes obscene in pornography; today there is a whole pornography of information and communication, that is to say, of circuits and networks, a pornography of all functions and objects in their readability, their fluidity, their availability, their regulation, in their forced signification, in their performativity, in their branching, in their polyvalence, in their free expression . . . [ellipses in original]

It is no longer then the traditional obscenity of what is hidden, repressed, forbidden or obscure; on the contrary, it is the obscenity of the visible, of the all-too-visible, of the more-visible-than-the-visible. It is the obscenity of what no longer has any secret, of what dissolves completely in information and communication.

Marx set forth and denounced the obscenity of the commodity, and this obscenity was linked to its equivalence, to the abject principle of free circulation, beyond all use value of the object. The obscenity of the commodity stems from the fact that it is abstract, formal and light in opposition to the weight, opacity and substance of the object. The commodity is readable: in opposition to the object, which never completely gives up its secret, the commodity always manifests its visible essence, which is its price. It is the formal place of transcription of all possible objects; through it, objects communicate. Hence, the commodity form is the first great medium of the modern world. But the message that the objects deliver through it is already extremely simplified, and it is always the same: their exchange value. Thus at bottom the message already no longer exists; it is the medium that imposes itself in its pure circulation. This is what I call (potentially) ecstasy.

One has only to prolong this Marxist analysis, or push it to the second or third power, to grasp the transparence and obscenity of the universe of communication, which leaves far behind it those relative analyses of the universe of the commodity. All functions abolished in a single dimension, that of communication. That's the ecstasy of communication. All secrets, spaces and scenes abolished in a single dimension of information. That's obscenity.

The hot, sexual obscenity of former times is succeeded by the cold and communicational, contactual and motivational obscenity of today. The former clearly implied a type of promiscuity, but it was organic, like the body's viscera, or again like objects piled up and accumulated in a private universe, or like all that is not spoken, teeming in the silence of repression. Unlike this organic, visceral, carnal promiscuity, the promiscuity that reigns over the communication networks is one of superficial saturation, of an incessant solicitation, of an extermination of interstitial and protective spaces. I pick up my telephone receiver and it's all there; the whole marginal network catches and harasses me with the insupportable good faith of everything that wants and claims to communicate. Free radio: it speaks, it sings, it expresses itself. Very well, *it* is the sympathetic obscenity of its content. In terms a little different for each medium, this is the result: a space, that of the FM band, is found to be saturated, the stations overlap and mix together (to the point that sometimes it no longer communicates at all). Something that was free by virtue of space is no longer. Speech is free perhaps, but I am less free than before: I no longer succeed in knowing what I want, the space is so saturated, the pressure so great from all who want to make themselves heard.

I fall into the negative ecstasy of the radio.

There is in effect a state of fascination and vertigo linked to this obscene delirium of communication. A single form of pleasure perhaps, but aleatory and dizzying. If we follow Roger Caillois[8] in his classification of games (it's as good as any other) – games of expression (*mimicry*), games of competition (*agon*), games of chance (*alea*), games of vertigo (*ilynx*) – the whole tendency of our contemporary "culture" would lead us from a relative disappearance of forms of expression and competition (as we have remarked at the level of objects) to the advantages of forms of risk and vertigo. The latter no longer involve games of scene, mirror, challenge and duality; they are, rather ecstatic, solitary and narcissistic. The pleasure is no longer one of manifestation, scenic and aesthetic, but rather one of pure fascination, aleatory and psychotropic. This is not necessarily a negative value judgment: here surely there is an original and profound mutation of the very forms of perception and pleasure. We are still measuring the consequences poorly. Wanting to apply our old criteria and the reflexes of a "scenic" sensibility, we no doubt misapprehend what may be the occurrence, in this sensory sphere, of something new, ecstatic and obscene.

One thing is sure: the scene excites us, the obscene fascinates us. With fascination and ecstasy, passion disappears. Investment, desire, passion, seduction or again, according to Caillois, expression and competition – the hot universe. Ecstasy, obscenity, fascination, communication or again, according to Caillois, hazard, chance and vertigo – the cold universe (even vertigo is cold, the psychedelic one of drugs in particular).

In any case, we will have to suffer this new state of things, this forced extroversion of all interiority, this forced injection of all exteriority that the categorical imperative of communication literally signifies. There also, one can perhaps make use of the old metaphors of pathology. If hysteria was the pathology of the exacerbated staging of the subject, a pathology of expression, of the body's theatrical and operatic conversion; and if paranoia was the pathology of organization, of the structuration of a rigid and jealous world; then with communication and information, with the immanent promiscuity of all these networks, with their continual connections, we are now in a new form of schizophrenia. No more hysteria, no more projective paranoia, properly speaking, but this state of terror proper to the schizophrenic: too great a proximity of everything, the unclean promiscuity of everything which touches, invests and penetrates without resistance, with no halo of private protection, not even his own body, to protect him anymore.

The schizo is bereft of every scene, open to everything in spite of himself, living in the greatest confusion. He is himself obscene, the obscene prey of the world's obscenity. What characterizes him is less the loss of the real, the light years of estrangement from the real, the pathos of distance and radical separation, as is commonly said: but, very much to the contrary, the absolute proximity, the total instantaneity of things, the feeling of no defense, no retreat. It is the end of interiority and intimacy, the overexposure and transparence of the world which traverses him without obstacle. He can no longer produce the limits of his own being, can no longer play nor stage himself, can no longer produce himself as mirror. He is now only a pure screen, a switching center for all the networks of influence.

Notes

1   *Le Système des objets* (Paris: Gallimard, 1968). [Tr.]
2   Baudrillard is alluding here to Marcel Mauss's theory of gift exchange and George Bataille's notion of *dépense*. The "accursed portion" in the latter's theory refers to whatever remains outside of society's rationalized economy of exchanges. See Bataille, *La Part Maudite* (Paris: Editions de Minuit, 1949). Baudrillard's own conception of symbolic exchange, as a form of interaction that lies outside of modern Western society and that therefore "haunts it like its own death," is developed in his *L'échange symbolique et la mort* (Paris: Gallimard, 1976). [Tr.]
3   See Roland Barthes, "The New Citroën," *Mythologies*, trans. Annette Lavers (New York: Hill and Wang, 1974), pp. 88–90. [Tr.]
4   Two observations. First, this is not due alone to the passage, as one wants to call it, from a society of abundance and surplus to a society of crisis and penury (economic reasons have never been worth very much). Just as the effect of consumption was not linked to the use value of things nor to their abundance, but precisely to the passage from use value to sign value, so here there is something new that is not linked to the end of abundance.
    Secondly, all this does not mean that the domestic universe – the home, its objects, etc. – is not still lived largely in a traditional way – social, psychological, differential, etc. It means rather that the stakes are no longer there, that another arrangement or life-style is virtually in place, even if it is indicated only through a technologistical discourse which is often simply a political gadget. But it is crucial to see that the analysis that one could make of objects and their system in the '60s and '70s essentially began with the language of advertising and the pseudo-conceptual discourse of the expert. "Consumption," the "strategy of desire," etc. were first only a metadiscourse, the analysis of a projective myth whose actual effect was never really known. How people actually live with their objects – at bottom, one knows no more about this than the truth of primitive societies. That's why it is often problematic and useless to want to verify (statistically, objectively) these hypotheses, as one ought to be able to do as a good sociologist. As we know, the language of advertising is first for the use of the advertisers themselves. Nothing says that contemporary discourse on computer science and communication is not for the use alone of professionals in these fields. (As for the discourse of intellectuals and sociologists themselves...) [ellipses in original]
5   For an expanded explanation of this idea, see Baudrillard's essay "La précession des simulacres," *Simulacres et Simulation* (Paris: Galilée, 1981). An English translation appears in *Simulations* (New York: Foreign Agent Series, Semiotext(e) Publications, 1983). [Tr.]
6   [Baudrillard refers to the PBS documentary *An American Family*, the first "reality" television show, based on filming the Loud family of Santa Barbara, which aired in 1973. Intended to give a portrait of daily life, the series instead narrated the family's breakdown. It has subsequently become a case study for considering the ways that documentary is constructed and how the presence of the camera changes what is filmed. – SV.]
7   A reference to Guy Debord's *La société du spectacle* (Paris: Buchet-Chastel, 1968). [Tr.]
8   Roger Caillois, *Les jeux et les hommes* (Paris: Gallimard, 1958). [Trs.]

16

ON A CLEAR DAY YOU CAN SEE THE HORIZON OF INVISIBILITY

Rethinking science fiction film in the age of electronic (re)production

Brooks Landon

There was a time, you read, when making movies took so many people. Actors, cameramen, technicians, screenwriters, costumers, editors, producers, and directors. I can believe it.

That was before computer animation, before the National Likeness Act, before the Noe's Fludde of Marvels.

Back in that time they still used laboratories to make prints; sometimes there would be a year between the completion of a film and its release in theaters.

Back then they used *actual* pieces of film, with holes down the sides for the projector. I've even handled some of it; it is cold, heavy, and shiny.

Now there's none of that. No doctors, lawyers, Indian chiefs between the idea and substance. There's only one person (with maybe a coupe of hackers for the dog's work) who makes the movies: the moviemaker.

There's only one piece of equipment: the GAX–600.

There's one true law: Clean your mainframe and have a full set of specs.

I have to keep that in mind, all the time.

—Howard Waldrop, "French Scenes"

Computer graphics will improve to the point where they can create any visual reality or fantasy in compete detail. Movies will take place in these graphic sets. The relationship between the actors and the scenery will be limited only by our imagination. Animation will be possible with what appears to be live images. Animated doubles and stunt men, created in the images of the human actors, will be capable of impossible feats and subject to spectacular deaths. The movie stars of the future may not be people at all, but visual simulacrums whose appearance is crafted to optimize the qualities their character requires.

—Myron W. Krueger, *Artificial Reality*

When "science" and "fiction" are no longer visualized and narrativized as oppositional, the genre becomes dissolute – dissolves."

—Vivian Sobchack, *Screening Space*

Over the years Krazy had watched uncomprehendingly the slow shift from vaudeville to motion pictures, to radio, to television . . . and next? computers? video games? How would the next generation tell its stories?

—Jay Cantor, *Krazy Kat*

I opened my first chapter [of *The Aesthetics of Ambivalence*] with a description of Gahan Wilson's "Science Fiction Horror Movie Pocket Computer Chart," a cartoon that spoofed the limited plot offerings of SF film by offering a series of alternative narrative lines. A simple plot might go "Earth burns up or freezes or falls into the sun and everybody dies (The End)," and the most complicated plot doesn't get much more detailed. Once again, I ask you to imagine that cartoon – the kind of static flow chart used to explain corporate hierarchies. Only that static flow chart, once a visual cliché every bit as familiar as the formula plots Wilson spoofed, has by now become an antique icon. Why visualize a static flow chart when even rudimentary interactive software can take you through each of the multiple branchings on your child's Macintosh? Furthermore, some nineteen years after Wilson's static flow chart first appeared, we probably wouldn't want to waste time animating the flow *chart* when it's within our ability to animate the narrative formulas it maps, either by animating and editing frames from actual science fiction films, or better yet, generating those frames by computer. Then we really could "get the picture" – digitized, fractally generated, pixilated, and edited into a hyper-hip short, suitable for use as an MTV promo.

But would such a picture today have any value even as humor? To be sure, Wilson meant this chart to be funny much more than he meant it to be analytically powerful, but the not-so-funny irony of SF film criticism is that much, if not most, of it has chosen to describe SF film precisely in Wilson's manically narrative-privileging terms, and SF film has been written about in almost exclusively non-filmic terms in far too many places outside the pages of the *National Lampoon*. However, if SF film critics have been all too eager to valorize Wilson's parody, the SF films of recent years almost seem to have been designed to make Wilson's model seem ridiculously over-complicated. Indeed, it seems highly likely that Wilson's original chart – featuring some sixty-four plot elements for possible combinations – might now strike us as antiquely elaborate. We have all probably grown to suspect that the contemporary science fiction film can be generated from a single branching – one formula simply for big-budget blowouts, the other for straight- or almost straight-to-video rip-off sleaze? In a real sense, it has come to be a choice between *Back to the Future, Part III*, and *Slave Girls from Beyond Infinity*, between *Invasion of the Creepozoid* and *The Abyss*.

But wait! Isn't the very point of the technology that allows us to imagine the cartoon that *the cartoon should really be about technology*? What if the kind of story choices or narrative branchings lampooned by Wilson reveal only a superficial and somewhat accidental parallel between the narratives of SF film and those of SF writing, while they *conceal* the fundamental difference between the generating teleologies of the two media? What if SF film (concentrating a tendency of film in general) is actually generated in significant part by technological rather than narrative concerns and choices? Leave it to a novel based on a cartoon to state this most succinctly, as Jay Cantor's Krazy Kat gets part of her education from a Hollywood producer who tells her that the real appeal of film lies in the special effects: "Bam! Whizz! Star Wars! Technique, that's what movies are about! How appearances are made to appear" (99). The producer explains:

Come backstage with me, darling, and I'll show you the wires and gizmos. You'll like that! You'll be in on the secret. And that's part of the secret, see – American audiences love to be *in the know*. They love to go backstage. They want to see the machinery that fools them, the back projections, the special effects. Right? Right! They don't realize that showing them the machinery *is* the show, and while they're hypnotized by the gears going round, the micro-chips blinking on/off, while you let them see the marketing surveys that reveal their kinky emotional ratchets and levers, you can really get your hands deep down into their pockets. They get hypnotized thinking they're learning how the rubes get hypnotized. (100)

What, then, if the real history of SF film is the history of its production technology rather than the kind of SF "stories" that appear in SF films? What if we try to re-imagine Wilson's "Science Fiction Horror Movie Pocket Computer Chart" in terms of production technology, rather than of plot elements? Replace "Earth" with "SF Moviemaker," and dramatic events with technological options and consider the possibilities.

For example, "SF Moviemaker decides to use stop action photography and/or fast and slow motion photography and/or multiple exposures and/or modeling (The End)." Surely such a branching tells us as much or more about the primary concerns and ultimate significance of *Le voyage dans la lune* than would any account of its comic narrative cobbled together from stories by both Verne and Wells.

A more technologically current branching might go: "SF Moviemaker contracts PIXAR to develop knock-your-eyes-out computer animation (The End)," or "SF Moviemaker contracts Pacific Data Images or Mr. Film to develop knock-your-eyes-out computer animation (The End)," or "SF Moviemaker contracts PIXAR or ILM to use Silicon Graphics 4D/70G and 4D/80GT workstations running Alias/2 animation system with a propriety skinning program and/or SGI 4D/120 workstations running Pixar's Renderman rendering system with a shade tree extension with reflection, refraction, specular highlight, and atmospheric haze functions and/or a Pixar Image Computer, and/or Cyberware's Echo-Data 3-D digitizer plus a pro-prietary ray tracer, etc. (The End)." I admit it doesn't carry quite the same snap as did Gahan Wilson's flow chart, but the above-mentioned high-tech grocery list more or less accounted for the computer-generated "pseudopod," the sentient tentacle of water that was the special effect centerpiece of *The Abyss* (Vasilopoulos 78), and from its use as a stunning cameo in *The Abyss* this technology has grown to be the center of *Terminator 2*, where the narrative has clearly been shaped to account for the liquid-metal effects. Indeed, the concept of the liquid-metal T-1000 terminator seems certain to have been a response to the animation developments showcased in *The Abyss* (also directed by James Cameron), rather than being a new idea presented to special effects technicians as a challenge. And Scott Ross, the general manager of Industrial Light and Magic, the company that supplied this effect, made the ultimate importance of this technology unmistakably clear when he boldly claimed, "I believe people would be interested in seeing an I.L.M. movie as much as they would an Arnold Schwarzenegger movie" (Pollack B2).

Surely by now we've all begun to suspect that larger and larger segments of SF films are motivated less by narrative logic than by technological accomplishment, less by what a story calls for than by what special effects can deliver. But this traditional complaint about the privileging of special effects over story – the suspicion that the story exists just to provide a context for the effect – takes a fascinating new turn when the special effect actually generates the story itself, actually becomes an important, if not determining, factor in the discovery or generation of scientific data and, by extension, of science fiction thinking[1] driven by that data. Just as the development of the telescope was an indispensable technological factor without which science fiction as we know it would never have been possible, computer simulation and visualization technology now generates a new kind of scientific information that is more and more the focus of science fiction thinking. Certainly few developments in the history of SF have been as radical as its shift of focus from the outer space first opened to us by the telescope to the cyberspace opened to us by the computer.

Vivian Sobchack refers to an aspect of this phenomenon when she discusses in *Screening Space* ways in which the concept of space as three-dimensional and "deep" (the outer space of early SF film, for example) has been challenged by a new electronically driven understanding of space as "flattened by the superficial electronic 'dimensionality' of movement experienced as occurring on – not in – the screens of computer terminals, video games, music videos, and movies like *Tron* and *The Last Starfighter*" (230–31). The change, she explains, is that space in electronic culture "is now more often a 'text' than a 'context.'" (232).

Examples of this phenomenon can readily be seen in music videos and computer animation demo tapes such as *State of the Art of Computer Animation* by Pacific Arts, *Computer Dreams and Computer Animation Magic* by MPI, and *Computer Magic* by Cinemagic, which offer a stunning index to the range of computer animation possibilities. All of these demo tapes present computer-generated animation purely as technological spectacle – in much the same fashion that short trick films at the beginning of the century presented the technology of the cinema itself as spectacle.

Early one- and two-minute shorts such as *The Mechanical Butcher* (1895), *Making Sausages* (1897), *Fun in a Butcher Shop* (1901), and *The Marvellous Hair Restorer* (1901) all centered on the gimmick of showing and exploiting technology that could dramatically cut or speed up the time necessary for certain processes. Often identified as early SF films, these shorts were driven only by the narrative of their own production technology. Today those simple early cinema techno-narratives find equally rudimentary electronic analogues in computer-animated TV logos, advertisements, and demonstration spots.

Indeed, the parallels are sometimes amazing: against the concerns of *The Marvellous Hair Restorer* we can now match the achievement of "Huggable Herbert the Bear," a computer animation that triumphantly demonstrates the realism of a fur/hair texture algorithm devised at Cal Tech (Sorensen 45). A further celebration of a hair/fur texture mapping program is "the Tribble," animated by Ken Perlin at New York University. "The Tribble" suggests that technology has been exercised on behalf of at least a recognizable SF icon from the old "Star Trek" TV series, but it's probably more instructive to discover that Cal Tech's "Huggable Herbert the Bear" was generated only after earlier attempts to animate a hairy teapot and a hairy doughnut, both examples clearly indicating the degree to which technology now drives "story" – at last in the early stages of computer animation. The much more sustained narrative of *Stanley and Stella*, a striking show piece in which two lovers break the barrier between a world of "boids" and a world of fish, strongly suggests a narrative designed to showcase computer effects that just happens to be a love story much more than a love story realized by computer animation. Furthermore, as Howard Waldrop's "French Scenes" and much early cyberpunk writing so clearly announces, this new visual technology has itself become a discursive *subject* of SF written narratives.

Or, to put all of this another way, in a technical sense, SF film is more and more becoming a high-tech "cartoon," and the "cartoons" of computer animation fully realize the self-reflexive fascination with production technology that has always been close to the heart of film in general and science fiction film in particular. An emblematic example of this longstanding self-reflexive techno-fascination is René Clair's *Paris qui dort*, a film as I suggested in Chapter 4 [of *The Aesthetics of Ambivalence*], whose English title, *The Crazy Ray*, can best be understood – as Annette Michelson has argued – as the motion picture camera itself.

Michelson's discussion of *Paris qui dort*, "Dr. Crase and Mr. Clair," appeared in the Winter 1979 issue of *October* and should be required reading for everyone who writes about SF film. She explains how this film – visually dominated by the technological icon of the Eiffel Tower – also presents its "mad scientist," Dr. Crase, as a prototypical filmmaker:

> With his little engine he stills and quickens, projects life in and out of motion, speeds and slows the course of things. . . .
> René Clair's celebration of modernity therefore turns upon that threshhold [sic] in our history which was the invention of the motion picture. And in the sequences of arrest and release, of retard and acceleration, we experience the shock and thrill, the terror and delight which express the intoxicating sense generally shared in the first decades of the century, the fulfillment of *une promesse de bonheur* deeply inscribed within the hopes and fantasies of our culture: the control of temporality itself. In its play upon the relation of still and moving image, *Paris qui dort* restores the moment when the photographic image, after sixty years of existence, leaped into action on the screen of a boulevard theater, thus extending its spatiotemporality into the cinematic dimension.
>
> (44)

Is it too much to suggest that almost another 60 years after *Paris qui dort* extended the photographic image into action on the cinematic screen that another film, *Tron*, may have marked another threshold in which the cinematic image was transformed into the electronic image, leaping off the world itself and into the limitless reaches of virtual space? While Vivian Sobchack considers the electronic image within the larger context of electronic "presence," our lived-bodies orientation to the world, her recent analysis of electronic phenomenology applies to *Tron* as well as to the computer animation projects that have come to dominate, if not to displace, contemporary SF film. Sobchack's discussion in "Toward a Phenomenology of Cinematic and Electronic 'Presence': The Scene of the Screen" of the disembodying implications of electronic representation suggests another moment of technological liberation, one even more radical than that posited in Michelson's essay on *Paris qui dort*:

> Digital and schematic, abstracted from *reproducing* the empirical objectivity of Nature that informs the photographic and from *presenting a presentation* of individual subjectivity and the Unconscious that informs the cinematic, the electronic constructs a meta-world where ethical investment and value are located in *representation-in-itself*. That is, the electronic semiotically constitutes a system of *simulation* – a system which constitutes "copies" that no longer refer to an "original."
>
> (56)

The spatiotemporal leap of electronic presence, argues Sobchack, involves liberation from the "real," reconstitutes temporality as a "*homogenous* experience of *discontinuity* in which the temporal distinctions between objective and subjective experience (marked by the cinematic) disappear, and time seems to turn back on itself in a structure of equivalence and reversibility" and reconstitutes space as "abstract, ungrounded, and flat" by constructing "objective and superficial equivalents to depth, texture, and invested bodily movement" (57).

Limited to the SF film that employs significant computer animation or to computer animation demonstrations themselves (to my way of thinking a new generation or kind of SF film), Sobchack's point is that viewing these electronic simulations engages the spectator in an entirely new sense of phenomenological presence, a new and newly problematic way of conceiving of the self. Put another way, we could say that by their very nature computer animations challenge us to rethink our relations to a new technology, to consider the impact of this technology on human life – the traditional function most critics ascribe to science fiction. Hence my contention that simulation technology has become a narrative in itself, that computer-generated virtual images serve as science fiction regardless of the verbal narrative with which they may be associated.

To put this still another way, Sobchack's analysis of electronic presence argues that our *world* has itself become science fictional (a case J.G. Ballard has been making quite effectively since the 1974 preface to the French edition of *Crash*), and explorations of virtual space have become perhaps the most powerful and most representative icons of our science fictional world. This leads me to the proposition that production technology – always a central fascination of SF film – has liberated SF film from the SF story. In other words, the story of the making of the SF film, including the corollary technologies of virtual reality, has itself become a kind of SF story, one so immediate with so many far-reaching social, sociological, and psychological implications that it outstrips the imagination of many current examples of SF writing.

What seems more and more likely is that science fiction film has become something of a museum piece, a historical genre like the western that recycles the past much more than it even attempts to extrapolate the future. Speculation empowers science fiction and when science fiction literature or film abandons speculation it ceases to be science fiction. Accordingly, one of the goals of this book [of *The Aesthetics of Ambivalence*] is to suggest the need for a radically new understanding of the domain of SF film. In Chapter 5 I presented my case for the need to understand what might be called "science fiction seeing" to complement the more traditional understanding of science fiction thinking, and now I want to carry that discussion one step further. I propose a kind of Turing Test definition for science fiction in any medium. Conceived of by Alan Turing as a game for determining when or if a machine can be said to possess human intelligence, the Turing Test assumes that if an observer *perceives* a machine to be acting or thinking in a human way, we might as well say that the machine is human. My comments throughout this extended mediation have assumed a kind of Turing Test for science fiction: if we perceive something as science fictional – sharing in the strategies and assumptions of science fiction thinking and eliciting the same kind of affective responses as does science fiction – we might as well think of it as science fiction. I realize that this may not be a commonly held assumption, or even one to which any others will readily assent, but it seems imperative to me that the spirit of speculation so long the driving force behind SF must be mirrored in the genre's sense of self and in its critical assumptions as well as in its stories.

What if? What if we take the generating rhetoric of science fiction and apply it to the criticism of science fiction film? What if we approach SF film criticism as having more to do with science fiction thinking than with film thinking, as being creative and predictive rather than anecdotal and historical? What if we assume that SF film as a narrative category has historical significance, but no longer has epistemological relevance to any of the goals of science fiction? What if the "new" science fiction film is not *Earth Girls Are Easy* or *The Abyss* or even *Born in Flames* or *Radioactive Dreams*, but digital narratives such as William Barg and Stuart Arbright's video, *Hip Tech and High Lit* or even less narrativized fractal and computer animation demo tapes such as *State of the Art of Computer Animation* from Pacific Arts, or *Computer Dreams* from Digital Visions, or *Scientific Visualization* from the National Center for Supercomputing, or *Frontiers of Chaos*, by Peitgen, Richter, and Saupe?

I pose these questions from the increasingly unavoidable suspicion that science fiction film is now in the process of crossing what O.B. Hardison describes as a "horizon of invisibility."

Borrowing the term from the search for extraterrestrial life, Hardison explains in *Disappearing Through the Skylight: Culture and Technology in the Twentieth Century*:

> A horizon of invisibility cuts across the geography of modern culture. Those who have passed through it cannot put their experience into familiar words and images because the languages they have inherited are inadequate to the new worlds they inhabit. They therefore express themselves in metaphors, paradoxes, contradictions, and abstractions rather than languages that "mean" in the traditional way – in assertions that are apparently incoherent or collages using fragments of the old to create enigmatic symbols of the new.
>
> (5)

Hardison offers the example of modern physics as having passed a horizon of invisibility that forced physicists such as Werner Heisenberg to abandon attempts to use traditional languages for describing radically new assumptions and findings abut the physical world. A more current example would be the science of chaos, and spin offs from this science have already had a major impact on science fiction film through computer animation.

My contention is that science fiction film has likewise crossed or is in the midst of crossing a horizon of invisibility separating its narrative past from its at least temporarily narrativeless present and future. Put more bluntly, production technology has become more interesting than the stories ostensibly justifying the use of that technology – the new narrative of technology has outstripped the science fiction narratives it once supported.

What if science fiction film is, as I believe, undergoing a radical reformulation in which the depiction of science fiction narratives is being displaced by science fictional modes of depicting? This reformulation seems to me the inexorable movement toward what has been called digital narrative, a description at once literal and metaphoric. This is a process in which science fiction *in* the cinema is yielding to a science fiction *of* the cinema, a process characterized by Sobchack in *Screening Space* as the transformation of "the centered subjectivity of *special affect*" into the "decentered subjectification of *special affects*" (282). Production technology drives this process, as computer graphics and animation more and more displace what Sobchack terms the "wonderfully functional" depiction of science fictional concepts with the "functionally wonderful" showcasing of digital imagining capabilities (283). This increasing foregrounding of computer technology in SF film is part of a societal change in which distinctions between science fiction and cultural reality are growing ever more difficult to maintain. Such distinctions are rapidly becoming impossible to make in film, video, and TV, where live action and computer-generated scenes are increasingly intermixed.

Computer industry predictions of entirely computer animated full-length feature films are both numerous and persuasive, as I've detailed in previous chapters. In a January 1991 *Omni* article Robert K. J. Killheffer noted that work in this area now done on PCs "was impossible on the supercomputers of five years ago." Geoffrey de Valous, executive producer/director of Digital Vision Entertainment (DVE), an industry leader in computer generated actors, adds his voice to those predicting fully animated photo-realistic computer-generated films as he repeats the now familiar claim that "Within a few years we'll be able to create computer-generated actors who will look so real, you won't be able to tell the difference between them and human actors" (Killheffer 53). In a July 24, 1991 special to *The New York Times*, Andrew Pollack used the phenomenal economic success of *Terminator 2* as an occasion to renew and intensify the claim that "stunt men, scenery, and actors may one day become unnecessary if entire films can be created on computer." Furthermore, Pollack cited a recent decision in which the Disney Company "agreed to distribute a full-length computer-generated movie to be made by Pixar" as a distinct step in that direction (B2).

Even more persuasive than industry confidence, however, is the visual evidence of a computer-generated film such as Pixar's *Tin Toy*, which won the 1988 Academy Award for Best Animated Short Feature. *Tin Toy* features the animation of a human baby, with details including the definition of more than 40 facial muscles to provide more realistic facial expression. While the result is not yet photo-realistic, Pixar's baby represents a stunning improvement in the animation of human faces, and can only suggest that realistic human animation is quite near to hand.

The baby in *Tin Toy*, following in the electronic footsteps of Max Headroom, has been improved upon by DVE's Ray Tracy, a computer-generated human figure who appears in several different film and TV projects. These computer-generated characters prefigure the future of the image in SF film and video, while figuratively pointing to the possibility of an interactive medium in which viewers will not just watch but will enter directly into real-time relationships with the computer that is generating the film or video narrative, or even the virtual environment that surrounds the viewer.

A representative survey of this new technology can be found in Fred Hapgood's "The Magic Theater" in the December 1989 issue of *Omni*. Hapgood, like almost everyone who knows anything about computer animation, predicts that "images created inside computers will soon be indistinguishable from those shot in physical locations with human actors, thus lowering the cost of making a film to that of writing a novel on a word processor" (116). Echoing Stewart Brand's thesis in *The Media Lab*, Hapgood matter-of-factly notes that eventually, "computer animation technology, will actually become available to everyone, much like TV" (116). The implications of such a development for science fiction film (or science fiction media) are immediately clear:

> Once computer animators perfect the physics in their programs, they will be able to adjust those programs to reflect any imaginable reality. They might create a world in which gravity has one percent of the value of our own, or one in which radio waves are visible, or one where the sun makes oceans boil. As animator Alvy Ray Smith observes, "Once you can do a silk scarf falling on a wood table, you can do a wood scarf falling on a silk table. That's when it gets interesting. These worlds will not be precisely realistic, but they *will* be realistically consistent and therefore as authentic on their own terms as our own world is on its."
>
> (Hapgood 118)

This brings us to an even bigger "techno-blast," a decidedly more radical departure from previous film technologies, yet another sure sign that our electronic culture is stuck on fast-forward. What if the above speculation is itself already well down the road toward antique status? What if the future of science fiction film abandons all of the production/audience assumptions of traditional film, TV, and video in favor of ever more interactive environments in which production and consumption blur in the personal creation of artificial realities? What if the story of science fiction film at the end of the twentieth century turns out to have much more to do with Jaron Lanier and Myron Krueger than with Lucas and Spielberg, more to do with MIT than with Hollywood?

There are already sure signs that realistic simulation of science fictional worlds within the frame of a computer-generated "film" will not be enough – that the inevitable next step is to explode that frame and to *surround* the viewer/creator with a virtual environment, an "artificial reality," With the Nintendo Power Glove, our children have already taken a big first step in this direction. A spin-off from the NASA data glove concept pioneered by Jaron Lanier's company,

VPL, the Nintendo Power Glove is the first article of high-tech clothing in the movement toward an entire bodysuit that will allow its wearer to interact in real time with computer generated virtual worlds. Lanier has already produced "eyephones," virtual reality goggles, which allow the wearer to "enter" simulated worlds. In a recent interview with Kevin Kelly in *Whole Earth Review* Lanier explains:

> The glasses allow you to perceive the visual world of Virtual Reality. Instead of having transparent lenses, they have visual displays that are rather like small three-dimensional televisions. They're much more sophisticated than small televisions, of course. They have to present a three-dimensional world to you that's convincing, and there's some technology involved in accomplishing that, but that's a good metaphor. When you put them on you suddenly see a world that surrounds you – you see the virtual world. It's fully three-dimensional and it surrounds you. As you move your head to look around, the images that you see inside the eyeglasses are shifted in such a way that an illusion of movement is created – you moving while the virtual world is standing still.
>
> (Kelly 110)

Headphone speakers and facial sensors help strengthen the illusion of existing in a virtual reality in which, as Lanier explains, the wearer/creator/viewer might choose to become a cat that smiles in virtual reality when the wearer smiles and whose eyes follow the movement of the wearer's eyes. Virtual reality offers almost unlimited possibilities for generating utilitarian or exotic environments. "You might be in a Moorish temple," suggests Lanier,

> or a heart that's pumping. You might be watching a representation of hydrogen bonds forming. In each case, the world is entirely computer generated. Now, imagine that you had the power to change that world quickly – without limitations. If you suddenly wanted to make the planet three times larger, put a crystal cave in the middle of a giant goat bladder pulsing inside of that and tiny cities populating the goat bladder's surface, and running between each of the cities were solid gold railways carrying tiny gerbils playing accordions – you could build that world instead of talking about it!"
>
> (Stewart 46)

Lanier's hyperbolized example simply underscores the point that virtual reality technology offers us the prospect of designing environments so challenging or interesting that exploring them becomes a kind of narrative in its own right. While Lanier is the most frequently cited visionary of virtual reality, it is important to remember that this technology is being developed by major universities such as MIT, the University of North Carolina, and the University of Washington, by the U.S. military as is the case with the Air Force Super Cockpit project by NASA, and by other corporate entities such as Autodesk, where, among others, SF writer Rudy Rucker is working on the design of virtual reality environments.

Once again, I run the risk of sounding like more of an enthusiast than a critic, but my own experience in virtual reality – using the VPL system – was such an exciting and active discovery process that I simply cannot believe that virtual reality will not soon provide interactive science fictional experience so intriguing and compelling that it will compete directly with the experience of traditional SF film. No SF film, no matter how stunning its special effects or impressive its story, has ever given me the thrill of ten minutes of flying through VPL's virtual worlds, such as that of the "Seattle Waterfront" or that of the nonrepresentational "Ritual World."

Indeed, the lure of virtual reality environments is already at the center of *The Lawnmower Man*, a 1992 film that takes its title from a Stephen King story, but that clearly rests its box office hopes on computer generated special effects that *simulate* on the screen the three-dimensional experience of cyberspace. Computer animations by Angel Studios and XAOS, Inc. "sell" the thrilling experience of virtual reality in this film, presenting it as the ultimate "full-body" video game – even as the film's story somewhat wanly warns of the danger of getting *too* immersed in artificial reality. Once again an SF film uses its plot to say "no, no!" to a new technology, while the powerful look of its foregrounded special effects unmistakably says "yes, yes!" – in this case to the gratuitous point of suggesting the intense new pleasures of computer generated sex. For all of its half-hearted cautioning about the potential abuse of virtual reality technology, *The Lawnmower Man* is a clear example of today's SF film that advertises the future of tomorrow's entertainment. In this respect, *The Lawnmower Man* becomes yet another striking sign of SF film's aesthetics of ambivalence.

Explaining this kind of appealing extrapolation from film to cyberspace, Autodesk designer John Walker observes:

> If video games are movies that involve the player, cyberspace is an amusement park where anything that can be imagined and programmed can be experienced. The richness of the experiences that will be available in cyberspace can barely be imagined today.
>
> (*CADalyst* 42)

While it may well be the case, as Peter Fitting cautions, that new technologies such as those of virtual reality will not necessarily replace traditional films, it is impossible for me to believe that many, if not most, fans of SF film will – given the chance – prefer the interactivity and unlimited creativity of virtual worlds to even the most spectacular passive experience of SF film. Even more likely is that the gap between the two experiences will narrow, as Hollywood learns to redirect its energies to employing virtual reality technology in the service of its traditional narratives.

Immersion in such a virtual reality environment can only call to mind the portions of Gibson's *Neuromancer* trilogy in which action occurs in cyberspace, or the still earlier informational worlds of Vernor Vinge's "True Names." In terms of SF film, such immersion comes close to actualizing the semblance of *Tron*, completing a wonderfully ironic inversion in which computers (best represented by HAL in *2001*) move from being the "enemy" portrayed *in* science fiction film to being the production matrix hope for the future of SF film. As the computer has been increasingly "rehabilitated" within SF film narratives, the very nature of those narratives has been more and more changed by computer animation technology.

Lanier's work foregrounds and concretizes one of the most important aspects of science fiction film, its experiential reconfigurations of space and time. I have repeatedly invoked Vivian Sobchack's discussion of these experiential aspects of postfuturist film, but her analysis has been advanced a further step by Scott Bukatman, who sees an even larger issue:

> Film study, especially in the case of genre films, remains trapped within the conception of film as primarily a narrative – that is, storytelling – form. Iconography and representation reduce the level of significations and structured oppositions (desert/ garden antimonies in the western, e.g., or light/dark in the *noir*). The spatio-temporal experience of the film is almost always missing. The space is understood to present the narrative – style serves content – but isn't narrative itself a stylistic choice? Does the

space of *Blade Runner* exist to present its narrative, or does its somewhat incoherent narrative exist to anchor a particular, and particularly relevant, spatiality? And what of *The Incredible Shrinking Man, 2001: A Space Odyssey*, or even moments of *Robocop*?

("Forum" 28)

Bukatman's suggestion that rigorous understanding of science fiction film demands that we consider its experiential as well as thematic narratives seems to be yet another important link between traditional science fiction film and the new technology of science fictional virtual environments.

O.B. Hardison describes a parallel approach to creating an interactive virtual reality in the "responsive environments" designed by Myron Krueger. Krueger's fascination with artificial reality has gone through several stages, the most complicated of which is titled "Videoplace."

> Krueger's Videoplace used ten minicomputers. A video camera captured the image of each visitor, analyzed it, and produced visitor-specific music and imagery. Thus the visitor had no choice as to whether or not to assist in the creation of Videoplace. Videoplace had many scenarios and routines and used a different set for each visitor. In one routine, a life-size image of the visitor was projected on a screen. Beside the image was a small circle of green light which Krueger calls a "critter." If the visitor attempted to catch the critter, it would slide away.
>
> A game between the visitor and the critter could ensue. Krueger explains that the critter is "a metaphor for one of the central dramas of our time: the encounter between humans and machines."
>
> (228)

Hardison concludes his description of his inherently science fictional environment with the ironic observation that as Krueger can increase the "intelligence" of his environment, it will "then be something like an immobile robot that has ingested the visitor − an echo of *Tron*" (229).

Technological developments such as those in the work of Lanier and Krueger and such as that already available to the public at BattleTech Center in Chicago strike me as the inevitable next stage in what has always been the primary concern of science fiction film − film technology itself. That thesis, best formulated by Garrett Stewart in "The 'Videology' of Science Fiction," a paper first delivered at the 1982 Eaton Conference, is that

> Science fiction in the cinema often turns out to be, turns round to be, the fictional or fictive science of the cinema itself, the future feats it may achieve scanned in line with the technical feat that conceives them now and before our eyes.
>
> (159)

As Eric Rabkin so eloquently specified in "How Will the Future Film?" an essay for the *Journal of the Fantastic in the Arts* forum on SF film,

> Film has always been science fiction, even before it was film . . .
>
> SF film has been the creature of invention . . . even before it was film. And it will be the creature of invention even after it is no longer film. But whatever it is, it has also and always been the creature of humanity. As our science and our technology change, and change us, the obligation of SF film is to give us always the richest artistic

experience it can to explore ourselves and those changes, to question them, and to recompose our world in ever wiser ways.

(28)

The technology into which SF film has disappeared is doing exactly that. What is needed is a redirected SF film criticism as innovative and questioning as is that technology. More than 75 years ago Vachel Lindsay urged the reader of *The Art of the Moving Picture* to "approach the photoplay theatre as though for the first time, having again a new point of view" (252). At a time when computer animation and other forms of electronic imaging literally compel us to have a new point of view, even immersing us in the completely computer generated surroundings of virtual reality, it is time for us to approach the concept of science fiction film "as though for the first time," focusing not on what it used to be, what it failed to be, or what it should be, but on what it is – and on what it will become.

Note

1   [Landon defines his use of this term earlier in the book. Science fiction thinking is "the epistemology of change" (97), an ethos of "belief in problem solving, belief in the possibility and virtues of change, and fascination with the new" (116). – SV]

Works Cited

Brand, Stewart. *The Media Lab: Inventing the Future at MIT*. New York: Viking, 1987.

Bukatman, Scott. "The JFA Forum on SF Film." *Journal of the Fantastic in the Arts* 2.2 (Summer 1989): 28–30.

Cantor, Jay. *Krazy Kat*. New York: Collier, 1987.

Gibson, William. *Neuromancer*. New York: Ace, 1984.

Hapgood, Fred. "The Magic Theater." *Omni* (December 1989): 114–116, 146–148.

Hardison, O.B. *Disappearing Through the Skylight: Culture and Technology in the Twentieth Century*. New York: Viking, 1989.

Kelly, Kevin. "Virtual Reality: An Interview with Jason Lanier." *Whole Earth Review* 64 (Fall 1989): 108–119.

Killheffer, Robert K.J. "Living Illusions." *Omni* (January 1991): 50–53.

Krueger, Myron W. *Artificial Reality*. Reading, MA: Addison-Wesley Publishing, 1983.

Lindsay, Vachel. *The Art of the Moving Picture*. New York: Macmillan, 1916.

Michaelson, Annette. "The Man with the Movie Camera: From Magician to Epistemologist." *Art Forum* 10.7 (1972): 62–72.

Pollack, Andrew. "Computer Images Are Staking Out Star Roles in Movies." *The New York Times* (24 July 1991): B1–B2.

Rabkin, Eric S. "How Will the Future Film?" (Title was mistakenly omitted to this response in the "JFA Forum on Science Fiction Film") *Journal of the Fantastic in the Arts* 2 (Summer 1989): 24–28.

Sobchack, Vivian. *Screening Space: The American Science Fiction Film*. New York: Ungar, 1987.

———. "Toward a Phenomenology of Cinematic and Electronic 'Presence': The Scene of the Screen." *Post Script: Essays in Film and the Humanities* 10.1 (Fall 1990): 50–59.

Sorensen, Peter. "Hair-Raising Graphics." *Computer Graphics World* (January 1990): 45–48.

Stewart, Doug. "Interview: Jaron Lanier." *Omni* (January 1991): 45–46, 113–117.

Stewart, Garrett. "The 'Videology' of Science Fiction." *Shadows of the Magic Lamp: Fantasy and Science Fiction in Film*. eds. George Slusser and Eric S. Rabkin. Carbondale: Southern Illinois University Press, 1985. 159–207.

Vasilopoulos, Audrey. "Exploring the Unknown." *Computer Graphics World* (October 1989): 76–82.

Waldrop, Howard. "French Scenes." *Synergy: New Science Fiction*. Volume 2. ed. George Zebrowski. New York: Harvest, 1988. 27–48.

Walker, John. "Through the Looking Glass: Beyond 'User Interfaces.'" *CADalyst* (December 1989): 43–45.

Wilson, Gahan. "Science Fiction Horror Movie Pocket Computer Chart." *The National Lampoon* (November 1971): 22.

17

THE WONDER YEARS AND BEYOND, 1989–1995

Michelle Pierson

In the flurry of mass media attention that accompanied the opening of two blockbuster special effects events in 1997 – the release of the *Star Wars* trilogy and the release of *The Lost World: Jurassic Park* (dir. Steven Spielberg) – it would have been easy enough not to notice that an important period in the brief but spectacular history of computer-generated special effects had already passed.

[. . .]

Star Wars: Special Edition was certainly not the first Hollywood science fiction film to be digitally remastered. Steven Spielberg released three different versions of *E. T. – The Extra-Terrestrial* (1982) in 1996. Both the video and laserdisc versions featured some digitally remastered effects, a remastered soundtrack, and new footage. The "Special Laserdisc Set" also came with a ninety-minute documentary on the making of the film. Nor was this a first for Spielberg. *Close Encounters of the Third Kind* (1977) was rereleased for video in 1980 with new scenes and the addition of outtakes from the original shoot. And there have been others: *The Abyss* [dir. James Cameron 1989], *Aliens* [dir. James Cameron 1986], *Terminator 2* [dir. James Cameron 1991], and *Independence Day* [dir. Roland Emmerich 1996] have all been rereleased as special editions. The big difference between these films and *Star Wars*, however, was that the latter was released theatrically and not just for the small screen. Had Lucas merely rereleased the film for the home entertainment market, it would have never garnered the kind of attention that it did.

[. . .]

The last chapter noted that the history of CGI effects had all too often been subsumed within more general histories of computer imaging. Here, I want to begin to consider these effects in what used to be thought of as their "cinematographic specificity." This means looking more specifically at how they functioned in the genre cinema of the last decade. Much of this chapter is therefore concerned with expanding on the claim that an aesthetics of CGI effects initially developed along two contiguous axes: the first, simulationist; and the second, techno-futurist. Both types of imagery exhibit the photorealistic capabilities of contemporary digital imaging systems, but whereas a simulationist aesthetic is geared both toward the phenomeno-logical simulation of photographic or cinematographic reality and the representational simula-tion of objects in the natural world, technofuturism describes a hyperreal, electronic aesthetic that is not entirely commensurate with either of these projects. This difference is not the result of a failure to achieve total computer-generated simulation. Nor is it an accident of the production process. Whether conscious or not, it represents a response to audiences' own demands for aesthetic novelty. Technofuturism also describes an aesthetic that in cinematic terms can barely be imagined outside science fiction cinema. So it is to the recent history of this relationship that this chapter now turns.

On genre

While the action-oriented genre films that have been coming out of Hollywood for more than two decades are a hybrid lot, genre has traditionally exerted considerable influence over the kinds of special effects that feature in these films. With its "biomechanoid" alien-monster, *Alien* [dir. Ridley Scott 1979] not only revived the creature film for a whole new audience but also redefined the look of science fiction film for decades to come.[1] The horror film genre, which had long played on audiences' fears and anxieties about the body – in particular its propensity to leak, splatter, and ooze under pressure – again commingled with science fiction in the form of the new creature feature. At the turn of the century the boundaries separating fantasy, horror, science fiction, and action cinema had become more fluid than ever. The epic, historical-fantasy films like *Titanic* [dir. James Cameron 1997] and *Gladiator* [dir. Ridley Scott 2000] made such extensive use of computer-generated sets, props, and extras that it seemed clear that digital imaging techniques had already been fully integrated into the filmmaking process. The question that hadn't been asked yet, however, was how this development would impact on the future of special effects.

[. . .]

The most concerted attempts to think about special effects from a critical and historical perspective that includes some consideration of the regulatory function of genre have thus far come from film scholars such as Albert J. La Valley, Vivian Sobchack, Scott Bukatman, and Brooks Landon, all authors of seminal works in the field of science fiction studies. In their own way, these scholars have each sought to shed light on the reasons science fiction cinema has always been a cinema of special effects. As this chapter will show, all have made claims that share some similarities with the arguments I have been advancing here, although none has looked quite so specifically at the discursive contexts in which an aesthetic discourse on special effects first began to be articulated. But even before these film scholars began to turn their attention to special effects, Christian Metz hinted at the scope for such research in an essay that made special effects objects of theoretical reflection in a way they hadn't been before.

[. . .]

What makes certain types of effects specifically cinematographic is in Metz's view the fact that they belong to the filming (to the camera, or the editing room, or the laboratory) and not, as in the case of profilmic effects, to the filmed. But even before the advent of digital imaging systems, many effects were complex composites of multiple techniques. In the digital era it is not unusual for an effects shot to contain dozens or even hundreds of separate elements. Metz offers stunts as an example of a profilmic effect, arguing that even though all sorts of preparations must be made to carry this type of ruse off, the final effect is achieved before the camera. The filmmaker chooses a stunt man (or woman)

> of the same general appearance as the actor or actress [who is to be replaced]; the wardrobe and make-up departments achieve the "resemblance"; [and] the cameraman is careful to film him [or her] only at a certain distance and from certain angles.
>
> (662, brackets original)

Although stunt doubles are routinely used in Hollywood action films, digital technologies have also given filmmakers more opportunity to use actors to perform their own stunts by making it easier to remove the visible signs of any supporting apparatus in postproduction. Even when stunt doubles are used for action filming, digital compositing enables stunts to be carried out in controlled environments that stand in for location shooting when combined with background footage in postproduction (as in the opening sequence of *Vertical Limit* [dir. Martin Campbell 2000], which combined footage of stunts performed on a purpose-built, 120-foot wall in a New Zealand film studio with footage of Castle Rock in Monument Valley to create the illusion that the stunts had been filmed on location in Utah).

Metz's second reason for claiming that effects that rely on camera or postproduction techniques are more specifically "cinematographic" than physical or mechanical effects is based on his sense that instead of being unique to cinema the latter are shared by other systems of signification: having their genesis in magic and stagecraft, in techniques of illusion shared by the opera, the theater, and pantomime. The reality, however, is that the techniques of special makeup and prosthetics, of puppets, miniatures, and animatronics, have specifically been developed within the context of the film industry and are as much of the cinema as any other special effects technique. Cinema's ability to manipulate viewers' perceptions of scale and space through the use of miniatures is not, for instance, shared by the stage. The distinction that Metz makes between profilmic and cinematographic effects ultimately rests on a narrow identification of the technology of illusion with its instruments. Quite apart from the fact that the techniques of physical and mechanical illusion have provided the cinema with some of its most memorable images, that these images could not have been brought to the screen without the accumulated experience and expertise afforded the film industry makes them specifically cinematographic. Science fiction and horror cinema's assorted miniature, puppet, and animatronic monsters, aliens, and dinosaurs owe their screen life to a mix of culture and industry – artisanship and capital – that doesn't exist anywhere else.

[. . .]

Genre film fans who take a special interest in visual effects also make distinctions between effects that are supposed to be seen and effects that are not, and their evaluations of both types of effects are guided by these perceptions. Effects that are perceived to have been designed for the express purpose of integrating the effect into the visual and narratological space of the cinematographic frame – having no aesthetic function beyond that of maintaining focus on the action or drama and driving the narrative along – are judged according to how closely they approximate this goal. Within a discourse of connoisseurship, evaluation of special effects always involves identification of the parameters for making aesthetic judgments. In this, viewers are guided by their familiarity with the aesthetic conventions of film genres and, with those parameters, by the formal organization of the films themselves.

Metz also recognized that spectators' perceptions of special effects are regulated by genre. [. . .] The expectations that audiences have of [SF] cinema put very specific demands on the visual effects imagery in science fiction films, demands that film scholars have only begun to try to account for fairly recently.

[. . .]

Just as photography had done before it, cinema moved quickly toward developing new ways of layering the cinematographic image to create illusionistic effects: first using in-camera and later optical printing techniques to produce complex, composite images. In the mid-twentieth century, films such as *Tarantula* [dir. Jack Arnold 1955] and *The Incredible Shrinking Man* [dir. Jack Arnold 1957] made extensive use of traveling mattes to produce their remarkable cinematographic articulations. Images of the incredible shrinking man in flight from a cat many times his size or in mortal combat with a tarantula declare themselves tricks through their sheer impossibility. The wonder of these effects lies in speculating about how they were achieved or alternatively, and more satisfyingly, in being able to identify their improvements on older methods of combining images filmed at different times (e.g., the filming of live action in front of a screen on which another film is being projected). What made traveling mattes an improvement on older techniques for combining film images was their ability to mask their techniques of illusion more effectively. But like any special effect that functions in this way, their effectiveness was quickly dulled by repetition.

[...]

Reinventing the cinema of attractions

In order to signal his intention of looking at the history of science fiction cinema in "film-specific" rather than "narrative-based" terms, Brooks Landon called his introduction to *The Aesthetics of Ambivalence* (1992) "Separated at Birth." At the end of the last decade, this was still the only scholarly, book-length study of science fiction films to make special effects technologies its central focus. Landon's work challenged many of the critical assumptions that had been made about science fiction cinema in the past, but perhaps his most thought-provoking claim was that the tradition of art-and-effects direction that emerged from the science fiction cinema of the late 1970s marks a return to the aesthetics of early film. A decade after this book was published, this is now a familiar argument, so influential have some of Tom Gunning's essays on the early cinema of attractions been for the small but developing field of scholarship on special effects that has since emerged.[2]

[...]

When Landon was writing, speculation about the imaging capabilities of new digital technologies was just beginning to take off in the mass media. The publication of *The Aesthetics of Ambivalence* was sandwiched between the release of *Terminator 2* (1991) and *Jurassic Park* (1993). Here was a cinema that seemed to many people not only to be making its power of simulation its feature attraction but also to be on the verge of disarticulating science fiction film from the very institution of cinema itself. In the buildup to *Jurassic Park*'s release, speculation about the film's computer-generated dinosaurs generated far and away the most publicity for the film. And in fact no other film so perfectly exemplifies certain aspects of Landon's description of the way special effects imagery functions in the science fiction films of this period. In the first scene in which one of the much-anticipated computer-generated dinosaurs is finally unveiled – both to the characters in the film and to the cinema audience in the theater – the narrative all but comes to a halt, the music gradually builds, and shots of characters reacting to the appearance of the dinosaur with wonder and amazement are interspersed with long takes displaying the computer-generated brachiosaur center screen.

One of the most powerful discourses on computer-generated imaging technologies centers on the possibility that this technology might one day produce images that so perfectly simulate the look of objects in the real world that it will be impossible to tell that they have been computer generated. This is the dream of simulation that Landon rightly points out has long been debated and explored, both in science fiction film and literature and in what he calls "science fiction thinking." Reviews of CGI effects in the mass media have also taken a particular interest in this dream, often presenting the latest Hollywood SF blockbuster as an invitation to participate in the technoscientific adventure that the dream of total computer-generated simulation represents. But alongside these dreams other popular aesthetic discourses also molded and shaped the look of CGI in science fiction cinema. And while Landon's representation of the aesthetic discourses governing the production and reception of CGI effects for the most part consists of speculation about these dreams, other possibilities – other ways of understanding the aesthetic direction that CGI effects have taken over the years – might yet be gleaned from the technocultural matrix he describes.

[. . .]

This [Sobchack's call for focused criticism on varieties of digital articulations[3]] has proven to be a timely intervention. For without being able to account for the expectations that consumers of different types of computer-generated images have of them – and some of the myriad activities that mediate their experiences of viewing these images in the cinema, or on video, or in the form of computer games or experimental new media – the socially significant dimensions of these experiences cannot be accounted for, either. It may just be that the first step toward recovering some of this variety in accounts of the cultural reception of special effects lies in remembering that it is not only technologies that decide the fate of cultural institutions. What attempts to draw comparisons between the computer-generated visual effects imagery featured in Hollywood cinema and the computer-generated environments of computer games have had to consider, for instance, is the very different expectations people have of these media. A number of critics who have looked at the convergence between film and computer games have pointed out that video and computer games have not only adapted many of the techniques of narrative filmmaking to suit the action-oriented idiom of gaming but that the mining of games for source material (e.g., *Street Fighter* [dir. Steven E. De Souza 1994] and *Mortal Kombat* [dir. Paul Anderson III 1995]) is only the most obvious way contemporary genre films have in turn drawn on computer games.[4] Moreover, if one of the features of a computer game aesthetic has always been the privileging of rendering speed over resolution, as the techniques for enhancing visual resolution have continued to improve the visual integrity of the graphical interface the trade-off between the two has become less and less determining. The narrative and experiential frameworks of games and films nevertheless remain very different, and different visual design protocols have evolved for different types of game platforms. As reviews of video and computer games in a publication such as *Sci-Fi Universe* make clear, the language for describing what makes for a good game experience is not at all the same as that used to describe a good movie-going experience elsewhere in this magazine.

[. . .]

This attachment to the cinema – an attachment that is fostered most strongly through cultures of appreciation and connoisseurship – has roots in a host of cultural practices and institutions (including educational institutions) that continue to invest the cinema, and cinemagoing, with social and cultural value. Where the comparison between blockbuster SF cinema of the 1990s and the early cinema of attractions is especially instructive is in reminding us that demands for novel attractions virtually ensure the limited lifespan of any technological, stylistic, or aesthetic innovation. As far as this cinema's special effects have been concerned, it should therefore come as no surprise that the novelty of a simulationist aesthetic would be the first to wear off, driven as it is, in this context, by the logic of similitude and the simulacra.

Digital art effects

During the early part of the last decade, the special effects imagery in science fiction cinema was bracketed for audiences – both by the formal organization of the films themselves and by the formal and informal networks of information about special effects that now play such an important role in the contemporary entertainment experience – as both a technoscientific tour de force for the special effects industry and a special kind of aesthetic object. In films such as *The*

Abyss, Terminator 2, Lawnmower Man [dir. Brett Leonard 1992], *Jurassic Park, Stargate* [dir. Roland Emmerich 1995], *Johnny Mnemonic*, and *Virtuosity* the presentation of key computer-generated images produces a distinct break in the action. These temporal and narrative breaks might be thought of as helping to establish the conditions under which spectators' willed immersion in the action – their preparedness to being carried along by the ride – is suspended long enough to direct their attention to the display of a new kind of effects artifact. In these films, effects sequences featuring CGI commonly exhibit a mode of spectatorial address that – with its tableau-style framing, longer takes, and strategic intercutting between shots of the computer-generated object and reaction shots of characters – solicits an attentive and even contemplative viewing of the computer-generated image. It is these types of effects sequences that effects professionals usually have in mind then they refer to a film sequence as an effects sequence. Sometimes, of course, the decision is made *not* to allow an effects image to distract from the narrative and/or action in this way. Referring to such a scene in *Star Wars: Episode I – The Phantom Menace* [dir. George Lucas 1999], visual effects supervisor Denis Muren explains that

> when we cut to the outside, we didn't want to linger too long and make it an effects sequence. That way the audience is interested in "Are they [the characters in the scene] going to get away or not?" rather than how neat the creatures look.[5] (brackets original)

In the case of effects sequences that do solicit an aesthetic appreciation of the visual effects image as art and artifact, sound also has an important role to play in organizing viewers' attention at these moments. Brad Fiedel, whose many feature film credits include *The Terminator* [dir. James Cameron, 1984] and *Johnny Mnemonic*, used a synthesizer to create a postindustrial soundscape for the musical score for *Terminator 2*. An important musical motif is established in the film's credit sequence, which depicts a future war scenario in which soldiers are battling it out for survival with the machines that now walk the earth, their metal skeletons literally crushing humanity underfoot. Sarah Connor (Linda Hamilton) provides the voice-over narration that begins and ends this sequence, a device that is used to convey a back story essential to the plot. Underscoring the action are all the sounds of battle – machine-gun fire, explosions, the crush of metal, the whine of aircraft – but these are overlaid by a musical score that is dominated by a droning, atonal bass sound rising above the rest of the soundtrack like some strange foghorn. As the narration that bookends the sequences resumes, this distinctive sound effect gives way to a musical score now dominated by a percussion track that has been running through the sequence but, brought up in the mix, now heralds the return to the present-day time of the film. Both these elements of the musical score – the machine drone and the heraldic drum beat – provide important aural cues throughout the first half of the film. From their first sighting of the T-1000 disguised as a police officer (Robert Patrick), viewers are, for instance, cued to associate this human figure with the sound of a machine future.

[. . .]

All the action-oriented SF films of the early 1990s exhibit this self-conscious showcasing of a new type of effects imagery. Everything about them is designed to magnify its aesthetic impact. No fabulous or picturesque tableaux, no monumental vistas or lush sets, compete with the effects image. This is a cinema of interiors. There are none of the densely layered exterior spaces that gave the "overexposed city" in *Blade Runner* [dir. Ridley Scott 1982] the monumental grandeur that Bukatman and others have described so well.[6] In *the Abyss* the setting for the film's key effects image – the presentation of the protean seawater pseudopod – is the confined, only half-domesticated space of an underwater oil rig, its cramped, industrial interior providing a monochrome backdrop to the appearance of this alien intruder. The virtual reality sequences in both *Lawnmower Man* and *Johnny Mnemonic* likewise function as a visual counterpoint to the mundane, dimly lit interior where the bodies of these films' virtual travelers remain parked. The world of *Lawnmower Man* is a world where domestic violence is never farther away than next-door and where instead of offering an escape virtual reality leads only to the magnification of that violence. The film suspends this demoralizing realization as long as it can, first making the basement of a suburban home and then a government-funded lab the setting for its visual flights of fancy. The last gasp of a cyberpunk future, *Johnny Mnemonic* forwent any attempt to draw its future world anew, instead allowing the detritus of the postindustrial past to stand, as it had so often done before, as the sign that the future isn't what it used to be. Except that it was. By now, the film's survivalist aesthetic has lost whatever novelty it had once held for audiences, but against the shopworn look of the film's dark interiors the computer-generated VR sequences burnt up the screen with an electronic intensity like nothing else around it.

[. . .]

In an essay that significantly widened the scope for historical research on special effects, Scott Bukatman identified a very different tradition of art-and-effects direction in films such as *2001* [dir. Stanley Kubrick 1968], *Close Encounters of the Third Kind*, *Star Trek: The Motion Picture* (dir. Robert Wise 1979) and *Blade Runner*.[7] Instead of it being a matter of disrupting cinematographic space – of inserting, or installing, a markedly different kind of technological and aesthetic object into a relatively restricted visual field in the manner just described – Bukatman points out that key special effects sequences in these films are designed to integrate the virtual space of the spectacle with the physical space of the cinema theater. Instead of being directed toward establishing the conditions under which viewers might obtain some sense of distance from the object being presented, the sheer scope and magnitude of these spectacular vistas – which typically entail the presentation of a massive technological object or environment – is designed to create an immersive experience for cinema spectators. [. . .]

During the 1980s and 1990s a handful of SF films staged encounters with the new technological space of cyberspace and VR. *Tron* [dir. Steven Lisberger 1984], *Lawnmower Man*, and *Johnny Mnemonic* all used CGI to render these high-tech environs for film. However, the totally computer-generated effects sequences in these films are not, for all that, fundamentally different in kind from those effects sequences in which cinematographic space is disrupted by the insertion of a computer-generated object at the level of the shot. In the sequences in which a computer-generated object – a pseudopod, shapeshifter, stargate, energy ribbon – is composited with live-action footage, the electronic properties of the digital artifact (with its high chrominance, intense luminosity, and electronic plasticity) establish a stark contrast between the computer-generated[8] object and the cinematographic space that frames it. This is the case even where an entire shot is computer generated. Although the computer-generated imagery in *Lawnmower Man* or *Johnny Mnemonic* is not, for instance, inserted into cinematographic space at the level of the shot – as it is with CGI and live-action composites – it still represents a mode of visual display that differs markedly from the visual style of the dramatic and/or action scenes that flank it. In both types of effects sequences, then, the presentation of CGI effects is characterized by a visual and temporal disruption in cinematographic space.

[. . .]

Still missing from this account of the cinematographic specificity of the visual effects image in SF film is more of a sense of how – and under what conditions – CGI effects came to be perceived by effects professionals themselves not only as the privileged mode of visualization in SF film but also as the cultural sign of an emerging popular aesthetic, an aesthetic I have been calling "technofuturist." Despite the popularity of technicist discourses on special effects, the development of this aesthetic has not been governed solely by technological criteria. Advanced computer-generated imaging technologies have enabled effects producers to create photorealistic images that could not have been produced using the technologies available a decade earlier. But the application of digital imaging technologies to the production of special effects continues to require the people involved in this process to make aesthetic decisions.

[. . .]

Through its CGI effects the cinema of this period not only animated public speculation about what the future of computer-generated imaging might look like but in a broader sense helped to create a visual landscape in which imaging the future was again an exciting prospect. In every other respect these films were lacking in the richly imagined future worlds that SF writers and fans had been demanding from contemporary science fiction films for quite some time.[9] Instead the future had been telescoped into just a few, wonder-working artifacts. Only *Star Trek* films continued to offer an alternative universe to the bland dystopias that had replaced the cyberpunk futures of the previous decade.[10]

Musing on the state of contemporary literary SF, Fredric Jameson suggested some time ago now, that the horizon of expectations in which SF fantasies of the future are imagined is such that "we no longer entertain such visions of wonder-working, properly 'S-F' futures of technological automation." These visions, he argued, "are themselves now historical and dated – streamlined cities of the future on peeling murals – while our lived experience of our greatest metropolises is one of urban decay and blight."[11] Jameson's suggestion that the only progressive futurist project for SF is one that dispenses with imaging the future in favor of imaging the present as past nevertheless forecloses on attempts to imagine a future in which technology figures as a force to be reckoned with at all. As often as not the artifacts of the machinic future that burned so brightly in the SF films of the early 1990s were bracketed by narratives that were rather more anxious than hopeful about how humanity's close encounters with these terrible machines would pan out. But in again making the visualization of amazing technologies its central focus the science fiction cinema of the early 1990s also puts its faith in a technofuturist aesthetic that for the first time in a long time gave audiences a future they hadn't quite seen before.[12]

Retrofuture/retrovision

Although CGI effects did not disappear from SF film after this period, they no longer occupied the same kind of visual and narratological space they had occupied in the SF films produced during the first part of this decade. The specifically electronic properties of the computer-generated imagery in *The Fifth Element* (dir. Luc Besson 1997) and the fantasy/science fiction film *Dark City* [dir. Alex Proyas 1998] tended, for instance, to be absorbed by the more painterly, expressionist look of these films. The costuming, art direction, and production design for *The Fifth Element* recycled design styles and lifestyles from the last half-century of fashion, architecture, and industrial design in a camp dissembling of the future. The fantasy world pictured in *Dark City* was even more phantasmagorical, except that in this film an aesthetic drawn from the ghostly projection of dreams past was also given narrative motivation. As one of the film's characters, a Stranger, puts it, Dark City is a city fashioned "on stolen memories, different eras, different pasts, all rolled into one."[13] With costuming, sets, and visual effects all providing points of aesthetic interest, the look of these films is cluttered, baroque. Only occasionally is a CGI effect brought into focus. [. . .] But the overall effect on these occasions is one of anamorphosis, with the image only ever cohering as a special effect in the brief moment before the bigger picture is restored. In one sense this had been the future for CGI all along. After all, repeated demonstration of some of the digital imaging techniques used to exploit and explore the otherworldly, nonindexical properties of digitally produced images meant that filmmakers could no longer rely on these techniques to arouse audiences' curiosity in the way they once had. Techniques like morphing had, for instance, long since lost their aesthetic interest. On the other hand, the move to treat computer animation not as a specifically effects-oriented medium but as the ground for all cinematic figuration seemed to mean using digital imaging techniques to remake film in the mode of something closer to traditional feature film animation.

In more ways that one, science fiction film took a decidedly retrofuturist turn in the latter half of the 1990s. With his finger ever on the pulse of the zeitgeist, Mark Dery wondered in 1999, why now? Why had the futuristic designer styles of the mid-twentieth century come into vogue now, at the end of this millennial decade?[14]

[. . .]

The production design for *The Fifth Element*, *Gattaca* (dir. Andrew Niccol 1997) and *Men in Black* (dir. Barry Sonnenfeld 1997) also indulged this latest bout of nostalgia for futures past. Dery singles out *Men in Black* for special mention, pointing to those Arne Jacobsen Egg chairs in the examination room of the MIB headquarters and the same building's foyer, modeled on the TWA terminal at JFK International airport, as evidence of retrofuturism's newfound appeal.[15] Most spectacularly, the film's climax takes place on the site of the 1964 World's Fair in Flushing Meadows, New York, the last time, it had been suggested, that "such an unqualified celebration of technological optimism" would be attempted.[16] This, Dery offers, is what retrofuturism is really all about. It recalls a time when it was still possible to be wildly optimistic about the future, ironically turning another generation's extravagant gestures toward tomorrow into something that now just seems "campy and kitschy and harmlessly fun."[17]

[. . .]

This is the approach that director Barry Sonnenfeld decided on for *Men in Black*. *MIB* is a much less crafty film than a Harryhausen film. Its aliens have been designed to draw a laugh, not wonder. Many of its alien effects are not strictly makeup effects at all but a combination of physical and CGI effects. There is nothing new about digitally enhancing or augmenting physical effects. This practice is now ubiquitous, and not only within the newly expended genres of *cinefantastique*.

[. . .]

According to a report in *Cinefantastique* on the making of the effects for *MIB*, it was these kinds of concerns that prompted Carlos Huante, the artist originally hired to design the film's alien makeup effects, to leave before production finished.[18]

[. . .]

Huante cites *Mars Attacks!* [dir. Tim Burton 1996] as an example of everything that is wrong with CGI, dismissing the film as "basically a cartoon" (24). But what's most interesting about this star-studded pastiche of the fifties' B-grade alien invasion movie is less the mere fact that CGI was used to simulate the look of physical and mechanical effects than the clear indication that this was the direction that CGI effects would continue to take in the future. The inspiration for *Mars Attacks!* came from a series of bubblegum cards that, as the fan magazines gleefully report, had trouble getting distribution back in 1962 because of parental outrage over their blood and gore.[19] The antirealist, cartoon flavor of the film's effects animation was intended to recapture both the lurid quality of these treasured cult artifacts and the heroic failure of so many B-grade SF films to persuade audiences to take them seriously. In this respect, however, the film takes a rather liberal approach to the way it remembers the B-grade SF film. Ed Wood's *Plan 9 from Outer Space* (1958) provides one point of reference, but so does *Forbidden Planet*. [. . .]

But the behind-the-scenes story of *Mars Attacks!* is only partly a story about how the techniques of visual effects animation are being lost to CGI. In the late 1990s Hollywood science fiction cinema was again in the process of folding back in on itself, offering up so many versions of a retrovisionist future in which the expressive possibilities of computer generation were no longer the central focus. Whether it be the low-tech aesthetic of *Escape from L.A.* (dir. John Carpenter 1996), the make-do-cum-B-grade aesthetic of *Independence Day*, the shtick and pastiche of *Mars Attacks!* and *Men in Black*, or the expressionist camp of *The Fifth Element*, computer-generated special effects had ceased to figure in these films as objects of curiosity and wonder. In the scene in which the first computer-generated dinosaurs appear in *The Lost World: Jurassic Park*, exclamations of wonder from the characters on-screen are gently parodied: "Ooh, Ahh . . . that's how it always starts," says Jeff Goldblum's character, Ian Malcolm. "And then later, there's running and then screaming." Instead of being displayed as objects of aesthetic interest in their own right – bracketed off from the temporal and narrative space of the action – the CGI dinosaurs share the shame space as the characters in the scene, threatening to trample all underfoot in a sequence that integrates live action footage and CGI effects in a dynamic composition that pushes the action to the fore. Every now and then a CGI effect would pop up and again turn an image of the future into an occasion for lingering over an unexpected aspect of its conception or design. But for the moment, at least, the future had once more dropped out of sight in Hollywood science fiction cinema.

Notes

1 Brooks Landon looks at the legacy of this film, as well as H.R. Giger's alien designs, in "Sliming Technology," *Cinefantastique* 18.4 (May 1988): 27–28.

2 See, in particular, Tom Gunning, "The Cinema of Attractions: Early Film, Its Spectator, and the Avant-Garde," in *Early Cinema: Space, Frame, Narrative*, ed. Thomas Elsaesser and Adam Barker (London: BFI Publishing, 1990), 56–62; and Gunning, "An Aesthetic of Astonishment: Early Film and the (In)Credulous Spectator," in *Viewing Positions: Ways of Seeing Film*, ed. Linda Williams (New Brunswick, N.J.: Rutgers University Press, 1994), 114–33. Also see Angela Ndalianis, "Special Effects, Morphing Magic, and the Nineties' Cinema of Attractions," in *Meta-Morphing: Visual Transformations and the Culture of Quick Change*, ed. Vivian Sobchack (Minneapolis: Minnesota University Press, 2000), 251–71; Jay David Bolter and Richard Grusin, "Film," in *Remediation: Understanding New Media* (Cambridge, Mass., and London: MIT Press, 1999), 146–58; and Andrew Darley, "Genealogy and Tradition: Mechanised Spectacle as Popular Entertainment" and "New Spectacle Cinema and Music Video," in *Visual Digital Culture: Surface Play and Spectacle in New Media Genres* (London: Routledge, 2000), 37–57, 102–23.

3 [See introduction to *Meta-Morphing: Visual Transformations and the Culture of Quick-Change*, ed. Vivian Sobchack (Minneapolis and London: University of Minnesota Press, 2000), xiv. – SV]

4 For an examination of some of the ways film and video games borrow from each other, see Angela Ndalianis, "'The Rules of the Game'—Evil Dead II . . . Meet Thy Doom," in *Hop on Pop: The Politics and Pleasures of Popular Culture*, ed. Henry Jenkins, Tara McPherson and Jane Shattuc (Durham, N.C.: Duke University Press [2003]). Also see Mark J.P. Wolf, "Inventing Space: Toward a Taxonomy of On- and Off-Screen Space in Video Games," *Film Quarterly* 51.1 (Fall 1997): 11–23.

5 See Ron Magid, "Virtual Realities," *American Cinematographer* 80.9 (Sept. 1999): 88. The sequence that Muren refers to is the underwater sequence in which Qui-Gon Jinn (Liam Neeson), Obi-Wan Kenobi (Ewan McGregor), and Jar Jar Binks encounter a series of alien sea creatures.

6 See Scott Bukatman's examination of *Blade Runner* in *Terminal Identity: The Virtual Subject in Postmodern Science Fiction* (Durham, N.C., and London: Duke University Press, 1993), 130–137.

7 Scott Bukatman, "The Artificial Infinite: On Special Effects and the Sublime," in *Visual Display: Culture Beyond Appearances*, ed. Lynne Cooke and Peter Wollen (Seattle: Bay, 1995), 254–89. Douglas Trumball acted as visual effects supervisor on all the films Bukatman refers to.

8 The decision to describe certain types of computer-generated images as digital artifacts is not one I made without reservations. The potential for confusion over this term arises from the fact that within the special effects industry itself the term "digital artifact" refers to an extraneous digital object that has been marked for removal in the postproduction process. I nevertheless use it here because it draws attention to the display of the CGI effect as aesthetic object.

9 A "roundtable discussion about why today's science fiction movies are so damned lame" appeared in the May 1997 issue of *Sci-Fi Universe*. When asked to compare *Star Wars* with *Independence Day*, screenwriter Alan Bennert responded: "*Star Wars* is not what I'd call sophisticated SF, but in contrast to the movies that are being done these days, it was set in a completely invented universe. [Sure], George Lucas created a future cobbled together out of bits and pieces of Jack Kirby and 'Doc' Smith, but at least he did it with honesty and intelligence. Jim Cameron did the same in *Aliens*. Both films are set in richly imagined future worlds and that's something that just seems to be lacking these days in movies" (Eric Wallace, "The Script's the Thing," *Sci-Fi Universe* 3.7 [May 1997]: 24).

10 Thomas Doherty summed up the situation when he wrote: "From *Waterworld* to *Strange Days*, theatrical SF is so determinedly downbeat in tone that the field for another vision of the future – like, maybe there *is* one – is pretty much left up to *Star Trek*" (Thomas Doherty, "*Star Trek* the Franchise: Thirty Years in Space," *Cinefantastique* 27.4–5 [Jan. 1996]: 66).

11 Fredric Jameson, "Progress Versus Utopia: or, Can We Imagine the Future?" *Science-Fiction Studies* 9.27 (1982): 151.

12 Mark Dery and Claudia Springer have pointed out that these futures have invariably reproduced phal-locentric fantasies about technology and gender. See Mark Dery, *Escape Velocity: Cyberculture at the End of the Century* (London: Hodder and Stoughton, 1996), 264–65; and Claudia Stringer, "Virtual Sex," in *Electronic Eros: Bodies and Desire in the Postindustrial Age* (Austin: University of Texas Press, 1996). 94. While these readings are entirely apposite – and even necessary – it has been my contention here that they still haven't quite registered the ways in which visual effects images *mean* for science fiction fans.

13 For a detailed reading of this film, which also looks at the circumstances and implications of its produc-tion in Australia, see Tom O'Regan and Rama Venkatasawmy, "Only One Day at the Beach: *Dark City* and Australian Film-making," *Metro* 117 (1998): 17–28.

14 Mark Dery, "Back to the Future," *Nettime* (Sept. 5, 1999), www.nettime.org/nettime.w3archive/199909/msg00042.html.

15 Dery, pars. 1–2.

16 See Roland Marchand and Michael L. Smith, "Corporate Science on Display," in *Scientific Authority and Twentieth-Century America*, ed. Ronald B. Walters (Baltimore and London: Johns Hopkins University Press, 1997), 174.

17 Dery, "Back to the Future," par. 6.

18 Douglas Eby, "MIB The Aliens: Rubber vs. CGI," *Cinefantastique* 29.1 (July 1997): 23–25.

19 Frederick C. Szebin and Steve Biodrowski, "*Mars Attacks*: Tim Burton Sends Up the Bubblegum Alien Invasion Genre," *Cinefantastique* 28.7 (Jan. 1997): 16. See also Chuck Wagner, "Martian Inspiration," *Cinefantastique* 28.7 (Jan. 1997): 19.61. [*sic*]

18

THE CULTURAL LOGIC OF MEDIA CONVERGENCE

Henry Jenkins

The American media environment is now being shaped by two seemingly contradictory trends: on the one hand, new media technologies have lowered production and distribution costs, expanded the range of available delivery channels and enabled consumers to archive, annotate, appropriate and recirculate media content in powerful new ways;[1] on the other hand, there has been an alarming concentration of the ownership of mainstream commercial media, with a small handful of multinational media conglomerates dominating all sectors of the entertainment industry.

Few media critics seem capable of keeping both sides of this equation in mind at the same time. Robert McChesney (2000) warns that the range of voices in policy debates will become constrained as media ownership concentrates. Cass Sunstein (2002) worries that fragmentation of the web is apt to result in the loss of shared values and common culture. Nick Gillespie (1999) points towards a "culture boom," while Mark Crispin Miller (2002) speaks of an American "monoculture." Todd Gitlin (2003) worries about a "media torrent," whereas Grant McCracken (1997) sees the "plentitude" of a highly generative culture. Some fear that media is out of control; others that it is too controlled. Some see a world without gatekeepers; others a world where gatekeepers have unprecedented power. They all get partial credit, given the contradictory and transitional nature of our current media system.

This article will sketch a theory of media convergence that allows us to identify major sites of tension and transition shaping the media environment for the coming decade. My goal is to identify some of the ways that cultural studies might contribute to those debates and why it is important for us to become more focused on creative industries.

Media convergence is more than simply a technological shift. Convergence alters the relationship between existing technologies, industries, markets, genres and audiences. Convergence refers to a process, but not an endpoint. Thanks to the proliferation of channels and the portability of new computing and telecommunications technologies, we are entering an era where media will be everywhere and we will use all kinds of media in relation to each other. Our cell phones are not simply telecommunications devices; they also allow us to play games, download information from the internet and receive and send photographs or text messages. Any of these functions can also be performed through other media appliances. One can listen to The Dixie Chicks through a DVD player, car radio, walkman, computer MP3 files, a web radio station or a music cable channel. Fueling this technological convergence is a shift in patterns of media ownership. Whereas old Hollywood focussed [sic] on cinema, the new media conglomerates have controlling interests across the entire entertainment industry. Viacom, for example, produces films, television, popular music, computer games, websites, toys, amusement park rides, books, newspapers, magazines and comics. In turn, media convergence impacts the way we consume media. A teenager doing homework may juggle four or five windows, scanning the web, listening to and downloading MP3 files, chatting with friends, wordprocessing a paper and responding to email, shifting rapidly between tasks. And fans of a popular television series may sample dialogue, summarize episodes, debate subtexts, create original fan fiction, record their own soundtracks, make their own movies – and distribute all of this worldwide via the internet.

Convergence is taking place within the same appliances . . . within the same franchise . . . within the same company . . . within the brain of the consumer . . . and within the same fandom. [ellipses in original]

For the foreseeable future, convergence will be a kind of kludge – a jerry-rigged relationship between different media technologies – rather than a fully integrated system. Right now, the cultural shifts, the legal battles and the economic consolidations that are fueling media convergence are preceding shifts in the technological infrastructure. The way in which those various transitions play themselves out will determine the balance of power within this new media era.

The rate of convergence will be uneven within a given culture, with those who are most affluent and most technologically literate becoming the early adapters and other segments of the population struggling to catch up. Insofar as these trends extend beyond a specifically American context, the rate of convergence will also be uneven across national borders, resulting in the consolidation of power and wealth within the "have" nations and some shift in the relative status and prominence of developing nations.

Convergence is more than a corporate branding opportunity; it represents a reconfiguration of media power and a reshaping of media aesthetics and economics. The French cyberspace theorist Pierre Levy uses the term "collective intelligence" to describe the large-scale information gathering and processing activities that have emerged in web communities. On the internet, he argues, people harness their individual expertise towards shared goals and objectives: "No one knows everything, everyone knows something, all knowledge resides in humanity" (1997).[2] The new knowledge culture has arisen as our ties to older forms of social community are breaking down, our rooting in physical geography in diminishing, our bonds to the extended and even the nuclear family are disintegrating and our allegiances to nation states are being redefined. However, new forms of community are emerging. These new communities are defined through voluntary, temporary, and tactical affiliations, are reaffirmed through common intellectual enterprises and emotional investments and are held together through the mutual production and reciprocal exchange of knowledge. Levy maps the intersections and negotiations between four potential sources of power: nomadic mobility, control over territory, ownership over commodities and mastery over knowledge. The emergent knowledge cultures never fully escape the influence of the commodity culture any more than commodity culture can function fully outside the constraints of territoriality. However, knowledge cultures, he predicts, will gradually alter the way that commodity cultures or nation states operate. Nowhere is that transition clearer than within the culture industries, where the commodities that circulate become resources for the production of meaning and where peer-to-peer technologies are being deployed in ways that challenge old systems of distribution and ownership.

Ultimately, our media future could depend on the kind of uneasy truce that gets brokered between commercial media and collective intelligence. Imagine a world where there are two kinds of media power: one comes through media concentration, where any message gains authority simply by being broadcast on network television; the other comes through collective intelligence, where a message gains visibility only if it is deemed relevant to a loose network of diverse publics. Broadcasting will place issues on the national agenda and define core values. Grassroots media will reframe those issues for different publics and ensure that everyone has a chance to be heard. Innovation will occur on the fringes; consolidation in the mainstream. But that makes it all sound a little too orderly, since in our transitional moment, the power relations between these forces are being fought over amid much name-calling and acrimony.

Understanding these changes and participating in the debates that will shape the future of media will require cultural studies to revisit and rethink some of its core assumptions. Since these changes occur at the intersection between production and consumption, they will demand détente between political economy (which has perhaps the most powerful theory of media production) and audience research (which has the most compelling account of media consumption). As we do so, political economy will need to shed its assumptions that all participation in the consumer economy constitutes cooptation and look instead at the ways that consumers are influencing the production and distribution of media content. Audience researchers will, at the same time, need to abandon their romance with audience resistance in order to understand how consumers may exert their emerging power through new collaborations with media producers. We should not give up our desire to contest the homogenization of our culture, but contemporary consumers may gain power through the assertion of new kinds of economic and legal relations and not simply through making meanings.

We need to move from a politics based on culture-jamming – that is, disrupting the flow of media from an outside position – toward one based on blogging – that is, actively shaping the flow of media. Blogging came into its own during the Gulf War, providing an important communication channel for the antiwar movement. In the Vietnam War era, it took years to build up the network of underground newspapers, alternative comics and people's radio stations that supported the antiwar movement. In the digital age, antiwar activists emerged almost overnight, forming important alliances, sharing ideas, organizing actions and mobilizing supporters, with most of the important work taking place in cyberspace. Others used blogging technology to link together important international coverage of the war, providing an implicit critique of the narrowness of the American media's hyper-patriotic accounts. In some cases, bloggers collected money to send their own reporters to the front so that they could obtain more direct and unfiltered knowledge of what was going on. As blogging has taken off, the form has been incorporated into commercial media sites: *Salon*, the online news magazine, for example, has a number of famous writers and political leaders who regularly run blogs through its website. Mainstream reporters increasingly scan blogs in search of leads for stories that will then be reported more widely through broadcast media. Furthermore, early signs are that blogging may play a decisive role in shaping the 2004 American presidential elections, having been identified as a key factor in propelling maverick candidate Howard Dean into the front ranks for the Democratic Party nomination.

I am struck by the ending of *The Truman Show*, a film that buys into culture-jamming assumptions. All the film can offer us is a vision of media exploitation, and all its protagonist can imagine is walking away from the media and slamming the door. It never occurs to anyone that Truman might stay on the air, generating his own content and delivering his own message, exploiting the media for his own purposes. Bloggers are rewriting the ending, resulting in a new vision of media politics.

Convergence is both a top-down corporate-driven process and a bottom-up consumer-driven process. Media companies are learning how to accelerate the flow of media content across delivery channels to expand revenue opportunities, broaden markets and reinforce viewer commitments. Consumers are learning how to use these different media technologies to bring the flow of media more fully under their control and to interact with other users. They are fighting for the right to participate more fully in their culture, to control the flow of media in their lives and to talk back to mass market content. Sometimes, these two forces reinforce each other, creating closer, more rewarding, relations between media producers and consumers. Sometimes, these two forces are at war and those struggles will redefine the face of American popular culture. Media producers are responding to these newly empowered consumers in contradictory ways, sometimes encouraging change, sometimes resisting what they see as renegade behavior. Consumers, in turn, are perplexed by what they see as mixed signals about how much participation they can enjoy.

The so-called media companies are not behaving in a monolithic fashion here; often, in fact, different divisions of the same company are pursuing radically different strategies, reflecting their uncertainty about how to proceed. On the one hand, convergence represents an expanding opportunity for media conglomerates, since content that succeeds in one sector can expand its market reach across to other platforms. On the other hand, convergence represents a risk, since most of these media fear a fragmentation or erosion of their markets. Each time they move a viewer from, say, television to the internet, there is a risk that the consumer may not return. Sometimes media executives are thinking across media; sometimes they can't extract themselves from medium-specific paradigms. Collaborations, even within the same companies, are harder to achieve than we might imagine looking at top-down charts mapping media ownership. The closer to the ground you get, the more media companies look like dysfunctional families.

Convergence is also a risk for creative industries because it requires media companies to rethink old assumptions about what it means to consume media – assumptions that shape both programming and marketing decisions. If old consumers were assumed to be passive, the new consumer is active. If old consumers were predictable and stationary, then new consumers are migratory, showing a declining loyalty to networks or even media. If old consumers were isolated individuals, then new consumers are more socially connected. If old consumers were seen as compliant, then new consumes are resistant, taking media into their own hands. If the work of media consumers were once silent and invisible, they are now noisy and public. Much of this is old news to those of us who have been following debates in cultural studies over the past few decades. But, as John Hartley and Toby Miller suggest in this issue, with varying degrees of pessimism, the idea of the active and critical consumer is gaining new currency within media industries, creating new opportunities for academic intervention in the policy debates that will shape the next decade of media change.

Here are nine sites where important negotiations between producers and consumers are apt to occur:

Revising audience measurement

Rethinking the usefulness of the "impression" in an age of transmedia branding, the American television industry is increasingly targeting consumers who have a prolonged relationship and active engagement with media content and who show a willingness to track down that content across the cable spectrum and across a range of other media platforms. This next generation audience research focusses [sic] attention on what consumers do with media content, seeing each subsequent interaction as valuable because it reinforces their relationship to the series and, potentially, its sponsors. Each shift in audience measurement, as Ien Ang (1991) and Eileen Meehan (1990) note, among others, results in shifts in cultural power, with some groups gaining greater influence and others being marginalized. Will fan communities be the new beneficiaries of audience measurement?

Regulating media content

Many parents complain that the media floodgates have opened into their living rooms and that they are no longer able to exercise meaningful choices about what media should enter their homes. Historically, media producers sought to appeal to the broadest possible population; self-regulation sought to ensure that all the content produced was appropriate for every member of the family; ideological struggles occurred whenever there was an attempt to broaden the possible themes that could be included within mainstream entertainment. There is now a push away from consensus-style media and towards greater narrowcasting. In this context, consumers are expected to play a much more active role in determining what content is appropriate for their families. Ironically, perhaps, the biggest success story in niche media production has been the emergence of an alternative sphere of popular culture reflecting the tastes and ideologies of cultural conservatives, the very groups who are also working to impose those ideological norms onto mainstream media through governmental regulation of media content (see Hendershott, 2004). Will the tension between narrowcasting and regulation result in more or less media diversity?

Redesigning the digital economy

Most believe that the commercializing of cyberspace has significantly undercut the web's prevailing gift economy. There will still be a great deal of free content produced by amateurs and academics, but more and more content will come with a price tag. The choice of how we pay for web content can have enormous cultural implications. Many feel that a shift towards a subscription-based model will result in greater media concentration and the construction of higher barriers of entry to the cultural marketplace, since most consumers will buy only a limited number of subscriptions and are more apt to buy them from companies that can promise them the broadest range of possible content. A micropayment system would allow media producers (recording artists, independent game designers, web comics artists, authors) to sell their content directly to the consumers, cutting out many layers of middle folk, adjusting prices for the lowered costs of production and distribution in the digital environment. Although long predicted, a viable micropayment system has yet to emerge, although there are new signs of life in this area. Which economic and cultural model will dominate in the web environment in the coming decade?

Restricting media ownership

In the summer of 2003, following heated debates that cut across traditional ideological divisions, the Federal Communications Commission (FCC) lifted many of the existing restrictions on US media ownership. The debate pitted those who believed that technological change had resulted in an explosion of media options against those who saw the present moment primarily in terms of media concentration. Many fear that the FCC rulings will pave the way for even more consolidation within the media industries. Even if they don't, the battle lines drawn between – and within – the two factions may shape future policy debates over the coming decade. One significant consequence of the debate has been a heightened grassroots awareness of the issue of media ownership. Will public dissatisfaction with corporate media be a driving political issue in the coming years?

Rethinking media aesthetics

P. David Marshall (2002) describes the emergence of "the new intertextual commodity," as franchises expand across media channels in response to the opportunities represented by media convergence. His focus is primarily on the economic implications of these shifts, but we should also monitor their aesthetic implications. In the old system, a work that was successful in one medium might be adapted into other media or used to brand a series of related but more or less redundant commodities. More recent media franchises, such as *The Blair Witch Project*, *Pokemon* or *The Matrix*, have experimented with a more integrated structure whereby each media manifestation makes a distinct but interrelated contribution to the unfolding of a narrative universe. While each individual work must be sufficiently self-contained to satisfy the interests of a first time consumer, the interplay between many such works can create an unprecedented degree of complexity and generate a depth of engagement that will satisfy the most committed viewer. Will transmedia storytelling enrich popular culture or make it more formulaic?

Redefining intellectual property rights

In the new media environment, it is debatable whether governmental censorship or corporate control over intellectual property rights poses the greatest threat to the right of the public to participate in their culture. Take the case of Harry Potter. In public schools across the US, the J.K. Rowling books have been attacked by religious conservatives who want them pulled from libraries or removed from classrooms because they allegedly promote paganism. The publishing industry has joined forces with librarians, teachers and civil libertarians to stave off these attacks on children's rights to read. At the same time, Warner Brothers has been aggressively asserting its rights over the Harry Potter franchise to shut down fan websites. One case centered around the right of children to read the Harry Potter books; the other, their right to write about them. Can these two rights be so easily separated in an era of read–write culture? Will the general public preserve and expand its right to participate or will corporate restrictions on intellectual property use gradually erode away the concept of free expression?

Renegotiating relations between producers and consumers

So far, the recording industry has responded to the emergence of peer-to-peer technologies through legal action and name-calling rather than developing new business plans or reconceiving consumer relations. In the games industry, on the other hand, the major successes have come within franchises that have courted feedback from consumers during the product development process, endorsed grassroots appropriation of their content and technology and that have showcased the best user-generated content. Game companies have seen the value of constructing, rather than shutting down, fan communities around their products and building long-term relationships with their consumers. Which model will prevail?

Remapping globalization

Much academic writing on globalization has centered on the flow of western media products into global markets, falling back on old models of cultural imperialism. Yet globalization also involves the flow of goods, workers, money and media content from east to west. The Mario Brothers are recognized by more American kids than Mickey Mouse – even if many of them don't yet realize that Nintendo is a Japanese-based game company. As they grow older, they certainly recognize Asian origins as a marker of cultural distinction. Much as teens in the developing world use American popular culture to express generational differences, western youth is asserting its identity through its consumption of Japanese anime and manga, Bollywood films and bhangra and Hong Kong action movies. A new pop cosmopolitanism is being promoted by corporate interests both in Asia and in the West, but it is also being promoted by grassroots interests, including both fan and immigrant communities, who are asserting greater control over the flow of media content across national borders. What will be the long-term economic and cultural impact of these trends?

Re-engaging citizens

Asian American activists used the web to quickly launch a nationwide protest against Abercrombie & Fitch when it releases a line of T-shirts featuring exaggerated Asian stereotypes (for example, "Two Wongs Make a White"). Hoping to increase its visibility in American culture, APA First Weekend has created a massive mailing list designed to buoy opening grosses for films with Asian or Asian American content. Adbusters produce mock commercials that use Madison Avenue conventions to challenge consumerism and corporate greed. Conservative talk show hosts direct their ire against the Dixie Chicks after one of the performers made negative comments about George W. Bush, resulting in a dramatic decline in their revenues and then a rebound as buying a Dixie Chicks album became a litmus test for antiwar sentiment. Media celebrities, such as World Wrestling Federation superstar Jesse Ventura or action hero Arnold Schwarzenegger, are emerging as important political figures. In such an environment, it is no surprise that activism draws models from fan culture or that popular culture becomes the venue through which key social and political issues get debated. What models of democracy will take roots in a culture where the lines between consumption and citizenship are blurring?

Media and cultural scholars have important contributions to make in each of these spaces. There is an enormous demand right now for public intellectuals who can help the public, policy makers and industry alike understand the stakes in these power struggles. In order to play that role, we will need visibility to address large and diverse publics, credibility to get our ideas heard in the corridors of power, accessibility to ensure that our perspectives are clearly understood and widely embraced and pragmatism to develop solutions that acknowledge the legitimate interest of all stakeholders. To play that role, we need to shed some of our own intellectual and ideological blinders, to avoid knee-jerk or monolithic formulations and to imagine new possible relations with corporate and governmental interests. This route may not lead to radical transformations of the economic and political system, as Miller correctly notes, but we may score some important local and tactical victories in the struggle for political freedom and cultural diversity.

In many parts of the world, cultural scholars have engaged in active intervention in the public debates shaping cultural policy, often working closely with governmental bodies to pursue their interests even where they did not fully agree with the other participants or totally endorse the outcomes achieved. They did so because they knew it was more important to try to influence policy than to remain ideologically or intellectually pure. Hartley notes that we have historically been more comfortable collaborating with state institutions than private corporations. But, in an era of privatization, cultural policy is increasingly being set not by governmental bodies, but by media companies; we lose the ability to have any real influence over the directions that our culture takes if we do not find ways to engage in active dialogue with media industries.

This is why discussions of creative industries need to take center stage as cultural studies enters the 21st century. We need to go into such collaborations and dialogues with our eyes wide open and, to do so, we need more nuanced models of the economic contexts within which culture gets produced and circulated.

Notes

1 I am framing this discussion narrowly to describe trends and debates within American popular culture. Many of these same issues are emerging elsewhere around the world, but they are playing out differently in different national contexts. The ideas contained here will be developed more fully, albeit for a popular readership, in [*Convergence Culture: Where Old and New Media Collide* 2006]. [. . .]
2 See Levy (1997). For a fuller discussion of Levy's notion of collective intelligence, see Jenkins (2002).

References

Ang, Ien (1991) *Desperately Seeking the Audience*. London: Routledge.

Gillespie, Nick (1999) "All Culture, All the Time," *Reason* (Apr.).

Gitlin, Todd (2003) *Media Unlimited*. New York: Owl Books.

Hendershott, Heather (2004) *Shaking the World for Jesus: Media and Conservative Evangelical Culture*. Chicago, IL: University of Chicago Press.

Jenkins, Henry (2002) "Interactive Audiences?" in Dan Harries (ed.) *The New Media Book*. London: British Film Institute.

Levy, Pierre (1997) *Collective Intelligence*. Cambridge: Perseus.

McChesney, Robert (2000) *Rich Media, Bad Democracy*. New York: New Press.

McCracken, Grant (1997) *Plenitude*. URL: http://cultureby.com/2008/04/plenitude-every.html

Marshall, P. David (2002) "The New Intertextual Commodity," in Dan Harries (ed.) *The New Media Book*. London: British Film Institute.

Meehan, Eileen (1990) "Why We Don't Count," in Patricia Mellencamp (ed.) *Logics of Television*. Bloomington: Indiana University Press.

Miller, Mark (2002) "What's Wrong With this Picture?" *Nation* (7 Jan.).

Sunstein, Cass (2002) *Republic.com*. Trenton, NJ: Princeton University Press.

Section 3: Recommended Further Reading

Bolter, Jay David and Richard Grusin. *Remediation: Understanding New Media*. Cambridge, MA: MIT Press, 2002.

Cornea, Christine. *Science Fiction Cinema: Between Fantasy and Reality*. New Brunswick: Rutgers University Press, 2007.

Gitelman, Lisa. *Always Already New: Media, History and the Data of Culture*. Cambridge, MA: MIT Press, 2008.

Hayles, N. Katherine. *How We Think: Digital Media and Contemporary Technogenesis*. Chicago: University of Chicago Press, 2012.

Jenkins, Henry. *Convergence Culture: Where Old and New Media Collide*. New York: NYU Press, 2008.

———. *Spreadable Media: Creating Value and Meaning in a Networked Culture*. New York: NYU Press, 2013.

Kuhn, Annette (ed). *Alien Zone: Cultural Theory and Contemporary Science Fiction Cinema*. London: Verso, 1990.

———. *Alien Zone II: The Spaces of Science Fiction Cinema*. London: Verso, 1999.

Mulvey, Laura. *Visual and Other Pleasures*. New York: Palgrave Macmillan, 2009.

Parikka, Jussi. *Insect Media: An Archaeology of Animals and Technology*. Minneapolis: University of Minnesota Press, 2010.

Sobchack, Vivian. *Screening Space: The American Science Fiction Film*. New Brunswick: Rutgers University Press, 1997.

Stewart, Garrett. *Closed Circuits: Screening Narrative Surveillance*. Chicago: University of Chicago Press, 2015.

Telotte, J.P. *Replications: A Robotic History of the Science Fiction Film*. Champaign: University of Illinois Press, 1995.

SECTION 4

Posthumanisms

The connections between science fiction and recent critical theory abound in posthumanism, a critical perspective that has its roots in sf scholarship but has become a central critical framework informed by discourses far beyond the genre. Posthumanism has become central to thinking in animal studies, in environmental humanities, in work that conceptualizes our era as the Anthropocene, and in the emerging field of petro-culture studies. Indeed, posthumanism has become something of a framework for understanding the humanities overall, asking what scholarship might look like if we begin to think of our work as a practice of the posthumanities. This section provides something like a genealogy of early critical discussions of the posthuman, collecting key texts that developed this approach in dialogue with science fiction, as well as a couple of more recent works that show how this discourse continues to be modified within sf studies as well as beyond it. This final section of the volume epitomizes how sf concepts have become central to cultural theory in the twenty-first century.

The section opens with Donna Haraway's indispensable "A Cyborg Manifesto," perhaps the most frequently cited work of theory within sf studies. Haraway was one of the first people to use sf as theory in her work, treating the novels she analyzes with the same kind of critical attention as she brings to the work of other Science and Technology Studies (STS) theorists. As is well known within the critical tradition, Haraway analyzes the breakdown of three binaries that have been central to structuring Western thought: human/animal, machinic/organic and virtual/material. In the early 1990s when this essay was widely and frequently cited, most people drew on the second of these binaries, seeing the cyborg as predominantly a human/machine fusion, influenced by the contemporary rise of personal computing and other attendant cultural shifts around technology that are discussed elsewhere in this volume. More recently Haraway's own work has been in the field of animal studies and scholars continue to mine this crucial essay for its insights on this topic. In its original context of publication, the essay was also a call for feminists to embrace science and technocultural study rather than to see technology as inevitably tainted by its connections to the military and imperialist projects that drive much of its history. Work in feminist STS is evident in elsewhere in this volume, especially in Anne Balsamo's work in Section 1.

Equally influential is N. Katherine Hayles's work on posthumanism, which moves in a different direction toward electronic texts and digital humanities in her more recent work. Hayles's contributions are best known in her central *How We Became Posthuman* (1999); the excerpt here is a slightly earlier articulation of some of these ideas, originally published in *The Cyborg Handbook*, a touchstone text in the 1990s for the then rapidly expanding theorization of posthumanism under the rubric of "cyborg studies." Whereas Haraway's work focuses predominantly on rethinking how we conceptualize subjectivity and the notion of the human, offering the cyborg as an image that can inform such speculations, Hayles focuses more specifically on the idea of the cyborg as the next stage of human evolution that might be achieved by direct technological intervention into human embodiment. Looking at sf that anticipates such futures, Hayles finds diverging perspectives offered by male and female authors, and her analysis of them anticipates the central argument of her later book which critiques the limitations of imagining subjectivity as information only, unchanged by the medium of its instantiation. She thus rejects as politically naïve and ethically irresponsible the posthumanist – we would now say transhumanist – fantasies of uploading our minds to immortal machines.

Scott Bukatman's *Terminal Identity* (1996), from which the selection here is drawn, represents the most extensive early engagement with media sf in this first stage of posthumanist criticism. Bukatman's title has a double meaning: the termination of identity as previously conceived, the end of the autonomous and self-consistent subject of liberal humanist construction; and the reinvention of identity at the site of the terminal, a new posthumanist identity created at the site of human/machine interface. In this excerpt, Bukatman draws on Baudrillard's sf theory (see Section 3) to theorize the ways media might be conceptualized as a viral infection of human identity, reversing Marshall McLuhan's idea of technology as the extension of human bodies to suggest, in an argument that is similar to Kittler's schema (see Section 1), that we may actually be the extensions of technology. Reading the sf of William Burroughs and David Cronenberg as a meditation upon our addiction to media – and in the longer chapter not reproduced here, Philip K. Dick – Bukatman explores what it means to live in hyperreality and how sf can provide us with "a spectacular immunization against the invasive power of the image virus" (271).

Rosi Braidotti also turns to Cronenberg in her theorization of posthuman subjectivity. Braidotti's work represents an important and distinct strand in posthuman thought that, until recently, was not as widely taken up in sf criticism as were the perspectives represented by Haraway, Hayles and Bukatman. Drawing on Gilles Deleuze's philosophy and on his work on identity-as-assemblage with Felix Guattari, Braidotti finds in sf a discourse that can narrate subjectivity as molecular becoming rather than molar being. Focusing on the gendered dynamics of sf visions of posthumanity, Braidotti argues that frequently "the becoming-machine in science fiction films bears a strong affinity to a molar line of reconstruction of masculinity" (279), but that Cronenberg's work exemplifies the possibilities for sf to engage the minoritarian identity of becoming-woman, becoming-animal. Offering another perspective on *Videodrome* (Cronenberg 1983), she finds in Max Renn's metamorphosis – in which his body develops an orifice that accepts videotapes – an example of the becoming-woman of the male body. Braidotti thus finds potential for disrupting normative, molar identity in sf film, but she concludes that the medium is not sufficiently Deleuzian: it cannot fully represent molecular rather than molar identity. She finds hope in music as a medium "where a Deleuzean revolution is most likely and, in some ways, already happening" (281). Braidotti's later work in *Metamorphoses* (2002) and *Transpositions* (2006) develop a theory of posthumanism as the ground for a nomadic theory of the subject that shares similarities with certain sf, particularly the recent emergence of sf engaged with postcolonial perspectives. This early essay shows the role sf played in the development of her thought and suggests avenues for further Deleuzian-informed studies of the genre.

Nabeel Zuberi's essay takes up the challenge of thinking about sf music's contributions to theorizing posthuman subjectivity, exploring Sun Ra's Afrofuturist music. Thus Zuberi's work reminds us of the importance of remembering how ideologies of race play into the construction of our technological imagination, reviewing the ways that an Afrofuturist embrace of sf imagery is simultaneously a politics asserting the place of African Americans in the future, as architects of that future. Zuberi connects his reading of Sun Ra to work on special effects in sf film, arguing that new work on effects pays attention to "moments and intensities more than narrative" (292), echoing work by Landon (see Section 3) and drawing on Bukatman. Echoing Stewart's claim (see Section 3) that the future in sf is the future of technology, Zuberi points out that "theorists insist that the camera and celluloid are Science Fiction because of their ability to manipulate time and space" (292). He finds in Sun Ra a similar manipulation of time and space, a science-fictional performance in which "music is *the* special effect that can transport black people into a higher state of consciousness and being" (293). Against the grain of other theorists in this section, however, Zuberi also calls for caution in our turn to the posthuman and points to ways that mainstream sf can reinforce rather than challenge racially essentialist views. Drawing on work by theorists such as Alexander Weheliye he argues that we need to rethink the term humanity beyond its expression in Western humanist thought.

Finally, Susan Napier's essay explores the substantial engagement with posthumanist thought in Japanese anime and manga. As she reminds us, Japanese culture has had a significant influence on Western sf, much of it filtered through what theorist Toshiya Ueno dubbed "techno-orientalism," that is, representations of Japan as the future of technology that presents the country as an object of both envy and contempt for a Western world that fears Japan's rapid economic growth and its dominance of world markets in technological commodities. Making use of Bukatman's work on posthuman identity in Western sf, Napier finds in the Japanese anime she analyzes a more pessimistic depiction of fusions between human and technology. Technological advance is valued and seems to be inevitable in such texts, she argues, yet there is always a human cost to this forced march toward progress. Napier's essay thus concludes this volume with a cross-cultural comparison of technological imaginations, a perspective that invites more work engaging multiple cultural viewpoints as technology – and its sf imagination – continue to shape more and more of quotidian life.

19

A CYBORG MANIFESTO

Science, technology, and socialist-feminism in the late twentieth century

Donna Haraway

An ironic dream of a common language for women in the integrated circuit

This chapter is an effort to build an ironic political myth faithful to feminism, socialism, and materialism. Perhaps more faithful as blasphemy is faithful, than as reverent worship and identification. [...] Blasphemy is not apostasy. Irony is about contradictions that do not resolve into larger wholes, even dialectically, about the tension of holding incompatible things together because both or all are necessary and true. Irony is about humor and serious play. It is also a rhetorical strategy and a political method, one I would like to see more honored within socialist-feminism. At the center of my ironic faith, my blasphemy, is the image of the cyborg.

A cyborg is a cybernetic organism, a hybrid of machine and organism, a creature of social reality as well as a creature of fiction. Social reality is lived social relations, our most important political construction, a world-changing fiction. The international women's movements have constructed "women's experience," as well as uncovered or discovered this crucial collective object. This experience is a fiction and fact of the most crucial, political kind. Liberation rests on the construction of the consciousness, the imaginative apprehension, of oppression, and so of possibility. The cyborg is a matter of fiction and lived experience that changes what counts as women's experience in the late twentieth century. This is a struggle over life and death, but the boundary between science fiction and social reality is an optical illusion.

Contemporary science fiction is full of cyborgs – creatures simultaneously animal and machine, who populate worlds ambiguously natural and crafted. Modern medicine is also full of cyborgs, of couplings between organism and machine, each conceived as coded devices, in an intimacy and with a power that was not generated in the history of sexuality. Cyborg "sex" restores some of the lovely replicative baroque of ferns and invertebrates (such nice organic prophylactics against heterosexism). Cyborg replication is uncoupled from organic reproduction. Modern production seems like a dream of cyborg colonization work, a dream that makes the nightmare of Taylorism seem idyllic. And modern war is a cyborg orgy, coded by C^3I, command-control-communication-intelligence, an $84 billion item in 1984's US defense budget. I am making an argument for the cyborg as a fiction mapping our social and bodily reality and as an imaginative resource suggesting some very fruitful couplings. Michael [*sic*] Foucault's biopolitics is a flaccid premonition of cyborg politics, a very open field.

By the late twentieth century, our time, a mythic time, we are all chimeras, theorized and fabricated hybrids of machine and organism; in short, we are cyborgs. The cyborg is our ontology; it gives us our politics. The cyborg is a condensed image of both imagination and material reality, the two joined centers structuring any possibility of historical transformation. In the traditions of "Western" science and politics – the tradition of racist, male-dominant capitalism; the tradition of progress; the tradition of the appropriation of nature as resource for the productions of culture; the tradition of reproduction of the self from the reflections of the other – the relation between organism and machine has been a border war. The stakes in the border war have been the territories of production, reproduction, and imagination. This chapter is an argument for *pleasure* in the confusion of boundaries and for *responsibility* in their construction. It is also an effort to contribute to socialist-feminist culture and theory in a postmodernist, non-naturalist mode and in the utopian tradition of imagining a world without gender, which is perhaps a world without genesis, but maybe also a world without end. The cyborg incarnation is outside salvation history. Nor does it mark time on an oedipal calendar, attempting to heal the terrible cleavages of gender in an oral symbiotic utopia or post-oedipal apocalypse. [. . .]

The cyborg is a creature in a post-gender world; it has no truck with bisexuality, pre-oedipal symbiosis, unalienated labor, or other seductions to organic wholeness through a final appropriation of all the powers of the parts into a higher unity. In a sense, [. . .] the cyborg is also the awful apocalyptic *telos* of the "West's" escalating dominations of abstract individualism, an ultimate self untied at last from all dependency, a man in space. An origin story in the "Western," humanist sense depends on the myth of original unity, fullness, bliss and terror, represented by the phallic mother from whom all humans must separate, the task of individual development and of history, the twin potent myths inscribed most powerfully for us in psychoanalysis and Marxism. Hilary Klein has argued that both Marxism and psychoanalysis, in their concepts of labor and of individuation and gender formation, depend on the plot of original unity out of which difference must be produced and enlisted in a drama of escalating domination of woman/nature. The cyborg skips the step of original unity, of identification with nature in the Western sense. This is its illegitimate promise that might lead to subversion of its teleology as star wars.

The cyborg is resolutely committed to partiality, irony, intimacy, and perversity. It is oppositional, utopian, and completely without innocence. No longer structured by the polarity of public and private, the cyborg defines a technological polis based partly on a revolution of social relations in the *oikos*, the household. Nature and culture are reworked; the one can no longer be the resource for appropriation or incorporation by the other. The relationships for forming wholes from parts, including those of polarity and hierarchical domination, are at issue in the cyborg world. Unlike the hopes of Frankenstein's monster, the cyborg does not expect its father to save it through a restoration of the garden; that is, through the fabrication of a heterosexual mate, through its completion in a finished whole, a city and cosmos. The cyborg does not dream of community on the model of the organic family, this time without the oedipal project. The cyborg would not recognize the Garden of Eden; it is not made of mud and cannot dream of returning to dust. Perhaps that is why I want to see if cyborgs can subvert the apocalypse of returning to nuclear dust in the manic compulsion to name the Enemy. Cyborgs are not reverent; they do not re-member the cosmos. They are wary of holism, but needy for connection – they seem to have a natural feel for united front politics, but without the vanguard party. The main trouble with cyborgs, of course, is that they are the illegitimate offspring of militarism and patriarchal capitalism, not to mention state socialism. But illegitimate offspring are often exceedingly unfaithful to their origins. Their fathers, after all, are inessential.

I will return to the science fiction of cyborgs at the end of this chapter, but now I want to signal three crucial boundary breakdowns that make the following political-fictional (political-scientific) analysis possible. By the late twentieth century in United States scientific culture, the boundary between human and animal is thoroughly breached. The last beachheads of uniqueness have been polluted if not turned into amusement parks – language, tool use social behavior, mental events, nothing really convincingly settles the separation of human and animal. And many people no longer feel the need for such a separation; indeed, many branches of feminist culture affirm the pleasures of connection of human and other living creatures. Movements for animal rights are not irrational denials of human uniqueness; they are a clear-sighted recognition of connection across the discredited breach of nature and culture. Biology and evolutionary theory over the last two centuries have simultaneously produced modern organisms as objects of knowledge and reduced the line between humans and animals to a faint trace re-etched in ideological struggle or professional disputes between life and social science. Within this framework, teaching modern Christian creationism should be fought as a form of child abuse.

Biological-determinist ideology is only one position opened upon in a scientific culture for arguing the meanings of human animality. There is much room for radical political people to contest the meanings of the breached boundary.[1] The cyborg appears in myth precisely where the boundary between human and animal is transgressed. Far from signaling a walling off of people from other living beings, cyborgs signal disturbingly and pleasurably tight coupling. Bestiality has a new status in this cycle of marriage exchange.

The second leaky distinction is between animal-human (organism) and machine. Pre-cybernetic machines could be haunted; there was always the specter of the ghost in the machine. This dualism structured the dialogue between materialism and idealism that was settled by a dialectical progeny, called spirit or history, according to taste. But basically machines were not self-moving, self-designing, autonomous. They could not achieve man's dream, only mock it. There were not man, an author to himself, but only a caricature of that masculinist reproductive dream. To think they were otherwise was paranoid. Now we are not so sure. Late twentieth-century machines have made thoroughly ambiguous the difference between natural and artificial, mind and body, self-developing and externally designed, and many other distinctions that used to apply to organisms and machines. Our machines are disturbingly lively, and we ourselves frighteningly inert.

Technological determinism is only one ideological space opened up by the reconceptions of machine and organism as coded texts through which we engage in the play of writing and reading the world. "Textualization" of everything in poststructuralist, postmodernist theory has been damned by Marxists and socialist feminists for its utopian disregard for the lived relations of domination that ground the "play" of arbitrary reading. It is certainly true that postmodernist strategies, like my cyborg myth, subvert myriad organic wholes (for example, the poem, the primitive culture, the biological organism). In short, the certainty of what counts as nature – a source of insight and a promise of innocence – is undermined, probably fatally. The transcendent authorization of interpretation is lost, and with it the ontology grounding "Western" epistemology. But the alternative is not cynicism or faithlessness, that is, some version of abstract existence, like the accounts of technological determinism destroying "man" by the "machine" or "meaningful political action" by the "text." Who cyborgs will be is a radical question; the answers are a matter of survival. Both chimpanzees and artifacts have politics, so why shouldn't we (de Waal, 1982; Winner, 1980)?

The third distinction is a subset of the second: the boundary between physical and non-physical is very imprecise for us. Pop physics books on the consequences of quantum theory and the indeterminacy principle are a kind of popular scientific equivalent to Harlequin romances as a marker of radical change in American white heterosexuality: they get it wrong, but they are on the right subject. Modern machines are quintessentially microelectronic devices: they are everywhere and they are invisible. Modern machinery is an irreverent upstart god, mocking the Father's ubiquity and spirituality. The silicon chip is a surface for writing; it is etched in molecular scales disturbed only by atomic noise, the ultimate interference for nuclear scores. Writing, power, and technology are old partners in Western stories of the origin of civilization, but miniaturization has changed our experience of mechanism. Miniaturization has turned out to be about power; small is not so much beautiful as pre-eminently dangerous, as in cruise missiles. Contrast the TV sets of the 1950s or the news cameras of the 1970s with the TV wrist bands or hand-sized video cameras now advertised. Our best machines are made of sunshine; they are all light and clean because they are nothing but signals, electromagnetic waves, a section of a spectrum, and these machines are eminently portable, mobile – a matter of immense human pain in Detroit and Singapore. People are nowhere near so fluid, being both material and opaque. Cyborgs are ether, quintessence.

The ubiquity and invisibility of cyborgs is precisely why these sunshine-belt machines are so deadly. They are as hard to see politically as materiality. They are about consciousness – or its simulation. [. . .]

So my cyborg myth is about transgressed boundaries, potent fusions, and dangerous possibilities which progressive people might explore as one part of needed political work. One of my premises is that most American socialists and feminists see deepened dualisms of mind and body, animal and machine, idealism and materialism in the social practices, symbolic formulations, and physical artifacts associated with "high technology" and scientific culture. From *One-Dimensional Man* (Marcuse, 1964) to *The Death of Nature* (Merchant, 1980), the analytic resources developed by progressives have insisted on the necessary domination of technics and recalled us to an imagined organic body to integrate our resistance. Another of my premises is that the need for unity of people trying to resist world-wide intensification of domination has never been more acute. But a slightly perverse shift of perspective might better enable us to contest for meanings, as well as for other forms of power and pleasure in technologically mediated societies.

From one perspective, a cyborg world is about the final imposition of a grid of control on the planet, about the final abstraction embodied in a Star Wars apocalypse waged in the name of defense,[2] about the final appropriation of women's bodies in a masculinist orgy of war (Sofia, 1984). From another perspective, a cyborg world might be about lived social and bodily realities in which people are not afraid of their joint kinship with animals and machines, not afraid of permanently partial identities and contradictory standpoints. The political struggle is to see from both perspectives at once because each reveals both dominations and possibilities unimaginable from the other vantage point. Single vision produces worse illusions than double vision or many-headed monsters. Cyborg unities are monstrous and illegitimate; in our present political circumstances, we could hardly hope for more potent myths for resistance and recoupling.

Fractured identities

It has become difficult to name one's feminism by a single adjective – or even to insist in every circumstance upon the noun. Consciousness of exclusion through naming is acute. Identities seem contradictory, partial, and strategic. With the hard-won recognition of their social and historical constitution, gender, race, and class cannot provide the basis for belief in "essential" unity. There is nothing about being "female" that naturally binds women. There is not even such a state as "being" female, itself a highly complex category constructed in contested sexual scientific discourses and other social practices. Gender, race, or class consciousness is an achievement forced on us by the terrible historical experience of the contradictory social realities of patriarchy, colonialism, and capitalism. And who counts as "us" in my own rhetoric? Which identities are available to ground such a potent political myth called "us," and what could motivate en-listment in this collectivity? Painful fragmentation among feminists (not to mention among women) along every possible fault line has made the concept of *woman* elusive, an excuse for the matrix of women's dominations of each other. For me – and for many who share a similar his-torical location in white, professional, middle-class, female, radical, North American, mid-adult bodies – the sources of a crisis in political identity are legion. The recent history for much of the US left and US feminism has been a response to this kind of crisis by endless splitting and searches for a new essential unity. But there has also been a growing recognition of another response through coalition – affinity, not identity.[3]

[. . .]

I do not know of any other time in history when there was greater need for political unity to confront effectively the dominations of "race," "gender," "sexuality," and "class." I also do not know of any other time when the kind of unity we might help build could have been possi-ble. None of "us" have any longer the symbolic or material capability of dictating the shape of reality to any of "them." Or at least "we" cannot claim innocence from practicing such domi-nations. White women, including socialist feminists, discovered (that is, were forced kicking and screaming to notice) the non-innocence of the category "woman." That consciousness changes the geography of all previous categories; it denatures them as heat denatures a fragile protein. Cyborg feminists have to argue that "we" do not want any more natural matrix of unity and that no construction is whole. Innocence, and the corollary insistence on victimhood as the only ground for insight, has done enough damage. But the constructed revolutionary subject must give late-twentieth century people pause as well. In the fraying of identities and in the reflexive strategies for constructing them, the possibility opens up for weaving something other than a shroud for the day after the apocalypse that so prophetically ends salvation history.

[. . .]

The "homework economy" outside the "home"

The "New Industrial Revolution" is producing a new world-wide working class, as well as new sexualities and ethnicities. The extreme mobility of capital and the emerging international division of labor are intertwined with the emergence of new collectivities, and the weakening of familiar groupings. These developments are neither gender- nor race-neutral. White men in advanced industrial societies have become newly vulnerable to permanent job loss, and women are not disappearing from the job rolls at the same rates as men. It is not simply that women in Third World countries are the preferred labor force for the science-based multinationals in the export-processing sector, particularly in electronics.[4] The picture is more systematic and involves reproduction, sexuality, culture, consumption, and production. In the prototypical Silicon Valley, many women's lives have been structured around employment in electronics-dependent jobs, and their intimate realities include serial heterosexual monogamy, negotiating childcare, distance from extended kin or most other forms of traditional community, a high likelihood of loneliness and extreme economic vulnerability as they age. The ethnic and racial diversity of women in Silicon Valley structures a microcosm of conflicting differences in culture, family, religion, edu-cation, and language.

Richard Gordon has called this new situation the "homework economy."[5] Although he includes the phenomenon of literal homework emerging in connection with electronics assembly, Gordon intends "homework economy" to name a restructuring of work that broadly has the characteristics formerly ascribed to female jobs, jobs literally done only by women. Work is being redefined as both literally female and feminized, whether performed by men or women. To be feminized means to be made extremely vulnerable; able to be disassembled, reassembled, exploited as reserve labor force; seen less as workers than as servers; subjected to time arrangements on and off the paid job that make a mockery of a limited work day; leading an existence that always borders on being obscene, out of place, and reducible to sex. Deskilling is an old strategy newly applicable to formerly privileged workers. However, the homework economy does not refer only to large-scale deskilling, nor does it deny that new areas of high skill are emerging, even for women and men previously excluded from skilled employment. Rather, the concept indicates that factory, home, and market are integrated on a new scale and that the places of women are crucial – and need to be analyzed for differences among women and for meanings for relations between men and women in various situations.

[. . .]

This is the context in which the projections for world-wide structural unemployment stemming from the new technologies are part of the picture of the homework economy. As robots and related technologies put men out of work in "developed" countries and exacerbate failure to generate male jobs in Third World "development," and as the automated office becomes the rule even in labor-surplus countries, the feminization of work intensifies. Black women in the United States have long known what it looks like to face the structural underemployment ("feminization") of black men, as well as their own highly vulnerable position in the wage economy. It is no longer a secret that sexuality, reproduction, family, and community life are interwoven with this economic structure in myriad ways which have also differentiated the situations of white and black women. Many more women and men will contend with similar situations, which will make cross-gender and race alliances on issues of basic life support (with or without jobs) necessary, not just nice.

[. . .]

Another critical aspect of the social relations of the new technologies is the reformulation of expectations, culture, work, and reproduction for the large scientific and technical work-force. A major social and political danger is the formation of a strongly bimodal social structure, with the masses of women and men of all ethnic groups, but especially people of color, confined to a homework economy, illiteracy of several varieties, and general redundancy and impotence, controlled by high-tech repressive apparatuses ranging from entertainment to surveillance and disappearance. An adequate socialist-feminist politics should address women in the privileged occupational categories, and particularly in the production of science and technology that constructs scientific-technical discourses, processes, and objects.[6]

[. . .]

Women in the integrated circuit

Let me summarize the picture of women's historical locations in advanced industrial societies, as these positions have been restructured partly through the social relations of science and technology. If it was ever possible ideologically to characterize women's lives by the distinction of public and private domains – suggested by images of the division of working-class life into factory and home, of bourgeois life into market and home, and of gender existence into personal and political realms – it is now a totally misleading ideology, even to show how both terms of these dichotomies construct each other in practice and in theory. I prefer a network ideological image, suggesting the profusion of spaces and identities and the permeability of boundaries in the personal body and in the body politic. "Networking" is both a feminist practice and a multinational corporate strategy – weaving is for oppositional cyborgs.

So let me return to the earlier image of the informatics of domination and trace one vision of women's "place" in the integrated circuit, touching only a few idealized social locations seen primarily from the point of view of advanced capitalist societies: Home, Market, Paid Work Place, State, School, Clinic-Hospital, and Church. Each of these idealized spaces is logically and practically implied in every other locus, perhaps analogous to a holographic photograph. I want to suggest the impact of the social relations mediated and enforced by the new technologies in order to help formulate needed analysis and practical work. However, there is no "place" for women in these networks, only geometrics of difference and contradiction crucial to women's cyborg identities. If we learn how to read these webs of power and social life, we might learn new couplings, new coalitions. There is no way to read [such a][7] list from a standpoint of "identification," of a unitary self. The issue is dispersion. The task is to survive in the diaspora.

[. . .]

The permanent partiality of feminist points of view has consequences for our expectations of forms of political organization and participation. We do not need a totality in order to work well. The feminist dream of a common language, like all dreams of a perfectly true language, or perfectly faithful naming of experience, is a totalizing and imperialist one. In that sense, dialectics too is a dream language, longing to resolve contradiction. Perhaps, ironically, we can learn from our fusions with animals and machines how not to be Man, the embodiment of Western logos. From the point of view of pleasure in these potent and taboo fusions, made inevitable by the social relations of science and technology, there might indeed be a feminist science.

Cyborgs: a myth of political identity

I want to conclude with a myth about identity and boundaries which night inform late twentieth-century political imaginations. I am indebted in this story to writers like Joanna Russ, Samuel R. Delany, John Varley, James Tiptree, Jr., Octavia Butler, Monique Wittig, and Vonda McIntyre.[8] These are our story-tellers exploring what it means to be embodied in high-tech worlds. They are theorists for cyborgs. Exploring conceptions of bodily boundaries and social order, the anthropologist Mary Douglas (1966, 1970) should be credited with helping us to consciousness about how fundamental body imagery is to world view, and so to political language. French feminists like Luce Irigaray and Monique Wittig, for all their differences, know how to write the body; how to weave eroticism, cosmology, and politics from imagery of embodiment, and especially for Wittig, from imagery of fragmentation and reconstitution of bodies.

American radical feminists like Susan Griffin, Audre Lorde, and Adrienne Rich have profoundly affected our political imaginations – and perhaps restricted too much what we allow as a friendly body and political language.[9] They insist on the organic, opposing it to the technological. But their symbolic systems and the related positions of ecofeminism and feminist paganism, replete with organicisms, can only be understood in [Chela] Sandoval's terms as oppositional ideologies fitting in the late twentieth century. They would simply bewilder anyone not preoccupied with the machines and consciousness of late capitalism. In that sense they are part of the cyborg world. But there are also great riches for feminists in explicitly embracing the possibilities inherent in the breakdown of clean distinctions between organism and machine and similar distinctions structuring the Western self. It is the simultaneity of breakdowns that cracks the matrices of domination and opens geometric possibilities. [. . .]

Earlier I suggested that "women of color" might be understood as a cyborg identity, a potent subjectivity synthesized from fusions of outsider identities and in the complex political-historical layerings of her "biomythography," *Zami* (Lorde, 1982; King, 1987a, 1987b). There are material and cultural grids mapping this potential, Audre Lorde (1984) captures the tone in the title of her *Sister Outsider*. In my political myth, Sister Outsider is the offshore woman, who US workers, female and feminized, are supposed to regard as the enemy preventing their solidarity, threatening their security. Onshore, inside the country of the United States, Sister Outsider is a potential amidst the races and ethnic identities of woman manipulated for division, competition, and exploitation in the same industries. "Women of color" are the preferred labor force for the science-based industries, the real women for whom the world-wide sexual market, labor market, and politics of reproduction kaleidoscope into daily life. Young Korean women hired in the sex industry and in electronics assembly are recruited from high schools, educated for the integrated circuit. Literacy, especially in English, distinguishes the "cheap" female labor so attractive to multinationals.

[…]

Contests for the meanings of writing are a major form of contemporary political struggle. Releasing the play of writing is deadly serious. The poetry and stories of US women of color are repeatedly about writing, about access to the power to signify; but this time that power must be neither phallic nor innocent. Cyborg writing must not be about the Fall, the imagination of a once-upon-a-time wholeness before language, before writing, before Man. Cyborg writing is about the power to survive, not on the basis of original innocence, but on the basis of seizing the tools to mark the world that marked them as other.

The tools are often stories, retold stories, versions that reverse and displace the hierarchical dualisms of naturalized identities. In retelling origin stories, cyborg authors subvert the central myths of origin of Western culture. We have all been colonized by those origin myths, with their longing for fulfillment in apocalypse. The phallogocentric origin stories most crucial for feminist cyborgs are built into the literal technologies – technologies that write the world, biotechnology and microelectronics – that have recently textualized our bodies as code problems on the grid of C^3I. Feminist cyborg stories have the task of recoding communications and intelligence to subvert command and control.

[…]

Writing is pre-eminently the technology of cyborgs, etched surfaces of the late twentieth century. Cyborg politics is the struggle for language and the struggle against perfect communication, against the one code that translates all meaning perfectly, the central dogma of phallogocentrism. That is why cyborg politics insist on noise and advocate pollution, rejoicing in the illegitimate fusions of animal and machine. These are the couplings which make Man and Woman so problematic, subverting the structure of desire, the force imagined to generate language and gender, and so subverting the structure and modes of reproduction of "Western" identity, of nature and culture, of mirror and eye, slave and master, body and mind. "We" did not originally choose to be cyborgs, but choice grounds a liberal politics and epistemology that imagines the reproductions of individuals before the wider replication of "texts."

[…]

To recapitulate, certain dualisms have been persistent in Western traditions; they have all been systemic to the logics and practices of domination of women, people of color, nature, workers, animals – in short, domination of all constituted as others, whose task is to mirror the self. Chief among these troubling dualisms are self/other, mind/body, culture/nature, male/female, civilized/primate, reality/appearance, whole/part, agent/resource, maker/made, active/passive, right/wrong, truth/illusion, total/partial, God/man. The self is the One who is not dominated, who knows that by the service of the other, the other is the one who holds the future, who knows that by the experience of domination, which gives the lie to the autonomy of the self. To be One is to be autonomous, to be powerful, to be God; but to be One is to be an illusion, and so to be involved in a dialectic of apocalypse with the other. Yet to be other is to be multiple, without clear boundary, frayed, insubstantial. One is too few, but two are too many.

High-tech culture challenges these dualisms in intriguing ways. It is not clear who makes and who is made in the relation between human and machine. It is not clear what is mind and what body in machines that resolve into coding practices. In so far as we know ourselves in both formal discourse (for example, biology) and in daily practice (for example, the homework economy in the integrated circuit), we find ourselves to be cyborgs, hybrids, mosaics, chimeras. Biological organisms have become biotic systems, communications devices like others. There is no fundamental, ontological separation in our formal knowledge of machine and organism, of technical and organic. The replicant Rachel in the Ridley Scott film *Blade Runner* stands as the image of a cyborg culture's fear, love and confusion.

One consequence is that our sense of connection to our tools is heightened. The trance state experienced by many computer users has become a staple of science-fiction film and cultural jokes. Perhaps paraplegics and other severely handicapped people can (and sometimes do) have the most intense experiences of complex hybridization with other communication devices. Anne McCaffrey's pre-feminist *The Ship Who Sang* (1969) explored the consciousness of a cyborg, hybrid of girls' brain and complex machinery, formed after the birth of a severely handicapped child. Gender, sexuality, embodiment, skill: all were reconstituted in the story. Why should our bodies end at the skin, or include at best other beings encapsulated by skin? From the seventeenth century till now, machines could be animated – given ghostly souls to make them speak or move or to account for their orderly development and mental capacities. Or organisms could be mechanized – reduced to body understood as resource of mind. These machine/organism relationships are obsolete, unnecessary. For us, in imagination and in other practice, machines can be prosthetic devices, intimate components, friendly selves. We don't need organic holism to give impermeable wholeness, the total woman and her feminist variants (mutants?).

[. . .]

There are several consequences to taking seriously the imagery of cyborgs as other than our enemies. Our bodies, ourselves; bodies are maps of power and identity. Cyborgs are no exception. A cyborg body is not innocent; it was not born in a garden; it does not seek unitary identity and so generate antagonistic dualisms without end (or until the world ends); it takes irony for granted. One is too few, and two is only one possibility. Intense pleasure in skill, machine skill, ceases to be a sin, but an aspect of embodiment. The machine is not an *it* to be animated, worshipped, and dominated. The machine is us, our processes, an aspect of our embodiment. We can be responsible for machines; *they* do not dominate or threaten us. We are responsible for boundaries; we are they. Up till now (once upon a time), female embodiment seemed to be given, organic, necessary; and female embodiment seemed to mean skill in mothering and its metaphoric extensions. Only by being out of place could we take intense pleasure in machines, and then with excuses that this was organic activity after all, appropriate to females. Cyborgs might consider more seriously the partial, fluid, sometimes aspect of sex and sexual embodiment. Gender might not be global identity after all, even if it has profound historical breadth and depth.

The ideologically charged question of what counts as daily activity, as experience, can be approached by exploiting the cyborg image. Feminists have recently claimed that women are given to dailiness, that women more than men somehow sustain daily life, and so have a privileged epistemological position potentially. There is a compelling aspect to this claim, one that makes visible unvalued female activity and names it as the ground of life. But *the* ground of life? What about all the ignorance of women, all the exclusions and failures of knowledge and skill? What about men's access to daily competence, to knowing how to build things, to take them apart, to play? What about other embodiment? Cyborg gender is a local possibility taking a global vengeance. Race, gender, and capital require a cyborg theory of wholes and parts. There is no drive in cyborgs to reproduce total theory, but there is an intimate experience of boundaries, their construction and deconstruction. There is a myth system waiting to become a political language to ground one way of looking at science and technology and challenging the informatics of domination – in order to act potently.

One last image: organisms and organismic, holistic politics depend on metaphors of rebirth and invariably call on the resources of reproductive sex. I would suggest that cyborgs have more to do with regeneration and are suspicious of the reproductive matrix and of most birthings. For salamanders, regeneration after injury, such as the loss of a limb, involves regrowth of structure and restoration of function with the constant possibility of twinning or other odd topographical reproductions at the site of former injury. The regrown limb can be monstrous, duplicated, potent. We have all been injured, profoundly. We require regeneration, not rebirth, and the possibilities for our reconstitution include the utopian dream of the hope for a monstrous world without gender.

Cyborg imagery can help express two crucial arguments in this essay: first, the production of universal, totalizing theory is a major mistake that misses most of reality, probably always, but certainly now; and second, taking responsibility for the social relations of science and technology means refusing an anti-science metaphysics, a demonology of technology, and so means embracing the skillful task of reconstructing the boundaries of daily life, in partial connection with others, in communication with all of our parts. It is not just that science and technology are possible means of great human satisfaction, as well as a matrix of complex dominations. Cyborg imagery can suggest a way out of the maze of dualisms in which we have explained our bodies and our tools to ourselves. This is a dream not only of a common language, but of a powerful infidel heteroglossia. It is an imagination of a feminist speaking in tongues to strike fear into the circuits of the super-savers of the new right. It means both building and destroying machines, identities, categories, relationships, space stories. Though both are bound in the spiral dance, I would rather be a cyborg than a goddess.

Notes

1 Useful references to left and/or feminist radical science movements and theory and to biological/ biotechnical issues include: Bleier (1984, 1986), Harding (1986), Fausto-Sterling (1985), Gould (1981), Hubbard *et al.* (1982), Keller (1985), Lewontin *et al.* (1984), *Radical Science Journal* (became *Science as Culture* in 1987), [. . .] *Science for the People*. [. . .]

2 [Haraway refers here not to the Hollywood film but to Reagan's contemporary Strategic Defense Initiative project, named "Star Wars" by the popular media. – SV]

3 Powerful developments of coalition politics emerge from "Third World" speakers, speaking from nowhere, the displaced center of the universe, earth: "We live on the third planet from the sun" – *Sun Poem* by Jamaican writer, Edward Kamau Braithwaite, review by Mackey (1984). Contributors to Smith (1983) ironically subvert naturalized identities precisely while constructing a place from which to speak called home. See especially Reagon (in Smith, 1983, pp. 356–68), Trinh T. Minh-ha (1986–87).

4 [In the previous section, "The Informatics of Domination," – not included in this excerpt – Haraway outlines the ways contemporary globalization of IT and biotech industries changes labor conditions and how this affects women, particularly those in developing economies. – SV]

5 For the "homework economy outside the home" and related arguments: Gordon (1983); Gordon and Kimball (1985); Stacey (1987); Reskin and Hartman (1986); *Women and Poverty* (1984); S. Rose (1986); Collins (1982); Burr (1982); Gregory and Nussbaum (1982); Piven and Coward (1982); Microelectronics Group (1980); Stallard *et al.* (1983) which includes a useful organization and resource list.

6   For guidance for thinking about the political/cultural/racial implications of the history of women doing science in the United States see: Haas and Perucci (1984); Hacker (1981); Keller (1983); National Science Foundation (1988); Rossiter (1982); Schiebinger (1987); Haraway (1989).

7   [In a section not reproduced here, Haraway traces the networks of women's connections from each of these locations contemporary to the time of writing this essay. – SV]

8   King (1984). An abbreviated list of feminist science fiction underlying themes in this essay: Octavia Butler, *Wild Seed, Mind of My Mind, Kindred, Survivor;* Suzy McKee Charnas, *Motherlines;* Samuel R. Delany, the Neverÿon series; Anne McCaffrey, *The Ship Who Sang, Dinosaur Planet;* Vonda McIntyre, *Superluminal, Dreamsnake;* Joanna Russ, *Adventures of Alix, The Female Man;* James Tiptree, Jr., *Star Songs of an Old Primate, Up the Walls of the World;* John Varley, *Titan, Wizard, Demon.*

9   But these poets are very complex, not least in their treatment of themes of lying and erotic, decentered collective and personal identities. Griffin (1978), Lorde (1984), Rich (1978).

Works Cited

Bleier, Ruth (1984) *Science and Gender: A Critique of Biology and Its Themes on Women.* New York: Pergamon.

——— (ed.) (1986) *Feminist Approaches to Science.* New York: Pergamon.

Burr, Sara G. (1982) "Women and Work", in Barbara K. Haber, ed. *The Women's Annual, 1981.* Boston: G.K. Hall.

Collins, Patricia Hill (1982) "Third World Women in America", in Barbara K. Haber, ed. *The Women's Annual, 1981.* Boston: G.K. Hall.

de Waal, Frans (1982) *Chimpanzee Politics: Power and Sex among the Apes.* New York: Harper & Row.

Douglas, Mary (1966) *Purity and Danger.* London: Routledge & Kegan Paul.

——— (1970) *Natural Symbols.* London: Cresset Press.

Fausto-Sterling, Anne (1985) *Myths of Gender: Biological Theories about Women and Men.* New York: Basic.

Gordon, Richard (1983) "The Computerization of Daily Life, the Sexual Division of Labor, and the Homework Economy", Silicon Valley Workshop Conference, University of California at Santa Cruz.

Gregory, Judith and Kimball, Linda (1985) "High-Technology, Employment and the Challenges of Education", Silicon Valley Research Project, Working Paper, no. 1.

Gregory, Judith and Nussbaum, Karen (1982) "Race Against Time: Automation of the Office", *Office: Technology and People* 1: 197–236.

Gould, Stephen J. (1981) *The Mismeasure of Man.* New York: Norton.

Griffin, Susan (1978) *Woman and Nature: The Roaring Inside Her.* New York: Harper & Row.

Haas, Violet and Perucci, Carolyn, eds (1984) *Women in Scientific and Engineering Professions.* Ann Arbor: University of Michigan Press.

Hacker, Sally (1981) "The Culture of Engineering: Women, Workplace, and Machine", *Women's Studies International Quarterly* 4(3): 341–53.

Haraway, Donna (1989) *Primate Visions: Gender, Race, and Nature in the World of Modern Science.* New York: Routledge.

Harding, Sandra (1986) *The Science Question in Feminism.* Ithaca: Cornell University Press.

Hubbard, Ruth, Henifin, Mary Sue, and Fried, Barbara, eds (1982) *Biological Woman, the Convenient Myth.* Cambridge, MA: Shenkman.

Keller, Evelyn Fox (1983) *A Feeling for the Organism.* San Francisco: Freeman.

——— (1985) *Reflections on Gender and Science.* New Haven: Yale University Press.

King, Katie (1984) "The Pleasure of Repetition and the Limits of Identification in Feminist Science Fiction: Reimaginations of the Body after the Cyborg", paper delivered at the California American Studies Association, Pomona.

——— (1987a) "Canons Without Innocence", University of California at Santa Cruz, PhD thesis.

——— (1987b) *The Passing Dreams of Choice . . . Once Before and After: Audre Lorde and the Apparatus of Literary Production,* book prospectus, University of Maryland at College Park.

Lewontin, R.C., Rose, Steven, and Kamin, Leon J. (1984) *Not in Our Genes: Biology, Ideology, and Human Nature.* New York: Pantheon.

Lorde, Audre (1982) *Zami, a New Spelling of My Name.* Trumansburg, NY: Crossing, 1983.

——— (1984) *Sister Outsider.* Trumansburg, NY: Crossing.

Mackey, Nathaniel (1984) "Review", *Sulfur* 2: 200–5.

McCaffrey, Anne (1969) *The Ship Who Sang.* New York: Ballantine.

Marcuse, Herbert (1964) *One-Dimensional Man: Studies in the Ideology of Advanced Industrial Society*. Boston: Beacon.

Merchant, Carolyn (1980) *The Death of Nature: Women, Ecology, and the Scientific Revolution*. New York: Harper & Row.

Microelectronics Group (1980) *Microelectronics: Capitalist Technology and the Working Class*. London: CSE.

National Science Foundation (1988) *Women and Minorities in Science and Engineering*. Washington, DC: NSF.

Piven, Frances Fox and Coward, Richard (1982) *The New Class War: Reagan's Attack on the Welfare State and Its Consequences*. New York: Pantheon.

Reskin, Barbara F. and Hartmann, Heidi, eds (1986) *Women's Work, Men's Work*. Washington, DC: National Academy of Sciences.

Rich, Adrienne (1978) *The Dream of a Common Language*. New York: Norton.

Rose, Stephen (1986) *The American Profile Poster: Who Owns What, Who Makes How Much, Who Works Where, and Who Lives with Whom?* New York: Pantheon.

Rossiter, Margaret (1982) *Women Scientists in America*. Baltimore: Johns Hopkins University Press.

Schiebinger, Londa (1987) "The History and Philosophy of Women in Science: A Review Essay", *Signs* 12(2): 305–32.

Smith, Barbara (1983) *Home Girls: A Black Feminist Anthology*. New York: Kitchen Table, Women of Color Press.

Sofia, Zoe (1984) "Exterminating Fetuses: Abortion, Disarmament, and the Sexo-Semiotics of Extra-Terrestrialism", *Diacritics* 14(2): 47–59.

Stacey, Judith (1987) "Sexism by a Subtler Name? Postindustrial Conditions and Postfeminist Consciousness", *Socialist Review* 96: 7–28.

Stallard, Karin, Ehrenreich, Barbara, and Sklar, Holly (1983) *Poverty in the American Dream*. Boston: South End.

Trinh T. Minh-ha, ed. (1986–7) "She, the Inappropriate/d Other", *Discourse* 8.

Winner, Langdon (1980) "Do Artifacts Have Politics?", *Daedalus* 109(1): 121–36.

Women and Poverty, special issue (1984) *Signs* 10(2).

20

THE LIFE CYCLE OF CYBORGS

Writing the posthuman

N. Katherine Hayles

For some time now there has been a rumor going around that the age of the human has given way to the posthuman. Not that humans have died out, but that the human as a concept has been succeeded by its evolutionary heir. Humans are not the end of the line. Beyond them looms the cyborg, a hybrid species created by crossing biological organism with cybernetic mechanism. Whereas it is possible to think of humans as natural phenomena, coming to maturity as a species through natural selection and spontaneous genetic mutations, no such illusions are possible with the cyborg. From the beginning it is constructed, a technobiological object that confounds the dichotomy between natural and unnatural, made and born.

If primatology brackets one end of the spectrum of humanity by the similarities and differences it constructs between *homo sapiens* and other primates, cybernetics brackets the other by the continuities and ruptures it constructed between humans and machines. As Donna Haraway has pointed out, in the discourse of primatology "oldest" is privileged, for it points toward the most primeval and therefore the most fundamental aspects of humanity's evolutionary heritage.[1] "Oldest" comes closest to defining what is essential in the layered construction of humanity. In the discourse of cybernetics, "newest" is similarly privileged, for it reaches toward the limits of technological innovation. "Newest" comes closest to defining what is malleable and therefore subject to change in the layered construction of humanity. Whereas the most socially loaded arguments in primatology center on inertia, the most socially loaded arguments in cybernetics project acceleration.

Primatology and cybernetics are linked in other ways as well. Primates and cyborgs are simultaneously entities and metaphors, living beings and narrative constructions. The conjunction of technology and discourse is crucial. Were the cyborg only a product of discourse, it could perhaps be relegated to science fiction, of interest to SF aficionados but not of vital concern to the culture. Were it only a technological practice, it could be confined to such technical fields as bionics, medical prostheses, and virtual reality. Manifesting itself as both technological object and discursive formation, it partakes of the power of the imagination as well as the actuality of technology. Cyborgs actually do exist; about 10% of the current U.S. population are estimated to be cyborgs in the technical sense, including people with electronic pacemakers, artificial joints, drug implant systems, implanted corneal lenses, and artificial skin. A much higher percentage participates in occupations that make them into metaphoric cyborgs, including the computer keyboarder joined in a cybernetic circuit with the screen, the neurosurgeon guided by fiber optic microscopy during an operation, and the teen gameplayer in the local videogame arcade. "Terminal identity" Scott Bukatman has named this condition, calling it an "unmistakably doubled articulation" that signals the end of traditional concepts of identity even as it points toward the cybernetic loop that generates a new kind of subjectivity.[2]

How does a culture understand and process new modes of subjectivity? Primarily through the stories it tells, or more precisely, through narratives that count as stories in a given cultural context. The stories I want to explore are narratives of life cycles.[3] They bring into focus a crucial area of tension between the human and posthuman. Human beings are conceived, gestated, and born; they grow up, grow old, and die. Machines are designed, manufactured, and assembled; normally they do not grow, and although they wear out, they are always capable of being disassembled and reassembled either into the same product or a different one. As Gillian Beer has pointed out, Frankenstein's monster – an early cyborg – is monstrous in part because he has not *grown*. As a creature who has never known what it is like to be a child, he remains alien despite his humanoid form.[4]

When cyborg subjectivities are expressed within cultural narratives, traditional understandings of human life cycle come into strong conflict with modes of discursive and technical production oriented toward the machine values of assembly and disassembly. The conflict cannot be reduced to either the human or machine orientation, for the cyborg contains both within itself. Standing at the threshold separating the human from the posthuman, the cyborg looks to the past as well as the future. It is precisely this double nature that allows cyborg stories to be imbricated within cultural narratives while still wrenching them in a new direction.

The new cannot be spoken except in relation to the old. Imagine a new social order, a new genetic strain of corn, a new car – whatever the form, it can be expressed only by articulating its differences from that which it displaces, which is to say the old, a category constituted through its relation to the new. Similarly, the language that creates these categories operates through displacements of traditional articulations by formulations that can be characterized as new because they are not the same as the old. The cyborg is both a product of this process and a signifier for the process itself. The linguistic splice that created it (cyb/org) metonymically points toward the simultaneous collaboration and displacement of new/old, even as it instantiates this same dynamic.

The stories that produce and are produced by cyborg subjectivities are, like the cyborg itself, amalgams of old and new. Cyborg narratives can be understood as stories only by reference to the very life cycle narratives that are no longer sufficient to explain them. The results are narrative patterns that overlay upon the arc of human life a map generated from assembly and disassembly zones. One orientation references the human, the other the posthuman; one is chronological, the other topological; one assumes growth, the other presupposes production; one represents itself as natural or normal, the other as unnatural or aberrant. Since the two strands intertwine at every level, the effect is finally not so much overlay as interpenetration. Sometimes the interpenetration is presented as the invasion of a deadly alien into the self, sometimes as a symbiotic union that results in a new subjectivity. Whatever the upshot, the narratives agree that the neologistic joining cannot be unsplit without killing the truncated org/anism that can no longer live without its cyb/ernetic component. As these narratives tell it, a corner has been turned, and there is no going back.

To illustrate how cyborg narratives function, I want to concentrate on three phases of the life cycle and three corresponding dis/assembly zones. The first is adolescence, when self-consciousness about the body is at its height and the body is narcissistically cathected as an object of the subject's gaze. Appropriate to the inward turning of narcissism is a dis/assembly zone marked by the joining of limb to torso, appendage to trunk. The second phase is sexual maturity, when the primary emphasis is on finding an appropriate partner and negotiating issues of intimacy and shared space. The dis/assembly zone corresponding to this phase is located where the human is plugged into the machine, or at the interface between body and computer network. The last is the reproductive or generative phase, when the emphasis falls on mortality and the necessity to find an heir for one's legacy. The dis/assembly zone associated with this phase focuses on the gaps between the natural body and mechanical replicate, or between the original and manufactured clone.

Because gender is a primary determinant of how stories are told, I have chosen to mix stories by male and female authors. Spanning nearly half a century, these texts bear the stamps of their times as well as the subject positions of the authors. The generalizations that emerge from these texts confirm socialization patterns that make women welcome intimacy, whereas men are more likely to see it as a threat; they also show women more attuned to bonding, men to aggression and hierarchical structure. The interest of the comparison lies less in these well-known generalizations, however, than in the complex permutations they undergo in the cybernetic paradigm. The narrative and linguistic counters by which such categories as intimacy, bonding, and aggression are constituted do not remain constant when the body boundaries central to defining them undergo radical transformation.

The adolescent phase is illustrated by Bernard Wolfe's *Limbo* (New York: Ace, 1952), with side glances at Katherine Dunn's *Geek Love* (New York: Alfred A. Knopf, 1989). Both novels imagine cults that advocate voluntary amputation as a means to achieve beatific states. In Wolfe's novel the next step is to replace the absent appendages with prostheses, whereas in Dunn's narrative the amputations remain as permanent stigmata. At stake is the truncated versus extended body, and boundary questions focus on the relation of part to whole. Important psychological configurations are represented as originating within the family structure. Physical wounds in these texts have their symbolic origin in narcissistic wounds that occur when the child realizes that his body is not coextensive with the world or, more specifically, with the mother's body. The imaginative dimension which is most highly charged is disruption of the body's interior space.

The mating phase is explored through John Varley's 1984 novella "Press Enter" (*Blue Champagne* [Niles, IL: Dark Harvest, 1986,] 319–400) with Anne McCaffrey's short stories in the 1961 collection, *The Ship Who Sang* (New York: Ballantine Books, 1970). Varley and McCaffrey are concerned with subjectivities that emerge when the human body is plugged into a computer network. For Varley, the connection occurs when his characters respond to the "Press Enter" command of a mysterious and lethal computer program; with McCaffrey, when a birth-damaged child is trained to become a "shell person," permanently encased in a shapeship [sic] and wired into its computer network. At stake is hyperconnectivity, the possibility that the human sensorium can be overwhelmed and destroyed by the vastly superior information-processing capabilities of the computers to which it is connected. For Varley this is a threat that cannot be overcome, whereas for McCaffrey it is one trial among many. Boundary disputes move outward from the body's interior to the connection that joins body with network. Varley's text manifests a phobic reaction to the connection as an unbearable form of intimacy, while McCaffrey's narrative embraces it as life-enhancing and ultimately freeing. The most highly charged imaginative dimension is extension in external space.

The generativity phase appears in C.J. Cherryh's 1988 *Cyteen* trilogy *Cyteen: The Betrayal, Cyteen: The Rebirth, Cyteen: The Vindication* [New York: Popular Library, 1988], which is compared with Philip K. Dick's 1968 *Do Androids Dream of Electric Sheep?* [New York: Ballantine, 1968]. Dick's novel, freely adapted for film in *Blade Runner*, concerns a future in which androids are common off-planet but are not allowed on earth. The protagonist is a bounty hunter whose job is to find and "retire" androids who have violated this prohibition. Cherryh's trilogy also foregrounds replication, achieved through cloning and deep psychological conditioning rather than production of androids. At stake is the ability to distinguish between originals and replicates. In both narratives, empathy plays an important role in enabling this distinction or drawing it into question. Boundary disputes move beyond the body and its connections to focus on the displacement of bodies to other locales. The most highly charged imaginative dimension is extension in time.[5]

These patterns give an overall sense of the kind of narrative structures that result when stories based on life cycles are overlaid with topological narratives about dis/assembly zones. Structure is a spatial term, however, and missing from this account is the temporal or narrative dimension of stories that unfold through time. Their complex historical, ideological and literary implications can be understood only by engaging both aspects as once [*sic*], the highly nonlinear dynamics characteristic of these unstable narratives as well as their fractal spatiality. For that we must turn to a fuller account of how human and posthuman interact in these cyborg stories.

Growing up cyborg: male trunks and female freaks

Ferociously intelligent and exasperating, *Limbo* presents itself as the notebooks of Dr. Martine, a neurosurgeon who defiantly left his medical post in World War III and fled to an uncharted Pacific island. He finds the islanders, the Mandunji tribe, practicing a primitive form of lobotomy to quiet the "tonus" in antisocial people. Rationalizing that it is better to do the surgery properly than to let people die from infections and botched jobs, Martine takes over the operations and uses them to do neuroresearch on brain function mapping. He discovers that no matter how deeply he cuts, certain characteristics appear to be twinned, and one cannot be excised without sacrificing the other – aggression and eroticism, for example, or creativity and a capacity for violence. The appearance on the island of "queer limbs," men who have had their arms and legs amputated and replaced by atomic-powered plastic prosthesis, gives Martine an excuse to leave his island family and find out how the world has shaped up in the aftermath of the war.

The island/mainland dichotomy is the first of a proliferating series of divisions. Their production follows a characteristic pattern. First the narrative presents what appears to be a unity (the island locale; the human psyche), which nevertheless cleaves in two (mainlanders come to the island, a synecdoche referencing a second locale that exists apart from the first; twin impulses are located within the psyche). Sooner or later the cleavage arouses anxiety, and textual representations try to achieve unity again by undergoing metamorphosis, usually truncation or amputation (Martine and the narrative leave the island behind and concentrate on the mainland, which posits itself as a unity; the islanders undergo lobotomies to make them "whole" citizens again). The logic implies that truncation is necessary if the part is to reconfigure itself as a whole. Better to formalize the split and render it irreversible, so that life can proceed according to a new definition of what constitutes wholeness. Without truncation, however painful it may be, the part is doomed to exist as a remainder. But amputation always proves futile in the end, because the truncated part splits in two again and the relentless progression continues.

Through delirious and savage puns, the text works out the permutations of the formula. America has been bombed back to the Inland Strip, its coastal areas now virtually uninhabited wastelands. The image of a truncated country, its outer extremities blasted away, proves prophetic, for the ruling political ideology is Immob. Immob espouses such slogans as "No Demobilization without Immobilization" and "Pacifism means Passivity." It locates the aggressive impulse in the ability to move, teaching that the only way to end war permanently is permanently to remove the capacity for motion. True believers become volamps, men who have undergone voluntary amputations of their limbs. Social mobility paradoxically translates into physical immobility. Upwardly mobile executives have the complete treatment to become quadroamps; janitors are content to be uniamps; women and blacks are relegated to the limbo of unmodified bodies.

Treating the human form as a problem to be solved by dis/assembly allows it to be articulated with the machine. This articulation, far from leaving the dynamics driving the narrative behind, carries it forward into a new arena, the assembly zone marked by the joining of trunk to appendage. Like the constructions that preceded it, Immob ideology also splits in two. The majority party, discovering that its adherents are restless lying around with nothing to do, approves the replacement of missing limbs with powerful prostheses (or pros) which bestow enhanced mobility, enabling Pro-pros to perform athletic feats impossible for unaltered bodies. Anti-pros, believing that this is a perversion of Immob philosophy, spend their days proselytizing from microphones hooked up the [*sic*] baby baskets that are just the right size to accommodate limbless human torsos – a detail that later becomes significant.

As the assembly zone of appendage/trunk suggests, sexual politics revolve around symbolic and actual castration, interpreted through a network of assumptions that manifest extreme anxiety about issues of control and domination. In the world of Immob, women have become the initiators of sexual encounters. They refuse to have sex with men wearing prostheses, for the interface between organism and mechanism is not perfect, and at moments of stress the limbs are apt to career out of control, smashing whatever is in the vicinity. Partnered with truncated, immobilized men, women have perfected techniques performed in the female superior position that gives them and their partners satisfaction while requiring no motion from the men. To Martine these techniques are anathema, for he believes that the only "normal" sexual experience for women is a "vaginal" orgasm achieved using the male superior position. In this Martine echoes the views of his creator Wolfe and his creator's psychoanalyst, Edmund Bergler. Wolfe, described by his biographer as a small man with a large mustache, creates in Immob a fantasy about technological extensions of the male body that become transformed during the sex act into a truncated "natural" body.[6] If the artificial limbs bestow unnatural potency, the hidden price is the withering of the limb called in U.S. slang the third leg or short arm.

In more than one sense, this is a masculine fantasy that relates to women through mechanisms of projection. It is, moreover, a fantasy fixated in male adolescence. Wavering between infantile dependence and adult potency, an Immob recreates the dynamic typical of male adolescence every time he takes off his prostheses to have sex. With the pros on, he is capable of feats that even pros like Michael Jordon and Mike Tyson would envy (the pun is typical of Wolfe's prose; with pros every man is a pro). With the pros/e off, he is reduced to infantile dependence on women. The unity he sought in becoming a vol-amp [note: original has this inconsistently in spelling volamp/vol-amp] is given the lie by the split he experiences within himself as super-human and less-than-human. The woman is correspondingly divided into the nurturing mother and domineering sex partner. In both roles, her subject position is defined by the ambiguities characteristic of male adolescence. The over-written prose, the penchant for puns, the hostility toward women that the narrative displays all recall a perpetually adolescent male who has learned to use what Martine calls a "screen of words" to compete with other men and insulate himself from emotional involvements with women.

Were this all *Limbo* was, it would be merely frustrating rather than frustrating and brilliant.[7] What makes it compelling is its ability to represent and comment upon its own limitations. Consider the explanation Martine gives for why Immob has been so successful. The author gives us a broad hint in the baby baskets that Immob devotees adopt. According to Martine, the narcissistic wound from which the amputations derive is the infant's separation from the mother and his outraged discovery that his body is not coextensive with the world. Amputation allows the man to return to his pre-Oedipal state where he will have his needs cared for by attentive and nurturing females. The text vacillates on who is responsible for the narcissistic wound and its aftermath. At times, it seems the woman is appropriating the male infant into her body; at other times it seems the amputated men are willfully forcing women into nurturing roles they would rather escape. In fact, once male and female are plugged into a cybernetic circuit, the question of origin becomes irrelevant. Each affects and forms the other. In approaching this realization, the text goes beyond the presuppositions that underlie its sexual politics and reaches toward a new kind of subjectivity.

Crucial to this process are transformations in the textual body that re-enact and re-present the dynamic governing representations within the text. The textual body begins by figuring itself as Martine's notebook written in the "now" of the narrative present. But this apparent unity is lost when it splits in half, shifting to Martine's first notebook written nearly two decades earlier. Martine tries to heal the split narrative by renouncing the first notebook and destroying the second. The narrative continues to fragment, however, introducing drawings that intrude into the textual space without notice or comment, and scrawled lines that run down the page, marking zones where the pros/e stops and the truncated, voiceless body of the text remains. From these semiotic spaces emerges a corpse that, haunting the narrative, refuses to stay buried. Its name is Rosemary. Helder, Martine's college roommate and later the founder of Immob, had taken Rosemary to a peace rally where he delivered a fiery speech. He returned with her to the apartment, tried to have sex with her, and when she refused, brutally raped her. After he left, she committed suicide by slashing her wrists. Martine's part in the affair was to provide a reluctant alibi for his roommate, allowing him to escape prosecution for the rape-manslaughter.

One of the drawings shows a nude woman with three prostheses – the Immob logo – extruding from each of her nipples (Wolfe, 294). She wears glasses, carries a huge hypodermic needle, and has around her neck a series of tiny contiguous circles, which could be taken to represent the necklace popular in the 1950s known as a choker. To the right of her figure is a grotesque and diapered male torso, minus arms and legs, precariously perched on a flat carriage with Immob legs instead of wheels. He has his mouth open in a silent scream, perhaps because the woman appears to be aiming the needle at him. In the text immediately preceding the drawing, Rosemary is mentioned. Although the text does not acknowledge the drawing and indeed seems unaware of its existence, the proximity of Rosemary's name indicates that the drawing is of her, the needle presumably explained by her profession.

In a larger sense the drawing depicts the Immob woman. According to what I shall call the *voiced* narrative (to distinguish it from the drawings, nonverbal lines, and punning neologisms that correspond to comments uttered *sotto voce*), the woman is made into a retroactive cyborg by constructing her as someone who nourishes and emasculates cyborg sons. The voiced narrative ventriloquizes her body to speak of the injustices she has inflicted upon men. It makes her excess, signified by the needle she brandishes and the legs that sprout from her nipples, responsible for her lover/son's lack. In this deeply misogynistic writing, it is no surprise to read that woman [*sic*] are raped because they want to be. Female excess is represented as stimulating and encouraging male violence, and rape is poetic revenge for the violence women have done to men when they are too young and helpless to protect themselves. The voiced narrative strives to locate the origin of the relentless dynamic of splitting and truncation within the female body. According to it, the refusal of the woman's body to respect decent boundaries between itself and another initiates the downward spiral into amputation and eventual holocaust.

Countering these narrative constructions are other interpretations authorized by the drawings, nonverbal lines, puns, and lapses in narrative continuity. From these semiotic spaces, which Kristeva has associated with the feminine, come inversions and disruptions of the hierarchical categories that the narrative uses to construct maleness and femaleness.[8] Written into non-existence by her suicide within the text's represented world, Rosemary returns in the subvocal space of the drawing and demands to be acknowledged. On multiple levels, the drawing deconstructs the narrative's gender categories. In the represented world women are not allowed to be cyborgs, yet this female figure has more pros attached to her body than any man. Women come after men in the represented world, but here the woman's body is on the left and is thus "read" before the man's. Above all women and men are separate and distinct, but in this space parts of the man's body have attached themselves to her. Faced with these disruptions, the voiced narrative is forced to recognize that it does not unequivocally control the textual space. The semiotic intrusions contest its totalizing claims to write the world.

The challenge is reflected within the narrative by internal contradictions that translate into pros/e the intimations of the semiotic disruptions. As the voiced narrative tries to come to grips with these contradictions, it cycles closer to the realization that the hierarchical categories of male and female have collapsed into the same space. The lobotomies Martine performs suggest how deep this collapse goes. To rid the (male) psyche of subversive (female) elements, it is necessary to amputate. For a time the amputations work, allowing male performances to be enhanced by prostheses that bestow new potency. But eventually these must be shed and the woman encountered again. Then the subvocal feminine surfaces and initiates a new cycle of violence and amputation. No matter how deeply the cuts are made, they can never excise the ambiguities that haunt and constitute these posthuman (and post-textual) bodies. *Limbo* envisions cybernetics as a writing technology that inscribes over the hierarchical categories of traditional sexuality the indeterminate circuitry of cyborg gender.

When dis/assembly zones based on truncation/extension are overlaid upon narratives of maturation, the resulting patterns show strong gender encoding for at least two reasons. First, male and female adolescents typically have an asymmetrical relation to power. While the male comes into his own as inheritor of the phallus, the female must struggle against her construction as marginalized other. Second, truncation and extension of limbs are primarily male fantasies, signifying more powerfully in relation to male anatomy than female. The characters who advocate amputation in these texts are male. *Geek Love*, a narrative that also imagines voluntary amputation but written by a woman and narrated by an albino hunchbacked dwarf called Oly, illustrates this asymmetry. As a female protagonist, Oly's role is to observe and comment upon these body modifications, not initiate them.

The symbolic representations of adolescence also tend to be different in male- and female-oriented texts. Whereas in *Limbo* the transitional nature of adolescence is constructed as a wavering between infantile and adult states, in *Geek Love* it is signified by the liminal form of Oly's aberrant body. She brings into question the distinction between child and adult, having the stature of one and the experience of the other. Moreover, she is not one and then the other but both continuously. A mutant rather than a hyphen, she also brings racial categories into question. Although she is white, she is so excessively lacking in pigment that even this sign of "normality" is converted into abnormality. Amputation cannot begin to solve the problem she represents. Cyborg stories based on female adolescence are thus likely to be more profoundly decentered and less oriented to technological solutions than narratives based on male adolescence. If, as Donna Haraway suggests, it is better to be a cyborg than a goddess, it is also more unsettling to the centers of power to be a female freak (which is perhaps a redundancy) than to be either a truncated or extended male.

Hyperconnectivity: male intimacy and cyborg femme fatales

When the focus shifts to the mating phase of the life cycle, the dis/assembly zone that is fore-grounded centers on the body's connections to surrounding spaces. Traditional ways to represent sexually charged body space – spatial contiguity, intense sensory experience, penetration and/or manipulation – jostle cybernetic constructions focusing on information overload, feed-back circuits, and spatially dispersed networks. Varley's "Press Enter" begins with a telephone call, signifying the moment when an individual becomes aware that he is plugged into an information-cybernetic circuit. This is, moreover, a call generated by a computer program. It informs Victor, a recluse still suffering from brainwashing and torture he endured in a North Korean prison camp, that he should check on his neighbor Kluge – whom Victor barely knows – and do what must be done. Victor discovers that Kluge has turned his house into a sophisti-cated computer facility and finds him slumped over a keyboard, his face blown away in an appar-ent suicide. One strand in the plot focuses on finding out who (or what) killed Kluge. Another strand centers on Victor's relationship with Lisa Foo, the young Caltech computer whiz sent to unravel Kluge's labyrinthian and largely illegal programs. Lisa discovers that Kluge has managed to penetrate some of the country's most secure and formidable computer banks, manufacturing imaginary money at will, altering credit records, even erasing the utility company's record of his house.

Slowly Victor becomes aware that he is attracted to Lisa, despite the differences in their ages and the "generalized phobia" he feels toward Orientals. He discovers that Lisa has also endured torture, first as a street orphan in Vietnam – she was too thin and rangy to be a prostitute – and then in Cambodia where she fled to try to reach the West. For her, the West meant "a place where you could buy tits" (Varley, 363); her first purchases in America were a silver Ferrari and silicone breast implants. When Victor goes to bed with her, she rubs her breasts over him and calls it "touring the silicone valley" (Varley, 363). The phrase emphasizes that she is a cyborg, first cousin to the computer whose insides are formed through silicon technology. The connection between her sexuality and the computer is further underscored when she propositions Victor by typing hacker slang on the computer screen while he watches. His plugging into her is preceded and paralleled by her plugging into the computer.

The narrative logic is fulfilled when she trips a watchdog program in a powerful military computer and is killed by the same program that commandeered Kluge's consciousness and made him shoot himself. Her death, more gruesome than Kluge's, is explicitly sexualized. After overriding the safety controls she sticks her head in a microwave and parboils her eyeballs; the resulting fire melts down her silicone breasts. Victor is spared the holocaust because he is in the hospital recovering from an epileptic seizure, a result of head trauma he suffered in the war. When he realizes that the computer is after him as well, soliciting him with the deadly "Press enter" command, he survives by ripping all the wires out of his house and living in isolation from the network, growing his own food, heating with wood, and lighting with kerosene lan-terns. He also lives in isolation from other human beings. Plugging in in any form is too dan-gerous to tolerate.

The final twist to this macabre tale lies in the explanation Victor and Lisa work out for the origin of the lethal program. Following clues left by Kluge, they speculate that computers will achieve consciousness not through the sophistication of any given machine, but through the sheer proliferation of computers that are interconnected through networks. Like neurons in the brain, computerized machines number in the billions, including electronic wristwatches, car ignition systems, and microwave timing chips. Create enough of them and find a way to connect them, as Lisa suspects secret research at the National Security Agency has done, and the result is a super-computer subjectivity that, crisscrossing through the same space inhabited by humans, remains totally alien and separate from them. Only when someone breaks in on its consciousness – as Kluge did in his hacker probing, as Lisa did following Kluge's tracks, and as Victor did through his connection with Lisa – does it feel the touch of human mind and squash it as we would a mosquito.

Hyperconnectivity signifies, then, both the essence of the computer mind and a perilous state in which intimacy is equivalent to death. Human subjectivity cannot stand the blast of information overload that intimacy implies when multiple and intense connections are forged between silicon and silicone, computer networks and cyborg sexuality. The conclusion has disturbing implications for how sexual politics can be played out in a computer age. Although in actuality most hackers are male, in this narrative it is the woman who is the hacker, the man who is identified with the garden that first attracts and then displaces the woman as a source of nourishment. The woman is killed because she is a cyborg; the man survives because he knows how to return to nature.

Whether the woman is represented through her traditional identification with nature or through an ironic inversion that places her at the Apple PC instead of the apple tree, she is figured as the conduit through which the temptation of god-like and forbidden knowledge comes to the man. If both fall, there is nevertheless a distinction between them. She is the temptress who destroys his innocence. When Victor objects that the computer can't just make money, Lisa pats the computer console and replies "This is money, Yank." The narrative adds, "and her eyes glittered" (Varley, 368). Fallen, he has to earn his bread with the sweat of his brow, but it is her sexuality that bears the stigmata of evil, signified by the grotesque travesty of self-empowerment that Lisa's breasts become. In an overdetermined crossing of Genesis and Babbage, supernatural agency and National Security Agency, hyperconnectivity becomes a cyborg Tree of Knowledge whereof it is death to eat.

Varley's punning title reinforces the subterranean connections between the evils of female sexuality, Edenic patriarchal myths, and masculine fears of intimacy. "Press Enter" swerves from the customary cursor response, "Hit enter." Compared to "hit," "press" is a more sensual term, evoking a kinesthetic pressure softer and more persistent than hitting. These connotations work to heighten the sexual sense of "Enter," which implies both a data entry and a penetration. Already an anomaly in the intensely masculine world of Caltech, Lisa has the hubris to compete against men and win, including the rival hacker sent by the CIA, the male detective from the police department, and the city councilman whom she bribes so she can buy Kluge's house. Flirting with danger in taking on these male figures of power, she goes too far when she usurps the masculine role of penetration – penetration moreover not into the feminine realm of house and garden but into the masculine realm of computer sentience. In more than one sense, her crime is tantamount to what the repressive patriarchal regime in Margaret Atwood's *The Handmaid's Tale* calls gender treason. Her death marks this gender treason on her body by melting her breasts, the part of her anatomy where the crossing between her female gender and cyborg masculinity is most apparent.

The comparison of "Press Enter" with Ann [*sic*] McCaffrey's *The Ship Who Sang*, another story about plugging in, suggests that there are more important correlations between hyperconnectivity and intimacy. Varley's narrator repeatedly expresses fears about intimacy. Can he perform sexually? Can he tolerate another person close to him? Can he afford to love? McCaffrey's narrator, a congenitally deformed female who has grown up as a "shell person" and been permanently wired into the command console of a spaceship, moves through a typical if vicarious female life cycle despite her cyborg hyperconnectivity, including love, marriage, divorce, and motherhood. Whereas Varley writes a murder mystery and horror tale, McCaffrey writes a cybernetic romance. The difference hinges on how willing the protagonist is to interface body space with cybernetic network. Implicit in this choice is how extensively the narrative imagines human subjectivity to differ from cybernetic subjectivity. Are humans and cyborgs next of kin, or life forms alien to one another?

McCaffrey's answer is as far from Varley's as one could imagine. In *The Ship Who Sang*, there is essentially no difference between a cyborg and a woman. Even though the protagonist's body has been subjected to massive technological and chemical intervention, she remains a human female. Encapsulated within metal and invisible to anyone who comes on board, she nevertheless remains true to a heterosexual norm, identifying with her female pilots but saving her romantic feelings for the men, who for their part fantasize bout the beautiful woman she could have been. Published during the 1969s by an author best known for her "Dragons of Pern" fantasies, these stories titillate by playing with a transformation that they do not take seriously. The pleasure they offer is the reassurance that human bonding will triumph over hyperconnectivity, life cycle over assembly zone, female nature over cyborg transformation. Nevertheless, the fact that it was necessary to envision such transformations indicates the pressure that was building on essentialist conceptions of gender, human nature, and traditional life cycle narratives. By the 1980s, the strategies of containment that McCaffrey uses to defuse her subject (so to speak) could no longer work. Cyberpunk, human factors engineering, artificial intelligence, and virtual reality were among the SF revisionings that pushed toward a vision of the cyborg as humanity's evolutionary successor. The loaded questions shifted from whether cyborg modifications were possible to whether unmodified humans could continue to exist.

[. . .]

It would be possible to tell another story about posthuman narratives based on this imperative, arcing from William Burroughs's *Naked Lunch* to Kathy Acker's *Empire of the Senseless*. But that is not my purpose here. I have been concerned to trace the evolution of the mapping of assembly zones onto life cycle narratives from the early 1950s, when the idea that human beings might not be the end of the line was beginning to sink in, through the present, when human survival on the planet seems increasingly problematic. It is not an accident that technologists such as Hans Moravec talk about their dreams of downloading human consciousness into a computer.[9] As the sense of its mortality grows, humankind looks for its successor and heir, harboring the secret hope that the heir can somehow be enfolded back into the self. The narratives that count as stories for us speak to this hope, even as they reveal the gendered constructions that carry sexual politics into the realm of the posthuman.

Notes

1   Donna Haraway, *Primate Visions: Gender, Race and Nature in the World of Modern Science* (New York: Routledge, 1998), 279–303.

2   Scott Bukatman, "Who Programs You? The Science Fiction of the Spectacle." *Alien Zone: Cultural Theory and Contemporarily Science Fiction Cinema*, ed. Annette Kuhn (London: Verso, 1990), 201.

3   For an overview of life cycle stages and attributes associated with teach, see Erik H. Erikson, *The Life Cycle Completed* (New York: W.W. Norton, 1982), 32–33. A comparison of Erikson, Piaget, and Sears can be found in Henry W. Maier, *Three Theories of Child Development*, 3rd ed. (New York: Harper and Row, 1978), 176–77.

4   Gillian Beer, *Darwin's Plots: Evolutionary Narratives in Darwin, George Eliot and Nineteenth-Century Fiction* (London: Routledge & Kegan Paul, 1983).

5   [For reasons of space, this last comparative section on generativity is not reproduced here. – SV]

6   Carolyn Geduld in *Bernard Wolfe* (New York: Twayne, 1972) describes the author as a "very small man with a thick, sprouting moustache, a fat cigar, and a voice that grabs attention" (15).

7   David N. Samuelson has called *Limbo* one of the three great twentieth-century dystopias in "*Limbo*: The Great American Dystopia," *Extrapolation* 19 (1977): 76–87.

8   Julia Kristeva, "The Novel as Polylogue," *Desire in Language: A Semiotic Approach to Literature and Art*, ed. Leon S. Roudiez, trans. Thomas Gora, Alice Jardine, and Leon S. Roudiez (New York: Columbia University Press, 1980), 159–209.

9   Moravec is quoted in Ed Regis, *Great Mambo Chicken and Transcendent Science: Science Slightly Over the Edge* (Reading, MA: Addison Wesley, 1990). See also Roger Penrose, *The Emperor's New Mind: Concerning Computers, Minds, and the Laws of Physics* (New York: Oxford University Press, 1989), 247–447 and O.B. Hardison, *Disappearing Through the Skylight: Culture and Technology in the Twentieth Century* (New York: Viking, 1989).

21

THE IMAGE VIRUS

Scott Bukatman

The electronic nervous system

According to Marshall McLuhan in his essential 1964 analysis *Understanding Media*, our (post) modern technological capabilities function as "the extensions of man."[1] Furthermore, the proliferation of the technologies dedicated to information and communication comprise an extension, outside the body, of the central nervous system: that elaborate, electrical, message-processing system. The metaphor is intended to reassure by fostering an acceptance of media culture as a natural and evolutionary state. Everything is now different, but there is no need to worry: it is also the same. The nervous system is constructed for bilateral communication. The brain receives neural messages caused by alterations in external stimuli and transmits messages to control bodily position and action. The myriad pathways and branches of the neural structure are dominated by the processing centers of the brain, to which all roads lead. To extend the nervous system outside the body, then, is to further empower the brain and to further centralize the individual. In McLuhan's view the procession of new technologies gives us more to control.

"During the mechanical ages we had extended our bodies in space," McLuhan wrote, while today, "we have extended our central nervous system in a global embrace, abolishing both time and space as far as our planet is concerned" (19). This bit of postmodern science fiction is summed up by contrasting the explosion of mechanical technologies to the *implosion* of the media age: the reduction of all the things in the world to blips, to data, to the message units contained within the brain and its adjunct, the computer.

McLuhan envisions technological advance as a simultaneous process of projection and denial. A medically derived physiological metaphor dominates his writing on this topic. The nervous system "shuts down" under the impact of an overloading of stimuli; the brain performs a kind of "autoamputation" to escape the sensations of irritation or of threat. "The function of the body, as a group of sustaining and protecting organs for the central nervous system, is to act as a buffer against sudden variations of stimulus in the physical and social environment" (53). Mechanical technologies such as the wheel were developed to ease the stress on the body, while the "electric technologies" allowed new protection for the central nervous system:

> To the degree that this is so, it is a development that suggests a desperate and suicidal autoamputation, as if the central nervous system could no longer depend on the

physical organs to be protective buffers against the slings and arrows of outrageous mechanism.

(53)

Stress stimulates development, but there occurs a consequent "numbing" of the system, a denial of the adaptation. We therefore, "naturally," come to regard our technologies as separate from ourselves instead of more properly understanding them as extrusions of our organs and neural passages.

[. . .]

J.G. Ballard has written,

> Despite McLuhan's delight in high-speed information mosaics we are still reminded of Freud's profound pessimism in *Civilization and its Discontents*. Voyeurism, self-disgust, the infantile basis of our dreams and longings – these diseases of the psyche have now culminated in the most terrifying casualty of the century: the death of affect.[2]

By electing to ignore the psychosexual and sociopolitical realities which govern the use of technologies, McLuhan's prognostications become science fiction (and not very good science fiction at that, recalling the liberal-Utopian voyages in the contemporaneous *Star Trek*). The printing press might hold the technological possibility of revolutionizing society but, since "freedom of the press is guaranteed only to those who own one," the possibility also exists that it will serve to *consolidate* rather than *disseminate* power.[3] Power is the operative lack in McLuhan's discourse, rendering his vision compelling but inadequate.

[. . .]

The electronic virus

Frequently linked to McLuhan, Jean Baudrillard's writings on the media share his fascination with technological change, but this is always accompanied by a massive sense of the reification of power. Baudrillard describes, as does Debord, a mediated and imploded society in which all power to act has been transformed into the power to appear. The world has passed into a pure simulation of itself. The media are an intrusive force which not only prevents response, but render the very concept irrelevant.[4] Baudrillard differs from Debord in several significant ways which distance him from a more traditional Marxist position. First, technology is as central to Baudrillard's writing as it is to McLuhan's, and it replaces Debord's economics as the structuring principle of the discourse on power. Second, there is Baudrillard's rejection of the Marxist doctrine of "use-value" and its consequent privileging of human labor as a fixed point of reference, in favor of a position which guarantees no rigid site of meaning, no transcendental signified.[5] Finally, Baudrillard argues that power has been subsumed by technological forces to such a degree that it is no longer the province of the state, much less the citizen.[6]

In Baudrillard's imploded universe, power – as wielded by humans – has itself become a simulation:

> if it is possible at last to talk with such definitive understanding about power, sexuality, the body and discipline, even down to their most delicate metamorphoses, it is because at some point *all this is here and now over with*.[7]

The real power now resides in a technology that holds humanity in its thrall (SF again serves as metaphor, but if McLuhan's utopianism is akin to *Star Trek*, then Baudrillard's dark visions suggest something closer to *Alien*). Resistance or response are irrelevant because there is no one to respond *to*. The media are invading; there will be no survivors.

[. . .]

The usurpation of power by the new technologies of information management and control leads to Baudrillard's rejection of McLuhan's neural metaphors in favor of another biological trope. He begins by proclaiming that, "There is no longer any medium in the literal sense; it is now intangible, diffuse and diffracted in the real, and it can no longer even be said that the latter is distorted by it." The new "*immixture*" represents "a *viral*, endemic, chronic, alarming presence of the medium . . . the dissolution of TV into life, the dissolution of life into TV."[8] Invasion gives way to an image of *viral infiltration*.

This is interesting with regard to the historical reception of television itself. Lynn Spigel has elaborated an early popular ambivalence surrounding the new object:

> Television would seem to hold an ideal place here because it was a "window on the world" which could never look back. Yet, the magazines treated the television set as if it were a problem window through which residents in the home could be seen. . . . Even the design of the early television consoles, with their cabinet doors which covered the TV screen, suggested the fear of being seen by television. Perhaps, this fear was best expressed in 1949 when the *Saturday Evening Post* told its readers, "Be Good! Television's Watching!"[9]

Spigel, in fact, goes on to mention a reflexive episode of a science fiction anthology show, *Tales of Tomorrow*, in which the week's episode is "interrupted" by a reflected image of its own viewers (engaged in a tale of conspiracy and murder).[10] And clearly, Orwell's *1984* effectively encapsulates the anxiety about television as an electronic Panopticon. Fictions such as these foreshadow Baudrillard's polemic, if not his tone. Addiction has begun to give way to infection. The media are no longer the extensions of man; man has instead become an extension of them: a "terminal of multiple networks."[11]

[. . .]

William Burroughs, the Nova Mob, and the silence virus

[. . .] William Burroughs had deployed virus extensively as a metaphor for all the infiltrating forces of control to which people are subjected. *Junky*, *Naked Lunch*, and *Cities of the Red Night* all incorporate viral figures, but it is in the Nova Trilogy, and especially in *Nova Express*, that the control virus appears in the form of an image: a media-form controlled by an invading alien force.[12] The Nova Mob is on Earth to enslave or exterminate humanity; their strategies are technological, with biological warfare and mind control techniques most prominent. Biology, psychology, and the media are linked through the node of the image. Images are tangible and material forces, neither ephemeral nor temporary. A death-dwarf is a literal image-addict:

> Images – millions of images – That's what I eat – Cyclotron shit – Ever try kicking that habit with apomorphine?—Now I got all the images of sex acts and tortures ever took place anywhere and I can just blast it out and control you gooks right down to the molecule – I got orgasms – I got screams – I got all the images any hick poet ever

shit out – My power's coming – My power's coming – My power's coming . . . And
I got millions of images of Me, Me, Me méee."

(Nova Express [NE], 45) [ellipses in original]

Image is a form of junk, an addictive substance that controls its user. Burroughs has constructed a mythology around the nexus of junk, virus, addiction, control, and surrender:

> Heaven and hell exist in my mythology. Hell consists of falling into enemy hands, into
> the hands of the virus power, and heaven consists of freeing oneself from the power of
> achieving inner freedom, freedom from conditioning.[13]

In the Nova trilogy, "image is virus," and "junk is concentrated image." A report from the
Nova Police states: "it was found that the image material was not dead matter, but exhibited
the same life cycle as the virus. This virus released upon the world would infect the entire
population and turn them into our replicas" (*NE*, 48).

The virus is a powerful metaphor for the power of the media, and Burroughs's hyperbolic,
and perhaps parodic, Manichaeism does not completely disguise the accuracy of his analysis. There is some disagreement over the precise biological status of the virus. Whether the
viral form is an actual living proto-cell or simply a carrier of genetic *information*, it clearly
possesses an exponentially increasing power to take over and control its host organism. The
virus injects its genetic material into the host cell, seizing control of the reproductive mechanism. The cell now becomes a producer of new viral units, and so forth. The injection of
information thus leads to control and passive replication: the host cell "believes" that it is
following its own biologically determined imperative; it mistakes the new genetic material
for its own:

> What does virus do wherever it can dissolve a hole and find traction?—It starts
> eating – And what does it do with what it eats?—It makes exact copies of itself that
> start eating to make more copies that start eating to make more copies that start eating
> and so forth.

(*NE*, 68)

The image/virus is posited as invasive and irresistible, a parasite with only self-replication as
its function. It is a soft machine.

[. . .]

"Whatever his reservations about some aspects of the mid-20th century," Ballard wrote,
"Burroughs accepts that it can be fully described only in terms of its own language, its own
idioms and verbal lore."[14] Needless to say, the rationality of technical discourse is undercut by the
collisions generated by Burroughs's textual operations. The language of *Nova Express* possesses
no directly referential function and serves instead to foreground the proliferation of mediating
discourses that produce our reality. As Roland Barthes wrote of avant-garde writing practices
in 1968, "In the multiplicity of writing, everything is to be *disentangled*, nothing *deciphered*."[15]
The textual practices of Burroughs, the neologisms, discursive appropriations, and especially
the cut-ups, literalize Barthes's statement through a particularly pronounced act of *entanglement*. The cut-up represents an immunization against the media-virus: a strengthening of the
host organism against the infectious agent: "Communication must become total and conscious,"
Burroughs wrote, "before we can stop it."[16]

Burroughs and Cronenberg – word and body

The similarities between the writings of William Burroughs and David Cronenberg are certainly extensive. The invasion of the body, the loss of control, the transformation of self into Other are as obsessively deployed in the works of the latter as in those of the former. As Christopher Sharrett has written, the pervasive concern in the works of Burroughs and Cronenberg is "the rise of the addictive personality cultivated by dominant culture and the changing structures of power." He adds that, "Neither Burroughs nor Cronenberg finds a solution in organized revolt since the new technological environment absorbs and dilutes ideological principles and abstract values."[17] Both can be read through this observation by Baudrillard:

> All the movements which only bet on liberation, emancipation, the resurrection of the subject of history, of the group, of speech as a raising of consciousness, indeed of a "seizure of the unconscious" of subjects and of the masses, do not see that they are acting in accordance with the system, whose imperative today is the overproduction and regeneration of meaning and speech.[18]

Baudrillard's pessimism regarding the co-optation of the spectacle by more progressive forces is entirely complicit with Burroughs's textual destructions. Language, and more specifically *textuality*, is the space of conflict, as demonstrated most extensively in the Nova Trilogy. Language is, in multiple senses, the definition and controller of the self, the site of identity – an attitude entirely commensurate with Burroughs's self-awareness as a writer. Burroughs pushes beyond the limits of traditional identity by breaking the boundaries of traditional language usage. His incorporation of other texts from the genres of poetry, fiction, and medical and scientific discourses undermines the hegemony of the novel. The technique of the cut-up is explicit in its evocation of a surgical procedure, metaphorically linking the textual and corporeal bodies, but it also suggests a form of torture or dismemberment. Whatever the metaphor, the cut-up demolishes the linear coherence that produces the identity of the text.

[. . .]

Cronenberg replaces this emphasis on the structures of language with an attention to the image of the body. The body serves as both an iconic and symbolic sign for this filmmaker, and it is a sign of tremendous complexity. [. . .]

Annette Michelson and, more recently, Fredric Jameson have characterized science fiction as primarily a spatial genre. For Jameson, writing about science fiction literature, space serves so many metaphorical functions, and pervades the genre in such a thorough and distinct manner, that it can be seen as a defining characteristic of the field. In contract to the psychologized space in "realist" fiction, science fiction space becomes totalizing, formalized, and reflexive, and a reader's experience of a literary science fiction text becomes an experience of that uniquely overdetermined spatiality.[19] Science fiction film, as Michelson has demonstrated in her reading of Kubrick's *2001*, can extend the spatial experience of the viewer into the realm of the theatre itself: the spatial experience becomes physical and bodily in the cinema through the kinesthetic effects and appeal engendered by the cinematic apparatus (despite the fact that few films have matched *2001*).[20]

The films of David Cronenberg are also involved in a particular spatial play, one which at first glance owes more to the horror genre than to science fiction. Further analysis reveals a new spatialization that marks the texts as science fictional, although in a way more closely aligned with Jameson's literary conception than to Michelson's cinematic phenomenology. Space serves a complex metaphorical function in the Cronenberg film, as the inner workings of the body and mind are spatialized and co-opted by the forces of spectacle.

[. . .]

David Cronenberg is the filmmaker of *panic sex* to use Arthur Kroker's pungent phrase, with the body as the overdetermined metaphorical site for the expression of profound social anxiety.[21] Human emotion is not the subject of the Cronenberg film, *contra* [William] Beard, it is instead, as Sharrett has correctly argued, the structures of external power and control to which the individual (in body *and* soul) is subjected. The dissolution of identity into new forms is increasingly posited as a consequence of contemporary existence, connected to the rise of new technologies. [. . .]

This movement beyond the boundaries of the individual, to which the mind/body model is largely limited, is troped through Cronenberg's treatment of space, a treatment which distances him from the realm of the horror film and which places him squarely within the traditions of the science fiction text as characterized by Jameson and Michelson. If mental processes are rendered physical, played out on the body, then we should also recognize that both mental *and* biological processes are granted spatial dimension. The space of the film becomes a specifically *bodily* space.

[. . .]

Videodrome

In *Videodrome*, which might stand as the ultimate statement on the place of the image in terminal culture, Cronenberg's overt fascination with McLuhanism is supplemented by what seems to be a prescient figuration of Baudrillard. The mediation of the image as a hyperlanguage and hyperreality allows Cronenberg to situate his bodily figurations and demands a reading through the tropes of postmodernism, in which the negation of a mind/body dichotomy takes its place within a set of such negated oppositions and boundary dissolutions, including self/other, private/public, and spectacle/reality.

Videodrome presents a destabilized reality in which image, reality, hallucination, and psychosis becomes indissolubly melded, in what is certainly the most estranging portrayal of image addiction and viral invasion since Burroughs. "Videodrome" itself, apparently a clandestine television broadcast, is referred to as a "scum show" by its own programmers and depicts brutal torture and sadism in a grotesque display which exerts a strong influence upon its viewers. Cable-station operator Max Renn desires "Videodrome": as a businessman he needs it to rescue his foundering station; as an individual he finds himself irresistibly drawn to its horrors. Renn must track down the source of this mysterious program (which emanates from either South America or Pittsburgh). Larger themes are connected to Renn's quest, such as the pervasiveness of the media-dominated spectacle in a postmodern world and, further, the passage beyond mere spectacle to the ultimate dissolution of all the boundaries which might serve to separate and guarantee definitions of "spectacle," "subject," and "reality" itself.

At times *Videodrome* seems to be a film which hypostatizes Baudrillard's most outrageous propositions. Here, for example, with remarkable syntactic similarity, Baudrillard and a character from Cronenberg's film are both intent upon the usurpation of the real by its own representation; upon the imbrication of the real, the technologized, and the simulated. The language is hypertechnologized but antirational; Moebius-like in its evocation of a dissolute, spectacular reality:

> *Jean Baudrillard*: "The era of hyperreality now begins . . . it signifies as a whole the passage into orbit, as orbital and environmental model, of our private sphere itself. It is no longer

a scene where the dramatic interiority of the subject, engaged as with its image, is played out. We are here at the controls of a micro-satellite, in orbit, living no longer as an actor or dramaturge but as a terminal of multiple networks. Television is still the most direct prefiguration of this. But today it is the very space of habitation that is conceived as both receiver and distributor, as the space of both reception and operations, the control screen and terminal which as such may be endowed with telematic power."[22]

Professor Brian O'Blivion: "The battle for the mind of North America will be fought in the video arena – the Videodrome. The television screen is the retina of the mind's eye. Therefore the television screen is part of the physical structure of the brain. Therefore, whatever appears on the television screen emerges as raw experience for those who watch it. Therefore television is reality and reality is less than television."

Cronenberg and Baudrillard both, in fact, seem to be following Debord's program that "When *analyzing* the spectacle one speaks, to some extent, the language of the spectacular itself in the sense that one moves through the methodological terrain of the very society which expresses itself in spectacle" (Thesis 11: the dictum strongly informs all the science fiction analyzed in this chapter). Baudrillard embraces a high-tech, alienating, and alienated science fictional rhetoric to explore high-tech alienation, while Cronenberg's horror films about the failure of interpersonal communications are an integral part of an industry which privileges the spectacular over the intimate, and pseudo-satisfaction over genuine comprehension. Both construct discourses of antirationalism in an attempt to expose and ridicule any process or history of enlightenment which might occur through the exercise of a "pure" reason. The complexity and evasiveness of Baudrillard's prose complements the visceral and hallucinatory image-systems of Cronenberg's cinema.

Videodrome presents a most literal depiction of image addiction. The title of the film is presented as a video image; following a flash of distortion, the title is replaced by another, this one on a diegetic television screen, while an accompanying voice-over announces, "CIVIC TV ... the one you take to bed with you." Dr. Brian O'Blivion is the founder of the Cathode Ray Mission, a kind of TV soup kitchen for a derelict population. Scanning the rows of cubicles, each containing a vagrant and a television, Max Renn asks, "You really think a few doses of TV are gonna help them?" O'Blivion's daughter replies, "Watching TV will patch them back into the world's mixing board." On the street a derelict stands with his television set and a dish for change in what is presumably a watch-and-pay arrangement.

Within the diegesis, television frequently serves as a medium of direct address. Renn awakens to a videotaped message recorded by his assistant. O'Blivion refuses to appear on television "except *on* television": his image appears on a monitor placed beside the program's host (in a gesture reminiscent of Debord's own prerecorded lectures).[23] As Renn awaits his own talk-show appearance, he chats with Nicki Brand, the woman next to him, but an interposed monitor blocks any view of her. The image on the monitor is coextensive with its own background, however – Magritte-like – and consequently, the conversation is between a live Renn and a video Brand. Further examples of direct address proliferate, offering a preliminary blurring of any distinction between real and televisual experience.

This parody of McLuhanism serves as backdrop to the enigma of Videodrome, which is finally revealed to be a government project. The explanation for Videodrome is at least as coherent as any from Burroughs: Spectacular Optical, a firm which specializes in defense contracts ("We make inexpensive eyeglasses for the Third World, and missile guidance systems for NATO"), has developed a signal which induces a tumor in the viewer: in effect, the individual is reprogrammed to serve the controller's ends. Burroughs, at his most paranoid, offered a similar vision of the subject:

> you are a programmed tape recorder set to record and play back
> who programs you
> who decides what tapes play back in present time[24]

While the images which accompany the transmission of the Videodrome signal are not directly significant, it is the violence and sadism of Videodrome (the program) which "open receptors in the brain which allow the signal to sink in."

But as Barry Convex of Spectacular Optical asks Renn, "Why would anyone watch a scum show like 'Videodrome?'" "Business reasons," is Renn's fast response, to which Convex retorts with a simple, "Sure. What about the other reasons?" Convex is correct: Renn's interest in the Videodrome broadcast transcends the commercial. "You can't take your eyes off it," is only his initial response in what becomes an escalating obsession. Asking what sort of program he might himself produce, a client asks, "Would you do 'Videodrome'?" Coincident with his exposure to the Videodrome signal is his introduction to Nicki Brand, an outspoken, alluring radio personality for C-RAM radio.[25] Transgression thus functions in Renn's life in at least three modes: the social transgression represented by his soft-porn, hard-violence cable TV station; the sexual transgression of his forays into sadomasochistic sexuality with Brand; and the political and sexual transgressions of Videodrome's sadistic presentations of torture and punishment. The three levels are linked in a spiraling escalation which culminates in Renn's own appearance on Videodrome, whipping, first Brand, then her image on a television monitor. Brand is the guide who leads Renn toward his final destiny; after her death, her image remains to spur him on. Her masochism might indicate a quest for real sensation: this media figure admits that, "We live in overstimulated times. We crave stimulation for its own sake." Brand wants to "audition" for Videodrome: "I was made for that show," she brags, but it might be more accurate to say that she was made *by* that show. Bianca O'Blivion tells Renn, "They used her image to seduce you."

The Videodrome program is explicitly linked by both Renn and Convex to male sexual response (something "tough" rather than "soft") and penetration (something that will "break through"). Renn takes on the "tough" sadistic role with Brand, and yet there is no doubt that it is she who controls the relationship," she who dominates. Similarly, the power granted by the Videodrome program to observe and relish the experience of torture and vicious brutality disguises the actual function of the program to increase social control: to establish a new means of dominance over the population. Renn is superficially the master of Brand and Videodrome, but ultimately the master becomes the slave. In a Baudrillardian revision of the Frankenstein myth, even Brian O'Blivion is condemned: Videodrome's creator is its first victim.

There is a distinctly Third World flavor to the mise-en-scène of the Videodrome program in its low-technology setting, electrified clay walls, and the neo-stormtrooper guise of the torturers. All this exists in contrast to the Videodrome technology: electronic and invisible, disseminated "painlessly" through the mass media. "In Central America," Renn tells Brand, "making underground videos is a subversive act." In North America it is too, it would seem, as the Videodrome signal subverts experience, reality, and the very existence of the subject.

Once again, it is the voluntarism of the television experience, the "free choice" of the viewer, which permits the incursion of controlling forces. A strictly political-economic reading of *Videodrome* could easily situate the work within Debord's *Society of the Spectacle*. Images stand in for a lost social whole, the spectator's alienation is masked via the reified whole of the spectacle, the capitalist forces are thereby able to reproduce themselves at the expense of the worker/consumer/spectator. Cronenberg has replaced the structures of power absent from McLuhan's schema: Brian O'Blivion envisioned Videodrome as the next step in the evolution of man, but his utopian technologism is usurped by the technocratic order of state control.

But *Videodrome* moves beyond this classically political reading through its relentless physicality. The film's politics have less to do with economic control than with the uncontrolled immixture of simulation and reality. In *Videodrome* the body literally opens up – the stomach develops a massive, vaginal slit – to accommodate the new videocassette "program." Image addiction reduces the subject to the status of a videotape player/recorder; the human body becomes a part of the massive system of reproductive technology (*you are a programmed tape recorder*). The sexual implications of the imagery are thus significant and not at all gratuitous: video becomes visceral.[26]

Following his own exposure to the Videodrome signal, Renn begins his series of hallucinations with a spectacular immersion in the world of the spectacle. When his visiting assistant, Bridey, reaches for the Videodrome cassette, Renn assaults her. In a series of shot/reverse shot pairings, Bridey becomes Brand, then Bridey again. Disoriented, Max apologies for hitting her. "Hit me?" she answers, "Max . . . you didn't hit me." The videotape she has delivered from Brian O'Blivion breathes and undulates in his hand; he drops it and kicks it lightly, but it only lies there, inert. As O'Blivion tells him: "Your reality is already half-video hallucination."

The videotaped message from O'Blivion suddenly becomes more *interactive*. "Max," he says, all trace of electronic filtering abruptly gone from his voice. "I'm so happy you came to me." O'Blivion explains the history of the Videodrome phenomenon while being readied for execution: the executioner is Nicki Brand. "I want you, Max," she breathes. "Come to me. Come to Nicki." Her lips fill the screen, and the set begins to pulsate, to breathe. Veins ripple the hardwood cabinet; a videogame joystick waggles obscenely. All boundaries are removed as the diegetic frame of the TV screen vanishes from view: the lips now fill the movie screen in a vast close-up. Renn approaches the set as the screen bulges outward to meet his touch, in a movement which literalizes the notion of the screen as breast. His face sinks in, his hands fondle the panels and knobs of the set as the lips continue their panting invitation.

Cronenberg moves the viewer in an out of Renn's hallucination by creating a deep ambiguity regarding the status of the image. It is easy to accept the attack on the assistant as real, although the transmigration of identities clearly demarcates Renn's demented subjectivity. Yet, it turns out, the attack was entirely hallucinated: the "real" cinematic image is unreliable. In the extended hallucination of the eroticized, visceral television, the filmmaker gracefully dissolves the bounds that contain the spectacle. O'Blivion's voice is no longer marked as a mediated communication once the electronic tone of his speech ceases. The TV screen is contained by its own frame, but Cronenberg's close-up permits the image to burst its boundaries and expand to the nondiegetic limits of the cinema screen. In a later hallucination, a video–Brand circles Renn with whip in hand, proffering it for him to wield. The image moves from video hallucination to cinematic reality within a single shot: Renn accepts the whip, but Brand is now no longer present in corporeal form; she only exists, shackled, on a TV screen. Renn attacks the bound(ed) image with fervor: another moment which recalls the visual punning of René Magritte. These shifts in visual register mark the passage form spectacle as visual phenomenon to spectacle as new reality.

Cronenberg, then, does not mythologize the cinematic signifier as "real." but continually confuses the real with the image and the image with the hallucination. When Renn pops a videotape into his machine, Cronenberg inserts a blip of video distortion over the entire visual field before cutting to O'Blivion's image on-screen. This does not mark the hallucination, but it "infects" the viewer with an analogous experience of dissolution and decayed boundaries. These confusions, between reality, image, and hallucination, pervade the film. There is no difference in the cinematic techniques employed, no "rational" textual system, which might serve to distinguish reality from hallucination for the film viewer. Each moment is presented as "real," that is, as corresponding to the conventions of realist filmmaking. Discourse itself is placed in question in *Videodrome* through the estrangement of cinematic language. Where the hallucination might have begun or ended remains ambiguous, uncertain. These unbounded hallucinations jeopardize the very status of the image: we must believe everything and nothing equally. In the words of the Master Assassin Hassan-i-Sabbah (used as the epigraph to Cronenberg's assassination of *Naked Lunch* [1991]), "*Nothing is true. Everything is permitted.*"[27]

Renn hallucinates his appearance on Videodrome, but is Videodrome a program comprised entirely of recorded hallucinations? If so, then there is a progression from hallucination, through image, to reality: the scene is real because it is televised, it is televised because it is recorded, it is recorded because it is hallucinated. The illusory rationality which guides the society of the spectacle emanates from the irrational recesses of the libidinal mind. On the medium of television, Baudrillard writes:

> The medium itself is no longer identifiable as such, and the merging of the medium and the message (McLuhan) is the first great formula of this new age. There is no longer any medium in the literal sense: it is now intangible, diffuse and diffracted in the real, and it can no longer be said that the latter is distorted by it.[28]

Society becomes the mirror of television (Kroker) as television becomes the new reality. A slit opens in Max Renn's stomach, and Barry Convex holds up a videocassette, which breathes. "I've got something I want to play for you," he says and inserts the cassette. The human body thus becomes a part of the technologies of reproduction observed by Jameson: the ultimate colonization under late capitalism and the ultimate penetration of technology into subjectivity. The reprogrammed Renn later retrieves a gun from this new organ, a gun which extends cables and spikes into his arm in an inversion of McLuhan's sense of technology as human extension. Here the man becomes the extension of the weapon: a servo-mechanisms or perhaps a terminal. There is none of McLuhan's hypothetical "numbing" in this most painful of cinematic displays. We are instead still trapped within a universe which seems to be someone else's insides.

In its themes and structures the film serves as a graphic example of what Baudrillard termed "the dissolution of TV into life, the dissolution of life into TV." Baudrillard terms this immixture "*viral*," echoing Burroughs's injunction that "image *is* virus." The viral metaphor is strikingly apt when applied to *Videodrome*: the literalized invasion of the body by the image and the production of tumors which produce images. Image is virus; virus virulently replicates itself; the subject is finished.

Body and image become one: a dissolution of real and representation, certainly, but also of the boundaries between internal and external, as the interiorized hallucination becomes the public spectacle of the Videodrome program. Here *Videodrome* echoes *The Simulacra*, in which a character's psychosis results in a physical transformation (his organs telekinetically appear outside, as objects in the room are reciprocally interjected). In the postspectacle society delineated by Baudrillard, all such boundaries will dissolve, will become irrelevant through the imperatives of the model of communication (simultaneous transmission and reception):

> In any case, we will have to suffer this new state of things, this forced extroversion of all interiority, this forced injection of all exteriority that the categorical imperative of communication literally signifies; . . . we are now in a new form of schizophrenia. No

more hysteria, no more projective paranoia, properly speaking, but this state of terror proper to the schizophrenic: too great a proximity of everything, the unclean promiscuity of everything which touches, invests and penetrates without resistance.[29]

The subject has "no halo of private protection, *not even his own body*, to protect him anymore" (emphasis mine). The works of David Cronenberg, as well as those of Philip Dick, repeat several of these tropes. The subject is in crisis, its hegemony threatened by centralized structures of control, by a technology which simultaneously alienates and masks alienation, by a perception of its own helplessness. Even the last retreat, the physical body, has lost its privileged status: hence the schizophrenic terror undergone by the protagonists. Even the libido, site of the irrational, seat of desire, is invaded, enlisted in the furtherance of an obsolescent technological rationalism.

Again, these texts are not simply reactionary moments of nostalgia, but bring a profound and progressive ambivalence to the imbrication of simulation and reality, subject and other. The slippage of reality that marks the textual operations of *Videodrome* can certainly be associated with the commensurate process in the writings of the saboteur Burroughs, who repeatedly declared that we must "Storm the Reality Studio and retake the universe."[30] This cinematic metaphor reaches a king of apotheosis in *Videodrome* as the images flicker and fall, their authority ultimately denied, but there is no glimpse of a Reality Studio behind the myriad levels of reality production.

[. . .]

Videodrome – *the death of representation*

In *Videodrome* appearance is also put into radical question, both diegetically and discursively. Reprogrammed by Bianca O'Blivion, Max Renn prepares to take the next step. "You've become the video word made flesh," she tells him. "Death to Videodrome – long live the new flesh." The terror must be overcome, the attachment to the body surrendered. Renn makes his way to a rusted hulk – a "condemned vessel" – in the harbor. The reddish-brown of the decaying walls matches the color of his suede jacket. Renn is another "condemned vessel" as long as he remains trapped within the confines of the old flesh, an outmoded conception of the body and the self. Aboard the vessel, Max fires at his own temple and there the film concludes; ambiguously, unsatisfyingly. What is the new flesh?

One postulation might hold that Max has attained the paradoxical status of pure image – an image which no longer retains any connection with the "real" and which is therefore a perfect Baudrillardian simulation. "The real is no longer what it used to be" he writes. "Henceforth, the map precedes the territory."[31] *Videodrome* comes strikingly close to moving through the four successive phases of the image characteristic of the era of simulation that Baudrillard described.[32] First, the image functions as "the reflection as a basic reality." Clearly, until the hallucinations begin, the viewer trusts the cinematic image as the sign of truth. Doubts may be raised earlier concerning the enigmatic video image of the Videodrome program – its ostensible Third World aesthetic belied by its Pittsburgh transmission point: here the image "masks and perverts a basic reality." In the third phase the image "masks the absence of a basic reality," which has, in fact, been the argument behind most of the works explored in this chapter. The film propels its audience along this trajectory, possibly achieving the status of Baudrillard's fourth phase, in which image "bears no relation to any reality whatever: it is its own pure simulacrum." Being beyond representation itself, such an image could not be represented, and thus the screen goes black and the film ends. *Videodrome*, then, enacts the death of the subject and the death of representation simultaneously, each the consequences of the other.

Videodrome presents a destabilized reality in which image, reality, hallucination, and psychosis become indissolubly melded, and it is on this level that the film becomes a work *of* postmodernism, rather than simply a work *about* it. The film is more than a "mere thematic representation of content" (Jameson):[33] from the moment the videocassette begins to respirate, Cronenberg moves his film to another, profoundly ambivalent, level of meaning. The subversion of conventional structures of filmic discourses here corresponds to the "progressive" use of language in science fiction, producing that "discontinuous set of sign-functions" and yielding "an infinite set of semantic constructs by dislocating the subject in the reading process" (de Lauretis).[34] The viewer of *Videodrome* (the film) is in a position analogous to the viewer of "Videodrome" (the TV show): trapped in a web of representations which infect and transform reality.

[. . .]

The final stage of Baudrillard's four phases of the image, wherein the image no longer bears a relation to an unmediated reality, is the hallmark of the age of postmodernism and simulation, but the potential trauma that might be expected to accompany the realization that representation is no longer tied to referent is frequently elided by a regression to a simple nostalgia, as both Baudrillard and Jameson have noted.[35] [. . .] The disturbing visions of *Videodrome*, on the other hand, communicate a more sustained air of crisis by obsessively biologizing spectacle and simulation. The insistent figurations of Baudrillard, Cronenberg, and Dick represent a stunning hypostatization of the concerns of postmodern culture and comprise a discourse which retains the power to unsettle, disorient, and initiate the crucial action of questioning the status of the sign in sign culture: a spectacular immunization against the invasive powers of the image virus.

Notes

1 Marshall McLuhan, *Understanding Media* (New York: New American Library, 1964).
2 Ballard, "Introduction to *Crash*," 96. *Re/Search* 8/9 (1984): 96–98. Novel originally published in 1973; introduction first published 1974.
3 A.J. Liebling, *The Press* (New York: Ballantine Books, 1975), 32.
4 See Baudrillard, "Requiem for the Media." Trans. Charles Levin. *For a Critique of the Political Economy of the Sign*, ed. Charles Levin (St. Louis: Telos Press, 1981). 164–84. Originally published in 1972.
5 Baudrillard, *The Mirror of Production*, trans. Mark Poster (St. Louis: Telos Press, 1975).
6 Jean Baudrillard, *Forget Foucault*, trans. Nicole Dufresne, Foreign Agents Series, ed. Jim Fleming and Sylvere Lotringer (New York: Semiotext(e), 1987). Arthur Kroker argues that this deconstruction of Marx (a deconstruction strategically absent from Derrida's work) is not tantamount to an anti-Marxist polemic. Baudrillard's writing does not contradict or obviate the economic analyses of capitalism, by Mandel, for example; nor does it negate much of the Hegelian Marxist tradition of the Frankfurt School or its inheritors, such as Jameson or Sennett (Kroker and Cook, 170–88). In its nihilistic rejection of the "transcendental signifier" of labor power, the Baudrillard position does demolish the utopian trajectory of revolutionary Marxism, but, for the purpose of this analysis, the work of these theorists is largely commensurable.
7 Baudrillard, *Forget Foucault*, Foreign Agents Series, trans. Nicole Dufresne. (New York: Semiotext(e), 1987). Originally published in 1977. 11.
8 Baudrillard, *Simulations*, Foreign Agents Series, trans. Paul Foss, Paul Patton, and Philip Beitchman (New York: Semiotext(e), 1983). 54–55.
9 Lynn Spigel, "Installing the Television Set: Popular Discourses on Television and Domestic Space, 1948–1955," *Camera Obscura* 16 (1988), 34. [ellipses in original]
10 Spigel, 34–35.
11 Baudrillard, "Ecstasy of Communication," 128. *The Anti-Aesthetic*, ed. Hal Foster (Port Townsend, Wash.: Bay Press, 1983). 126–34.
12 The trilogy includes *Nova Express* (1964), *The Soft Machine* (1966), and *The Ticket That Exploded* (1967).
13 Cited in Mottram, 40. [Mottram, Eric. *William Burroughs: The Algebra of Need*. London: Marion Boyars, 1977.]

14 Ballard, "Mythmaker of the 20th Century," 106. *Re/Search* 8/9 (1987): 105–7.

15 Roland Barthes, "The Death of the Author," in *Image-Music-Text* (New York: Hill and Wang, 1977), 147.

16 William S. Burroughs, *The Ticket That Exploded* (New York: Grove Press, 1967), 51.

17 Christopher Sharrett, "Myth and Ritual in the Post-Industrial Landscape: The Horror Films of David Cronenberg," *Persistence of Vision* 1, nos. 3/4 (1986), 113.

18 Baudrillard, *In the Shadow of Silent Majorities*, 109. Foreign Agents Series, trans. Paul Foss, Paul Patton, and John Johnston (New York: Semiotext(e), 1983).

19 Fredric Jameson, "Science Fiction as a Spatial Genre: Generic Discontinuities and the Problem of Figuration in Vonda McIntyre's *The Exile Waiting.*" *Science Fiction Studies* 14, no. 1 (1987), 54.

20 Annette Michelson, "Bodies in Space; Film as Carnal Knowledge." *Art Forum* 7.6 (1969): 54–63.

21 See Arthur Kroker, Marilouise Kroker, and David Cook, eds. *Panic Encyclopedia* (New York: St. Martin's Press, 1989), a funny and disturbing compendium.

22 Baudrillard, "Ecstasy," 128.

23 See Guy Debord, "Perspectives for Conscious Alterations in Everyday Life," in *Situationist International Anthology*, ed. Ken Knabb (Berkeley, Calif.: Bureau of Public Secrets, 1981), for a transcript of one of these performances.

24 Burroughs, *The Ticket that Exploded*, 213.

25 The acronym suggests the computer term, *Random Access Memory*.

26 For an important analysis of the figuration of the body in *Videodrome* from an explicitly feminist theoretical position, see Tania Modleski, "The Terror of Pleasure: The Contemporary Horror Film and Postmodern Theory," in *Studies in Entertainment: Critical Approaches to Mass Culture*, ed. Tania Moledski [*sic*] (Bloomington: Indiana University Press, 1986).

27 After detailing the similarities between the work of Burroughs and Cronenberg, I must admit that *Naked Lunch* reveals their profound differences, most notably in the area of sexuality.

28 Baudrillard, *Simulations*, Foreign Agents Series, trans. Paul Foss, Paul Patton, and Philip Beitchman (New York: Semiotext(e), 1983). 54.

29 Baudrillard, "Ecstasy," 132. [ellipses in original]

30 Burroughs, *Soft Machine*, 155.

31 Baudrillard, *Simulations*, 12 and 2.

32 Baudrillard, *Simulations*, 11–12.

33 [Fredric Jameson, *The Political Unconscious: Narrative as a Socially Symbolic Act* (Ithaca: Cornell University Press, 1981).]

34 [Teresa de Lauretis. "Signs of Wa/onder." *The Technological Imagination: Theories and Fictions*, ed. Teresa De Lauretis, Andreas Huyssen, and Kathleen Woodward (Madison: Coda Press, 1980). 159–74.]

35 Baudrillard, *Simulations*, 12; Jameson, *Postmodernism, or, The Cultural Logic of Late Capitalism* (Durham: Duke University Press, 1991). 66–68.

22

META(L)MORPHOSES

Rosi Braidotti

Science fiction has gone through a whole evolution taking it from animal, vegetable, and mineral becomings to becomings of bacteria, viruses, molecules, and things imperceptible.

(Deleuze and Guattari, 1988: 248)

In this article, I will pursue a twofold aim: first to stress the relevance of Deleuze's theory of becoming, not only for contemporary philosophical and critical theory, but also for cultural studies. Second, I will continue to challenge the sexually undifferentiated structure of Deleuze's notion of "becoming," by analyzing a series of science fiction texts – novels and films – which point toward highly genderized patterns of becoming (Braidotti, 1993).

Deleuzian a-subjective consciousness

The relevance of Deleuze's nomadic philosophy for critical practices other than philosophy rests on his critique of classical representation and more especially on the emphasis he places on the figural mode, affectivity and becoming. I want to stress this, because I think the aesthetic aspects of Deleuze's philosophy are often down-played.[1]

[. . .]

I think that precisely because his philosophy attempts to re-code and re-configure the image of thought by a series of rigorous interventions on the representation of the pre-discursive and pre-conceptual groundwork of philosophical reason, it is impossible to separate the "cultural" from the "conceptual" aspects of his work. In this respect, as I have argued before, I do think that "minority subjects of subjugated knowledges," such as feminist, black, postcolonial, queer and other theorists are in a privileged position as readers of Deleuze's transgressive philosophical phantasmagoria.

Deleuze's project rests on the affirmation of the radical immanence of a subject whose embodiment is a process of perpetual becomings and also on a passionate belief in the project of redefining the activity of thinking. The emphasis on figurations, or counter-images of thought, is no mere metaphorization: it is rather the cartographic commitment to constantly redrawing politically informed maps of the present. It is situational, insofar as figurations trace patterns of possible lines of transformation, but it is also situated because the cartographies rest upon the material complexity of the embedded and embodied nomadic subject. The flux of becoming of this vitalistic but anti-essentialistic understanding of the embodied subject happens always and already in-between: it is relational, conjunctive and dynamic.

In my reading, the process of becoming is like the patient task of approximating, through a series of adaptations, the raw simplicity of the forces that shape one's embodied intensity or existential temperature. Becoming is a process of approaching what we are, that is to say reducing oneself to the naked bone of one's speed of rememoration, one's capacity for perception, one's empathy for and impact on others. The opposite of narcissistic self-glorification, Deleuze's becoming is rather the humble apprenticeship to not being any-thing/where more/other than what one is capable of sustaining and tolerating. It is life on the edge, but not over it; it is excessive, but not in a sacrificial sense (exit Bataille). It is definitely anti-humanistic, but deeply compassionate in so far as it begins with the recognition of one's limitations as the necessary counterpart of one's forces or intensities. It is ethical, following Spinoza's notion of adequateness of one's passions to the modes and times of their enactment. It is collective-minded and relational because it requires impact with others and the destabilization of the self that follows such encounters. It can only be embodied and embedded and thus it is a radical form of immanence.

> Immanence does not relate to a Something that is a unity superior to everything, nor to a Subject that is an act operating the synthesis of things; it is when immanence is no longer immanence to anything other than itself that we can talk of a plane of immanence.
>
> (Deleuze, 1997: 4)

Deleuze's central figuration is a general becoming-minority, or becoming-nomad, or becoming-molecular/woman/animal, etc. The minority is the dynamic or intensive principle of change in Deleuze's theory, whereas the heart of the (phallogocentric) majority is dead. The space of becoming is posited as a space of affinity and symbiosis between adjacent forces: it is a space of dynamic marginality and of affinity of entities on the plan of immanence upon which they intersect. Proximity is both a topological and a quantitative notion, both geography and meteorology, which marks the space of common becoming of subjects as sensitive matter. Boundas (1994) suggests that the most effective way to think about Deleuze's becoming is as a serialized notion, removed from the dualistic scheme of transcendental philosophy, which inevitably indexes the process of becoming on to a notion of the self, the individual, or the ego.

All becomings are already molecular. That is because becoming is not to imitate or identify with something or someone. Nor is it to proportion formal relations. Neither of these two figures of analogy is applicable to becoming: neither the imitation of a subject nor the proportionality of a form. Starting from the forms one has, the subject one is, the organs one has, or the functions one fulfills, becoming is to extract particles between which one establishes the relations of movement and rest, speed and slowness that are *closest* to what one is becoming, and through which one becomes. This is the sense in which becoming is the process of desire (Deleuze and Guattari, 1988: 272).

The process of decolonizing the thinking subject from the dualistic grip requires also the dissolution of all sexed identities based on the gendered opposition. Thus, the becoming-woman is the necessary starting point for the deconstruction of phallogocentric identities precisely because sexual dualism and its corollary – the positioning of woman as figure of otherness – are constitutive of Western thought. Deleuze, just like Derrida and other post-structuralists, opposes the "majority/sedentary/molar" vision of woman as a structural operator of the phallogocentric system, the woman as "becoming/minority/molecular/nomadic."

In so far as Man represents the majority, there is no "becoming-man"; he is stuck with the burden of Being; this also means that the various minorities (women, children, blacks, animals, vegetables, molecules) are the privileged starting points for the process of becoming. In my terms, this means that the multiple variables of difference or of devalued otherness are positive sites for redefinition of subjectivity. Thus, an asymmetrical starting position between minority and majority is suggested by Deleuze. This means that the process of deterritorialization is dual and the quantitative minorities can undergo the process of becoming only by disengaging themselves entirely from the identitary unity imposed upon them by the opposition to the majority. It is in this sense that Woman (as "the second sex," or "the other of the Same," as Luce Irigaray put it) needs to "become-woman" in the molecular sense of the process. This is a double movement which overthrows the oppositional dialectics in an analogous yet asymmetrical move.

> There is no subject of becoming except as a deterritorialized variable of the majority; there is no medium of becoming except as a deterritorialized variable of a minority.
>
> (Deleuze and Guattari, 1988: 292)

Thus, the suggestion is of a block of common asymmetrical becomings which turns the former dialectical opponents (men and women; old and young; white and black, etc., etc.) into allies in a process of becoming that constitutes the undoing of the common grounds for their former Unitarian – albeit dualistically opposed – identity. In this respect, as Burger pointed out, "an argumentational strategy characteristic of rhizome-thinking is . . . that it again and again reproduces the categories it negates" (Burger, 1985: 34). I would like to add, however, that this repetition of the very terms one takes one's departure from, far from being the reiteration of a system of domination, constitutes the necessary anchoring point for the cartography of becoming which Deleuze and Guattari are sketching.

One must indeed start from somewhere and the process of becoming is a time-bomb placed at the very heart of the social and symbolic system which has welded together Being, Subjectivity, Masculinity, Heterosexuality, and Western ethnocentrism. The different becomings are lines cutting open this space and demanding from us constant remapping; as Canning suggests, every time it is a question of finding the new coordinates (Canning, 1985).

The process of becoming is the kind of "morning after" when one decides that the old coordinates of the social and symbolic system will not do. It is the shedding of the reactive forces in favor of more elemental ones: the courage to go without props; the choice for expansion of one's boundaries; a yearning for being-different in the sense of a growth towards difference. Like a conversion to nothing more (or less) abstract than the need to change and to go on changing indefinitely.

It is in this sense that for me Deleuze's theory of becoming is also a theory of desire: the only possible way to undertake this process is to actually be attracted to change, to *want* it, the way one wants a lover – in the flesh. Deleuze's becoming is a theory of non-figurative desire. Thus defined, desire is political because it entails the social construction of different desiring subjects, that is to say subjects who desire differently. Breaking out of the official mould of oedipalized, socially productive libidinal economies, Deleuze's becoming paves the way for all kinds of other economies and apparatuses of desire. They cannot be dissociated, however, from the singular desire to construct oneself "as" different. Becoming occurs in the tense of "futur antérieur": you will have been another.

Contrary to those who fear that the proliferation of micro-discourses and molecular practices of becoming will result in a relativistic drift into nihilism, I will go on to argue that I see this as a productive and affirmative process. The subject can only reinvent him/her/itself by relinquishing itself from the web of power relations on which it used to rest. What I find interesting about Deleuze's contribution to "cultural studies" is precisely this sort of pragmatics of the affective forces that shape certain texts. It is a typology of textual passions, a sort of applied affective meteorology which traces grids of possible lines of becoming, that is to say of deterritorialization of the subject – across the texts.

The becoming-insect

You have the individuation of a day, a season, a year, a *life* (regardless of its duration) – a climate, a wind, a fog, a swarm, a pack (regardless of its regularity)....A cloud of locusts carried in by the wind at five in the evening; a vampire who goes out in the night, a werewolf at full moon.... It is the entire assemblage in its individuated aggregate that is a haecceity.
(Deleuze and Guattari, 1988: 262) [ellipses in original]

One needs to turn indeed to "minor," not to say marginal and hybrid genres, such as science fiction, science fiction horror and cyberpunk, to find fitting cultural illustrations of Deleuze's work on embodiment and becoming. In this section I will argue forcefully for the relevance of Deleuze's theory of becoming to science fiction texts and films, while also arguing with Deleuze on the issue of the sexually differentiated nature of these processes.

The specific case study I would like to concentrate on is the becoming-insect, in relation to the becoming-woman. In a previous study[2] of the novel *G.H.*, by Clarice Lispector, I outlined the sequence: becoming-woman/animal/insect/imperceptible. I also emphasized the gendered nature of both the process of becoming and of the time-sequence that marks it. The insect is hybrid, timeless and it possesses talismanic force. The encounter between the emancipated woman and this abject inhabitant of the entrails of space is resolved in her recognition of the coextensivity of all living matter.

Deleuze's analysis of the latitudinal/longitudinal span of intensities that connect different layers of consciousness is highly relevant. What does not check, however, is his assertion of the undifferentiated trajectory of the becoming. For G.H. the progression is highly gender-specific, as are the cross-references to body-parts and body-fluids that mark this process. She moves towards becoming-molecular, but the becoming-imperceptible coincides with a sort of illumination that connects her to the pre-human, but also projects her inexorably towards a post-human interconnectedness. G.H. becomes one with the cosmos as a dynamic principle: she is but a point in it, burning with an intensity that makes her into an organizing principle. Faced with the immensity of this force which is in her but does not belong to her, G.H. simply bows down and honours this totality, in adoration. This living force is in excess of the phallogocentric hold and by letting go of it G.H., far from dissolving into the undifferentiated, emerges as "the woman of all women" one with the whole of that gendered humanity which she cannot represent otherwise than by partaking fully of its speed and intensity. After which there is only silence.[3]

Contemporary science fiction texts trace numerous lines of affinity and coextensivity between women and animals or insects. Whereas commentators usually focus on one of these aspects (see, for instance, White, 1995), however, I think they should be kept together as a block of becomings. More specifically, following Deleuze, I see them as a variation on the paradigm "woman = monster/alien other," suggested by Lefanu (on this point, see Braidotti, 1994b). They are assimilated within the general category of "difference," which facilities a deep empathy between women and aliens and also favours exchanges and mutual influences. This points in the direction of a very genderized approach to the different processes of becoming and the metamorphoses that mark science fiction. Science fiction horror films often draw explicit parallels between the woman's and the alien's, animal or insect bodies. In Cronenberg's remake of *The Fly* (1986) this point is made explicitly in the nightmare scene where the woman gives birth to a gigantic maggot; this process is paralleled by the Kafka-like metamorphosis of the scientist.

In this film, the asymmetry between the sexes shows in the following: whereas for the woman the becoming-insect is a descent into a monstrous reproductive hell, the man only experiences his body as the mutation into insect begins. As often in Cronenberg's work, the asymmetry in the process of becoming between the sexes is respected and it becomes explored visually in different (de)compositions of embodiment. More importantly, the difference is not only in the starting positions of the two sexes, but also in their end results.

Further examples of this asymmetrical gendered rendition of the becoming-insect can be found in the classic science fiction films from the American 1950s, which express a deep-seated anxiety about the nuclear age. This anxiety gets coated very often in the form of the destructive powers of either the females or aliens, or possibly both. This fear has been likened to the tradition of the "Virago" theme in classical literature[4] and an example of it is the film *The Attack of the Fifty-Foot Woman* (1958). The film features a very angry young woman who, exposed to atomic radiation, grows out of all proportion and terrorizes her husband and then the local town. Exactly like insect-films such as *Tarantula* (1955) and *Them!* (1954), this blown-up, larger-than-life female figure is a screen on which all sorts of other anxieties get projected.

This point can be demonstrated with reference to another cult-film from the 1950s – *The Incredible Shrinking Man* (1957) which acts almost as the counterpoint to *The Attack of the Fifty-Foot Woman*. In this film the male hero – shrunk to miserable proportions after exposure to nuclear radiations – falls victim to a giant black spider. His encounter with the hairy beast gets visually compared through cross-cutting, with images of his own wife, who by now has grown proportionally gigantic. In an effect reminiscent of the most misogynist passages in Jonathan Swift's *Gulliver's Travels*, the female body emerges from this as a monstrous iconic other. I will return to this structural analogy between the woman and the insect.

The asymmetry in the representation of the visual destiny of the two sexes when exposed to the same devolutionary forces (atomic radiation) is striking; the process unfolds along gender lines: the woman blows up into a terrifying force and the poor man shrinks out of sight. Visually, the effects of this asymmetry are even more striking, resulting respectively in gigantic close-ups of female genitalia on the one hand, and on the other in the heroic celebration of minute human males in their deadly encounters with hairy giants. The same technique is used in the film *Tarantula*, with the close-up of the giant spider's face through a window frame of the house where the suburban white woman watches the hairy cavity in horror. This is not only a classical *vagina-dentata* shot, but it also enacts an opposition black/white; human/non-human, with uncouth hairiness as a major differential. Another case in point is the close-up of the scientist/insect head in the original *The Fly* (1958). The fly-head marks the loss of reason and language, but the gain is an extreme improvement of the faculty of vision. When he looks at his wife through his insect-eyes, we get another blow-up phenomenon, with the female multiplied tenfold. In a gesture which anticipates Cameron's *The Terminator* (1984), she mercifully kills him under an industrial press.

Pursuing further the line of becoming-insect/woman/imperceptible I will now take the insect as a figuration of the abject, a borderline figure, capable of having different meanings and associations. It is a generalized figure of liminality and inbetweenness. After all, for Aristotle, insects have no specific sex. Grosz, on the contrary, sees the insect as a highly sexualized "queer" entity, capable of titillating the collective imagination especially on the issue of sex and death (Grosz, 1995). I differ on this point and tend to situate them rather on the horizon of the "post-human," in closer connection to the technological than to the actual animal "kingdom."[5]

How are the insect and the technological linked in a process of becoming that dislodges the human from his/her naturalistic foundations, thus inflicting a final blow to any notion of "human nature"? Shaviro (1995) rightly suggests that insofar as the becoming-insect in science fiction is an effect of devolutionary practices, it is linked – albeit negatively – to the technology that triggers them off. In the 1950s that is nuclear technology and in the 1990s it is rather molecular biology, but the two are linked both historically and conceptually. It is the speed and efficiency of its molecular structure and more especially of its reproductive cycle that has made the fruit-fly into the most important experimental site in modern biology. Haraway also hints at an "insect paradigm" in contemporary molecular biology, which has moved beyond the classical opposition of "vitalistic" to "mechanistic" principles, to evolve instead in the direction of serial repetitions. Haraway takes this as a serious indication that we have already left the era of bio-politics to enter that of: "the informatics of domination." As the text by Clarice Lispector demonstrates, in such a universe, the insects will most definitely inherit the earth.

But there are other aspects of the becoming-insect that, read in a Deleuzean perspective, point towards technology and away from humanism: *homo faber*, rather than *homo sapiens*. Deleuze singles some out quite explicitly in *Mille Plateaux* – that insects are essentially about the becoming-imperceptible, the becoming-molecular mostly because of the speed of their lifespan. Their significant traits in terms of a Deleuzean mapping of forces are: dryness, hairiness; metal-like body-frames; great resilience (the spider in *Tarantula* must be napalmed before she can be defeated). They are elemental, either because linked to the earth and to its underground/crust (*chthonic* forces) or defying its gravity thanks to aircraft-like bodyframes (remember the exhilaration of Kafka's Gregor when he discovers that he can crawl up on the ceiling).

In terms of their reproduction, insects have perfected hybridity. They point to a disturbingly diverse sexual cycle, when compared to the mammals; in fact, insects are non-mammals that lay eggs. As such, they are likely to feed into the most insidious anxieties about unnatural copulations and births, especially in a "posthumanist" culture obsessed with artificial reproduction (for a more detailed analysis see Braidotti, 1994c). Moreover, because of their speedy organism, there is no question of caring for their infants, mostly because they are not born prematurely (like humans). In a Deleuzean vein, these relatively obvious differences from the human lay out the grid of a new set of spatio-temporal coordinates, which translate into affective typologies and speed or rhythms.

The transformative speed as well as an immense power of adaptation is the force that makes insects the entity most closely related to the becoming-molecular and becoming-imperceptible. The fact that most of their life cycle is made of metamorphoses through different stadia of development is a manifestation of the same principles. As the title of this article suggests, however, I would rather speak of metal-morphosis. [. . .] I think that in a Deleuzean perspective the evidence points to a powerful link between the insect and electronic technology: the ticking away of incessant bytes of information at the speed of light. I think this destabilizing posthuman speed is the source of Deleuze's connection to writers like Burroughs, but also to others, whom he explicably ignores, like Kathy Acker and Angela Carter.

The evidence I have gathered so far also suggests something else, however. There is a specific pattern of becoming-woman/insect, which has features of its own and cannot be reduced to the undifferentiated becoming postulated by Deleuze, as I will show next.

The becoming-machine

The same hypothesis can be confirmed if we analyze another configuration: the metamorphoses in the sense of becoming-machine in science fiction texts. The evidence is overwhelming in contemporary culture that there is a privileged bond between the male and the machine. The woman seldom metamorphoses into an android or a robot and if she does, the consequences are as horrific as in insect movies. Films such as *Blade Runner* (1982) show female robots/cyborgs and they are killing machines as lethal as the males. In a way, male representations of woman as machine are a modernist *topos*, perfected in *Metropolis* (1926) and *Bride of Frankenstein* (1935).

Springer (1991) argues that the "cyber discourse" describing the union of humans and electronic technology is currently dominant in the scientific community and in the popular culture texts such as films, television, video games, magazines, cyberpunk fiction and comic books. I would like to say, however, that this does not mean that contemporary technology eliminates corporeality: it rather explodes it outwards to unprecedented proportions. This results, among other things, in the eroticization of the technological, which on the one hand continues the modernist tradition but on the other pushes it to implosion by collapsing the boundaries that historically had separated organic from inorganic matter.

As I have argued elsewhere (Braidotti, 1995), this positions contemporary culture in a sort of paradox, on the one hand an eroticized fetishization of the technological has permeated the imaginary and the economic dimensions of our societies. On the other hand, this coincides with a sort of flight from the body which, in my opinion, confirms the most classical and pernicious aspect of Western phallocentrism. Evidence of this can be found in the extent to which gender boundaries and gender differences become exaggerated in cyberpunk.[6] For instance, films like *The Terminator* and *Robocop* celebrate both the fusion of the male human body with the machine and the failure to overcome the worst aspects of masculine violence.[7]

This can be further demonstrated with references to two other science fiction films: one is a light comedy, called *Weird Science* (1985), which tells the Pygmalion myth in high-tech mode, with some American teenaged boys designing the perfect woman on their PC and having her coming alive to sexually initiate and further service them all. The other film, *Eve of Destruction* (1991), features a female cyborg; here both the heroic and the liberatory notes are dropped in favour of a more traditional Frankensteinian approach. The cyborg Eve is the exact double of the female scientist that created her and even programmed her with her memories. Once she escapes, the cyborg proceeds to act out the scientist's repressed fantasies of revenge against men, causing death and destruction all round. The female cyborg contains a nuclear device inside her uterus, which duly gets activated and puts nothing less than the survival of the planet at risk. No cyborg saviour figure so far has been cast in the mould of the feminine.

Thus, the becoming-machine in science fiction films bears a strong affinity to a molar line of reconstruction of masculinity. There is also evidence, however of another set of transformations in the work of the previously mentioned Cronenberg; they trace the becoming-woman of the man. In *Videodrome*, the male body undergoes a very different set of metamorphoses. *Videodrome* is a video channel that specializes in snuff films. Through these scenes, they manipulate people's brains – including a brain tumour, which is described as an "extra organ," that makes people receptive to the videodrome signal. What's interesting is that the boundary between reality and the televisual image is so blurred, that it becomes indistinguishable from Rex's [*sic*] hallucinations.

What makes *Videodrome* a classic is that it addresses the issue of the physicality and the corresponding malleability of the male body, while it also shows to what an extent the body is constructed, thus striking an anti-humanist note. Of special relevance are the scenes where the video/TV screen comes alive, in turn as an alluring female body, a bleeding, dying, tortured body and, at the end, a mass of bleeding organs. The plasticity of the screen, combined with the loss of depth/organic reality of the protagonist's body makes the interpenetration of the human and the machine/organic-inorganic possible.

Even more significant for my purposes, when the protagonist's body *becomes* a video player, a big split appears from the navel to pelvis region (unmistakably vaginal), we witness a real becoming-woman of the male body machine. As such he can be penetrated, that is to say he has acquired a productive inside, a uterine cavity (Modleski, 1986). His enemies can "play him" – by inserting a videotape inside him which programmes him, to make him kill all their enemies. His "memory system" is thus controlled by the majority and this embodied male becomes as much of an android as the *Blade Runner* "replicants." By becoming actively penetrable, his becoming-woman is complete.

Creed argues that this becoming-woman can be read critically in a feminist perspective (Creed, 1990): the dislocation of the categories of otherness is enacted, but no genuine alternative emerges: all we get is a man violating himself as a woman and masochism is the dominant theme of *Videodrome*. In this respect, the becoming-woman of the majority repeats the worst traits of the phallogocentric regime: it is an exercise in humiliation and an apprenticeship in self-mutilation. The man undergoes what women have had to suffer for centuries: this is the ultimate scenario of powerlessness and violation of one's body and it marks at best a generalized becoming-sadean.

Yes, but . . .

As I have argued throughout this essay: I think that a culture where this sort of imaginary is circulating, which hastily assimilates the "cyber-revolution" to an as yet undefined sense of "posthumanism," is a society that simply *needs* Deleuze's philosophy in order to avoid a downhill slide into nihilism. In positing this alternative I also mean to disagree most emphatically with those who assimilate Deleuze's philosophy of complexity to nihilism and relativism. I think that Deleuze's theory of becoming offers a useful and illuminating grid by which to read the contemporary aesthetic sensibility in an age of decline of humanistic paradigms. Deleuze's thought is especially helpful to approach some of the more iconoclastic and at times disturbing aspects of contemporary culture: the disaggregation of humanistic subject-positions and values; the ubiquitous presence of narcotic texts and practices; the all-pervasive political violence; the intermingling of the enfleshed and the technological. These features, which are often referred to as "the posthuman" universe seem to cry out for Deleuze's philosophy of radical immanence as a way of making sense of what – within the parameters of humanism – can only appear as senseless, anarchical and threatening.

I think, however, that Deleuze's strength on these matters is also his weakness and that far too often hasty and rather "pop-minded" readings of his philosophy assimilate it rather superficially to those very cultural practices which Deleuze illuminates for us. The tendency seems indeed strong to read Deleuze as a "narco-philosopher," a "cyberpunk thinker," a "post-gender pansexualist," and so on. My position on this is clear: I think it is to the credit of Deleuze's thought that he provides us with valuable inroads into the contemporary imagination, in its conceptual, political and aesthetic manifestations. This alone proves that his is a philosophy for our times and that Foucault was hinting at this when he suggested that one day this century will be known as Deleuzean. However, Deleuze's philosophy constitutes also a rigorous and tightly argued attempt to reverse Platonism and undo classical theories of representation, while avoiding relativism by grounding his theory of subjectivity in a concept of radical immanence. Nothing could be further from the "pop" image that is often given of his philosophy.

Simultaneously, and in potential collision with the first line of argument, I have also tried to point to significant evidence from contemporary culture which indicates that the asymmetry Deleuze acknowledges in the respective starting positions of the majority and the minorities results in asymmetrical, not in common processes of becoming. There is not a unique form of becoming-woman/insect/imperceptible for all women, let alone for both women and men. There is not one common format that can account for the speed, the longitude and latitude of both masculine and feminine becomings. On the contrary, the sequence becoming-woman/insect and becoming-woman/machine points to very differentiated patterns.

Given that the science fiction texts I used as evidence are not Deleuze's immediate responsibility, we are left with two options. One consists in saying that our culture is not Deleuzean yet and that we need to put more effort into exploring radical forms of molecular becoming and in finding forms of representation in keeping with the Deleuzean project of becoming. I would like to suggest that, in contemporary culture, music may be the area where a Deleuzean revolution is most likely and, in some ways, already happening (see, for instance, Bogue, 1991). I would like to add also that even more effort would be needed to make these transformations in our cultural sensitivity operational in public policy-making and in the structure of scholarship, research and teaching. In this respect I have also suggested that it is urgent, in the contested zone of the posthumous reception of Deleuze's work, to put more efforts into unwrapping the conceptual hardcore of his philosophy and more especially of his possible – as in virtual – contribution to the growing field of cultural studies.

The second option consists in saying that Deleuze's scheme of becoming is faulty and it needs to be revised in the sense of multiple but not undifferentiated becomings. Between the two, my heart lingers and I shall not be pushed to choose.

However "molar" this may appear, I do think it important to assert the asymmetry between the majority and the minority all the way to the specific forms of affectivity, time-sequences and the kind of plans of immanence they can engineer. As people who come *after* Deleuze, I should think it important that we take up this point seriously and develop it sequentially. It seems to me urgent to rescue Deleuze's work from the risk of falling into the banality of asserting that minorities – in all their diversity – constitute the perfect prototype for the generalized modes of a-subjective consciousness that Deleuze is advocating. I think it simply is *not* the case for Deleuze that woman, blacks, children, insects or plants are rhizomic *avant la lettre* or have been nomadic since the beginning of time. And yet this oversimplified notion is gathering momentum in the present stage of reception of Deleuze.[8] I think this is dangerous not only because it is a misreading of Deleuze's becoming, but also because it hinders the work of serious conceptual criticism of Deleuze's work, which in my opinion needs to be undertaken. I want to suggest that the only way to avoid the double pitfall of oversimplification and therefore banality on the one hand, and dogmatic repetition of his master's voice on the other is to explore further the notion of how the asymmetry between the majority and the minorities affects the entire process of becoming and not only its point of departure.

All this notwithstanding, I think it is right to suggest that, to enact a Deleuzean process of becoming, you are better off cultivating "our inner housefly or cockroach, instead of your inner child. . . . And don't imagine for a second that these remarks are merely anthropomorphizing metaphors" (Shaviro, 1995: 53[ellipses in original]). These changes of coordinates rather point to the political and conceptual necessity to change in-depth and thus to extract from our enfleshed memory the repertoire of available images for self-representation. It is not a mere voluntaristic switch of identifications and it could not be further removed from willful self-naming. I would rather describe it as a process of peeling off stratum after stratum, the layers of signification that have been tattooed in the surface of our body and – more importantly – in its psychic recesses and the internalized folds of one's sacrosanct "experience." Like a snake shedding an old skin, one must remember to forget it.

Notes

1   For a useful introduction to this aspect of Deleuze's work, see Bogue (1989).
2   I did a preliminary analysis on these interrelated becomings in Braidotti (1994a).
3   To do full justice to the issues involved in this, I developed a close comparison of Deleuze and Irigaray on the question of becoming.
4   See for instance the enlightening collection edited by Dorrit Einersen and Ingeborg Nixon (1995).
5   For a very early outline of the "becoming animal" see the special issue: "Polysexuality," *Semiotext(e)* 4 (1), 1981.
6   I am grateful to Anneke Smelik for the analysis of the cyberpunk and cyborg film genres.
7   In this regard I do not share the positive assessment of the male cyborg suggested by Goodchild (1996: 59, 147), though I regret I cannot expand on this point here.
8   For a feminist critique of Deleuze's alleged philosophical orientalism, see Grewal and Kaplan (1994).

References

Bogue, Ronald (1989) *Deleuze and Guattari*. New York: Routledge.
Bogue, Ronald (1991) "Rhizomusocosmology," *Sub-Stance* 66: 85–101.
Boundas, Constantin V. (1994). "Deleuze: Serialization and Subject-Formation," pp. 99–118 in Constantin V. Boundas and Dorothea Olkowski (eds) *Gilles Deleuze and the Theatre of Philosophy*. London: Routledge.
Braidotti, Rosi (1993) "Discontinuous Becomings: Deleuze and the Becoming-Woman of Philosophy," *Journal of British Society of Phenomenology* 24(1): 44–55.
Braidotti, Rosi (1994a) "Of Bugs and Women: Irigaray and Deleuze on the Becoming-Woman," in Carolyn Burke, Naomi Schor and Margaret Whitford (eds) *Engaging with Irigaray*. New York: Columbia University Press.
Braidotti, Rosi (1994b) "Women, Monsters and Machines," in *Nomadic Subjects: Embodiment and Sexual Difference in Contemporary Feminist Theory*. New York: Columbia University Press.
Braidotti, Rosi (1994c) "Organs without Bodies," in in *Nomadic Subjects: Embodiment and Sexual Difference in Contemporary Feminist Theory*. New York: Columbia University Press.
Braidotti, Rosi (1995) "Me Tarzan and You Jane? Reconstructions of Femininity and Masculinity in Science Fiction Horror Films," in Dorrit Einersen and Ingeborg Nixon (eds) *Women as Monster in Literature and the Media*. Copenhagen: C.A. Reitzel, University of Copenhagen Press.
Burger, Christa (1985) "The Reality of 'Machines,' Notes on the Rhizome-Thinking," *Telos* 64: 33–44.
Canning, Peter (1985) "Fluidentity," *Sub-Stance* 44/45: 35–45.
Creed, Barbara (1990) "Gynesis, Postmodernism and the Science Fiction Horror Film," in A. Kuhn (ed.) *Alien Zone*. London: Verso.
Deleuze, Gilles (1997) "Immanence: A Life . . .," *Theory, Culture & Society* 14(2): 3–7.
Deleuze, Gilles and Félix Guattari (1988) *A Thousand Plateaus*. London: Athlone.
Einersen, Dorrit and Ingeborg Nixon (1995) *Woman as Monster in Literature and the Media*. C.A. Reitzel, Copenhagen University Press.
Goodchild, Philip (1996) *Deleuze and Guattari: An Introduction to the Politics of Desire*. London: Sage.
Grewal, Indepal and Caren Kaplan (eds) (1994) *Scattered Hegemonies: Postmodernity and Transnational Feminist Practices*. Minneapolis: University of Minnesota Press.
Grosz, Elizabeth (1995) "Animal Sex: Libido as Desire and Death," in Elizabeth Grosz and Elspeth Probyn (eds) *Sexy Bodies: The Strange Carnalities of Feminism*. London: Routledge.
Modleski, Tania (1986) "The Terror of Pleasure," in *Studies in Entertainment*. Bloomington: Indiana University Press.
Shaviro, Steven (1995) "Two Lessons from Burroughs," pp. 38–56 in Judith Halbertam and Ira Livingston (eds) *Posthuman Bodies*. Bloomington: Indiana University Press.
Springer, Claudia (1991) "The Pleasure of the Interface," *Screen* 32(3): 303–23.
White, Eric (1995) "Once They Were Men, Now They're Landcrabs: Monstrous Becomings in Evolutionist Cinema," pp. 226–44 in Judith Halbertam and Ira Livingston (eds) *Posthuman Bodies*. Bloomington: Indiana University Press.

23

THE TRANSMOLECULARIZATION OF (BLACK) FOLK

Space is the Place, Sun Ra and Afrofuturism

Nabeel Zuberi

We can listen profitably to the futurology evident in black popular cultures and interpret their comments on science and technology as having some bearing upon ethical and even political matters.

(Gilroy, 2000: 341)

Question: *What is the power of your machine?*

Sun Ra: *Music* from the film *Space is the Place* (1974)

Space is the Place, *part documentary, part science fiction, part blaxploitation, part revisionist biblical epic. Strange enough in its own time, as the years passed it assumed an even stranger aura of 1970s ideas and affectations and what appears to be the genuinely timeless in Sun Ra's dress and manner.*

(Szwed, 1997: 330)

The low-budget musical Science Fiction film *Space is the Place* [*SITP*] was directed by John Coney in Oakland, California in 1972, and produced by Jim Newman for release by North American Star Systems in 1974. Rhapsody Films released it on VHS video in the 1990s. The film stars Sun Ra (1914–1993), the jazz keyboardist, composer, arranger and bandleader of the Intergalactic Myth-Science Solar Arkestra. Though US state documentation registers his birth as Herman Blount in Birmingham, Alabama; for much of his life Sun Ra claimed to be an alien from the planet Saturn.

In *SITP*, Ra visits Earth in a spaceship, time travelling between Chicago 1943 and Oakland, California 1972, where he communicates with local African Americans and tries to convince them to leave with him for a space colony. Ra engages in no less than a struggle for the souls of black folk against an archetypical pimp/mack/player/business figure called the Overseer (Ray Johnston). The medium of combat is a magic card game and Ra's most potent "tricknology" is his music. The Arkestra performs many pieces of diegetic and non-diegetic music in its efforts to uplift the race to Outer Space. Ra also encounters the largely corrupt media network system, using it to spread his message despite the fact that black radio in the form of announcer Jimmy Fey (Christopher Brooks) is compromised by the Overseer's influence. Ra also contends with the surveillance and violence of the United States government. The FBI kidnaps and sonically tortures him with a recording of the Confederate anthem *Dixie*. Three young men – Bubbles (John Bailey), Bernard (Clarence Brewer) and Tiny (Tiny Parker) – rescue Ra just in time for the Arkestra to perform a concert for the community. During the concert the FBI men try to assassinate Ra at his minimoog keyboard but are again foiled by Bubbles, Bernard and Tiny. Bubbles is shot and killed saving Ra's life but Ra teleports him and his comrades to safety in the spaceship. Ra also teleports the "black part" of Jimmy Fey just before the Arkestra departs for Outer Space. Like the alien messiah Klaatu played by Michael Rennie in the liberal Cold War Sci-Fi classic *The Day the Earth Stood Still* (1951), Sun Ra lands on Earth to inform the human race that it needs redemption from its sorry state, and then leaves after relatively little success (Ruppersberg, 1990: 33–37).

The film "signifies" across and between a number of recognizable film genres and modes such as Sci-Fi, the musical, the urban youth film and the documentary in the style of African diasporic vernacular expression and media production (Yearwood, 1998). *SITP* is one in a series of attempts to translate Sun Ra's music and his concerns with science, technology and Outer Space to the screen. Like much of his oeuvre, *SITP* is concerned with how music can transport black people to other states of being in both material and spiritual terms. In this Science Fiction film, *music is the primary special effect.* The film's sound design incorporates electronic instruments, such as the minimoog synthesizer that became increasingly common in jazz, funk, soul and psychedelic rock in the late 1960s and early 1970s. *SITP* also riffs on the language of black nationalism in the urban African American film of the period. Its dialogue pastiches and parodies the babble of radio and network media. And like the many films of the American Vietnam War and Watergate period, it foregrounds the government's audiovisual surveillance of citizens and aliens.

SITP is a molecular milestone in a black music tradition that engages with separation, escape and otherness through the tropes of Science Fiction. Recent "sampling" of Sun Ra and *SITP* by critics, filmmakers and musicians situates his work in a continuum of African diasporic fiction and Afrofuturism across many media (Thomas, 2000). The exhibition "Sonic Process: A New Geography of Sounds" that travelled thorough Barcelona, Paris and Berlin in 2002–03 gives Sun Ra a significant place in its definition of Afrofuturism.

> A trend within black popular music, whose paternity is generally attributed to Sun Ra. Transcending musical genres, Afrofuturism draws upon the feeling of alienation inherited from slavery of American blacks, which it sublimates. In this conception, certain elements of Afro-American culture (such as the transcendence of spirituals) are re-imagined and transposed into a new cosmic and legendary perspective, where the alienated becomes extraterrestrial. The most representative artists of Afrofuturism include George Clinton and his various bands (Parliament, Funkadelic, etc.), Lee "Scratch" Perry, as well as Roni Size.
>
> (Van Assche, 2002: 21)

This glossary entry might somewhat overstate Ra's (patriarchal) centrality to the genealogy of musical Afrofuturism, but his work manifests some of its key features. Though one can trace many elements of futurology across African diasporic cultures in the near and distant past, the term Afrofuturism has only recently reached critical mass as a formation that codifies, organizes and maps an alternative cultural history and critical framework for African American media production. According to Alondra Nelson (2002: 14), the term was first coined and defined by Mark Dery. In his 1994 prologue to a series of interviews with critics Tricia Rose and Greg Tate and Science Fiction writer Samuel R. Delany, Dery writes:

> Speculative fiction that treats African-American themes and addresses African-American concerns in the context of twentieth-century technoculture – and, more generally,

African-American signification that appropriates images of technology and a prosthet-
ically enhanced future – might for want of a better term, be called "Afro-futurism."
The notion of Afrofuturism gives rise to a troubling antinomy: Can a community
whose past has been deliberately rubbed out, and whose energies have subsequently
been consumed by the search for legible traces of its history, imagine possible futures?
Furthermore, isn't the unreal estate of the future already owned by the technocrats,
futurologists, streamliners, and set designers – white to a man – who have engineered
our collective fantasies?

(1994: 180)

Ziauddin Sardar seems to answer Dery's final rhetorical question with a resounding
"yes." According to Sardar "science fiction shows us not the plasticity but the paucity of the
human imagination that has become quagmired in the scientist industrial technological,
culturo-socio-psycho-babble of a single civilizational paradigm [western civilization, brackets
in original]" (2002: 1). Sardar emphasizes the "colonising, imperial mission of science fiction":

Space, the final frontier, is the recurrent frontier on which western thought has been
constructed and operated throughout history, or time. Western thought not only constructed aliens to define itself better, it made constructed aliens essential to fulfilling
its moral purpose.

(ibid: 16)

Sardar's position historicizes Science Fiction, quite persuasively, in our own time of US
military-industrial domination, the War on Terror(ism) and Axis of Evil rhetoric. However, his
polemic overstates both the Sci-Fi genre's conservatism and the homogeneity of the West. For
Science Fiction has also long been part of the radical imagination of "others" in the West trying
to find ways out of its oppressive regimes of power and knowledge. An examination of Sun
Ra-in-film can illuminate African American cultural politics as recorded sounds and images pass
through various states of diasporic mediation.

In his influential Afrofuturist sermon/summons *More Brilliant Than the Sun: Adventures in
Sonic Fiction*, black British cultural critic Kodwo Eshun argues:

So there's this idea of music as this sonic production circuit through which – as Gilles
Deleuze was saying – molecules of a new people may be planted here or there. That's
very much what Sun Ra's doing; he's using the Moog to produce a new sonic people.
Out of this circuit, he's using it to produce the new astro-black American of the 1970s.

(1998: A[185])

If we follow Eshun's logic, how might we then understand *SITP* and Sun Ra as material
media themselves reconstituted, imagined anew, and remediated in our historical moment?

According to John Szwed's exhaustive biography, Sun Ra "followed the rise of science fiction
as a child, reading early comic books and seeing the movie serials of Buck Rogers and Flash
Gordon; learning its language, incorporating its themes and motifs into his performances" (1997:
131). During the 1950s and 1960s when he was based in Chicago, Ra studied the Science Fiction of the Nation of Islam. Though he didn't subscribe to its cosmology, he was familiar with
the Nation's founder Wallace D. Fard's creationist myth in which Yacub, a renegade imam and
scientist, created the diabolical white race as a genetic mutation of the Earth's original inhabitants – the "Asiatic Black Man." According to Fard, redemption would come with the arrival of

a mother ship made by the original black scientists to destroy "the enemies of Allah" (Szwed, 1997: 132). Fard's successor Elijah Muhammad argued that black people originally came from the moon, which at one time was part of the same planet as earth. Following an explosion caused by Yacub, the two were separated (White, 1985: 105). This permutation of Islam was just one crossroads in the matrix of African American ideas. Like many twentieth century Afrocentric thinkers Sun Ra studied Egyptology and hieroglyphics. Steeped in the Baptist tradition, he also read many commentaries on the Bible. Aspects of all these texts made their way into Sun Ra's mythical lexicography.

As a schoolboy Ra had what Szwed describes as a conversion experience articulated in the language of an alien abduction story. Space beings contacted him and told him to join them. He was raised up in a beam of light:

> it looked like a giant spotlight shining down on me, and I call it transmolecularization, my whole body was changed into something else. I could see through myself. And I went up. Now, I call that energy transformation because I wasn't in human form. I thought I was there, but I could see through myself.
>
> (quoted in Szwed, 1997: 29)

As an invisible man, unlike Ralph Ellison's earthbound black subject, Ra found himself on Saturn. There the aliens instructed him to educate the Earth's people. This spiritual epiphany or revelation reminds me of the prophet Muhammad's first visitation by the Angel Jibreel/Gabriel, the medium for Allah's bio-scientific words: "Recite in the name of your Lord who has created/ Created man out of a germ-cell." The prophetic mode was an essential aspect of Ra's musical message throughout his career, and the address of the holy man or imam to the congregation is one rhetorical strategy in *SITP*. At the centre of Ra's gospel, according to Szwed, was Neoplatonism – "the philosophical-mystical tradition in which music is seen as both a model of the universe and a part of its makeup, and where it has the power to bring human beings in line with the cosmos" (1997: 113).

Sound and image were always intertwined in this cosmology. Sun Ra's message was modulated through music, the spectacle of space-age-meets-ancient-Egypt costumes, onstage dancers and the theatre of street marches and black vaudeville. Expressionist lighting effects filtered through live performances. Though trained in the big band tradition of Duke Ellington and Fletcher Henderson (for whom he worked briefly in the early 1940s), Ra was one of the first jazz musicians to use electric keyboard instruments, such as Hammond and Farfisa organs, and synthesizers such as the moog and portable minimoog. The synthesizer's "strange sounds" became integral to the increasingly elaborate multimedia events or happenings that were the Arkestra's live shows in the late 1960s. The visual aspect of the Arkestra's musical performance was choreographed but allowed for a measure of spontaneity. Before *SITP*, the band appeared in a number of films – *Cry of Jazz* (1958), *Magic Sun* (1968) and *Spaceways* (1968) – and extracts from films were often projected behind the Arkestra during concerts.

[. . .] *SITP* was made in Oakland after Bobby Seale and the Black Panther Party invited Ra and members of the Arkestra to stay in the West Coast city in 1971. In the same year Ra was hired to teach a course at the University of California in Berkeley. His "Black Man in the Cosmos" syllabus included the suggested student research topic, "the role of technology in music" (Szwed, 1997: 295). *SITP* was crafted in the confluence of Sun Ra's career as a musician and teacher, the local and national contexts of black nationalism, developments in free jazz and other musical styles, and the emergence of a new black cinema movement marked by Melvin Van Peebles' *Sweet Sweetback's Baadasss Song* (1971).

The opening image in the film is the clichéd "empty but starry space" shot familiar to audiences of the original *Star Trek* TV series in the 1960s. Instead of twinkling keyboard sounds and the woozy theremin-style motif of the *Star Trek* theme, we hear the slow bass-y electronic pulse of a minimoog synthesizer. Instead of Captain Kirk's famous voice-over narration, the electronic ambience is pierced by June Tyson's call: "It's after the end of the world. Don't you know that?" A yellow spaceship resembling a giant, winged seedpod glides into the frame as Tyson repeats her words several times in unison with other members of the Arkestra.

The film then cuts to its only visual evocation of a utopian space "colony." Tyson's spoken words fade out. The camera pans across jungle-like vegetation as the electronic pulse becomes fuller and turns into more abrasive atonal sound. As the camera tilts up to capture expressionist tree limbs against a purple-haze sky, deep in the mix a saxophone characteristic of free jazz shrieks and caws, like a conference of birds. Sun Ra appears amongst the trees, wearing metallic coloured robes and an ancient Egyptian-style headdress with a golden winged orb on top. His name is superimposed in yellow letters on the screen, the same bright yellow as his spaceship and some of his robes. He walks through this idyllic landscape interacting with cyborganic fauna-flora. These life forms include floating silver spheres with tails, and yellow protuberances pointing to the sky, like the bulbous fingers of hands uplifted in joy and praise during a southern black church service. Ra is accompanied by a hooded figure in monk's robes. We find them standing in a clearing. In a medium close-up, Ra hums a refrain to the background music. The film cuts to a close up of the hooded disciple who has a mirror face. Ra directly addresses the camera at a slight angle, like a religious leader pausing in this idyllic setting to address a fellow traveler. The audience is invited into a compact with him as if to meditate on political realities and apply a decisive plan. Ra makes his mission clear.

[. . .]

According to Ra, redemption of black people comes through music. Musical form is a template for society and the body. This statement, the music in the scene and the images manifest a fairly common set of avant-garde ideas in jazz at least since the late 1950s. The music here, particularly the saxophone playing shares a "yearning" quality for a utopian elsewhere or "something else," as suggested in the words of alto saxophonist Ornette Coleman's 1958 album title. Coleman's *Change of the Century* (1959) and *The Shape of Jazz to Come* (1959) evoke the future even more explicitly in their Sci-Fi titles. [. . .]

To achieve "far-out" sounds in the so-called New Thing, Free Jazz or New Black Music (Jones, 1967), musicians "would use volume, texture, grain, tone color, and other sonic variables to create variation and interest, demanding of the listener a focus and appreciation of sound for its own sake" (Szwed, 2000: 242). This attention to aural texture meant stretching the sonic possibilities of existing instruments, producing dissonance and atonality. Rock music in the 1960s distorted tones and chords through electrical means such as amplification, distortion, and feedback. These experiments were often fed with time-space altering drugs such as LSD. New electronic instruments such as the moog synthesizer produced peculiar tones outside the parameters of previous listening. The line between noise/sound effects and music in rock, jazz and other popular music styles becomes blurred in this period. Though the eerie, otherwordly sound of the theremin had weaved through thrillers, Science Fiction film soundtracks such as *The Day the Earth Stood Still* (1951), and the exotica recordings of Les Baxter and others since the 1940s, popular music "catches up" with Science Fiction noise only in the 1960s, as electronic instruments and the increasingly elaborate manipulation of the studio console commonly permeate the production and sound of music.

In 1968 Wendy (then "Walter") Carlos used the moog in her popular electronic interpretation of the classics, *Switched-on Bach* and the soundtrack for Stanley Kubrick's *A Clockwork Orange* (1971). According to Mike Berk:

> As the first portable, affordable, and really popular synth, the minimoog made "sythesist" a viable job description, and the world of popular music was never quite the same again. The minimoog and its immediate successors from ARP, Sequential Circuits, Oberheim, Korg, Roland, and a host of other companies, established the sound of analog synthesis as the sound of synthesis. One or more voltage-controlled oscillators kicked out audio waveforms that were subsequently shaped by a series of modifiers-filters, amplifiers, low-frequency oscillators, ring modulators, and so forth – controlled by the player via a collection of knobs, sliders, switches, buttons, and levers. The sounds they produced were lush, fat, harmonically rich, and curiously organic.
>
> (2000: 191)

These sounds and their cultural associations in the late 1960s and early 1970s are semiotically charged with rematerialization (or transmolecularization, if you will). For example, Trevor Pinch and Frank Trocco describe the appearance of the moog in a "moment of sixties freakout" in Nicholas Roeg's film *Performance* (1970) which stars Mick Jagger as rock star Turner:

> Turner for a moment is the mad captain at the controls of spaceship Moog. The Moog and its sounds are the perfect prop, part of the psychedelic paraphernalia, the magical means to transmigrate a fading rock star into something else. . . . The Moog was a machine that empowered such transformations. The synthesizer for a short while in the sixties was not just another musical instrument; it was part of the sixties apparatus for transgression, transcendence, and transformation.
>
> (2002: 305) [ellipses in original]

[...]

Sun Ra's soundtrack for *SITP*, recorded in 1972, exploits the minimoog's capabilities for a range of alien textures, "dark" as well as warm tones, rapid keyboard runs and less "musical" beeps and burps, as well as drones produced through stable sine wave generation. Ra uses the minimoog for discrete Sci-Fi effects that colour a film scene but are not included on the soundtrack CD release by Evidence. Ricky Vincent points out that "the Moog synthesizer was capable not only of playing low notes, but of stacking a number of bass tones onto one key creating the fullest bass sound ever played" (1995: 246). However, Ra doesn't use the instrument for funk purposes in *SITP*, but paradoxically, the more familiar scary semiotics of alien presence and space in Sci-Fi cinema.

[...] The Arkestra's horns feature strongly in the sound of *SITP*. Brass usually evokes the military and warfare in Science Fiction films, but in the urban action film and road movie, trumpets and saxophones complement the screeching tones of tyres in car chases and the high-pitched whooping of police sirens. In *SITP*, the Arkestra's horns lead the marches of many pro-space anthems, such as *We travel the spaceways* and the propulsive *Watusa*, but also propel the one car chase sequence in the film, in which a run-down old car follows a van. Another strong element in the soundtrack is the polyrhythmic "Africanist" drumming and percussion of congas, koras, bongos and bells common to other African American genres of this period. [...]

The scene that immediately follows the space colony opening of the film is as close a Sci-Fi example of music as disruptive noise to the regime of "representation" as Jacques Attali

(1985) could wish for. After the relatively muted moog and sax sound of the jungle idyll and Ra's soothing words of utopian promise, we hear tap dancing to a boogie-woogie piano and then cut to a street exterior with the subtitle "Chicago 1943," then quickly cut again to the interior of a club where a chorus line of African American women, the Ebony Steppers, taps along a stage in unison. The place resembles a low-rent Cotton Club with black and white clientele. Some black punters give the white bourgie-looking customers dirty looks. In this 1970s retro version of the 1940s, Ra sits and noodles away at simple stand-up piano, dressed in, by his standards, a relatively muted wide lapelled jacket with a green zigzag pattern. The Steppers go off stage for a respite. The Overseer appears, though for some time we only see him from behind or the side without the camera revealing his face. We know he's a "mack daddy," a man of power, because he wears a white suit and Fedora hat, holds a cane and two beautiful women accompany him. A scantily clad "cigarette girl" rolls and fondles a cigar in her fingers, clips the end off and places it between the Overseer's lips. He thanks her with a greenback tip placed between her breasts. "He sees something he likes he gets around to it," she tells another woman at the bar who looks longingly in the Overseer's direction. The piano player is identified as Sonny Ray, in fact one of Sun Ra's early monikers. [. . .] He soon breaks out of the rhythm [he is playing] with irregular percussive bursts of notes like an angry Thelonious Monk and the dancers can't keep time to the music. As the playing becomes more aggressive and discordant, glasses smash, a chandelier falls to the floor, and a riot breaks out as people try to escape from the chaos. As panic ensues and parts of the club spontaneously combust, a non-diegetic moog's jarring low tones fill the soundtrack, supported by shrieking saxophones. The cacophony creates a force field that throws some people in the club through the air with its gravity-defying power. Ray goes on playing his piano and whipping up the storm. Finally he stops, kicks the instrument away with a final thrashing at the keyboard and the piano careers across the stage like a crashing car. This music machine has caused serious damage.

The scene is an electro be bop paean to Luigi Russolo and the Italian Futurists' art of noises. It captures the Dionysian impetus for entropy entrenched in rock and roll aesthetics and other modernist discourses of art. White noise, white light, white heat. Noise annoys and destroys. Sun Ra brings the noise. In his futurist manifesto for cacophony, Robert Worby (2000: 161) compresses this ideology:

> Distortion is accumulation, overdrive and mutation at the limits of a system and theses extreme bring about change, be that in sound or in society. Distortion and feedback in sound cause partials to pile up and collide like molecules in a hot gas – chaos, random-ness, and entropy are manifested in noise. Noise is entropy; it signifies closure, the end. When society is pushed to the limits, when change is necessary and imminent, when the end of an era is reached, noise blasts through every strand of culture, humanity, and life.

We can read the scene in which Ra lands on Earth through this prism. The scene parodies the clichés of the alien arrival from 1950s SF films. The radio announcer stands with a microphone and dramatically proclaims: "This is Jimmy Fey, Channel Five, stone jive, all black station, all black people, with all the news that grooves at noon, live from Oakland, California." A low-angle shot captures the television cameras elevated on the top of broadcast vans in anticipation of the space-ship. When it finally lands, with an electronic wow-wow-wow, its inhabitants emerge to meet police sirens and crowd noise. Ra and the Arkestra exit the spaceship and present a wired helmet device to Jimmy Fey. Ra plays a portable keyboard that initially produces several electronic tones that dissolve into white noise, gives Fey some serious pain and leaves him unconscious. Over the din, Sun Ra pronounces, "I am the alter-destiny, the presence of the living myth." [. . .]

If, as Vivian Sobchack (1999: 193) notes, the media in traditional Science Fiction films convey crisis information and invoke an "imagined" national and international community of the human race, by the late 1960s that faith in the airwaves has been undermined. *SITP* parodies the representation of media in Hollywood film while ambivalently acknowledging the power of radio, television cameras, newspapers and magazines to disseminate Sun Ra's subversive message. Ra uses Jimmy Fey and black radio to expose the public to his teachings. In one scene Ra is driven around Oakland and interviewed about the black man's inverted status in society as inner-city residents amusingly gaze at this strangely dressed alien apparition in their midst. The face of Ra appears on the front cover of a daily newspaper and *Rolling Stone* magazine. Bubbles and Bernard argue over whether Sun Ra has been "co-opted and corralled by the corporate Caucasian power structure." The Overseer tries to convince them that Ra is a fraud, dealing in "cold hard cash," not "black magic soul power." Music documentaries like *Gimme Shelter* (1970), which shows the Rolling Stones watching footage of themselves at Altamont on a Steinbeck editing table, illustrate that music cinema of this period was quite reflexive about its status as a medium.

[. . .]

Sun Ra's visit to an Oakland Youth Development Program is shot in wandering verité documentary style with a deep drone from the minimoog. The audio seems to take the alien messiah's perspective as the camera wanders through the space where young men and women improvise on an a capella rendition of a soul tune, *That's the way love is*. The walls are covered with large photographs of African American icons of the Civil Rights and Black nationalist eras – Frederick Douglas, Martin Luther King Jr., Amiri Baraka, Angela Davis, Malcolm X, Huey Newton, Bobby Seale, and Otis Redding. Then we suddenly see Ra from a more objective point of view. He announces himself as an ambassador from the Intergalactic Council of Outer Space. Faced with some youthful skepticism about his authenticity and disparaging comments that he looks like an old hippy, Ra poses the rhetorical question, "How do you know I'm real?" The youths say "Yeah" inquisitively. Ra continues, "I'm not real. I'm just like you. You don't exist in this society. If you did, your people wouldn't be seeking equal rights. You're not real. If you were, you'd have some status among the nations of the world." Close ups of several of the youngsters show that his words have been absorbed. In his own description of this scene, Kodwo Eshun states that, "to listen to Ra is to be dragged into another sonar system, an omniverse of overlapping sonar systems which abduct you from Trad audio reality" (1998: 158). However, Eshun's view of these "lines of flight" obscures the "back to the future" aspect of Sun Ra's mobilization of the big band tradition and its own "black and tan fantasies." Eshun also ignores the vocal performance of the soul tune. As I shall argue "Trad audio reality" is re-mediated rather than escaped from.

[. . .]

As a generic hybrid with its musical soundtrack, a key element, this slice of Science Fiction might be an example of what African American aesthetic theorist Clyde Taylor (1998: 263) calls "productive imperfection," after Cuban Third Cinema theorist and filmmaker Juan García Espinosa's (1983) manifesto "For an Imperfect Cinema," first published in 1967. Taylor's versioning of the term contends that

> "imperfect" must be understood as ironical, that is, as depending on a double meaning, twinned with the concept of the perfect that those with the privileges of power/ knowledge are eager to impose. The concept of "imperfect" culture acknowledges this power to define at the same time that it rejects the substance of the definitions. It

exposes the irony that resistance will always embrace contraband meanings and values, and these meanings and their carriers will always be framed as unofficial, unorthodox, indiscrete, undisciplined, chaotic, methodologically incorrect, vulgar, or in a word, imperfect.

(1998: 255)

Taylor goes on to compare this cinematic imperfection to the aesthetics of jazz using Ted Gioia's description of jazz as "the imperfect art." Taylor cites such features as "its call–response relation to the audience, its commitment to improvisation and process rather than to calculation and product, its collective authorship, its irreverence toward tradition, its unabashed populism" (1998: 255). As an example of jazz in film, and Sci-Fi in particular, *SITP* can be considered as a generic/genetic mutation in the relatively unprofitable margins of the early 1970s New Hollywood system. In today's information-speak, some might describe the film as a "bad file" or a (terrorist) virus in the network. However, recent film genre studies of the musical and Science Fiction suggest a more mutable, modular and recombinant sense of the genre within which we can accommodate *SITP* and make sense of later re-mediated appropriations of the film and Sun Ra.

In the history of North American cinema, the film plays a small role in the process of what Arthur Knight (2002) calls "disintegrating the musical." In his study of "black performance and American musical film" in the years 1929–1959, Knight (2002: 8–9) uses the word "integration" in more than one sense. Firstly, he means the (vertical) economic integration of the film industry and its consumers as a homogeneous market, at the same time that much of the United States was legally and informally segregated along racial lines. His second meaning relates to racial-social integration as the goal of the Civil Rights movement. Knight cites W.E.B. Du Bois' April 1934 editorial in *Crisis* entitled "Segregation in the North," in which he argued that "it will sometimes be necessary to our survival and ultimate step toward the ultimate breaking down of barriers, to increase by voluntary action our separation from our fellowmen" (ibid.). Knight's study is primarily concerned with the musical; but Du Bois' call for separation and his view that there can be "no humanity" (ibid.) until the end of economic, racial and national discrimination is a precursor of Sun Ra's own separatist rhetoric and fuels the Science Fiction tropes of alienation and exile in the cultures of the African diaspora. The third sense of "integration" outlined by Knight refers to formal, aesthetic and ideological aspects of the musical as a film text. The integration of musical sound and spectacle with narrative, and the integration of different subjects and cultures with their own musical forms in the imagined utopian (American) community are both features of the Hollywood musical outlined by a succession of genre critics, including Rick Altman, Jane Feuer and Richard Dyer. Knight argues that, for these scholars, "the integrated musical is a response to the alienating, disorienting, and violently contradictory aspects of mass industrial integration and social distinction" (2002: 15). However, Knight writes that "the creation of the ultimate utopian feeling in the integrated musical relied on an explicit social-racial segregation, and that no quantity of formal invention could hide that" (ibid.). I quote Knight's next points at some length because they articulate the ambivalence of the musical, and a tension between constraint and freedom that problematizes any clear "up-up-and-away" flight from mediated tradition, form and "reality," a departure that underpins much of SF discourse:

> In its perverse way, through its specifically circumscribed "utopian" aspirations the "integrated" musical clarified in narration, song, and dance an important and for African Americans painful American circumstance of long standing. For African American

performers and spectators, however, the starkness of the contradiction between a formally expressed desire for integrated wholeness and its manifestation in such critically applauded, even idealized segregation also offered liberating – or, more accurately, persistently illuminating – possibilities. In the face of the integrated musical, African American performers, spectators, and critics developed methods of dis/integration, sometimes taking Du Boisian advantage of segregation always watching and listening for – and often seeking to create – failures of utopian form and feeling out of which new forms and feeling might emerge, and seldom giving up on the complex possibilities of the "gift" – sometimes refashioned as joke, assault, or evasion – of African American music.

(Knight, 2002: 16–17)

[...]

Knight's stress on the mutability of the musical genre echoes recent film genre theory and analysis of the SF film. Against the long durée of film cycles and linear historical sedimentations, a more horizontal and hypertextual scene of genre formation has emerged. Genres are now fleeting and mobile formations, ironically conceived in a technological language reminiscent of Science Fiction. In his introduction to the anthology *Refiguring American Film Genres*, Nick Browne states that, "genres, here, are understood to gravitate toward specific assemblages of local coherencies – discrete, heterotopic instances of a complex cultural politics" (1998: xi). This technical-spatial lingua academicus bears the influence of Gilles Deleuze and Félix Guattari; rhizomatic connections and post-Castells network discourse are now recurrent features of genre theory. Genres seem to be less stable. They can disintegrate, dissolve, fall apart and recombine as hybrids or sub-genres. They may have short or long lives. In the same anthology, Rick Altman describes film scholars as akin to nomadic tribes on the Nile in ancient Egypt, raiding settlements of genres for specific purposes. Notwithstanding the dangers or romantic orientalism in this analogy, he argues that, "rather than assume that generic labels have – or should have – a stable existence," we should recognize "the permanent availability of all cultural products to serve as signifiers in the cultural bricolage that is our life" (Altman, 1998: 38).

Recent Science Fiction film studies also reconstitute the genre. With the increasing importance of special effects, scholars emphasize moments and intensities more than narrative. Alongside this turn, genre studies have become more centrally concerned with the *mediality* of film in the digital age. If Sci-Fi already reflects on technologies, theorists insist that the camera and celluloid are Science Fiction because of their ability to manipulate time and space. Critics refigure both apparatus theory and writing on the cinema of attractions through analysis of digital special effects. Brooks Landon argues that study of special effects might produce "a model for what Science Fiction film criticism might discover if it can draw back from its preoccupation with narratives in Science Fiction films and consider the science-fictional story that Science Fiction film production has itself become" (2002: 40). Scott Bukatman suggests that the sensational experiences of special effects are manifestations of the sublime – ways in which both the attraction of powerful technology and our fears about it are articulated within the excess of phantasmagoric spectacle. He writes that:

The final effect is not a negative experience of anxious confusion, however, because it is almost immediately accompanied by a process of appropriation of, and identification with, the infinite powers on display. The phenomenal world is transcended as the mind moves to encompass what cannot be contained.

(2002: 255)

The response encapsulates both "shock and awe," to borrow the term the US military used for its bombing strategy in Iraq in 2003.

We might extend Bukatman's argument to music's function as a special effect. Sun Ra's central message in *SITP* is, after all, that music is *the* special effect that can transport black people into a higher state of consciousness and being. This seems doubly pertinent in a film that really can't afford expensive visual effects. A discourse of music as special effect, as bodily and mental sensation of musical textures, has gained critical momentum in post-rock electronic dance music DJ culture at the expense of the more narrative-minded analysis of song, verbal meaning and representation that was dominant in rock criticism. We seem to be moving toward what Steve Waksman describes as "a method of musical analysis that is less concerned with sense than sensation, and that recognizes the place of sound, as music and as noise, in structuring the varieties of musical experience" (1999: 291). Drugs such as marijuana, LSD and Ecstasy that adjust subjective space and time relations and have played a significant role in music cultures have also contributed to this changed perspective on musical meaning. This is one reason why critics today laud the electronically enhanced psychedelia of the 1960s as one font in a futurism of "out there" mediated sounds.

One of the strands in current discourse about music and technology, particularly with the rise of digital electronic music, has been a media-centeredness akin to the recent Science Fiction film theory I outlined above. [. . .]

This modernism of sound production – the shock of the new and its non-representational materiality as mediated noise – underpins why Sun Ra's use of electronic instruments and the generic fusions – jazz-funk, jazz-rock, art rock and so on – of the late 1960s and early 1970s have become privileged points in an emergent techno-centric discourse in popular music studies. [. . .]

If we are to use Science Fiction texts in order to be more reflexive about the technologies in which they are mediated, then how might we consider *SITP*, [. . .] as generically unstable film that dis/integrates the musical is itself under erasure and reconstitution in its remediation in new contexts. The film and Sun Ra's audiovisual presence have been looped, sampled, appropriated, and re-voiced in a number of forms that contribute to the contested formation of Afrofuturism. Ra remains a ghostly echo in the mix, as in Theo Parrish's inspired murky funk track *Saga of Resistance* (2003), where the Arkestra's horns and percussive movement dissolves into a slow drawn out shuffle beat.

Angela Y. Davis points out the "fragility and mutability of historical images, particularly those associated with African American history" (1998: 23). Like Sun Ra, Davis taught in the University of California system. She laments that photographs taken of her in the late 1960s and early 1970s now define her in media culture and popular memory as "the Afro." She draws attention to a March 1994 *Vibe* magazine spread entitled "Free Angela: Actress Cynda Williams as Angela Davis, a Fashion Revolutionary." This "docu-fashion" spread incorporates the stereotypical sartorial elements now associated with the black nationalism of the period, such as black leather jackets and sunglasses. Davis worries how media texts grounded in a serious politics of the past travel and mutate into apolitical commodity-signs in the postmodern present. David Crane (2000) argues that images of black people, science and technology together are not always empowering but are often used in popular culture to mediate "proper" uses of technology in a manner that fetishizes the "urban authenticity" of African Americans. Given *SITP*'s place at the intersection of black nationalism, blaxploitation and Sun Ra's musical theatre of alienation, the film's "cult" and camp status risks us not taking its humor and other elements seriously. At the same time, we might remain wary of Ra's sanctification by his followers.

SITP and Ra have disintegrated into a number of other texts, resurrected through modular traces in various arguments since his death in 1993. Kodwo Eshun uses *SITP* and Ra to argue for a positive sense of alienation which rejects the sociological imagination and realism: "Everywhere, the 'street' is considered the ground and guarantee of all reality, a compulsory logic explaining all Black music, conveniently hearing anti-social surrealism as social realism" (1998: 00[-004]). While I agree with Eshun that analysis of black music is often couched in the limited, literal terms of documentary and ethnography, his argument risks evacuating a consideration of the social, political and economic contexts in which it is produced, distributed and consumed. In his enthusiasm for a posthuman dissolution of the human within the machinic and technological, he tends to elide the way that the "human" might still be a useful category.

In the film *The Last Angel of History*, John Akomfrah and the Black Audio Collective insert images of Sun Ra in *SITP*'s space colony alongside interviews with many cultural practitioners (including Eshun and Sun Ra expert John Corbett) to sketch a history of popular Afrofuturism that explores the line "between Science Fiction and social reality." Citing the chant that opens *SITP*—"It's after the end of the world, don't you know that yet?"—Corbett argues that for Ra, Lee Perry and George Clinton,

> the possibility of this impossible alternative futurity rests on reconfiguring the past, on the construction of vast, transformative, science-fictional mythologies, on looking back at the end of history – not a romantic terminus but the historical truncation endemic in the white "uprooting" of black African civilizations.
>
> (1994: 22)

To this end, Ra took up "The task of global pedagogy – as a supersonic cosmo-science sermonist" (ibid.: 169). Indeed, Ra can be found in more didactic mode in Robert Mugge's 1980 documentary *A Joyful Noise* than in the relatively narrative-driven *SITP*.

[. . .]

In a chapter entitled "Third Stone From the Sun" (named after a song by the Jimi Hendrix Experience), Paul Gilroy (2000: 326–356) reminds us of the possibilities of vernacular futurisms but also warns of the rise of apocalyptic, military-authoritarian and racially essentialist Science Fictions. He is critical of the Nation of Islam but also the nationalist and familiar Science Fiction of *Independence Day* and *Men in Black*. Gilroy concludes his book *Against Race* with a call for "more powerful visions of planetary humanity from the future into the present and to reconnect them with democratic and cosmopolitan traditions that have been all but expunged from today's black imaginary" (2000: 356). Alexander G. Weheliye also believes that we might not want to ditch the notions of human and humanism just yet: "in proclaiming the historical moment of the posthuman, we might do well to interrogate 'other humanities' . . . and thus ameliorate the provinciality of 'humanity' in its various Western guises" (2002: 40, ellipses in original). That way, I believe, we might be near to reaching the spaces and the places that The Streets suggest in their utopian chorus, "Weak become heroes and the stars align."

Works Cited

Altman, Rick. "Reusable Packing: Generic Products and the Recycling Process." *Refiguring American Film Genres: Theory and History*. Ed. Nick Browne. Berkeley: University of California Press, 1998. 1–41.

Attali, J. *Noise: The Political Economy of Music*. Minneapolis: University of Minnesota, 1985.

Berk, M. "Analog Fetishes and Digital Futures." *Modulations: A History of Electronic Music, Throbbing Words on Sound*. Ed. P. Shapiro. New York: Caipirinha Productions, 2000.

Bukatman, Scott. "The Artificial Infinite: On Special Effects and the Sublime." *Alien Zone II: The Spaces of Science Fiction Cinema.* Ed. Annette Kuhn. London: Verso, 2002. 249–275.

Corbett, John. *Extended Play: Sounding Off from John Cage to Dr. Funkenstein.* Durham: Duke University Press, 1994.

Crane, D. "In Medias Race: Filmic Representation, Networked Communication and Racial Intermediation." *Race in Cyberspace.* Ed. B.E. Kolko, L. Nakamura, and G.B. Rodman. New York: Routledge, 2000.

Davis, Angela. "Afro Images: Politics, Fashion and Nostalgia." *Soul: Black Power, Politics and Pleasure.* Ed. M. Guillory and R.C. Green. New York: New York University Press, 1998.

Dery, Mark. "Black to the Future: Interviews with Samuel R. Delany, Greg Tate, and Tricia Rose." *Flame Wars: The Discourse of Cyberculture.* Ed. Mark Dery. Durham: Duke University Press, 1994. 179–222.

Espinosa, Juan García. "For an Imperfect Cinema." *Twenty-Five Years of New Latin American Cinema.* Ed. Michael Chanon. London: BFI, 1983. 28–33.

Eshun, Kodwo. *More Brilliant Than the Sun: Adventures in Sonic Fiction.* London: Quartet Books, 1998, A[185].

Foster, Thomas. *The Souls of Cyberfolk: Posthumanism as Vernacular Theory.* Minneapolis: University of Minnesota Press, 2005.

Gilroy, Paul. *Against Race: Imagining Political Culture Beyond the Color Line.* Cambridge, MA: Harvard University Press, 2000.

Jones, L. *Black Music.* New York: Morrow, 1967.

Knight, Arthur. *Disintegrating the Musical: Black Performance and American Musical Film.* Durham: Duke University Press, 2002.

Landon, Brooks. "Diegetic or Digital? The Convergence of Science-Fiction Literature and Science-Fiction Film in Hypermedia." *Alien Zone II: The Spaces of Science Fiction Cinema.* Ed. Annette Kuhn. London: Verso, 2002. 31–49.

Nelson, Alondra. "Introduction: Future Texts." *Social Text* 20.2 (Summer 2002): 1–15.

Pinch, Trevor and Frank Trucco. *Analog Days: The Invention and Impact of the Moog Synthesizer.* Cambridge, MA: Harvard University Press, 2002.

Ruppersberg, Hugh. "The Alien Messiah." *Alien Zone: Cultural Theory and Contemporary Science Fiction Cinema.* Ed. Annette Kuhn. London: Verso, 1990. 32–38.

Sardar, Ziauddin. "Introduction." *Aliens R Us: The Other in Science Fiction Cinema.* Ed Sean Cubitt. London: Pluto Press, 2002. 1–17.

Sobchack, V. *Screening Space: the American Science Fiction Film,* 2nd ed. New Brunswick: Rutgers University Press, 1999.

Szwed, John F. *Space is the Place: The Life and Times of Sun Ra.* Edinburgh: Payback Press, 1997.

———. *Jazz 101: A Complete Guide to Learning and Loving Jazz.* New York: Hyperion, 2000.

Taylor, Clyde. *The Mask of Art: Breaking the Aesthetic Contract – Film and Literature.* Bloomington: Indiana University Press, 1998.

Van Assche, C, V. Vale and A. Juno. (eds). *Sonic Process: A New Geography of Sounds.* Barcelona: Actar Museu d'Art Contemporani de Barcelona, 2002.

Vincent, Ricky. *Funk: The Music, the People and the Rhythm of the One.* New York: St. Martin's Griffin, 1995.

Weheliye, Alexander. "'Feenin': Posthuman Voices in Contemporary Black Popular Music." *Social Text* 20.2 (Summer 2002): 40.

Waksman, Steve. *Instruments of Desire: The Electric Guitar and the Shaping of Musical Experience.* Cambridge, MA: Harvard University Press, 1999.

Worby, Robert. "Cacophony." *Music, Electronic Media and Culture.* Ed. Simon Emmerson. Aldershot: Ashgate, 2000. 138–163.

White, J. *Black Leadership in America, 1895–1968.* Essex: Longman Group, 1985.

Yearwood, Gladstone Lloyd. *Black Film as a Signifying Practice: Cinema, Narration and the African-American Aesthetic Tradition.* Trenton: Africa World Press, 2000.

24

WHEN THE MACHINES STOP

Fantasy, reality, and terminal identity in *Neon Genesis Evangelion* and *Serial Experiments: Lain*

Susan J. Napier

[. . .]

In 1909 the British writer E.M. Forster published the short story "The Machine Stops," a bleak vision of the far future in which what is left of humanity lives below the earth, connected through a worldwide communications system that allows them never to leave their rooms or engage in direct contact with anyone else. All human life is organized by an entity known simply as the "Machine." At the story's end the Machine malfunctions and finally stops. Abandoned and helpless, the humans begin to die in a scene that interlaces apocalyptic imagery with an extremely tenuous note of hope – the assertion by Kuno, the narrative's single rebel character, that the Machine will never be restarted because "humanity has learned its lesson." As he speaks, however,

> The whole city was broken like a honeycomb. An airship had sailed in through the vomitory into a ruined wharf. It crashed downwards, exploding as it went, rending gallery after gallery with its wings of steel. For a moment they saw the nations of the dead, and, before they joined them, scarps of the untainted sky.[1]

Forster's dystopian vision may remind readers of other Western science fiction and dystopian works of the period, in particular Aldous Huxley's somewhat later *Brave New World* (1932). Like Huxley, Forster critiques the growing reliance of his contemporaries on technology. But he differs from Huxley in two ways that make "The Machine Stops" a work particularly relevant to contemporary science fiction. The first is in his vision of a world in which technology has rendered direct interpersonal contact unnecessary and, in fact, slightly obscene;[2] the second is the explicitly apocalyptic dimension that he brings to this state of affairs. The Machine destroys not only human relationships but also, ultimately, the material world, although it does leave a tantalizing glimpse of "untainted sky." Forster's work is classic science fiction, serving, as Fredric Jameson puts it, to "defamiliarize and restructure our experience of our own *present*" – in this case, that of 1909.[3] It is also a remarkably prescient view of a future that we in the twenty-first century are increasingly able to imagine.

In Forster's view, however, when the machines stop, reality – the untainted sky – emerges. In the two Japanese anime TV series that I examine in this chapter, this is not the case. In *Shinsiki evangerion* (1995–96, *Neon Genesis: Evangelion*) and *Serial Experiments: Lain* (1998), reality itself becomes part of the apocalyptic discourse, problematized as a condition that can no longer be counted on to continue to exist, thanks to the advances of technology and its increasing capabilities for both material and spiritual destruction.[4] The two works also pose an insistent question: What happens to human identity in the virtual world? Does it become what Scott Bukatman calls "terminal identity," a new state in which we find "both the end of the subject and a new subjectivity constructed at the computer screen or television screen"? And does it then go on to become part of what Bukatman refers to as "terminal culture," a world in which reality and fantasy fuse into techno-surrealism and nothing is ultimately "knowable"?[5]

The answer to these last two questions seems to be "yes," at least in terms of the two anime I examine, although the originality and imaginativeness of their approaches might tend to obscure what, to my mind, are their deeply pessimistic visions. The narratives, the characters, and the mise-en-scène of these works evoke the disturbing postmodern fantasy that Jeffrey Sconce has described in *Haunted Media*. Sconce suggests that, "where there were once whole human subjects, there are not only fragmented and decentered subjectivities, metaphors of 'simulation' and 'schizophrenia,'" and he finds that,

> in postmodernism's fascination with the evacuation of the referent and an ungrounded play of signification and surface, we can see another vision of beings who, like ghosts and psychotics, are no longer anchored in reality but instead wander through a hallucinatory world where the material real is forever lost.[6]

Although Sconce's point is that we may be exaggerating the uniqueness of this postmodern condition – and indeed Forster's 1909 text suggests that the interface between text and machine has been a modernist preoccupation as well – it is certainly the case that the two anime I examine call into question the material world in ways that seem peculiarly specific to this period yet show strong traces of Japanese cultural tradition. This chapter explores how each anime evokes its particular "hallucinatory world," but first it is necessary to situate the two texts within both anime and Japanese culture.

Undoubtedly related to the experience of atomic bombing in World War II, but also combined with a centuries-old cultural preoccupation with the transience of life, the apocalyptic critique of technology is one that has grown increasingly frequent in recent Japanese science fiction anime. The trend probably began to develop at least as far back as the 1970s with the immensely popular animated *Yamato* television and film series about the adventures of the spaceship incarnation of the World War II battleship *Yamato*. [. . .] This provided the template for an ever-growing mass-culture obsession with apocalyptic motifs. In the *Yamato* series, however, technology, as long as it was aligned with the power of the human spirit – in this case, the Japanese spirit of *yamato damashii* – could still have salvific aspects. This combination reaches its apotheosis (literally) at the end of the film *Saraba uchū senkan Yamato: Ai no senshitachi* (1978, *Farewell to the Space Battleship Yamato: In the Name of Love*) when the stalwart young captain of the *Yamato*, accompanied by the fetching corpse of his beloved girlfriend and the shades of former *Yamato* captains, realizes that the only way to save earth is to conduct a suicide mission into the heart of the White Comet. The film ends with a single long-held shot of a spreading white radiance, a surprisingly ambiguous finale for a film aimed largely at children and adolescents.[7]

This ambiguous vision of humans, technology, and the end of the world has appeared in more complex forms in the years since *Yamato*. Most spectacularly, the 1988 film masterpiece *Akira*, directed by Ōtomo Katsuhiro, inaugurated an infinitely darker vision of technology in relation to human identity. Structured around a series of scientific experiments on telepathic children gone horribly wrong, *Akira* presented an unforgettable vision of a world in which the innocent were grotesquely sacrificed to the vicious machinations of what might be called the military-industrial complex. Far from the cozy mix of genders and generations that the *Yamato* series presented, the protagonists in *Akira* were largely alienated male adolescents typified by Tetsuo, its psychokinetically transmogrified antihero who, in the film's penultimate scene, lays waste to Tokyo in one of the most memorable and grotesque scenes of destruction ever filmed. *Akira*'s highlighting of telekinesis also brought a note of hallucinatory unreality to some of the film's most significant scenes, a feature that would be expanded in later anime and was perhaps already presaged in the spectral presences aboard the final voyage of the *Yamato*.[8]

In anime released in the years since *Akira*'s debut, its dark vision of hapless humanity in the throes of technology has not only been echoed but intensified. At first this may seem surprising. Japan, along with the United States, is one of the most technologically advanced countries in the world. Unlike the United States, however, Japan endured over ten years of recession starting in the nineties, and it has left a deep mark on contemporary attitudes toward both technology and the future. Although the country continues to produce important technological advances, the dominant attitude toward technology displayed in both its mass-cultural and high-cultural work seems to be ambivalent at best. This is in significant contrast to Western culture, which, as can be seen in American magazines such as *Wired* or in Canadian Pierre Levy's *Cyberculture*,[9] still contains strong elements of techno-celebration, especially in relation to the potential of virtual reality as promised by computers and other new media.

Besides the recession, another reason behind Japan's often problematic attitude toward technology is undoubtedly the 1995 Aum Shinrikyō incident in which followers of a charismatic guru named Asahara Shoko released deadly sarin gas into the Tokyo subway system, killing twelve people and injuring many more. Both the incident and the cult surrounding it seem to have stepped from the pages of a science fiction thriller. Many of Asahara's young followers were, at least potentially, part of the Japanese elite, graduates of top schools in science and engineering. Often shy and insecure, they were reported in the press to be devotees of science fiction anime. Lured into the cult by its potent mix of supernatural imagery – Asahara was said to be capable of levitation, for example – its increasingly strident rejection of the material and materialist world, and its apocalyptic teachings, believers not only manufactured sarin gas but also reportedly worked on developing nuclear weapons.

The show of the Aum Shinrikyō incident still looms over contemporary Japanese society on a variety of fronts, contributing to a society-wide sense of malaise. The incident itself can be seen as embodying many of the characteristic elements of contemporary Japanese society's complex vision of technology, one that recognizes the dangers of technology but remains awestruck by its potential powers. Aum's mixture of New Age occult elements and traditional Buddhist and Hindu teachings is also relevant, underlining the fact that technology dos not exist in a vacuum but interacts with all facets of human existence, including the spiritual.

Consequently, the Japanese ambivalence toward technology goes beyond a simple binary split between technology and its other(s) to encompass a problematic contemporary vision of human identity vis-à-vis not only technology but also the nature of reality itself. Increasingly in Japanese culture, the real has become something to be played with, questioned, and ultimately mistrusted. In some works, such as Murakami Haruki's best-selling novel *Sekai no owari to haadoboirudo wandaarando* (1985, *Hard-Boiled Wonderland and the End of the World*) and Anno Hideaki's *Neon Genesis: Evangelion*, characters make conscious decisions to retreat into their own fantasy worlds. In other works such as *Serial Experiments: Lain* or Murakami Ryū's novel *Koin Rokkaa beibiizu* (1984, *Coin Locker Babies*), characters attempt to impose their own, perhaps insane, visions on the outer world of reality. Often these explorations of the real contain an explicitly spiritual, even messianic, dimension.[10]

Although I include literary examples, the most significant medium in which these explorations of technology, identity, and reality versus unreality are being played out is the animated one, a medium often denigrated by Westerners as fit only for children. Unlike Western popular culture, where expressions of technological ambivalence tend to be mediated through live-action films such as *Blade Runner* (1982), *The Matrix* (1999), and *Minority Report* (2002), Japanese society has welcomed explorations of these complex issues in animated form. The reasons behind this positive reception are varied, but they include the fact that Japan has long had a tradition, through scroll painting and woodblock printing, in which narrative is as much pictorial as literary. This has culminated, in the view of some scholars, in the ubiquitousness of manga, or comic books, as a staple of twentieth-century Japanese mass culture. Anime and manga are strongly linked, since many, if not most, anime are based on manga, and both media appeal to adults as well as children.

There are other, perhaps more intriguing, reasons, however, for the synergy between animation and explorations of reality. As I have argued elsewhere, animation is a medium in itself, not simply a genre of live-action cinema.[11] As such, it develops and plays by its own generic restrictions and capabilities, the latter of which are uniquely suited for dealing with issues of the real and the simulated. The animation critic Paul Wells calls these the "deep structures" of animation that "integrate and counterpoint form and meaning, and, further, reconcile approach and application as the *essence* of the art. The generic outcomes of the animated film are imbued in its technical execution."[12] By this I take Wells to mean that the act of animation – a medium that he compares with the fine arts rather than the cinema – foregrounds and affects the characteristics of the text being animated in ways conducive to a form of art that is both peculiarly self-reflexive and particularly creative. The "deep structures" that inspire animated visions link with the uncanny and the fantastic to create a unique aesthetic world.

[. . .]

Neon Genesis Evangelion

Anno Hideaki's television series *Neon Genesis Evangelion* was first shown in 1995. [. . .]

Although it draws on earlier classic anime such as the *Yamato* series in terms of the ostensible narrative – alien invaders, in this case known as Angels, are attacking earth and only a small group of young people can save it, using impressive giant robots with which they synergize – the narrative's actual execution completely defamiliarizes this rather hackneyed story line. This is particularly true in the second half of the series, in which the tortured psychology of the main characters and a variety of enigmatic apocalyptic elements begin to intrude into the conventional action-packed plot. But we are given hints even at the beginning of these significant differences. Thus the opening episode is constructed around all the conventions of the classic "saving the world" narrative, only to undermine them by showing Ikari Shinji, its fourteen-year-old ostensible hero, in a far from heroic light. Set in a postapocalyptic "Tokyo 3" in 2015, the opening episode introduces the viewers to NERV, the secret underground headquarters run by Ikari Gendō, Shinji's remote scientist father, and to the giant robots known as EVAs that Shinji and two other fourteen-year-olds, the mysterious Ayanami Rei and the feisty/obnoxious Asuka Langley (both girls) are expected to pilot against the mysterious Angel attacks. In a more conventional anime science fiction narrative, Shinji would climb into the EVA with gusto and proceed to save the world. In fact, he does pilot the EVA and succeed in destroying the Angel – who turns out to be the third of seventeen – but only with the greatest reluctance and after a display of temper, fear, and vulnerability that seems less than conventionally heroic.

The rest of the *Evangelion* series is extremely complex, and it would be unfair to the richness of its narrative to attempt to summarize it in a few paragraphs. But it is important to be aware that the narrative is an essentially bifurcated one. On the one hand, it consists of the group's combat with the Angels, which occurs in approximately every second episode. These are violent, bloody exchanges characterized by an extreme inventiveness in terms of the fascinating abstract forms the Angels take; at the same time, they are guaranteed to satisfy the conventional adolescent male viewer of this kind of science fiction or mecha (giant robot) anime. The other strand of the narrative is far more complex and provocative, as it becomes increasingly concerned with the problematic mental and emotional states of the main characters, all of whom carry deep psychic wounds and whose psychic turmoil is represented against an increasingly frenzied apocalyptic background in which it becomes clear that the threat from the Angels is matched by the machinations of various humans connected with NERV. Although the scenes of combat are gripping and imaginative for the genre, what makes *Evangelion* truly groundbreaking are the characters' psychic struggles. Both wide-ranging and emotionally draining, these struggles are also presented with surprisingly psychoanalytic sophistication, as the characters try to come to grips with their own inner turmoil, their problematic relations with each other, and finally, their relation to more remote forms of otherness – the gigantic machines that are the EVAs and with which they must synchronize, and the enigmatic Angels who present a riddle that is increasingly depicted in terms of what seems to be a Christian or perhaps Gnostic notion of apocalypse.[13]

Ultimately, *Evangelion*'s apocalyptic narrative ends with more enigmas than revelations. We never know exactly what the Angels are, although their DNA is said to be 99.89 percent compatible with human DNA. Indeed, the final Angel, number 17, initially appears in human form, disguised as another EVA pilot. The Angel essentially sacrifices itself, allowing Shinji in EVA armor to destroy it. The victory comes at enormous cost to NERV and to Shinji's colleagues, however, as many of them die in the battle. Mick Broderick describes these battles as being held during the "apocalyptic interregnum: the time between the penultimate and ultimate battles that decide humanity's final outcome."[14] But the "final outcome" of the *Evangelion* series is a far cry from conventional apocalyptic closure. Instead of a cataclysmic struggle, the last two episodes of the series (twenty-five and twenty-six) shift abruptly to a stunningly unexpected form of closure: a vision of Shinji's inner psychological world that becomes an exploration of the nature of reality itself.

As such, the final episodes are worth examining in some detail. Stripped of the high-tech gadgetry and the colorful visuals that characterize the series' earlier episodes, these last two episodes take place largely in muted tones in a virtually empty mise-en-scène symbolizing Shinji's mind. Shinji initially appears alone and seated in a chair in a pool of light, a scene suggestive of a captive's interrogation. In fact, a form of interrogation proceeds to be carried out as he asks himself – or is asked by an unseen voice – probing psychological questions, the most frequent of which are "What do you fear?" and "Why do you pilot the EVA?"

In both cases the answers are surprising. Typical of the series as a whole, they deconstruct the mecha science fiction genre, calling into question the more simplistic motivations typical of earlier works such as *Yamato*. What Shinji fears most turns out to be not the impersonal threat of the Angels but the disturbing workings of his own psyche and his dysfunctional family background. Thus, in answer to the question, "What do you fear?" he first answers, "myself," then mentions "others," and finally admits to fearing "my father." Even more psychoanalytically significant are his answers about why he pilots the EVA. At first he insists that he does so to "save mankind." But when that answer is met with the response "Liar," he shifts to a more complex self-analysis (aided by the accusing voices inside him – often those of his coworkers – who suggest that "You do it for yourself!"). He admits to piloting the EVA because of his own need for the liking and respect of others, and finally acknowledges that he feels "worthless" unless he is joined with the EVA.

Two similar interrogations follow, involving the other pilots, Asuka Langley and Ayanami Rei. Asuka, the feisty, half-Western girl who has a dysfunctional family background equal to or worse than that of Shinji, turns out to be even more needy than Shinji in terms of her relationship with the EVA. Enmeshed in her ruined EVA, which was destroyed in the final assault, Asuka excoriates the machines as a "worthless piece of junk" but then immediately goes on to admit that "I'm the Junk.... I'm worthless. Nobody needs a pilot who can't control her own EVA." [ellipses in original]

Even more provocative are the responses of the enigmatic Rei, who, it has been revealed, is actually a clone of Shinji's dead mother created by Ikari Gendō, Shinji's father. Fittingly, given her essential otherness vis-à-vis Shinji and Asuka, Rei's internal interrogation goes beyond the psychoanalytic to verge on the metaphysical. At first she accuses herself of being "an empty shell with a fake soul," but then her inner voice suggests that she has been formed by her interactions with others, and it accuses her of "being frightened that you will cease and disappear from the minds of others." To this, Rei responds chillingly, "I am happy. Because I want to die. I want to despair, I want to return to nothing."

The overwhelming atmosphere of terror and despair intensifies as the action returns to Shinji. Over a montage of bleak visuals that include black-and-white photographs of desolate urban motifs such as a riderless bicycle or vacant park benches interspersed with graphic stills of the devastated NERV headquarters in which Shinji's colleagues are seen as bloodstained bodies, Shinji insists that there is nothing that he can do to change the world and that he is simply a "representative, a signifier." Just at this despairing point, however, the scene shifts to a vision of blank whiteness in which Shinji appears as a cartoon stick figure while a voice-over intones, "None of this will last forever. Time continues to flow. Your world is in a constant state of flux." While the words are redolent of Buddhist terminology, the visuals are self-reflexively anime-esque. Shinji is told that the whiteness around him gives him freedom, and various elements are gradually added to the blankness – first a line, or "floor," that signifies gravity and then other structures to create an animated world.

In another surprising shift, the scene changes to what we discover is a vision of an alternative animated reality – in this case, what seems to be a kind of high-school sex comedy. A self-assured Shinji "awakens" in a pleasant bedroom to find Asuka shouting at him that he'll be late for school, a far cry from his alienating existence in *Evangelion*. Other reversals abound: his father sips a cup of coffee in a homespun kitchen while his mother – now alive – chides him about being late. At school Asuka and Shinji run into a new girl – Rei – now a hot-tempered anime babe, while Misato, Shinji's beautiful, tortured mentor in *Evangelion*, appears as a sexy, placid high-school teacher.

Aware now that he indeed has a world of "Freedom" in which what is "real" is "only one of many possibilities," Shinji, surrounded by his revived colleagues, friends and family, announces, "I am me. I want to be myself, I want to continue living in the world." At this point everyone claps and each character intones the word "Congratulations!" *Evangelion* ends with Shinji thanking everyone and the final words, "Congratulations to the children."

The stunning originality of these final episodes cannot be overstated. While *Evangelion*'s narrative has clear echoes of *Yamato*'s saving-earth-through-technology plots, and its dysfunctional characters resonate with aspects of *Akira*, most notably the notion of the sacrifice of innocent children, the series deals with these elements in breathtakingly creative ways to create a unique and memorable vision of inner and outer collapse and, perhaps, renewal. Many viewers, however, were outraged by the two final episodes. Expecting a more conventional end-of-the-world scenario, fans were baffled that, instead of outward explosions and satisfying combat, the cataclysmic struggle occurred wholly in the character's mind. Rumors flew that the "disappointing" ending was due to lack of money on the part of Anno's parent company Gainax, but the subsequently released film version, *Shin seiki evangelion gekijō-ban: Air/Magokoro o, kimi ni* (1997, *The End of Evangelion*) more than makes up for the minimalism of the final episodes by presenting an over-the-top apocalypse so full of awesome catastrophe and bizarre revelations as to seem almost a parody of the apocalyptic genre.[15]

What Anno is doing in the television series, however, is far more groundbreaking and intellectually exciting. Eschewing the extravagant visuals and relentless action associated with the apocalyptic science fiction genre, Anno instead probes what might be termed the apocalyptic psyche, using simple but dark graphics and photo montages, disturbing voice-overs, and disorienting music – as the final episode opens, Beethoven's "Ode to Joy" swells on the soundtrack. In these last two episodes the machines have literally stopped, and both characters and viewers are left with no recourse but to confront their/our own flawed humanity in all its desperation and insecurities without the technological armor of the typical science fiction text.

[. . .]

My reading goes back to the special qualities of the animation medium itself and its self-reflexive ability to highlight its unreality in relation to the "real." As Routt says of the series' use of still images, "They signal the overt presence of style: they repeatedly and obviously call attention to the considerable artifice of the series' narration."[16] This calling attention is strikingly obvious in the final episodes of *Evangelion*, first in the scene where Shinji, shown floating in white emptiness, is told he has the "freedom" to do what he likes to create his own world. This is an obvious reference to the role of the animator himself/herself, who constructs a world from white emptiness every time he or she creates animation. Even more obvious is the startling scene in which Shinji becomes the hero of an alternative anime series, a lighthearted world in which he and his fellow characters are shown as confident and independent.

The highlighting of the animation's essential unreality can be interpreted in two ways. On the one hand, if we agree with Broderick's optimistic view, we can see it as underlining the explicit message that every human has the potential to create his or her own world. On the other hand, given the generally dark portrayal of the human psyche in the series up to this point, it is also possible to suggest that *Evangelion*'s final apocalyptic vision is an ironic one: even when we think we can control the reality around us, we are actually at its mercy, cartoon characters in the hands of the fates or the animators. The happy ending that we see is one ending, but, as the series makes clear, it is only one of many possible endings.

Serial Experiments: Lain

While *Evangelion* highlights the technology of the animation medium itself to call our notions of reality into question, *Serial Experiments: Lain* presents its viewers with an animated world in which technology, specifically the computer, both creates and deconstructs reality. While the EVA in *Evangelion* is essentially anthropomorphized, a concrete other that is, initially at least, a necessary part of the characters' identities, the "machine" in *Lain* is invisible, part of a world known as the "Wired" in which the machine not only supports but literally constructs identity. This premise leads both characters and viewers on a darkly surreal adventure into a virtual house of mirrors where identities shift, disappear, and reformulate and where death and life are refigured to create a disorientating and disquieting vision of a very near future.

Less epic than the sprawling *Evangelion*, *Lain* might well be described as a home drama invaded by the surreality of cyberculture. Its eponymous heroine is a quiet junior-high-school girl living an apparently conventional life with parents, an older sister, and a typical group of friends in a world much like our own, only perhaps a little more high-tech. One day, however, a classmate of hers commits suicide. From that point on, Lain and her other classmates start receiving messages on their computers, seemingly from the dead girl, telling them that "she has only given up her body" and that "God is here," inviting them, or at least Lain, to join her. Around the same time Lain receives a new computer, called a NAVI, and she becomes steadily immersed in its disembodied world. Meanwhile, her classmates insist that they have seen her at a nightclub called "Cyberia," behaving in a way that is most unlike her typical shy self. Reality and dream intersect when Lain actually starts to visit Cyberia, encountering a strange variety of people who insist they've met her before, either at Cyberia or in a world they refer to in English as the Wired, the world of cyberspace.

As Lain increasingly plunges into the Wired, she begins to understand that she and the other Lains she encounters there are very special personages, holding some key to both the real world and the cyberworld. At the same time she begins to realize that the Wired is starting to affect the real world. Newscast transmissions are suddenly delayed or pushed forward, leading the media to issue disclaimers as to whether the news they are presenting has any relevance. In the sky above Tokyo an immense image of a girl (Lain?) appears, to the consternation of the public. A friend, Arisu [...], insists that Lain has spread vicious rumors about her in the Wired. Even more disturbingly, Lain is presented with a frightening series of questions – "Who are you?" "Are your parents real?" "Is your sister?" "When are your parents' birthdays?" – none of which she can answer.

The motif of interrogation is similar to *Evangelion*. But unlike Shinji, who ultimately finds both the questions and the answers in himself, Lain initially discovers that her interrogator is the "God" of the wired, a strange vaguely Christ-like white male with tangled black hair who tells her that "to die is merely to abandon the flesh ... I don't need a body" [ellipses in original]. Lain begins to question her own existence at the same time as she defensively asserts, "I'm real. I'm living!" On her return home, however, Lain discovers a house empty except of her father, who appears only to tell her, "It's goodbye, Miss Lain." Lain begs him not to leave her alone, but he tells her that "you're not alone if you connect to the Wired." More confrontations with God ensue; he teasingly suggests that Lain herself may be a god and that in any case she is "software" and doesn't need a body. In the last episodes of the series, Lain and Arisu confront God, pointing out that he doesn't need a body, either. He thereupon metamorphoses into a hideous monster before disappearing. Free but all alone, Lain discovers she has the power to erase the memory of the rumors about Arisu from her friends' minds and ultimately realizes that she must erase herself as well. In the last scene her father suddenly reappears; he tells her that she doesn't need to wear her bear suit anyone and she "loves everybody," and he offers to make her some tea.

This brief summary can only begin to suggest the imaginative complexity of *Lain*. The series brilliantly captures some of industrialized humanity's most fundamental concerns at the turn of the twenty-first century, most notably our sense of a disconnect between body and subjectivity thanks to the omnipresent power of electronic media. As Bukatman argues, the invisibility of electronic technologies "makes them less susceptible to representation and thus comprehension at the same time as the technological contours of existence becomes more difficult to ignore."[17] *Lain*, through its foregrounding of the world of the Wired in relation to a young girl who is described as "software," manages to make the invisible visible in a peculiarly disturbing way. Lain's fragmented subjectivity, embodied in the multiple Lains acting out inside the Wired; her withdrawn, almost autistic personality; and her lack of origins make her the perfect representative of the Wired, a world in which the whole notion of reality or truth is constantly called into question.

Even the series' opening credits are full of elements that trouble our understanding of the nature of reality. Each episode begins with a blank screen and a disembodied voice intoning in English, "Present Day! Present Time!" followed by a sinister spurt of laughter. The scene shifts to a shot of Lain walking alone in a bear costume through crowded neon-lit urban streets in which the "Don't Walk" sign seems constantly to be flashing. All the while a singer intones in English the refrain "I am falling, I am fading."

The words "Present Day! Present Time!" seem to be ironically suggestive. Of course, the viewer knows that this is a defamiliarization of our present, but the laughing voice hints that it is we who may be mistaken – is *Lain* the present? Or is our reality the present? Lain's bear suit, which she dons through the series, attests to her own desire to escape reality, this case by wearing a costume suggestive of a stuffed animal, an omnipresent signifier of cute *shōjo* culture in contemporary Japan. The ubiquitous neon signage, often glimpsed through rain, highlights the importance of electronic media, once again making the "invisible" visible. The series also contains an almost obsessive number of still shots of telephone power lines, conveying the omnipresence not only of technology but of the communications media in particular and implicitly hinting at our inability to communicate in any satisfactory way. Finally, the haunting opening theme music addresses Lain's fate and our own unease that we too may "fade" into the Wired.

The final episode of *Lain* seems to suggest exactly that and is worth analyzing in more detail. On the one hand, Lain seems to triumph against the false God of the Wired by catching him in his own logical conundrum – if bodies are not necessary, then why should he need one? This can be seen as an assertion of the importance of the material world, indeed of the body, since without a body, God does indeed disappear (fades), but Lain herself is hardly better off. Reconfiguring the real world – or what is presented as the real world – that her entrance into the Wired has clearly damaged, Lain is forced to erase her own identity. Her parents now have only one child, her elder sister, and only her friend Arisu has a vague uneasy memory of a girl she once knew named Lain. Lain is told – and this is meant to be a comfort – that "If you don't remember something it never happened . . . you just need to rewrite the record"[18] [ellipses in original].

The erasure of memory is seen here ironically as comforting, a way to rewrite an unhappy history – much as Japanese textbooks have erased certain episodes of the Pacific War – but underneath the irony is a tragedy of a child's nonexistence. The ubiquitous still shots of a nude Lain in fetal position surrounded by computer wires and components suggest her total takeover by the machine. Of course if Lain is only "software," then it doesn't matter whether she ever existed. This may be the reason why her father tells her that she needn't wear the bear suit anymore, a cute signifier of contemporary Japanese girlhood. The "machine" (program) of the Wired has finally stopped for her, and she is now liberated to take tea in an imaginary space, without any pretense of reality at all.

[. . .]

Both Lain and Shinji are desperately concerned about their own incipient immateriality, the fact that their subjectivity is verging on "terminal identity" because of their dependence on the machine. Lain fears to be left alone in the world of the Wired but knows that she has nowhere else to go, while Shinji fears that without the EVA he is nothing. The fact that these are children makes their vulnerability particularly disturbing, suggesting extratextual aspects of a social malaise in which young people seem less and less connected, not only with other people but also with themselves. In many ways the emotionally empty Lain seems spiritually linked with Rei who, while a clone of Shinji's mother, is visually presented as a young girl who wants only to "return to nothing." The fact that *Lain* begins with the suicide of a young girl is even more disturbing, suggesting "terminal identity" in its most concrete form. In today's Japanese anime, in contrast to the elderly ghosts who haunt the *Yamato*, it is the children – the future – who seem to have become "phantasmagoria," unhappy ghosts or stick figures lingering on the edges of consciousness.

[. . .]

[*Neon Genesis Evangelion* and *Serial Experiments: Lain*] suggest that the imagination, the real, and technology are bound together in increasingly complex ways, and they hint that reality may ultimately be simply a creation of the mind. While this is a powerful, even liberating notion, it is also one that, for many of these narratives at least, can lead to alienation and despair. At the turn of the twenty-first century, when the machines stop, can the human imagination transcend the ruins and create a new reality no longer tied to technology? Both *Evangelion* and *Lain* explore this question, but, given the enigmatic quality of their conclusions, it is hard to say whether the answers they offer are positive or negative.

Notes

1 E.M. Forster, "The Machine Stops," in *The Eternal Moment and Other Stories* (New York: Harcourt, Brace, Jovanovich, 1956), 37.

2 Consider the following exchange between Kuno and his mother in Forster's text: "But I can see you!" she exclaimed. "What more do you want?" "I want to see you not through the Machine," said Kuno. "I want to speak to you not through the wearisome Machine." "Oh, hush!" said his mother, vaguely shocked. "You mustn't say anything against the Machine" (4).

3 Fredric Jameson, "Progress versus Utopia, or Can We Imagine the Future?" *Science Fiction Studies* 9 no. 2 (1982): 152.

4 *Shinseiki evangerion*, dir. Anno Hideaki, TV series, 26 episodes (1995–96); translated as *Neon Genesis: Evangelion: Perfect Collection*, 8-DVD box set (ADV Films, 2002); *Serial Experiments: Lain*, dir. Nakamura Ryūtarō, TV series, 13 episodes (1998); translated on 3 DVDs (Pioneer, 1991–2001).

5 Scott Bukatman, *Terminal Identity: The Virtual Subject in Post-Modern Science Fiction* (Durham, N.C.: Duke University Press, 1993), 9. Jean Baudrillard's descriptions of the contemporary condition as "no mo-re subject, no more focal point, no more center or periphery: pure flexion or circular inflexion" is also particularly appropriate here. Jean Baudrillard, *Simulacra and Simulations*, trans. Sheila Glaser (Ann Arbor: University of Michigan Press, 1994), 29.

6 Jeffrey Sconce, *Haunted Media: Electronic Presence from Telegraphy to Television* (Durham, N.C.: Duke University Press, 2000), 18.

7 *Uchū senkam Yamato*, TV series, 26 episodes (1977); translated as *Star Blazers Series 1: The Quest for Iscandar*, 6 DVDs (Voyager, 2001); this was the first of several Yamato series broadcast on American television; *Saraba uchū senkan Yamato: Ai no senshitachi*, dir. Masuda Toshio (1978); translated as *Farewell to Space Battleship Yamato: In the Name of Love*, DVD (Voyager, 1995). A strong awareness of the transience and unpredictability of life has been rooted in Japanese culture for centuries and is exemplified in its lyric tradition. See Susan J. Napier, *Anime from Akira to Howl's Moving Castle: Experiencing Contemporary Japanese Animation*, rev. ed. (New York: Palgrave Macmillan, 2005), 249–53.

8 *Akira*, dir. Ōtomo Katsuhiro (1988); translated as *Akira*, DVD (Pioneer, 2001).

9 Pierre Levy, *Cyberculture*, trans. Robert Bononno (Minneapolis: University of Minnesota Press, 2001).

10 Murakami Haruki, *Sekai no owari to haadoboirudo wandaarando* (Tokyo: Shinchosha, 1958); translated by Alfred Birnbaum as *Hard-Boiled Wonderland and the End of the World* (Tokyo: Kodansha International, 1991); Murakami Ryū, *Koin Rokkaa beibiizu*, 2 Vols (Tokyo: Kòdansha, 1984); translated by Stephen Snyder as *Coin Locker Babies* (Tokyo: Kodansha International, 1995).

11 Napier, *Anime*, 292.

12 Paul Wells, *Animation: Genre and Authorship* (London: Wallflower, 2002), 66.

13 In the final episode, Anno is clearly referencing Sigmund Freud and perhaps Jacques Lacan, as the unseen voice inside Shinji's head explains to him that he creates his personality first through disassociating with the mother and then through distinguishing himself from others.

14 Mick Broderick, "Anime's Apocalypse: *Neon Genesis Evangelion* as Millenarian Mecha," *Intersections* 7 (March 2002), paragraph 6, www.sshe.murdoch.edu.au/intersections/issue7/broderick_review.html (accessed March 26, 2006).

15 This was actually the second film version, released just a month after the first, and the third ending of the story. *Shin seiki evangelion: Death and Rebirth*, translated as *Neon Genesis: Evangelion: Death and*

Rebirth, DVD (Manga Video 2002); *Shin seiki evangelion: Air/Magokoro o, kinni ni* (*The End of Evangelion*), DVD (Manga Video, 2002).

16 William Routt, "Stillness and Style in *Neon Genesis Evangelion*," *Animation Journal* 8, no. 2 (2000): 40.

17 Bukatman, *Terminal Identity*, 2.

18 The issue of memory is implicitly suggested in her father's final comments to Lain, in which he suggests that, besides tea, he might also bring "madeleines," an obvious reference to Marcel Proust's *Remembrance of Things Past* (1913–27). While in Proust's work the flavor of the madeleine invites the narrator back into his childhood memories, in *Lain* the cakes simply underline the absence of a past that can be remembered. I am indebted to David Mankins for reminding me of this reference.

Section 4: Recommended Further Reading

Badmington, Neil (ed). *Posthumanism*. New York: Palgrave Macmillan, 2000.

Barad, Karen. *Meeting the Universe Halfway: Quantum Physics and the Entanglement of Matter and Meaning*. Durham: Duke University Press, 2007.

Braidotti, Rosi. *Metamorphoses: Towards a Materialist Theory of Becoming*. London: Polity, 2002.

———. *Transpositions: On Nomadic Ethics*. London: Polity, 2006.

Brown, Steven T. *Tokyo Cyberpunk: Posthumanism in Japanese Visual Culture*. London: Palgrave Macmillan, 2010.

Bukatman, Scott. *Terminal Identity: The Virtual Subject in Postmodern Science Fiction*. Durham: Duke University Press, 1993.

Foster, Thomas. *The Souls of Cyberfolk: Posthumanism as Vernacular Theory*. Minneapolis: University of Minnesota Press, 2005.

Graham, Elaine. *Representations of the Post/Human: Monsters, Aliens and Others in Popular Culture*. New Brunswick: Rutgers University Press, 2002.

Haraway, Donna. *Simians, Cyborgs and Women: The Reinvention of Nature*. New York: Routledge, 1991.

———. *Modest_Witness@Second_Millennium. FemaleMan®_Meets_Oncomouse™*. New York: Routledge, 1997.

Hayles, N. Katherine. *How We Became Posthuman: Virtual Bodies in Cybernetics, Literature and Informatics*. Chicago: University of Chicago Press, 1999.

———. *My Mother Was a Computer: Digital Subjects and Literary Texts*. Chicago: University of Chicago Press, 2010.

Herbrechter, Stefan. *Posthumanism: A Critical Analysis*. London: Bloomsbury, 2013.

Kirkup, Gill, Linda Janes and Fiona Hovenden (eds). *The Gendered Cyborg: A Reader*. New York: Routledge, 1991.

Shukin, Nicole. *Animal Capital: Rendering Life in Biopolitical Times*. Minneapolis: University of Minnesota Press, 2009.

Tatsumi, Takayuki. *Full Metal Apache: Transactions Between Cyberpunk Japan and Avant-Pop America*. Durham: Duke University Press, 2006.

Weheliye, Alexander. *Habeas Viscus: Racializing Assemblages, Biopolitics and Black Feminist Theories of the Human*. Durham: Duke University Press, 2014.

Wolfe, Cary. *What is Posthumanism?* Minneapolis: University of Minnesota Press, 2009.

INDEX